SCOTLAND

2019

16th Edition

By Stephen Brewer
& Lucy Gillmore

Ferns and mosses grow in abundance in the rainy climate of Argyll Forest Park in western Scotland. Forest trails are at their most lush in the early spring and summer, and hiking options range from easy pathways to challenging peaks. See p. 205.

CONTENTS

With its snug harbor lined with a row of brightly painted houses Portree is the Isle of Skye's largest and prettiest town, and an excellent base for exploring the rest of the island. See p. 374.

A LOOK AT SCOTLAND

Images of Scotland are etched into the psyche of most travelers. But that imagery changes depending on the kind of Scotland they seek. Those setting off to discover their own heritage may find a family surname carved into an ancient gravestone or their clan colors emblazoned on tartan, and walk the battlefields where their ancestors fought and died. History buffs will swoon over its hulking castles, either pristinely preserved or crumbling in picturesque piles of ivy-covered stone. Culture-seekers will revel in world-class festivals of music, theatre, art and literature, ranging from traditional to the farthest brinks of cutting-edge. Nature lovers will fix their binoculars on puffin, whales, and roe deer, while hikers will find themselves immersed in misty, fern-covered fairy forests and rolling green landscapes and cliffside trails, their solitude interrupted only by the sounds of crashing waves or bleating sheep. Golfers will tee off on the very greens where the game was born, while whiskyphiles will sample drams at the industry's most hallowed distilleries. Scotland is all these things and much, much more, and in these pages, our expert authors guide readers through the best of this bonny, bonny land.

Set near Inverarary, the moody ruins of Kilchurn Castle seem to rise from the water of the aptly named Loch Awe. The 15th-century castle belonged to the Campbell Clan, and featured a barracks that could house 200 troops. See p. 208.

EDINBURGH

Edinburgh, the capital of Scotland, as seen from the city's Calton Hill. Dominated by Edinburgh Castle, the city is composed of small neighborhoods and packed to the gills with options for sightseeing, culture and recreation.

In the shadow of Edinburgh Castle, Princes Street Gardens separate Old and New Towns, and provide a green space in the heart of the city, for relaxing on one of Scotland's coveted sunny days.

The famous Royal Mile (p. 69) forms the spine of the Old Town, connecting Edinburgh Castle to the Palace of Holyroodhouse. Today it's lined with shops, pubs and cafes.

Cherry blossoms in bloom at the Meadows, a sprawling park on Edinburgh's Southside, near the campus of Edinburgh University.

Book your lodging well in advance to attend the Royal Edinburgh Military Tattoo, which takes place every August and features precision marching, Highland dancing, and heart-stirring pipe and drum bands.

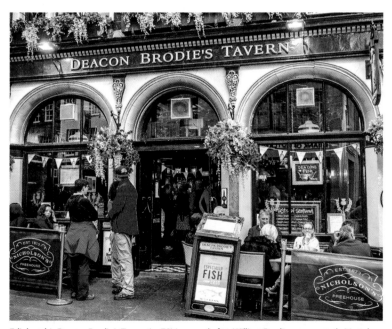

Edinburgh's Deacon Brodie's Tavern (p. 78) is named after William Brodie, a respected citizen by day and thief by night, whose notorious double life inspired Robert Louis Stevenson's tale of Dr. Jekyll and Mr. Hyde.

Nearly 1,000 years of history unfold at Edinburgh Castle, the imposing fortress that is home to an active military garrison, the Scottish Crown Jewels and former royal apartments. See p. 72.

Controversial and contemporary, the Scottish Parliament Building (p. 75) is generally loved or loathed by those who set eyes upon it. Either way, it makes a strong statement about Scotland's future.

Set high on Calton Hill, the Dugald Stewart Monument (p. 80) provides a picturesque vantage point for surveying the Edinburgh skyline.

GLASGOW

As Glasgow expanded in the 1700s, George Square and the blocks around it became the city center, and remain so today. Shopping streets, including several broad pedestrian thoroughfares, spread out from this statue-lined square.

Looking skyward in the main hall of Glasgow Cathedral (p. 163). The city's oldest structure and Scotland's only complete medieval cathedral was consecrated in 1197 and dedicated to St Mungo, the city's patron saint.

Street artist Smug created one of Glasgow's most beloved murals, a painting of a modern-day, stocking-capped version of city patron St Mungo, holding the robin that he allegedly brought back to life.

The dazzlingly modern Glasgow Science Centre (p. 172) houses exhibits on marine invertebrates, ship engineering, health and the human body, and much more. There's also a planetarium and IMAX theater.

Mainstay department stores and one-off specialty shops line Buchanan Street (here decorated for Christmas), Glasgow's main commercial artery.

The campus may be a 19th-century neo-Gothic design, but the graceful cloisters of Glasgow University look straight out of Hogwarts.

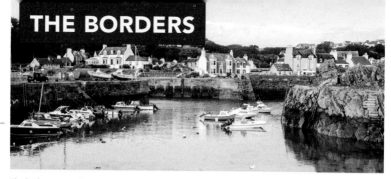

THE BORDERS

The harbor town of Portpatrick still exudes the briny flavor of an old Scottish fishing village, with rugged seascapes, bracing sea air, and pastel-colored houses surrounding its snug harbor. See p. 152.

Built on the banks of the River Tweed, novelist and national hero Sir Walter Scott's Abbotsford House (p. 121) was designed and constructed in what became known as Scottish baronial style, and set the standard for Scottish architecture for the rest of the 19th century.

In a land filled with picturesque castles, they don't come much more archetypal than moated Caerlaverock Castle (p. 143), once the seat of the Earl of Nithsdale and now set amid 21 square miles of wildlife-filled wetlands.

No golf carts are allowed on the Old Course, the oldest golf course in the world and the most famous of the seven courses that make up St Andrews Links. See p. 237.

Built in 1214 as a defense against the Danes, Eilean Donan (p. 344) was destroyed by clan fighting and lay in ruins for centuries, until it was restored in the early 1900s. Today it's a clan war memorial and museum, and featured prominently in the first *Highlander* film.

Though it's the capital of the Highlands, Inverness retains a small-town feel and offers a pretty historic center. Most visitors use it as a base for exploring nearby Loch Ness, Culloden Battlefield, and Cawdor Castle. See p. 308.

Offering stunning scenery at any time of year, the Scottish Highlands are ablaze in color during the cooler, less-crowded months of autumn.

Young Highland dancers perform in Stonehaven, site of one of Scotland's many annual Highland Games, which celebrate Scottish and Celtic culture and traditions.

At the historic distilleries along the Malt Whisky Trail, you can watch barrels being made, witness the whisky-making process and, of course, sample the final products (see p. 299).

ARGYLL & THE HEBRIDES

The American Monument in the Oa Nature Reserve on the Isle of Islay (p. 217) commemorates two accidents at sea near the end of WWI. The area is a reserve for golden eagles and a good place for spotting Highland cattle and longhorn sheep.

Hiking near the Old Man of Storr, part of a series of jagged volcanic outcroppings in the Storr section of the Trotternish Ridge, Isle of Skye. See p. 375.

The Skye Museum of Island Life preserves thatched-roof cottages once common in the Hebrides, with peat fires, box beds and farming implements (p. 376).

Boats bob in the sheltered harbor of Tobermory, the Isle of Mull's largest village and its unofficial capital, home to a museum, a theatre and a whisky distillery. See p. 360.

Ponies and horses compete at a show on the Isle of Lewis in the Outer Hebrides. Once the realm of Vikings and their far earlier predecessors, Lewis is known for its outstanding archaeological monuments. See p. 387.

The Northern Lights dance behind the standing stones at Callanish (p. 389), a series of 13 stones dating to about 1800 B.C.E. and laid out in a circle to depict a Celtic cross, with a burial cairn at the center.

ORKNEY & SHETLAND

Lighthouses such as this one on Bressay Sound dot the craggy, perilous seascape of the Shetland Islands, which mark the northernmost reaches of the British Isles.

Orkney's Skara Brae archaeological site, sometimes called "the Pompeii of Scotland," preserves the remains of 10 houses, which, about 5,000 years ago, were home to a community of farmers, hunters, and fishermen (p. 408).

Founded in the 1100s, Kirkland's St Magnus Cathedral (p. 398) honors a pacifist Viking who was axed in the head for refusing to take part in a raid of the island.

The door of St Magnus Cathedral, notable for its colorful, patterned yellow and red sandstone.

A puffin at Sumburgh Head, site of one of several large puffin colonies on the Shetland Islands, which is home to hundreds of thousands of nesting seabirds. See p. 431.

THE BEST OF SCOTLAND

By Stephen Brewer

D eciding where to go in Scotland is really not such a big dilemma after all, because you really can't go wrong. Strike out in just about any direction and you'll find yourself amid woodlands, in green glens, on heathery moors, and along dramatic coastlines. Really, you will, because Scotland is small and densely packed with magnificent scenery. You'll probably discover that these landscapes are just as beautiful as you imagined them to be, maybe after reading Sir Walter Scott or watching *Outlander* or some other film or television show shot in Scotland.

Not that Scotland is all about Highland scenery and bagpipes and lairds in tartans and fluttering kilts. While, yes, again and again in your travels you'll come upon ridiculously romantic-looking castles next to brooding lochs, Scotland is also contemporary and vibrant. This becomes evident not just in Edinburgh and Glasgow, with their galleries and snazzy shops and some in-your-face new architecture, but also in places as far-flung as Lerwick in the Shetlands and Stornoway on the Isle of Lewis.

Chances are you'll begin your Scottish travels in **Edinburgh** or **Glasgow.** These age-old rivals are vastly different—one is traditionally the elegant center of government, the other a gritty industrial powerhouse, though that sort of oversimplification certainly doesn't do justice to either. It might come as a surprise just how close together these cities are geographically. Edinburgh developed as an east coast port and Glasgow as a gateway to the western seas, but since Scotland is narrow, the nation's two largest cities are only about 40 miles apart. Dunedians (that's what residents of Edinburgh are called) and Glaswegians probably wouldn't want to hear it, but you can approach these two cities in one go, with a couple or a few days in each. You'll enjoy their heady mix of medieval, Georgian, and Victorian architecture and some of those stunning new architectural landmarks, along with pubs, restaurants, shopping, and many other urbane diversions. To the south are the **Borders,** with their famous ruined abbeys that attest to years of strife with England, and **Galloway and Dumfries,** with a long, salt-tinged, estuary-indented

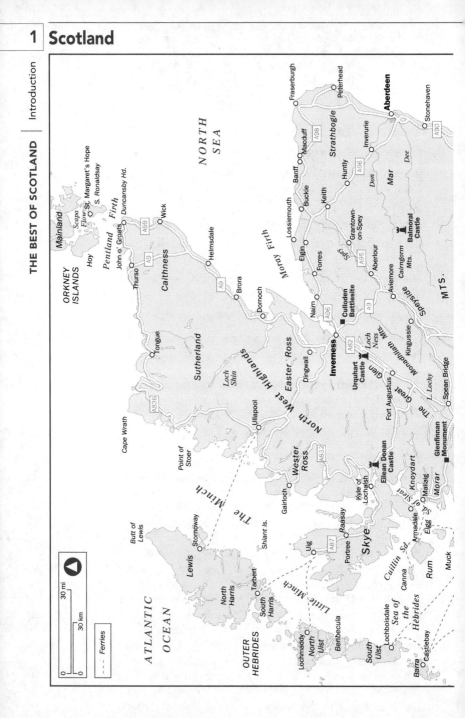

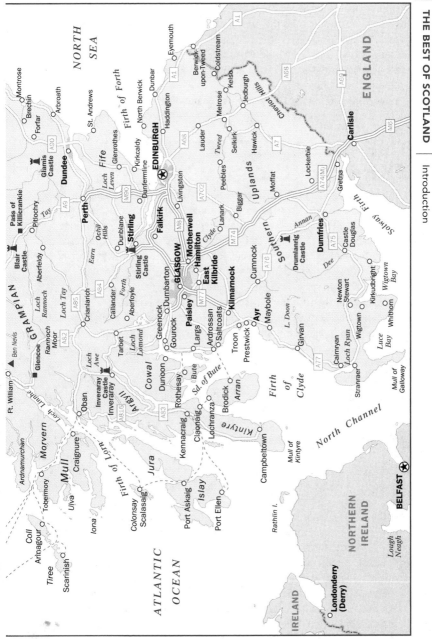

coastline and inland forests. To the north stretch the moody glens and stark mountains of the **Highlands,** and farther north, the **Tayside** and **Grampian Regions,** near **Aberdeen.** Then there are the islands. Scotland has close to 800 of them, but the ones that will probably most capture your attention are rugged (and whisky-rich) little Islay and its neighbors just off the beautiful western **Argyll** coast, the wild and scenery-saturated **Hebrides,** also off the west coast, and the windswept **Orkney** and **Shetland** archipelagos off the northernmost mainland.

Now, in the following few pages, we share what we like most about these places, and how you can best enjoy them.

THE best AUTHENTIC EXPERIENCES

o **Sipping single malts at the source:** Scotland has more than 120 whisky distilleries, so do a few site visits before debating with locals if the best drams come from the island of Islay (Laphroaig and Bowmore, among others) or Spayside (Glenlivet and Glenmorangie). Or maybe someplace else altogether, like Orkney (Highland Park) or Clydeside (Auchentoshan and Glengoyne). As you delve into single-malt science, remember that it's whisky here, never whiskey, and please don't ask for ice.

o **Watching burly guys hurl logs:** That's during the Highland Games, which take place all across the Highlands and other parts of Scotland during the summer, with one of the most famous in Braemar. Lots of squealing bagpipes and flapping kilts accompany the tossing, tugs-o-war, and other he-man events, said to have originated about 1,000 years ago to test the mettle of warriors. See p. 296.

o **Getting into the swing of Edinburgh at festival time:** Every August, the not-really-so-stuffy city erupts in a spectacular celebration of theater, art, dance, music, street performance, and every other known variation of culture, headed up by the Edinburgh International Festival, the Fringe, and the Military Tattoo. See p. 80.

o **Eating haggis:** You may wince at the recipe—the liver, heart, and lungs of a sheep, minced and mixed with suet and oatmeal and seasoned with onion and other spices, then stuffed into a sheep's stomach and boiled. But haggis is the national dish, served everywhere, usually accompanied by neeps and tatties (turnips and mashed potatoes), and washed down with whisky. Maybe you'll want to throw back a few of the latter before digging in. See p. 28.

o **Cruising across Loch Lomond:** Boats depart from Balloch, Balmaha, and other lochside towns, and once on the shimmering waters you're surrounded by a spectacle of moors, woodlands, and mountains, the very essence of a Scottish landscape. Landlubbers can enjoy the scenery from the many paths that plunge into Loch Lomond and the Trossachs National Park or on an amble around Aberfoyle, where Sir Walter Scott set his romantic poem *Lady of the Lake.* See p. 254.

- **Keeping an eye out for the Loch Ness monster:** It might be wishful thinking, but many are those who swear to have witnessed the long-neck and ink-black hump of Nessie emerging from the frigid depths. So keep a lookout during your Highland travels, and while you're at it, don't be surprised to come upon wee folk as you explore misty glens and dark forests anywhere in Scotland. Fairy Glen on the Isle of Skye is one place you're likely to encounter them. See chapters 9 and 11.
- **Looking over the Tweed Valley from Scott's View:** Sir Walter himself used to climb up here to sit and regard the Eildon Hills rising and falling before him. The outlook fired the author's imagination as he sat in his book-lined study in nearby Abbotsford Manor and extolled the beauty of the Scottish countryside in one romantic novel and narrative poem after another. See p. 124.
- **Walking along the Royal Mile:** You'll be following in the footsteps of royalty, economist Adam Smith, poet Robert Burns, and just about every other notable Scot as you make the trek through Old Town between Edinburgh Castle and Holyrood Palace on this legendary stretch of paving stones. You can walk the length in well under half an hour, but with so many diversions along the way—St Giles Cathedral, the John Knox House, Scottish Parliament, to name but a few—the journey could take days. See p. 69.

THE best HOTELS

- **The Dunstane Houses, Edinburgh:** A Victorian mansion has been stylishly redone with lots of traditional tweed mixed with sumptuous velvet, smartly executed contemporary and vintage flair, and a surplus of luxury. The result is a cozy and stylish bolthole. See p. 88.
- **The Witchery, Edinburgh:** It's like bedding down in a historical drama set. Theatrical rooms overlooking Edinburgh's higgledy-piggledy rooftops drip in luxurious fabrics and are done up with chunky four posters, antiques, and deep roll-top bathtubs. All in all, the perfect antidote for travelers bored with bland beige minimalism. See p. 90.
- **Grasshoppers Hotel, Glasgow:** This welcoming and stylish sixth-floor lair high above Central Station is geared to tasteful, pared-down luxury, with handmade Scandinavian furnishings and clean-lined, Italian lighting. Breakfast and weeknight dinners are served family-style in a kitchen-dining room that's as warm and inviting as everything else about this place. See p. 178.
- **Ship Inn, Elie, Fife:** No doubt about it: You're definitely at the seashore in this chic little pub and guest house, with blue and green colorful schemes, nautical motifs, and big views of the golden sands and sea across the way. Open fires in the armchair-filled lounges and hearty pub fare are all the more reason to linger a while. See p. 230.

- **Clint Lodge Country House, near Melrose, the Borders:** The former hunting lodge of the duke of Polwarth is the perfect country inn, with five comfortable, heirloom-filled bedrooms looking across a generous sweep of countryside to the River Tweed and a welcoming lounge and conservatory well-suited to tea and whisky sipping. An excellent dinner is served on request in the refined family dining room. See p. 125.

- **Torrisdale Castle Estate, near Campbeltown, Argyll:** Niall and Emma Macalister Hall share their romantic, meadow-surrounded 19th-century castle on the Kintyre Peninsula with guests they house in a castle apartment and four lodges and cottages on the extensive wooded grounds. Amenities include a wood-fired hot tub and sauna next to a gurgling stream and Kintyre's first gin distillery. See p. 215.

- **Scalloway Hotel, Scalloway, Shetland:** The island's most pleasant rooms are simply but carefully done with exquisite touches that include hand-fashioned, locally crafted furniture and island woolens and, from a choice few, views over the harbor. Downstairs, chef Colin Maclean's renditions of island shellfish, fish, and lamb make the friendly bar room and slightly more formal dining room the island's top places for a meal. See p. 429.

THE best RESTAURANTS

- **21212, Edinburgh:** The name tells you how to order from the five course menu, with your choice of one of the two starters, one of the two entrees, and one of the two desserts, with set soup and cheese courses. However the numbers add up, chef Paul Kitching's innovative offerings are served amid subdued, candlelit elegance in a Georgian townhouse, and if you don't want to dispel the mood, you can settle into one of the luxurious guest rooms upstairs. See p. 96.

- **Aizle, Edinburgh:** The name rhymes with hazel and is the old Scots word for spark, or glowing ember. You'll be shown a list of seasonal ingredients, but you have no say in what's going to arrive at your table in the stylishly simple dining room. You're in the capable hands of Chef Stuart Ralston, who will create an imaginative five-course tasting menu for you. See p. 95.

- **Timberyard, Edinburgh:** A giant red door opens into what was once a costume and props warehouse, now all rough-hewn floors and metal columns, with a stove and tartan rugs for warmth and a bit of softness. The menu is as eclectic as the surroundings, vaguely Nordic and decidedly modern Scottish, with lots of seafood, beef, game, and local produce, all enjoyed in the sunny south-facing Yard on a fine day. See p. 94.

- **Stravaigin, Glasgow:** Haggis—you have to try it sooner or later, and no better place to do so than this attractive, straightforward room with plain wood tables and straight-backed chairs where the menu focuses on all things Scottish, with some exotic global flourishes thrown in. See p. 185.

- **Ubiquitous Chip, Glasgow:** The name is a snide reference to what at one time passed as haute cuisine in Glasgow, but the kitchen's superb, straight-forward Scottish cuisine, as in Aberdeen beef and Orkney salmon, shows just how far the city has come. The plant-filled, stonewalled nooks and crannies of a former undertaker's stables give off an easygoing vibe that make good on the premise's claim that "we're so solidly good we don't have to put on airs." See p. 185.
- **The Seafood Hut, Oban:** You may never feel the need to sit down to eat a seafood meal again, because unless you're lucky and grab a seat at the one table here (and outdoors, at that), you'll probably devour your crab sandwich, scallops, or langoustines while standing, and the maritime snack will be nothing less than transporting. Oban, after all, is the seafood capital of Scotland. See p. 357.
- **The Ninth Wave, Fionnphort, Isle of Mull:** Your waiter may be John Lamont, who spends part of the day in his little fishing boat landing the catch that's appears on your table in imaginative innovations like smoked crab cheesecake and soups made with dandelion leaves and nettles from the cottage garden, served on set menus. The name is from mythology, and a meal in this handsomely decorated cottage will indeed transport you to otherworldly realms. See p. 362.

THE best ARCHITECTURE

- **The Borders Abbeys:** The evocative ruins of four great ruined abbeys—Kelso, Dryburgh, Jedburgh, and Melrose—are rich reminders of the monastic communities that once thrived along the border with England but were laid asunder over a few turbulent centuries by armies and religious reformers. Elaborate carvings, faded frescoes, and moss-covered stonework attest to the abbeys' onetime wealth and power. See chapter 6.
- **Bridges across the Firth of Forth:** Romans lined up 900 boats to get across this almost 2-mile-wide, fjord-like waterway between Edinburgh and the Fife region, and in more recent times Scottish engineering has come to the fore with three spectacular spans. The Forth Rail Bridge was a marvel of Victorian achievement when it opened in 1890, and the Forth Road Bridge was the longest suspension span in the world outside the U.S. upon completion in 1964. Queensferry Crossing, opened 2017, now has the distinction of being the longest triple-tower cable-stayed bridge in the world. See p. 225.
- **The Scottish Parliament:** Love it or hate it, you won't leave Edinburgh without forming an opinion of the seat of the Scottish Parliament, opened in 2004 at the foot of the Royal Mile in front of the Salisbury Crags. The work of late Catalan architect Enric Miralles is said to reflect upturned boats, Scottish landscapes, even a famous 1790s oil painting, the *Skating Minister.* Inside the debating hall, 129 Scottish MPs exercise their newly acquired (as of 1998) powers to legislate. See p. 75.

o **Rosslyn Chapel, Roslin:** What from the outside looks like just another pleasant country church reveals a world of magic in the stone-carved nave, where farmers dance with skeletons, angels play the bagpipes, and green men peer out of foliage. Making the place all the more intriguing are the Holy Grail and a piece of the cross on which Christ was crucified, alleged to be hidden deep within a sealed vault. Little wonder the chapel was the setting for the final scene of the blockbuster book and film *The Da Vinci Code.* See p. 110.

o **Skara Brae:** Scotland has no shortage of quaint old homesteads, but none have the provenance of this cluster of eight houses that Neolithic farmers erected on the island of Mainland, Orkney, roughly 5,000 years ago—that's long before the pyramids or Stonehenge were built. Hearths, built-in stone seats and cupboards, even primitive toilets show off what were then all the modern comforts. See p. 408.

o **Old and New Towns, Edinburgh:** With wynds (alleyways), closes, and a jumble of leaning tenements and proud merchants' houses, the capital's medieval heart tumbles down a ridge from Edinburgh Castle. Your wanderings down narrow lanes may lead you into another world altogether, the elegant and orderly streets and squares of adjacent, Georgian-era New Town. See p. 66.

THE best MUSEUMS

o **Scottish Fisheries Museum, Anstruther, Fife:** Fishing, of course, has long been a mainstay of life in Scotland, with an estimated 6,000 miles of coastline and 790 islands. A cluster of old harborside houses pays homage to this heritage with nets, models of sailing clippers, a recreated fisherman's cottage, tableaux of herring gutters, and in the waters just outside the door, a fleet of historic vessels. See p. 232.

o **Fort George, Highlands:** Talk about a living museum! You'll walk past soldiers stationed on active duty at one of the most massive and sturdiest fortifications ever built in Britain as you step into the 18th century barracks, chapel, and Grand Magazine. The grass-topped, cannon-lined battlements provide a great view of dolphins leaping in the waves of the Moray Firth far below. See p. 311.

o **Kelvingrove Art Gallery & Museum, Glasgow:** Where else but in this wonderfully eclectic treasure trove would you find an RAF spitfire suspended above an Asian elephant named Sir William? As you wander past working hives of bees and a leather pouch worn by medieval monks, you'll also come upon works by Rembrandt and local, 19th-century artists known as the Glasgow Boys. Your viewing will be all the more enjoyable if the Kelvingrove organ is pumping out some tunes. See p. 170.

o **Hunterian Museum & Art Gallery, Glasgow:** This oddball cabinet of curiosities, housed in high-vaulted, timber-roofed galleries, shows off Egyptian coins from the rule of Cleopatra, Viking plunder, and all sort of other oddities. Across the street is the world's largest collection of works by Scottish-American painter James McNeill Whistler, as well as the recreated home of architect Charles Rennie Macintosh and his designer wife, Margaret Macdonald. See p. 170.

o **Scottish National Gallery of Modern Art:** No old stiffs in wigs in these groundbreaking collections. The old masters here are the likes of pop artists David Hockney and Andy Warhol, while life-size figures by British art-star Antony Gormley rise out of the pavement in front, and a sculpture park is littered with abstract works by Henry Moore and Dame Barbara Hepworth. See p. 77.

o **Scalloway Museum, Shetland:** The Shetland Bus, a clandestine World War II maritime operation, takes center stage here in the headquarters village. Maps, artifacts, and portraits chronicle 215 missions that carried 192 agents and 389 tons of weapons into Nazi-occupied Norway and brought 73 agents and 373 refugees out. See p. 429.

THE best FAMILY EXPERIENCES

o **Exploring spooky underground Edinburgh:** Buried deep beneath the Royal Mile is the Real Mary King's Close, a warren of narrow, tenement-lined streets that was closed off long ago but in the 16th century bustled with hawkers and huskers. Costumed actors don't miss a trick in telling colorful, highly entertaining, and largely imaginative tales of ghosts and murderers and the sorry plights of plague victims. See p. 75.

o **Having a fun history lesson in Culloden:** The ins and outs of Jacobite history can be a tough slog for all of us, but snazzy timeline exhibits and 360-degree film projections at Culloden Battlefield will keep you and the kids riveted. Best part of all, a guide takes you out to the heather-clad moors to describe the battle on April 16, 1746 that brought a quick end to Bonnie Prince Charlie's campaign to regain the British throne for the Stuart dynasty. See p. 311.

o **Jumping on and off trams and buses on the banks of the Clyde:** Seeing all the vintage buses and streetcars at the Riverside Museum provides a walk down memory lane for older visitors and a few hours of fun for their young companions. In this age of driverless cars, you'll all be impressed by just how far motorized transport has come in just a few decades. See p. 172.

o **Indulging in monster madness at Loch Ness:** Is Nessie an elaborate hoax? Grainy film footage and photos of optical illusions in the kid-friendly galleries of the Loch Ness Centre & Exhibition in Drumnadrochit leave that question unanswered and don't debunk the myth. One thing for sure, monster hunting is serious business, judging by the mini-submarines, research vessels, and underwater cameras engaged in the search. See p. 320.

o **Discovering the Glasgow Science Centre:** A titanium-clad pod on the banks of the River Clyde (the resemblance to the hull of a boat is no accident) is filled with family-oriented attractions that enlighten us all on everything from ship engineering to the complex systems of the human body. Topping it all off is a trip up 100m (328-ft.) tall, rotating Glasgow Tower. See p. 172.

o **Taking a train ride:** Just about any rail journey in Scotland is packed with scenery, but the West Highland line, from Glasgow to Oban or Fort William, comes with a big bonus—this is the route, past Highland lochs and mountains, that Harry Potter took from Platform 9¾ to Hogwarts. Among other rides sure to have everyone clamoring for a window seat: the Borders Railway between Edinburgh and Tweedbank and the crossing over the Firth of Forth on the Forth Rail Bridge between Edinburgh and Fife. See p. 225.

THE best CASTLES & PALACES

o **Edinburgh Castle:** The ancient volcanic plug from which Scotland's most famous and important castle rises has been occupied since at least 900 B.C.E. and has witnessed many of the most momentous events in Scottish history. Almost as glittering as the Crown Jewels is the view over the city from the battlements. See p. 72.

o **Holyroodhouse, Edinburgh:** At the foot of the Royal Mile, this elegant and airy palace is the Queen's official residence in Scotland and the scene of her summertime garden parties. Finery-filled state apartments and a painting gallery show off just how far the surroundings have evolved since their founding as a monastery in 1128. See p. 74.

o **Doune Castle, Doune:** Feel you've been here before? That's because this stern medieval stronghold is Castle Leoch of *Outlander,* Winterfell in *Game of Thrones,* and well, a castle in the 1975 cult classic *Monty Python and the Holy Grail.* In fact, Monty Python's Terry Jones does the audio narration that guides you on a circuit of the royal apartments, great hall, kitchens, and cellars. See p. 245.

o **Stirling Castle, near Stirling:** You'll see one of the most imposing and impressive castles in Scotland from miles away, crowning a volcanic outcropping and looking ripe for being sieged, as it has been 16 times. This was probably not, as legend has it, Sir Arthur's Camelot, but a long succession of kings and queens have been born, crowned, died, and on occasion, murdered here. See p.244.

o **Castle of Mey, Caithness:** The late Queen Mother fell in love with this isolated estate looking out over the Pentland Firth toward the Orkney Islands, and she went to town redoing the dilapidated old place, from cellars to jutting towers and corbeled turrets. She had a green thumb, too, and her gardens are among the most beautiful in Scotland. See p. 340.

o **Eilean Donan Castle, near Dornie.** Scotland's most photogenic castle sits on an islet at the junction of three sea lochs. Warriors once dashed, kilts aflutter, along the picturesque causeway leading to the gates (at least according to the many historical dramas filmed here). A 20th-century restoration brought the banqueting hall and other nooks and crannies back to all their medieval grandeur, with some romantic embellishment. See p. 344.

o **Caerlaverock Castle, near Dumfries:** Medieval castles don't get much more romantic and picture-perfect than these red sandstone ruins, triangular in shape and approached over a moat and through a twin-towered gatehouse. Amid the mossy vaulted halls it's easy to imagine lairds in fur capes sitting around roaring fires. On walks in the surrounding wetlands you're like to encounter geese, seals, and other wildlife. See p. 143.

o **Mellerstain House, near Kelso:** This golden-hued seat of the earls of Haddington shows off the best work of father and son architects William and Robert Adam. Plaster reliefs, friezes, columns, and airy, formally aligned rooms are hallmarks of the pair's affinity for neoclassical simplicity, and their taste was perfection. See p. 117.

THE best TOWNS & NEIGHBORHOODS

o **Stockbridge, Edinburgh:** A slight bohemian edge, tidy workers' cottages turned expensive real estate, a farmer's market, and lots of gastropubs and galleries make this village within the city a preferred hangout of urbane Dunedians (as residents of Edinburgh are called). Adding to the charm of this seriously pretty neighbourhood is the gem on its doorstep, the 70-acre Royal Botanic Garden. See p. 67.

o **Culross, Fife:** This picture-postcard collection of medieval houses and quaint cottages on the Firth of Forth may be the fairest village in the land, and that's no accident—the National Trust for Scotland has painstakingly preserved this 17th-century time capsule to ensure that each step on the cobbled streets is a step back in time. See p. 227.

o **Pittenweem, Fife:** In the easternmost and most lively of Fife's historic fishing villages, jaunty trawlers chug out of to sea and unload their catch and lobster pots at a bustling morning fish market, the very one where Pittenweem Jo, "every fisher laddie's dream" of folk song fame "guts the herrin doon buy the quay." See p. 232.

o **Kirkcudbright, Galloway:** Generations of artists have been transported by the spectacle of the light playing off the sea in this pretty little seaside village on the Galloway coast. You will, too, while enjoying the works they've left behind in the Tolbooth Art Centre and a walk along the wharves. See p. 146.

o **Tobermory, Isle of Mull:** The pretty port, unofficial capital of the rugged island, is not much more than a row of brightly painted houses facing a flotilla of boats bobbing in a sheltered harbor. Adding to the romance of the isolated setting is the alleged presence of a Spanish treasure of gold bullion somewhere on the seabed. See p. 360.

o **Stromness, Mainland, Orkney:** In this picturesque port, wedged between the sea on one side and a tall granite ridge on the other, it's easy to imagine the masts of 19th-century clipper ships swaying above the slate rooftops of gabled houses and the longboats of Vikings floating in the sheltered anchorage. See p. 403.

THE best OF THE OUTDOORS

o **Getting moody in Glencoe:** A trek through this Highlands glen on foot or by car is one of the most dramatic outings in Scotland. The narrow valleys have a brooding, almost claustrophobic grandeur, and you might feel as if the bleak mountainsides are hemming you in. Or maybe that's just echoes of the most notorious massacre in Scottish history, still haunting these landscapes. See p. 348.

o **Trekking around the Treshnish Headland, Mull:** A relatively easy 7-mile hike past sea cliffs and shoreline caves comes with the company of deer, sheep, seals, and seabirds. When you can take your eyes off the immediate surroundings, scan the horizon for Dutchman's Cap, or Boc Mor, one of the Treshnish Islands just offshore. See p. 361.

o **Going ashore on Staffa:** The main reason to sail over to this tiny islet, really just a grass-covered outcropping, is to see and listen to Fingal's Cave, where the melodic sound of incoming surf has inspired poets and composers. Then find a perch on the grassy bluffs and observe the colony of enchanting puffins that breed and nest on the sea ledges. See p. 364.

o **Crossing the Sound of Sleat to the Isle of Skye:** Few places on earth are as transporting as this near-mystical island of heather-carpeted moors, weird rock formations, mossy glens, green headlands, boulder-strewn beaches, craggy saw-toothed mountains, and transformative seascapes. The only fly in the ointment? Legions of nature and scenery lovers feel the same way, so it's best to avoid the August crush. See chapter 12.

o **Having an adventure in the Cairngorms:** Nature goes on overdrive in Britain's largest national park, 4,528 sq. km (1,748 sq. miles) of wild mountain tundra, heather-carpeted moorland, ancient Caledonian pinewoods, and 55 summits over 900m (3,000 ft.). Hiking, kayaking, wildlife-watching—pick your pleasure. See p. 327.

o **Admire the daffodils in Threave Gardens:** Nearly 200 different varieties burst into bloom in April, and rhododendrons provide a riot of color in June.

But the 24 hectares (59 acres) overlooking the Galloway Hills are a delight almost any time, with a secret garden and a woodland with a pond and waterfall. See p. 145.

THE best THINGS TO DO FOR FREE

o **Bagging a Munro:** A "Munro," as designated by Sir Hugh Munro in the 1890s, is a Scottish mountain more than 900m (3,000 ft., more or less) high. The grand prize for Munro baggers is Ben Nevis, at 1,342m (4,403 ft.) the tallest mountain in the British Isles. That ascent might be a bit ambitious for non-mountaineers, but many other Munros are more approachable. For example, for Ben More on Mull, it's a relatively easy 3 hours up and 2 hours down—or so we've heard. See p. 60.

o **Making the hike up to Grey Mare's Tail:** Outside Moffat, one of the U.K.'s tallest waterfalls plunges down a mountainside from Loch Sheen amid moors and stark cliffs and tumbles into the Tail Burn, a swift-moving stream. A 2½-mile trail leads up the valley past the falls to the loch—look out for nesting peregrine falcons along the way. All you'll pay to witness the spectacle is small fee in the car park at the foot of the trail. See p. 139.

o **Traipsing around Kelso Abbey:** The oldest and largest of the Border abbeys, founded in 1128, was also one of the richest, and enough remains of the massive towers, turrets, and buttresses to suggest all this onetime might. Unlike other ruined abbeys in the Borders region, Kelso is free to enter, and among visitors who found the old stones inspiring was aspiring wordsmith Walter Scott, who attended grammar school down the lane. See p. 117.

o **Getting to know Robert Burns in Dumfries:** Scotland's national poet, who penned some of the most memorable lines in the English language, lived and worked in Dumfries from 1791 to 1796. The Robert Burns Centre, in a converted 18th-century water mill, honors the poet with manuscripts and other paraphernalia. His modest but comfortable house nearby contains many personal relics and mementos as well as much of the original furniture used by Burns during his creative years—including the chair he sat on to write the last of his poems. Admission to both is free. See p. 142.

o **Escaping into Edinburgh's greenery:** The capital is laced with parks, and you don't need to wander far off the beaten path to enjoy them. A climb up the grassy slopes of Arthur's Seat comes with views over the city from the top, while the Royal Botanic Garden is a haven of tranquility with a rock garden, Chinese plantings, and a steamy Victorian Palm House (the garden is free, but you must pay a fee to enjoy this glass-roofed paradise). See chapter 5.

THE best UNDISCOVERED SCOTLAND

o **Logan Botanic Garden, Port Logan, Galloway:** Touched by the warm currents of the Gulf Stream, an exotic paradise thrives in what seems to be the edge of the world amid these stark landscapes at Scotland's southernmost tip. It's all the work of the McDougall family, who over the years traveled the world to bring back the palms, ferns, and other semitropical species that thrive in this microclimate. See p. 153.

o **Colonsay, Hebrides:** This 20-square-mile island facing the open Atlantic— only a lighthouse stands between the western shores and Canada—is as remote, quiet, and wild as it gets, the domain of wild goats with elegant horns, and for most visitors, that's the appeal. See p. 365.

o **The Water of Leith, Edinburgh:** It's easy to forget that you're in the busy capital as you follow a 12-mile wooded trail along this ribbon-like river that tumbles from the Pentland Hills down to the docklands in Leith to meet the Firth of Forth. See p. 82.

o **The Trossachs:** Despite their proximity to Glasgow, these mist-shrouded lochs and wooded glens seem a world removed. The A821 from Callander to Aberfoyle is your entryway into the appealing landscapes, but get off the road as quickly as you can and onto a woodland trail or the deck of the 1890s steamer SS *Sir Walter Scott* for a cruise across Loch Katrine. See p. 248.

o **Fair Isle, Shetland:** Diehard birders flock to this small, remote island floating about halfway between Orkney and Shetland to observe an estimated 350 species known to stop over on their flight paths. Aside from spotting these winged attractions, the rewards for a trip to this hard-to-reach outpost, famous also for knitwear, are walks across moors ablaze with summertime wildflowers. Be mindful, though, foul weather can make it impossible to get off what becomes "Not So Fair Isle" for days at a time. See p. 436.

o **The Falkirk Wheel, Falkirk, near Edinburgh:** Another testament to Scottish engineering is the world's first and only rotating boat lift. Talk about old-fashioned know-how: Using the ancient Greek Archimedes' theory of water displacement, the giant, clawlike mechanism lifts and lowers boats between the Forth and Clyde Canal and the Union Canal. Visitors can board a boat to experience this new take on an age-old principle. See p. 108.

o **Kintyre Peninsula, Argyll:** The longest peninsula in Scotland seems like an island, surrounded by water except for a wee slip of land, and the quiet glens, woodlands, and pebbly shorelines are lost in a sleepy world of their own. At the southern tip, looking toward Ireland across 12 choppy miles of the Mull of Kintyre, you'll probably be humming along with local celeb Paul McCartney, "Oh mist rolling in from the sea/My desire is always to be here/Oh Mull of Kintyre." See p. 212.

SCOTLAND IN DEPTH

By Stephen Brewer

Of all the many influences that have shaped the national character of Scotland, perhaps the most relevant is the fact that this small country has 6,158 miles of coastline, comprises 787 islands, and is deeply indented with sea lochs. No Scot lives more than 40 miles from saltwater, and it's no wonder Scots have such a long tradition of seafaring, or that many famous seagoing explorers, among them Mungo Park and David Livingstone, set sail from Scotland. Vikings and other invaders have arrived by sea, Roman sailors rowed onto the shores, and the coasts have witnessed the comings and goings of the Spanish Armada, German U-boats, fleets of the Royal Navy, World War II spies, and present-day oil-drilling operations. The proximity of such great expanses of open sea also means that all sorts of weather blows in and out at any time, that many Scots have a strong character that might be described as being rather salty, and salmon and other seagoing creatures show up on menus even in landlocked places. However, and despite all these traditions, conditions, and achievements linked to the sea, it's a testament to the complex richness of the Scots' character that the most famous Scottish legend of all dwells in fresh water, the Loch Ness Monster.

SCOTLAND TODAY

Throughout Scotland, change is in the air. The great migrations of the 19th century—when many Scots went overseas to find a better life—are now starting to reverse. Slowly but surely, some of the estimated 20 million Scots who live outside the country are making the long trip home, where they find far more opportunities than they might have even 50 years ago. The country that gave us inventor Alexander Graham Bell and entrepreneur Andrew Carnegie is once again starting to turn a strong face to the world, with a powerful combination of innovation and tradition. Scotland's high-tech

THE singing butler DID IT

The most popular Scottish painting of all time is not a misty Highlands landscape or a romantic portrait of a fiery, tartan-wearing freedom fighter. No, it's a 1992 canvas, *The Singing Butler,* by onetime coalminer Jack Vettriano. A well-dressed couple, he in a tuxedo, she in a red ball gown and barefoot but wearing opera-length gloves, dance on a beach of smooth wet sand against a background of clouds and fog. A maid and a butler stand nearby, umbrellas at the ready. Art critics have had a field day deriding this work by a man, humphs one, who's "not even an artist"—the lighting is all wrong, and the wind is coming from the wrong direction! The painting has been derided as brainless, dimly erotic, even plagiaris-tic. Little matter, it seems. *The Singing Butler* has been compared to Grant Woods' *American Gothic* and the much beloved image has appeared on post-cards, jigsaw puzzles, cocktail napkins, calendars, and more than 12 million post-ers, making it the best-selling art print in the United Kingdom. The original, now in a private collection, sold at auction in 2004 for £744,800—then a record for a Scottish painting and, for that matter, any painting ever sold in Scotland. Other top contenders include *Waltzers* and *Road to Nowhere,* both also by Vettriano.

industries are playing an important role in the technological revolution, and today the country produces personal computers, workstations, and automated banking machines. Scotland is also at the forefront of the renewable energy industry, tapping into its considerable potential for wind and tidal power gen-eration. Meanwhile, exports of Scotland's time-tested crafts (woolen tweeds and knitwear) are thriving, the market for Scotch whisky has burgeoned around the world, and tourists are visiting in record numbers—to taste whisky, to golf, to fish for trout and salmon, to enjoy the wild landscapes of the High-lands and islands, and to partake of increasingly vibrant urban scenes in Edinburgh and Glasgow.

Much of the appeal of Scotland derives from the image the country projects to the world. These impressions of creativity, talent, industriousness, and, often, quirkiness have little to do with misty glens and verdant dales. No one has ever said "Shaken not stirred" with as much suave masculinity as Sean Connery. Since bursting onto the international scene as James Bond in the 1960s, the actor has been named the sexiest man of the 20th century and a national treasure, been knighted, and won many well-deserved awards. Singer Annie Lennox proved that the Scots' musical talents go well beyond playing the bagpipes, just as flower-power icon Donovan did in the 1960s. Danny Boyle's 1996 *Trainspotting,* high on the list of the great British films of all time, introduced us to squalor and poverty in the shadow of Edinburgh's Royal Mile, and Ian Rankin covers some of the same underbelly turf in his Inspector Rebus novels. Among other writers who have revealed the many sides of Scotland are Muriel Spark, who draws on her Edinburgh school days in *The Prime of Miss Jean Brodie.* Alexander McCall Smith, a noted professor of medical law, displays a Scottish propensity for wry humor and understate-ment in his *No. 1 Ladies' Detective Agency* series. While those sensationally popular novels take place in Zimbabwe, McCall Smith's gently satirical *44 Scotland Street* and *The Sunday Philosophy Club* series are set in Edinburgh. It's a point of pride in Scotland that the quintessential Londoner, Sherlock Holmes, is the creation of a Scot, Sir Arthur Conan Doyle, who was born in Edinburgh in 1859 and studied medicine at the city's university.

Scotland achieved literary acclaim again in 2009, when Carol Ann Duffy became Poet Laureate of the United Kingdom—the first Scot, the first woman, and the first openly LGBT person to be appointed to the position. Scotland has also broken away from tradition with the country's most important new building, the Scottish Parliament at the foot of Edinburgh's Royal Mile. This legislative body has met only since 1998, after voters in a 1997 referendum called for restoration of the Scottish Parliament that was dissolved in 1707, when the kingdoms of England and Scotland merged under the Act of Union. So, it's only fitting that the 129 members meet in a bold new landmark. Designed by the late Catalan architect Enric Miralles (1955–2000), the free-form assemblage of leaf-shaped wings is said to resemble Scottish landscapes, upturned boats, and even *The Skating Minister,* a 1790s oil painting by Henry Raeburn in the nearby Scottish National Gallery. Critics have called the mélange of abstract forms, grass roofs, and canoe-shaped skylights everything from an "architectural travesty" and a "symbol of government excess" to "an icon of organic resolution." Little wonder that Parliament has quickly become a major tourist attraction, as well as a topic of lively discussion among even the most typically taciturn Scots.

Whatever you think of this startling new presence, the debating hall will be the scene of some fiery sparring in the coming years, as Scotland deals with a dilemma. Scottish voters said "no" to independence in 2014 and "yes" to remaining in the European Union in 2016, when the rest of Britain opted for Brexit. Which means Scots are being forced to leave the European Union against their will, and time will tell how they deal with that.

THE MAKING OF SCOTLAND

Early Scotland

From the looks of it, early Scots were ardent builders. On the Orkney and Shetland islands and in the Hebrides, the ruins of farming settlements, tombs, and monuments litter windswept, treeless coastal plains. It's a sobering thought that the **Callanish Stones,** forming a monumental circle on the Isle of Lewis (p. 389), were set in place about 2,500 years before the Parthenon began to take shape on the Acropolis in Ancient Athens.

3000 B.C.E.   Chambered tombs and dwellings are built in Orkney. **Skara Brae,** a village on the Orkney island of Mainland, dates from 2500 B.C.E. (p. 408).

200 B.C.E.–C.E. 200   Brochs, circular stone towers that might have done double duty as dwellings and defense posts, appear throughout Scotland. One of the most impressive is the **Broch of Mousa,** in Shetland (p. 429).

C.E. 82   Romans attack northern tribes, but despite some spectacular blood-letting, they fail to conquer the country. **Hadrian's Wall** in northern England, erected in C.E. 122, comes to mark the northern limits of Roman influence.

200–500   The Scoti, or Scots, from Ireland establish themselves at what is known today as **Kilmartin Glen** in Argyll, where 800 forts, *cromlechs* (stone circles), and burial mounds litter their onetime kingdom of Dalriada (p. 206). Over time, the Scots intermarry with the Picts, or Painted Ones, as the Romans call the northern tribes because of their colorful tattoos.

Vikings & Christians

Vikings begin settling in the northern islands of Shetland and Orkney in the 8th century, and sail down the coast to the Hebrides and other islands and shores along the western mainland. The monasteries that early Christians establish in these remote outposts are easy targets and ripe for their plunder.

397   St. Ninian, an early Christian missionary, founds the first Christian church in Scotland in **Whithorn,** on the Galloway Peninsula in the southwest corner of the mainland (p. 151).

563   St. Columba arrives from Ireland and establishes a Christian community on the small Hebrides island of **Iona** (p. 363). This remote but large monastery helps preserve culture and learning through the Dark Ages. Elsewhere, in 552 St. Mungo, or St. Kentigern, founds a church on the site of present-day **Glasgow Cathedral** (p. 163). The Vikings raid Iona in 793 and over the next several centuries launch attacks on other monasteries on the Scottish coast and islands.

843   Scot chieftain Kenneth MacAlpin becomes King of the Scots and King of the Picts, unifying these groups within the kingdom of Alba.

1018   Malcolm II (1005–34) defeats the Northumbrians in a battle near the River Tweed, more or less establishing the modern border between Scotland and England, and further unifying the major tribes of Scotland into one broadly cohesive unit. Duncan I, Malcolm's son and heir, dies in battle with Macbeth of Moray in 1040—an event that, with much elaborate embellishment, provides the plotline for Shakespeare's "Scottish play." "Duncan's Hall" at **Glamis Castle** (p. 293), north of Dundee was for a long time, and quite imaginatively, claimed to be the scene of the murder.

1070   King Malcolm III (1031–1093) marries Margaret (later St Margaret, 1045–1093), a Saxon princess who takes refuge in Scotland after the Norman conquest and William the Conqueror's victory at the Battle of Hastings in 1066. Margaret imports English priests into Scotland and makes Saxon the language of the court, laying the groundwork for a common language that eases Scotland's eventual incorporation into England. She commissions **St Margaret's Chapel** in Edinburgh Castle (p. 72) and establishes a monastery at **Dunfermline** (p. 224) that that grows into a powerful abbey, the remains of which still dominate the town. While in Dunfermline, Margaret often prays in an underground shrine that is now known as **St Margaret's Cave.** Margaret dies of a broken heart upon hearing that Malcolm III and her eldest son are killed in battle against the English.

1124   David I (1081–1153), a son of Malcolm III and Margaret, becomes king and embarks on a lavish building spree that sees the rise of powerful, now-ruined abbeys at **Jedburgh, Kelso, Melrose,** and **Dryburgh** (chapter 6). Under David's rule, Northumberland and Cumbria in England come under Scot control and Scotland is recognized as an independent kingdom—though neither of these developments withstand the test of time.

1266   After centuries of Norse control and many skirmishes, the Norwegians cede the foggy and windswept **Western Isles** (also known as the Outer Hebrides) to Scotland. Islanders organize themselves around the Donald (or MacDonald) clan, who rule the islands as an independent state from castles at **Dunaverty** off the coast of Kintyre, **Kildonan** on Arran, and **Knock** on Skye. The honorary title of their chief, Lord of the Isles, is still used on state occasions by Britain's Prince of Wales. The Museum of the Isles, at **Armadale** on the Isle of Skye (p. 372), explores the colorful history of what's probably the most powerful clan in Scottish history.

1328   The Treaty of Edinburgh and Northampton inaugurates a short-lived period of full independence from England. Many of Scotland's legendary heroes lead the fight for independence: Sir William Wallace (1270–1305) drives the English out of Perth and Stirling (he's quite flatteringly portrayed by Mel Gibson in the 1995 film *Braveheart*); Sir James Douglas, the Black Douglas (1286–1330), repeatedly attacks the English along the borders; and Robert the Bruce (1274–1329), crowned Robert I in 1306, leads the war of independence that results in the truce. In the 1314 **Battle of Bannockburn,** near Stirling (p. 244), Bruce leads forces in Scotland's most celebrated military victory, in which 6,000 Scots force the withdrawal of a 25,000-man English army.

1468   The **Orkney** and the **Shetland** islands (chapter 13), Norse strongholds since the Vikings first rowed ashore in the 8th century, come under Scottish rule as part of the marriage dowry of the Norse princess Margaret to 18-year-old King James III (reigns 1460–88).

Stuarts, the Commonwealth & the Jacobites

The Stuart (or Stewart) monarchs are so-called because the family became powerful as stewards of the English king. They assume the Scottish throne under Robert II in 1371 and in 1603 become the first monarchs of the United Kingdom when James VI of Scotland also becomes James I of England. It would be hard to match the dynasty for sheer drama. Their reigns are marked by battles, uprisings, intrigues, treacherous plots, and cold-blooded murder, set against the religious reformation sweeping across Scotland in the latter years of their monarchy.

1513 The Scots lose 10,000 men out of an army of 25,000 in the Battle of Flodden Field in northern England. Among them are much of Scottish nobility, as well as King James IV (reigns 1488–1513), who, this catastrophe aside, is one of the most capable of the Stuart monarchs. The campaign at Flodden Field remains Scotland's worst military defeat and marks the last time a British monarch dies in battle. James ill-advisedly launches the campaign not to grab territory but out of allegiance to France, to divert the armies of King Henry VIII from attacks on the French.

1559 John Knox preaches sermons that reflect some of the ideas of the Protestant Reformation underway in England and on the Continent and lays out the basic outline of the Scottish Presbyterian Church. A devoted disciple of the Protestant John Calvin and a bitter enemy of both the Catholic Church and the Anglican Church, Knox displays a mixture of piety, conservatism, strict morality, and intellectual independence. You can learn more about this fiery reformer at the **John Knox House** (p. 72) in Edinburgh.

1561 Mary Stuart, Queen of Scots (1542–87), returns from France to take up her rule but is soon involved in intrigues, foments widespread dissention, riles John Knox and other protestants against her, and is eventually executed in England (p. 27).

1589 George Jamesone is born in Aberdeen (dies 1644). His self-portrait in the **Scottish National Portrait Gallery** (p. 77) is the most famous of his many works that launch a tradition of Scottish portrait painting. His portrait of businesswoman and philanthropist Mary Erskine hangs in the **Scottish National Gallery** (p. 76).

1603 James VI of Scotland, Mary Stuart's son (reigns as King of Scotland from 1567), also assumes the throne as king of England, Scotland, and Ireland as James I, successor to Queen Elizabeth I. He dies in 1625 and is succeeded by his son, Charles I.

1642 Parliament strips away much of the authority of Charles I, son of James I, and king from 1625 to 1649. Charles travels north to Edinburgh to organize an army against the Parliamentary forces and civil war ensues, with Oliver Cromwell (1599–1658) leading the forces of Parliament to victory. Charles flees to Scotland, but the Scots turn him over to Parliament. In 1649 Charles is convicted of treason and beheaded. Under the ensuing Commonwealth, Cromwell becomes Lord Protector in 1653 and rules England until his death.

1650–60 Cromwell's forces defeat Scottish opposition at **Dunbar** and Scotland comes under Commonwealth military occupation. The English found the garrison town of **Fort William** and build ramparts at Inverness, among other places.

1689 The English Parliament strips the uncompromising Catholic James II (also known as James VII of Scotland) of his crown, making him the last Roman Catholic monarch of Scotland, England, and Ireland. Parliament imports the Protestant William and Mary from Holland to replace him.

A stone OF MANY NAMES

After a rocky journey, the legendary Stone of Scone—or Stone of Destiny, or Coronation Stone—is firmly installed in Scotland, at least for the time being. Physically, the stone is a somewhat unprepossessing block of sandstone, measuring 66cm (26 in.) long and 40cm (16 in.) wide and weighing 152kg (336 lbs.). But this is no mere stone: Revered for centuries as a holy relic, the stone allegedly came from the Middle East, and in biblical times Jacob is said to have used the block as a pillow.

In the 6th and 7th centuries, monarchs of the Dalriada kingdom, whose peoples were the first to be known as Scots, sat on the stone for their coronations on the island of Iona and elsewhere. The stone was later moved to Scone (p. 273), where in 1292 John Balliol became the last king to be crowned there while seated in a hollow carved out of the rough surface. So powerful were the legends associated with the Stone of Scone that Edward I took it to England in 1296, believing possession gave him sovereignty over Scotland. There the stone stayed, positioned under the coronation chair in Westminster Abbey in London. In 1328, the Treaty of Northampton, recognizing Scotland's independence, called for the return of the stone to Scotland, but the revered heirloom was never removed from Westminster Abbey.

Until, that is, Christmas Day 1950, when a group of Scottish Nationalists stole the stone and hid it in Arbroath Abbey, near Dundee, where it was found 4 months later and returned to Westminster. A rumor spread that the retrieved stone was actually a replica, but this claim has never been proved. The Stone of Scone was last used for the coronation of Queen Elizabeth II in 1953.

In 1996, the Stone of Scone was officially returned to Scotland and installed, with all due ceremony, beside the Scottish Crown Jewels in Edinburgh Castle, where you can see it today (p. 72). As with most matters concerning Scottish heritage, a few dissenters have stepped forward. Is this not just a political ploy, and is the Queen not merely "lending" the stone to her Scottish subjects and might it be taken back to London for a future coronation? Does the stone really belong in Edinburgh Castle and not in Scone Castle? After all, it's not called the Stone of Edinburgh, is it? In any case, for many the stone continues to be a bedrock of national pride, and little wonder. As a legend inscribed on a plaque once attached to the stone stated, "Where'er is found this sacred stone/The Scottish race shall reign."

1707   The Act of Union unites England and Scotland as Great Britain.

February 13, 1962   In what's known as the Glencoe Massacre, troops slaughter 38 members of the MacDonald clan for their loyalty to James II and alleged refusal to swear allegiance to William and Mary. Many others die of exposure when they flee into the hills.

The Jacobites

The Jacobites (the name comes from *Jacobus*, the Latin form of James) attempt unsuccessfully to place James II (also known as the Old Pretender) back on the English throne and restore the Stuart line. James II dies in exile in France, where he leads an austere, pious life, and his pleasure-loving son Charles Edward (the Young Pretender, 1720–1788), takes up the cause. Better known as Bonnie Prince Charlie, Charles does not share his father's piety but is ardent in his attempts to regain the crown. Raised in Rome, Charles has never set foot in Scotland until a French ship lands him on the Hebrides island of Eriskay in July 1745.

1714 Anne, niece of James II, Queen of Great Britain and Ireland and the last Stuart monarch, dies. Gout ridden and obese, she was astute and immensely popular and won widespread support with her pledge upon her coronation in 1702, "There is not anything you can expect or desire from me which I shall not be ready to do for the happiness and prosperity of England." She is succeeded by George I (1660–1727), the first monarch from the German House of Hanover. Arrogant and mean-spirited, George wins little favor in London, and certainly none in Scotland, partly because he speaks almost no English and is known to keep his wife, Princess Sophia, prisoner in a German castle.

1745–1746 Charismatic but with an alcohol-induced instability, Bonnie Prince Charlie launches the Jacobite Uprising. A French fleet sent to support Charles is scattered in a storm at sea so he assembles an army among the Highland clans, with whose support he raises his standard at the head of Loch Shiel (west of Fort William; p. 344); the **Glenfinnan Monument** marks the spot. The Jacobite army marches on Edinburgh and advances as far south as Derby, just 150 miles north of London. The Jacobites are then soundly defeated in just 40 minutes at the **Battle of Culloden,** near Inverness; you can walk the battlefield and a visitor center fills in the background (p. 311). Clans that support the Jacobite cause lose their lands, and, until 1782, the wearing of Highland dress is illegal.

1745–1790 The Young Pretender's gambit to regain the throne ends unceremoniously. Charles is smuggled out of the Highlands to the island of Benbecula then the Isle of Skye dressed as a maidservant, assisted by Flora MacDonald, one of the era's most popular heroines. The pair's adventures are romanticized in a popular 19th century folk tune, *The Skye Boat Song.* The **Kildonan Museum** near MacDonald's birthplace (marked by a monument) on South Uist honors the local heroine (p. 385). The Bonnie Prince soon escapes to France and leads a life of dissipation in Paris and Rome, where he dies of a stroke in 1788. Flora MacDonald is captured on Skye, interred briefly in the Tower of London, and later emigrates to the American colonies. She eventually returns to Skye, where she dies in 1790 and is buried in **Kilmuir** cemetery (p. 375).

An Age of Commerce & the Arts

Scottish literature blossoms in the 18th century. Joining the literary ranks with ploughman poet Robert Burns are other Scots who produce a spate of lucid and powerful prose. Economist Adam Smith (1723–1790) is best known for his *The Wealth of Nations,* published in 1776. Philosopher David Hume (1711–1776) examines human behavior in *Treatise on Human Nature,* published in 1739. James Boswell (1740–1795) writes about his friend and muse in the *Life of Samuel Johnson,* published in 1791 and considered to be one of the finest biographies ever written in the English language.

1750–1850 As trade with British overseas colonies and Europe increases, the great ports of Aberdeen, Glasgow, and Leith (near Edinburgh) flourish. The merchants of Glasgow grow rich on a nearly monopolistic tobacco trade with Virginia and the Carolinas, until the outbreak of the American Revolution.

1759 Robert Burns (dies 1796) is born in Alloway, Ayrshire. Scotland's national bard is revered throughout the world, famous for verses and songs ("Auld Lang Syne," "A Red, Red Rose") that combine the humor and vigor of Scottish speech with the lilt of Scottish melodies. In **Dumfries,** you can visit "Rabbie's" home, favorite drinking spot, and grave (p. 140); **Burns Cottage,** his birthplace in Alloway is now a museum (p. 197).

1760–1850s The Highland Clearances force crofters, or small-scale tenant farmers, off their lands in the Highlands and the Hebrides. Among other factors, the Clearances come about as large-scale sheep rearing is deemed to be more economically advantageous than farming, bringing about a wave of forced emigration to America and Australia. Largely as a result of the Clearances, the Highlands and the Hebrides are still among the least populated regions in Europe. As these populations disperse, much of the regions' Gaelic culture dies out. You can still see the ruins of deserted crofts, farmsteads, and villages all over the Highlands and in the islands.

1771 Sir Walter Scott (dies 1832), one of the most-read Scottish writers, is born in Edinburgh. His unbridled flair for medieval Romanticism (*Ivanhoe*) and perceptive description of character and misty, moody locales (*The Heart of Midlothian*), along with an ingenious knack for storytelling, ensure his place in the ranks of great national heroes. **Abbotsford,** his estate overlooking the River Tweed, is open to visitors and has been a site of literary pilgrimage since the author's death (p. 121). The stone manor, along with **Balmoral Castle** (p. 295), are splendid examples of the Baronial Revival style that became a popular choice for architects of country seats, courthouses, libraries, and other public buildings throughout Scotland and the British Empire.

1773 Samuel Johnson and James Boswell tour the **Hebrides** (chapter 12) together, and Boswell recounts their adventurous travels in *A Journal of a Tour to the Hebrides* (published in 1785). Johnson publishes his own account, *Journey to the Western Islands of Scotland,* in 1775. Boswell is a man of great intellect and sensual appetite. He is famous among his contemporaries for his many liaisons, often with streetwalkers, and frequent bouts of venereal disease, to which he eventually succumbs in 1795, exacerbated by drinking.

1826 The Royal Scottish Academy of Art is established, providing a forum where professional painters can exhibit and sell their works. Among the prominent artists who show at the new academy is Sir David Wilkie

> ### Distinctly Scottish
>
> Don't mention this, say, at the Royal Edinburgh Military Tattoo, but the bagpipe, that most Scottish of instruments, is not Scottish at all. Romans may have encountered the pipes in the Near East and brought them to their lonely northern outposts. Highlanders took to the bagpipes with relish, and battalions of pipers still show up at any Highland gathering, from weddings and funerals to political rallies and parades. The skirl of the pipes can certainly send a chill down the spine, just as intended, to instill fear in the enemy during times of clan warfare. In those days of yore, as romanticized in *Ivanhoe* and other novels by Sir Walter Scott, clansmen wore kilts woven in distinctive colors and patterns, to identify each other on the field
>
> of battle. The Scottish Tartans Authority has registered more than 5,000 different tartans, each subtly different from the others. Though tartan is used interchangeably these days with plaid, the word "plaid" originally referred specifically to a mantle of cloth draped over the back and shoulders. Woolen plaids, fashioned into kilts, tartans, and all sorts of other garments, are available for sale in shops and markets everywhere in Scotland. Just for the record, though, Queen Victoria long ago authorized only two Lowland designs as suitable garb for Sassenachs (the English and, more remotely, the Americans). And do remember, you should only wear the Balmoral tartan if you're a member of the Royal Family.

(1785–1841), best known for his genre paintings, or scenes of everyday life. *The Confessional* is one of his many works in the collections of the National Galleries of Scotland (p. 77). Alexander Nasmyth (1758–1840) is the first of a long line of Scottish landscape painters, and his romantic views of Highland lochs and castles create a moody, scenery-saturated image of Scotland that is still prevalent. *The Windings of the Forth* and many of his other evocative landscapes are in the collections of the National Galleries of Scotland. His portrait of Robert Burns, perhaps his most acclaimed work, is in the National Portrait Gallery (p. 77).

1850   The novelist Robert Louis Stevenson is born in Edinburgh. In his short life (he dies of a stroke in Samoa in 1894), the celebrity author pens such classics as *Treasure Island, Kidnapped,* and *The Strange Case of Dr. Jekyll and Mr. Hyde,* as well as poems, many for children. The Stevenson name appears throughout coastal Scotland, as members of several generations of the family, the author's father among them, were noted lighthouse engineers.

The Rise & Fall of an Industrial Nation

From the mid-19th century, great successes in science and engineering propel Scotland into the forefront of industrial know-how around the globe. Queen Victoria ushers in the era in 1850 when she opens the Royal Border Bridge, carrying main rail lines between England and Scotland across the River Tweed. Scots of the time have given us everything from Listerine to the Kelvin scale, and their technical accomplishments stack up rapidly. Meanwhile, the arts flourish. William McTaggart (1835–1910) brings an Impressionist sensibility to his celebrated paintings of Scottish landscapes and seascapes, many of which hang in the Scottish National Gallery (p. 76). The so-called Glasgow Boys, and their female cohorts, the Glasgow Girls, break away from tradition to create Impressionistic images of rural scenes and seascapes that are iconically Scottish. Their work can be seen at the Kelvingrove Art Gallery and Museum in Glasgow (p. 170).

1853 Queen Victoria is administered chloroform during the birth of Prince Leopold. The success ushers in widespread use of the anesthesia to relieve pain in childbirth, as pioneered by Sir James Young Simpson (1811–1870) at the University of Edinburgh.

1861 William Burrell (dies 1958) is born in Glasgow. He enters the family shipping firm at 14, amasses vast wealth with his remarkable business acumen, and spends his fortune and spare time assembling one of the world's great art collections. In 1944 he donates more than 6,000 pieces to the city of Glasgow, along with funds to build a gallery to house them (currently being rebuilt; p. 173).

1868 Charles Rennie Mackintosh (dies 1928) is born in Glasgow. He and his wife, glass and textile designer Margaret Macdonald (1864–1933), bring a particularly Scottish element to the Art Nouveau and Arts and Crafts movements. Among their finest creations in Glasgow are the **Lighthouse** (p. 167) and **House for an Art Lover** (p. 171).

1872 Explorer and missionary David Livingston, born near Glasgow in 1813, dies of malaria and dysentery while seeking the source of the Nile. No European has ventured as far into the African interior, and among his lasting legacies is the phrase "Dr. Livingston, I presume?" *New York Herald* reporter Henry Stanley issues this greeting upon meeting the explorer on the shores of Lake Tanganyika in 1871.

1876 Scottish-born Alexander Graham Bell (1847–1922) is issued a U.S. patent for the telephone.

1882 Oceanographer Sir Charles Wyville Thomas (born 1830), a professor of natural history at the University of Edinburgh, dies of exhaustion while compiling a 50-volume account of his 1872–76 expedition aboard the HMS *Challenger.* Thomas traveled 70,000 miles and recorded 450 new marine species; the NASA Space Shuttle *Challenger* is named after the ship to commemorate the historic voyage.

1889 The **Highland Games,** rooted deep in Scottish tradition, gain worldwide attention during a display at the Paris Exhibition. Two of the events, shot put and hammer throw, are incorporated into the Olympics. The games, with rugged sporting matches (along the lines of tossing tree trunks and running up mountainsides), music, and dance, are still held across Scotland from May through September and are staged across the world as well.

1890   Edward, Prince of Wales, inaugurates the 8,000-foot long Forth Rail Bridge, considered in its time to be the Eighth Wonder of the World and still massively imposing.

1896   A.J. Cronin (dies 1981), one of modern Scotland's most successful authors, is born. Cronin studied medicine at the University of Glasgow and became most famous for a novella, *Country Doctor,* made into a 1990s television series featuring small-town physician Dr. Finlay.

1914–1919   Scotland loses an estimated 80,000 to 110,000 men in World War I. Many of the troops wear kilts, and opposing Germans call them "Ladies from Hell." In 1919, German naval officers scuttle their fleet that has been impounded at **Scapa Flow,** in Orkney, sending 53 ships to the bottom of the sea (p. 406).

1939–1945   Just weeks into World War II, on October 14, 1939, the Germans sink the HMS *Royal Oak,* anchored in Scapa Flow, Orkney. Among the 833 men lost are 120 so-called "boy sailors" between 14 and 18. Clydebank near Glasgow and other cities around Scotland sustain heavy bombing, while factories turn to war production. The Shetland Bus, a clandestine maritime operation that aids the resistance movement in Norway, operates out of the fishing port of **Scalloway** (p. 428).

Mid-20th century   The decline of traditional industries reshapes Scottish society. Scotland finds that, like the rest of Britain, aging industrial plants can't compete with more modern commercial competition from abroad. The most visible decline occurs in the shipbuilding industries; the vast Glasgow shipyards that once produced some of the world's great ocean liners go bankrupt.

New Prosperity & an Undercurrent of Separatism

The talk in Scotland these days is all about independence—yes, still, after all these centuries. At issue now is the possibility of a second independence referendum, after voters elected to stay united with the rest of Britain in a 2014 vote. The other big concern is how to maintain a place in European markets after Great Britain voted to leave the European Market—and Scots overwhelmingly voted to stay in. Meanwhile, Scots are seeing signs of newfound prosperity around the country, in such places as the Clyde riverbank in **Glasgow** (chapter 7), where bold, design-statement museums and exposition halls have replaced shuttered shipyards.

1970   The discovery of North Sea oil deposits brings new prosperity to Scotland and provides jobs for thousands of workers. Oil has continued to play a prominent role in the Scottish economy. In 1981, the largest oil terminal in Europe opened at Sullom Voe in the Shetland Islands.

1999   Under Prime Minister Tony Blair's devolution reforms, Scotland is allowed to elect its own legislature for the first time since its 1707 union with England. A total of 129 Scots are elected to a newly formed Parliament that has the power to tax and make laws, as well as to pursue such matters as

Mary Stuart, the Soap Opera

When Mary Stuart, also known as Mary Queen of Scots, took her place on the Scottish throne, she had some serious strikes against her. She tried to impose Roman Catholicism on a country that favored Protestantism; she ruled an unruly group of subjects who did not trust her; and she was the great niece of King Henry VIII, making her a legitimate heir to the throne of England, occupied by Elizabeth I, and thus considered to be a big threat. Mary also had lousy taste in men, who, rather than aiding her cause, embroiled her in a thick web of political intrigue. Daughter of Scotland's James V and Mary of Guise, a French noblewoman, Mary became queen when her father died only 6 days after her birth. With her mother acting as regent, Mary was betrothed to Francis, the French Dauphin, at age 5 and sent to France, where she was well-educated and polished to a high shine in the court of Henri II. She was just 15 when she married 16-year-old Francis and became Queen of France. The two were supposedly passionately in love, but Francis died of a brain abscess two years later. Mary returned to Scotland and take up her royal duties in 1561. She barely remembered Scotland, spoke little English, hated the damp, chilly weather, missed the sophisticated French court, and grieved for her young husband. She found solace in the company of the politically ambitious Lord Bothwell, her closest advisor, and she soon married the tall, dashing, and arrogant Lord Darnley, with whom she was said to be "bewitched." The marriage quickly soured when Darnley and other conspirators stabbed Mary's trusted Italian secretary, David Rizzio, to death in front of her, and Mary begin describing her husband in letters to Bothwell as "this poxy fellow that troubleth me." Murder seems to have been the best way out of the marriage, and, according to reports, it appears that Bothwell arranged to have an explosion set off at a house where Darnley was staying, then had him stabbed and strangled as he tried to escape. Mary was implicated in the murder, then Bothwell adducted her, held her captive in Dunbar Castle, raped her, and forced him to marry him. Or so Mary said, though it's hard not to imagine she was complicit in the elaborate plot. Mary and Bothwell did not remain together long. Protestant lords denounced Mary as an adulteress and murderess and had her imprisoned. Bothwell went into exile in Denmark and died there after 10 years, reportedly insane. Mary escaped and sought refuge in England but, considered a threat to the English crown, spent the next 19 years in custody. She was beheaded in 1587, under an execution order reluctantly issued by her cousin, Queen Elizabeth I. You can follow these dramatic events at the **Mary Queen of Scots' Visitor Centre** in Jedburgh (p. 129).

healthcare, education, public transportation, and public housing. Scotland is still represented in the main British Parliament in London, and must bow to the greater will of London in matters of foreign policy. In the same year, and perhaps as a symbol of resurgence, salmon reappear in Glasgow's River Kelvin for the first time since 1852.

2002 Residents of **Gigha** buy their 1,375-hectare (3,400-acre) island, now administered by a Community Trust (p. 215). Islanders in **South Uist, Benbecula,** and **Eriskay** purchase their islands under similar community ownership arrangements in 2006, and portions of **Lewis, Harris,** and **Rum** come under similar administration. As a result, the **Hebrides** (chapter 12) and other islands are undergoing a process of social and economic regeneration.

2014   A Scottish Parliament does not necessarily satisfy the ever-present undercurrent of Scottish separatism. At sporting events, Scots can be heard singing "Flower of Scotland" instead of "God Save the Queen." The issue comes up for a vote with a referendum on Scottish independence. The "nays" win, with 55.3% of voters saying "no" to independence, with 44.7% in favor. Voter turnout is high, 84.6%. Meanwhile, Queen Elizabeth inaugurates the controversial new **Scottish Parliament Building** in Edinburgh (p. 75).

2016   Britain votes to leave the European Union. Scotland, however, votes to remain in the EU, with 62% of voters in favor of staying and 38% in favor of leaving. In effect, Scotland is being forced to quit the EU against popular will, and the implications of so-called "Brexit" for Scotland remain unclear. First Minister Nicola Sturgeon advocates for protection of Scotland's place in European markets as well as a second independence referendum.

2018   Restoration of the **Glasgow School of Art** in the wake of a devastating fire in 2014 is just about complete when a second, more destructive blaze roars through the early 20th-century landmark, designed by Charles Rennie Mackintosh.

EATING & DRINKING IN SCOTLAND

Shall we just cut to the quick and address the elephant in the room? Or, that is, the sheep's stomach in the room? The one filled with bits and pieces of sheep's lung, liver, and heart mixed with suet and spices, along with onions and oatmeal? Yes, we're talking about **haggis.** You'll encounter Scotland's favorite traditional dish on menus everywhere, and sooner or later, you really must try it. Because haggis is delicious, best when accompanied by **neeps and tatties** (turnips and potatoes), and washed down with a shot or two of smoky single malt whisky. Have a few of those malts and you might be moved to recite a verse or two from Robert Burns, who praised haggis as the "great chieftain o the puddin'-race!" Chefs are venturing into all sorts of variations of haggis, mixed with Indian spices, vegetarian versions, and small portions served tapas style as an appetizer. Haggis also often appears in a **full Scottish—** breakfast, that is, accompanied by baked beans, fried egg, sausage, and **tattie scones** (made with mashed potatoes). Yes, a full Scottish sends you into the day with a full human stomach.

It's probably not entirely surprising that a country that makes a national dish out of sheep offal also enjoys **black pudding.** That's pig's blood, mixed with pig fat and oatmeal, and stuffed sausage-like into a casing. One more dish that might have you scratching your head when perusing a menu in Scotland is **cullen skink.** Off-putting as the name might be (it's been suggested it sounds like the name of a villain in a novel by Charles Dickens), this rich fish soup is just the tonic for a winter night when the weather is *dreich* and the rain is beating against the windows. (This being Scotland, that might also be a summer's eve.) Cullen skink combines smoked fish (traditionally haddock), potatoes (usually mashed), onions, and wee bit of cream, how much depending upon the cook; the more cream, the richer the soup. **Scotch pie** is as easy as pie to find, and in some places still sold by street vendors (piemen or pie-wives), as it has been since the Middle Ages. Eaten hot or cold, often as a handy on-the-go snack, the pie consists of a double crust filled with minced mutton cooked with herbs.

The Scots also enjoy a lot of food that is not as exotic as haggis or pig's blood but is just plain delicious. **Aberdeen Angus beef,** from shaggy beasts that spend their lives outdoors feeding on grass, is rich, marbled, and tender. Depending on where you happen to be dining, **lamb** tastes of the heather-clad moors of the Highlands or the salt-tinged pasturelands and shores of the Shetland islands, with a wee hint of seaweed. **Salmon** seem to jump out of the sea and rivers right into the kitchen, best onto a grill and simply done with some herbs—or smoked over oak. The modest **herring** becomes quite regal when split from head to tail, salted, and smoked over wood chips to emerge as a kipper. The best are from Loch Fyne.

Among their other fine qualities, many Scots have a sweet tooth. You may or may not share their enthusiasm for **battered Mars bars** (as if the popular candy bar isn't unhealthful enough, in this version it's dipped in a sweet batter and deep fried). Only slightly less challenging to cholesterol levels are sweet buttery **shortbread,** a national treasure for centuries, and **sticky toffee pudding,** sweet sponge cake soaked in toffee sauce and topped with ice cream. A favorite on-the-go treat is **tablet,** the Scottish version of fudge.

Whisky & Beer

Sir Walter Scot praised **Scotch whisky** as the "only liquor fit for a gentleman to drink in the morning." A wee dram is satisfying just about any time of the day, and after dinner, sipped in front of a fire, is the best sleep tonic around.

Americans will make a much better impression on bar tenders if they can refrain from asking for Scotch. Here at the source, Scotch is simply whisky, and it's spelled without the "e" as it is across the Atlantic. It's also important to specify a **single malt** or a blend. You'll be taken more seriously if you ask for a single malt, especially if you can specify a point of origin: for example, Highlands, Lowlands, Islay, or Campbeltown on Kintyre. You can ruin your connoisseur credentials entirely with a single word: "ice."

Blended whiskies came into being because the single malts were for a long time too harsh for delicate palates and they were expensive and time-consuming to produce. A shortcut was developed: A portion of whisky could be mixed with such ingredients as American corn, Finnish barley, Glasgow city tap water, and caramel coloring. Not that there's anything wrong with blends. They're rich and tasty, and since they account for about 90% of

Scotland's whisky output, you've probably been drinking them for years. To be officially called Scotch whisky, single malts and blends alike must be made within the borders of Scotland and aged for at least 3 years.

Scots may have whisky in their veins, but they have been throwing back **beer** for about 4,000 years. Brewers had a tough time over the past few centuries, dealing with the consequences of a malt taxes and beer duties, but the brewing industry is making a comeback and breweries are opening all over Scotland.

USEFUL TERMS & LANGUAGE

The speech patterns of the Scots are famously rich and evocative. It's a special pleasure to hear Gaelic, the lingua franca from Scotland's earliest days and still spoken in parts of the Highlands and the Hebrides—especially on the Isle of Skye, where about 60% of the population still use this millennia-old language. Here are some words, Gaelic and otherwise, that you might encounter during your travels around Scotland.

aber   river mouth

ach   field

aird   promontory

alt   stream

auch   field

auld   old

baillie   magistrate

bal   hamlet or tiny village

ben   peak, often rugged

birk   birch tree

brae   hillside, especially along a river

brig   bridge

broch   circular stone tower

burn   stream

cairn   heap of stones piled up as memorial or landmark

ceilidh   Scottish hoedown with singing, music, and tall tales

clach   stone

clachan   hamlet

close   narrow passage leading from the street to a court or tenement

craig   rock

creel   basket

croft   small farm worked by a tenant, often with hereditary rights

cromlech, dolmen   prehistoric tomb or monument consisting of a large flat stone laid across upright stones

dram   ⅛ fluid ounce

drum   ridge

dun   fortress, often in a lake

eas   waterfall

eilean   island
factor   manager of an estate
fell   hill
firth   arm of the sea reaching inland
gait   street (in proper names)
gil   ravine
glen   a small valley
haugh   water meadow
how   burial mound
howff   small, cozy room or meeting place
inver   mouth of a river
kil, kin, kirk   church
kyle   narrows of ancient or unknown origin
land   house built on a piece of ground considered as property
larig   mountain pass
links   dunes
loch   lake
machair   sand dune, sometimes covered with sea grass
mon   hill
muir   moor
mull   cape or promontory
ness   headland
neuk   nose
pend   vaulted passage
provost   mayor
reek   smoke
ross   cape
schist   highly compact crystalline rock formation
strath   broad valley
tarbert   isthmus
tolbooth   old town hall (often with prison)
uig   sheltered bay
uisge   water
uisge beatha   water of life, whisky
way   bay
wynd   alley

SUGGESTED SCOTLAND ITINERARIES

By Stephen Brewer

3

To get the most out of your time in Scotland in 1 or even 2 weeks requires a little strategizing, and we offer some suggestions below. The first two itineraries cover the highlights—how many you see depends on how much time you have—and the other two are more specialized, one looking at some places we consider to be distinctly Scottish. The other one is for families, who will discover that Scotland can be a heck of a lot of fun for young travelers. The scenery and other sights may leave you feeling a bit breathless, but we don't want the pace of your touring to do so. Take it slow in places, and be sure to allow time for some well-deserved relaxation. And finally, make room in the itinerary to sit in a pub or two, or on the side of a mountain watching the mist rising from the glens below—after all, these are time-honored Scottish pursuits.

THE REGIONS IN BRIEF

Scotland is small, about the same size as South Carolina, but looms large with an astonishing variety of scenery. Adding to all this geographic abundance, the lochs (lakes), glens (valleys), mountains, far-flung islands, and history-saturated towns and cities are all the richer for the many stories attached to them, from sagas of Viking seafarers to centuries' worth of accounts of battles with the English on the fact-based side of the ledger, to tales of wee folk and giants on the "who's to say?" side. All in all, Scotland is an almost mythical place in all its variety and grandeur, and your travels will only enhance the magic.

EDINBURGH & THE LOTHIAN REGION   **Edinburgh** is one of Europe's most beautiful capitals, half medieval and half Georgian, with elegant towers and spires rising against an enticing natural stage setting of crags, cliffs, and green hillsides. The city is at its liveliest every August during the **International Festival,** when diversions include the acclaimed Military Tattoo and avant-garde Fringe Festival, but Edinburgh puts on a pretty good show any time of the year. Packed with history and filled with art, the capital also has a fun side that you only need to wander into a pub to experience. Strike out from the center in almost any direction and you'll come upon a landmark or two set amid enticing landscapes. On the coast to the north, medieval **Dirleton Castle** once guarded sea approaches to Edinburgh, and to the west, **Linlithgow Palace** was the birthplace of Mary Queen of Scots.

THE BORDERS & GALLOWAY REGIONS   Southern Scotland sweeps across these two scenic, history-drenched neighboring regions, each with a distinct character all its own. The gently rolling landscapes of the **Borders** form the age-old divide between England and Scotland, and hulking castles and sturdy stone towers, along with a string of ruined abbeys in **Jedburgh** and other Borders towns, attest to this often-turbulent past. **Kelso** and other pretty villages and grand estates are tweedy not just because of the fashion choices of the city folk who like to weekend here—the River Tweed cuts a course through the green valleys, and novelist and poet Sir Walter Scott felt so at home in the gentle terrain that he built a baronial estate, **Abbotsford,** on the river banks outside **Melrose.** Meanwhile, sea-washed **Dumfries and Galloway** is where poet Robert Burns lived and wrote his best work. The ruggedly beautiful coast-line, etched with coves and tidal estuaries, cradles beautiful gardens at **Threave** and **Port Logan,** and some appealing seaside villages. **Kirkcudbright** is still an artists' colony, as it has been for more than a century, while out-of-the-way **Wigtown** is Scotland's National Book Town. The vast **Galloway Forest Park** sweeps across much of the mountainous interior.

GLASGOW & THE STRATHCLYDE REGION   There's a lot of talk these days that Scotland's onetime industrial powerhouse is undergoing a renaissance, but Scotland's largest city never really lost its edge. Yes, many of the 19th- and 20th-century shipyards and factories are shuttered, but elegant Georgian merchants' houses, Victorian monuments, and Scotland's oldest **medieval cathedral** have long lent the city a distinctive presence. Glaswe-gians shows off an unpretentious worldliness in their shops, bars and clubs, and outstanding museum collections, as well as a taste for fine dining. Mean-while, a strikingly modern exhibition center and auditorium, along with the bold new **Glasgow Science Centre** and the **Riverside Museum,** have all taken shape along the banks of the Clyde and signal the city's move beyond the industrial past. When Glaswegians and their visitors want to take in some sea air they only need to make the short trip to the **Ayrshire Coast,** where they can also pay homage to poet Robert Burns at his birthplace in **Alloway.**

ARGYLL & THE SOUTHERN HEBRIDES   The lands of Argyll comprise much of the west of Scotland, a generous sweep of forests, mountains, and a long coastline deeply etched with sea lochs. To the south the green **Kintyre peninsula** stretches toward Ireland, and clustered in the seas around this long, scenic sliver of mainland are a cluster of beautiful islands. **Arran** rises and falls across wild moor-and-mountain landscapes that justify the nickname "Scotland in miniature," and **Islay** is the source of single malts that put the island on the "must visit" list of all serious whisky drinkers. Islanders on little **Gigha** nurture a world-class garden, while deer and wild sheep scramble across moors and glens on **Jura.** Much of the mainland is no tamer, especially in the vast **Argyll Forest Park,** carpeting some 24,300 hectares (60,000 acres) just to the east of **Loch Fyne** and its waterside, stage-set town of **Inveraray.** Some 1,500 years ago these landscapes gave rise to the Kingdom of Dalriada, at **Kilmartin Glen.** Life may have been tough for these Dark Age inhabitants, but enjoyed some good weather: the North Atlantic drift blows in balmy temperatures that ensure nearby **Arduaine Gardens** thrive.

FIFE & THE CENTRAL HIGHLANDS   The region was long known as the "kingdom" of Fife," and while that sounds very grand indeed, this now-sleepy realm of softly rolling hills and picture-perfect **East Neuk** fishing villages does have many royal associations. **Dunfermline** is the erstwhile capital of Scotland, seat of the Stuart monarchy, and resting place of 22 royals. Mary Queen of Scots lived as an infant monarch at **Stirling Castle** and was crowned in the chapel in 1543, and later she took time off from her duties as embattled queen to hunt at **Falkland Palace.** In recent times, the duke and duchess of Cambridge (William and Kate) met at the **University of St Andrews,** the oldest and most prestigious in Scotland. The surrounding town is, of course, also famous for its golf links, the oldest in the world, but to put things in perspective, **St Andrews Castle and Cathedral** were already hundreds of years old when some sporty types started hitting balls around in 1552. The region goes green and wild in the moors, mountains, and lochs to the west, where **Loch Lomond** and the **Trossachs** mountains are protected as a national park.

ABERDEEN & TAYSIDE & GRAMPIAN REGIONS   The Royal Family helps put these northern lands on the map with their fondness for **Balmoral Castle,** the "beloved paradise" of Queen Victoria and still the Queen's summer getaway. Other castles and palaces also pepper green landscapes watered in places by the trout- and salmon-rich River Tay. **Glamis Castle** has been linked to British royalty for 10 centuries (though the most famous noble resident, Macbeth, dwelt here only courtesy of William Shakespeare's literary license) and **Scone Palace** was built in 1580 near hallowed ground where Scottish kings were crowned for 10 centuries. Meanwhile, aficionados of single malts follow the well-worn **Speyside Whisky Trail** to taste the output of Glenlivet, Glenfiddich, and other esteemed distillers at the source. **Aberdeen,** Scotland's third-largest city, anchors the northeast coast, and solidly so, as this North Sea oil center is known as "Granite City" for the gray stone in which much of the town is clad.

INVERNESS & THE HIGHLANDS   It says a lot about this near-mythic region that the most famous resident is the monster who's said to dwell in **Loch Ness.** As befits this elusive mascot, the Highlands is a region of stark beauty where lonely landscapes suggest mysterious, even otherworldly doings on the moors of **Glencoe**, in the misty woodlands of **Black Isle,** and on the stark flanks of **Ben Nevis,** topping out at 1,345m (4,411 ft.) to hold the title as the highest peak in the British Isles. Monsters, savage landscapes, and a turbulent history of clan warfare aside, the Highlands is a favorite retreat for hikers, climbers, fishermen, and other outdoors enthusiasts who relish some of Britain's wildest terrain. Civilization intrudes gently in the inviting regional capital of **Inverness,** near the mouth of the River Ness. Some remarkable manmade wonders include the **Caledonian Canal,** begun in 1803 and stretching for 60 miles to join several natural lochs, and **Cawdor Castle,** an altogether pleasant lordly seat despite some purely fictional bloodletting from the pen of Shakespeare (the residents have said they wish the Bard had never written that "damned play"). The Highlands ends with a bang, that is, with lots of dramatic scenery, at **Dunnet Head,** the northernmost point on the British mainland.

THE HEBRIDES   A spirit of adventure descends the moment you step onto the breezy deck of an outbound ferry for these any of the dozen or so main isles, and dozens of other smaller islands, off the West Coast (or for that matter, even zip across the road bridge that connects the **Isle of Skye** with the mainland). The shortlist of what to expect includes some of Europe's best beaches, with the best lining the coasts of **Barra** and **Harris** (though beachgoing in the Hebrides is usually a chilly undertaking); soaring mountains, none craggier and more dramatic than the **Cuillins** on **Skye**; an abundance of wildlife that flourishes on **Mull, South** and **North Uist**, and elsewhere in undisturbed habitats here at the western edge of Europe; and a palpable sense of history that, in the case of standing stones on **Lewis,** goes back three millennia or so and, on **Iona,** to the days of early Christianity. Seafood that seems to jump right out of the sea onto your plate also add a lot to the pleasure of island hopping, and in these wild, almost mystical landscapes it's quite alright to keep company with the "wee folk."

THE ORKNEY & SHETLAND ISLANDS   Windswept and largely treeless, these two northern archipelagoes are almost savagely beautiful and unblemished in many places, the domain of seals and seabirds. Not that the islands are anything less than highly civilized—they had been inhabited for about 4,000 years by the time Vikings rowed their longboats into the surrounding seas. Neolithic farmers, Pictish tribes, Norse clans, and generations of Celtic-influenced islanders have all left a legacy on both archipelagoes. The **Orkneys,** separated from the mainland by the choppy Firth of Pentland, are flat, fertile, and notably and generously littered with the tombs, houses, and monuments of early peoples who farmed here 5,500 years ago. The more northerly **Shetlands** are bleaker, wilder, and more rugged. They, too, were settled early, and a lavish settlement at **Jarlshof** dates to 2500 B.C.E. But most likely to fire the imagination up here is the coastline, battered by both the Atlantic Ocean and the North Sea into weird and wonderfully shaped cliffs and sea stacks.

SCOTLAND IN 1 WEEK

Seeing Scotland in a week seems like a tall order. In your favor is the fact that easy-to-navigate cities are jam-packed with attractions, and Scotland is small enough that getting to farther-flung places is relatively easy. The down side is that wherever you go you will want to see more, spend more time, stay longer to settle into these beautiful and storied landscapes. Which is all the more reason to come back.

Days 1 & 2: Edinburgh

In the morning, head for Old Town's **Royal Mile** (p. 69). Scotland's two most august landmarks, steeped in lore and history, anchor either end of this storied stretch of pavement, **Edinburgh Castle** (p. 72) to the west and the **Palace of Holyroodhouse** (p. 74) to east. After a couple of hours in the castle, take your time ambling up the Royal Mile to Holyroodhouse, stopping for a bite and a look at the shops that seem to sell all the cashmere, tweed, and whisky in Scotland. After touring the palace, step into the nearby **Scottish Parliament** (p. 75); guided tours show off this architectural masterpiece (or travesty, depending upon who you talk to). After all this sightseeing you can clear your head with a stomp up nearby **Arthur's Seat** (p. 69) for a good workout along with panoramic views of the city and coastline. In the evening, find your way to **Stockbridge** or one of Edinburgh's other village neighborhoods for dinner (restaurant reviews begin on p. 93).

You can see a bit more of the city on **Day 2** without rushing. The **Scottish National Gallery of Modern Art** (p. 77) and the **National Museum of Scotland** (p. 73) show off a good selection of national treasures and will nicely fill the morning. In the afternoon, enjoy some more of the city's considerable greenery by clambering up the Greek-inspired **Calton Hill** (p. 79) and wandering around the tranquil **Royal Botanic Garden** (p. 80), one of Britain's finest. For dinner, head down to the revamped docklands in **Leith** (p. 83), where the buzzing waterfront is lined with pubs and fish restaurants.

Days 3: Glasgow

On the morning of **Day 3,** take the train or bus to Glasgow, only 40 miles west of Edinburgh. Even without too early a start you should arrive in time for a walk around **George Square** (p. 166) and a bite in **Merchant City** (p. 183), then a walk or bus ride over to the medieval quarter around **Glasgow Cathedral** (p. 163), for a look at Glasgow's oldest structure and the Victorian-era Necropolis across the street. From here take the bus or subway (that's what they call it here, not the underground, and the closest stop to the cathedral is Buchanan Street) to the **Kelvingrove Art Gallery and Museum** (p. 170) in the West End (Kelvinbridge stop). This

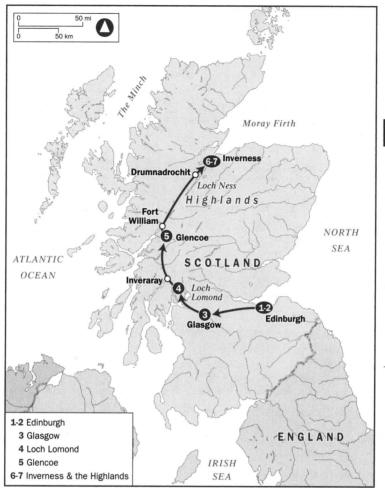

magnificent faux Spanish baroque palace is crammed with an appealing collection that ranges from Rembrandt's *Man in Armour* to an RAF spit-fire hanging from the ceiling of the main hall, above an elephant. At the nearby **Hunterian Museum & Art Gallery** (p. 170) a standout is the recreation of the Glaswegian house of noted architect Charles Rennie Mackintosh and his designer wife, Margaret. The West End is the place to be in the evening, with a great selection of pubs and restaurants on and around Byres Road (reviews begin on p. 190).

Day 4: Loch Lomond

You'll be picking up a rental car and heading out of town today, but you'll have time in the morning to explore the restored riverbanks along the Clyde. At the **Riverside Museum** (p. 172), designed by the late Zaha Hadid, trolleys, buses, and other conveyances and accompanying audio commentary richly evoke Glasgow's 20th-century history. You don't have far to drive today— just 20 miles northwest to an overnight in **Balloch** (p. 255), on the shores of Loch Lomond, where Ben Lomond rises above the shimmering waters. The best way to get a look at the scenery is from the deck of one of **Sweeney's Cruisers** (p. 255).

Day 5: Loch Lomond to Glencoe

This is a day of easy driving through mountain and lake scenery. From Balloch, the road leads north through **Loch Lomond and the Trossachs National Park** (p. 254), where the forests and glens have been called the realm of "elves, fawns, and fairies." At **Arrochar,** 19 miles north of Balloch, take a side trip 22 miles west on A83 to **Inveraray** (p. 204). The road passes over the "Rest and Be Thankful" pass with wonderful views across Glen Kinglass and Glen Coe then drops down to wind along the shores of Loch Fyne, with Inveraray slowly taking shape as a tidy collection of white houses tucked onto a little finger of land at one end of the loch. Tour **Inveraray Castle** and **Inveraray Jail,** then backtrack toward Arrochar and the A82 to continue north. First though, stop for lunch at the famous **Loch Fyne restaurant** (p. 207) on the shores of the loch about 8 miles east of Inveraray, for some fish and mussels just hauled out of the waters across the road. From Arrochar, it's another 53 miles north to **Glencoe** (p. 348), your stop for the night. Set amid brooding Highland landscapes, Glencoe is the scene of the infamous 1692 massacre in which members of the Campbell clan murdered men, women, and children of the Macdonald clan, and the event is commemorated in a memorial and the visitor center. The village today is a pretty backwater set amid moors and mountains.

Days 6–7: Inverness & the Highlands

After a drive around Glencoe, across wild and windswept Rannoch Moor to Loch Leven, follow the shores of Loch Linnhe north on A82 16 miles to **Fort William** (p. 344). While there's no reason to linger in town, you'll want to stop long enough to take in the views of **Ben Nevis,** the highest mountain in the British Isles, rising 1,344m (4,408 ft.) from the shores of Loch Linnhe. As you continue to Inverness, another 68 miles north on A82, stop at the ruins of **Old Inverlochy Castle** (p. 346), just outside Fort William. Another stop is **Fort Augustus** (p. 322), 32 miles north of Fort William, where the **Caledonian Canal** passes through a series of stepped locks. For a good part of the rest of the drive into

Inverness the road follows the western bank of **Loch Ness** (p. 319), and drivers and their passengers are advised to keep an eye out for the elusive monster. The official **Loch Ness Monster Exhibition** (p. 320) is at Drumnadrochit, where you can also explore the ruins of **Urquhart Castle** (p. 321).

On **Day 7,** after a walk around the pretty center of **Inverness,** set out on a leisurely drive to see some of the surrounding sights. Topping the list is **Culloden Battlefield** (p. 311), where on April 16, 1746, Bonnie Prince Charlie and his Jacobite army lost their crusade to place the Roman Catholic dynasty back on the throne of Great Britain. The pretty village of **Beauly** (p. 318) surrounds a picturesquely ruined abbey. Either spend the night in Inverness or head back to back to Edinburgh on the A9. The drive of 160 miles will take you about 3½ hours and the first leg takes you through **Cairngorms National Park** (p. 327), a glorious landscape of mountain tundra, pinewoods, and 55 summits climbing more than 900m (2,970 ft.).

SCOTLAND IN 2 WEEKS

A 2-week itinerary tacks on some island hopping. First, you'll travel to the far north and the fascinating Orkneys, where your attention will probably be divided between the spectacle of 5,000-year old ruins and the antics of seabirds and other wildlife. Then it's onto the Isle of Skye, just maybe the most beautiful place in all of Scotland.

Days 1–7

Follow the itinerary outlined above in "Scotland in 1 Week."

Day 8: Inverness to Orkney

Inverness is temptingly close to **Orkney** (chapter 13), the island chain that trails north off the northernmost coast. The green, fertile, mostly low-lying islands are spellbinding, littered with the tombs, houses, and monuments of early peoples who farmed here 5,500 years ago and are also a haven for sea birds, otters, seals, and other wildlife. Set off north on the A9 for the 111-mile trip to **Scrabster,** where you will catch the ferry; see p. 341 for details on getting to Orkney. Break up the drive in **Dornoch** (p. 333), 43 miles north of Inverness, with a famous golf club, ancient cathedral, and a beach backed by dunes where you can stretch your legs. If you're not rushing to catch a ferry, pull off the A9 again at **Golspie,** 12 miles north, and tour **Dunrobin Castle** (p. 336), set in formal gardens and, with turrets and towers, looking like it was cut out of the pages of an illustrated storybook. The Scrabster ferry lands you in **Kirkwall** (p. 395), a good base for exploring the islands.

Days 9–11: Orkney

A walk around Kirkwall on the morning of **Day 9** provides a glimpse into Orkney's Norse past at **St Magnus Cathedral** (p. 398) and the ruined **Bishop's Palace and Earl's Palace** (p. 396) across the road. Then it's time to delve into the even more distant past at the so-called **Heart of Neolithic Orkney** (p. 406), 13 miles west of Kirkwall. Standing stones, tombs, and a village (Skara Brae) attest to the presence of a community that was thriving here as long as 5,000 years ago.

On **Day 10,** make the drive 25 miles southwest to the salty old port town of **Stromness** (p. 403), where sailors who accompanied Captain Cook on his voyages once caroused. The **Stromness Museum** takes in a generous sweep of local history, with Buddo, a 5,000-year-old figurine, and artifacts from the German fleet that sank in nearby **Scapa Flow** in 1919. The road from Stromness drops south across the **Churchill Barriers** (p. 409), causeways built during World War II to provide a safe harbor for the British fleet, to **St Margaret's Hope,** a quaint port and fishing village on the island of South Ronaldsay. Along the way, pull over onto the little islet of Lamb Holm to see the **Italian Chapel** (p. 409), two conjoined Nissen huts that Italian POWs imprisoned here during World War II painted with dazzling biblical scenes. A trip to the southern tip of South Ronaldsay brings you to another millennia-old sight, the **Tomb of the Eagles** (p. 409), so-called because the giant birds were put into service to peck the flesh and viscera off the interred. Claustrophobics be warned: To enter, it's necessary to lie flat on a trolley to traverse a low tunnel,

On **Day 11** it's time to see more of the islands, so take the ferry to **Westray** (p. 417). The 500 or so residents share their island with an estimated 100,000 seabirds, many of whom nest on the sea cliffs at **Noup Cliffs Nature Reserve,** known as "Seabird City" for obvious reasons. The island is also home to the **Orkney Venus,** the oldest known representation of the human form found in Scotland. A visit to Westray comes with an added attraction—a 2-minute jaunt on the world's shortest commercial airplane trip to little **Papa Westray** (p. 419). You can walk or bike around the little island, or join a ranger guided tour (p. 420) to see the **Knap of Howar,** one of the oldest structures in Europe, and enjoy the wilds of the **RSPB North Hill Nature Reserve** and its sea cliffs teeming with bird life. On some days you can take a ferry directly back to Kirkwall from Papa Westray or you will make the connection in Westray.

Days 12–14: Isle of Skye

Day 12 is spent traveling as you make the scenic trip back through the Highlands to the **Isle of Skye.** Begin with the short ferry crossing from St. Margaret's Hope to Gill's Bay, then follow the A9 south from there toward Inverness then the A832 west to Kyle of Lochalsh and the bridge crossing to Skye; the drive from Gill's Bay to Kyle is about 200 miles,

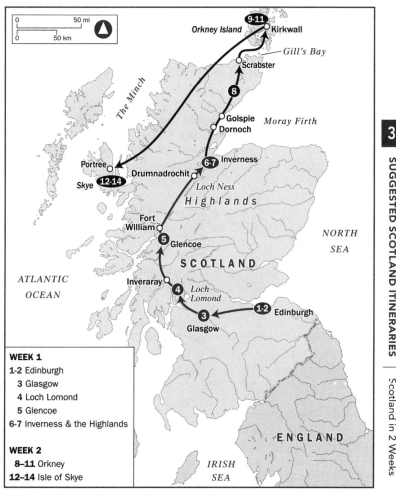

Scotland in 2 Weeks

WEEK 1
1-2 Edinburgh
3 Glasgow
4 Loch Lomond
5 Glencoe
6-7 Inverness & the Highlands

WEEK 2
8–11 Orkney
12–14 Isle of Skye

4 hours. With a good choice of lodging and proximity to many sights, **Portree** (p. 374) is a handy base on Skye.

A good way to see a lot of Skye in a short time is with a small-group minibus tour with **Real Scottish Journeys** or many other operators (p. 372). Most leave from Portree. This option spares you the wear-and-tear of driving on Skye's single-track roads and cuts down on summer-time congestion that's a growing concern on the popular island. Whether traveling on your own or with a tour, the must-see agenda for **Day 13** includes the **Fairy Pools** (p. 374) and **Neist Point** (p. 377), in the far west, **Fairy Glen** (p. 374), a domain of wee folk in the north, and the

41

almost ridiculously scenic splendor on the **Trotternish Peninsula,** including the peaks and bluffs of the **Quiraing** (p. 375) and the rocky pinnacles around the **Old Man of Storr** (p. 375).

You can enjoy a final adventure on **Day 14** on one of the island's most scenic outings (and that's saying a lot) with **Bella Jane Boat Trips** (p. 381), from **Elgol** across Loch Scavaig into the craggy **Cuillin mountains,** where you're left at the base of the hills to make a short trek across the rock-strewn landscape to freshwater **Loch Coruisk**. A less strenuous outing in the afternoon takes you to **Dunvegan Castle** (p. 376), home to the Macdonald clan, where diversions include a stroll through the gardens and short boat trip onto **Loch Dunvegan** for a look at seals and herons, and of course, the spectacle of the castle rising across the shimmering waters. The trip back to Edinburgh from Kyle of Lochalsh is 201 miles, 4½ hours on the A9.

SCOTLAND FOR FAMILIES

Young travelers love Scotland, and why not? Castles, boat rides, beaches, magical landscapes—what is there not to like? Here are some suggestions to help you and your kids get the most out of a trip, and to have a great time, too.

Days 1 & 2: Edinburgh

Though elegant Edinburgh shows off quite a bit of grown-up pomp and circumstance in places, for young travelers the city can seem like a big amusement park. Top stop on **Day 1** is **Edinburgh Castle** (p. 72), with its dank 18th-century prisons and the batteries of cannons that used to protect the fortress. The reward for patiently accompanying you through the castle's **Crown Jewels** exhibit can be a descent into the nearby **Real Mary King's Close** (p. 75), a long-ago bricked up warren of 17th-century houses; costumed guides tells some whopping good tales of hauntings. Maybe a brighter outlook is in order, and that comes with a climb up **Edinburgh's Camera Obscura** (p. 69), where the city views and optics are usually a big hit with curious youngsters. A scramble up at least the lower flanks of **Arthur's Seat** (p. 69) is a good way to get some fresh air, run off any extra steam, and get another view of the Edinburgh from on high.

On **Day 2** in Edinburgh, head first for the harbor in **Leith** (p. 83) to go aboard the Royal Yacht *Britannia* (p. 83), once owned by Queen Elizabeth II. From there head a few miles down the coast to **Portobello** (p. 81), Edinburgh's beach strip, where you can walk along the promenade and stop at a standup counter for some fish and chips then relax a bit on the sand. Spend the rest of the afternoon at **Craigmillar** (p. 82), Edinburgh's other castle, a fascinating medieval labyrinth well suited to a couple of hours of exploring. You can reach all these places on the city's efficient bus network (p. 65).

1-2 Edinburgh
3-4 Glasgow
5-7 Loch Lomond, Oban, & the Islands

Days 3 & 4: Glasgow

Day 3 begins with a train ride (only about 45 min.) to Scotland's largest city. After a walk around atmospheric, 17th to 19th-century **Merchant City** (p. 166) and lunch at kid-friendly **Café Gandolfi** (p. 183), walk over to George Square and board a **City Sightseeing** hop-on hop-off bus (p. 173); this is an easy way to get around the far-flung city while seeing the sights along the way. Your first stop is **Glasgow Cathedral** (p. 163), the city's oldest structure and unchanged since its completion in 1197. The real attraction for youngsters might be the **Necropolis** across the way, a Victorian city of the dead where, provided you don't find the exercise to be too ghoulish, they can wander amid elaborate tombs that litter a green hillside. From there go across town to the **Kelvingrove Art Gallery and Museum** (p. 170) in the West End. Young museumgoers will find plenty to amuse themselves in this faux-baroque palace, from beehives and Eskimo artifacts to a plane and a stuffed elephant. End the afternoon with a walk in **Kelvingrove Park** (p. 174), from where the spires and towers of **Glasgow University** poking above the trees look like something out of Hogwarts.

Spend **Day 4** along the **banks of the River Clyde.** First, take a good look at the enormous, out-of-commission **Finnieston Crane** (p. 171), once used to load trains and other heavy cargo onto ships and now a monument to the city's industrial heritage. Then step into the nearby **Riverside Museum** (p. 172), the city's transit collection, a riveting assemblage of buses, trams, cars, and just about anything else that moves, including the three-mast tall ship *Glenlee,* moored along the quay out back. The gleaming titanium-clad, crescent-shaped **Glasgow Science Centre** (p. 172) is across the river. Here, kids can learn all about marine invertebrates, the human body, ship engineering, and just about anything else having to do with science and technology and see a show in the adjacent Planetarium and IMAX theaters. The biggest thrill for many visitors is a trip up the 100m (328-ft.) tall rotating **Glasgow Tower.**

Day 5: Loch Lomond to Oban

You'll be picking up a rental car and doing some driving on **Day 5,** but distances aren't great and some fun stops will keep your young passengers from getting too squirmy in the backseat. First stop is **Balloch** (p. 255), on the shores of Loch Lomond, just 20 miles northwest of Glasgow. Kids might be disappointed not to be seeing the Loch Ness monster, but let them know that the forests and glens of surrounding **Loch Lomond and the Trossachs National Park** (p. 254) are said to be the realm of "elves, fawns, and fairies" and they'll love getting onto the open water on a **Sweeney's Cruise** (p. 254). From Balloch, it's a scenery-filled drive of 41 miles through glens and mountains and along loch shores on the A82 and A83 to **Inveraray** (p. 204). Kids, and you, too, will enjoy the views across the loch to the town, with tidy rows of white houses that look like they're part of a Lego village. Spare your young companions the trudge through the fussy staterooms of **Inveraray Castle** and settle instead for a view of the towers and turrets from the grounds. A tour of **Inveraray Jail,** complete with screams and other sound effects, is a surefire hit. Back in the car, it's only another hour, about 37 miles, to **Oban.** You should arrive in time for a pre-dinner walk along the seaside promenade.

Days 6 & 7: Oban

On **Day 6,** get a taste of the Hebrides on a **Three Isles Day Adventure** cruise with Caledonian MacBrayne (p. 358), the ferry operator that connects the islands. You'll make a short crossing to **Mull** (p. 358), and kids and adults alike should keep an eye out for the picture-book vision of seaside **Duart Castle** as the boat pulls into **Craignure.** From there, a bus takes you across the island, through moorland in the shadow of **Ben More** and past lochs with artificial islets where medieval lairds once took refuge from their enemies. At **Fionnphort,** you'll board a small boat for the short sail over to **Staffa** (p. 364). A easy hike leads past fantastic geological formations to the mouth of **Fingal's Cave,** where inrushing surf creates an eerily melodious sound (ask the kids if they recognize the tune). The island's grassy hillsides provide a good perch for observing nesting puffins. The next stop is **Iona** (p. 363), an outpost of early Christianity; young travelers might not be too enthusiastic about touring the abbey, but they will enjoy the island's sheep-filled meadows and sandy beaches. The return trip takes you back to Mull, across the island again, and from there to Oban. All the sea air and tromping across remote islands should ensure a good night's sleep for everyone.

Day 7 allows some welcome leisure time. In the morning take a look around town and walk up to **McCaig's Tower** (p. 354), a weird memorial monument that was meant to resemble the Coliseum in Rome; it provides great views up and down the coast and out to sea, all the way to Mull. An afternoon drive (or seaside hike if the troops are up for it), takes you a few miles north of town to the ruins of **Dunstaffnage Castle** (p. 355), one side of which seems to rise right out the sea; the nearby **Ocean Explorer Centre** (p. 355) has kids-oriented displays of marine life in the surrounding waters. Just down the coast, back toward town, is another castle, **Dunollie** (p. 354), also mostly in ruins but with a little exhibit in the Laird's House chronicling the days when it was a matter of survival to live in a well-defended fortress like this (complete with a staircase that could be dismantled in times of trouble). From Oban, it's a 2 hour and 15 minute direct drive back to Glasgow, about 96 miles; and 3 hours to Edinburgh, 123 miles.

ICONIC SCOTTISH LANDSCAPES IN A WEEK

This tour combines beautiful scenery, historic towns, palaces and castles, quaint fishing villages, the homes of Robert Burns—that is, everything you want to discover in Scotland. If you have the time for some extended Scottish travel, this itinerary is a great add-on to "Scotland in 1 Week" or "Scotland in 2 Weeks."

Day 1: Arran

With its forests, glens, moors, and rocky coasts the little island of **Arran** (p. 208) is often called "Scotland in Miniature." Remote and otherworldly as the island can seem, it's only a 45 minute ferry crossing from the west coast port of Ardrossan, 33 miles southwest of Glasgow. Arrive in the morning, settle into **Brodick** (p. 210), and spend the rest of the day enjoying the 60-mile circuit of the island. The road skirts pebble beaches along quiet bays where you'll want to pull over, and some other stops along the way are **Glenashdale waterfall; Arran distillery,** next to the bay at Lochranza; and **Brodick Castle,** a grand Victorian hunting lodge.

Days 2 & 3: Ayr & Wigtown

On the morning of **Day 2,** take the ferry back to Ardrossan, then follow the West Coast south on A78 and A77 for 24 miles to the resort of **Ayr** (p. 196). The poet Robert Burns was baptized here in the **Auld Kirk,** and the humble cottage where he was born and a memento-filled gallery are part of the **Robert Burns Birthplace Museum** (p. 197) in **Alloway,** 2 miles south. You can pay homage to the "ploughman poet" at the grandiose **Burns Monument.** From Ayr it's a 50 mile drive, about 1½ hours on A77 and A714, to **Wigtown** (p. 149). This quirky little place, officially known as Scotland's National Book Town, with bookshops and book-lined pubs, is a good base for exploring the mountains and coasts of the Galloway region. You should arrive in time for a late afternoon stroll through the surrounding wetlands.

On **Day 3,** a nice outing begins with a drive 10 miles south to **Whithorn** and the nearby **Isle of Whithorn** (p. 151), where St Ninian established a beachhead of Christianity in 397, and a now-ruined pilgrim's chapel and monastery have weathered the centuries. A drive back north through Wigtown takes you into **Galloway Forest Park** (p. 150). Cross through the vast tracts of forests on A712 then drop down to **Kirkcudbright** (p. 146), a seaport and artists' colony. Painters set their easels up on the salt-tinge wharves, and the works of their famous predecessors, colorists known as the Glasgow Boys, hang in the **Tolbooth Art Centre**. The A72 heads 40 miles west back to Wigtown, but make one more stop just west of Kirkcudbright at the **Marrbury Smokehouse** (p. 148) to pick up some smoked scallops. Total length of this **Day 3** drive is about 100 miles.

Day 4: Dumfries into the Borders

Leave Wigtown on the morning of **Day 4** and make the 54-mile drive east on A75 to **Dumfries** (p. 140). Spread out along the banks of the River Nith, Dumfries was the longtime home of poet Robert Burns, who is still very much in residence, in spirit at least. His statue stands above High Street, and you can visit his home, grave, favorite pub, and a museum devoted to the author of "My love is like a red, red rose" and other memorable verse. It's only fitting that a town so wholeheartedly immersed in poetry should have an outlying castle as romantic as **Caerlaverock** (p. 143); this picture-perfect compilation of red sandstone ruins rises amid wetlands along the Solway Firth 8 miles southeast of town. Now drive 20 miles north of Dumfries to **Moffat** (p. 138), a bucolic country town and onetime spa. Make a five-mile detour north up A701 toward **Peebles** to a viewpoint over the **Devil's Beef Tub** (p. 139), a sheer-sided hollow in the hills where cattle rustlers who raided farms across the English border would rest and water their stock as they traveled north to Edinburgh. Storied and scenic as the spot is, even better scenery lies ahead: Backtrack to Moffat then take the A708 route toward **Selkirk,** past

moody moors, stark hillsides with jagged outcroppings, and patches of woodland, making this one of Scotland's most scenic drives. **Grey Mare's Tail** (p. 139), one of Britain's highest waterfalls, tumbles down a mountainside about 10 miles north of Moffat, then the road skirts **St Mary's Loch** (p. 139), said to be so deep it has no bottom. From Selkirk, 35 miles northeast of Moffat, the A7 and A6091 lead the remaining 9 miles into **Melrose** (p. 120), a lovely little town and a good base for exploring the Borders region.

Days 5 & 6: Melrose & the Other Abbey Towns

At the edge of town, **Melrose Abbey** reposes in splendid ruin (the British laid waste to this and other nearby, once-thriving monastic communities in the 15th and 16th centuries), and on a morning visit on **Day 5** make sure to climb the narrow, stone spiral staircase for a view over the town, meadows, River Tweed, and surrounding Eildon Hills. It's a pleasure to stroll around the shop-filled town square then down country lanes to the banks of the River Tweed, where the narrow **Gattonside Suspension Bridge** sways above the torrent. The Tweed also flows past your next stop, **Abbotsford House** (p. 121), the baronial manor that Sir Walter Scott built 2 miles upstream in 1821; the rich interiors are a fine tribute to the author, who romantically evokes his beloved Scotland in verses and novels. Scott is buried in **Dryburgh Abbey** (p. 124), on the river bank 4 miles east of Melrose and your final stop for the day. Surrounded by yew trees and cedars of Lebanon, the mossy old stones and crumbling walls stand in splendid isolation and invite some quiet contemplation, perhaps continued over a pint in the Dryburgh Abbey Hotel (p. 126), an atmospherically faded country house next door.

Another day, another abbey or two: **Day 6** takes you first to **Kelso** (p. 116), at confluence of the River Teviot and River Tweed 15 miles east of Melrose. Towers, turrets, and buttresses suggest the onetime might of **Kelso Abbey,** the largest and richest of the Border abbeys, and visits to two grand estates at the edge of town show off secular wealth: **Floors Castle** (p. 116), at the center of a 21,000-hectare (52,000-acre) estate, is Scotland's largest inhabited castle, while golden-hued **Mellerstain** (p. 117) is the best work of 18th-century father and son architects William and Robert Adam. There's one more abbey to visit, the best preserved of them all, in **Jedburgh** (p. 127), 12 miles south of Kelso on the A698. While in town, step into the Mary Queen of Scots' Visitor Centre, a short-term residence of the young queen, whose turbulent life unfolds in the informative galleries. Melrose is 13 miles north of Jedburgh on the A68.

Day 7: East Neuk Fishing Villages

Edinburgh is just 37 miles northwest of Melrose. Whether you're heading home from the capital or nearby Glasgow, enjoy one more look at scenic Scotland by making a short excursion out to the coast of Fife and the country's most beautiful and unspoiled fishing villages, known collectively as **East Neuk.** In **Elie** (p. 230), the westernmost village, 45 miles northeast of Edinburgh, step-gabled houses surround a picture-postcard harbor. You might even be tempted to take a swim from one of the golden-sand beaches, but don't linger too long, because you want to be in **Pittenweem** (p. 232), 4 miles east on the A917, before the morning fish market shutters (Monday through Saturday); this is where, according to the song, Pittenweem Jo "guts the herrin' doon by the quay, and saves her kisses just for me." **Anstruther** (p. 232), just 1½ miles east, is a good spot for lunch, followed by a visit to the **Scottish Fisheries Museum** (p. 232), down by the harbor, and a seaside walk over to the tiny hamlet of **Cellardyke** (p. 233). The stop for the final night is **Crail** (p. 234), another 4 miles northwest, where you can cap off the day with a harborside stroll and a dinner of fish and chips. From Crail, it's 53 miles back to Edinburgh.

THE ACTIVE TRIP PLANNER

By Stephen Brewer

With a surfeit of lochs, glens, river, mountains, and coastlines, Scotland is the promised land for outdoor enthusiasts. Even that infamously wet weather rarely gets in the way of outdoor fun in this land where it's considered to be a fine day when the mist turns warm and the rain falls straight.

TEEING OFF: GOLFING IN SCOTLAND

4

Scotland is proud to call itself "the home of golf," though the game hasn't always been so well received. Monks around St Andrews weren't applauded when they diverted themselves from a schedule of daily chores and praying to play *gowf,* and in 1457 James II churlishly issued edicts prohibiting play throughout Scotland, preferring the population to hone its archery skills instead. The ban was upheld until 1502 when James IV became a golfer himself, and by the mid-1700s golf was firmly entrenched in Scotland, enjoyed by commoners and royalty alike.

Scotland has more than 550 golf courses, many of which are among the world's most famous and challenging, and scenic, too. Even Mark Twain, who groused that "golf is a good walk spoiled," would probably agree that playing a round on a Scottish golf course places you amid some spectacular landscapes, often with the surf raging along the fairways and a mountain or two rising beyond the greens. Seasoned golfers from across the globe make pilgrimages to courses such as the hallowed Old Course in St Andrews and relative newcomers enjoy the Torrance and the Kittocks, also at St Andrews. Most of Scotland's courses are municipal and therefore open to everyone and, although they can be found all over the country, many are located in the central and southern regions around Fife, Ayrshire, and East Lothian.

You don't need to lug your own set of clubs across the Atlantic, because many courses rent full or half sets. If you're female or plan on playing golf with someone who is, be aware that some courses are still restricted to men only, while others limit female players to

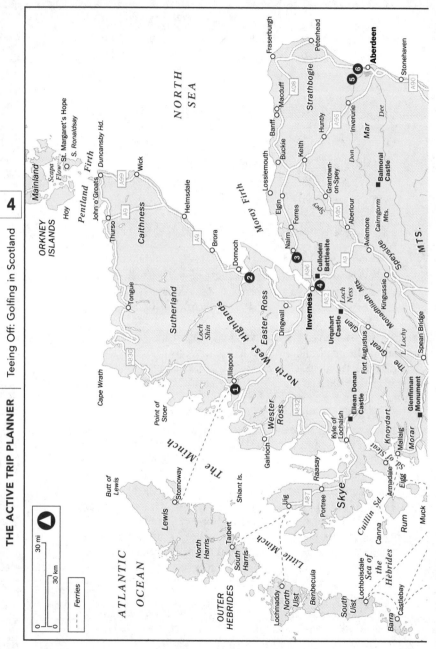

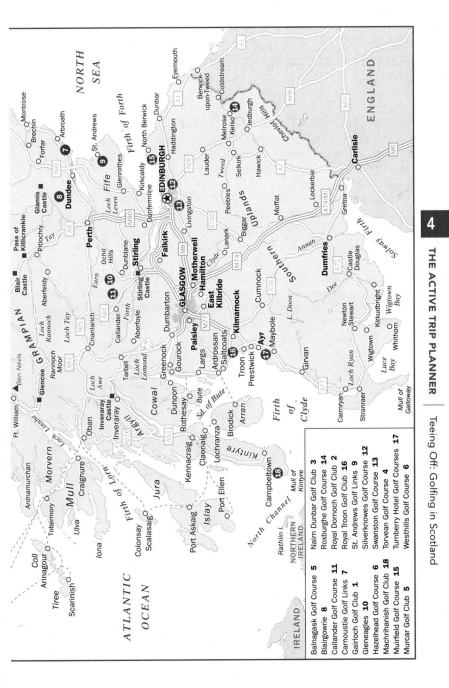

IRELAND

Balnagask Golf Course **5**
Blairgowrie **8**
Callander Golf Course **11**
Carnoustie Golf Links **7**
Gairloch Golf Club **1**
Gleneagles **10**
Hazelhead Golf Course **6**
Machrihanish Golf Club **18**
Muirfield Golf Course **15**
Murcar Golf Club **5**

Nairn Dunbar Golf Club **3**
Roxburghe Golf Course **14**
Royal Dornoch Golf Club **2**
Royal Troon Golf Club **16**
St. Andrews Golf Links **9**
Silverknowes Golf Course **12**
Swanston Golf Course **13**
Torvean Golf Course **4**
Turnberry Hotel Golf Courses **17**
Westhills Golf Course **6**

VisitScotland Golf Guide

VisitScotland provides a wealth of information for anyone planning a golfing trip or the odd round at www.visit scotland.com.

designated days. Despite this old-fashioned tradition, women's golf thrives in Scotland and the **Scottish Ladies' Golfing Association Ltd** (www.slga.co.uk) has thousands of members; its website helps women find female golfing partners.

Any serious golfer who's planning to stay in the country for a while should consider joining a local club. Membership makes it easier to bag coveted tee times. If you're not staying long, you might not bother, but remember to bring a letter from a golf club in your home country—it can open doors otherwise closed to the general public.

Access to many private clubs can be difficult, particularly those boasting so much tradition and history that waiting lists for tee-off times stretch on for up to a year in advance. One solution is to stay in a hotel that has its own course—Gleneagles or Turnberry, for example—thereby guaranteeing the availability of tee times, or you can arrange a golf tour (see below).

Many of Scotland's courses are set among some of the country's most stunning scenery. However, the weather can often be as challenging as the courses and golfers can expect to brace themselves against brisk coastal breezes and sometimes fog, all of which have left their mark on the landscape of gorse and heather that epitomizes Scotland's coastal courses.

Knowing a term or two in advance might help in picking your course. The Scots make a strong distinction between their two types of courses: links and upland. **Links courses** nestle into the sandy terrain of coastal regions and, although years of cultivation have rendered their fairways and putting greens emerald colored, they're still wild around the edges. All links courses are on or near the sea and they include some of the most famous names, such as St Andrews, Royal Troon, Turnberry, Prestwick, and Muirfield. In contrast, **upland courses** are inland and invariably consist of hilly terrain. They're usually drier and less windy than links courses. Upland courses include Gleneagles, Loch Lomond, and Pitlochry. It rains a lot in Scotland, especially on the west side of the country, so a sweater and rain gear are recommended for *all* courses.

Golf Tours

Access for non-members to the country's many golf courses hasn't always been easy. All that changed, however, with the establishment of **Golf International** (www.golfinternational.com; © **800/833-1389** or 212/986-9176 in the U.S. and Canada). The company will guarantee its clients starting times at 40 or so of Scotland's most sought-after courses, including St Andrews, Carnoustie, Royal Troon, Prestwick, and Gullane.

Potential clients, in self-organized groups of 2 to 12, produce a wish list of the courses they'd like to play. Starting times are prearranged (sometimes rigidly) with an ease that an individual golfer would find impossible. Packages can include as much or as little golf on as many courses as you wish. Weekly prices, including hotels, breakfasts, car rentals, green fees, and the services of a greeter and helpmate at the airport, range from £1,100 to £5,300 a person.

Some other U.S.-based companies specializing in golf tours are **Adventures in Golf** (www.adventures-in-golf.com; ℂ **877/424-7320** or 603/424-7320); **ITC Golf Tours** (www.itcgolftours.com; ℂ **800/257-4981** or 562/595-6905); and **Perry Golf** (www.perrygolf.com; ℂ **800/344-5257** or 910/795-1048). A Scottish-based company is **Tayleur Mayde Golf Tours** (www.tayleurmayde.com; ℂ **800/847-8064** in the U.S., or 0131/524-9554).

The Classic Courses

Scotland is jam-packed with some of the best golf courses in the world; below are details on merely a few of the most famous. Reservations must be made in advance on all these courses. In addition to the big names listed here, many additional courses are detailed in the appropriate destination chapters of this book.

The **Carnoustie Golf Links,** Links Parade, Carnoustie, Angus (www.carnoustiegolflinks.co.uk; ℂ **01241/802-270**), claims three top courses including the par-72, 6,941-yard Championship Course. Green fees are £200, the use of a caddy at £40 for 18 holes is required, clubs can be hired for £45 per round, and a trolley costs £18 per round.

Golf was first played around 1400 at the par-72 **Old Course, St Andrews,** Golf Place, St Andrews, Fife (www.standrews.org.uk; ℂ **01334/466-666**). Many consider this 6,721-yard, 18-hole course to be the real home of golf and this fabled course witnessed yet more history when it hosted the 2000 British Open and Tiger Woods became the youngest golfer to complete a grand slam (and only the fifth golfer ever to perform the feat). Green fees are £88 to £180, a caddy costs £50 plus tip, and clubs rent for £30 to £40 per round. Electric carts aren't allowed, and you can rent a trolley on afternoons only, between May and October, for £5 (or £20 for battery powered).

The 18-hole Championship Course at the **Royal Dornoch Golf Club,** Dornoch, Sutherland (www.royaldornoch.com; ℂ **01862/810-219**), 40 miles north of Inverness, has a par of 70. At this 6,514-yard course, the green fees

---

A Warning for Beginners

Newcomers to golf simply **aren't allowed to play** the country's most legendary courses. Many courses require you to produce evidence of your familiarity with the game and level of competence before you're let loose on the links.

Depending on the setting and the season, this could include a letter from your club back home citing your ability and experience, or visual proof that you've mastered a basically sound swing and an understanding of golf-related etiquette.

are £90 to £160. Caddies cost £50 per round, club rental is £30 per round, and a trolley rents for £5 per round.

The par-71 Old Course at the **Royal Troon Golf Club,** Craigend Road, Troon, Ayrshire (www.royaltroon.co.uk; ☎ **01292/311-555**), is one of the largest courses in Scotland, with 7,175 yards of playing area. The green fees are £250 for a round on the Old Course. Caddies cost £40 per round, club rental is £40 per round or £55 per day, and a trolley rents for £5 per round, £20 for an electric caddy cart.

The **Turnberry** golf courses, Ayrshire (www.turnberry.co.uk; ☎ **01655/334-060**), give priority at its famous 6,976-yard, par-72 Ailsa course to guests of the hotel (see p. 200). The green fees for this course are £175 to £375 for non-guests. Clubs rent for £50 per round; and caddy service costs £50 plus tip.

FISHING

Scotland is an angler's paradise. The country's fast-flowing rivers harbor Atlantic salmon and other game fish such as brown trout. Fishing on these rivers, as well as on Scotland's many pristine lochs, allow anglers to enjoy some of Europe's most beautiful scenery as well as world-class sport. Your hotel can often arrange permits, though in some choice spots these can be expensive; for example, a week's permit for one of the grand beats on the River Tay or River Tweed can run into hundreds, even thousands, of pounds. That said, there are many lesser-known rivers where a permit costs a mere few pounds a day.

The **Tweed** and the **Tay** are Scotland's famous salmon-rich rivers. The Tweed flows through the Scottish Borders, while the Tay—Scotland's broadest and longest river—strikes a course through Perthshire. In Aberdeenshire, the **Dee** is fished by Britain's royal family; the Queen herself has been seen casting from these banks. Other anglers prefer the **Spey,** and this region has the added attraction of being home to many of Scotland's whisky distilleries. Some well-heeled anglers prefer the remote lochs and rivers of the **Outer Hebrides.** In general, Scotland's season for salmon fishing runs from late February until late October, but these dates vary from region to region.

Types of Fishing

Here's a breakdown of terms you're likely to hear even before you cast your first line into Scotland's glittering waters:

COARSE FISHING This covers any species of freshwater fish except salmon and trout. Especially prized trophies known for putting up a spirited fight are carp, tench, pike, bream, roach, and perch. Because few lochs freeze during winter, the sport can be practiced throughout the year. Local Tourist Information Centres all over the country can provide advice.

GAME FISHING Salmon and trout (brown, rainbow, or sea) are the most desired of the game fish and the ones that have inspired the image of a fly fisherman whipping a lure and line in serpentine arcs above a loch. Many travelers dream of donning bulky rubber waders up to their waists and trying their luck in streams and freshwater lochs. Fly-fishing for salmon and trout is subject to seasonal controls and sometimes requires a permit.

SEA FISHING   This term simply refers to fishing from a beach, a rocky shoreline, or a pier. Inshore fishing involves dropping a line into ocean waters within 3 miles of any Scottish coastline; deep-sea fishing is done from a boat, more than 3 miles offshore, in a style made popular by cigar-chomping tycoons and Hemingway clones. Offshore waters are also populated with several species of shark, including porbeagle, thresher, mako, basking, and blue shark. For info on what to expect from offshore waters and fishing in general across Scotland, contact **VisitScotland** (www.visitscotland.com/see-do/active/fishing).

Fishing Clubs

Getting permits and information on worthwhile places to fish is easier if you join one of the more than 380 fishing clubs headquartered in Scotland. The oldest angling club in the world, the Ellem Fishing Club, was founded in Scotland in 1829. The **Scottish Anglers National Association** (www.sana.org.uk) believes that newcomers should learn at the side of the more experienced and offers courses in the fine art of fishing around Scotland.

BIKING, WALKING & OTHER OUTDOOR ACTIVITIES

Biking

Cycling in Scotland is extremely popular with both locals and visitors, and new routes and cycle ways are opening up all over the country. Once you escape the main urban areas, roads are generally low on traffic and high on scenery, although, due to harsh winters, November through March can be an inhospitable time for all but the most seasoned of cyclists. Motorways and some main A roads that are also dual carriageways (divided highways) are out of bounds to cyclists, and a number of the more tourist-trodden routes can be busy with cars during July and August, although it's often possible to find quieter routes or to get off the road altogether.

Your first source of information should be **Cycling Scotland** (www.cycling.scot), a government-funded organization that dispenses cycling tips and info on events and organized rides online. Serious cyclists can glean information on mountain biking, cycle speedway, cyclocross, and track racing across Scotland through the **British Cycling** website (www.britishcycling.org.uk).

Sustrans (www.sustrans.org.uk; © **0131/346-1384** in Scotland) is a U.K. charity aimed at encouraging cycling; its online shop at www.sustransshop.co.uk is a good place to purchase route maps and books on cycling in Britain.

biking AREAS

What are the best places for two wheels? Here are our picks:

- **The Galloway Region.** Southwestern Scotland doesn't draw the most visitors, but its beauty is unrivaled. A land of fields, verdant forests, and mist-shrouded hills, Galloway offers endless biking possibilities. You can get maps and route information at tourist offices in the area and at www.dumgal.gov.uk.

- **The Isle of Arran.** The largest of the Clyde Islands, Arran has been called "Scotland in miniature." And indeed, if you don't have time to see the whole country, you can get a preview of its various regions by biking this island. The northern part is mountainous, like the Highlands, while the south, with scenery akin to the Borders, resembles the Lowlands. The full circuit around the island takes about 9 hours. The tourist office distributes information on the best routes, and you can also go to www.visitarran.com.

- **The Trossachs.** Scotland's most scenic stretch for biking (as well as for driving and bucolic walks) is the Trossachs, famed as Rob Roy MacGregor country. The ideal biking spot is along Loch Katrine, 16km (10 miles) long and 3km (1¾ miles) at its widest. See chapter 9.

- **Glencoe.** What maybe the most romantic glen in Scotland features stark and grandiose mountain scenery. Rent a bike in the village and embark on an adventure, though you're likely to get rained on, as some 100 inches of rain a year are recorded. But then again, Glencoe is at its most mystical in the rain. See chapter 11.

- **The Isle of Skye.** The Hebridean island rises high into the Cuillins, a brooding mountain range you see at every turn as you pedal along. An especially scenic place to bike is the Trotternish Peninsula, known for its odd rock formations. The coastal road passes beautiful rocky seascapes, opening onto Loch Snizort and the Sound of Raasay. See chapter 12.

In addition, all local Tourist Information Centres in Scotland can provide reams of information on routes, off-road trails, and bike rental outfits.

You may take your bike without restrictions on car and passenger ferries in Scotland. It's rarely necessary to make arrangements in advance, but the transport of your bike is likely to cost £2 to £10, plus the cost of your own passage. On trains, there's no charge for bicycles, but it's advisable to make a reservation at peak times.

Wilderness Scotland (www.wildernessscotland.com; ✆ **01479/898-518** or 844-549-1622 in U.S.) leads weeklong tours through the Highlands, from Inverness to Edinburgh, a 230-miles trip that comes with hotels, meals, guided tours, and support; the cost is £1,695 per person, bike rental is extra. Local rental shops offer a wide range of bicycles, from three-speeds to mountain bikes, and accessories such as child seats and tag-a-longs. They can also provide advice on organized trips, ranging from tours of several hours to full-fledged week-long itineraries. Some local rental shops are listed in the destination chapters of this book.

Bird-Watching & Nature Holidays

Partly because of their low human population density, the moors and Highlands of Scotland attract millions of birds. For reasons not fully understood by ornithologists, the Orkneys shelter absolutely staggering numbers of birds. Bird-watchers cite the Orkneys as even richer in native species than the more isolated Shetlands, with such species as the hen harrier, short-eared owl, and red-throated diver (a form of Arctic loon) not frequently seen in the Shetlands.

Any general tour of the Orkneys will bring you into contact with thousands of birds, as well as with Neolithic tombs and other ancient sites. A worthy tour operator is **Wildabout Orkney** (www.wildaboutorkney.com; © **01856/877-737**), which leads a number of tours and shore excursions taking in the history and bird-rich nature reserves of the region. Day-long tours cost £59 per person.

During winter and early spring, the entire Solway Firth shoreline in southern Scotland around Loch Ryan, Wigtown Bay, and Auchencairn Bay is an excellent location for observing wintering wildfowl and waders. Inland, Dumfries and Galloway has a rich and varied range of birdlife, including British barn owls, kestrels, tawnies, and merlins. A useful source of information on Scotland's many sea bird colonies is the **National Trust for Scotland** (www. nts.org.uk), because around one-fifth of all seabirds in the country nest on land belonging to this organization.

Those who are interested in observing Scotland's extraordinary wildlife beyond birds should check out the **Grant Arms Hotel** (www.grantarmshotel. com; © **0800/043-8585**), in Grantown-on-Spey in the Highlands. The hotel operates as a base for outings to observe birds, mammals, and flora. A much-loved but all too rare resident of Scotland is the otter; consult the website of the **International Otter Survival Fund** (www.otter.org) for news of day-long outings that allow you a privileged glimpse of this elusive species.

Canoeing & Kayaking

Scotland's lochs, seas, and rivers are popular spots for canoeing and kayaking, and several clubs around the country offer instruction and advice. Supervising these activities is the **Scottish Canoe Association** (**SCA;** www.canoescot land.org; © **0131/317-7314**), which offers advice on access and sells books on Scottish canoe touring and white-water rafting. A recommended tour operator for either guided or self-led canoe and kayak tours in Scotland is **Wilderness Scotland** (www.wildernessscotland.com; © **01479/898-518** or 844-549-1622 in U.S.).

Hiking & Walking

Scotland is unsurpassed for those who love to walk, and hikers can expect an abundant choice of terrain, including mountain slopes, river valleys, and woodland and coastal paths. Trails for all abilities lie across every region for hour-long jaunt to days of hiking.

Scotland boasts some excellent long-distance footpaths (see below). The **Scottish Borders** is one of the finest areas for walking, with the Pentland Hills and the Tweed Valley promising rolling terrain and scenic trails. The haunting coastline of **Dumfries and Galloway** around the Solway Firth is ideal for gentle walks, or head north into the Galloway National Forest for more challenging trails.

In central Scotland's **Cairngorms National Park** (www.visitcairngorms.com), rangers offer guided walks through forested land. In the west of the country, some of Scotland's most memorable walks are found along **Loch Lomond** and in the **Trossachs** (see chapter 9).

Whichever region of Scotland you choose to walk in, local Tourist Information Centres and the visitor centers of national parks and forests are filled with leaflets and books on trails and routes. The **Ramblers** (www.ramblers.org.uk; ℰ **0131/472-7006**) can put you in touch with local walking groups. A good online guide to walks throughout Scotland is www.walkhighlands.co.uk.

Walkers can arrange accommodation and luggage transfer, and obtain detailed advice on routes from **Easyways** (www.easyways.com; ℰ **01324/714-132**), who can manage your self-guided treks along the West Highland Way and other long-distance walks. **North-West Frontiers** (www.nwfrontiers.com; ℰ **01997/421-474**), specializes in both guided and self-guided walking holidays in Scotland that lead hikers through remote glens, magnificent mountains and lochs, and isolated islands and beaches where you're likely to encounter seals, deer, and many species of birds, including divers and golden eagles. **Walkabout Scotland** (www.walkaboutscotland.com; ℰ **0845/686-1344**) specializes in small-group walking holidays in the Highlands as well as day-long hiking outings. **C-N-Do Scotland** (www.cndoscotland.com; ℰ **01786/445-703**) has been organizing hiking tours since 1984 with independent and guided treks that show off good Scottish food and wildlife on tours that can be just for a day or stretch over a week. **Scot Mountain Holidays** (www.scotmountain.co.uk; ℰ **01479/831-331**) offers hiking and biking vacations as well as "skills" courses on mountain skills. **English Lakeland Ramblers** (www.ramblers.com; in the U.S. at ℰ **800-724-8801** or 703-680-4276) can book you on one of their tours of Skye, Lewis, and Harris.

Horseback Riding & Pony Trekking

Horseback riding and trekking through Scotland's panoramic countryside across both the Lowlands and the Highlands can be enjoyed by everyone, from novices to experienced riders.

Although more adventurous riders prefer the hillier terrain of the Highlands, the Scottish Borders in the southeast (chapter 6) is the best for

o **The Southern Upland Way:**
One of Scotland's great walks begins at Portpatrick and runs 212 miles along the southwest coast to Cockburnspath, on the east coast. The route passes through some of the most dramatic scenery in the Borders, including Galloway Forest Park. See chapter 6.

o **East Neuk:** Directly south of St Andrews lie some of Scotland's loveliest fishing villages, collectively known as East Neuk. The most enchanting walk is between the villages of Pittenweem and Anstruther. It's often breezy here, with wind from the sea, so dress accordingly. The path begins at the bottom of West Braes, a cul-de-sac off the main road in Anstruther. See chapter 9.

o **The Trossachs Trail:** Ever since Sir Walter Scott published *The Lady of the Lake* and *Rob Roy,* the area has attracted hikers in search of unspoiled natural beauty. This well-trod route extends from Loch Lomond, in the west, to Callander, in the east, and also from Doune to Aberfoyle and the Loch Ard Forest, to the south. In the north, it's bounded by the Crianlarich Hills and Balquhidder, the site of Rob Roy's grave. Our favorite start for walks is the village of Brig o' Turk, between lochs Achray and Venachar, at the foot of Glen Finglas. From here you can set out in any direction, including one signposted toward the Achray Forest. There's also the Glen Finglas circular walk; and many hikers leave Brig o' Turk heading for Balquhidder via Glen Finglas. See p. 249.

o **The West Highland Way:**
Unquestionably one of Scotland's great walks begins north of Glasgow, in Milngavie. The footpath stretches 95 miles northward along Loch Lomond, going through Glencoe to Fort William and eventually to Ben Nevis, Britain's highest mountain. See p. 344.

o **The Fife Coastal Path:** Taking in old fishing harbors, artists' communities, and rugged coastal cliffs, this route stretches for 117 miles, between the Firth of Forth in the south and the Firth of Tay in the north. Along the way the route passes through cosmopolitan St. Andrews. See p. 229.

o **Ben Nevis:** Just 4 miles southeast of the town of Fort William looms Ben Nevis, Britain's highest mountain. At 1,342m (4,403 ft.), the snow-capped granite mass dominates this entire region of Scotland. This ascent can be done in a day, but you'll need to massage your feet in the evening at a local pub. See p. 346.

4

THE ACTIVE TRIP PLANNER | Biking, Walking & Other Outdoor Activities

horseback riding—in fact, it's often called Scotland's horse country. (The equivalent in the United States is Kentucky.) On the western coastline, Argyll (chapter 8) is also recommended for riding amongst dramatic scenery. The Argyll Forest Park encompasses 24,300 hectares (60,000 acres) and contains some of the finest scenery in Scotland. Trails lead through forests to sea lochs that cut deep into the park.

Pony trekking is popular across both moorland and glen. Highland ponies have been trekking tourists for years and most centers lead treks from 2½ hours to a full day, and have ponies suitable for nearly all age groups. You'll find operators in Kirkcudbright and around Stirling as well as on Shetland, plus several in the Hebrides. Local Tourist Information Centres and **VisitScotland** (www.visitscotland.com) can provide full info on regional equestrian centers.

Mountaineering

Mountain climbing in Scotland ranges from moderate treks over heather-clad hilltops to demanding rock face climbs that bear the brunt of the country's harsh winter weather. Many Scots are avid Munro baggers—that is, they climb the 282 mountains in Scotland topping 3,000 feet that are known as Munros, named for Sir Hugh Munro (1856–1919), who compiled the list of summits in 1919. Those who climb all the Munros are known as "Compleat-ers" (5,000 men and women have achieved the feat) and Scottish offices are well-populated with weekend climbers plotting their next ascents. A good online guide to Munro-bagging and other climbs and walks in Scotland is www.walkhighlands.co.uk.

The **Southern Uplands,** the **Hebrides,** and the **Highlands** contain the best mountaineering sites. The weather can turn foul during any season with almost no advance notice, creating dangerous conditions. If you're climbing rock faces, you should be familiar with basic techniques and the use of such specialized equipment as carabiners, crampons, ice axes, and ropes. Don't even consider climbing without proper instruction and equipment.

Ben Nevis is the highest (but by no means the most remote) peak in Scotland and, in fact, in the British Isles. Despite its loftiness at 1,336m (4,383 ft.), the peak has attracted some eccentrics, including one who arranged to transport a dining table and formal dinner service and a grand piano to the top.

If you want to improve your rock-climbing skills, consider joining a club or signing on for a mountaineering course at a climbing center. **Sport Scotland** (www.sportscotland.org.uk) can provide advice on reputable centers, while the **Mountaineering Council of Scotland** (www.mountaineering.scot; ✆ **01738/493-942**) is also a mine of useful information and contacts. Membership of the Council allows overnight stays at the club's climbing huts located around the country. True rock-climbing aficionados looking to earn certification should consider getting in touch with **Mountain Training** (www.mountain-training.org), which organizes a range of training schemes and qualifications.

Sailing & Watersports

Scotland has a rich maritime heritage, so you have plenty of opportunities to get afloat. There are sailing schools and charter operations all around the coasts, as well as on inland lakes and rivers. The **Royal Yachting Association,** RYA House, Ensign Way, Hamble, Hants, SO31 4YA (www.rya.org.uk; ✆ **023/8060-4100**) can provide a list of suitable companies. You might also try the website **GetMyBoat.com.**

Wherever you travel in Scotland, you're never far from the water. Windsurfing, canoeing, water-skiing, and sailing are just some of the activities available at a number of sailing centers and holiday parks. You'll find it easy to rent boats and equipment at any of the major resorts along Scotland's famous lochs. Local Tourist Information Centres and **VisitScotland** (www.visitscotland.com) can provide information on regional operators.

AND SOME NOT-SO-ACTIVE TRIPS

Of course, you can also enjoy Scotland on trips that require no more exertion than eating, sipping whisky, and enjoying the scenery.

Among the many companies offering general escorted group tours of Scotland (the price usually includes everything from airfare to hotels, meals, tours, admission costs, and local transportation) are luxury-oriented **Abercrombie & Kent** (www.abercrombiekent.com; ✆ 800-554-7016 in the U.S.), with canal and loch cruises and rail journeys on the Royal Scotsman, among other tours, and **Tauck World Discovery** (www.tauck.com; ✆ 800-788-7885 in the U.S.), with a focus on Edinburgh and the Highlands; both provide lots of comforts with prices to match. For less expensive holidays, try **Wallace Arnold Worldchoice** (www.waworldchoice.com; ✆ 0845/365-6747), with pleasantly paced bus tours around the country; the U.S.-based **Trafalgar Tours** (www.trafalgartours.com; ✆ 866-544-4434), with some all-encompassing introductory tours to Scotland; and **Maupintour** (www.maupintour.com; ✆ 800-255-4266 in the U.S.), with tours of Edinburgh and Glasgow and day trips from each.

You can sip your way through the landscapes with **Whisky Tours Scotland** (www.whisky-tours-scotland.com) or **Distillery Destinations** (www.whisky-tours.com; ✆ 0141/429-0762). **McKinlay Kidd** (www.seescotlanddifferently.co.uk; ✆ 0844/804-0020) leads a whisky explorer tour and also puts together self-guided trips to the Hebrides, Orkney, and other islands and mainland regions. **McLean Scotland** (www.mcleanscotland.com; ✆ 01738/560-435) does small-scale whisky tours as well as driving circuits of castles and other scenic high points.

At **Solway Tours** (www.solwaytours.co.uk; ✆ 07789/794-142 or 07809/239-696), the personable and well-informed Mark Turner and Lesley Watson lead personalized historic and ancestral trips of one to several days or a week, and will help clients trace their Scottish roots. **Afternoon Tea Tour** (www.afternoonteatours.com; ✆ 07873/211-856) accompanies a look around Edinburgh with tea at a country house hotel and does highly personalized, individual tours to the Isle of Skye, the Highlands, and other Scottish regions.

EDINBURGH & THE LOTHIAN REGION

By Lucy Gillmore

5

At first sight, it's probably love. How could you not fall for such a cool, classic, and cultured beauty, one whose haughty reserve melts as soon as summer festival season starts? The Scottish capital has it all: culture, history, a tongue-tantalizing culinary scene, and dazzling good looks to boot. At times it can feel more like a historical film set than a contemporary political powerhouse. However, Edinburgh is not a city stuck in the past. In fact, there have been concerns over the last few years that it might be moving forward a little too quickly. Controversial developments in the center of the city have even threatened to put its World Heritage status in jeopardy.

Surprisingly compact and built around a series of hills, Edinburgh is peppered with tiny neighborhoods, each with its own distinct character and charm. Dipping in and out of these is one of the best ways to explore the city, and to shake off the crowds. Away from the main arteries there are pockets of peace where it feels almost sleepily provincial. All you can hear is the rumble of cars on cobbles as you breathe in the heady scent of hops and soak up the history seeping out of the stonework.

Edinburgh is also, of course, host to one of the biggest cultural shindigs in the world. Each summer, the city's famous reserve melts away and the low-key capital cranks it up a gear. Visitors from all over the world flock to the **Edinburgh Festival** and **Fringe Festival**, and the Royal Mile becomes a rippling river of ticket touts, street performers, and face-painters as the whole city turns into a vast open-air arena.

Edinburgh has layer upon layer of history to peel back. The city is crammed with world-class museums, crowned by the **National Museum of Scotland.** Art lovers can dip into the **Scottish National Galleries,** which showcase artwork from the medieval to the contemporary. Escape the city streets for the wild volcanic heights of **Arthur's Seat,** or meander the maritime shores of the Port of **Leith.**

Edinburgh is Scotland's culinary as well as its political capital, with an exciting and ever-diversifying restaurant scene. In the center, recent large-scale development has enticed the large chains up from London and restaurants such as the Ivy on St Andrews Square. Head out to neighborhoods like Stockbridge and Leith, where you can find Michelin-starred restaurants, local seafood eateries, and gastropubs.

Princes Street forms the city's backbone of high street brands and department stores, topped by old stalwart **Jenners.** A block north, **George Street** is lined with higher-end high street names; however, for independent boutiques you'll need to head to the **West End Village**. There's more eclectic shopping in the **Old Town,** where vintage clothing, cashmere, and tweed stores gather around Grassmarket. The Royal Mile is targeted at tourists with tacky tartan, whisky, and ginger wig shops.

Don't Leave Edinburgh Without . . .

Exploring Edinburgh Castle. This brooding castle is Edinburgh's most iconic landmark and must-see tourist destination for good reason. Amazing views, intriguing history, and a swath of Scotland's treasures are waiting to be experienced inside its mighty battlements. See p. 72.

Discovering Edinburgh's "village" neighborhoods. The center of the city can be a heaving mass of tourists. To see the real Edinburgh, head north to Stockbridge, with its delis and farmers' market, or south to Bruntsfield to wander its chic boutiques and cafes. See p. 66.

Taking in the view from Arthur's Seat. Take a walk on the wild side of Scotland's capital and hike the well-trodden path to the summit of this magnificent 251m (823-ft.) high natural landmark. The easy climb is a small price to pay for the views waiting at the top. See p. 69.

Descending into the underground vaults. Come face to face with the dark side of Edinburgh's history and many of its prominent ghosts on a tour into the long buried vaults of Old Town, which some claim are the most haunted places in Britain. See p. 75.

Taking a boat trip to Inchcolm. Escape to the sea onboard a boat bound for Inchcolm island in the heart of the Firth of Forth, home to Scotland's finest medieval abbey and local wildlife. See p. 110.

ESSENTIALS

GETTING THERE Edinburgh Airport (www.edinburghairport.com; ✆ **0844/448-8833**) is 7½ miles west of the city center. Double-decker **Airlink** buses (www.lothianbuses.co.uk; ✆ **0131/555-6363**. £4.50 one-way, £7.50 round-trip) make the round-trip from the airport to Edinburgh city center every 10 minutes, letting you on and off at Haymarket or Waverley train

Edinburgh's Old and New Towns have been designated a UNESCO World Heritage site, in recognition of their historical and architectural importance. **Edinburgh World Heritage** (www.ewh.org.uk) provides a wealth of information to help visitors make the most of their time here.

You can follow a range of themed trails, such as *Walk in the Footsteps of Robert Louis Stevenson*, around the Heritage Site; pick these up at the **VisitScotland iCentre** (p. 65) or download them from Edinburgh World Heritage's website, along with accompanying podcasts.

stations. You can buy a single or return ticket or pay contactless with a debit or credit card. The journey takes around 25 minutes. You can also take the smart new **tram** into town. They run every 7 to 12 minutes from the airport to York Place via Haymarket train station and Princes Street; the fare is £6 one-way, £8.50 return. You buy your ticket from the machine at the stop. There's a busy **taxi** stand at the airport and a ride into town costs around £25, depending on traffic.

Edinburgh has two **train** stations—**Haymarket** in the West End and **Waverley**, the main station in the city center at the east end of Princes Street. **Virgin Trains East Coast** (www.virgintrainseastcoast.com; ℂ **0345/722-5333**) link London's King's Cross with Waverley station, depart London every hour or so, take about 4½ hours, and cost from £143 round-trip, with frequent online promotions. There is also the **Caledonian Sleeper** (www.sleeper.scot; ℂ **0330/060-0500**) service, overnight trains from London with sleeper berths. One-way fares cost from £145. There's a taxi stand in Waverley station, and Edinburgh's bus station is only a short walk away.

The least expensive way to travel between London and Edinburgh is by **bus,** but it's an 8½ hour journey. **MegaBus** (uk.megabus.com; ℂ **0900/160-0900**) is the cheapest option, with one-way fares costing from £14.20. **National Express** (www.nationalexpress.com; ℂ **0871/781-8181**) has one-way fares costing anywhere between £10.50 and £82. Buses depart from London's Victoria Coach Station to Edinburgh's **St Andrews Square Bus Station.**

If you're **driving,** Edinburgh is 46 miles east of Glasgow and 105 miles north of Newcastle-upon-Tyne in England. No express motorway links Edinburgh with London, which lies 393 miles to the south. The M1 from London takes you part of the way north, and then becomes the A1—otherwise known as the "Great North Road"—leading drivers along the coast to enter Edinburgh from the east. Allow 8 hours or more if you're driving from London. A city bypass, the A720, circles Edinburgh and routes from all other directions meet this road, making it easy to enter the city from whichever point suits you. The M8 links Edinburgh with Glasgow and connects with the city on the west side of the bypass, while the M90/A90 travels down from the north over the Queensferry Crossing (www.theforthbridges.org), the longest three-tower, cable-stayed bridge in the world when it opened in 2017.

VISITOR INFORMATION Edinburgh's main **VisitScotland iCentre** (www.visitscotland.com; ✆ **0131/473-3868**: Mon–Sat 9am–7pm in summer, 10am–7pm on Sun and 9am–5pm winter, 10am–5pm Sun) is at the street level of Princes Street Mall, next to Waverley train station and the Balmoral Hotel. Staff can also help book a place to stay and sightseeing tickets. There's also an info desk at Edinburgh Airport (✆ **0131/473-3690**).

GETTING AROUND Many of Edinburgh's attractions are scattered around a small area along or around the Royal Mile, Princes Street, or one of the major streets in New Town. As such, it's easy to explore on foot.

Edinburgh's **bus** system is operated by **Lothian Buses** (www.lothianbuses. co.uk; ✆ **0131/555-6363**); its frequent, inexpensive service covers every corner of the city. The fare for a one-way journey of any distance is £1.70 for adults, 80p for children ages 5 to 15, free for children under 4. You need to have the exact change to buy tickets onboard. A **Day Saver Ticket** allows 1 day of unlimited travel on city buses and trams within the city zone at a cost of £4 for adults and £2 for children. Other options include the 1-week Rida-card, mobile ticketing via your phone and the Citysmart top-up card. The different ticket options are outlined on the website so you can choose the best one for you. Route maps and timetables can also be downloaded from the website or found at one their travel shops on either Waverley Bridge or Hanover Street. The latter is open Monday through Friday 9am to 6pm and Saturday 9am to 5:30pm. The Waverley Bridge Travel shop is open 9am to 7pm Monday and Thursday, 9am to 6pm Tuesday, Wednesday and Friday, 9am to 5:30pm Saturday and 10am to 5:30pm on Sunday.

You can hail a **taxi** or pick one up at any of Edinburgh's numerous taxi stands. Meters begin at £2.10 and increase £2 every ⅔ mile. Taxi stands are at Hanover Street, North St Andrews Street, Waverley Station, Haymarket Station, Lothian Road, and Lauriston Place. Fares are displayed in the front of the taxi, including extra charges for night drivers or destinations outside the city limits. To call a taxi, try **City Cabs** (✆ **0131/228-1211**) or **Central Taxis** (✆ **0131/229-2468**).

Many residents don't **drive** around the center of Edinburgh; public transport is very good, the city's traffic system is tricky, and parking is expensive and difficult to find. Metered parking is available (exact change required) but some zones are only for permit holders; vehicles with no permit are towed away and Edinburgh's traffic wardens are notoriously active in handing out tickets. A yellow line along the curb indicates no parking. Major parking lots are at Castle Terrace, convenient for Edinburgh Castle, Lothian Road, and the West End; and St John Hill, convenient for the Royal Mile.

The cobbled streets in the New and Old Towns can make **cycling** a challenge, as does the fact that the city is hilly. That said, there's a network of bike paths around the city that many love. Edinburgh has been a bit slow to join the party when it comes to bike share schemes, but a pilot program was set to launch in late 2018. At press time, no website was yet available. Bike rental companies include **Leith Cycles** (www.leithcycleco.com; ✆ **0131/467-7775**); their rentals start at £12 for a half-day and include a helmet, lock, map, and puncture repair kit. Children's bikes, trailers, and tag-alongs can also be rented.

CITY LAYOUT   Edinburgh is a compact city. At its center are the Old and New Towns, separated by the grassy divide of Princes Street Gardens. The **Royal Mile** forms the spine of the **Old Town,** snaking downhill from Edinburgh Castle to the Palace of Holyroodhouse. A labyrinth of ancient wynds (small lanes) and steep stone stairways spreads out on either side, while to the south is the **Grassmarket,** a wide, open street where criminals were once hung on the gallows. Today cafes, pubs, and shops line this historic thoroughfare, spilling out onto its pavements in summer.

To the north of Old Town is the Georgian **New Town,** a masterpiece of neoclassical town planning, its broad avenues, leafy squares and elegant crescents created between 1765 and 1850 in response to overcrowding in the dark and claustrophobic Old Town. Peppered with gourmet restaurants, buzzing bars, smart shops and attractions, such as the **National Portrait Gallery,** the New Town rolls down to the village-like **Stockbridge** with its cafes, delis and boutiques. From here you can walk along the city's narrow, meandering river, the Water of Leith to **Dean Village** (another rural pocket) and the **National Gallery of Modern Art.** Or head in the other direction and you'll emerge in the revamped docklands of Leith with its Michelin-starred restaurants and gastropubs.

Between the city center and Haymarket is the **West End,** where there are a cluster of performance spaces such as **Usher Hall** and the **Traverse Theatre.** Edinburgh's **Southside** is mostly residential, with the sprawling park known as the **Meadows,** Edinburgh University, and suburbs such as Marchmont.

Neighborhoods in Brief

OLD TOWN   The **Royal Mile** is the backbone of the Old Town, a medieval thoroughfare snaking along the spine of the volcanic crag that supports **Edinburgh Castle** to the flat land of Holyrood Park—home to the **Palace of Holyroodhouse** and the imposing **Arthur's Seat.** English author Daniel Defoe described the Royal Mile as "the largest, longest, and finest street for buildings and number of inhabitants in the world." Little has changed today, and you haven't really experienced Edinburgh until you've explored the Old Town's dark, history-soaked streets.

NEW TOWN   North of the Old Town, Edinburgh's New Town is one of the largest Georgian developments in the world, a network of elegant squares, terraces, and circuses. It stretches from Haymarket in the west to Abbeyhill in the east and from Canonmills at its northern perimeter to Princes Street, its main artery, along the southern tier. The **West End Village** north of Shandwick Place is peppered with chic shops and gastropubs. While technically

Neighborhoods in Brief

EDINBURGH & THE LOTHIAN REGION

Firth of Forth

0 1 mi
0 1 km

Golf Course
Lighthouse

NEWHAVEN
Royal Yacht Britannia

GRANTON

MUIRHOUSE
CRAMOND
Lauriston
Castle
LEITH
Ferry Rd.
A902
Water of Leith
Leith Walk
A199
Seafield Rd.

ROYAL
BOTANIC
GARDENS
Central Edinburgh

CLERMISTON BLACKHALL
Telford Rd.
Queensferry Rd.
RESTALRIG
Calton Hill
Holyroodhouse
PORTOBELLO
Willowbrae Rd.

MURRAYFIELD
Edinburgh Zoo
HAYMARKET
Princes St.
Edinburgh
Castle
HOLYROOD
PARK
Arthur's
Seat
DUDDINGSTON
St. John's Rd.
Corstorphine Rd.

CORSTORPHINE
Gorgie Rd.
Union Canal
CHURCH HILL
MARCHMONT
NEWINGTON
Braid Burn
NIDDRIE
CRAIGMILLAR

STENHOUSE
SIGHTHILL
Calder Rd.
A70
MERCHISTON
GRANGE
MORNINGSIDE
Craigmillar
Castle

CRAIGLOCKHART
A702
Royal
Observatory
Old Dalkeith Rd.
Gilmerton Rd.

Water of Leith
BRAID
LIBERTON

WESTER HAILES
A701

JUNIPER
GREEN
A70 A720
COLINTON
Comiston Rd.
FAIRMILEHEAD

SCOTLAND
Edinburgh

CURRIE
A720
A702
0 50 mi
0 50 km
ENGLAND

outside New Town, Edinburgh's **West End** leads along Lothian Road where you'll find many of the city's theatres, cinemas, and nightclubs.

BRUNTSFIELD   This suburb to the southwest of the Old Town is fringed by **Bruntsfield Links,** the park where James IV gathered his Scottish army before marching to their devastating defeat at Flodden in 1513. It's also the site of the mass graves of the city's plague victims. Today, the main thoroughfare, Bruntsfield Place, is lined with quirky boutiques and bustling cafes.

STOCKBRIDGE   Northwest of New Town, Stockbridge is one of Edinburgh's hidden gems. Once a village on the outskirts of the city, it was incorporated into Edinburgh in the 19th century, yet still retains a village feel. This is an upmarket area with a bohemian edge and is known for its delis, cafes and galleries, and its proximity to the **Water of Leith** and Edinburgh's **Botanic Gardens.**

LEITH   Once a down-at-heel area, the revamped **Port of Leith,** the city's major harbor, opens onto the Firth of Forth. The port might not flex the maritime muscle it used to, but the regeneration has given it a new lease of life, the waterfront now lined with fish restaurants and lively pubs. Today, cruise ships dock at Leith's Ocean Terminal, and although this isn't an area in which many visitors stay, it's one of the best places in the city to eat and a must-see for anyone wanting to glimpse the often overlooked maritime side of Edinburgh past and present.

[FastFACTS] EDINBURGH

ATMs There are ATMs all over Edinburgh, and most are open 24/7.

Babysitters A reliable service is provided by Super Mums (www.supermums.co.uk; ℂ 0131/225-1744).

Business Hours Banks are usually open Monday through Friday 9am to 5pm; some also open on Saturdays from 10am to 3pm. Stores generally open Monday through Saturday 9 or 10am to 6pm; on Thursday some stores open until 8pm. Many stores are open on Sunday from 11am to 4 or 5pm. Offices generally open Monday through Friday 9am to 5pm.

Doctors & Dentists If you have a dental emergency, go to the **Chalmers Dental Centre,** 3 Chalmers St. (ℂ 0131/536-4800), which has a walk in clinical service. Children under 16 will be treated at the Children's Department of the **Edinburgh Dental Institute** on Lauriston Place (ℂ 0131/536-1129). On evenings and weekends, call the **Lothian Dental Advice Line**

ℂ 0131/536-4800 or **NHS 24** on ℂ 08454/242424. You can seek advice from NHS Lothian's Lauriston Building, 1 Lauriston Place (ℂ 0131/536-1000). However, the city's 24-hour Accident and Emergency Department is located at the **Royal Infirmary of Edinburgh,** 51 Little France Crescent, Old Dalkeith Road (www.nhslothian.scot.nhs.uk; ℂ 0131/536-1000).

Emergencies Call ℂ 999 for the police, an ambulance, or firefighters.

Newspapers Published since 1817, *The Scotsman* is a daily newspaper. Along with national and international news, it has strong coverage of the arts.

Pharmacies There are no 24-hour pharmacies (also called chemists) in Edinburgh. The major one is **Boots,** 101–103 Princes St. (ℂ 0131/225-8331), open Monday through Friday 8am to 7pm (Thurs til 8pm) and Sunday 10am to 6pm. You can also try a 24-hour supermarket such as **Asda,** 2 Sandpiper Dr., Newhaven (ℂ 0131/561-2300).

Police See "Emergencies," above.

Post Office There are many post offices dotted around the city; a central option is located inside the St James Centre on Leith Street. It's open Monday through Saturday 9am to 5:30pm. For postal information and customer service, call ℂ 0845/722-3344.

Safety Edinburgh is generally a safe city to walk around any time of the day or night—in fact, it's one of Europe's safest capitals. However, like any city, crimes such as muggings do occur, so stay aware of your surroundings.

Toilets Don't hesitate to use Edinburgh's public toilets, often marked WC and located at strategic corners and squares throughout the city. They're perfectly safe and clean, but likely to be closed late in the evening. Toilets can also be found at railway and bus stations as well as in department stores, museums, and art galleries. Many cafes, pubs, and restaurants only allow patrons to use their toilets.

EXPLORING EDINBURGH
Along the Royal Mile

The Old Town's **Royal Mile ★★★** is, in fact, 1 mile and 107 yards long and stretches from Edinburgh Castle all the way down to the Palace of Holyroodhouse. It's made up of a chain of linked streets (Castlehill, Lawnmarket, High Street, and Canongate) and is lined with a mix of museums, churches and shops selling cashmere, tweed and whisky—and a fair bit of tartan tat—to the tourists who flock here. Walking its length you'll see some of the most fascinating parts of the old city, including a section of the **Flodden Wall** if you veer off along St Mary Street. Built in the 16th century, this 1.2m-thick (4-ft.) structure used to mark the city limits. The point where a fortified gateway once stood as it crossed the Royal Mile was known as the World's End. Today a pub of the same name now stands near the spot.

Holyrood Park, which opens out at the bottom of the Royal Mile, is a dramatic landscape, characterized by rocky crags, a loch, sweeping meadows, and a tiny ruined chapel. The 250m-high (820-ft.) peak of **Arthur's Seat ★★★** is the park's crowning glory, rewarding all who climb with heart-stopping views over Edinburgh, the Pentland Hills and Firth of Forth beyond.

Camera Obscura ★ OBSERVATION POINT   This quirky warren of wonders (from old-school to high-tech) is Edinburgh's oldest purpose-built tourist attraction. An optician, Maria Short, added the white Victorian Outlook Tower to the building in 1853 and topped it with a periscope, which throws a revolving image of Edinburgh's streets and buildings onto a circular table in the top chamber. You can pick people up on a piece of paper as they walk up to the castle—while the guide shares tales of the city's landmarks and history. The other five floors are crammed with interactive optical illusion exhibits—great fun for kids.

Castlehill. www.camera-obscura.co.uk. ℂ **0131/226-3709.** £16 adults, £14 seniors and students, £12 children 5–15. July–Aug daily 9am–10pm; Sept–Oct and Apr–June daily 9:30am–8pm; Nov–Mar daily 10am–7pm.

City Art Centre ★ GALLERY   Spread over six floors of an imposing former warehouse behind Waverley station, the City Art Centre boasts an impressive collection of Scottish art from the 17th century to the present day, including works by the Glasgow Boys, the Scottish Colourists, and the Edinburgh School. A changing program of exhibitions showcase paintings, drawings, photographs, sculpture, and installations from subjects as broad as Highland Art to human anatomy, alongside new work from local and international artists.

2 Market St. www.edinburghmuseums.org.uk. ℂ **0131/529-3993.** Free admission. Wed–Sat 10am–5pm; Sun noon–5pm.

Edinburgh Attractions

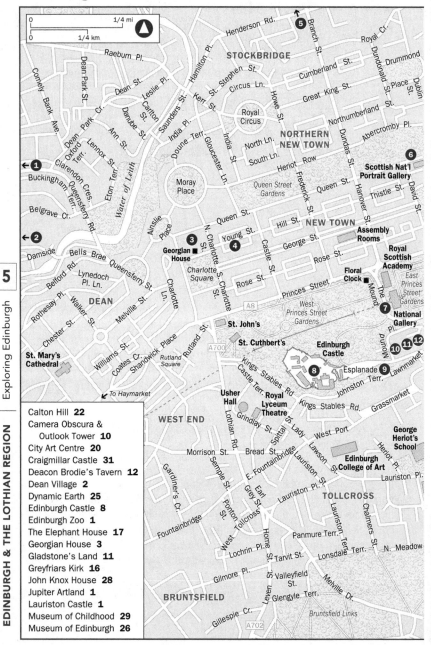

Calton Hill **22**
Camera Obscura &
    Outlook Tower **10**
City Art Centre **20**
Craigmillar Castle **31**
Deacon Brodie's Tavern **12**
Dean Village **2**
Dynamic Earth **25**
Edinburgh Castle **8**
Edinburgh Zoo **1**
The Elephant House **17**
Georgian House **3**
Gladstone's Land **11**
Greyfriars Kirk **16**
John Knox House **28**
Jupiter Artland **1**
Lauriston Castle **1**
Museum of Childhood **29**
Museum of Edinburgh **26**

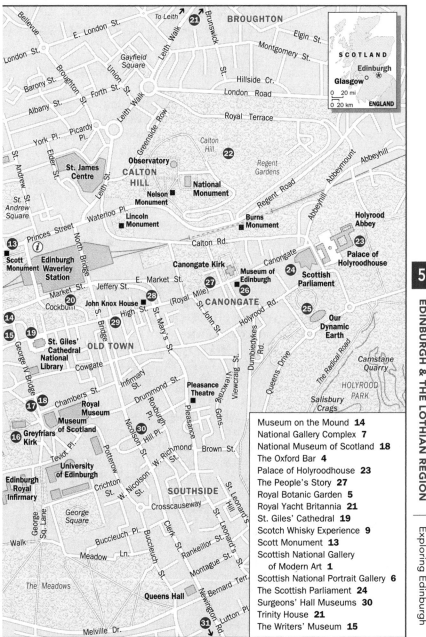

Museum on the Mound **14**
National Gallery Complex **7**
National Museum of Scotland **18**
The Oxford Bar **4**
Palace of Holyroodhouse **23**
The People's Story **27**
Royal Botanic Garden **5**
Royal Yacht Britannia **21**
St. Giles' Cathedral **19**
Scotch Whisky Experience **9**
Scott Monument **13**
Scottish National Gallery
   of Modern Art **1**
Scottish National Portrait Gallery **6**
The Scottish Parliament **24**
Surgeons' Hall Museums **30**
Trinity House **21**
The Writers' Museum **15**

Edinburgh Castle ★★★ HISTORIC SITE   Few locations in Scotland have lore equal to that of Edinburgh Castle. The very early history is somewhat vague, but in the 11th century, Malcolm III and his Saxon queen, later venerated as St Margaret, founded a building on this spot. There's only a fragment of their original pile in **St Margaret's Chapel,** which dates principally to the 1100s. After centuries of destruction, demolitions, and upheavals, the buildings that stand today are basically those that resulted from the castle's role as a military garrison over the past 300-odd years. It still barracks soldiers, and many of the displays are devoted to military history, which might limit the place's appeal for some. The castle vaults served as prisons for foreign soldiers in the 18th century, and these great storerooms held hundreds of Napoleonic soldiers in the early 19th century. Some prisoners made wall carvings still seen today.

However, it is not all about war. Visitors can see where Mary Queen of Scots gave birth to James VI of Scotland (later James I of England) in 1566. Scottish Parliaments used to convene in the Great Hall of the castle. Another highlight for visitors is the Scottish Crown Jewels, used at the coronations, along with the scepter and sword of the state of Scotland and the infamous Stone of Scone.

It's not the easiest attraction to navigate if you have a disability—there are cobblestones, steep hills, and the chapel and prisons have narrow entrances. But there is a mobility vehicle and a number of wheelchairs. There is a timed ticketing system in place so it is best to book your tickets online in advance to get the slot you would like and a cheaper price.

Castlehill. www.edinburghcastle.scot. ℗ **0131/225-9846.** £17 adults, £13.60 seniors (60+), £10.20 children 5–15, free for children under 5. Apr–Sept 9:30am–6pm, Oct–Mar 9:30am–5pm last admission 1 hr. before closing.

Gladstone's Land ★ HISTORIC SITE   Dip into this 17th-century merchant's house on the Royal Mile, one of the few surviving Old Town tenements (many were pulled down and rebuilt in the 1800s) to get a real feel for the living conditions at this time—of the wealthier classes. There's a reconstructed shop at street level and upstairs an apartment, decorated in the original style with period furnishings and a glorious painted ceiling dating back to 1620. Access is now only via guided tour, which must be booked in advance. Times vary so check the events page of the website. The top two floors can be rented through the National Trust for Scotland as a holiday apartment.

477B Lawnmarket. www.nts.org.uk. ℗ **0131/226-5856.** £7 adults, £5 seniors and children.

John Knox House ★ HISTORIC SITE   Wonky, wonderful, and possibly the prettiest dwelling in Edinburgh's Old Town, the John Knox House is characteristic of the "lands" that used to flank the Royal Mile. Its interior is a showcase of medieval craftsmanship, including a frescoed ceiling in The Oak Room. John Knox himself is an important figure, the acknowledged father of the Presbyterian Church of Scotland, the Protestant tenets of which he established in 1560. While some regard him as a prototypical Puritan, he actually proposed progressive changes in the ruling of the church and in education. Knox lived at a time of great religious and political upheaval; he spent 2 years as a galley slave and later lived in exile in Geneva. Upon his return, he became minister of St Giles and worked to ensure the Reformation's success in Scotland. Even if you're not overly interested in the firebrand reformer (who may never have lived here anyway), this late-15th-century house is well worth a visit just to learn about one man who definitely did: James Mossman, jeweler and goldsmith to Mary Queen of Scots, who resided here from the 1550s until his execution in 1573. Today Knox's house is joined to the Scottish Storytelling Centre, with its bright cafe and performance space.

43-45 High St. www.tracscotland.org. ℭ **0131/556-9579.** £5 adults, £4 seniors, £1 children 7 and up, under-7 free. Mon–Sat 10am–6pm (Sun 10am–6pm July–Aug).

Museum of Childhood MUSEUM   This small museum was the first in the world to devote itself solely to the history of childhood. Toys and games from the 18th to 21st centuries, including child-size pedal cars, dollhouses, and toy soldiers have taken visitors on a journey down memory lane since it opened in 1955. It had started to feel a little dated, however, and, with around 60,000 exhibits, a bit cluttered. A much-needed refurbishment was completed in 2018, to sweep away the Miss Havisham element and transform the space with a series of interactive zones.

42 High St. www.edinburghmuseums.org.uk. ℭ **0131/529-4142.** Free admission. Mon–Sat 10am–5pm; Sun noon–5pm.

Museum of Edinburgh MUSEUM   Across from the Canongate Tolbooth, the Museum of Edinburgh is housed in Huntly House, a restored 16th-century mansion that fans of the TV series Outlander might recognize as one of the locations in the third series. Today, this old-school, warren-like museum is dedicated to the history of Edinburgh and features faithfully crafted reproductions of rooms inspired by the city's traditional industries, including glassmaking and pottery. Original plans for New Town are also on display along with the National Covenant, a petition for religious freedom created in 1638, while quirky exhibits include Greyfriars Bobby's collar and bowl.

142 Canongate. www.edinburghmuseums.org.uk. ℭ **0131/529-4143.** Free admission. Mon and Thurs–Sat 10am–5pm, Sun noon–5pm.

National Museum of Scotland ★★ MUSEUM   There aren't many places where you roam around a room full of frocks, take in the odd dinosaur, and check out the jaw of a sperm whale. The subject matter might be broad and the collection a bit of a mish-mash, but it's still a great time wandering wide-eyed among the 12,000 objects that make up the museum of "Scotland" (don't miss the adorable Hillman Imp, one of the last automobiles manufactured in Scotland). It's a bit like a stroll through a living encyclopedia, but worth dipping into for the magnificent Victorian Grand Gallery alone. Plus there's a cafe, brasserie, shop, regular events, and, up on the roof, The Tower

Restaurant, a fine dining spot from restaurateur royalty James Thomson, with stunning views of the Castle.

Chambers St. www.nms.ac.uk. © **0300/123-6789.** Free. Daily 10am–5pm, closed Dec 25, Dec 26 noon–5pm, Jan 1 noon–5pm.

Palace of Holyroodhouse ★★★ HISTORIC SITE   The Royal Mile is topped and tailed by a castle and a palace. While the former is a fortress drenched in military history and housing an arsenal of weapons, Holyrood, the Queen's official residence in Scotland, is all lightness, grace, and charm. Holyrood started life as an Augustinian abbey built by King David I of Scotland in 1128. It morphed over the centuries into the elegant building you see today. The complimentary audio tour takes about an hour as you wind through the State Apartments heavy with tapestries and still used for official functions, but it's Mary Queen of Scots' apartments and the Darnley rooms that give the biggest thrill (you'll see the place where her lover Rizzio was murdered). In terms of access, the Great Staircase has 27 steps and there's a steep spiral staircase up to Mary Queen of Scots' bedchamber (with no wheelchair access). Other areas are accessible and manual wheelchairs are available.

Canongate. www.royalcollection.org.uk. © **0303/123-7306.** £14 adults, £12.70 seniors/students, £8.10 under 17, free under 5, £36.10 families, with complimentary audio tour. Nov–Mar 9:30am–4:30pm; Apr–Oct 9:30am–6pm.

The People's Story HISTORIC SITE   Housed in Canongate Tolbooth, which dates back to 1591 and was once the local jail and tax collection center, the People's Story celebrates the social history of Edinburgh from the late 18th century to the present day. There are no tales of royalty here; instead, the stories of ordinary people, how they worked, how they played, the hardships they endured, and the rights they fought for are presented in a series of staged tableaux. It's not a flashy place, but it has a real higgledy-piggledy, old-fashioned charm.

163 Canongate. www.edinburghmuseums.org.uk. © **0131/529-4057.** Free admission. Wed–Sat 10am–5pm; Sun noon–5pm.

St Giles' Cathedral ★★ CATHEDRAL   This moodily magnificent cathedral standing sentinel on the Royal Mile is also known as the High Kirk of Edinburgh, and is one of the most important churches in Scotland. Its oldest parts date to 1124, but after a fire in 1385, many sections were rebuilt and altered during its 19th-century restoration. The brooding stone exterior features a distinctive crowned spire and graceful flying buttresses. Don't skip Thistle Chapel. Built in 1911 and dedicated to the Knights of the Thistle, Scotland's order of chivalry, this intricate space houses beautiful stalls and detailed heraldic stained-glass windows. One of the other highlights is music. As well as offering two choral services each Sunday, the spectacular St Giles' Cathedral Choir has undertaken a series of concert tours in Europe and the U.S.

High St. www.stgilescathedral.org.uk. © **0131/226-0674.** Free (£3 donation suggested). May–Oct Mon–Fri 9am–7pm, Sat 9am–5pm and Sun 1–5pm; Nov–Apr Mon–Sat 9am–5pm and Sun 1–5pm.

underground EDINBURGH

Tall tales of an underground city have been circulating for years, not all of which are unfounded. Abandoned railway tunnels lead under New Town, a legacy of old train lines that once linked the ports along Edinburgh's coast with Waverley station. However, it's in Old Town that tales of underground Edinburgh take on a mythical status. It's long been rumored that a network of secret tunnels spread out from Edinburgh Castle, one of which leads under the Royal Mile to the Palace of Holyroodhouse. However, more grounded in the real world are stories of bricked over streets. In the late 18th and early 19th centuries, as the fortunes of Old Town declined, anyone with the funds to do so fled its cramped, unhygienic quarters for the wide-open streets of the blossoming New Town. Most of the dilapidated housing around the Royal Mile was demolished, and in the case of streets such as Mary King's Close, the lower levels were simply built over—and tales of underground streets with resident ghosts passed into urban legend.

In the late 1990s, the old street-level sections of Mary King's Close were rediscovered and are, today, one of Edinburgh's spookiest and most atmospheric tourist attractions. Hidden beneath the City Chambers, you enter **The Real Mary King's Close ★★** (www.real marykingsclose.com; ✆ **0131/225-0672**) via Warriston's Close off the Royal Mile. Costumed actors lead you back to the 17th century through a haunted underground warren of old houses where people lived and worked for centuries. You learn about Mary King herself and the last man to leave her close, whose ghost is believed to still occupy his old house (Dec–Mar Sun–Thurs 10am–5pm and Fri–Sat 10am–9pm, and Apr–Oct daily 10am–9pm, Nov Mon–Thurs 9am–5:30pm, Fri–Sat 9:30am–9pm, Sun 9:30am–6pm). Admission is £15.50 for adults, £13.50 seniors and students, and £9.50 for children 5 to 15.

The Scotch Whisky Experience ★ MUSEUM/ENTERTAINMENT COMPLEX   A theme-park-style barrel ride spins you through the whisky-making process at this popular attraction at the top of the Royal Mile. Tours range from "Silver," a fun introduction for whisky novices where you are taught how to sample a wee dram, and finishes in a bar housing the world's largest whisky collection, to a "Morning Masterclass" more suited to the whisky enthusiast, which includes comparative tastings and nosing of a new-make spirit.

354 Castlehill. www.scotchwhiskyexperience.co.uk. ✆ **0131/220-0441.** £15.50 adults, £13.50 seniors and students, £7.50 children 6–17, £38 families. Masterclass £40. Daily Sept–Mar 10am–5pm; Apr–July 10am–6pm; Aug Mon–Fri 10am–5pm, Sat and Sun 10am–5.40pm.

The Scottish Parliament ★★ ARCHITECTURE   Like it or loathe it, this bold and controversial modern building stands opposite the Palace of Holyroodhouse at the east end of the Royal Mile and embodies a strong statement on Scotland's past, present, and future. Designed by the late Spanish architect Enric Miralles, who died before his vision was completed, this unique building cost a cool US$893 million. The abstract motif repeated on the facade facing the Canongate was apparently inspired by Raeburn's painting of *Reverend Robert Walker Skating on Duddingston Loch*, which hangs in the National Gallery of Art. You can take a self-guided tour, but to understand the philosophy behind the architecture and to enter the debating chamber, a guided tour (choose from parliament, architecture, or literature themes) is a must. These are very popular, so advance booking is recommended.

Canongate. www.parliament.scot. ℂ **0131/348-5200.** Free and free guided tours. Mon–Sat 10am–5pm.

New Town

Georgian House ★ ARCHITECTURE Robert Adam designed this Georgian gem at the heart of Charlotte Square in 1796. The gracious drawing and dining rooms filled with antique furnishings, china, and artwork capture the elegance of the era, while the servants' quarters give a sense of below-stairs life. Don't miss the fascinating film "Living in a Grand Design" for an introduction to the family's story. The film sheds light on life at the time, while the guides in each room are also happy to share interesting anecdotes about the house and its history. If you would like to really immerse yourself, you can even dress up in period costume.

7 Charlotte Sq. www.nts.org.uk. ℂ **0131/226-3318.** £8 adults, £6 children, students, and seniors, £17.50 families. Mar daily 11am–4pm; Apr–Oct daily 10am–5pm. Closed mid-Dec until Mar.

National Gallery Complex ★ GALLERY To be honest, there are so many phenomenal museums and attractions in the Scottish capital, many of which have undergone multi-million pound revamps over the past few years, that this imposing museum complex does feel a little dowdy and old-fashioned. The grand columned buildings in the middle of Princes Street Gardens certainly have stage presence—and are a fitting home for Scotland's small but carefully chosen collection of fine art from the early Renaissance to the end of the 19th century, including important works from Raphael, Rembrandt, Rubens, Velazquez, El Greco, van Gogh, and Cézanne, as well as a dedicated Scottish collection.

The Mound. www.nationalgalleries.org. ℂ **0131/624-6200.** Free; fees for some temporary exhibitions. daily 10am–5pm; Thurs 10am–7pm.

Greyfriars Bobby

There's nothing like the tragic tale of a dog's devotion to bring a lump to your throat, even if it does stretch the truth a little. Greyfriars Bobby was a Skye Terrier whose master, police constable John Gray, died of tuberculosis in 1858. Bobby, faithful to the last, guarded his grave in 17th-century **Greyfriars Kirk** (www.greyfriarskirk.com), until he too died in 1872. There's a statue of Bobby near the entrance to the kirkyard, and there have been a number of books and films made about his story. You can see his collar and bowl in the Museum of Edinburgh on the Royal Mile.

The contemporary sculpture park **Jupiter Artland** (www.jupiterartland.org; ☏ **01506/889-900**) describes itself as a "garden of discovery," and it's an apt description for the whimsical installations here. The garden sits in the grounds of Bonnington House, on the outskirts of the city, and contains a growing number of specially commissioned pieces created in situ by the likes of Charles Jencks, Anish Kapoor, Antony Gormley, Cornelia Parker, and many more. Maps are provided and imaginations teased in this unique haven of hidden landscapes. Jupiter Artland is open mid-May to October daily 10am to 5pm. Admission is £8.50 for adults and £4.50 for students and children ages 6 to 16, £23.50 families, £6 seniors. **First** (www.firstgroup.com; ☏ **01324/602-200**) bus services nos. 27 and X27 depart from Regent Road and Haymarket train station in Edinburgh and drop off close to the entrance of Bonnington House.

Scottish National Gallery of Modern Art ★★ MUSEUM   A head emerges from the pavement at the entrance of Modern One, a grand Neoclassical building dating back to 1825. The head is one of Antony Gormley's six Times' sculptures, a series of cast-iron, life-size figures rising out of the Water of Leith—and the paving slabs outside the museum. Across the road is Modern Two, originally a 19th-century orphanage. Together, the galleries in both buildings showcase an impressive, sometimes off-the-wall, permanent collection, from works by Picasso and Matisse to Damien Hirst and Tracey Emin, along with a series of changing exhibitions. It's the sculpture park that's the biggest draw, however, featuring works by Henry Moore and Barbara Hepworth. Slightly off the beaten tourist track—not that anywhere in Edinburgh is much of a schlep—the Scottish National Gallery of Modern Art is just above the Water of Leith, the little river that tumbles through the city.

73-75 Belford Rd. www.nationalgalleries.org. ☏ **0131/624-6200.** Free; fees for some temporary exhibitions. Daily 10am–5pm.

Scottish National Portrait Gallery ★★ GALLERY   This grand red sandstone Arts and Crafts building dates back to 1889; it was the first purpose-built portrait gallery in the world. Today, its mix of intimate rooms and light-filled contemporary spaces are strung with images, from paintings to photographs, of famous and not-so-famous Scots. It's a wonderful place to dip into to marvel at the mesmerizingly ornate Great Hall, the detailed frieze of notable persons in chronological order and external decorative statues of Scottish poets and monarchs.

1 Queen St. www.nationalgalleries.org. ☏ **0131/624-6200.** Free; fees for some temporary exhibitions. Daily 10am–5pm.

Surgeons' Hall Museums ★ MUSEUM   This unusual museum medley, made up of the Wohl Pathology Museum, the History of Surgery Museum and the Dental Collection includes one of the most important surgical collections in the world and is well worth a visit. On the upper floors is the Pathology

5

EDINBURGH & THE LOTHIAN REGION

Exploring Edinburgh

EDINBURGH UNESCO CITY OF literature

From Robert Burns to Ian Rankin, Sir Walter Scott to J.K. Rowling, this is a city steeped in the written word. The city was named the world's first **UNESCO City of Literature** (www.cityofliterature.com) and is home to the biggest literary shindig in the world, the **Edinburgh International Book Festival** (www.edbookfest.co.uk) each August. At any time of year, here are some of Edinburgh's top literary places to visit:

IN OLD TOWN

Even the flagstones outside **The Writers' Museum ★** (www.edinburghmuseums.org.uk; ✆ **0131/529-4901**), a 17th-century hidden gem in Lady Stair's Close off the Lawnmarket, are inscribed with inspirational quotes from poets and authors. The treasure trove of portraits, relics, and manuscripts belonged to three of Scotland's greatest writers: Robert Burns (1759–96), Sir Walter Scott (1771–1832), and Robert Louis Stevenson (1850–94) and is open Wednesday to Saturday 10am to 5pm, and on Sundays noon to 5pm.

The Elephant House (www.elephanthouse.biz; ✆ **0131/220-5355**) cafe on George IV Bridge is where J.K. Rowling penned her early Harry Potter books. This popular spot opens daily from 8am (9am at weekends) until 11pm and dishes up picture-postcard views of Edinburgh Castle in rustic, elephant-themed surroundings along with a pizza, pasta and pie-style menu.

Deacon Brodie's Tavern (✆ **0131/225-6531**), on Lawnmarket opposite George IV Bridge, is named after William Brodie, a respected citizen by day and thief by night who was eventually caught and hung in 1788. His notorious double life inspired Robert Louis Stevenson's *The Strange Case of Dr. Jekyll and Mr. Hyde*, and the fictional protagonist of Muriel Spark's *The Prime of Miss Jean Brodie* was created as a direct descendant of Deacon Brodie himself.

Museum with cabinets of specimens dating back to the 1500s. The role of women in surgery as well as military surgery through the ages is also explained. The Dental Collection has every conceivable dentistry tool alongside 3,000-year-old dentures, while in the new History of Surgery Museum there is an anatomy theatre with an interactive dissection table. However, the must-sees of the museum's more macabre objects are a plaster cast of William Burke's head taken moments after his execution—you can still see the mark of the hangman's rope on his neck—and a small pocket notebook bound with a section of this notorious body snatcher's skin. Due to the medically graphic nature of some of the exhibits this museum isn't for the squeamish and not recommended for children under 10. Anyone under age 16 must be accompanied by an adult.

Nicolson St., opposite the Festival Theatre. www.museum.rcsed.ac.uk. ✆ **0131/527-1711**. Admission £7 adults, £4 children, seniors and students. Daily 10am–5pm.

Organized Tours

Every city seems to have a hop on, hop off open-top **bus tour** these days, and they can be a fun introduction to the main sights. **Edinburgh Bus Tours** (www.edinburghtour.com; ✆ **0131/220-0770**) has a range of routes and themes,

EDINBURGH & THE LOTHIAN REGION

IN NEW TOWN

The Oxford Bar (www.oxfordbar.co.uk; *C* 0131/529-4068) on Young Street is famous among crime fiction fans as the pub where Ian Rankin's Detective Inspector John Rebus would head to sup a pint. However, Scottish writers have favored this venerable bar since the 19th century, and it remains a popular locals' pub.

When Sir Walter Scott died in 1832, an architectural competition was launched to find the most fitting design for his memorial. The winner was an unknown architect, George Meikle Kemp, whose Gothic-inspired, elaborate spire soars over 60m high (200-ft.) At the center of the **Scott Monument** ★ (www.edin burghmuseums.org.uk; *C* 0131/529-4068), on the east end of Princes Street is a large statue of Sir Walter Scott and his dog, Maida, carved from one block of Carrara marble by Sir John Steell. Visitors can pay £5 to climb the spire's 287 steps to enjoy spectacular views of the city. The Monument is open daily 10am to 4pm. During the summer it stays open until 7pm.

Those seeking to tap into Edinburgh's prodigious literary inspiration by walking the city's streets have a number of tour choices. Ian Rankin has created a free iPhone app that leads walkers around his favored Edinburgh haunts and can be downloaded from his website, www.ian rankin.net. Other options include **Edin burgh Book Lovers Tour** (www.edin burghbooktour.com), which leads a day-time jaunt May to September, Wednesday to Sunday at 1:30pm with an extra tour at 11am during August. There's one tour a week on Sundays the rest of the year (£12 full price/£11 concessions) and an evening Lost World Literary Pub Crawl (£12 adult, £9 seniors/students); reserve via the website (www.edinburgh literarypubtour.co.uk).

starting on Waverley Bridge and lasting around an hour. Tickets cost £15 for adults, £14 for seniors and students, and £7.50 for children ages 5 to 15.

There's no shortage of literary and ghost tours nowadays, but back in 1985 when a group of history teachers set up **Mercat Tours** (www.mercattours. com; *C* 0131/225-5445), they were ground-breaking. Thirty years on and a clutch of awards later they're still going strong—as are two of the original tours: "Secrets of the Royal Mile" and "Ghosts and Ghouls." A more recent addition is the "Outlander Experience," taking in the locations used in the TV series. Tickets start at £13 for adults, £11 seniors and £8 for children 5 to 15 (no children under age 5).

Outdoor Activities

Calton Hill ★★★ MONUMENT   Edinburgh is said to have been built, like Rome, on seven hills—although which hills is disputed. Calton Hill is one, with its medley of monuments at the summit including the unfinished (the money ran out) 19th-century **National Monument,** designed to replicate the Parthenon in Athens and to commemorate Scottish soldiers who died in the Napoleonic Wars. It was subsequently nicknamed Edinburgh's Shame. The **Nelson Monument** contains relics of the man himself and is crowned by

EDINBURGH'S famous FESTIVALS

Summer in the city is a festival frenzy. However, there are festivals peppered throughout the year, kicking off with **Hogmanay** (www.edinburghshogmany.com; © 0131/510-0395) the capital's world-famous 3-day New Year's Eve revelries. Show-stopping events include a torchlight procession and one of the biggest street parties in the world on Princes Street (ticket-only—it's a sell-out so book early. The spectacular firework display at midnight over the castle can be seen all over the city).

The **Edinburgh International Science Festival** (www.sciencefestival.co.uk; © 0131/553-0320) takes place each April, though on the last day of the month scientific scrutiny gives way to pagan pyres, drums and theatrical performances when Calton Hill becomes the setting for the **Beltane Fire Festival** (www.beltane.org) a Celtic celebration to welcome in the summer. The **Leith Festival** spans 10 days in June (www.leithfestival.com; © 0131/555-4104) while the **Edinburgh International Film Festival** (www.edfilmfest.org.uk; © 0131/623-8030) takes place at the end of the month. July sees the **Edinburgh Jazz & Blues Festival** heralding the start of festival season proper (www.edinburghjazzfestival.com; © 0131/473-2000).

The summer's clutch of world-class festivals celebrating theatre, music, opera, dance, comedy, street theatre, literature, and art, to name but a few, all started with the **Edinburgh International Festival** (www.eif.co.uk; © 0131/473-2000) in 1947. It attracts major international stars in all those fields, from jazz artist Chick Corea to movie star Juliette Binoche in the title role of *Antigone*. The box office at **The Hub,** an old church on Castle Hill is open daily year-round.

---

a large time ball to enable vessels on the Firth of Forth to set their chronometers accurately, while the **Dugald Stewart Monument,** modeled after the Tower of the Winds in Athens, boasts one of the best views in the city. A visionary conservation project to restore the 1818 **City Observatory** and turn it into a contemporary visual arts space has recently been undertaken by the Edinburgh Council Collective, an arts organization with funding from Edinburgh World Heritage. **Calton Old Cemetery** (enter via Waterloo Place), dating from the 1700s, is also worth a detour. It's the resting place of many famous Scots including the philosopher David Hume. The **Scottish-American Soldiers Monument** is crowned with a statue of Abraham Lincoln, to remember the Scots who fought for the Union during the American Civil War.

Calton Hill can be entered via Waterloo Place and Royal Terrace. Free except for the Nelson Monument (£5). Mon–Sat 10am–4pm; open until 7pm during the summer.

Royal Botanic Garden Edinburgh ★★ PARK/GARDEN   Edinburgh is a green city dotted with parks, but the jewel in the crown is the Botanic Gardens. Established in the 17th century, today the 70-acre site is a haven of tranquility. Highlights include the **Chinese Hillside,** its slopes bushy with the largest collection of wild-origin plants outside China; the rock garden (5,000 plants at any one time); and the steamy **Victorian Palm Houses.** The cutting-edge, eco-designed visitors center houses a cafe upstairs that spills outside,

The **Edinburgh Festival Fringe** (www. edfringe.com; ✆ **0131/226-0026**), or "the Fringe," was created at the same time as an opportunity for anybody—professional or amateur—to put on a show wherever they can find an empty stage or street corner. The Fringe is the biggest arts festival in the world with street performers, comedy, offbeat theatre and late-night cabaret. The box office is at 180 High St. (the Royal Mile).

One of the most exciting August spectacles is the **Royal Edinburgh Military Tattoo** (www.edintattoo.co.uk; ✆ **0131/225-1188**), which takes place over 3 weeks every night except Sundays on the floodlit esplanade in front of Edinburgh Castle. First performed in 1950, the Tattoo features the precision marching of the Massed Band of Her Majesties Royal Marines and other regiments from around the world, along with Highland dancing, motorcycle displays, and the heart-stirring massed pipes and drums bands, concluding with the poignant spectacle of the Lone Piper playing high up on the castle ramparts. The Tattoo Office is at 1-3 Cockburn St. behind Waverley station.

Other festivals during August include the **Edinburgh International Book Festival** (www.edbookfest.co.uk; ✆ **0345/373-5888;** see the box on p. 78) and the **Edinburgh Art Festival** (www.edinburghartfestival.com; ✆ **0131/226-6558**).

Tickets for many shows at the International Festival and Military Tattoo sell out months in advance, so book early. Ways to save money include opting for lower-priced preview shows at the start of the festival and the Fringe's 2-for-1 ticket deals, which can be bagged on the first Monday and Tuesday of the festival. The Fringe also operates a Half Price Hut by the National Gallery Complex on the Mound.

and exhibition space, a shop, and a nursery. **Inverleith House,** an 18th-century mansion in the grounds, hosts temporary art exhibitions. There are guided garden tours at 11am and 2pm during the summer, or just while away an hour or two lying on the grass with a picnic.

Arboretum Place. www.rbge.org.uk. ✆ **0131/248-2909.** Gardens free; glasshouses £6.50 adults, £5.50 seniors, under 15 free. Daily (except for Dec 25 and Jan 1), Nov–Jan 10am–4pm, Feb and Oct 10am–5pm, Mar–Sept 10am–6pm.

Especially for Kids

There are dungeons, a castle or two, and giant pandas, what more could kids want? They can learn the value of money and how to crack open a safe (in an attraction that's free, but only open Tues–Fri from 10am–5pm); the **Museum on the Mound** is in what was once the headquarters of the Bank of Scotland (www.museumonthemound.com; ✆ **0131/243-5464**). And, when they need to let off steam, there are plenty of parks and beaches nearby. A wild scramble up **Arthur's Seat** is always a good bet or for a breath of salty air, head to the town beach at **Portobello** for fish and chips on the seafront or an ice cream on the sand. If the weather's bad they can head to the polar ice caps instead to touch an iceberg or plunge to the bottom of the ocean in a submarine. At the bottom of Arthur's Seat is **Dynamic Earth** (www.dynamicearth.co.uk;

© **0131/550-7800**), an attraction that takes kids on an interactive journey around the planet. Admission is £15.50 for adults and £9.75 for children.

Craigmillar Castle ★ CASTLE Dubbed Edinburgh's "other" castle, Craigmillar is one of Scotland's best preserved medieval castles, with battlements, gun-holes and a family chapel to explore, as well as large lawns for picnicking. At its heart is a late 14th-century tower, the interior of which is a maze of rooms, including a Great Hall and the room where Mary Queen of Scots is said to have stayed. A large complex of buildings grew around the tower, however, much of these are now merely picturesque ruins.

Craigmillar Castle Rd. www.historicenvironment.scot. © **0131/661-4445**. £6 adults, seniors £4.80, £3.60 children. Apr–Sept daily 9:30am–5:30pm; Oct–Mar Sat–Wed 10am–4pm. Take any bus to the Royal Infirmary; it is a ½ mile walk to the castle.

Edinburgh Dungeons ★ THEME PARK This 80-minute rollercoaster of a journey through 1,000 years of Scottish history with a cast of costumed actors is a highly staged, Disney-style attraction. From body snatchers Burke and Hare to cannibalism in the caves of Galloway, it's funny, scary, and a little corny, and not ideal for very young children.

31 Market St. www.thedungeons.com. © **0871/663-1670**. £14.25 adults, £11.50 children 5–15. Open daily. Hours vary; but usually from 10am–5 or 6pm. Check website to confirm.

Edinburgh Zoo ★★ ZOO Giant Pandas Tian Tian (Sweetie) and Yang Guang (Sunshine) lumbering around their bamboo-planted enclosure or simply snoozing is one of the main draws here. The penguins, splashing about in the largest outdoor penguin pool in Europe with a waterfall feature and water shoot, are also a big hit. Then there are the meerkats and monkeys, wallabies and wee beasties, with a daily program of talks and hands-on "keeper experiences" to add an educational element. Scotland's largest animal collection is on the western edges of the city and spreads over 32 hectares (79 acres) of hillside parkland with views toward the Pentland Hills. The zoo is home to more than 1,000 animals, including many endangered species. Book online in advance for the cheapest prices.

134 Corstorphine Rd. www.edinburghzoo.org.uk. © **0131/334-9171**. £17.50 adults, £15 seniors and students, £9.95 children 3–15. Apr–Sept daily 10am–6pm; Oct and Mar daily 10am–5pm; Nov–Feb daily 10am–4pm, Christmas Day 10am–1pm.

The Water of Leith ★

Meandering along the 12-mile wooded trail that hugs the **Water of Leith,** a ribbon-like river that tumbles from the Pentland Hills down to the now swank docklands in Leith to meet the Firth of Forth, you could easily forget that you were in the heart of the city (www.wateroflleith.org.uk). You can dip in and out, following the brown signposts from the visitor center in Balerno (pick up a map here or download it from the website) as the track passes landmarks such as Murrayfield Stadium, the Modern Art Galleries, Dean Village,

TRACING YOUR ancestral ROOTS

There are a number of avenues to explore if you want to trace the Scottish side of your family tree. In addition to the many books on clan histories, a number have their own museums throughout Scotland, and local tourist offices can provide details on where to find them. Staff at Historic Scotland properties are also well briefed on the most popular Scottish names related to their sites and are more than happy to share information.

For anyone wanting to dig deeper, the **Scotlands People Centre** at General Register House, 2 Princes St. (www. scotlandspeople.gov.uk; ✆ **0131/314-4300**), helps researchers gain access to records held by the National Register of Archives for Scotland (www.nrscotland. gov.uk). The center is open Monday through Friday from 9am to 4:30pm. Free introductory sessions run most days, otherwise a day's research costs £15 and should be reserved in advance by phone or on the website. Also in Edinburgh on Victoria Place, the **Scottish Genealogical Society** (www.scots genealogy.com; ✆ **0131/220-3677**) can assist with research into Scottish family history.

Stockbridge, and the Royal Botanic Gardens. **Dean Village** is a picture-perfect little pocket, the old grain milling buildings converted into apartments, with the high arched **Dean Bridge** (1833) designed by Thomas Telford. Dip into **Warriston Cemetery** an overgrown oasis—now a designated nature reserve—designed in 1842 with catacombs, Gothic arches, and moss-blanketed war graves. Think tree-shaded pathways, scampering squirrels, and blackberry picking among the tombs.

Leith ★

Leith is the hub of Edinburgh's long maritime history. Archaeological excavations discovered medieval wharfs dating back to the 12th century, while today cruise ships still dock at the Ocean Terminal. For years a dilapidated area, over the last couple of decades the Shore has been revamped and is now a chic spot sprinkled with gastropubs, Michelin-starred restaurants, and even a boutique hotel, the cobbled waterfront scattered with interpretive boards depicting old harbor life. If you are interested in delving deeper into Edinburgh's maritime heritage, **Trinity House** is a museum open for pre-booked visits only (www. historicenvironment.scot; ✆ **0131/554-3289**). The old Georgian property is packed with seafaring memorabilia.

The biggest tourist draw is the **Royal Yacht Britannia ★** (www.royal yachtbritannia.co.uk; ✆ **0131/555-5566**) moored at Ocean Terminal. Launched on April 16, 1953, this 125m (410-ft.) luxury yacht sailed more than a million miles before she was decommissioned in 1997. Onboard, an atmospheric audio tour takes you around the five levels, including the decks where Prince Charles and Princess Diana strolled on their honeymoon, the Royal Apartments, engine room, and captain's cabin. It costs £16 for adults, £14 for seniors and students, £8.50 for children (5–17) and £45 for families and is open daily November to March 10am to 3:30pm; April to September 9:30am to 4:30pm and October 9:30am to 4pm.

Cramond

The small village of Cramond lies 4 miles west of the center of Edinburgh and is rarely discovered by visitors. Its edges push against the mouth of the River Almond as it tumbles into the Firth of Forth, and the pretty waterfront and riverside walkways are popular with Edinburgh families at weekends. The earliest evidence of human habitation in Scotland dates back to 8500 B.C.E. and was unearthed at this tranquil spot, which also boasts the scant remains of a Roman fort. Today, a waterfront cafe sells ice creams and teas, or you can sup a pint beside the fire in the cozy **Cramond Inn** (✆ **0131/336-2035**) before meandering along the banks of the Almond. This area is rich with bird life, and species such as curlews and oystercatchers can be spied along this shore. When the tide is out, you can cross an old causeway to explore tiny Cramond Island, which lies 1 mile offshore.

Lauriston Castle (www.edinburghmuseums.org.uk; ✆ **0131/336-2060**) stands inland on Cramond Road South and is one of the city's finest historical houses. The oldest section dates back to the 1600s and, following redecoration in the early 19th century, Lauriston shines with Edwardian elegance. Also take time to enjoy the castle's serene gardens, which include an award-winning Japanese Friendship Garden. The castle grounds are open daily from 8am to 5pm and are free to enter. Tours of the castle are scheduled at 2pm and 3pm Saturday and Sunday and 2pm Monday, Tuesday, and Wednesday and cost £5 for adults and £3 for children. Lothian bus no. 21, 41, and 42 link Cramond with the city center.

WHERE TO STAY

Bagging a bed in Edinburgh during its frenzy of festivals can be a tricky business. The race to keep pace with increasing visitor numbers has led to an influx of dull chains, but if you're pounding the pavements all day, a boutique bolthole might not be top of your list of requirements. It's also led to some interesting developments. The accommodation scene in the capital is constantly evolving and we're not just talking about a handful of new hotels bumping up the bed quota, but huge—and sometimes controversial—development projects. The re-designed St James Centre (www.edinburghst-james.com) at the top of Leith Walk will feature a 12-story hotel wrapped in metal ribbons (and nicknamed the Walnut Whip) when it is completed in 2020 and heralds the **W** brand's arrival to the city. There will also be a **Roomzzz** aparthotel in the complex.

Aparthotels are one of the most interesting growth sectors, in fact. The redevelopment of part of St Andrews Square saw the launch of the **Edinburgh Grand** (www.lateralcity.com; ✆ **0131/230-0570**) in 2018. This historic city landmark, once the global headquarters of the Royal Bank of Scotland, now houses 50 individually designed serviced apartments, a champagne and cocktail lounge, and restaurant. It's Lateral City's latest venture, the company that also owns two other aparthotels in the capital, Old Town Chambers and Merchiston Residence. At the budget end of the market, another design-led aparthotel arrived in the capital in 2017. **Eden Locke** (www.lockeliving.com; ✆ **0330/056-3363**) is a stylish 72-room property on George Street with studios from £105.

The lower end of the market has real design-cred as well. There are two outposts of German budget design chain, **Motel One** (www.motel-one.com; ✆ **0131/220-0730**), both just a stone's throw from Waverley Station and with rooms from £59, while the Scottish-owned G1 stable has a cluster of funky, centrally located properties in the capital including **The Inn on the Mile** (www.theinnonthemile.co.uk; ✆ **0131/556-9940**), which has double rooms from £117; **The Grassmarket** (www.grassmarkethotel.co.uk; ✆ **0131/220-2299**) with double rooms from £54; and **Stay Central** (www.staycentral. co.uk; ✆ **0131/622-6801**). Double rooms are categorized small, medium, large with XL (quad) and XXL (six-bedded) and there's a private dorm. Double rooms from £86, including a complimentary bottle of prosecco on arrival. The same group has bought the historic—but tired—Scotsman Hotel and set about refurbishing it in 2018.

Hostels are no longer a bare-bones option. Check out **Code Pod Hostel** at 50 Rose Street (www.codehostel.com; ✆ **0131/659-9883**) with its cool minimalist design, secure keypad entry system, high-quality linens, healthy breakfasts, and beds from £26. Many traditional hostels have been spruced up, and are now sleek alternatives to the traditional guesthouse, with private rooms as well as dorms. **Edinburgh Central,** a five-star hostel and part of the Scottish Youth Hostel Association, at 9 Haddington Place along Leith Walk (www.syha. org.uk; ✆ **0131/524-2090**), has double and twin en suite rooms from £44.

Added to this the meteoric rise of **Airbnb** (www.airbnb.co.uk) and rival **HomeAway.co.uk,** and there's never been so much choice for visitors. Of course, during the busiest times of the year—the summer festival season from July to early September and Hogmanay (New Year)—you still need to book as far in advance as possible and prepare for sharp price rises. Other useful sites include **Edlets** (www.edlets.com; ✆ **0131/297-1429**) and **Festival Flats** (www.festivalflats.net; ✆ **0131/235-2044**).

If you have an early flight and want a more characterful option than an airport hotel, **The Bridge Inn** in the conservation village of Ratho (27 Baird Rd., EH28 8RA; www.bridgeinn.com; ✆ **0131/333-1320**) is an award-winning gastropub with rooms overlooking the Union Canal. It feels a million miles away from the city but is actually just 20 minutes by car from the center of Edinburgh and 10 minutes from the airport. They grow much of the produce on the menu themselves, while the four charming country-chic rooms start at £110 with breakfast.

Edinburgh Hotels & Restaurants

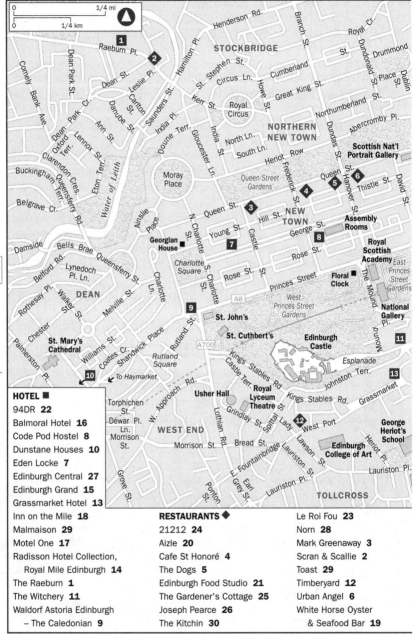

HOTEL ■

94DR **22**
Balmoral Hotel **16**
Code Pod Hostel **8**
Dunstane Houses **10**
Eden Locke **7**
Edinburgh Central **27**
Edinburgh Grand **15**
Grassmarket Hotel **13**
Inn on the Mile **18**
Malmaison **29**
Motel One **17**
Radisson Hotel Collection,
    Royal Mile Edinburgh **14**
The Raeburn **1**
The Witchery **11**
Waldorf Astoria Edinburgh
    – The Caledonian **9**

RESTAURANTS ◆

21212 **24**
Aizle **20**
Cafe St Honoré **4**
The Dogs **5**
Edinburgh Food Studio **21**
The Gardener's Cottage **25**
Joseph Pearce **26**
The Kitchin **30**

Le Roi Fou **23**
Norn **28**
Mark Greenaway **3**
Scran & Scallie **2**
Toast **29**
Timberyard **12**
Urban Angel **6**
White Horse Oyster
    & Seafood Bar **19**

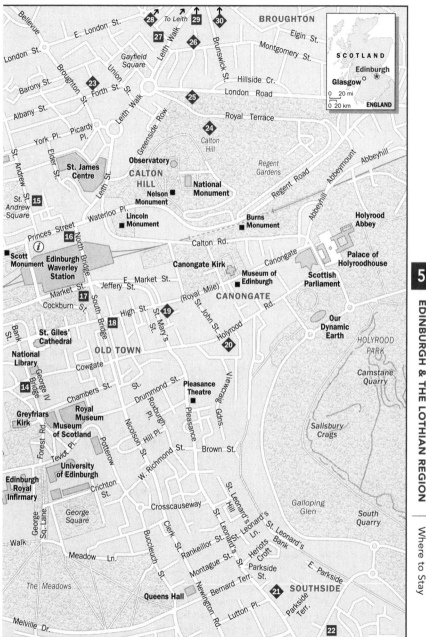

NEW TOWN
Expensive

The Balmoral ★★★　With an unruly litter of new hotels nipping at her heels, Edinburgh's grand dame might have taken umbrage. Instead she simply upped her game with a dazzling, multimillion-pound refurbishment. Since it first opened in 1902, this Victorian railway hotel next to Waverley Station has been the place to stay. The grand new signature Scone & Crombie suite is one of the largest in Scotland with a serene color palette reflecting the soft tones of the Scottish glens, a working fireplace, and floor-to-ceiling windows framing spectacular views of the Old Town. The castle view rooms—including 552 with its owl door knocker and vintage typewriter where J.K. Rowling completed the Harry Potter series—now have a sylvan woodland theme. The hotel is classic elegance, a chic cocoon away from frenetic Princes Street. It boasts a Michelin-starred restaurant, Number One, as well as new brasserie headed up by culinary royalty, the Roux brothers, a light, airy Palm Court where harp music soothes away city cares over afternoon tea, and a sleek spa. Scotch, the whisky bar, is daubed in the earthy amber tones of the 400 or so drams available here. What new hotels?

1 Princes St. www.roccofortehotels.com. ⓒ **0131/556-2414.** Doubles £220–£800, suites £875–£4000. **Amenities:** 2 restaurants; 2 bars; spa; sauna; steam room; gym; indoor pool; valet parking £35; free Wi-Fi.

Waldorf Astoria Edinburgh—The Caledonian ★★　Its name might be a bit of a mouthful, but this grand sandstone Victorian railway hotel will always be the Caley to locals. In its glittering heyday, Elizabeth Taylor swanned down its corridors. Today, it still gets the Hollywood seal of approval, Eva Longoria Baston has been a guest. The hotel mirrors the perks of The Balmoral at the opposite end of Princes Street—although it was the first to head-hunt a pair of gastronomic brothers: Chris and Jeff Galvin founded The Pompadour by Galvin, the hotel's fine dining restaurant, as well as the relaxed ground-floor brasserie. Then there's Peacock Alley for afternoon tea, the Caley Bar for cocktails and the Guerlain Spa for a spot of pampering. Bedrooms, some with castle views, come in a cool color palette of smoky grey, silver, and blue.

Princes Street. www.waldorfastoriaedinburgh.com. ⓒ **0131/222-8888.** Doubles £175–£689, suites £255–£2,249. **Amenities:** 2 restaurants; bar; lounge; spa; swimming pool; sauna; steam room; Jacuzzi; gym; beauty salon; free Wi-Fi.

Moderate

The Dunstane Houses ★★　In an increasingly homogenized city, overrun by anonymous chain hotels, the Dunstane Houses is that rare find: a family-run, friendly, small independent boutique hotel—which doesn't skimp on luxury. It also has a parking lot—never underestimate the joy of free parking in the Scottish capital. The hotel is split between two properties on either side of the road, just a 10-minute stroll from the West End. Its Orkney island-born owners, Shirley and Derek Mowat (check out the wall covered in old black and white photos of life on the northerly archipelago) have created a cozy bolthole in Dunstane House, a Victorian mansion designed by renowned architect William Playfair in 1852 and Hampton House, another grand pad opposite. Design-wise, think traditional tweed sofas and oversize headboards mixed with sumptuous velvet. Rooms in the recently refurbished Dunstane House have Orkney-inspired names, the Scapa Suite boasting a freestanding copper bathtub beside the dramatic black four-poster bed. Downstairs, the stylish Ba'Bar (named after the Orcadian street football game) blends into a laidback lounge–dining area where you can tuck into wee bites or bigger plates that champion Scottish produce, or maybe sip a dram from the glamorously backlit whisky cabinet. Added extras? Book a private tour of Edinburgh or over to the Kingdom of Fife in one of Derek Mowat's vintage cars.

4 West Coates. www.thedunstane.com. ℰ **0131/337-6169.** Doubles £139–£379, suites £375–£525. **Amenities:** Restaurant; bar; free parking; free Wi-Fi.

The Raeburn ★ Stockbridge is one of Edinburgh's village neighborhoods. Just down the hill from the New Town, a 15-minute walk to the center, it's a world away from the tourist scrum. This area is quaint, creative and crammed with character, independent delis, restaurants and bars, and this boutique hotel in a 19th-century building. The rooms are sleek, with fabulous bathrooms with roll-top tubs in the deluxe doubles. The stair runner is Anta (tasteful tartan), as are fabrics and throws, the walls painted in moody Farrow and Ball hues. Downstairs, however, there is a little lack of individuality. The bar feels a bit like a chain pub, albeit with a splash of tweed. The "library" has no books—instead the mock bookshelves have a theme pub–vibe. There's a specialist secondhand bookshop a few doors down. Stacking the shelves with well-thumbed volumes would have added real character.

112 Raeburn Place. www.theraeburn.com. ℰ **0131/332-7000.** 10 units. Doubles £122–£320. **Amenities:** Restaurant; bar; library; free Wi-Fi.

Inexpensive

Eden Locke ★★ The aparthotel concept has been shaking up the capital's accommodation scene. This cool 72-room property opened in 2017 and describes itself as a cross between a stylish boutique hotel and an Airbnb apartment. Design-wise it's all sorbet hues, bright yellow doors, and the signature L-shaped, mint-green sofa. It has a young vibe and enviably central New Town location. New York architects Grzywinski+Pons are responsible for converting this elegant heritage listed Georgian townhouse into a pioneering "lifestyle" hub and private sanctuary in the city. Studio rooms feature a contemporary kitchen and living area with thoughtful touches, from organic teas to cocktail kits. In the bedroom you'll find a yoga mat—for the twice-weekly complimentary yoga classes downstairs in the sprawling "social space," an open-plan botanical-themed lounge and cafe area, flooded with light and peppered with potted plants. Hyde & Son serves coffee and pastries by day morphing into an artisan wine and cocktail bar at night.

127 George St. www.lockeliving.com. ℰ **0330/056-3363.** Studio room £105–£235. Eden Suite £135–£325. **Amenities:** Lounge; cafe; bar; free Wi-Fi.

OLD TOWN
Expensive
The Witchery ★★★   If you've harbored secret Rapunzel fantasies since childhood you can step into the pages of a fairytale here, bedding down in a 16th-century turret with views over Edinburgh's rooftops. Or maybe you've been spellbound by the swashbuckling romp, Outlander? This fabulously flamboyant, historical hideaway, in the shadow of the castle, is the nearest you'll get to traveling back in time to Scotland's past. Created by James Thomson as a restaurant with rooms in 1979, there are nine sumptuous suites sprinkled through a warren of ancient buildings. Think gothic romance, oak-paneled bathrooms, tapestries and antiques, ornately carved four-posters draped in rich silks and brocades and even the odd suit of armor. You can traipse down to breakfast in the equally dramatic restaurant (all wood paneling and candlelight at night), but why bother when you can have breakfast in bed? A gourmet breakfast hamper is delivered to your suite. If it's fully booked, try Prestonfield (www.prestonfield.com; ✆ **0131/225-7800**) Thomson's second hotel and mini country estate on the outskirts of the city.

Castlehill, The Royal Mile. www.thewitchery.com. ✆ **0131/225-5613.** Doubles £345–£560, includes breakfast and a bottle of champagne. **Amenities:** Restaurant; free Wi-Fi.

Moderate
Radisson Collection Hotel, Royal Mile Edinburgh ★★   This five-star, modern design hotel has reinvented itself more times than Madonna. It launched onto Edinburgh's catwalk under the Missoni label, its signature stripes and zigzags even adorning the doormen's zany kilts and free-flowing Prosecco on tap. When the Italian fashion house skipped town it was re-crowned the G&V (George & Victoria) with a nod to the area's royal heritage. Kilt-designing legend Howie Nicholsby refashioned the doormen's uniform, while Glasgow-based duo Timorous Beasties gave Cucina, the restaurant, a flamboyant new look. The top suites were also revamped by a group of Scottish artists and fashion designers, while the ground floor was totally remodeled. A new bar, Epicurean, was created, mixing cocktails sweetened with honey from the rooftop hives. In 2017 it was time for a change again, but in name only. It might sound more corporate, less individual, but the Radisson Collection is a group of hotels curated for their sense of flair.

1 George IV Bridge. www.radissoncollection.com. ✆ **0131/220-6666.** 136 units. Doubles £165–£496, suites £415–£746. **Amenities:** Restaurant; lobby bar; spa; room service; free Wi-Fi.

Inexpensive
The Grassmarket Hotel ★★   If there's one thing Edinburgh has got right recently it's the bottom end of the market. There's no need to sacrifice style if your wallet won't stretch to one of the swankiest design hotels. Just make a beeline for the bumper crop of budget boltholes. Bland, boring and beige are out, funky and fun is in. At the Grassmarket Hotel a wall in reception

is hung with old keys while shelves are stacked with games and comic books. Designer Jim Hamilton was on a roll with the comic theme decorating rooms with Dandy wallpaper and adding a giant magnetic city map for the geographically challenged. Rooms come in cosy (single), snug (double), and comfy categories—double, triple, and quad. All the amenities that hotel-savvy guest expects are here (rainfall showers and iPod docking stations), along with a few they probably don't, such as free Tunnock's teacakes, for the big kid in you and a complimentary bottle of Prosecco for the fully-formed adults (if you book direct). You can grab a cappuccino in reception, but for breakfast you need to stumble next door to Biddy Mulligans pub.

94-96 Grassmarket. www.grassmarkethotel.co.uk. © **0131/220-2299.** 42 units. Doubles £54–£285. **Amenities:** Free Wi-Fi.

LEITH
Moderate

Malmaison ★★   Location, location, location. For some, its position on the waterfront in Leith's gentrified docklands is a plus point; for others the schlep into the center is a disadvantage. However, transport links are quick and easy, and Leith is now a destination in its own right. It's one of the city's culinary hotspots, with Michelin-starred restaurants rubbing shoulders with innovative new wine bars and traditional pubs, and you can sleep in a magnificent 19th-century Scottish baronial style Seaman's mission—now a sleek design hotel. Its history is a colorful one: it was home to 56 sailors and at one time was also a "house of ill-repute." Today, its brasserie and bar are buzzing, with guests spilling out onto the cobbled street. Opt for a room at the front overlooking the port, if possible, as rooms at the back are darker, and with no view to speak of.

1 Tower Place. www.malmaison.com. © **0131/468-5000.** 100 units. Doubles £175–£205, suites £245–£295. Bus 16 or 22. **Amenities:** Restaurant; bar; gym; room service; free parking; free Wi-Fi.

SOUTHSIDE
Moderate

94DR ★★   The rooms in this boutique B&B are all named after whiskies. Even the room for children with its bunk-beds, books, games, DVDs and Xbox is called the Wee Dram. 94DR—that's 94 Dalkeith Road—is a Victorian townhouse in the Blackett Conservation Area. As a B&B it's a cut above: Paul Lightfoot and John MacEwan have created a designer haven with a cool grey color scheme, wool and tweed fabrics and a scattering of reindeer skins. The Bowmore room has a giant button-backed grey headboard, a cast-iron claw-foot tub and under-floor heating, with bay windows looking out onto Salisbury Craggs and Arthur's Seat. Rooms at the back have views of the walled garden and Pentland Hills. It's not exactly central, but nowhere in this compact capital is far away. It's just a 5-minute walk to Arthur's Seat and a 10-minute bus ride to Princes Street. Paul is also a chef, so breakfast is a

Edinburgh has a vibrant cafe culture and there's no shortage of artisan micro-roasters, hipster baristas, and third-wave coffee hotspots where you can grab a flat white or macchiato and marvel at the latte-art. **Cairngorm Coffee** (www.cairngormcoffee.com) has two branches in the New Town, starkly different in design to differentiate them from the one-style-fits-all chains. The cafe at 1 Melville Place is all high copper-and-wood tables and bright, light interiors, open weekdays from 8am to 6pm and 9am to 6pm at weekends. The cozy basement cafe at 41a Frederick Street, meanwhile, is more rugged mountain-chic and is open weekdays from 8am to 5pm, opening at 9am weekends. You could imagine holing up here among the sacks of coffee, nursing a latte as a blizzard raged outside. Another basement bolthole is **Lowdown Coffee,** the pared-back minimalist design Japanese in inspiration, the beans from Swedish roaster, Koppi, the moreish cakes homemade. The cool kitchen counter layout was designed to encourage you to chat as if you're in a friend's apartment. At 40 George Street (no website; ✆ **0131/226-2132**), it's open 8am to 6pm weekdays, from 9am Saturday and 10am Sunday.

In the Old Town **Brew Lab Coffee** deserves a shout out (www.brewlab coffee.co.uk; ✆ **0131/662-8963**). Coffee connoisseurs Tom Hyde and Dave Law converted an old university office on South College Street near the National Museum of Scotland into a specialty coffee bar with an industrial vibe, concrete counter and retro reclaimed furniture. This is the real deal. Each day there are four rotating single origin, micro-lot coffees to choose from, two filtered using the Kalita Wave pour-over and two used for espresso-based coffees. You can even take a barista course in the basement. The training lab offers two- and three-hour masterclasses in espresso-making, latte art and filter brewing as well as cupping sessions with tasting notes. It's open weekdays from 8am and weekends from 9am until 6:30pm.

Edinburgh's homegrown coffee empire **Artisan Roast** kick-started the capital's caffeine craze with the opening of its Broughton Street branch and on-site roastery in 2007 (www.artisanroast. co.uk; ✆ **07858/884-756**). They now have a separate roastery and lab, three hipster hangouts (Stockbridge, Broughton Street, and Bruntsfield) and pop-up cafes each summer. The Bruntsfield branch began life as a pop-up in fact during the Fringe Festival. Broughton Street is open weekdays from 8am and weekends from 9am until 6:30pm and 6pm on Sunday.

Tea lovers need a brew too, of course. **Eteaket,** at 41 Frederick Street (www.eteaket.co.uk; ✆ **0131/226-2982**), is a specialty teahouse with a tea menu as long as your arm, open daily from 9am until 6pm. Choose from black teas including Second Flush Darjeeling, Lapsang Souchong and Royal Earl Grey, Oolong teas, Green teas, Rooibos, flowering and herbal teas. They also mix tea cocktails. Move seamlessly from teatime to cocktail hour with a Royal Earl Grey G&T. You can even get a cappuccino. (The coffee comes from Artisan Roast.) Why go to Starbucks when you can patronize these home-grown cafes?

gourmet feast—although if you want a lie-in, ask for a breakfast box in your room.

94 Dalkeith Road. www.94dr.com. ✆ **0131/662-9265.** 7 units. Doubles £80–£200 including breakfast. **Amenities:** Concierge service; loaner bikes; free Wi-Fi.

WHERE TO EAT

Chefs in Edinburgh perform gastronomic acrobatics with the country's overflowing natural larder. There are a handful of Michelin-starred restaurants: **21212** (www.21212restaurant.co.uk; © **0131/523-1030**), **Martin Wishart** (www.restaurantmartinwishart.co.uk; © **0131/553-3557**), **The Kitchin** (www.thekitchin.com; © **0131/555-1755**) and **Number One** at The Balmoral (www.roccofortehotels.com; © **0131/557-6727**), but it's not the star count that sets pulses racing. It's the innovation and experimentation of the fine supporting cast who are pushing the gastronomic boundaries: Chefs such as Stuart Ralston at **Aizle** (see p. 95) who has scrapped the menu altogether, and Ben Reade and Sashana Souza Zanella who founded another wild card, the **Edinburgh Food Studio** (www.edinburghfoodstudio.com; © **0131/258-0758**) which walks a fine line between supper club, restaurant, and culinary workshop.

With all the homegrown talent in the capital, the arrival on the scene of anonymous chains is a worrying trend. The city's independent restaurants and chefs need supporting—and it's a win-win situation: diners get to experience the real flavor of Scotland. That flavor that comes from a natural larder stocked with wild venison from ancient Highland estates, heather-fed lamb, Aberdeen Angus beef, and salmon from its rushing rivers. Add shellfish from the chilly waters off the Scottish coast—langoustines (aka Dublin Bay Prawns), oysters, mussels, and plump hand-dived scallops along with fish such as halibut, bream, and sea bass.

A good guide to grab for more dining ideas is *The List* magazine's comprehensive *Eating & Drinking Guide* updated annually and featuring reviews of hundreds of restaurants, bars, and cafes in Edinburgh. It is available to buy or check out the reviews online.

NEW TOWN
Expensive

Mark Greenaway ★★★ PROGRESSIVE BRITISH Award-winning chef, Mark Greenaway, a TV cooking show and food festival regular and a proud champion of Scottish produce, heads up his eponymous restaurant in the New Town. His exquisite dishes are Instagram-perfect, the signature Loch Fyne crab cannelloni with smoked cauliflower custard, lemon pearls, herb butter, and baby coriander is a jaw-dropping crowd-pleaser. The setting, a moody blue teal dining room with crisp, white tablecloths and statement brass cluster chandelier is pure class—as are the deconstructed desserts. Greenaway is justifiably famous for his puddings. Another signature is the Knot Chocolate tart, composed of custard jelly, frozen cookies, crème fraiche parfait, salted caramel, and kumquat puree. The presentation is precise perfection, the flavors fabulous.

69 North Castle St. www.markgreenaway.com. © **0131/226-1155.** Mains £21–£29, 3-course market menu £30, 4-course tasting menu £50, 8-course tasting menu £75. Tues–Sat noon–2:30pm, 5:30–10pm.

Moderate

Cafe St Honoré ★★ BRITISH BISTRO   Hidden down a cobbled alley in the New Town is a cozy bistro that catapults you straight to the Left Bank. Style-wise it's old-school Parisian brasserie, the walls lined with mirrors, a black-and-white tiled floor, and starched white tablecloths. The classic cooking style might be French, but the ingredients showcase the best of Scotland's natural produce. The menu changes daily (there are also gluten-free and dairy-free menus) and features dishes such as organic beetroot and red onion tarte tatin, endive, Blue Murder cheese, and candied Californian walnuts; and Perthshire venison with roast beetroot, Stornoway black pudding, and organic kale.

34 North West Thistle St. www.cafesthonore.com. ℂ **0131/226-2211.** Mains £17–£25, 2-course express lunch £14.50. Daily noon–2pm, Mon–Fri 5:15–10pm, Sat–Sun 6–10pm.

Inexpensive

The Dogs ★★ BRITISH REVIVAL   You can't beat this eclectic eatery for kitsch style, a smattering of dog-themed memorabilia, and a quirky menu at wallet-hugging, not mugging, prices. David Ramsden's shabby-chic little joint on the first floor of a Georgian townhouse dishes up old-school favorites with a twist: think fried ox liver on Scotch broth with crispy kale, or soused herring in oatmeal with potato salad. If you have room for dessert, don't miss the whisky-laced rice pudding. Ramsden also launched a cool wine bar in 2017 in the Old Town, The Fat Pony (www.thefatpony.com; ℂ **0131/229-5770**), in his inimitable style, with cheese and charcuterie platters to go with a wine list that includes orange, biodynamic, organic, and vegan.

110 Hanover St. www.thedogsonline.co.uk. ℂ **0131/220-1208.** £12–£15. Weekdays noon–2:30pm, weekends noon–4pm daily 6–10pm.

Urban Angel ★ CAFE   Before it became fashionable, Gilly Macpherson was pioneering the seasonal, sustainable, and local ethos in her independent cafe in an old bakery in the city center. She's a woman on a mission to cut down food miles while creating mouth-watering, healthy food (there are vegan, vegetarian, and gluten-free options every day). All cozy, country-chic with old stone floors and chapel chairs, you can tuck into delicious all-day brunch options such as a peanut butter and maca bowl (a smoothie bowl of banana, peanut butter, maca, chia seeds, dates, and almond milk topped with cacao nibs and granola), or ripe avocado on toast with slow-roasted tomato, feta, chili flakes, mint, and lime. Popular lunch options include baked little goats' brie with fig, walnuts, and endive salad.

121 Hanover St. www.urban-angel.co.uk. ℂ **0131/225-6215.** Breakfast £4–£10.50, mains £8.80–£9.90. Mon–Fri 8am–5pm; Sat–Sun 9am–5pm.

OLD TOWN
Expensive

Timberyard ★★★ MODERN BRITISH   Behind a giant red door on Lady Lawson Street is one of the capital's most inventive culinary spaces. Once a costume and props warehouse, at another time—you guessed it—a timber yard, the industrial-scale dining area is all rough-hewn floors, bare light bulbs suspended from the rafters, metal columns and wood-stacks, a traditional stove, and bundles of tartan rugs to add coziness. There's also a butchery, a smokehouse, a kitchen garden, private dining in the Shed, an old brick outhouse, and open-air seating in the sunny south-facing Yard. A family affair, Andrew and Lisa Radford set up their latest venture with their children Ben, Jo, and Abi. Ben is the chef, the menu featuring inventive plates such as pigeon, endive, salt plum, rowan along with veal sweetbreads, truffle, artichoke, sea purslane, hazelnut. Lunch and pre-theatre menus are a la carte, but in the evening the choice is between a four-course or eight-course menu, a six-course fish menu also available for lunch and dinner. Wines are natural and sourced from small artisan European producers, cocktails courtesy of Jo, a mean mixologist who also creates herbal tonics and cordials from the kitchen garden.

10 Lady Lawson St. www.timberyard.co. ⓒ **0131/221-1222.** Mains £13; 4-course set menu £55, paired drinks an extra £40; 8-course set menu £77, paired drinks an extra £70. Tues–Sat noon–2pm, 5:30–9:30pm.

Moderate

White Horse Oyster & Seafood Bar ★★ SEAFOOD   Oyster Happy Hour is from 4 to 6pm Monday to Thursday, the salty crustaceans shucked at the bespoke green marble bar of this sleek seafood restaurant in what was the oldest inn on the Royal Mile (1742 is etched in stone above the door). It's a "buck a shuck"—well, £1. Hammering home the seafood theme, there's a custom-designed lobster tank, and even the bread is served with seaweed butter. This is the latest venture from the team that brought the capital's carnivores to their knees with the Chophouse Bar & Butchery steakhouses (www.chophousesteak.co.uk). The design here also has wow factor with a moody industrial vibe, leather banquettes, and exposed stonework. As for the food? You remember those jokes about the seafood diet? It's a challenge not to go crazy and order everything on the menu—especially as the small plates are designed for sharing. Special shout-outs have to go to the chargrilled octopus—soft, smoky, and succulent tentacles with crispy kale and citrusy ponzu sauce, and the rich monkfish satay with toasted nuts. There are seafood platters of course, mains such as crab linguine and whole lemon sole, and on Sunday they do a special Surf & Turf lunch with rib-eye steak, half a lobster, and fries for a weekend blow-out.

266 Canongate. www.whitehorseoysterbar.co.uk. ⓒ **0131/629-5300.** Mains £19–£26. Daily noon–late.

SOUTHSIDE

Moderate

Aizle ★★ MODERN SCOTTISH   Have you the courage to take a culinary leap in the dark? That's the pre-requisite for booking a table at Aizle (rhymes with hazel—and is the old Scots word for spark or glowing ember). Diners put themselves in Chef Stuart Ralston's hands—not exactly a risky move. Ralston worked with Gordon Ramsay in New York. But you do have to surrender to the experience. There's no menu, just a list of seasonal ingredients used to create the imaginative five-course tasting menu. The Spring Harvest's highlighted produce includes maitake mushroom, wild garlic, lobster, beetroot, squid ink and sorrel—not all in the same dish. Or maybe they are . . . Everything is made in-house, from the sourdough bread to hand-churned butter and the aged kombucha in the cocktails. They do a mean cocktail . . .

107-109 St Leonard's St. www.aizle.co.uk. ℂ **0131/662-9349.** 5-course tasting menu £55 paired drinks an extra £40. Wed–Sat 5–9pm.

STOCKBRIDGE
Moderate
The Scran & Scallie ★★ GASTROPUB   When two of the capital's top chefs—Tom Kitchin and Dominic Jack—open a gastropub, chances are they know what they're doing. The fact that the Scran & Scallie was awarded a Michelin guide Bib Gourmand in 2017 proves that they do. This is posh pub grub (*scran* means grub and *scallie* is scallywag) and hearty and wholesome comfort food. You can tuck into homemade beef sausage and potato mousseline (that's bangers and mash goes gourmet), fish and chips with chunky tartar sauce or braised lamb shoulder, peas, pancetta and lettuce. Design-wise, it's Scotland meets Scandinavia (Tom's wife Michaela is Swedish), with a shabby-chic vibe, a medley of mismatched chairs, exposed brickwork, rough-hewn floors, a wood-burning stove, Scottish tweeds, and sheepskin rugs.

1 Comely Bank Road. www.scranandscallie.com. ℂ **0131/332-6281.** Mains £13–£20. Mon–Fri noon–3pm, bar food 3–5pm, 5–10pm; Sat, Sun 8:30–11am noon–10pm.

EAST END
Expensive
21212 ★★★ CONTEMPORARY FRENCH   This is Edinburgh's only Michelin-starred restaurant with rooms: an inspired idea allowing dazed diners to stumble upstairs to their boutique-hotel bed in this heritage-listed Georgian townhouse, after experiencing Paul Kitching's alchemy in the open-kitchen theater. There's drama in the decor too, a giant moth-themed carpet, crystal chandeliers, and private dining "pod" with a pink marble table, circular cream leather banquette and kitsch cherub-laced Caravaggio print wallpaper. It's a whirlwind for the senses, but taste is at the forefront, of course. Each dish is a work of art and explosion of flavors, giddying invention and experimentation. BBC 2 for instance is a starter of brown barley, crab bisque, beets, and celeriac. You won't be bored. Book a table.

3 Royal Terrace. www.21212restaurant.co.uk. ℂ **0131/523-1030.** 5-course dinner £85, 2-course lunch £20 on weekdays. Tues–Sat noon–1:45pm; Tues–Thurs 7–9pm; Fri–Sat 6:45–9:30pm.

Moderate
The Gardener's Cottage ★★ BRITISH   When chefs around the country were jumping on the local, seasonal bandwagon and chattering about cutting down food miles, two young chefs, Edward Murray and Dale Mailley,

If you're foot-sore and famished, there's no shortage of independent little eateries where you can pick up a quick bite or lunch on the go, many so popular they've spawned off-shoots. Swedish success story **Soderberg,** started life on the southern outskirts of the Old Town at Quartermile (www.soderberg.co.uk; (**0131/228-5876**), as a bakery and cafe selling artisan sourdough breads and cardamom buns along with steaming bowls of soup and Scandinavian-style high-stacked open sandwiches. There are now six sprinkled across the city (varying opening times). The original, Soderberg The Meadows, is open from 7:30am weekdays and 9am weekends until 7pm. Also on the south side of the city is German bakery and kaffeehaus, **Falko & Konditormeister,** at 185 Bruntsfield Place (www.falko.co.uk; (**0131/656-0763**), famous for its German breads, cakes, and pretzels, Wednesday through Saturday from 9am, Sunday from 9:30am until 6pm. There's another outpost of this popular cafe and bakery in the historic East Lothian market town of Haddington.

Just off Leith Walk at 90 Brunswick Street **Twelve Triangles** is a tiny gem, a bakery and cafe (www.twelvetriangles.com; (**0131/629-4664**), specializing in slow-fermented doughs and doughnuts (oozing custards of caramel, pistachio, peanut or lemon ricotta) and open daily 9:30am until 5pm. You can pick up artisan breads (charcoal anyone?) and pastries here or in the second branch in Portobello. The third, called Twelve Triangles Kitchen Table, is a place to gather, eat—and take a fermentation workshop and is open daily 9:30am to 4:30pm. Also in the East End at 22

Easter Street is locals' favorite, the **Manna House Bakery & Patisserie** ((**0131/652-2349**) with its deli-style lunches and artisan breads—and there's now a second branch in Queensferry. In New Town, another old-timer is still going strong after more than 50 years. **Hendersons** (www.hendersonsofedinburgh.co.uk; (**0131/225-2131**) shop and deli on Hanover Street is a vegan and vegetarian deli and cafe, open Monday to Saturday from 8:30am until 5:30pm, with a vegan restaurant round the corner on Thistle Street (think tofu teriyaki Buddha bowl with coconut, lime, and coriander rice, Asian veg, pickled shitake and candied radish) open Sunday to Thursday noon to 9pm, Friday and Saturday noon until 10pm. Also on Hanover Street, locals queue out the door at **Urban Angel** (www.urban-angel.co.uk; (**0131/225-6215**) for brunch. The eggs benedict is legendary while the French toast comes with bacon and maple syrup for traditionalists or berries, aniseed sugar and orange yoghurt. It's open weekdays from 8am, weekends from 9am until 5pm. The new kid on the block, meanwhile, is Rowan Taylor or the **Bearded Baker** (www.thebeardedbaker.co.uk; (**0131/281-9285**) whose bagels were such a hit he opened a little cafe in Canonmills at 46 Rodney Street. Choose from a classic smoked salmon, cream cheese, pickled cucumber, and dill, or go wild with a Reuben: pastrami, sauerkraut, gruyere and mustard mayo. The homemade doughnuts aren't bad either (white chocolate and pecan, lemon meringue, cinnamon maple . . .). It's open weekdays from 7:30am until 5pm and 9am to 4pm at the weekend.

5

EDINBURGH & THE LOTHIAN REGION | Where to Eat

went out and found a real gardener's cottage on the edge of Royal Terrace Gardens and planted a vegetable patch. They converted the rundown 19th-century stone cottage into one of the hottest dining spots in the capital. The long communal wooden tables are decked out with jars of wildflowers and mismatched china, while an old record player fills the rooms with jazz. The blackboard at the door is scrawled with the daily changing menu, featuring dishes such as lamb, heritage potato, wild garlic, and smoked ricotta. The sourdough comes from their bakery and cafe down in Leith, Quay Commons Pony (www.quaycommons.co; ℂ 0131/677-0244), opened in 2017 in an old warehouse.

1 Royal Terrace Gardens. www.thegardenerscottage.co. ℂ **0131/677-0244.** 7-course set dinner menu £30, 4-course set lunch £21 lunch a la carte mains £14–£22. Daily noon–2:30pm; 5–10pm; Sat–Sun 10am–2:30pm.

Le Roi Fou ★★ FRENCH The broad-beamed men of Edinburgh breathed a collective sigh of relief when Jerome Henry blew into town. A chef with solid credentials delivering dishes they'd actually heard of, man-size portions and none of that flower-sprinkling nonsense: fancy—but not too fancy. Henry was the head chef of Anton Mosimann's Dining Club and Le Trois Garcons in London. Now he has his own kingdom. This is classic high-end cooking with flashes of genius. The spiced fish soup with gurnard and tomato is a deep, dark, rich, velvety bisque of such intensity you'll have to stop yourself licking the bowl. Mains such as roasted guinea fowl with braised leg, olive and preserved lemon sauce and grilled dry-aged beef fillet with market vegetables, pommes frites and four-pepper sauce don't try to reinvent the wheel but do caress your taste buds. And you can never go wrong with a side of pommes frites.

1 Forth St. www.leroifou.com. ℂ**0131/557-9346.** Mains £16–£31. 2-course pre-theater menu £19, 3-course pre-theater menu £23, 6-course tasting menu £50 with paired wine £40. Tues–Wed 5–10pm; Thurs–Sat noon–2:30pm; 5–10:30pm.

Inexpensive
Joseph Pearce ★★ SWEDISH GASTROPUB Swedish couple Anna and Mike Christopherson's bohemian bar and eatery empire just keeps growing. There are now six eclectic spots scattered across the capital, from the original bijoux Boda Bar to Akva, which boasts the biggest beer garden in Edinburgh. All have a quirky menu of extras from knitting nights to jogging clubs, language cafes to crayfish parties—check out the website for events. Joseph Pearce is a gastropub with retro chic vibe, comfy sofas and frilly lampshades, and bottomless Bloody Marys. Food-wise the menu includes Scandi favorites such as Swedish meatballs with mustard mash and lingonberry jam and spicy crayfish pasta with red chili and onion along with a range of gourmet burgers and smorgasbord platters. It's also family-friendly: in the back there's a stack of high chairs, toys, and games.

23 Elm Row. www.bodabar.com. ℂ**0131/556-4140.** Mains £10–£12. Sun–Thurs 11am–midnight, Fri–Sat 11am–1am.

LEITH
Expensive
The Kitchin ★★★ MODERN BRITISH A vocal champion of Scotland's natural larder, "Nature to Plate" has been Tom Kitchin's philosophy since

opening his restaurant on Leith's revamped waterfront in 2006. (He was awarded a Michelin star just 7 months later). It's also the name of his first book (he's now got three under his belt including *Kitchin Suppers* and *Meat & Game*). The space includes a dining area, kitchen, and butchery and a whisky snug with exposed stonework from the building's previous incarnation as a whisky warehouse. Textures and fabrics (tweeds of course) conjure up the colors of the Scottish landscape. Add sheepskins from the Isle of Skye and bespoke tableware in earthy tones and the result is a relaxed, natural atmosphere. The restaurant might be Michelin-starred, but it's not stiff or stuffy, the produce Scotland's best, the cooking style French. Don't miss the signature surf and turf starter, pig's head and langoustine. Main courses include Roe Deer from the Scottish Borders (with root vegetable mash, fresh apple, and red wine sauce) and Monkfish from Scrabster on the north coast (with diced spring vegetables, squid ink pasta, capers, and saffron sauce).

78 Commercial St. www.thekitchin.com. ✆ **0131/555-1755.** 3-course set lunch £33, 3-course a la carte dinner £75, the Chef's surprise tasting menu and vegetarian surprise tasting menu £85. Tues–Sat noon–2pm; Tues–Thurs 6–9:15pm; Fri–Sat 6–9:30pm.

Norn ★★★ MODERN SCOTTISH   Leith is no stranger to gastronomic gravitas. The once down-at-heel docklands boasts not one but two of the capital's Michelin-starred venues (Martin Wishart's eponymous restaurant and The Kitchin) while just round the corner, the lively waterfront is peppered with gastropubs and fish restaurants. Edinburgh's appetite for excellent eateries in insatiable, however, and Norn was a welcome addition in 2016. In shades of grey and beige, the decor is neutral and unassuming, the perfect plain canvas on which to showcase chef-owner Scott Smith's inventive and experimental four- and seven-course tasting menus. Even the bread and butter is a work of art. The bread is made from not one, but two starters and Orcadian beremeal, a native grain from Orkney, while the butter is churned fresh in the kitchen. The wine, much of it natural and biodynamic, is sourced from small artisan winemakers.

50-54 Henderson St. www.nornrestaurant.com. ✆ **0131/629-2525.** 4-course set menu £40, paired drinks £35, 7-course menu £65 paired drinks £60. Tues–Wed 7pm–late; Thurs–Sat 5:30pm–late.

Inexpensive

Toast ★★ WINE CAFE   Customers cram into this funky, jazz-filled cafe in a former art gallery on Leith's vibrant waterfront, and spill out of the door onto the pavement tables. Inside it's all exposed brickwork, granite-grey paintwork, and a mix of high-table perches and turquoise velvet banquettes in the picture windows. The atmosphere is bustling, the menu mouth-wateringly simple and wholesome with avocado toast, huevos rancheros, and platters of local cheeses. The carefully curated wine list is the main draw, of course. About 30 of the 100 wines are organic or biodynamic. Wines by the glass are changed every week, and there are regularly scheduled tastings.

65 The Shore. www.toastleith.co.uk. ✆ **0131/467-6984.** Mains £6.50-8. Mon–Wed 8am–10pm; Thurs 8am–11pm; Fri 8am–midnight; Sat 9am–midnight; Sun 9am–9pm.

SHOPPING

After a spot of retail therapy? Three main shopping drags run parallel to each other in the city center: In the New Town, Princes Street is the main high street, the stately homegrown department store, **Jenners,** at one end; while George Street is more of a high-brow high street, bookended by Charlotte Square and St Andrews Square with its London interlopers: design-led department store **Harvey Nichols** and a cluster of designer shops within teetering distance along **Multrees Walk.**

Across Princes Street Gardens, in the Old Town, the **Royal Mile** is strung with shops selling cashmere, kilts, tweed, and tartan tat along with a few specialist whisky stores, but swing down **Cockburn Street** and **Victoria Street** to the **Grassmarket** and you'll stumble upon quirky boutiques and vintage clothing stores.

As part of the £150-million New Waverley development the Waverley Arches, 19 listed Victorian arches on East Market Street have also been renovated and opened as a quirky new retail and dining spot, the vaulted spaces tempting in independent boutiques. And the elephant in the room is the £850-million redevelopment of the St James Centre, the shopping mall at the top of Leith Walk, which was an ugly '60s eyesore. The new development is due to be completed in 2020.

It's Edinburgh's "village" neighborhoods, however, where you'll find the most interesting independent stores. **Bruntsfield** has chic boutiques and a vibrant cafe culture as does the **West End Village,** a string of Georgian streets between the Waldorf-Astoria hotel and Haymarket which even has its own website: www.edinburgh-westend.co.uk. **Stockbridge,** meanwhile, is peppered with cafes and specialist food stores, such as old-school deli **Herbie** (www.herbieofedinburgh.co.uk; ✆ **0131/332-9888**); French patisserie and artisan bakery, **La Barantine** (www.labarantine.com; ✆ **0131/332-8455**); **Raeburn Fine Wines** (www.raeburnfinewines.com; ✆ **0131/343-1159**); and not just one, but two specialty cheesemongers: **George Mewes Cheese** (www.georgemewescheese.co.uk; ✆ **0131/332-5900**) and **I.J. Mellis** (www.mellis cheese.net; ✆ **0131/226-6215**): it's a real hub for food lovers. It's also home to an increasingly popular farmers market every Sunday (www.stockbridge market.com), giving the jauntily striped stalls of the original Saturday **farmers market** (www.edinburghfarmersmarket.co.uk) on Castle Terrace every Saturday morning a run for its money.

ACCESSORIES & GIFTS

Alistir Tait ★ An Aladdin's cave of a jewelry shop down a tiny cobbled alley in the New Town, you can sift through rare Scottish freshwater pearls from the Spey and Tay rivers, renowned for their unique luster and colors, quartz jewels from the Cairngorm mountains, Scottish gold and antique jewelry from Georgian to Victorian, Art Nouveau and Art Deco. 116A Rose St. www. alistirtaitgem.co.uk. ✆ **0131/225-4105.**

Fabhatrix ★★ Tricorns and bicorns, top hats and flat caps, bowlers, fedoras, trilbies, pork pies and homburgs: and that's just for men. In the basement workshop of this modern-day millinery, handmade creations are sculpted and pinned from soft wools and felts, Scottish tweeds, velvets and vintage fabrics, from over-sized peak caps to feather-trimmed berets and Harris Tweed fascinators. 13 Cowgatehead, off Grassmarket. www.fabhatrix.com. 🕾 **0131/225-9222.**

Homer ★★ This eclectic homeware emporium is spread through five rooms of a grand Georgian townhouse in the New Town, roughly themed around the kitchen and dining room, bathroom and bedroom, garden and living room. There's a mix of vintage shabby chic furniture, ceramics, rustic linens, velvet bedspreads, and bespoke Fair Isle blankets. 8 Howe St. www.athomer.co.uk. 🕾 **0131/225-3168.**

Life Story ★★ When Susan Doherty took over this lifestyle concept store with its focus on Scandinavian design, crafts, and gifts in Edinburgh's East End she added coffee and cake—a touch of hygge in the Scottish capital. You can browse the cushions, cozy blankets, prints, and jewelry before tucking into a salted caramel brownie and matcha latte or flat white in the cafe at the back. 53 London St. www.lifestoryshop.com. 🕾 **0131/629-9699.**

The Method ★★ This Zen-like lifestyle store and therapy room is an artfully arranged, calm space in Stockbridge. Sparse shelves showcase a range of natural seaweed scrubs, soaps and potions, lotions and balms, candles and incense, tactile ceramics and concrete bowls. If mindfulness could be packaged this is where you'd find it. Downstairs you can indulge in Ayurvedic massage and facials. 9 St Stephen St. www.themethod.life. 🕾 **0131/225-4770.**

Red Door Gallery ★ Championing artisan makers and local artists, Red Door is a popular gallery packed with bespoke jewelry, quirky one-off pieces and affordable artworks. It's a carefully curated exhibition space, the team all artists and designers themselves, where you can while away an hour browsing the collection of prints and paintings. 42 Victoria St. www.edinburghart.com. 🕾 **0131/477-3255.**

FOOD & DRINK

Demijohn ★★ The demijohns (large glass bottles) in this self-styled liquid deli are full of fragrant oils, vinegars, liqueurs, artisan wines, and meads, which are decanted into an Italian glass bottle of your choice. You're encouraged to try before you buy. You might not want to sip Perthshire rapeseed oil or Gooseberry Vinegar, but Sloe Gin or Bramble Scotch Whisky Liqueur? 32 Victoria St. www.demijohn.co.uk. 🕾 **0131/225-4090.**

I.J. Mellis ★★★ Follow your nose to this specialist cheese monger to discover a world of fine farmhouse Scottish, Irish, and French cheeses. There are often queues out of the door of the Old Town branch, where locals also pick up artisan breads, olives, and pickles. At the back of the Morningside store, they've opened a Cheese Lounge where customers can tuck into simple cheese plates and wine. 30A Victoria St. www.mellischeese.net. 🕾 **0131/226-6215.**

Valvona & Crolla ★★   The Contini family are Edinburgh deli royalty—and this local institution, established in 1934, is reassuringly old school. It feels like stepping back in time, with hams hanging from the high ceiling, old wooden shelves crammed with Scottish and Italian delicacies that include artisan Tuscan honey and the family specialty, a spicy fonteluna sausage, the recipe created in their Italian mountain village a thousand years ago. At the back of the long, narrow shop is a cafe where you can tuck into traditional rustic fare, made from recipes handed down over the years. 19 Elm Row. www.valvonacrolla.co.uk. ℂ **0131/556-6066.**

CASHMERE, TARTANS & KILTS

21st Century Kilts ★★   From camouflage to Harris Tweed, PVC to denim, owner Howie Nicholsby designs contemporary kilts in his tiny New Town store. Passion for men's skirts runs in the family: his father, Geoffrey is one of the most famous kiltmakers in Edinburgh, counting Sean Connery and Mel Gibson among past clients. For a traditional hand-sewn, made to measure kilt head to his High Street store, Geoffrey's Kilts. 48 Thistle St. www.21stcenturykilts.com. ℂ **0131/220-9450.** 57 High St. www.geoffreykilts.co.uk. ℂ **0131/557-0256.**

Anta ★★★   In 2012 designers Annie and Lachlan Stewart opened their sleek flagship store on George Street over in the New Town. Provenance is key for this brand and everything from the cushions to the capsule clothing collection is made in Scotland: the yarn for the tweeds, carpets, and tartan cabin bags comes from the Western Isles and is woven in the Borders, the furniture is made from Scottish oak, while the signature ceramics are hand-decorated in the Highlands. 117-119 George St. www.anta.co.uk. ℂ **0131/225-9096.**

Hawico ★★★   This cashmere company might have been producing the finest woolens in its Scottish Borders mills for over a century, but there's not a whiff of the heritage brand about this bright, light, sleekly minimalist store which oozes class and has price tags to match. The collections and accessories are displayed with precision and artistry. 71 Grassmarket. www.hawico.com. ℂ **0131/225-8634.**

Walker Slater ★★   "Specialists in Scottish tweed" sounds stuffy and old-fashioned. However, this is anything but. Think a Ralph Lauren vibe in the stylishly bare-boarded stores on Victoria Street. Contemporary bespoke tailoring sits alongside rugged knitwear and linens. 18-20 Victoria St. (Menswear), 46 Victoria St. (ladieswear). www.walkerslater.com. ℂ **0131/220-2636.**

ENTERTAINMENT & NIGHTLIFE

Edinburgh sizzles through summer with a frenzy of festivals, but the capital has a thriving year-round cultural scene with a rich array of theatre, film, dance, and music events across the city's venues. The West End around Lothian Road is where you'll find a cluster of theatres and cinemas, while in the Old Town the area around Cowgate and Grassmarket has a vibrant, student-focused nightlife. In the New Town, George Street is buzzing after dark with clubbers and partygoers, while Rose Street and West Register Street are packed with bars and traditional pubs.

Entertainment & Nightlife

EDINBURGH & THE LOTHIAN REGION

THE PERFORMING ARTS

BALLET, OPERA & CLASSICAL MUSIC   Performances by the **Scottish Ballet** and the **Scottish Opera** can be enjoyed at the **Edinburgh Playhouse** (see below). The **Scottish Chamber Orchestra** (www.sco.org.uk) performs at the **Queen's Hall,** Clerk Street (www.thequeenshall.net; ✆ **0131/668-2019**). Edinburgh's other major music venue is the **Usher Hall** (www.usherhall.co.uk; ✆ **0131/228-1155**), which presents mainly classical concerts but also some jazz, rock, and pop.

COMEDY   Open 7 nights a week, **The Stand** (www.thestand.co.uk; ✆ **0131/558-7272**) on York Place in Edinburgh's New Town is regarded by many as one of the world's best comedy clubs and is the place to catch both raw talent and established acts.

FILM   Edinburgh's Lothian Road has more than its fair share of cinemas. At the Princes Street end, the **Filmhouse,** 88 Lothian Rd. (www.filmhousecinema.com; ✆ **0131/228-2688**), is Edinburgh's arthouse cinema, showing a diverse range of mainstream, independent, and repertory titles. Heading south, the Art Deco **Cameo,** 38 Home St. (www.picturehouses.com; ✆ **0871/902-5723**), is one of Edinburgh's best-loved cinemas and the place to catch new, mainly mainstream releases. Midway between the two is a multi-screen **Odeon,** 18 Lothian Rd. (www.odeon.co.uk; ✆ **0871/2244-007**). There's also a multi-screen **Vue** cinema at the Edinburgh Omni Centre (www.omniedinburgh.co.uk; ✆ **0131/524-7770**) at the top of Leith Walk.

FOLK MUSIC   Folk music is performed in a number of pubs around the city such as the legendary **Sandy Bell's** (www.sandybells.co.uk; ✆ **0131/225-2751**), 25 Forrest Rd. There are live sessions here every night, from Scottish and Irish folk to blues and bluegrass. Many make a pilgrimage to this pub where the likes of Gerry Rafferty, Barbara Dickson and Billy Connolly once performed. **The Royal Oak** (www.royal-oak-folk.com; ✆ **0131/557-2976**) is another popular venue, 1 Infirmary St. The **Leith Folk Club** (www.leithfolkclub.com; ✆ **07833/135-399**) holds regular folk, blues, and country music sessions at the Victoria Park House Hotel, 221 Ferry Rd. Also look out for information on the **Scots Music Group** (www.scotsmusic.org; ✆ **0131/555-7668**), which organizes regular ceilidhs in the city.

THEATRE   At the mainstream end of the market, you've got the **Edinburgh Playhouse,** 18–22 Greenside Place (www. playhousetheatre.com; ✆ **0844/871-3014**), the city's largest theatre dating back to the 1920s (it was saved from demolition by a petition in the 1970s and was decreed a listed building) whose program focuses on large-scale touring musicals, comedy, and dance; and the **Festival Theatre,** 13–29 Nicolson St., and **King's Theatre,** 2 Leven St., both managed by the same company. Tickets for their wide repertoire of classical entertainment can be booked by phone or online (www.capitaltheatres.com; ✆ **0131/529-6000**). The resident company of the **Royal Lyceum Theatre,** 30b Grindlay Street (www.lyceum.org.uk; ✆ **0131/248-4848**), produces a strong program of work from both established and new playwrights. The

EDINBURGH & THE LOTHIAN REGION

Entertainment & Nightlife

Traverse Theatre, 10 Cambridge Street (www.traverse.co.uk; ✆ **0131/228-1404**), is dedicated to presenting new work by contemporary Scottish writers. The **Scottish Story Telling Centre,** 43 High St. (www.tracscotland.org; ✆ **0131/556-9579**), presents a regular program of storytelling, theatre, and music events in its small performance space.

BARS, PUBS & CLUBS

The bar and pub scene is equally vibrant, from olde-worlde pubs to glitzy cocktail bars. And it's not just all about whisky; gin is now basking in the spotlight. Under the city's pavements at the west end of Princes Street is a distillery where Edinburgh Gin is created in copper stills (1a Rutlant Pl.; www.edinburghgin.com; ✆ **0131/656-2810**). During the day you can take a tutored tasting; at night it turns into a funky cocktail bar, Heads & Tales (www.headsandtalesbar.com; ✆ **0131/656-2811**).

When it comes to **bars and pubs,** the **Grassmarket** in Old Town and **Broughton Street** in New Town are buzzing, as is the waterfront in the rejuvenated docklands of **Leith.** There's no shortage of traditional pubs where you can sup a pint or take a nip of whisky with locals propping up the bar. A couple of old stalwarts include the **Barony Bar** on Broughton Street (www. thebarony.co.uk; ✆ **0131/556-9251**) and the **Cumberland** in the New Town (1-3 Cumberland Street; www.cumberlandbar.co.uk; ✆ **0131/558-3134**) which has one of the best beer gardens in the city. The cocktail is now king, however, in Edinburgh, and one of the best places to sip one in the New Town is **Bramble ★★** (16A Queen St.; www.bramblebar.co.uk; ✆ **0131/226-6343**). This tiny boho basement bar is all exposed brickwork, dimly lit nooks and crannies, and bartenders conjuring up margaritas in teacups and delicate lavender martinis.

There's no distinct gay quarter in Edinburgh, but the city's oldest gay bar is **CC Blooms** (22-24 Greenside Place; www.ccblooms.co.uk; ✆ **0131/556-9331**), while **The Regent** (2 Montrose Terrace; no website; ✆ **0131/661-8198**) is a cozy traditional pub. Also check out Edinburgh's "Pink Triangle" around the top end of Leith Walk and **Broughton Street.**

Cafe Royal Circle Bar ★★   This historic, Parisian-style Edinburgh institution (now a listed building), opened its doors in 1863 and is one of the city's most famous bars. Its ornate interiors feature a series of stunning ceramic tile artworks and glorious stained glass. Cafe Royal is also renowned for its opulent oyster bar and haunted by its very own ghost. 19 W. Register St. www.cafe royaledinburgh.co.uk. ✆ **0131/556-1884.** Sun–Wed 11am–11pm, Thurs 11am–midnight, Fri–Sat 11am–1am.

Goya 23 ★★   A wine and sherry bar in the heart of Stockbridge transports you straight to Andalusia. With its rustic-chic decor this funky little bar is hung with Iberico hams and offers sherry tastings from the cask, craft beers, and fine wines, along with a range of tapas. 30 North West Circus Place. www. goya23.co.uk. ✆ **0131/220-0984.** Mon, Wed & Thurs 4–11pm, Fri–3pm Sat noon–10pm, Sun noon–8pm.

There's no shortage of whisky bars in the Scottish capital or period pubs with an eye-watering selection of single malts. Serious whisky connoisseurs should make the pilgrimage to one of the **Scotch Malt Whisky Society's** (www.smws.co.uk; ✆ **0131/516-4822**), venues in Edinburgh. Annual membership is pricey (from £65), but the new **Kaleidoscope Whisky Bar** at 28 Queen Street is open to non-members too, there's a restaurant and shop, and it stocks more than 200 single malts. It's open 11am to 11pm Monday to Wednesday, Thursday to Saturday 11am to midnight and Sunday 11am until 10pm. If you do want to splash out for membership, the **Vaults** bar, is in a centuries-old warehouse, tucked away on Giles Street in Leith, with roaring fires, leather sofas, and olde-worlde ambience, and stocks around 1,300 single malts that can be sampled by the dram. The Vaults opens Tuesday to Saturday from 11:30am (12:30am on Sun) until late. **The Scotch Whisky Experience** (354 Castlehill; www.scotchwhiskyexperience.co.uk; ✆ **0131/220-0441**), also boasts a restaurant, Amber, and bright, backlit whisky bar stocked with nearly 450 single malts from the five main whisky producing regions: the Lowlands, Speyside, Islay, the Highlands, and Campbeltown. They also offer a whisky and cheese pairing. At the west end of a cobbled alley behind Princes Street, **The Black Cat** (168 Rose St; www.theblackcatbar.com; ✆ **0131/225-3349**), is a cool hangout with church chairs, retro radiators, metal bar, regular folk sessions, and around 100 different malts above the bar. It's open daily from 10:30am to 1am. The clue is in the name for a traditional bar and restaurant on the Royal Mile. **Whiski** ★ (119 High St; www.whiskibar.co.uk; ✆ **0131/556-3095**) has over 300 malts and live music every night. It's open Monday to Thursday 11am until midnight and Friday to Sunday 10am until 1am. Just round the corner on the Mound, teetering above Princes Street, its sleeker sister establishment is the **Whiski Rooms** ★★ (4-7 North Bank St.; www.whiskirooms.com; ✆ **0131/225-7224**), all exposed stonework and a mural of a stag. Its shop stocks around 500 whiskies, and there's a bar, bistro, and tasting room—where along with traditional tastings, whisky is matched with cheese and chocolate. You can take a whisky flight in the bar or try a whisky cocktail or just relax with the perfect dram. It's open 10am every day, closing at 1am.

The Jazz Bar ★ Soak up some jazz at this intimate subterranean club—or funk, fusion, soul or blues acoustic sessions. The club's had a checkered history, but has risen from the rubble Phoenix-style. Drummer and jazz scene regular Bill Kyle opened the original bar round the corner, but the fire that swept through Cowgate in 2002 destroyed the building. It was thanks to the generosity of loyal regulars that he was able to scrabble together the money to re-open again in this basement bar in 2005: a cool, dimly lit, late-night hangout with an extension to 5am during the festival. 1A Chambers St. www.thejazzbar.co.uk. ✆ **0131/220-4298.** Mon–Fri 5pm–3am, Sat 1:30pm–5am, Sun 12:30pm–3am. Covers vary but go directly to the musicians £3–£10.

Kay's Bar ★ Boudoir chic is not what you'd expect from an old boozer in the New Town, but the velvet banquettes are a deep ruby red. This bijoux

Victorian pub also has its original wood paneling and old barrels, there's rugby on the TV, board games in the tiny back room, and a good selection of real ales and single malts behind the bar. 39 Jamaica St. www.kaysbar.co.uk. ℗ **0131/225-1858.** Mon–Thurs 11am–midnight, Fri–Sat 11am–1am, Sun 12:30–11pm.

The Lucky Liquor Co ★★ Bar impresarios Mike Aikman and business partner Jason Scott own a string–well a trio–of New Town bars with a cult following among the city's cocktail connoisseurs and educated drinkers. Lucky Liquor was a departure from the Speakeasy vibe of underground drinking den, Bramble just a few doors down, the inspiration the cafe bars of France with their black and white tiled floors. The bar is American white oak, while the bentwood seats came from local antiques fairs. While Bramble is a late-night hangout, Lucky Liquor has a small patio area for daylight drinking. 39a Queen St. www.luckyliquorco.com. ℗ **0131/226-3976.** Daily 4pm–1am.

Queens Arms ★ The Queens Arms is a cozy basement pub in the New Town with a library of old books and comforting leather Chesterfields to curl up on with the newspaper. There's a good selection of wines, whiskies, hand-picked cask ales, and cocktails. The Sunday Roast is legendary. 49 Frederick St. www.queensarmsedinburgh.com. ℗ **0131/225-1045.** Daily 11am–1am.

Smith and Gertrude ★★ The wine bar revival is a story that just keeps rolling. And in Stockbridge, no stranger to demon drinking dens, old-world pubs and gastropubs this is one of the new brigade. With its reclaimed wooden flooring, painted chairs, and vintage radiators, it's retro cool in design. In terms of the concept it's pure and simple: wine, cheese, company. And great wine at that, many organic, biodynamic, and natural. 26 Hamilton Pl. www.smithandgertrude.com. ℗ **0131/629-6280.** Tues–Thurs 4–11pm, Fri–Sat noon–midnight, Sun 10am–9pm.

Voodoo Rooms ★ Think live music, cabaret, cocktails, and 60 specialty tequilas in a string of bars and ballrooms in a historic building down a little alley just off Princes Street. The main first-floor bar and restaurant is a glamorous affair with booths, banquettes, huge arched windows, and soaring ceilings ornately decorated with gold leaf. You can also book yourself in to learn the art of mixology or take a burlesque class. 19a West Register St. www.thevoodoorooms.com. ℗ **0131/556-7060.** Bar open Mon–Thurs 4pm–1am, Fri–Sun noon–1am. Event tickets £5–£15.

Spectator Sports

FOOTBALL There are two local football (soccer) teams—the Heart of Midlothian (www.heartsfc.co.uk), otherwise known as "Hearts," and Hibernian (www.hibernianfc.co.uk), also known as "Hibs"—who battle each other and other national and European teams. Hearts' home ground is **Tynecastle Stadium,** McLeod St (℗ **0333/043-1874**), and Hibs' home ground is **Easter Road Stadium,** 12 Albion Place (℗ **0131/661-2159**). Games are traditionally played on Saturday afternoons and often televised in pubs throughout Scotland. Tickets are around £26 for adults, £10 for under-18s.

HORSE RACING   Place your bets at the **Musselburgh Racecourse,** Linkfield Road (www.musselburgh-racecourse.co.uk; $\mathcal{C}$ **0131/665-2859**), about 4 miles east of Edinburgh. In summer, the races are on a flat circular track, but in winter, the more elaborate National Hunt format challenges horses and riders to a series of jumps and obstacle courses. Admission is £17 to £22 for adults, and free for under-17s.

RUGBY   Home of the Scottish Rugby Union, **Murrayfield Stadium,** Murrayfield (www.scottishrugby.org; $\mathcal{C}$ **0131/346-5250**), is about 1 mile west of Edinburgh. Matches mainly take place from September to April, usually on Saturdays. The top fixtures are those of the Six Nations Championship between Scotland, Wales, England, Ireland, Italy, and France. Other matches are usually between Edinburgh or Glasgow and other U.K. teams. Ticket prices range from £20 for adults and £5 for under-18s to £25 for adults and £10 for under-18s.

SIDE TRIPS FROM EDINBURGH

Armed with a road map or a train timetable, it's easy to explore historic towns, tourist attractions, and seaside resorts just a day trip from Edinburgh. If you don't fancy the DIY method, tour companies for everything from a 1-day trip to Rosslyn Chapel and the Scottish Borders to a 5-day tour of the Highlands or a 17-day island hopping extravaganza include **Rabbie's** (www.rabbies.com; $\mathcal{C}$ **0131/226-3133**) and the **Highland Experience** (www.highlandexperience.com; $\mathcal{C}$ **0131/226-1414**). For a very personal experience, book an **Afternoon Tea Tour** (www.afternoonteatours.co.uk; $\mathcal{C}$ **07873/211-856**); one of Scotland's top tour operators, this Edinburgh-based company offers set guided tours or will create bespoke itineraries focusing on individual interests and providing a unique glimpse at the more unusual and intimate side of Scotland.

Callendar House ★ HISTORIC SITE   All the usual suspects slept here over the centuries: Bonnie Prince Charlie (who seems to have bedded down in most of Scotland's grand houses), Mary Queen of Scots, and Oliver Cromwell. The house, which looks like a sumptuous French chateau, is cradled by Callendar Park, 170 acres of sweeping parkland, and dates back to the 14th century. It contains a number of interesting exhibitions including a display outlining the history of the house from the 11th to 19th century and one on the Antonine Wall built by the Romans across the central belt of Scotland in 142 C.E. as the northernmost frontier of their empire, sections of which can be seen in the park. In the kitchen, costumed guides dish up samples of 19th-century delicacies and regale visitors with tales of life in a stately home.

Callendar Park, Falkirk. www.callendarestate.co.uk. $\mathcal{C}$ **01324/503-770.** Free. Wed–Sun 10am–5pm. Approximately 25 miles from Edinburgh, with frequent train service between Edinburgh and Falkirk and regular buses from the town center.

East Lothian is a golfer's heaven and boasts the highest number of links courses in close proximity in the world. You can choose from 21 courses, including **Muirfield Golf Course** (www. muirfield.org.uk; ℰ **01620/842-123**), one of the greatest courses on the planet. Check out **www.golfeastlothian.com**, for info on the East Lothian Visitor Golf Pass, and where to play and stay in the region.

Falkirk Wheel ★★★ ARCHITECTURE   When an ambitious project was proposed to re-link the Union and Forth & Clyde canals, the major obstacle to overcome was the fact that one canal lay 35m (115 ft.) below the other, and the flight of 11 locks that once joined them had been demolished. The solution, the Falkirk Wheel, is an impressive feat of modern engineering. Boats enter from one canal and the wheel, which operates according to Archimedes' principle of water displacement, rotates and discharges them into the other canal. Visitors can hop aboard a boat to experience this, the world's only rotating boat wheel, or spend time in the visitor center to find out how it was created and how it works.

Lime Rd., Tamfourhill, Falkirk. www.scottishcanals.co.uk. ℰ **0870/050-0208**. Boat rides £13.50 adults, students and seniors £11.50, £7.50 children 3–15. Mar–Oct daily 10am– 5:30pm; Nov–Mar Wed–Sun 11am–4pm. Approximately 23 miles from Edinburgh, with frequent train service between Edinburgh and Falkirk and regular buses from the town center.

Hopetoun House ★★ HISTORIC SITE   Surrounded by spectacular landscaped grounds, *a la* Versailles, Hopetoun has been in the Hope family since the late 1600s and is Scotland's greatest Robert Adam mansion and a stunning example of 18th-century architecture (note its resemblance to Buckingham Palace). Seven bays extend across the slightly recessed center, and the classical style includes a complicated tympanum, as well as hood molds, quoins, and straight-headed windows. A rooftop balustrade with urns completes the ensemble. You can wander through elegant reception rooms, filled with 18th-century furniture, paintings, and statuary, before checking out the panoramic view of the Firth of Forth from the roof. After touring the house, take the nature trail, explore the deer parks, see the Stables Museum, or stroll through the formal gardens.

1¾ miles from the Forth Road Bridge near South Queensferry, 10 miles from Edinburgh off the A904. www.hopetoun.co.uk. ℰ **0131/331-2451**. £10.50 adults, £9 seniors, £5.50 children 16 and under, £28 families. Easter–Sept daily 10:30am–5pm (last admission 4pm).

Newhailes ★ HISTORIC SITE   Often called "The Sleeping Beauty," this impressive late-17th-century Palladian mansion has largely survived intact thanks to the fact that it lay dormant for years. The house is a testament to early 18th-century decorative Rococo interiors which, a National Trust official explained, is because "nobody in this house earned a penny after 1790 and subsequent owners couldn't afford to change anything." Expect a feast of

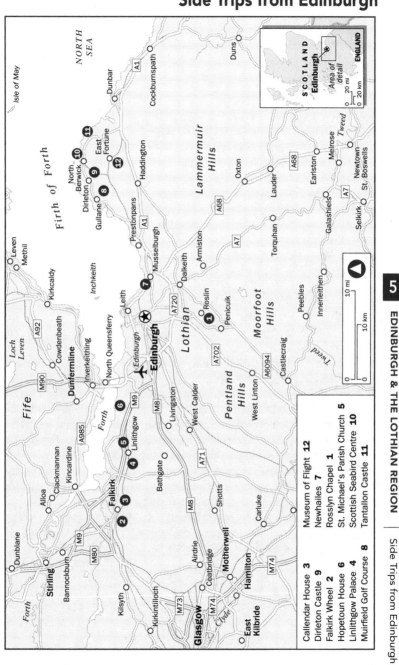

Callendar House 3
Dirleton Castle 9
Falkirk Wheel 2
Hopetoun House 6
Linlithgow Palace 4
Muirfield Golf Course 8

Museum of Flight 12
Newhailes 7
Rosslyn Chapel 1
St. Michael's Parish Church 5
Scottish Seabird Centre 10
Tantallon Castle 11

5

EDINBURGH & THE LOTHIAN REGION | Side Trips from Edinburgh ornate decoration including rich furnishings, gilding, antique wallpaper, damask, and needlepoint, as well as a 7,000-volume library hailed by Samuel Johnson as "the most learned room in Europe." Make time to explore the surrounding parkland with its woodland walks, summerhouse, and grotto.

Newhailes Road, Musselburgh. www.nts.org.uk. ⒸⒸ **0131/653-5599.** Tours of the house take 1¼ hours. £13 for adults, £10 seniors, £5 children 5–15, £35 families. Apr–June and Sept–Oct Thurs–Mon noon–3:30pm, July–Aug daily noon–3:30pm. Musselburgh is 4 miles to the east of Edinburgh. Bus no. 44.

Rosslyn Chapel ★★★ CHAPEL   Catapulted into the limelight by Dan Brown's international bestseller *The Da Vinci Code* and the subsequent movie, this 15th-century chapel is one of the alleged sites of the Holy Grail and is still a place of worship. Every inch of this historic masterpiece, founded by Sir William St Clair in 1446, is adorned with elaborate stonework, depicting everything from devils to dragons, knights to farmer's wives, and angels playing the bagpipes. By far the most celebrated piece is the Apprentice Pillar, carved by an apprentice mason after being inspired by a dream.

Chapel Loan, Roslin (6 miles south of Edinburgh). www.rosslynchapel.com. ⒸⒸ **0131/440-2159.** £9 adults, £7 seniors, children 18 and under free. Sept–May Mon–Sat 9:30am–5pm, Sun noon–4:45pm; June–July Mon–Sat 9:30am–6pm.

South Queensferry ★

It's a bit of a tongue-twister, but if want to cross the Firth of Forth to the Kingdom of Fife there are now three iconic bridges across the water: the Forth Bridge, the Forth Road Bridge, and the Queensferry Crossing (www.theforthbridges.org). The **Forth Bridge ★★★**, a marvel of Victorian engineering and a rail bridge, first opened in 1890 and gained UNESCO World Heritage status in 2015. When the **Forth Road Bridge** opened in 1964, it was the largest long-span suspension bridge in the world outside the United States. With the increase in traffic and corrosion to the cables, a new bridge was mooted at the turn of the century. **The Queensferry Crossing** is the result and opened in 2017 as the longest three-tower, cable-stayed bridge in the world.

Historically, of course, boats were the means of transport, which is how this tiny settlement got its name. Saint Margaret, Queen of King Malcolm III, used to cross the water here in the "Queen's Ferry." Another boat will take you from here to wildlife-rich **Inchcolm Island ★★**, home to the ruins of a 13th-century abbey. Three-hour trips aboard *The Maid of the Forth* (www.maidoftheforth.co.uk; ⒸⒸ **0131/331-5000**) with island landing depart from Hawes Pier from April to October (check the website for times); £20 for adults, £10.60 for children ages 5 to 15. If you're peckish, the **Hawes Inn** (www.vintageinn.co.uk; ⒸⒸ **0131/331-1990**) on the waterfront in South Queensferry was featured in Robert Louis Stevenson's *Kidnapped*. Catch a bus from Edinburgh's St Andrews bus station to South Queensferry, or a train from Waverley to Dalmeny station, a short walk from the High Street.

The coastline heading east from Edinburgh is strung with pretty dune-backed beaches and guarded by fairy-tale castles. **Gullane, Bents,** and **Yellowcraig** are lovely sweeps of sand, but **Seacliff,** a couple of miles from North Berwick, comes with a burnt-out mansion dating back to 1750, a tiny harbor carved out of the rocks in 1890 and said to be the smallest in Scotland and a ruined 14th-century castle. Perched above a sheer cliff face, **Tantallon Castle** ★ (www.historic environment.scot; ✆ **01620/892-727**) dates back to the 1350s. It has endured a number of sieges, and the sturdy gun in the east tower is an exact replica of the one used to defend the castle in the 15th and 16th centuries. It is open April to September daily 9:30am to 5:30pm, October-March daily 10am to 4pm; £6 adults, £4.80 seniors and £3.60 children.

Midway between North Berwick and Gullane is **Dirleton,** one of the prettiest villages in Scotland and home to a 13th-century castle (www.historicenvironment.scot; ✆ **01620/850-330**). Abandoned in 1663, **Dirleton Castle** ★ looks like a fairy-tale fortification with its towers, arched entries, and oak ramp mimicking the old drawbridge. The castle was partially destroyed by Cromwell in 1650, but you can still see the remains of the Great Hall and kitchen, as well as the Lord's Chamber. The gardens date from the late 19th and early 20th century and are one of its highlights. Dirleton Castle is open April to September daily 9:30am to 5:30pm and October to March daily 10am to 4pm; £6 adults £4.80 seniors and £3.60 children.

Linlithgow ★

Mary Queen of Scots was born in **Linlithgow Palace** in 1542. Today, it's an eerily evocative ruin surrounded by sweeping parkland on the side of a loch while Linlithgow itself, a royal burgh, is one of West Lothian's most picturesque historic towns and an easy day trip from Edinburgh, 18 miles to the east. **Trains** run every half-hour between Edinburgh and Linlithgow; the journey takes 20 minutes, and a round-trip fare costs £8.40 adults and up to two children go for free with the Kids Go Free ticket.

Linlithgow Palace ★★ HISTORIC SITE A devastating fire swept through the palace in 1745 and today it stands a magnificent roofless ruin, yet still imbued with a haunting power and grandeur. Wander the old royal rooms and Great Hall, gaze up at the pink-tinged walls soaring five stories high and supported by flying buttresses. From the ramparts there are panoramic views over the loch, and for a picture-perfect walk round the loch the palace forms a majestic backdrop.

Kirkgate, Linlithgow. www.historicenvironment.scot. ✆ **01506/842-896.** £6 adults, £4.80 seniors, £3.60 children 16 and under. Apr–Sept daily 9:30am–5:30pm; Oct–Mar daily 10am–4pm.

St Michael's Parish Church CHURCH South of the palace stands the medieval kirk of St Michael the Archangel, site of worship of many a Scottish monarch since its consecration in 1242. Despite being ravaged by the disciples of John Knox (who then chided his followers for their "excesses") and temporarily transformed into a stable by Cromwell, this remains one of Scotland's best examples of a parish church and features a striking contemporary "crown" on top of the church's tower.

Adjacent to Linlithgow Palace. www.stmichaelsparish.org.uk. ✆ **01506/842-188.** Free admission. May–Sept daily 10:30am–4pm; Oct–Apr daily 10:30am–1pm.

North Berwick ★

Once dubbed the Biarritz of the North, this little seaside town, hugging a rocky promontory where the Firth of Forth meets the North Sea, might not have the old-world glamour of the French Atlantic resort, but it was once a tourist hotspot. Today, it's still popular with weekenders in search of fish and chips and bracing sea air. It's just a 44-minute drive from Edinburgh along the coastal strip lined with dune-backed beaches, wildlife reserves, and golf courses.

Gazing seawards the volcanic **Bass Rock,** emerges wild and white from the waves, the breeding ground each spring for the world's largest colony of gannets. Boat trips on the old wooden boat, Sula, chug out of the little harbor each day or you can spy on the birds via the live webcams in the state-of-the-art **Scottish Seabird Centre ★** (www.seabird.org; ✆ **01620/890-202**) on the seafront. The center opens daily year-round from 10am closing at 6pm in the summer and between 4 and 5:30pm in winter. Admission is £8.95 for adults and £4.95 for children ages 3 to 15.

Another nearby attraction is the **Museum of Flight ★** (www.nms.ac.uk; ✆ **0300/123-6789**), 6 miles south at East Fortune Airfield. This low-key attraction showcases the history of aviation from the First World War to the present day. Climb onboard a Concorde and wander among fighter planes in the Military Aviation Hangar. During the summer (from Apr to the end of Sept) East Coast Buses (www.eastcoastbuses.co.uk) lays on a special service, the number 121. The museum is open daily from April through October from 10am to 5pm and from November to March on Saturdays and Sundays from 10am to 4pm. Admission is £12 for adults, £10 for seniors, £7 for children ages 5 to 15, and families £31.

Trains between North Berwick and Edinburgh run roughly every hour. The journey takes a half-hour and a day-trip costs £7.10 for adults, £3.55for children.

If you overnight in the area, **Greywalls Hotel ★★** is an elegant country house hotel designed by Edwardian architect Edward Lutyens in 1901 and visited by Edward VII, who is said to have admired the views across the Firth of Forth. A stroll in the beautiful gardens created by Gertrude Jekyll helps work up an appetite for dinner in gourmet French restaurant, **Chez Roux** (Muirfield, Duncur Rd., Gullane; www.greywalls.co.uk; ✆ **01620/842-144.** Doubles £240–£335)—the twice-baked cheese soufflé is legendary. Georgian **Glebe House ★** (4 Law Rd; www.glebehouse-nb.co.uk; ✆ **01620/892-608;** doubles £120) dates back to 1780 and was originally the home of the pastor of the nearby Presbyterian Church. Today it's an elegant bed-and-breakfast near the center of town and close to the sea.

THE BORDERS & DUMFRIES & GALLOWAY

By Stephen Brewer

Southern Scotland packs a one-two punch with these two scenic, history-drenched regions. The gently rolling landscapes of the Borders form the age-old divide between England and Scotland, and hulking castles and sturdy stone towers, along with a string of ruined abbeys, attest to this often-turbulent past. Meanwhile, sea-washed Dumfries and Galloway is where poet Robert Burns lived and wrote his best work. The ruggedly beautiful coastline cradles some of Scotland's most appealing seaside villages, while the vast Galloway Forest Park sweeps across much of the interior.

The two regions are rather unlikely neighbors. The Borders is gentle terrain, with pretty villages and grand houses that seem right out of the pages of *Country Life* magazine and are tweedy in more ways than one—the River Tweed, one of Scotland's legendary fly-fishing streams, cuts a path through green valleys. Dumfries and Galloway, meanwhile, is briny and a bit rougher around the edges, with a rocky, cove-etched coastline to the south and west, shimmering tidal flats along the estuaries, and forest-clad interior mountains.

Varied as these southern lands are, distances are fairly short, and it's easy to work a lot into sightseeing while still finding time to relax in the beautiful settings—there are only 150 miles between Kelso, at the eastern side of the Borders, and Portpatrick, at the far western edge of Dumfries and Galloway.

Don't Leave the Borders & Dumfries & Galloway Without . . .

Taking time out for some quiet reflection in Dryburgh Abbey. Of all the ruined Borders abbeys, this enchanting place is the most peaceful, set amid a grove of yew trees on the banks of the River Tweed. Sir Walter Scott chose to spend eternity here, and it's easy to see why.

Encountering Mary Stuart at Hermitage Castle. The ghost of the ill-fated queen is said to haunt these dark, gloomy, mist-shrouded ruins, where she had a rendezvous with her lover, the Earl of Bothwell.

Soaking in small-town country life in Melrose. The prettiest of the Borders towns surrounds a lively Market Square, and nearby are gardens, the town's evocatively ruined abbey, and riverside walks along the Tweed.

Making the hike up to Grey Mare's Tail. One of the U.K.'s tallest waterfalls plunges down a mountainside outside Moffat, amid moors, stark cliffs, bubbling brooks, and shimmering lochs.

Taking in the sea air and art in Kirkcudbright. Generations of artists have been transported by the spectacle of the light playing off the sea in this pretty little seaside village, and you will, too, while enjoying the works they've left behind and a walk along the wharves.

Being transported to the tropics in Logan Botanic Garden. Of all the gardens that flourish in southern Scotland, this enchanting bower is the most exotic, blooming with rare Southern Hemisphere species.

THE BORDERS

Once tagged the "debatable lands," the Borders rise and fall across the age-old Anglo-Scottish divide in the southeast corner of Scotland. Some of the great moments of Scottish history have played out in the abbeys, castles, great houses, and gardens that line the banks of River Tweed as it flows through gentle valleys and past a string of appealing Borders towns. The long-ago ruined abbeys at Jedburgh, Melrose, Kelso, and Dryburgh are the romantic shells of once-thriving monastic communities. Mary Queen of Scots had a rendezvous with her lover, Lord Bothwell, at Hermitage Castle, near Jedburgh; Bonnie Prince Charlie was a guest at Traquair House, outside Peebles; and the novelist Sir Walter Scott created a baronial manor, Abbotsford, above the Tweed near Melrose. These worthy connections aside, the Borders is also a region of great natural beauty. The Eildon Hills, rising from the Tweed Valley above Melrose, and the Pentland Hills, around Peebles, are fine walking country, and the Tweed is one of Scotland's best fly-fishing rivers.

Our coverage moves from east to west, following the River Tweed upstream, from Kelso through the other abbey towns to Peebles. Any of the towns along the Tweed are handy bases for exploring the Borders, as distances are not great and the drives are scenic. Public transport between the towns is

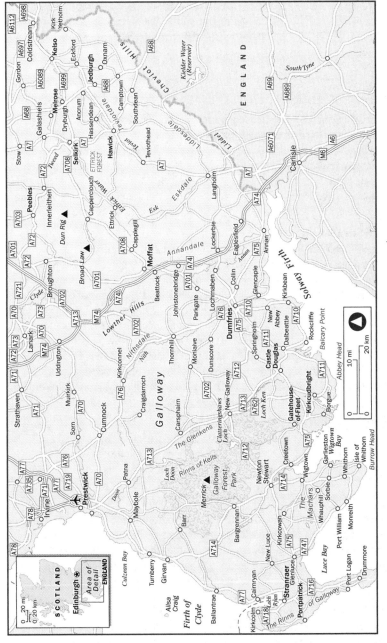

also fairly good, so with a little planning you can explore the region without a car. Melrose and Kelso are especially attractive, and they offer some of the best accommodation and are well poised for seeing the sights. The Borders Railway handily connects the region with Edinburgh in about an hour, with high-speed service to stations at Galashiels and Tweedbank, where buses connect to most towns.

Kelso ★★

44 miles SE of Edinburgh

Sir Walter Scott, who attended grammar school in Kelso, spoke a bit nostalgically of the town of his youth as "the most beautiful, if not the most romantic, village in Scotland." You may well agree as you wander around the pleasant streets of pastel-colored houses and along riverside walks to regard the confluence of the River Teviot and River Tweed. Just off a pretty, cobbled central square is the town's famous and very ruined abbey, and two of Scotland's great estates, Floors Castle and Mellerstain House, are at the edge of town.

ESSENTIALS

GETTING THERE   The nearest train station is Tweedbank, 17 miles west and a stop on the **Borders Railway** (www.scotrail.co.uk; ✆ **0344/811-0141**), with trains running about every half hour for the hour-long journey. **Borders Buses** (www.bordersbuses.co.uk; ✆ **01289/308-719**) service no. 67 links Kelso with Tweedbank. Buses depart roughly every 2 hours and take 40 minutes to reach Kelso. Borders Buses also operates a direct bus service, the no. 51/52, between Edinburgh and Kelso. The service runs hourly from Edinburgh bus station and the trip takes a little more than 2 hours. The fare is £6.50 one-way.

If you're driving from Edinburgh, join the A68 at the east side of the city bypass (A720), and then fork left north of Lauder onto the A697. At Whitburn, fork right onto the A6089, which leads to Kelso.

EXPLORING THE AREA

A stroll along Cobby Riverside Walk offers a close-up look at the Kelso Bridge across the Tweed. Architect/engineer Sir John Rennie used this span, with wide arches separated by columns, as a model for his more famous work, London's Waterloo Bridge. In the background are the towers of the ruined abbey and a forest of turrets and pepper pots atop Floors Castle, just upstream.

Floors Castle ★★ CASTLE   The grandiose home of the 10th Duke of Roxburghe and Scotland's largest inhabited castle was created in 1721 by neoclassical architect William Adam and sits above the banks of the Tweed at the center of a 21,000-hectare (52,000-acre) estate. While a few elements of Adam's hallmark restrained style remain in place, the palatial residence is largely the unrestrained fantasy of a Victorian, William Playfair, who remodeled Floors in the middle of the 19th century as a fairytale castle with cupolas, turrets, pinnacles, and crenellated parapets. The dozen or so of the castle's hundreds of rooms on view to the public show off a lot of lavish ostentation and a fine collection of Gobelin tapestries and paintings by Matisse and Gainsborough. These are the legacy of one of the wealthiest American heiresses of her day, Mae Goelot, who became the 8th duchess in 1903 and, with her skills at fly fishing and down-to-earth demeanor, soon endeared herself to the county folk, who affectionately called her Duchess May. Walks through the beautifully landscaped grounds lead to views across the water to the ruins of Roxburgh castle, strategically tucked between the Rivers Tweed and Teviot. A holly tree marks the spot where Scottish King James II was killed during a British attack on the fortress in 1460.

Off the A697, 1¾ miles north of Kelso. www.floorscastle.com. ⓒ **01573/223-333.** Castle, gardens, and grounds £12 adults, £6 children 5–16, under 5 free, £29 families of 2 adults and 3 children; gardens and grounds £6.50 adults, £3.50 children 5–16, under 5 free, £16 families of 2 adults and 3 children. Easter weekend and May–Sept daily 10:30am–5pm. Oct weekends only 10:30am–3:30pm.

Kelso Abbey ★ ABBEY The oldest and largest of the Border abbeys, founded in 1128, was also one of the richest, collecting revenues and rents from granges, fisheries, mills, and manor houses throughout the region. The library was one of the finest in medieval Britain, and the abbot of Kelso was one of the most powerful men in Scotland. Enough remains of the massive towers, turrets, and buttresses to suggest all this onetime might, though during the so-called "Rough Wooing," Henry VIII's war on Scotland from 1543 to 1551, English forces launched the last of a series of attacks on the abbey, ripping off the roofs and reducing the huge church and domestic quarters to the romantic ruins they are today. Among those who found the old stones inspiring was aspiring wordsmith Walter Scott, who attended grammar school down the lane.

Bridge St. www.historic-scotland.gov.uk. No phone. Free. Apr–Sept daily 9:30am–5:30pm, Oct–Mar Mon, Wed, Sat–Sun 10am–4pm.

Mellerstain ★★ HISTORIC SITE This golden-hued seat of the earls of Haddington shows off the best work of father and son architects William and Robert Adam. William built two wings in 1725, while his son, Robert, designed the main house 40 years later. Plaster reliefs, friezes, and columns show off the pair's affinity for neoclassical simplicity in airy, formally aligned rooms filled with light and still painted in their original colors. One of Mellerstain's enduring legacies is the "Household Book" of Lady Grisell Baillie (1665–1746), an accomplished poet, songwriter, and diarist who left a detailed account of 18th-century customs and social life on the estate. Her 1,000-plus pages of entries have yielded a wealth of information about the cost of household goods and even the daily caloric intake of servants. Lady Grisell's beloved gardens and parkland sweep across 40 hectares (100 acres), with beautiful terraces that overlook the Cheviot Hills. Tucked away amid lakes and copses is a thatched-roof tea cottage where lords and ladies, in the fashion of Marie-Antoinette, could get a taste of rural simplicity.

5 miles northwest of Kelso off the A6089. www.mellerstain.com. ⓒ **01573/410-225.** £9 adults, £4 children, under 5 free. Easter weekend, May–Sept Fri–Mon, house 12–5pm, gardens 11am–5pm.

Robert Adam (1728–92), whose adaptations of the Italian Palladian style have been duplicated around the world, is Britain's most prestigious neoclassical architect. He once rather immodestly but accurately claimed that he revolutionized the principles of English aesthetics, and the Adam style, a richly detailed yet airy interpretation of neoclassicism, was indeed a radical and refreshing departure from the more ponderous styles that preceded it.

Adam's genius derived from his synthesis of the decorative traditions of the French and Italian Renaissance with those of ancient Greece and Rome. His designs are notable for their lavish use of color, inspired by Grecian vase paintings and artifacts uncovered from Pompeii and other archaeological digs.

Adam also demonstrated a shrewd business sense and had the knack of decorating the right house at the right time for rich clients who helped propel him into the spotlight.

Throughout much of his career Robert collaborated with his capable but less talented younger brother, James (1730–94), who handled many of the everyday details of the commissions they executed together, which often included every aspect of a property's interior decoration and furnishings. The brothers' education in the visual arts began early thanks to their father William Adam (1689–1748), who was the leading Scottish architect of his day and designed many manor houses in what's been described as a crude but vigorous Palladian style.

AROUND KELSO

The small town of **Coldstream,** on the boundary between Scotland and England 12 miles northeast of Kelso via the A698, is on the north banks of the Tweed, at a spot where the river is easily forded. This convenient location has put Coldstream in the path of some of big events in Scottish history. The Battle of Flodden Fields, Scotland's worst military defeat, was fought just across the border in England in 1513, when 10,000 Scottish troops were slaughtered along with the monarch, James IV. In 1660, a regiment based in Coldstream marched to London to take part in restoring Scottish King Charles II as monarch of England, Scotland, and Ireland. The regiment became known as the Coldstream Regiment of Footguards and is still part of the Queen's personal troops. Their story comes to light at the **Coldstream Museum ★** (www.scotborders.gov.uk; ✆ **01890/882-630**) on Market Square. The museum is free and open March to September Monday to Saturday 9:30am to 12:30pm and 1 to 4pm and Sunday 2 to 4pm, and October Monday to Saturday 1 to 4pm.

OUTDOOR ACTIVITIES IN KELSO

Designed by Dave Thomas, one of Britain's leading golf-course architects, the par-72, 7,111-yard **Roxburghe Golf Course** (www.roxburghe-golf.com; ✆ **01573/450-333**) is open to non-members. Greens fees are £65 for 18 holes. The village of **Kirk Yetholm,** 8 miles southeast of Kelso on the B6352, is at one end of the **Pennine Way,** a 266-mile hike with the southern terminus at

Edale in Yorkshire, England. Even a short trek from Kirk Yetholm takes walkers through some beautiful rural Borders scenery.

WHERE TO EAT & STAY IN KELSO

The Cross Keys Hotel ★   James Dickson, founder of this Kelso landmark, allegedly fled town in shame when, as a saddler's apprentice, he broke the fountain in the marketplace out front. But he returned as a rich man to open this legendary coaching inn in 1769. The plain but still-appealing guest quarters were an especially welcome stop on the route from Edinburgh, at a time when half-frozen passengers had to be carried from their coaches and placed in front of the hearths to thaw, and the lounges have long been the scene of balls and hunt breakfasts. There's still a center-of-the-action air to the place, even though it's been modernized down to the last old timber. The woody Oak Room is the town's favorite spot for coffee or light meal, and the choicest of the good-size guest rooms overlook the lively cobbled marketplace.

36 The Square, Kelso. www.cross-keys-hotel.co.uk. ✆ **01573/223-303.** 28 units. £80–£140 double, includes breakfast. **Amenities:** Restaurant; bar; free Wi-Fi.

Ednam House Hotel ★★   A Georgian mansion from 1761 is tucked away off a courtyard in the center of town and set on a grassy riverside hectare (3 acres). The house became a hotel in 1928, but it doesn't seem like even a high-backed wing chair was moved out of place; marble fireplaces, plastered ceilings, and acres of rich paneling spruce up the atmospheric, fire-warmed public rooms and many of the bedrooms upstairs. High-ceilinged Principal Bedrooms, the original master suites, face the river through tall sash windows, while a two-bedroom suite is tucked away in the riverside orangery. Attic bedrooms, nestled under the eaves, are a lot less grand but cozy and atmospheric. Antiques and historic provenance aside, this is a well-known fisherman's retreat, accounting for the friendly, informal ambience and onsite smokehouse that supplies the delicious smoked salmon served at breakfast.

Bridge St., Kelso. www.ednamhouse.com. ✆ **01573/224-168.** 32 units. £115–£160 double, includes breakfast. **Amenities:** Restaurant; bar; free Wi-Fi.

The Old Priory B&B ★★   This wonderful, rambling family home, just around the corner from the abbey, dates back to 1796 and is full of character and welcoming atmosphere. Guests can relax in the large, airy drawing room, where comfy sofas rest on polished wood floors, and in good weather, a walled garden. Guest rooms show off shuttered windows, antiques, comfy old family pieces, and in two of them, fireplaces; a large family suite is especially grand, with a twin room linked to a master double bedroom.

Woodmarket, Kelso. www.theoldpriorykelso.com. ✆ **01573/223-030.** 4 units. Doubles £90–£120, includes breakfast. No credit cards. **Amenities:** Free Wi-Fi.

The Waggon Inn ★★ PUB FOOD   A couple of busy, bright, and decidedly homey rooms from the early 19th century overlook the square where cattle and coals were once traded (a waggon was a sturdy coal cart). They're a favorite Kelso spot for reliably good informal meals, with burgers, fish and chips, chops, and other standard pub grub fare elevated a notch or two with the freshest ingredients and expert preparations. A popular carvery lunch is a Sunday afternoon tradition in town.

10 Coalmarket, Kelso. www.thewaggoninn.com. ℂ **01573/224568.** Main courses £8.85–£11. Daily 11am–9pm.

Melrose ★★

15 miles W of Kelso, 37 miles SE of Edinburgh

The romantic novelist Sir Walter Scott, who spent most of his life in the Borders, was especially fond of this lively market town in the valley of the River Tweed. In fact, Scott liked Melrose so much that he commissioned a suitably atmospheric manor, Abbotsford House, nearby, and he's not the only local person of fame: The heart of Robert the Bruce is encased in a sealed casket beneath the rose-tinged ruins of Melrose Abbey, and, it's said, albeit with a twinkle in the eye, that King Arthur is buried in the surrounding Eildon Hills. Aside from all this history, with an enticing complement of castles, great houses, and ruins, Melrose is a lovely little place, with a clutch of shops and hostelries around the town square and some delightful walks through meadows and woodland alongside the River Tweed. The town fields a famous rugby club, founded in 1877 and winners of many national championships. Any diehard fan recognizes the Melrose Club (www.melroserugby.org) as the first to play seven-a-side rugby, in 1883.

ESSENTIALS

GETTING THERE   The Tweedbank stop on the **Borders Railway** (www. scotrail.co.uk; ℂ **0344/811-0141**) is just 2 miles outside Melrose at the Tweedbank station. The trip down from Edinburgh takes an hour on trains that run every half hour. A lot of city clickers prefer the easy walk into town along a nice path to launch their country getaways, and Borders Buses (www.bordersbuses.co.uk; ℂ **01289/308-719**) nos. 60, 62, and 68 connect the station and town with runs about every 10 minutes.

If driving from Edinburgh, join the A68 at the east side of the city bypass (A720) and follow this road until the junction with the A6091, which leads west into Melrose.

VISITOR INFORMATION   **Melrose Tourist Information Centre** is at **Abbey House,** 4 Abbey Street (www.visitscottishborders.com; ℂ **01896/822-283**). It's open daily 10am to 5pm.

EXPLORING MELROSE

At the fringes of town, just beyond the bookshops and antique stores on and around Market Square, are two pleasant patches of greenery. The colorful flowers and fragrant herbs of **Priorwood Garden,** on Abbey Street, are grown to be dried, while an orchard yields more than 70 varieties of apples. **The Harmony Garden,** across from the abbey on St Mary's Road, surrounds a

Georgian manor house with herbaceous borders and pristine lawns. From both, views of the abbey enhance the natural spectacle. Both gardens (www. nts.org.uk; ℭ **01896/209-504**) are open April through October, daily 10am to 5pm, and admission is free.

A walk south from the abbey through pastureland brings you to the river banks and the iron **Gattonside Suspension Bridge,** from 1826. You can make the scenic crossing to admire the swift-flowing Tweed, but heed the posted warning: "Not more than 8 persons should be on the bridge at one time. Passengers are requested not to cross the bridge in a heavy gale."

The Melrose **railway station,** at the northern edge of town off Palma Place, has not seen a train roll in since 1969 but is now a vintage attraction, and signs advertising tea and household products from the 1960s still line the canopy of the deserted platform. You can get a quick glimpse of the signs from the A6091 bypass road that skirts the old station.

Abbotsford House ★★★ HISTORIC HOME   Sir Walter Scott was at the height of his success in 1821. His historical novels were bestsellers, he was a respected judge, and he had been named president of the Royal Society of Edinburgh. It was only fitting that the house he built on the banks of the River Tweed should be a showplace. He chose what came to be known as Scottish baronial style and for the rest of the 19th century set the standard for national architecture. Wandering through the rooms, to the accompaniment of Scott in a corny-yet-charming audio-guide narration, it's easy to see how the author-historian could have felt at home in his double-height study with an overhanging gallery, the paneled library with 7,000 books lining the shelves, and the richly plastered dining room with a gas-lit chandelier, one of the first made for domestic use in Scotland. Comfortable and welcoming as the surroundings are, Scott could not have led a relaxed life in these rooms. In 1825, the publishing concern in which he had a controlling interest collapsed, leaving Scott with close to today's equivalent of $10 million in debt. Over the next 7 years he literally wrote himself to death to meet his financial obligations, and, exhausted and in failing health, he succumbed to typhus in 1832, reclining in the dining room looking out to the Tweed.

Off the B6360, 2 miles west of Melrose. www.scottsabbotsford.co.uk. ℭ **01896/752-043.** £11 adults, £10 seniors, £5 child 5–17, £28 families of 2 adults and 3 children. Mar 10am–4pm; Apr–Oct 10am–5pm; Nov 10am–4pm.

Melrose Abbey ★★ ABBEY   Sir Walter Scott once wrote, "If thou would'st view fair Melrose aright, go visit in the pale moonlight." However, it's in the sunshine that the abbey's sandstone shell has a rosy glow, highlighting still-standing facades, elongated windows, carvings, and delicate tracery, along with walls of the nave and the outlines of two large cloisters. The setting is especially magical when viewed from the top of the tower, reached by a steep, spiral stone staircase, with meadows and town gardens running down to the glistening waters of the River Tweed and the three peaks of the Eildon Hills rising in the near distance.

These picturesque ruins are all that's left of the ecclesiastical community that Cistercian monks established in 1136, making a fortune trading wool and hides with their brothers on the Continent. While the British did a good job of laying waste to the abbey, putting it out of commission entirely in 1545, many evocative details remain in place (and the free audio guide points them out): a stone *pulpitum* (screen) still separates the monks' choir and, quite charmingly, stone angels wield musical instruments around window frames and a gargoyle pig plays a bagpipe. A plaque marks the spot where a silver casket believed to contain the heart of Robert the Bruce (1274–1329) lies buried. Bruce, who fought valiantly against English rule and for his own right to be king of an independent Scotland, wanted his heart to be buried in the Holy Land, though it's hard to imagine he would object to any part of himself spending eternity here. Nearby is the alleged tomb of Michael Scott the Wizard, a 13th-century astrologer, alchemist, and astronomer who curried favor with popes and emperors across medieval Europe by addressing such issues as the distance from earth to Heaven. Sir Walter Scott tapped into local legends with his claim that Michael "cleft the Eildon Hills in three and bridled the River Tweed with a curb of stone." Everyday objects from the abbey are on display in the adjoining 16th-century Commendator's House and include the piss pots that enabled the monks to endure hour after hour of prayer.

Abbey St. www.historic-scotland.gov.uk. (✆) **01896/822-562.** £6 adults, £4 seniors, £3 children 5–15. Apr–Sept daily 9:30am–5:30pm; Oct–Mar daily 9:30am–4:30pm.

Thirlestane Castle ★ CASTLE The Maitland family has owned this estate since 1218, and with connections to William the Conqueror and King William I of Scotland, have traveled in powerful circles. Their upward mobility has shaped their ancestral home over the centuries, from dank tower to an enormous castle with circular towers at each corner, begun in 1590, when the first Lord Maitland became chancellor of James IV, to a grand palace, built in 1670, when another Maitland, the second earl of Lauderdale, became secretary of state of Scotland. Around 1840, the 9th earl of Lauderdale decided to give the old place another redo, adding some new wings and many turreted towers that today rise above the Leader Valley like a vision from a fairy tale. Some of the drawing rooms are an ostentatious feast of ornamental plasterwork and ancestral portraits, but nurseries crammed with Victorian toys, a much-used billiards room, and the old kitchens filled with gargantuan old cast-iron ranges lend a rather homey touch. Among visitors to the castle over the centuries was Bonnie Prince Charlie, who showed up on the doorstep unannounced one day in 1745 with most of his Jacobite army, on their way to wage an unsuccessful uprising to restore the Stuarts as monarchs of England and Scotland. Charlie slept comfortably in one of the many bedrooms, while his troops camped out in the lovely meadows that surround the castle.

10 miles north of Melrose off the A68. www.thirlestanecastle.co.uk. (✆) **01578/722-430.** £8 adults, £7 seniors, £4 children 5–15, £20 families. June Tues–Thurs 10am–3pm; July–Aug Sun–Thurs 10am–3pm. Grounds open until 5pm.

Sir Walter Scott was born in Edinburgh in 1771, and as he said, "My birth was neither distinguished nor sordid." He had relatives from the Borders, and as a boy listened rapturously to their stories of the region's history and folklore. He became even more fascinated with the Borders landscapes when he attended grammar school in Kelso. Though Scott studied and practiced law, his passions were German romanticism and Borders ballads, and these influences soon appeared in several long poems, including *Lady of the Lake* and *Lord of the Isles*. A long string of historical novels that followed were immensely popular, and it's easy to see why. In the Waverley novels, *Rob Roy*, and others, Scott seems to effortlessly wield all the ingredients of a great read: a knack for relating history in a gripping, colorful way; acute observations of everyday life; an ear for dialogue; a love of misty landscapes; and a flair for storytelling, complete with the trials and tribulations of lovely lasses and gallant lairds. Readers around the world know Scotland, and specifically the Borders, through Scott's works, and for Scots the beloved author remains a national hero. Residents of the Borders are justly proud of the author, who elevated their region into an exalted realm. Scott died at Abbottsford, his manor house overlooking the River Tweed near Melrose, in 1832.

Trimontium Heritage Centre ★ MUSEUM   A modest collection tells a big story, that of a nearby Roman camp, the largest in Scotland, where more than 1,500 soldiers were once posted to guard crossings on the River Tweed. The name, translating to "Three Hills," refers to the three Eildon peaks that rise nearby. Many of the more spectacular finds, including helmets and armor, have been carted off to larger museums, but on display here are a hoard of silver coins, tools, and shards of pottery on which officers once dined—often on pork chops, as excavations of the kitchen trash pits indicate. Guided walks to Trimontium are led from late spring through early autumn and come with views, tea, engaging chatter, and a chance to see the outlines of the 2,000 seat amphitheater, the remains of a bath, and an officials' guest house.

The Square. www.trimontium.org.uk/wb. © **01896/822-651.** £2 for adults, £1.50 for seniors and children, and £5 for families. Apr–Oct daily 10:30am–4:30pm. Walks: Apr–Oct, Thurs 1:30pm–5:15pm; also Tues in July–Apr. £4 adults, £1 children.

WALKS AROUND MELROSE

The **Southern Upland Way,** a 212-mile coast-to-coast route (see p. 153), passes through Melrose, and an especially scenic section follows the River Tweed just outside of town. The 62½-mile **St Cuthbert's Way** stretches from Melrose Abbey across the border into England to the Holy Island of Lindisfarne on the Northumberland coast, passing prehistoric relics, Roman ruins, and historic castles along the way. St Cuthbert began his ministry in Melrose in about 650 and was later appointed Bishop of Lindisfarne, where he died and was buried in 687. Following Cuthbert's death, the community he created on the island produced one of the greatest legacies of the Anglo-Saxon period, the Lindisfarne Gospels. On an easy trek you can meander along the first part of the route from the abbey into the nearby Eildon Hills. You might want to set your sights on the middle of the three peaks, Eildon Hill, at 422 meters (1,392 feet) the highest, where a monument honors Sir Walter Scott. Stop by the Melrose Tourist Information Centre for information on these and other local walks.

A SIDE TRIP TO DRYBURGH ABBEY

Drive 4 miles southeast of Melrose along A68 to St Boswells, then follow the B6356 another 3 miles to the ruins of the Borders' fourth great abbey, **Dryburgh.** Houses in St Boswells are built of pink stone that seems to glisten even on a gray day. They surround what's said to be the largest village green in Scotland, which for the past 350 years or so has been the setting of an annual sheep and horse fair in July. Off B6356 just outside town, a well-signposted lane climbs up to **Scott's View ★**, a lookout point above the Tweed Valley where Sir Walter used to come to reflect while admiring the prospect of the river flowing beneath his beloved Eildon Hills.

Dryburgh Abbey ★★ ABBEY   The most secluded of the ruined Borders abbeys stands in peaceful solitude on a wide loop of the River Tweed. The ancient headstones and crumbling walls are surrounded by gnarled yew trees and cedars of Lebanon said to have been planted by knights returning from the Crusades. Sir Walter Scott is buried in Dryburgh's north transept, so for eternity he's soaking up the peace and solitude of a monk's life that's richly evoked here in the ruined dormitories, novice's refectory, and warming room (monks were allowed to spend an hour a day in the only heated space in the abbey). Faint frescoes still appear on the remaining walls of the Chapter House—so called because in the morning monks gathered in the large hall, common to most abbeys, as a chapter of the monastic rule was read aloud. Among the many generations of monks who worked and prayed at Dryburgh was wealthy landowner Hugh de Morville, who helped finance the founding of the abbey in 1150 and, perhaps to ensure his salvation, became a novice and died in his habit in 1162.

Off the B6356, Dryburgh. www.historic-scotland.gov.uk. ✆ **01835/822-381.** £6 adults, £4 seniors, £3 children 5–15. Apr–Sept daily 9:30am–5:30pm; Oct–Mar daily 9:30am–4:30pm.

WHERE TO EAT & STAY IN MELROSE

Apples for Jam (✆ **01896/823-702**) at 14 High Street makes its own, much-appreciated scones and other pastries, and the selection often includes Selkirk bannock, a sweet concoction resembling fruitcake, from the neighboring town; sandwiches and soups are also served in an airy white room. If you're packing a picnic, stop at **Millers of Melrose,** at 2 High Street (✆ **01896/822-015**) and stock up on beef and haggis pies—the chicken and haggis is also delicious.

In St Boswells, 5 miles south of Melrose, stylish **Mainstreet Trading Company** (www.mainstreetbooks.co.uk; ✆ **01835/824-087**) is part bookshop, part rustic cafe, and part deli, and the scent of coffee wafts down aisles of enticing books.

Top choices for a meal in and around Melrose are in many cases the hotels, where Borders beef and Tweed salmon are served next to roaring fires. One of the grandest lodgings in Melrose isn't an inn but **Harmony House,** a Georgian manor now owned by the National Trust of Scotland (www.nts.org.uk; ⓒ **01314/580-305**); up to 12 guests can reside in splendor amid oil paintings and old furnishings, with a chance to stroll in the adjoining gardens (see p. 120) once the gates close and the hoi-polloi departs. Weekly rentals begin at about £3,000. If **Abbotsford,** Sir Walter Scott's manor outside town (see above), seems like the sort of place you might want to settle into for a spell, you're in luck: a wing that was added in the late 19th century to afford the family some privacy when the house opened to the public is now a lavish rental, with seven bedrooms, formal dining room that seats 16, billiard room, and many other luxuries. Weekly rentals begin at about £3,000.

Buccleuch Arms ★★   The location on the busy Edinburgh road shouldn't be a drawback at all, since this attractive, welcoming inn from 1836 is relaxingly bucolic, near the south banks of the River Tweed and just outside Melrose in a postcard-perfect little village, St Boswell's. Polished wood floors, glowing hearths, and inviting sofas encourage many hours of lingering in the public rooms downstairs, while the guest rooms on the floor above are cozily done up with plush headboards and matching fabrics and wallpapers. The relaxed Blue Coo Bistrot and adjoining bar room serve a hearty breakfast and locally sourced Scotch rib-eye and sirloin at lunch and dinner, with an especially memorable steak pie.

The Green, St Boswells, Melrose. www.buccleucharms.com. ⓒ **01835/822-243.** 19 units. Doubles £110–£130, includes breakfast. **Amenities:** Restaurant; bar; free Wi-Fi.

Burts Hotel ★   Facing the market place with a black-and-white 18th-century facade that bursts with colorful flowerboxes in season, this pub and inn is everything a historic market town hostelry should be—cheerful, welcoming, and usually filled with appreciative guests, many of whom are walkers and anglers who come back time and again. Windsor chairs and an old fireplace are atmospheric trappings for a pub lunch, casual supper, or on a drizzly afternoon, a dram of one of the carefully selected 90 single-malt whiskies. Guest rooms are smallish but comfy, with a tasteful smattering of plaids and stripes to make them stylish.

Market Square, Melrose. www.burtshotel.co.uk. ⓒ **01896/822-285.** 20 units. £130 double, includes breakfast. **Amenities:** Restaurant; bar; room service; free Wi-Fi.

Clint Lodge Country House ★★★   The search for the perfect Scottish country retreat ends here, in the utterly charming former hunting lodge of the duke of Polwarth, still owned by the Duke of Sutherland, and home to the hospitable Walker family of mother, father, daughter innkeepers. Their five bedrooms are filled with comfortable old heirlooms and look across a generous sweep of countryside and the River Tweed, framed by gentle hills in the distance. Dryburgh Abbey is just down the road and a nice country walk away. Lounges and a conservatory are done with great taste but manage to be relaxed enough that you won't feel like a bumpkin if you put your feet up in front of the fire and sip a whisky, and an excellent dinner is served on request on a beautifully set table in the refined family dining room. Heather and daughter Suzie are accomplished chefs and bakers and work magic with locally sourced ingredients. A rather luxurious and well-equipped three-bedroom cottage is tucked into the beautiful gardens.

Off the B6356 at St Boswells, Melrose. www.clintlodge.co.uk. ℂ **01835/822-027.** 5 units. £100–£110 double, includes breakfast. **Amenities:** Restaurant; free Wi-Fi.

Dryburgh Abbey Hotel ★   It's said this atmospheric mid-19th-century manor on the banks of the River Tweed, set in 4 hectares (10 acres) of parkland at the edge of the abbey ruins, is haunted by the so-called Gray Lady. As the story goes, the ill-fated woman occupied an older house on the estate and had the misfortune of falling in love with a monk. The pair was discovered and the cleric was hung within view of his lover's window—an ordeal that led her to drown herself in the Tweed. If the lady is indeed roaming the halls, and a harmless spirit she's said to be, she might be a bit distressed by the tired interiors and some decidedly threadbare carpets and worn furnishings, though many guests find that the parkland setting and the chance to stroll and lounge beside the river overcome any shortfalls.

Dryburgh Abbey, off the B6356. www.dryburgh.co.uk. ℂ **01835/822-261.** 38 units. Doubles £125–£180, includes breakfast. **Amenities:** Restaurant; bar; pool (indoor); sauna; room service; free Wi-Fi.

Marmion's Brasserie ★ MODERN SCOTTISH   This cross between a brasserie and tea shop occupies a 150-year-old building close to the abbey ruins and is busy from morning into the evening. The kitchen ventures into some rather unlikely Turkish fare as well as Scottish classics, though the bright room is at its best as a place to linger over coffee, homemade scones, or a sandwich.

2 Buccleuch St., Melrose. www.marmionsbrasserie.co.uk. ℂ **01896/822-245.** Main courses £9–£20. Daily 10am–9pm.

Roulotte Retreat ★★   Seven French and Dutch *roulottes* (wooden wagons) arranged in a wide circle in a wildflower meadow outside town offer a "glamping" alternative to coaching inns and country houses and might appeal to the inner gypsy in all travelers. Deep hues, rich fabrics, Persian carpets, and lots of carved wood envelop guests in a funky Bohemian style that extends to many creature comforts, including plush couches and chairs, good beds, well-designed en suite bathrooms, and wood stoves. A former stable has been converted into a two-bedroom suite, with its own gypsy caravan hideaway tucked into the woodland out front.

Bowden Mill, Melrose. http://roulotteretreat.com. ℂ **08450/949-729.** 8 units. From £235 double. **Amenities:** Pond; free Wi-Fi.

Townhouse Hotel ★   Though this handsome white house has been commandeering one side of the marketplace for 300 years or so, the large guest rooms are sleek and contemporary, with flamboyant patterns playing against soothing neutrals to provide a welcome break from the tweed and tartan circuit. Even the bathrooms, often an afterthought in these historic inns, are showcases. Downstairs, similar design flair shows up in the brasserie and dining room and is matched with an innovative menu.

Market Square, Melrose. www.thetownhousemelrose.co.uk. © **01896/822-645.** 11 units. £125–£135 double, includes breakfast. **Amenities:** Restaurant; bar; free Wi-Fi.

SHOPPING IN MELROSE

Melrose's long tradition as a market town is still much in evidence around the pretty Market Square. Step into **Mason's of Melrose,** an old-fashioned bookshop at 9 Market Square (© **01896/822-196**) and you might lose track of time browsing the well-stocked shelves. The **Abbey Mill** (© **01896/822-138**), close to the abbey ruins on Annay Road, carries all things tartan, Scottish knitwear, and lots of clothing made from amazingly soft local lambswool. **The Country Kitchen** (www.countrykitchendeli.co.uk; © **01896/822-586**) is the place to stock up on local cheeses, as well as many from England and France.

Jedburgh ★

13 miles S of Melrose, 48 miles SE of Edinburgh

A location only about 10 miles from the English border, and the largest place of any size between Edinburgh and Newcastle-upon-Tyne in England, has put this quiet, low-key little market town in harm's way since 1138. That's when King David ordered construction of a magnificent priory on the site where a church has stood since the 9th century. His intention was to create an edifice that would impress upon the British that the Scots were capable of great achievements, and the abbey that took shape on a hillside above the river certainly proved him right. Jedburgh was thriving when England's King Edward I and his troops marched peaceably into town in 1296. The troops of later British monarchs did not come as amicably and attacked time and again, looting, burning, and stealing lead from the abbey roof. When Mary Queen of Scots arrived in 1566, the abbey was already mostly a ruined shell, home to just a few monks. She spent a month in the town, laid low with a fever she caught during a tiring ride from a visit to her lover, the Earl of Bothwell. Her remembered presence, along with the evocative abbey ruins, are the main draws, but Jedburgh is an appealing place in its own right, with the Jed rushing below the stone houses on cobbled lanes and forested hills beckoning in the near distance.

ESSENTIALS

GETTING THERE   Hourly buses (www.bordersbuses.co.uk; © **01289/308-719**) run between Jedburgh and Edinburgh, and the journey takes about 2 hours. An alternative is the train to Galashiels on the Borders Railway (www.

scotrail.co.uk; © **0344/811-0141**), a journey of about an hour, and the number 68 Borders Bus from there; buses run about every 2 hours and the trip takes 50 minutes. If you're **driving** from Edinburgh, follow the A68 down to Jedburgh.

VISITOR INFORMATION The **Tourist Information Centre (TIC)** (www.visitscottishborders.com; © **01835/863-170**) is at Murray's Green, adjacent to the town's main car park and across the road from the abbey ruins. It's open year-round daily from 10am to 5pm. You can get a quick snack at the adjacent coffee shop.

EXPLORING JEDBURGH

Castle Jail ★ HISTORIC SITE When Jedburgh's Georgian jail opened on the edge of town in 1820, the facilities were groundbreaking, the most progressive in Scotland, designed to the plans of 18th-century prison reformer John Howard. After being captured by French pirates and left to languish in the filth of a French cell, Howard escaped, returned to England, and spent the rest of his days working to improve the physical and mental health of prisoners. The cells here have central heating and, with windows, bunks, and a few other pieces of simple furniture, were a far cry from the dank dungeons that, as Foster experienced firsthand, were the norm of the day. Some visitors say that a walk around the cellblocks comes with the chilling, ghostly accompaniment of Edwin McArthur, a murderer executed here in 1855. The towers, stone walls, and moat-like entrance were built to mimic Jedburgh's Castle, destroyed in 1409, and are a fitting setting for the jail's repository of local artifacts. Among the curious bits and bobs are the pottery and other fragments found along Dere Street, a Roman road that survived into the Middle Ages as the main route between Jedburgh and Edinburgh.

Castle Gate. www.scotborders.gov.uk. © **01835/864-750.** Free. Apr–Oct Mon–Sat 10am–4:30pm; Sun 1–4pm.

Jedburgh Abbey ★★★ ABBEY The best-preserved abbey in the Borders is roofless, but even in splendid ruin is majestic. Tiers of arches, long rows of columns, and a peaceful cloister evoke the prosperity and power of the Augustinian monks from France whose community flourished here for a couple of medieval centuries. The Augustinians made it their mission to travel in influential secular circles, and it's no accident that Malcolm IV chose to be crowned and Alexander III married Yolande de Dreux in the vast nave with its semicircular apse, a European influence unusual in British churches. The mood of the elaborate royal marriage ceremony was dampened a bit when a spectral figure appeared on horseback near the entrance, portending the king's untimely death—which came to pass a year later when his horse stumbled and he was pitched over a cliff. The English sacked the abbey repeatedly in the 16th century and most of the complex fell out of use, though a small section of the transepts were put into service as the town's parish church. A walk through the vast ruins, to the accompaniment of an excellent audio guide, shows off the Romanesque and Gothic architecture of the main church—best appreciated by a climb up a narrow spiral staircase of rough stones to an overhanging balcony—and on the slope below, the refectory, Chapter House, and domestic quarters where at one time as many 100 monks lived, prayed, and worked. The visitor's center nicely chronicles the construction of the abbey, its turbulent history, and day-to-day monastic life. Among the artifacts unearthed at the site are an altar stone from a Roman shrine and a fine-looking, delicately carved ivory comb from the 11th century. Not on display are the remains of a body found next to the comb, said to be that of Eadwulf Rus, who, according to a largely unfounded story, killed the bishop of Durham and fled to Jedburgh, where townsfolk tore him apart limb by limb and left his remains to rot in a ditch.

Abbey Place. www.historicenvironment.scot. ✆ **01835/863-925.** £6 adults, £4 seniors, £3 children 15 and under. Apr–Sept daily 9:30am–5:30pm; Oct–Mar daily 10am–4pm.

Mary Queen of Scots' Visitor Centre ★ HISTORIC HOME   Mary Stuart spent a month in this attractive tower house in 1566. For part of the time she hovered close to death after coming down with a fever on a 50-mile horseback ride to and from Hermitage Castle, where her lover and later husband, the Earl of Bothwell, was recovering from battlefield wounds. Given what lay in store for the young queen, it's understandable that she later wrote, "Would that I had died at Jedburgh." Four floors of the tall, narrow house, once heavily fortified to fend off British attacks on the town, are crammed with paintings, engravings, and artifacts relating to Mary's life and death, including a lock of her hair, her death mask, and a watch that she supposedly lost when she fell in a marsh on that ill-fated horseback ride. Her life unfolds here like a soap opera and is well-documented in narrative panels—her ascension to the throne of Scotland in absentia when still an infant, her childhood in France, short-lived teenage marriage to French king Francis II (who died of an ear infection a year after the nuptials), her return to Scotland as monarch and, as a Roman Catholic, her struggles to win support of her Protestant subjects. Mary was only 25 when she was forced to abdicate the throne in favor of her infant son, later James I of England. She was soon arrested for treason after allegedly plotting against her cousin Elizabeth I and imprisoned for 18 years, before being executed in 1587 at age 44. After all this cloak-and-dagger history it's refreshing to stroll in Mary's footsteps in the pear tree garden that adjoins the house—a reminder of the days when Jedburgh was famous for its fruit.

Queen St. www.scotborders.gov.uk. ✆ **01835/863-331.** Free. Mar–Nov Mon–Sat 9:30am–4:30pm; Sun 10:30am–4:30pm.

NEAR JEDBURGH

Hermitage Castle ★★ CASTLE   Few places in Scotland seem more sinister than this isolated medieval castle, just 5 miles from the Anglo-Scottish border. The mostly windowless walls with blind arches and the dark, gloomy, ruined rooms can seem as brutally unwelcoming as the bleak surrounding moorland. In fact, it's been said the castle is the physical embodiment of the phrase "sod off," as befits a place so often mired in misty gloom and steeped in stories of murder and intrigue. One of the original owners, or so the story goes, was the infamous Lord William de Soules, who was boiled alive in molten lead by angry tenants whom he'd brutalized. A 14th-century owner, Sir William Douglas, allegedly lured a colleague who was given a royal position he coveted into the cellars, imprisoned him, and starved him to death. The castle's one famously romantic moment came in 1566 Mary Queen of Scots traveled from Jedburgh to the bedside of her lover, the Earl of Bothwell (1535–78), who lay wounded by English troops. It was an ill-fated trip: Mary was then married to Lord Darnley, her second husband, attractive, scheming and universally despised, and largely responsible for turning the political tide against Mary. Her association with the Earl of Bothwell was likewise unpopular, all the more so when he was later implicated in the murder of Darnley, and Mary sealed her fate and eventual deposition when she married Bothwell and lost her last vestiges of support. Mary spent only a few hours at Hermitage, though her restless ghost is said to haunt the eerie ruins.

On an unclassified road (the castle is signposted) between the A7 and B6399, 10 miles south of Hawick. www.historicenvironment.scot. ℂ **01387/376-222.** £5 adults, £4 seniors, £3 children 15 and under. Apr–Sept daily 9:30am–5:30pm.

Monteviot House & Gardens ★ GARDEN A refreshing antidote to Jedburgh's many associations with the intrigues of Mary Queen of Scots is the utterly charming home of the Marquess of Lothian, dripping in wisteria, roses, and clematis. If you visit in July, the only month the house is open to the public, you'll have the pleasure of wandering through lived-in rooms that seem like homey spaces where you might plop down and put your feet up (not condoned), with the addition of a painting or two by the likes of Van Dyck, Bellini, and Reynolds. From Easter to October, you can enjoy a leisurely hour or two enjoying the 12-hectares (30 acres) of gardens perched above a curve in the River Teviot, divided into "rooms" that include a rose garden and river garden, with ponds, woodlands, and soothing views.

Off the B6400, which leads east off the A68 north of Jedburgh. www.monteviot.com. ℂ **01835/830-380.** Garden £5 adult, under 16 free; house £5 adult, under 16 free. Garden open Apr–Oct daily noon–5pm; house July only daily 1–5pm.

WHERE TO EAT & STAY IN JEDBURGH
Capon Tree Townhouse ★★ You might think you're in London rather than little Jedburgh in this stylish townhouse near the center of town. The name, though, is firmly rooted in Jedburgh and is a reference to a beloved landmark—a centuries-old tree in the woodlands just outside of town that is a remnant of the ancient forests that once carpeted this part of Scotland; a little the worse for wear these days, and supported by timber supports, the noble old tree continues to grow. Bedrooms in this urbane retreat are done in soft colors and artfully sparse-yet-comfortable furnishings and filled with light filtering through tall windows. The ground floor dining room takes some innovative

twists and turns with Scottish classics—as in loin of venison in a red wine and veal reduction, served by candlelight in casually sophisticated surroundings.

61 High St. www.thecapontree.com. © **01835/869-596.** 8 units. From £105 double, includes breakfast. **Amenities:** Restaurant; bar; free Wi-Fi.

Glenbank House ★   A Georgian manor of cream-colored stone is one of the finest houses in town and puts guests up in high-ceilinged, sometimes cavernous rooms fashioned out of old salons and gracious old master bedrooms. Furnishings don't quite match the surroundings and are decidedly more toward homey than luxe, but enough carved woodwork and elaborate plasterwork remains to lend a rather grand air to the place. The abbey and other town attractions are short stroll away on the stone streets, while a large garden is a leafy retreat.

Castle Gate, Jedburgh. www.jedburgh-hotel.com. © **01835/862-258.** 8 units. From £75 double, includes breakfast. **Amenities:** Bar; garden; free parking; free Wi-Fi.

Selkirk ★

17 miles NW of Jedburgh, 40 miles SE of Edinburgh

The residents of this attractive, breezy town, spread out along a ridge above the Ettrick Valley, are known as *souters,* for cobblers, because that is how they famously earned their livings for centuries. They then took up weaving, producing tweed in now-closed Victorian-era stone mills below town on the Ettrick Water. You'll probably pass through Selkirk on the way to Melrose or Kelso, just to the north, or the beguiling landscapes to the southwest along a spectacular route past St Mary's Loch and the Grey Mare's Tail waterfall to Moffat (p. 138), or northwest into the gentle countryside of the Tweed Valley. Take time to stop long enough to enjoy the views of the surrounding valleys and forests—a good place to regard the scenery is from the mossy graveyard of the ruined Kirk o' the Forest, just off the medieval marketplace—and to soak in some colorful local history.

ESSENTIALS

GETTING THERE   The Borders Railway (www.scotrail.co.uk; © **0344/811-0141**) gets you down to Galashiels in about an hour, and the number 73 Borders Bus (www.bordersbuses.co.uk; © **01289/308-719**) continues from there to Selkirk, with hourly departures for the 15-minute trip. If you're driving from Edinburgh, take the A720 south to the A7 and continue on that to Selkirk.

EXPLORING SELKIRK

Sir Walter Scott was a lawyer among his many other accomplishments, and he served as the sheriff of Selkirk from 1799 to 1832. His statue stands in the marketplace in front of the faux-medieval 1803 **courthouse** where he listened to local cases and dealt out justice, supposedly fairly, as he was immensely popular. A little farther along the High Street is a monument to the great explorer/physician Mungo Park, who was born near Selkirk in 1771 and became famous for exploring the River Niger, where he drowned in 1806. The small **Sir Walter Scott's Courtroom** museum (www.liveborders.org.uk; ℂ 1750/720-761) inside the courthouse pays homage to both men, as well as the town's other great man of letters, poet and novelist James Hogg. A contemporary of Scott's, and his biographer, Hogg was the author of *The Private Memoirs and Confessions of a Justified Sinner*, a strange, dark, Gothic thriller published in 1824. Hogg was also known as the Ettrick Shepherd, a reference to his lowly birth and work as a farmhand in the valleys below Selkirk. Despite his self-education through reading and his considerable acclaim, Hogg was never able to shake his reputation as a country bumpkin, and even the gentlemanly William Wordsworth opined, "He was undoubtedly a man of original genius, but of coarse manners and low and offensive opinions." The museum is open April to September Monday through Friday 10am to 4pm and Saturday 11am to 3pm plus Sunday May to August 11am to 3pm, and October Monday through Saturday noon to 3pm. Admission is free.

Another town statue honors Fletcher, a young man who was the sole survivor among the 80 Selkirk men who fought in the Battle of Flodden Field in 1513, when 10,000 Scots died alongside James IV in a fierce battle against the forces of England's Henry VIII. As legend has it, the boy returned to town carrying a bloodied English standard he had captured and dipped it to the ground, signaling the fate of his fellow townsmen. The event is commemorated in the Selkirk Common Riding in June, when 400 horse riders race on a circuit around the town. **Halliwell's House Museum** (www.liveborders.org. uk; ℂ 01750/200-96), an atmospheric ironmonger's shop in a close off Market Square, chronicles Selkirk's role in the battle along with other local history. Admission is free, and a visit also includes a tour of the **Robson Gallery,** which exhibits contemporary art and local crafts. The museum is open April to October Monday through Saturday 11am to 4pm and Sunday noon to 3pm.

Bowhill ★★ HISTORIC SITE   The Scotts of Buccleuch have been avid collectors for the past 500 years, and works by Canaletto, Gainsborough, and Reynolds, rare rugs and tapestries, and fine French furniture fill the rooms of their onetime hunting lodge, built in 1708 and vastly expanded over the years. The stately facade extends almost 450 feet, set against some of the Borders' most stunning scenery on a 22,000-hectare (55,000-acre) estate laced with lochs and woodlands. The deep surrounding forests befit the family name: During the 10th century King Kenneth III was hunting in the forest when he was charged by a deer, or "buck," in a ravine, or "cleuch." John Scott saved the king's life by grabbing the beast by the antlers and ever since the Scotts have had Buccleuch appended to the family name.

Off the A708, 3 miles west of Selkirk. www.bowhillhouse.co.uk. ℂ **01750/222-04.** House: £11 adults, £10 seniors, £6 children 3–16, £30 families of 2 adults and 2 children; Estate: £5.50 adults, £4.50 seniors and children, £18 families of 2 adults and 2 children. House by guided tour: July daily 11:30am–5pm, Aug and Sept weekends 11:30am–3pm. Estate: July–Aug Fri and Mon 10am–5pm, Sat and Sun 11am–5pm.

WHERE TO STAY IN SELKIRK
Philipburn Country House Hotel ★   Built in 1751, the former dower house of the Philiphaugh Estate has been home to a long line of baronets and commands high ground outside Selkirk, surrounded by 1.6 peaceful hectares (4 acres) of gardens and woodlands overlooking the Ettrick Valley. The paneled lounges, bar, and bistro are probably a bit more causal than they were in the lords' and ladies' days, and the nicely done bedrooms are well-suited to a country stay, with balconies and garden views, and several conform to the quirks of the old house with alcoves and mezzanines. Four cozy wooden lodges are comfortably rustic.

Linglie Rd., Selkirk. www.philipburnhousehotel.co.uk. © **01750/207-47.** 16 units. £120–£170 double. Lodges £50 per person per night. **Amenities:** 2 restaurants; bar; free Wi-Fi.

Peebles ★
22 miles NW of Selkirk, 23 miles S of Edinburgh

Cradled by the Pentland Hills, this small, appealing town is skirted by the swift-moving waters of the River Tweed flowing from the west and the Eddleston Water from the north. Forests and pasture-carpeted valleys run right up to the outskirts and are easy to reach via riverside walks along the Tweed. Before setting out, though, take a stroll down High Street, which becomes Eastgate, and is lined with a handsome assemblage of Victorian-era shops.

ESSENTIALS
GETTING THERE   Borders Bus no. 62 (www.bordersbuses.co.uk; © **01289/308-719**) provides a direct service from Edinburgh to Peebles that runs roughly every half-hour; the journey takes about an hour. If you're **driving** from Edinburgh, follow the A703 south to Peebles. The A72 heads west to Peebles from Selkirk and the other Borders towns

VISITOR INFORMATION   The **Tourist Information Centre** (www.visitscotland.com; © **01721/723-159**) is on High Street. It's open daily 9am to 5pm most of the year, with reduced hours in winter.

EXPLORING PEEBLES
Peebles' exotic-looking World War I **memorial,** with mosaics and an elaborate roof that resembles an onion dome, stands amid flowers and greenery in a courtyard off High Street and bears the names of the 225 men from Peebles who lost their lives in World War I. Just opposite is the charming **John Buchan Story ★** (www.johnbuchanstory.co.uk; © **01721/723-525**), a quirky tribute to Sir John Buchan, Baron Tweedsmuir (1875–1940), a diplomat, intelligence officer, and eventually Governor-General of Canada. Sir John spent his spare hours writing thrillers and is best remembered for his good-natured spy novel, *The 39 Steps,* which Alfred Hitchcock made into a film in 1935. His sister, Anna Masterton Buchan, is also honored, as well she should be:

under the name O. Douglas, she wrote *Pink Sugar* and other novels about life in Peebles between the wars, and the worst thing anyone's ever found to say about these light-hearted reads is that the characters are just too pleasant, as actually, Peebleans (who are traditionally known as *gutterbluids*) tend to be. The town is linked less flatteringly with adventure novelist Robert Louis Stevenson (1850–1894). The fledgling author came to Peebles with his parents and nanny on a summer holiday when he was 13, and in the petulant manner of an adolescent wrote an unflattering account of the residents in the style of Thackeray's *Book of Snobs*.

A walk west along the Tweed to the edge of town leads to **St Andrews Tower,** rising from a jumble of spooky-looking tombstones. The squat stone structure is the sole remnant of an 11th-century church destroyed in the 1560s during the Reformation. A little farther along is 12th-century **Neidpath Castle ★**. The romantic old pile standing above the river is the home of the Earl of Wemyss and closed to the public. Even so, views from the riverbank and surrounding pastures show off the tall, almost-windowless facade, rounded corner towers, and balcony-like sentry walks. It's easy to see why such a forbidding, storybook house is reputed to be haunted by the ghost of early-17th-century resident Jean Douglas. Her father forbade his only daughter to marry a boy he considered to be common and had him sent away. Jean pined away into such a pitiful state that when her lover returned he did not recognize her, and she died of a broken heart.

Dawyck Botanic Garden ★ GARDEN   A 4-century-long passion for gardening shines through on these 25 hectares (61 acres) of azaleas, rhododendrons, and other woodland plants. An especially picturesque display pops up when the springtime snowdrops blossom alongside Scrape Burn, a spry little waterfall. The Veitch family planted the beeches and many of the other trees in the 17th century, though the Douglas firs are slightly younger—owner Sir John Murray Naesmith helped fund the 19th-century plant-hunting expeditions of David Douglas (1799–1834), who returned from America's Pacific Northwest with specimens of these attractive evergreens later named for him (Douglas died on an exhibition to Hawaii, when he fell into a bull trap and a bull tumbled in after him). Royal Botanic Garden Edinburgh (p. 80) owns and runs Dawyck and leads guided walks throughout the spring and early summer.

Stobo, off the B712 near Bellspool, 8 miles south of Peebles. www.rbge.org.uk. ⓒ **01721/760-254.** £6.50 adults, £5.50 seniors, children free. Feb and Nov 10am–4pm; Mar and Oct 10am–5pm; Apr–Sept 10am–6pm.

Kailzie Gardens ★ GARDEN   Walled gardens are a common feature of Scottish country houses, laid out behind high walls that block the wind and radiate the warmth of the sun. Walls of this garden, laid out on the south banks of River Tweed in 1812, are 18 feet high, and within them are grassy paths that meander between glorious displays of roses, including many climbers, and greenhouses fragrant with wisteria and exotic fuchsias. Beyond the garden walls, pathways lead through woodlands carpeted in spring with daffodils and bluebells, and riverside groves are home to kingfishers, herons, and osprey.

Kailzie, on the B7062, 2½ miles southeast of Peebles. www.kailziegardens.com. ℂ **01721/720-007.** May–Oct £5 adults (£4 Nov–Mar), £4 seniors £1 children 5–16. Apr–Oct daily 11am–5:30pm; Nov–Mar daily daylight hours.

Little Sparta ★★ GARDEN   Artist, poet, and gardener Ian Hamilton Finlay (1925–2006) created what has been called the "only original garden" to take shape in Britain since 1945. The 7 acres wrap around ponds and a loch and are enhanced with more than 275 sculptures and other permanent art works, referred to as "poem-objects." "Sparta" is a play on Edinburgh's moniker, Athens of the North—the stark surrounding peaks and wild hillside on which the garden is perched suggest Athens' austere rival city-state. Finlay, an agoraphobic who allegedly never left the property in 30 years, liked to refer to himself as an avant-gardener, and it's easy to see why when coming upon whimsical temples created from an old barn, a golden head of Apollo, and stones painted with the different names for boat (wherry, keel, yawl). Some of the references in the garden may seem a bit obscure, but who cares? This artful, playful creation is mesmerizing.

Stonypath (off the A702), 17 miles northwest of Peebles. www.littlesparta.org.uk. ℂ **07826/495-677.** £12.50, students £7.50. June–Sept Thurs–Sun 12:30–5pm.

Traquair House ★ HISTORIC HOME   The famous "Bear Gates" of this former hunting lodge of the kings of Scotland have been closed since 1745, when Bonnie Prince Charlie passed through them after a short visit. The earl of Traquair, whose ancestors had lived at the house since 1495 and whose descendants still do, said the gates would remain closed until a Stuart monarch was crowned in London. That's one of many historically notable tidbits surrounding Scotland's oldest inhabited house, since 1107, and visited since then by 27 Scottish kings and queens. Mary Queen of Scots rocked the infant James VI in an ornately carved oak cradle in the King's Room. Tucked along the tapestry-hung halls are secret escape routes used by the priests the family hid during the Reformation. Traquair Ale has been brewed on the estate since the time of Mary's visit in 1566, and is still made the old-fashioned way in oak vessels and copper vats installed beneath the chapel in 1739. A modern addition to the estate is a maze that confounds visitors in a 1/4-mile-long labyrinth of hedges.

Off the A72 at Innerleithen, 6 miles east of Peebles. www.traquair.co.uk. ℂ **01896/830-323.** £9 adults, £8 seniors, £4 children 3–16, £25 families. Apr–Sept daily 11am–5pm; Oct daily 11am–4pm; Nov Sat–Sun only 11am–3pm.

WALKS NEAR PEEBLES

Peebles is close to some of southern Scotland's most picturesque countryside, including the **Pentland Hills** to the northwest (www.pentlandhills.org). More than 60 miles of signposted trails thread their way past the remains of ancient forts and cairns; visitor centers are off the A702 north of Penicuik and east off the A70 near Balerno. **Glentress Forest** (www.glentressforest.com) immediately northeast of Pebbles is also good hiking and mountain-biking country.

WHERE TO EAT & STAY IN PEEBLES

Mary Queen of Scots and Bonnie Prince Charlie slept at Traquair House (see above), and you can, too, in one of three delightful bedrooms offered on a bed-and-breakfast basis. Once visiting hours are over, you'll have the grand place to yourself and can wander in the grounds and lounge in one of the drawing rooms. Rates begin at £200 a night (www.traquair.co.uk; ✆ **018696/830-232**).

Cringletie House Hotel ★★ The towers and turrets crowning this manor from 1666 are the result of a Victorian redo, when society architect David Bryce rebuilt the house in his hallmark style that ensured the well-to-do would feel baronial in a faux-medieval fantasy. Another enlargement in the 1920s fine-tuned the swanky lounges that are tailor-made for sipping a cocktail in style. Distinctively designed guest rooms, no two alike, overlook 11 hectares (28 acres) of well-manicured grounds and are a pleasant mix of traditional and contemporary, with nice perks that include original fireplaces and freestanding tubs. A spa cottage sleeps two to six and has a hot tub. Dinner is served in an elegant room beneath a spectacular painted ceiling, commissioned as a wedding gift for the offspring of two early-20th century aristocratic families.

Edinburgh Rd, Peebles, off the A703 2½ miles north of Peebles. www.cringletie.com. ✆ **01721/725-750**. 13 units. Doubles £100–£200, includes breakfast. **Amenities:** Restaurant; bar; croquet lawn; putting green; free Wi-Fi.

Osso ★ MEDITERRANEAN/SCOTTISH A popular daytime gathering spot serves coffee, pastries, and sandwiches in a bright, comfortable room. Three nights a week the lighting is dimmed to create a more intimate setting and the kitchen shows off with a short and ambitiously inventive dinner menu. Offerings change frequently, depending on season and market freshness, but they reliably feature seafood from the southern coast, pork from local farms, and Borders beef.

Innerleithen Rd., Peebles. www.ossorestaurant.com. ✆ **01721/724-477**. Main courses £8–£22. Mon–Sat 10am–4:30pm, Thurs–Sat 6–9pm, Sun 11am–4:30pm.

Stobo Castle ★ A stay at this luxurious countryside spa can make any guest feel like a princess or prince, with comfortable accommodation in a 19th-cenury manor built to look like a fairytale castle, complete with towers and crenellations, and an almost endless supply of indulgent pampering. Guest quarters are decidedly old world, clubby and cozy, done up with rich colors and acres of plaids and tartans; a couple of the gracious rooms have private balconies from which to soak in the beautiful, bucolic surroundings. State-of-the-art spa facilities in a new wing include a beautiful swimming pool facing the surrounding terrain through a wall of glass, along with mud rooms, outdoor torch-lit hot tubs, and all sorts of amenities designed to coddle guests.

Stobo, off the B712, 7 miles southeast of Peebles. www.stobocastle.co.uk. © **01721/725-300.** 24 units. Doubles from £280, includes breakfast. Packages with meals and treatments available. **Amenities:** Restaurant; bar; pool; spa; gym; tennis courts; free Wi-Fi.

Tontine Hotel ★★ This proud old Georgian landmark behind a forecourt on High Street has been the town gathering spot of two centuries. The fire-warmed lounges do a brisk business with morning coffees and afternoon teas, and the 1808 ballroom is now a grand dining room (the same menu is served in a more casual bistro to the side). Most guest rooms are in a rear modern wing that, though they lack the historic provenance of the front of the house, overlook the River Tweed and are nicely done in a contemporary style with bits of tartan here and there to add a touch of tradition.

High St., Peebles. www.tontinehotel.com. © **01721/788-139.** 36 units. Doubles from £70, includes breakfast. **Amenities:** Restaurant; bar; free Wi-Fi.

Windlestraw Lodge ★★★ Country living seems awfully appealing in this warm and relaxing redo of a secluded Edwardian manor house set in sweeping lawns above the banks of the Tweed. A sun room, sitting areas grouped around glowing hearths, and good-weather terraces create a convivial "country weekend" atmosphere, though all sort of nooks and crannies, indoors and out, afford the privacy you'd expect from a getaway like this. At the top of the carved wooden staircase, charming guest rooms are done in a restrained and soothing country chic style with brass beds, chaise lounges for reclining while gazing at the countryside, and deep tubs for soaking. Set menu dinners make the most of the offerings of local farmers and homegrown herbs.

Off the A72 (Galashiels Rd.), Walkerburn, 8½ miles east of Peebles. www.windlestraw. co.uk. © **01896/870-636.** 6 units. Doubles £175–£210, includes breakfast. **Amenities:** Restaurant; bar; free Wi-Fi.

DUMFRIES & GALLOWAY

The lands of Scotland's southwestern corner sweep across green mountain-sides and along rugged coastlines, embracing castles, country houses and gardens, dark forests, charming seaside villages, and history-saturated locales linked to everyone from Mary Stuart to Robert Burns. With no disrespect to royalty, Rabbie Burns is the region's hero, and the largest town, Dumfries, is where the poet spent many of his most creative years and is the best place in Scotland (aye, the world!) to appreciate Burns' legacy and colorful life. Kirk-cudbright, on the coast to the west, is a bohemian artists' colony, as it has been since the late 19th century, while Wigtown, farther along the coast, is Scotland's official National Book Town. Nearby Whithorn is the cradle of some of Scotland oldest settlements and also the beachhead of early Christianity. This seriously scenic region takes in one of Scotland's highest waterfalls, Grey

Mare's Tail, and highest upland loch, Loch Skeen, both near Moffat, and to the west, Britain's largest tract of protected woodland, Galloway Forest Park. The Mull of Galloway is Scotland's southernmost point of land and juts into the Irish Sea from a Gulf Stream-warmed stretch of coast known, a tad hyperbolically, as the Scottish Riviera.

Our coverage moves from the mountainous boundary with the Borders region around Moffat in the northwest down to Dumfries then west all the way out to pretty seaside Portpatrick, at Scotland's southwestern edge.

Moffat ★

33 miles S of Peebles, 61 miles S of Edinburgh, 60 miles SE of Glasgow

In the late 18th and early 19th centuries, this small sheep-farming town at the head of the Annandale Valley was thronged with visitors who came to take the waters. Among them was Robert Burns, who found the local beer to be a lot more restorative than water, so much so that while in Moffat the poet was inspired to compose the drinking song "O Willie Brewd a Peck o' Maut." He also became enamored of a beautiful, petit woman whom he used to see riding past with a much more portly, less attractive companion. Seeing the pair while drinking at the still-operating Black Bull Inn, he etched a verse into the glass, "Ask why God made the gem so small, and so huge the granite? Because God meant man to set the higher value on it." Tsar Nicholas I of Russia visited Moffat in 1816, saw the verse, and took the pane as a souvenir with him home to St. Petersburg, where it remains.

The allegedly healing waters were channeled into the town square from a well in the hills 1½ miles away (an easy walk on a well-signposted path). Along with the erstwhile spa goers, no longer in evidence is the overpowering odor of sulfur that once wafted down the little cobblestone lanes, though a Greek Revival pump room now houses the town hall. Another holdout from Moffat's cure-all days is the oldest continuously operating pharmacy in Scotland. The reason to come to Moffat these days is to enjoy the surrounding mountains and moors that roll across some of southern Scotland's most stunning scenery.

ESSENTIALS

GETTING THERE   If you're traveling down to Moffat from the Borders by **car,** you have a choice of two especially scenic routes. From Selkirk, the A708 heads south though moors and stark hill country past beautiful St Mary's Loch then Grey Mare's Tail Waterfall. From Peebles, the A701 drops through the mountains past a particularly scenic and historic patch around the Devil's Beef Tub. The nearest train station is in Lockerbie, 15 miles south of Moffat (www.scotrail.co.uk; ✆ **0344/811-0141**), where you can catch the frequent **Stagecoach** (www.stagecoachbus.com) bus no. 380 service to Moffat; the bus journey takes around 35 minutes.

VISITOR INFORMATION   The privately owned **Tourist Information Centre** (www.visitmoffat.co.uk; ✆ **01683/221-210**) is at 9 High St. and open daily 10am to 5pm (hours vary).

EXPLORING AROUND MOFFAT

The countryside surrounding Moffat is a walkers' paradise. The **Southern Upland Way** (p. 123) skirts the east shore of **St Mary's Loch** then heads towards Moffat and west into the Lowther Hills. Moffat is also a prime spot for golfers with 11 courses lying within a 25-mile radius. For more information, visit the Tourist Information Centre (see above) or see the town's website (www.visitmoffat.co.uk).

The Valleys Northeast of Moffat

The Moffat Water, Yarrow, and Ettrick valleys spread out on either side of the A708 route between Selkirk and Moffat. Moody moors, stark hillsides with jagged outcroppings, patches of woodland, and glimmering lochs and streams create magical landscapes, making this one of Scotland's most scenic drives. Ten miles north of Moffat, and 25 miles southwest of Selkirk, the **Grey Mare's Tail** ★, one of Britain's highest waterfalls, cascades 60m (200 ft.) from **Loch Skeen.** High in the hills at 500m (1,640 ft.), Skeen is Scotland's highest upland loch. The cascade spills down a spectacular rock face before tumbling into the **Tail Burn** (a swift-moving stream) then emptying into Moffat Water. From the car park (£2 fee) at the foot of the waterfall off the A708, a well-trodden 2.5-mile trail leads up the valley past the falls to Loch Skeen— look out for nesting peregrine falcons along the way.

About 4 miles north the road begins to skirt **St Mary's Loch** ★, a large stretch of water which, local legend has it, has no bottom. Gazing across the southern end of the loch, in the guise of a statue, is the poet and novelist James Hogg, who worked these valleys as a shepherd and whose grandfather Will o' Phaup is credited with being the last man who could speak with fairies; if you're heading north up to the valley to Selkirk (see p 131), you can learn more about Hogg in the town's Sir Walter Scott's Courtroom museum. He seems especially at home in this rural setting, since he never wanted to shake off his rural roots. Lore has it that he turned down an invitation to attend the coronation of King George IV in London because doing so would have meant missing the annual livestock fair in St Boswells (see above). A day's angling can be arranged through **St Mary's Angling Club** (www.sites.google.com/site/stmarysloch; ✆ **07980/350-031**).

The Devil's Beef Tub

A sheer-sided hollow in the hills 5 miles northwest of town was once the refuge of cattle thieves. Formed by the flanks of four steep-sided hills, this dramatic formation, 152m (500-ft.) deep and 1¾-mile-wide, provided a handy natural corral for rustlers who would raid farms across the English border then herd their prizes north to the cattle market in Edinburgh, pausing here outside Moffat to rest and water the stock. The Devil's Beef Tub can be viewed from a well-marked turnoff on the A701, the road you'll likely take if you're driving south from Peebles to Moffat; to reach the tub on foot from town, follow the **Annan Water Valley Road,** a rural route with little traffic.

WHERE TO EAT & STAY

Annandale Arms Hotel ★   This 250-year-old coaching inn opened to serve weary passengers on the London to Edinburgh run and is right in the center of town, off the tree-lined square. The suit of armor standing guard over the reception gives a good idea of the sort of traditional comforts extended to legions of guests who have included Tsar Nicholas I of Russia and World War I poet Rupert Brooke. The intimate oak-paneled pub rooms still exude old-world hospitality, while the comfortable guest rooms are stylishly modern. The kitchen will pack a lunch when the surrounding hills beckon.

High St., Moffat. www.annandalearmshotel.co.uk. ✆ **01683/220-013.** 16 units. £110 double, includes breakfast. **Amenities:** Restaurant; bar; free Wi-Fi.

Dumfries ★

20 miles S of Moffat, 80 miles SW of Edinburgh, 79 miles SE of Glasgow

Southwest Scotland's largest town grew up around the banks of the River Nith just north of the point where its wide estuary merges with the Solway Firth. Dangerously close to the border with England, and a thriving seaport since the Middle Ages, Dumfries was an irresistible target for British armies, who attacked again and again. Robert the Bruce came to Dumfries in 1306 to murder John III Comyn, his rival for the Scottish crown, a maneuver that got him excommunicated but put him on the throne until his death in 1329. In the 17th century, Doonhamers, as residents are called, turned on themselves and accused nine women of being witches and burned them at the stake.

For all this turbulent history, Dumfries is cheerful in appearance and disposition, with many fine red sandstone landmarks and some graceful spans across the River Nith. Dumfries is immensely proud to have been the home of the poet Robert Burns, whose spirit seems to inhabit every street and square.

ESSENTIALS

GETTING THERE   **ScotRail** (www.scotrail.co.uk; ✆ **0344/811-0141**) operates direct service between Glasgow's Central Station and Dumfries. The journey takes 1¾ hours. From Edinburgh, take a train to Lockerbie, 12½ miles south of Dumfries, and then catch Stagecoach (www.stagecoachbus.com) bus service no. 81 to Dumfries. Stagecoach bus service X74 connects Glasgow's Buchanan Street station with Dumfries. The journey takes 2 hours.

If you're driving from Edinburgh, follow the A701 southwest through Moffat to Dumfries. From Glasgow follow the M74/A74 to Moffat and then the A701.

VISITOR INFORMATION   The **Tourist Information Centre** is at 64 Whitesands (www.visitdumfriesandgalloway.co.uk; ✆ **01387/253-862**). It's open December to June and October Monday through Friday 9:30am to 5pm, plus Saturday April to June and Sunday in October 10:30am to 4pm; and September and November Monday through Saturday 9am to 5pm and Sunday 10:30am to 4pm. Dumfries-based **Solway Tours** (www.solwaytours.co.uk;

ⓒ **07789/794-142** or 07809/239-696) provides excellent and highly enjoyable in-depth day and multi-day tours of the region, along with ancestral tours for visitors tracing their Scottish roots (see p. 61).

EXPLORING DUMFRIES

Whitesands, a riverside esplanade, follows the north bank of the River Nith past the town's four bridges. The oldest, Devorgilla, has stood here in one form or the other since the 1260s and has been rebuilt many times, for the last time in 1620 (and clumsily shortened in 18th century to make way for a roadway). The stone crossing is these days for pedestrians only, as is the Suspension Bridge just upstream, from 1875. This delicate-looking Victorian creation was once off limits to men in the early morning and late afternoon, so women working at mills along the south banks could make the crossing without unwanted attention.

Robert Burns makes two appearances on High Street, as a happy and proud looking statue, and in spirit in the Globe Inn, opened in 1610 and still a working pub, where the poet spent many of his evenings. Burns's favorite seat is still in place, but you'll be cajoled into reciting a verse or two of his poetry if you sit in it. The poet's mausoleum is in **St Michael's Churchyard,** on St Michael's Street (cemetery is usually open). This large neo-Grecian shrine-like monument seems a bit pompous and formal for a poet who sang the virtues of a simple life. But his figure, with a muse hovering above him, leans on a plough, and if you look carefully you can see some touching references to his verse—the little field mouse he celebrated in his poem "To a Mouse" and the rose of which he wrote in the song, "My love is like a red, red rose."

Burns died in 1796 and was originally buried in a corner of the churchyard. Local officials decided the national poet deserved a more suitable resting place and, after funds poured in from around the world, his remains were moved here in 1815 and now he rests in peace alongside his wife, Jean Armour, and five of their nine children. Workmen who undertook the transfer supposedly had quite an ordeal, more worthy of Edgar Allan Poe than of Burns. The casket in which the poet had been buried more or less disintegrated upon being moved, exposing the well-preserved corpse: high forehead, scalp still covered with hair, and teeth firm and white. Then, with a slight jostle, the head detached from the body and the poet crumbled into dust. Or so the story goes.

Burns House ★ HISTORIC HOME   Burns lived in this stone house off St Michael's Street for the last 3 years of his life, succumbing to rheumatic fever here in 1796 at the age of 37. His modest but comfortable home contains many personal relics and mementos as well as much of the original furniture used by Burns during his creative years—including the chair he sat on to write the last of his poems. His wife, Jean Armour, continued to live in the house until her death in 1834. Jean became a respected celebrity in her own right as the widow of the celebrated poet and she and her children lived on a charitable

A Hero with Feet of Clay

Robert (Rabbie) Burns was sometimes called the "heaven-taught ploughman," a reference to his humble roots and supposed lack of a formal education. He perpetuated the myth by referring to himself as a "simple bard, unbroken by the rules of art." The poet, of course, was no clodhopper. Though he was forced to leave school at an early age, Burns was encouraged by his farmer parents to study and read voraciously, continued to do so throughout his life, and was probably better versed in the classics, literature, and world affairs than most well-educated men of his day. Probably because of his playful drinking songs, Burns is often thought to have been a heavy drinker, though his fondness for libation was typical of the times, when beer and gin were considered healthier than water and consumed at most meals. Burns's one weakness appears to have been woman: He fathered 13 children, 4 with his wife, Jean Armour, before they were married, and several more with Jean and other women once they were married; his last child was born the day he was buried. Burns's fondness for women inspired some fine art, including the love song "Ae Fond Kiss."

trust raised for their continued support. A statue of Jean stands near St Michael's Kirk, behind which she's buried alongside her husband.

Burns St. www.dumfriesmuseum.demon.co.uk. ✆ **01387/255-297.** Free. Apr–Sept Mon–Sat 10am–5pm, Sun 2–5pm; Oct–Mar Tues–Sat 10am–1pm and 2–5pm.

Dumfries Museum & Camera Obscura ★ MUSEUM   A converted 18th-century windmill is quite literally stacked to the rafters with quirky bits and pieces that do justice to Dumfries' long and colorful history, from Roman altar stones to bicycles made by local blacksmith Kirkpatrick Macmillan (see Drumlanrig Castle, below). At the very top is the crowning achievement, a camera obscura installed in 1836, when the windmill became an observatory from which to study the night sky and watch the passage of Halley's Comet as it streaked over Dumfries. To demonstrate the camera obscura, an attendant maneuvers ropes to operate a contrivance of mirrors and lenses that project images of Dumfries, spreading out below the windmill, onto a circular white table in the center of the room. Jaded as we are with computer graphics and selfies, seeing church towers, rooftops, and the gleaming river come into view via this precursor to the camera is a magical experience.

Church St. www.dumgal.gov.uk. ✆ **01387/253-374.** Museum free; camera obscura £2.30 adults, £1.15 children 5–16 and seniors. Apr–Sept Mon–Sat 10am–5pm; Oct–Mar Tues–Sat 10am–1pm and 2–5pm; camera obscura closed Oct–Mar.

The Robert Burns Centre ★ MUSEUM   A converted 18th-century water mill honors the poet with manuscripts and other paraphernalia. A scale model of Dumfries in 1796 depicts the town in which Burns lived and worked for some of his most productive years, and a rich portrait emerges of Burns and his life in Dumfries. Scotland's national poet, who penned some of the most memorable lines in the English language, was also a dutiful bureaucrat who rose in the ranks of the Excise Office, charged with calculating and collecting tax on silk, tobacco, and spirits. He often covered 200 miles a week on horseback in pursuit of these duties. The center also houses an art-film theater.

Mill Rd. www.dumgal.gov.uk. ⓒ **01387/264-808.** Free. Apr–Sept Mon–Sat, 10am–5pm, Sunday 2–5pm; Oct–Mar Tues–Sat, 10am–1pm and 2–5pm.

EXPLORING THE AREA
In the hills near Dumfries, landscape artist Andy Goldsworthy has created **Striding Arches** ★ (www.stridingarches.com), three striking red sandstones arches that seem to "stride" across the landscape. The road leading to this dramatic piece of landscape art is signposted from the center of Moniaive, 23 miles northwest of Dumfries via the B729.

Caerlaverock Castle ★★★ CASTLE Medieval castles don't come much more romantic and picture perfect than these red sandstone ruins, triangular in shape and approached over a moat and through a twin-towered gatehouse. Amid the mossy vaulted halls it's easy to imagine lairds in fur capes sitting around roaring fires, though the most imposing remnant of domestic life within the battlements is an elaborate Renaissance facade from the 1630. The earl of Nithsdale had this bit of finery installed when he tried to convert the old pile into a proper country seat, though this wild frontier was not yet ready for such refinement. Nymphs and satyrs cavort around window frames and doorways that, during the religious wars, were rendered empty shells just 6 years after they were crafted. The castle sits amid 21 square miles of wetlands along the Solway Firth, and walks usually include an encounter or two with geese, seals, and other wildlife.

8 miles southeast of Dumfries off the B725. www.historicenvironment.scot. ⓒ **01387/770-244.** £6 adults, £4.80 seniors, £3.60 children 5–15. Apr–Sept daily 9:30am–5:30pm, Oct–Mar daily 9:30am–4:30pm.

Drumlanrig Castle ★★ CASTLE One of Scotland's finest lordly seats is the creation of 31 masons and eight builders who toiled for a decade, between 1679 and 1689, to create a proud, pink Renaissance facade that has always seemed a bit too fine for its rugged surroundings amid moors and stark mountains. At least the writer Daniel Defoe thought so, and visiting in 1726 he wrote that the great house was "like a fine picture in a dirty grotto, or like an equestrian statue set up in a barn." One of the resident dukes of Queensbury made the place seem even starker when toward the end of the 18th century he had all the trees on the estate cut down and sold as timber to pay off his gambling debts. Bonnie Prince Charlie added a colorful episode when he spent a night on his way to fight the Battle of Culloden in 1745 and left in such a hurry that his servants didn't have time to unscrew his money box from the bedroom floor. Among the family portraits—and interestingly, paintings of beloved chefs and other faithful retainers—are many old masters, minus Leonardo da Vinci's *Madonna with the Yarnwinder.* In 2004, thieves posing as sightseers matter-of-factly took the painting off a wall and climbed through a window with it. Recovered in a dramatic sting operation in 2007, the painting is now in the Scottish National Gallery in Edinburgh. The Scottish Cycle Museum occupies the former stable yard and is dedicated to Kirkpatrick Mac-Millan, a blacksmith on the estate who in 1839 invented the rear-wheel-driven bicycle.

16 miles north of Dumfries, 3 miles north of Thornhill off the A76. www.drumlanrig.com. © **01848/331-555.** Castle and gardens: £10 adults, £8 seniors, £5 children 3–16, £28 families; gardens: £6 adults, £4.50 seniors, £3.50 children 3–16, £16 families; gardens Castle: by guided tour only, some weekends in May and Jul–Aug daily 11am–4pm. Gardens: Apr–Sept 10am–5pm.

Ellisland Farm ★ FARM/MUSEUM   From 1788 to 1791, Robert Burns rented this small farm from landlord Patrick Miller (1731–1815), a wealthy banker and inventor whose interests included modern farming methods and steamship travel. Burns wrote some of his most famous work at Ellisland, including "Auld Lang Syne," often while walking in the countryside. Two of his children were born here, including a daughter by a young woman with whom he had an affair. Burns's wife, Jean Armour, was obviously an understanding soul and adopted the child, who was born 9 days before she delivered her third child, a son, with Burns. The soil was sorely depleted with years of overplanting and the farm was, as Burns said, "ruinous." The family returned to Dumfries, where Burns, though in fragile health, continued to work successfully as a tax collector and to write prodigiously. Ellisland is still a working farm and a cottage is filled with Burns memorabilia. One of the best things to do here is retrace the poet's steps along scenic trails to the banks for the River Nith where Burns often walked.

6 miles north of Dumfries off the A76. www.ellislandfarm.co.uk. © **01387/740-426.** £5 adults, £4 seniors, under-15s free. Apr–Sept Mon–Sat 10am–1pm and 2–5pm, Sun 2–5pm; Oct–Mar Tues–Sat 10am–1pm and 2–4pm.

Sweetheart Abbey ★ ABBEY   Devorguilla Balliol, one of Europe's wealthiest women of the Middle Ages, founded this abbey in 1273 in memory of her husband, John Balliol the Elder. Lady Balliol also endowed the college at Oxford that has proven to be a more famous testament to the family name. Even so, the red sandstone abbey prospered for almost 400 years, and the formidable remains of the church remain a tribute to the pair's enduring love. Lady Balliol never went anywhere without her husband's embalmed heart, encased in a silver box, so it's only fitting that the cherished organ still lies next to her, near the place where the altar would have stood.

Off the A710 at New Abbey 6¾ miles south of Dumfries. www.historicenvironment. scot. © **01387/850-397.** £5 adults, £4 seniors, £3 children 5–15. Apr–Sept daily 9:30am–5:30pm; Oct–Mar daily 10am–4pm.

Threave Castle ★ CASTLE   The moniker of Archibald the Grim, a 14th-century lord of Galloway, says a lot about his demeanor and the way he treated his tenant farmers and enemies alike. He built this now-ruined stronghold on a small island in the River Dee, and quite fittingly, over the doorway of the massive five-story tower house is the gallows knob from which Archibald and successive lords hanged their enemies. Stacked on the floors above were a hall, apartments, and a defensive redoubt to which weapons and supplies could be lifted via winches. Forbidding as the place is, getting there is a delight, via a half-mile walk through farmland to a dock, from which a boatman/ guide ferries visitors across to the island.

Off the A75 19 miles southwest of Dumfries. www.historicenvironment.scot. ©**07711/223-101.** £5 adults £4 seniors, children 5–15 £3; includes ferry ride. Apr–Sept daily 10am–last sailing at 4:30pm, Oct 9:30am–last sailing at 3:30pm.

Threave Gardens ★ GARDEN   William Gordon, a Liverpool business-man, built this baronial estate in 1872, placing the house and gardens so they would get the best vantage points of the Galloway Hills to the west. Nearly 200 different varieties of daffodil burst into bloom in April, and rhododen-drons provide a riot of color in June, but the 24 hectares are a delight almost any time, with a secret garden, a peat garden, and a woodland with a pond and waterfall. The walled garden once provided the house with cut flowers, fruit, and vegetables well into the chillier months, and coal-heated greenhouses extended the growing season even further. The house is now occupied in part by students of the National Trust for Scotland's School of Practical Garden-ing, who keep the grounds in tiptop shape.

Off the A75 17 miles southwest of Dumfries. www.nts.org.uk. ©**0844/493-2245.** £8.50 adults, £7 seniors and children 15 and under, £18.50 families of 2 adults and 2 children, £12 families of 1 adults and 2 children. Mar–Oct 10am–5pm.

WHERE TO EAT & STAY IN DUMFRIES

Cavens Arms ★★ PUB FOOD   The most popular pub in Dumfries is almost as legendary as the nearby Globe, where Robert Burns used to hang out, though the fame is not for any literary provenance . . . but who's to say? One of the regulars may well be scribbling a masterpiece. Rather, this conviv-ial place is top choice in town for a pub meal—with some distinctive twists to the usual offerings, such as haggis topped with melted cheese—or a pint of one of the many ales on tap.

20 Buccleuch St. © **01387/852-896.** Main courses £8–£12. Sun–Tues 11am–11pm, Wed–Sat 11am–midnight.

Cavens Country House Hotel ★   Sir Richard Oswald, who lived for a time in America and was a friend of Benjamin Franklin, built this country house in 1752. Among those who have visited over the years is Robert Burns, who wrote unflatteringly of the lady of the house as having a "bursting purse" and "hands that took but never gave." Burns' quibbles aside, the present hosts could not be more gracious, and it's a sheer delight to settle into these 2.4 hectares (6 acres) of landscaped gardens in rolling countryside south of Dum-fries, with the Solway Firth sparkling in the near distance. Fires burn in the book-lined sitting rooms and three of the six bedrooms are especially large, with cozy sitting areas, and all are done up nicely and overlook the beautiful grounds.

Kirkbean, 13 miles south of Dumfries off the A710. www.cavens.com. ✆ **01387/880-234.** 8 units. £110–£190 double, includes breakfast. **Amenities:** Restaurant; bar; free Wi-Fi.

Huntingdon House ★   While the great Scottish essayist and philosopher Thomas Carlisle was busy writing his treatises on the French Revolution and other matters, his sister, Jean Aitkin Carlyle, was settling into this commodious, gabled Victorian house. Much of the grandeur of that era remains in the atmospheric lounges and up-to-date guest rooms, with modern concessions that include a beer garden and, should you be a biker, parking for motorcycles and advice on seeing the region on two wheels, motorized or not.

18 St Mary's St. www.huntingdonhotel.co.uk. ✆ **01387/254-893.** 8 units. £85 double, includes breakfast. **Amenities:** Bar; free Wi-Fi.

Trigony House Hotel ★★   The notion that guests won't want to leave this shooting lodge from 1895 is more than a cliché, since the ivy-clad house was home for a full century to one resident, Scotland's longest-lived woman, who died peacefully in one of the character-filled bedrooms at the age of 107. Rich paneling, fireplace nooks, and many arts and crafts touches enhance the public rooms, and large guestrooms overlook the beautiful gardens and surrounding countryside. Dogs are welcome, a testimony to the casual, relaxed ambience that extends to the appealing dining rooms where what's modestly referred to as "simple European peasant dishes" are served.

Off the A76 just south of Thornhill, 12 miles north of Dumfries. www.trigonyhotel.co.uk. ✆ **01848/331-211.** 10 units. £105–£155 double, includes breakfast. **Amenities:** Restaurant; bar; free Wi-Fi.

Kirkcudbright ★★

28 miles SW of Dumfries

Despite a name that seems tailor-made to thwart correct pronunciation (it's Kir-*coo*-bree) this little seaport at the head of Kirkcudbright Bay on the Dee estuary is an inviting and utterly delightful place, with pretty pastel houses surrounding a lively harbor. Just about the only person who's ever gone on record as not liking Kirkcudbright is 18th-century novelist Daniel Defoe, who must have been having a bad travel day when he noted "nothing pleasant to be seen." Generations of artists have found plenty to see in Kirkcudbright, especially the play of light on water, and the color-washed town has long been an artists' colony and a favorite of weavers, potters, and painters, who still bring a bohemian ambience to the broad streets and salt-tinged wharves.

ESSENTIALS

GETTING THERE   The nearest train station is at Dumfries. **Stagecoach** (www.stagecoachbus.com) bus service no. 501/502 departs from Whitesands in Dumfries to Kirkcudbright throughout the day; the trip takes about an hour.

If you're driving from Dumfries, follow the A75 west past Castle Douglas until you come to the junction with the A711, which takes you into Kirkcudbright.

VISITOR INFORMATION The **Tourist Information Centre** is at Harbour Square (www.kirkcudbright.co.uk; ☎ **01557/330-494**). It's open February to March and November Monday through Saturday 10am to 4pm and Sunday 11am to 4pm; April to June and September to October Monday through Saturday 10am tɔ ʂpm and Sunday 11am to 4pm; and July to August Monday through Saturday 9:30am to 6pm and Sunday 11am to 5pm.

EXPLORING KIRKCUDBRIGHT

Though Kirkcudbright has endured pirate attacks and other setbacks, hulking **MacLellan's Castle** (www.historicenvironment.scot), off High Street, was made to look like a fortress only for show and was actually a refined country seat, one of the finest houses in Scotland when completed in 1582 (and built in part with stone from the ruined Greyfriars Monastery). The MacLellans burned through their lands and fortune and by 1742 the laird, working as a glover in Edinburgh, was forced to sell off the furnishings, lead roof, and window panes, and the tall gabled manor has been a shell ever since. A large staircase still leads to a Banqueting Hall, where a massive fireplace has a built-in "lairds lug"—a secret spy hole through which the laird could eavesdrop on his guests—and in the old vaults are the castle's kitchens, where legions of servants toiled away. The castle is open April through September daily, 9:30am to 5:30 pm, and admission is £4, £3.20 seniors, and £2.40 children 5–15.

The former court and debtors' prison on High Street is now the hospitable **Tolbooth Art Centre** (www.dumgal.gov.uk; ☎ **01557/331-556**), with an impressive collection of colorful renderings of Kirkcudbright by the artists who began spending summers and weekends in town in the late 19th century. As you'll see, the headlands and grassy shores of estuaries around town became as much a favorite subject for them as romantic landscapes of the Highland were for earlier painters. They became known as the Glasgow Boys, as most had studied at the Glasgow School of Art, and not all the members were "boys": The ephemeral illustrations of Jessie M. King (1875–1949) are among the works by a female contingent labeled the Glasgow Girls. The center is open Monday through Saturday 11m to 4pm (Sun 1–4pm from mid-Apr–Sept), and admission is free.

Around the corner on St Mary Street, the **Stewartry Museum** (www.dum gal.gov.uk; ☎ **01557/331-556**) is a charmingly eclectic showcase of the distinctive culture of this part of Dumfries and Galloway, known as Stewartry. Victorian-era glass classes are filled with watch fobs, stuffed specimens of waterfowl, cigarette cases, and other paraphernalia that engagingly capture local life. It's easy to imagine the quandary of a resident encountering WWI posters posing such questions as, "Who's Absent, Is It You?" or "Am I justified in using my good field glasses for pleasure when I might send them to Lady Roberts for the troops at the front?" With a little poking around you'll also learn the origin of the town's name —it's for Kirk of St Cuthbert, from a long-vanished monastery that flourished here a thousand or so years ago. The museum is open from mid-April through September, Monday to Saturday, 11am to 5pm and Sunday, 2 to 5pm, and October to mid-April, Monday to Saturday, 11am to 4pm. Admission is free.

Broughton House ★ HISTORIC HOME   The artist Edward Atkinson Hornel (1864–1933) spent most of his life in Kirkcudbright and became one of the better-known artists among the so-called Glasgow Boys. Bessie MacNicol, a member of the like-named Glasgow Girls, painted the portrait of Hornel in the dining room. The house the artist shared with his sister, as well as the adjoining studio, are filled with Hornel's colorful canvases as well as those of many of his colleagues. Hornel's 2,500-volume library of books by and about Robert Burns is one of the largest of its kind. Hornel traveled to the Far East several times, and one of the many charms of the house is a Japanese-style garden, with plantings and a pond that sometimes appear in his paintings.

12 High St. www.nts.org.uk. *C* **0844/493-2246.** £7.50 adults, £6.50 seniors and children 15 and under, £16.50 families of 2 adults and 2 children, £11 families of 1 adult and 2 children. Apr–Oct daily 10am–5pm.

AROUND KIRKCUDBRIGHT

Just west of Kirkcudbright, the A75 hugs the coast as it curls around Wigtown Bay for about 12 miles from Gatehouse of Fleet to Creetown. Along the way are some evocatively historic places. **Cardoness Castle** (www.historicenvironment.scot), just off the A75 a mile southwest of Gatehouse of Fleet, is a ruined 15th-century six-story tower house that's well-preserved enough to show off a massive fireplace and hidey hole where the family's best silver was kept, as well as a chillingly gruesome pit prison. The castle is open April through October, daily, 9:30am to 5:30pm, and admission is £5 adults, £4 seniors, and 3£ children 5 to 15. **Cairn Holy** (www.historicenvironment.scot), on a hillside overlooking Wigtown Bay about 7 miles west of Cardoness off the A75, comprises two haunting burial chambers from about 6,000 years ago. Though the top stones were removed several centuries ago to build dykes in the surrounding tidal flats, the tombs maintain a peaceful aura of mystery. Another 2 miles west, and 3 miles south of Creetown, are the roadside ruins of **Carsluith Castle** (www.historicenvironment.scot). This L-shaped tower house was built in 1420 and enlarged a few times since, and commands long views across Wigtown Bay. Carsluith Castle and Cairn Holy are free to enter and always open. At the **Marrbury Smokehouse** (www.visitmarrbury.co.uk; *C* **01671/820-476**), at the Carsluith Castle turnoff from the A75, you can pick up such delicacies as smoked Kirkcudbright scallops and wild Cree smoked salmon (perhaps the best smoked fish in the world).

WHERE TO EAT & STAY IN KIRKCUDBRIGHT
The Castle Restaurant ★ SCOTTISH/CONTINENTAL   The ruins of MacLellan's Castle (see above) loom just beyond the windows of this cozy little lair. The best of Galloway's bounty shows up in delicious preparations

of local duck and game, though it seems a shame to sit this close to the wharves and not indulge in the fresh seafood, including Kirkcudbright king scallops or just-caught monkfish. Full meals are available on some good-value set menus, and the kitchen often shakes up the standard offerings with pizza nights, tapas accompanied by Spanish music, or other specials.

5 Castle St. www.thecastlerestaurant.net. ✆ **01557/330-569.** Main courses £12–£20. Daily noon–3pm and 6:30–9:30pm.

Gladstone House ★ A carefully restored Georgian townhouse in the center of town maintains all of the gentility and grandeur of the era in which it was built, with a spacious drawing room and large gardens. The carefully appointed guest rooms, with a smattering of fine old pieces, show off architectural flare with dormers and tall sash windows that overlook the surrounding streets. A breakfast of home-baked bread, homemade preserves, and local produce is served in an elegant dining room.

48 High St., Kirkcudbright. www.kirkcudbrightgladstone.com. ✆ **01557/331-734.** 3 units. £75 double, includes breakfast. **Amenities:** Restaurant; bar; free Wi-Fi.

Glenmore Country House ★★ The center of town is only a short walk away along the banks of the River Dee, yet this fine old Victorian house seems like a country retreat, and a rather exotic one. Beyond the richly paneled hall is a library full of well-thumbed books, while the four, high-ceilinged bedrooms upstairs are filled with club chairs, and period furniture and look over the surrounding water meadows and distant hills. The former servants quarters have been transformed into an airy cottage that sleeps four.

Tongland Rd. www.glenholmecountryhouse.com. ✆ **01557/331-734.** 4 units and cottage. From £120–£135 double. **Amenities:** Restaurant; free Wi-Fi.

Selkirk Arms ★★ Behind the modest facade of this 18th century townhouse is a surprisingly stylish and sophisticated haven. Downstairs a friendly bar and bistro specialize in regional fare—scallops from Kirkcudbright and crab from Wigtown, along with Dumfries and Galloway steak. Upstairs, the small but stylish and bright guest rooms sport fabric wall coverings and a calming, contemporary look.

High St. www.selkirkarmshotel.co.uk. ✆ **01557/330-402.** 16 units. £95–£120 double, includes breakfast. **Amenities:** Restaurant; bar; free Wi-Fi. Meals daily noon–2pm and 6pm–9pm.

Wigtown ★

54 miles SW of Dumfries

This small town skirted by salt marshes at the edge of Wigtown Bay would be just another quiet, pretty, out-of-the-way place if it weren't for books. About 25 years ago, Wigtown officially became Scotland's National Book Town—and as a result, Wigtown is to the written word what nearby Kirkcudbright is to painting. At least a dozen bookshops surround the grand, triangular-shaped main square, books line the walls of pubs, and during 10 days in late

September, a vibrant book festival (www.wigtownbookfestival.com) floods the town with some of the U.K.'s top authors and a sea of bookworms who come to hear them speak. Visitors who manage to take their noses out of their books can also enjoy encounters with wildlife in the surrounding nature preserve, follow in the footsteps of early Christians at nearby Whithorn, and explore the trails of Galloway Forest Park.

ESSENTIALS

GETTING THERE   By **bus,** you can catch Stagecoach (www.stagecoach bus.com) service no. 500 from Dumfries to Newton Stewart, and then service no. 415 from Newton Stewart to Dumfries. If you're **driving** from Dumfries, head southwest along the A75 until Newton Stewart and then turn south along the A714, which leads directly into town.

VISITOR INFORMATION   There's no tourist information center in Wigtown, but you can pick up info at the **County Buildings** adjacent to the main square that also houses the town library. You can also get a lot of local info and learn about the Book Festival at the **Wigtown Festival Company,** 11 N. Main St. (www.wigtownbookfestival.com; ✆ **01988/403-222**).

EXPLORING WIGTOWN

It won't take long to explore this tiny town unless you're a book lover, in which case the plethora of bookstores will detain you for hours. Two especially enticing shops are **ReadingLasses,** 17 S. Main St. (✆ **01988/403-266**), where you can interrupt your pursuit of the many titles by and about women with a cup of coffee or snack in the excellent cafe, and **The Bookshop,** 17 N. Main St. (www.the-bookshop.com; ✆ **01988/402-499**), which claims to be the largest second-hand bookshop in Scotland, with 100,000 books lining more than a mile of shelving.

Wigtown buts up against the **Wigtown Bay Local Nature Reserve** (www. rspb.org.uk), 4,000 hectares (9,900 acres) that spread out over tidal flats along the River Cree and River Bladnoch to the east side of town. This evocative, silent landscape is a haven for bird-watchers, and from two public hides reached on well-marked trails around Wigtown Harbour you can expect to spy at various times of the year pink-footed geese, ducks, and wading birds.

A short walk through the flats at the east edge of town leads to the **Martyrs' Stake,** a haunting stone memorial to two women who were Covenanters, Scottish Presbyterians who opposed the crown's move toward Roman Catholicism, and were gruesomely executed in 1685; they were tied to stakes and left to drown in the rising tide of the River Bladnoch.

At the **Torhouse Stone Circle,** 4 miles west of town off the B733, 19 stones are arrange on a grassy platform, placed there for reasons that have not been determined perhaps 4,000 years ago.

AROUND WIGTOWN
Galloway Forest Park

Britain's largest forest park carpets 300 square miles of untamed landscape north of Wigtown. Trails and roads crisscross a terrain of forested glens, highest hills, and remote lochs, with viewing stations for wildlife that includes red deer and wild goats. Galloway is also the U.K.'s only **Dark Sky Park ★**, where measures are taken to minimize light pollution that dulls the night sky so stargazers (on guided tours in the company of astronomers) can feast on blankets of star-studded darkness. From Wigtown, a good way to see the park is to follow A75 about 8 miles north to the Kirroughtree Visitor Center, just east of Newton Stewart, and from there the A712 into the heart of the park.

East of Newton Stewart. www.gallowayforestpark.com. *©* **01671/402-420.**

Whithorn

From Wigtown, the A746 and several smaller roads head south down the Machars, a broad peninsula jutting into the Irish Sea. Whithorn, about 10 miles south of Wigtown, is one of the oldest settlements in Scotland, home to early settlers, who included the Novantae tribe that lived here around C.E. 100 and traded with the Romans. St Ninian, an early Christian missionary, founded the first Christian church in Scotland in Whithorn around 397.

The pretty little town is chockablock with reminders of this long past, nicely chronicled at the small **Whithorn Story** museum on George Street (www.whithorn.com; *©* **01988/500-508**). Just around the corner are the ruins of a monastery that grew up around the small, whitewashed stone church that St Ninian founded—and gave the town its name, from the Anglo-Saxon Huitaern, or White House. The monastery housed a shrine to Ninian that became a popular place of pilgrimage, and for a long time was a whistle stop for Scottish monarchs, including Robert the Bruce and Mary Queen of Scots. The **Priory Museum,** in a house to one side of the monastery grounds, displays an intriguing collection of early Christian carved stones and crosses, while excavations across the lane have unearthed copious evidence of a settlement from around 450 B.C.E. These early residents were farmers who prospered off the rich land for many following centuries. The boggy soil nicely preserved the timbers and other materials they used to build sophisticated round houses, one of which has been reconstructed and provides a fascinating look at to early domestic arrangements. The Whithorn Story museum, the Priory Museum, and monastery ruins are open from April through October daily, 10:30am to 5pm, and the roundhouse can be visited on an excellent guided tour offered at intervals during the museums' opening hours. Admission to all these sites is £5 adults, £4 seniors, £3 children 5–16, £12 families.

The windy, quiet seaside hamlet of the **Isle of Whithorn**—no longer an island and connected to the mainland by a short causeway—is 3 miles south of Whithorn. The Isle was a lively trading port well into the 19th century, and long before that was a major destination for pilgrims traveling to pay homage to St Ninian at his shrine in nearby Whithorn. They climbed out their boats after a rough sea voyage from England or Ireland onto the village beach and climbed up to say a prayer of thanks in tiny, ruined **St Ninian's chapel,** from around 1100. Another 3 miles across the windswept peninsula is **St Ninian's Cave,** where the saint allegedly retreated to lead a life of solitude. Both of these holy places are always open and free to enter.

WHERE TO EAT & STAY IN & AROUND WIGTOWN

If you've ever dreamed of having a small bookshop, here's your chance. The **Open Book** provides a bookshop holiday—with your rental apartment (sleeps 2) comes keys to the bookshop downstairs, which you operate during your stay. Volunteers with the Wigtown Festival Company come around to help keep things running smoothly. Rates begin at about £40, and the time you put in downstairs is not compensated. The apartment is rented through Airbnb, and you can contact the Wigtown Festival for more information (www.wigtownbookfestival.com; ✆ **01988/403-222**).

Bladnoch Inn ★ PUB FOOD   A junction in the countryside just outside Wigtown is bound to lift your spirits, with Bladnoch Whisky Distillery on one side of the road and this homey pub on the other. A good menu of traditional pub grub is served next to glowing hearths in chilly weather and on a flowery patio in warmer months and includes a Sunday lunch that's a local institution. Upstairs are six simple but comfortable bedrooms.

Bladnoch. www.the-bladnoch-inn.com. ✆ **01988/402-200.** Daily. Meals: noon–3pm and 6–9pm; pub noon–midnight. Rooms from £60.

Hillcrest House ★★   A local merchant and town official built this Victorian villa in 1875 with an eye to making sure that everyone could see he resided in the grandest house in town. Current residents/proprietors Andrew and Deborah have no such pretensions and instead have ensured their commodious rooms and grand hallways are a homey getaway. Most rooms look over the surrounding grasslands and tidal flats and several are equipped with armchairs strategically poised at the windows, plus binoculars for wildlife viewing. Dinner is served 5 nights a week, and Hillcrest's food wins many awards, and the drawing room and large garden are extremely well-suited to lounging.

Maitland Place, Station Rd., Wigtown. www.hillcrest-wigtown.co.uk. ✆ **01988/402-018.** 6 units. £80 double, includes breakfast. **Amenities:** Restaurant; free Wi-Fi.

The Steam Packet Inn ★ SEAFOOD/MODERN SCOTTISH   Right on the quayside, with wide views over the harbor through the big windows, these snug pub rooms pair simple and delicious preparations of the freshest seafood with a big choice of real ales, a winning combination. Seven bright rooms upstairs enjoy the same views and friendly atmosphere.

Harbour Row, Isle of Whithorn. www.thesteampacketinn.biz. ✆ **01988/500-334.** Daily. Meals noon–2pm and 6:30–9pm, pub 11am–11pm (to 12:30pm Sat/Sun). Rooms from £60.

Portpatrick ★

38 miles W of Wigtown, 80 miles W of Dumfries

This colorful tiny harbor town tucked beneath sea cliffs at the extreme edge of southwest Scotland exudes the briny flavor of an old Scottish fishing village. Once a thriving port between Scotland and Ireland, Portpatrick was the go-to place for Irish couples who wanted to marry quickly; they would land on Saturday, have the banns announcing the marriage called on Sunday, and wed on Monday. Today, visitors come for the rugged seascapes, to breathe in the bracing sea air, and to enjoy the postcard-like setting of pastel-colored houses surrounding the snug harbor, protected by a rocky islet.

ESSENTIALS

GETTING THERE The nearest train station (www.scotrail.co.uk; ℂ **0344/811-0141**) is at Stranraer, 8 miles north. **Stagecoach** (www.stage coachbus.com) bus service no. 367 connects Stranraer with Portpatrick. The service runs regularly throughout the day and the journey takes around 20 minutes. If you're driving from Wigtown, the most scenic route takes you south to the Isle of Whithorn then around the coast through Port William. It's a beautiful drive full of sea views and will take about an hour and a half.

EXPLORING PORTPATRICK & THE AREA

Perched atop Castle Bay, the dramatic ruins of **Dunskey Castle** command a cliff-top half a mile south of Portpatrick and can easily be reached on a seaside footpath. These cliffs are a haven for bird-watchers who can expect to be bombarded with black guillemots, herring gulls, and fulmars.

Portpatrick's cliffs are also the starting point of the **Southern Upland Way** (www.southernuplandway.gov.uk); see p. 123. From Portpatrick the footpath meanders for 212 miles through some of southern Scotland's most memorable landscapes, including the Galloway Forest Park (p. 150), to Cockburnspath on the east coast. Many walkers come to Portpatrick to enjoy the stretch from the cliff tops above town to Castle Kennedy, 13 miles east.

Portpatrick is a popular watering stop on the trip down to the Mull of Galloway, Scotland's most southerly point. The **Mull of Galloway Lighthouse** (www.mull-of-galloway.co.uk; ℂ **01776/830-682**) was first lit in 1830 and shoots out a powerful beam that on a clear night can be spied 28 miles away. The lighthouse opens its doors to the public from Easter until October, daily in July and August and on weekends in other months, from 10am to 4pm. Visitors can climb the 115 steps to the light room and balcony at the top of the tower for some spine-tingling views up and down the coast and far out to sea. Admission is £4 adults and £1 children under 14.

Some 10 miles south of Portpatrick is the little hamlet of Port Logan and **Logan House,** the seat of the ancient McDougall family. Their remarkable gardens are part of the Royal Botanic Garden Edinburgh and open to the public.

Logan Botanic Garden ★★ GARDEN Touched by the warm currents of the Gulf Stream, an exotic paradise thrives in these stark landscapes at Scotland's southernmost tip. In the mid-19th-century, Lady Agnes McDougall planted a eucalyptus tree her garden and continued to indulge her passion for exotic flora, and she passed her love of plantings from the Southern Hemisphere onto her sons, Kenneth and Douglas. They, in turn, traveled the world to bring back the palms, ferns, and other semitropical species that thrive in this microclimate. Many come from New Zealand and Australia, including a recent addition, a Wollemi pine, one of the rarest tree species in the world, only discovered in 1994. Warm Gulf Stream currents aside, the garden is susceptible to salt-laden gales from the Irish Sea and is quite ingeniously protected by a shelter-barrier of woodlands and a border of resilient shrubbery.

1½ miles north of Port Logan off the B7065. www.rbge.org.uk. ⓒ **01776/860-231.** £6.50 adults, £5.50 seniors, children under 16 free. Mar–Oct daily 10am–5pm and Nov 1–15 daily 10am–4pm (also Sundays in Feb 10am–4pm for snowdrop season).

WHERE TO EAT & STAY IN PORTPATRICK

Campbells ★ MEDITERRANEAN/SEAFOOD   Regulars come from all over southern Scotland for a meal in this relaxed, woody room overlooking the harbor, where fresh fish and shellfish from the waters glimmering beyond the big windows are stars of the show. Fresh crabs and grilled Solway Bay scallops top the must-have list on a menu that also strays south for a delicious Mediterranean fish soup and includes a beautifully done lamb that too long before was grazing on the green hillsides around town.

1 South Crescent, Portpatrick. www.campbellsrestaurant.co.uk. ⓒ **01776/810-314.** Main courses £11–£20. Tues–Sat noon–2:30pm and 6–9:30pm, Sun 12:30–2:30pm and 6:30–9:30pm.

Knockinaam Lodge ★★   Tucked into 12 hectares (30 acres) of seaside meadows beneath towering cliffs 5 miles southwest of town, this Victorian hunting lodge is an utterly enchanting place, with cozy fires and oak-paneled lounges inside and a generous strip of beach beyond the lawns in front. Sir Winston Churchill met General Eisenhower to plan the D-Day invasions of World War II, and guests can stay in the Churchill room where the man himself slept, with fireplace, a king-size sleigh bed, and a century-old deep soaking tub. Other accommodations are similarly distinctive and atmospheric and include an airy seaside cottage on the grounds. Whether lunch, dinner, or tea, dining at Knockinaam is informal and candlelit.

Portpatrick, signposted off the A77 west of Portpatrick. www.knockinaamlodge.com. ⓒ **01776/810-471.** 10 units. £220–£400 double, includes breakfast. **Amenities:** Restaurant; bar; beach; free Wi-Fi.

Portpatrick Hotel ★   It's hard to miss this huge, rambling white landmark on the cliffs above the harbor, a holdover from the days when a train from Glasgow arrived with city dwellers in need of sea air. A series of commodious lounges recall grander days and are light-filled and airy and spill out to sea-view patios. Bedrooms have been redone to the point of being blandly modern, though the extensive views from most certainly ensure a flutter of excitement.

Heugh Rd., Portpatrick. www.coastandcountryhotels.com. ⓒ **01942/417-859.** 55 units. £45–£80 double, some rates include breakfast. **Amenities:** Restaurant; bar; pitch-and-putt golf course; free Wi-Fi.

GLASGOW & THE STRATHCLYDE REGION

7

By Stephen Brewer

These days a lot of old industrial cities claim to be coming back from the brink to enjoy new life and vitality. In Glasgow, that's really true, though Scotland's largest city never really lost its edge. Many of the 19th- and 20th-century shipyards and factories are shuttered, but elegant Georgian merchants' houses and grand Victorian piles remain, as does Scotland's oldest medieval cathedral and rows of tenements built to house the working class. They all speak legions about this city's down-to-earth values and an unpretentious worldliness, as much in evidence in old pubs as it is in glitzy shops, sophisticated bars and clubs, and outstanding museum collections. Glaswegians are well aware that a lot of the world considers Edinburgh to be more elegant, but they really don't care. As they like to say, the only good thing to come out of Edinburgh is the train to Glasgow.

Don't Leave Glasgow Without . . .

Meeting Charles Renee Mackintosh. In the late 19th and early 20th centuries, the architect and his designer wife, Margaret Macdonald, graced the city with a forward-thinking Scottish style that you'll encounter in such places as the Lighthouse office building and Willow Tea Rooms.

Encountering the past and future along the Clyde. The river was the lifeblood of the industrial city, and along the banks rises a proud remnant of ship-building days, the Finnieston Crane, near the stunning contemporary creations of architects Sir Norman Foster and Zaha Hadid.

Having a wee dram or two. Glasgow is generously littered with snug locales for enjoying the national beverage, and you can also taste whisky at the source at several local distilleries. Do as the locals do and chase your spirit of choice down with a beer, preferably one from the city's own East End Tennent's Brewery.

Poking around the Kelvingrove. Your wanderings through this delightful treasure trove turn up one surprise after another—a medieval monk's satchel, a fighter jet, a Rembrandt masterpiece, all housed in an atmospheric, turn-of-the-20th-century pavilion.

Doing some time travel in the East End. Centuries of city history collide in the precinct where Glasgow began to take shape some 1,500 years. Medieval Glasgow Cathedral; Provand's Lordship, the oldest house in town; and the Necropolis, a Victorian city of the dead crown a rise above Glasgow Green, a centuries-old greensward where sheep once grazed.

ESSENTIALS

Glasgow is 47 miles W of Edinburgh, 216 miles N of Manchester, and 404 miles N of London.

Getting There

ARRIVING By Plane: Glasgow Airport (www.glasgowairport.com; ✆ 0870/040-0008) is 10 miles west of the city. The easy-to-use airport handles flights to and from London Heathrow and Gatwick and many other European hubs, with low-cost flights to and from many destinations on easyJet (www.easyjet.com) and Ryanair (www.ryanair.com), as well as nonstop service, in many cases summer only, to and from several U.S. and Canadian airports. These include New York (Delta; www.delta.com); Newark (United; www.united.com); Philadelphia (American; www.aa.com); Orlando (Virgin Atlantic; www.virginatlantic.com); and Toronto and Vancouver (Air Transat; www.airtransat.com). **First** (www.firstgroup.com; ✆ 0141/423-6600) operates shuttle bus no. 500 between the airport and several stops in the city center, with a final stop at Buchanan Street bus station. Service runs along Bothwell and Waterloo Streets at the southern edge of the city center, with convenient stops near many hotels. This 24-hour service runs up to every 10 minutes; the ride takes 20 minutes. Pay on the bus (cash or contactless credit/debit card): adults £8 one way, £12 round trip; kids £4 one way, £6 round-trip. A taxi to the city center costs about £24.

Glasgow's second airport, **Prestwick** (www.glasgowprestwick.com; ✆ 0871/223-0700) is on the Ayrshire coast, 33 miles southwest of the city center, and serves flights to and from European airports, often resort destinations, and many operated by easyJet and Ryanair. Connections to Glasgow include **ScotRail** trains to and from Central Station (www.scotrail.co.uk; ✆ 0845/601-5929), with up to 3 trains an hour making the 50-minute trip; the one-way adult fare is as low as £4 for passengers with airline tickets. The X77

Stagecoach bus (www.stagecoachbus.com; ✆ **01292/613-500**) connects the airport with Buchanan Street bus station; adult fare is £6.20.

Glasgow is also convenient to Edinburgh Airport, 39 miles west and 45-minutes by car. Bus connections to and from Glasgow's Buchanan Street station run every 30 minutes, via CityLink Air (www.citylink.co.uk; ✆ **0871/266-3333**) from Stance C outside the arrivals area; the trip takes about 1 hour and one way adult fare is £12; round trip is £20.

By Train: Virgin Trains (www.virgintrains.co.uk; ✆ **0871/977-4222**) and **ScotRail** (www.scotrail.co.uk; ✆ **0845/601-5929**) operate regular service at least hourly throughout the day and early evening between London Euston and Glasgow Central, on Gordon Street. The journey time is approximately 4½ to 5½ hours. ScotRail's **Caledonian Sleeper** (www.sleeper.scot; ✆ **0330/060-0500**) is an overnight train to and from London's Euston Station, with berths and reclining seats.

Glasgow's **Queen Street Station** is on the north side of George Square and serves the north and east of Scotland, with ScotRail trains arriving from and departing to Edinburgh every 15 minutes until 11:30pm. The journey takes 50 minutes. You can also travel to Highland destinations from this station as well as Aberdeen and Stirling. The station is undergoing extensive renovations, expected to be completed in mid-2020, but remains fully operational.

By Bus: Buchanan Street Bus Station is 2 blocks north of Queen Street Station on Killermont Street. **National Express** (www.nationalexpress.com; ✆ **08717/818-178**) service from London's Victoria coach station to Glasgow service is at night, with four trips taking from 8½ to 14 hrs., depending on the number of stops; Glasgow to London service operates three times during the day and once nightly. Low fares may compensate for the extra time and discomfort of an overnight journey. **Megabus** (www.megabus.com; ✆ **0900/160-0900**) also operates a service between London Victoria and Buchanan Street, with three daytime trips and one overnight. **Scottish CityLink** (www.citylink.co.uk; ✆ **0871/266-3333**) operates frequent bus service between Glasgow and Edinburgh on the M8; the journey is about an hour but can be longer during morning and evening commutes.

By Car: From England, Glasgow is reached via the M74, which becomes the A74 as it leads into the city. From Edinburgh, the M8 joins the two cities and travels directly through the heart of Glasgow.

Visitor Information

Glasgow City Marketing Bureau (GCMB) provides a wealth of info on its website, www.peoplemakeglasgow.com. In the city, stop by the Glasgow Information Centre in the Buchanan Galleries at 10 Sauchiehall St. (www.visitscotland.com; ✆ **0141/204-4400**), open May and June and September and October, Monday to Saturday from 9am to 6 and Sunday 10am to 4pm; July and August, Monday through Saturday 9am to 7pm and Sunday 10am to 5pm; and November through April, Monday to Saturday 10am–5pm and Sunday 10am to 4pm.

City Layout

Glasgow's neighborhoods can seem like lands apart, and city attractions are fairly far-flung. The **East End** surrounds the great Cathedral of St Kentigern, better known as St Mungo's or simply as Glasgow Cathedral and a perfect example of pre-Reformation Gothic architecture that dates in part to the 12th century. To the south of the cathedral precincts, on the banks of the River Clyde, is **Glasgow Green,** common land since 1178 and Britain's first public park. The Victorian **West End** surrounds Kelvingrove Park and the River Kelvin, and around these leafy precincts are the Kelvingrove and Hunterian museums, as well as many restaurants and bars on streets enlivened with the presence of students at the University of Glasgow. Other museums are clustered alongside the **River Clyde,** where the Riverside Museum is on the north banks and the Science Centre is on the south side. The commercial **city center** cuts a large swath between the East End and the West End and surrounds George Square, around which the broad pedestrian thoroughfares of **Buchanan, Argyle,** and **Sauchiehall streets** form the heart of Glasgow's main shopping district.

You can walk from the City Center into the East End, though it's a bit of a trek from the City Center out to the West End and to the cluster of museums along the River Clyde. If you want to see a good range of the attractions, you'll need to do a little planning and approach the city by sections—East End in one go, West End museums in another, and the riverside in another. A good transportation system, including a single-line subway and several cross-city bus routes, make it easy to get around, though you'll want to equip yourself with a city map (most hotels hand out them out). When navigating, keep in mind that Glasgow streets have a habit of running into a square with one name and emerging from the other side with another name, or of changing names inexplicably at an intersection.

The Neighborhoods in Brief

THE EAST END & MEDIEVAL GLASGOW   Most of Glasgow's history has transpired in what is now considered the East End. The city began here along the banks of the River Clyde and, in the Middle Ages, expanded up the hill where the **Cathedral of St Kentigern,** also known as St Mungo's or Glasgow Cathedral, was completed in 1197. **Glasgow Green,** common land since 1178, stretches from the riverbanks toward **Glasgow Cross,** the junction of High Street and four other main thoroughfares of the 17th-century city.

THE CITY CENTER & MERCHANT CITY   Glasgow spread west of High Street in the 18th century, and so-called tobacco barons built elegant townhouses and warehouses in what is now known as Merchant City. As the city expanded, George Square and the blocks around Central Station became the city center, and remain so today. Many of the shop-lined streets are for pedestrians only.

THE WEST END   In the Victorian era, Glasgow spread farther west, this time into what is now a lively neighborhood that is home to the University of Glasgow and the Kelvingrove and Hunterian Museums. These institutions are housed in grand neo-Gothic and baroque quarters on the edge of **Kelvingrove Park.** Just a few strides away is Byres Road, lined with bars, shops, and restaurants, while Glasgow's **Botanic Gardens** lie to the north off the Great Western Road.

ALONG THE CLYDE   Glasgow once shipped its manufactured goods around the world from docks on the River Clyde, amid shipbuilding yards and factories. These days the shoreline is being revitalized with museums, office complexes, and apartment blocks.

THE SOUTHSIDE   The Science Centre is on the south banks of the River Clyde, while the largely residential neighborhood gives way to Pollok Country Park about 3 miles south of the river. Highland Cattle graze within sight of beautiful Pollok House and the Burrell Collection, closed until 2020.

Getting Around

While it's easy to navigate the city center on foot, you'll probably rely on public transport to visit attractions in the West End and along the river.

BY BUS   Glasgow is serviced by **First** buses (www.firstgroup.com; Ⓒ **0141/423-6600**). Services run frequently throughout the day, but are greatly curtailed after 11pm. Pick up schedules at the Travel Centre at the **Buchanan Street Bus Station** on Killermont Street (Mon–Sat 6:30am–10:30pm, Sunday 7am–10:30pm) or download them from First's website at www.firstgroup.com/ukbus/glasgow. One-way fares are £1.20 for short journeys (usually up to 5 stops) and £2 for longer trips anywhere within the city. Pay on the bus, exact change required. A day pass for unlimited travel costs £4.50, and a week pass is £17. At stops, flag down your bus as it approaches, or the driver is likely to pass you by.

BY SUBWAY   The bright orange cars of Glasgow's single-line subway (and "subway" is what it's called here, not "underground") make a circular route with 15 stops. Hence the name, "Clockwork Orange." Trains run every 4 to 8 minutes and operate Monday through Saturday 6:30am to 11:30pm and Sunday 10am to 6pm. Tickets can be bought at any subway station and one-way fare is £1.50 adults and 75p children; all-day tickets are £2.90 adults, £1.45 children. Trains make the entire circuit in 24 minutes. Inner Circle trains travel in a counterclockwise direction, Outer Circle trains travel in a clockwise direction. Aside from spending some extra time underground, it doesn't really matter which direction you go in, as you'll get to your stop eventually. The stops you're most likely to use as a visitor are Hillhead, Kelvinbridge, and St George's Cross, for the Kelvingrove and Hunterian museums and other West End attractions, and Buchanan Street and St Enoch, for the City Center. For more information, go to www.spt.co.uk.

BY TAXI   You can hail taxis on the street or call **Glasgow Taxis** (www. glasgowtaxis.co.uk; ☎ **0141/429-7070**). When a taxi is available on the street, a "TAXI" sign on the roof is lit a bright yellow. Meters start at £2.80 and increase by £3.22 every mile.

BY CAR   Driving around Glasgow can be difficult, and really unnecessary for a sightseeing visit. The city is a warren of one-way streets, and parking is expensive and can be difficult to find. Pay-and-display street parking is available in the city center at 60p for every 12 minutes, 2 hours maximum, payable only with coins in some machines. A yellow line along the curb indicates no parking, and some zones are marked PERMIT HOLDERS ONLY—your vehicle will be towed if you have no permit. Some convenient car parks, open 24 hours a day, are Cathedral in the East End, Charing Cross and Waterloo Streets in the City Center, and Kelvin Grove in the West End. You'll pay £1.60 to £2.40 an hour for the first 6 hours, and an overnight flat rate of £2.50 to £3 from 6pm to 8am; for more information, go to www.cityparkingglasgow. co.uk.

BY BICYCLE   Bikes can be rented at **Gear of Glasgow,** 19 Gibson St. in the West End (www.gearbikes.com; ☎ **0141/339-1179**). Rates range from £15 for a half-day or £20 for a full day to £70 for a week; a driver's license or passport must be left as a deposit. You can also try the city's bike-sharing **Nextbike** system (www.nextbike.co.uk), available at stands throughout the city. You'll register via an app or hotline (☎ **020/816-69851**) and pay £1 for every 30 minutes, up to a maximum of £10 a day.

[Fast FACTS] GLASGOW

Business Hours   Most **offices** and **banks** are open Monday through Friday 9am to 5pm; some banks also open on Saturday. Many have 24-hour ATM machines, and withdrawals are often free (though you will still probably pay your bank's international withdrawal fees). **Shops** are generally open Monday through Saturday 9:30am to 6pm, with many city center shops remaining open until 7pm on Monday through Wednesday. On Thursdays, stores remain open until 8pm; many also open on Sundays from 11am to 5 or 6pm.

Currency Exchange   Most city center banks operate a *bureaux de change*. There are also currency exchanges at Glasgow Airport and Central Station, where you'll also find ATM machines.

Dentists   If you have an emergency, go to the Accident and Emergency Department of the University of Glasgow **Dental Hospital & School,** 378 Sauchiehall St. (www.gla. ac.uk/schools/dental; ☎ **0141/232-6323**). Appointments are necessary. Hours are Monday through Friday 8:30am to 5:15pm.

Doctors   The major hospital is the **Glasgow Royal Infirmary,** 82–86 Castle St. (www.nhsggc.org.uk; ☎ **0141/211-4000**).

Embassies & Consulates   See "Fast Facts: Scotland" (p. 454).

Emergencies   Call ☎ **999** in an emergency to summon the police, an ambulance, or firefighters.

Hot Lines   Some major contacts are: **Women's Aid** (www.glasgowwomensaid. org.uk; ☎ **0141/553-2022**) and the **Rape Crisis Centre** (www.rapecrisis centre-glasgow.co.uk; ☎ **08088/000-014**).

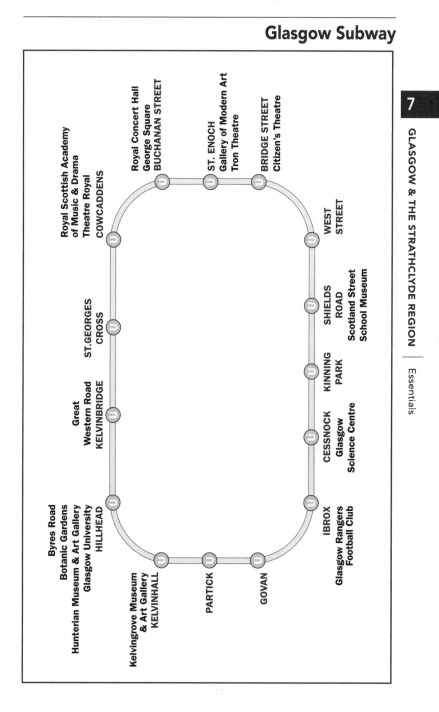

Laundry & Dry Cleaning **Laundrette Glasgow,** 1110 Argyle St. in the West End (www.majestic laundrette.co.uk; (*C*) **0141/334-3433**) is open Monday to Friday 8am to 6pm, Saturday 8am to 4pm, and Sunday 10am to 4pm.

Luggage Storage & Lockers **Buchanan Bus Station** has left luggage lockers. There are also a Left Luggage Departments at **Central Station** (www. left-baggage.co.uk) and **Queen Street Station**, (www.nationalrail.co.uk) open Monday through Saturday 6am to midnight and Sunday 7am to midnight. Rates are £6 for one hour, £9 per item for the first 24 hours. You can also use Bag-bnb (http://bagbnb.com), a service that locates a shop or other business where you can drop off and store luggage.

Newspapers & Magazines Published since 1783, the *Herald* (www.heraldscotland.com) is the major newspaper with national, international, and financial news, sports, and cultural listings; the *Evening Times* (www.eveningtimes. co.uk) covers local news.

Pharmacies There are branches of Boots (www. boots.com) in most of the main shopping malls and at 200 Sauchiehall St., City Center ((*C*) **0141/332-1925**), open Monday through Wednesday and Saturday 8am to 6pm, Thursday and Friday 8am to 7pm, and Sunday 10:30am to 5:30pm.

Police In an emergency, call (*C*) **999.** For other inquiries, contact police headquarters at (*C*) **0141 /532-2000.**

Post Office The main branch is at 47 St Vincent's St., City Center ((*C*) **0845/ 722-3344**). It's open Monday through Saturday 9:30am to 5:30pm.

Safety Glasgow is the most dangerous city in Scotland, but it's relatively safe when compared with cities of its size in the United States. Drug use is a big problem here, and with it comes muggings and other crimes. As in any big city stay alert and watch your wallet and other belongings.

Toilets Facilities can be found at train stations, bus stations, museums, and some department stores. Glasgow also operates some public toilets around the city, often marked "wc"; it usually costs 20p to use them.

EXPLORING GLASGOW

Glasgow's attractions are spread around the city. It's easiest to approach them in clusters: City Center, Merchant City, and East End in one go, West End in another, the riverside museums as a separate trip.

The East End & Medieval Glasgow

Glasgow's long history makes itself known in the eastern end of the city, rather spookily so in the Cathedral Precinct. The dark hulking mass of the medieval cathedral, the city's oldest structure, rises next to the oldest house in Glasgow, **Provand's Lordship ★** (www.glasgowlife.org.uk; (*C*) **0141/276-1625**) from 1471; the stone-walled rooms are filled with 17th-century Scottish furniture and portraits and are open Tuesday through Thursday and Saturday, 10am to 5pm, and Friday and Sunday, 11an to 5pm, and admission is free. Just beyond is a steep green hillside littered with the soaring monuments of the **Necropolis ★,** a Victorian city of the dead. If you're a Goth, you've found your place. Volunteers give free tours of the Necropolis three times a month, usually with a guided walk on a Friday, Saturday, and Sunday; go to www. glasgownecropolis.org for schedules, a list of major monuments, and to book a place; black attire is de rigueur, of course.

The medieval city stretched from here south to river, surrounding **Glasgow Green ★**. This sprawling greensward where sheep once grazed has, over the centuries played host to Bonnie Prince Charlie's 18th-century Jacobite army that tried to restore the Stuarts to the British throne, early-20th-century suffragette meetings, and 21st-century rock concerts. By city charter, Glaswegians who have been honored with "freedom of the city" have the right to graze cows and sheep on the green. Facing the green is the elaborate, vaguely Moorish-looking brick **Templeton Carpet Factory,** which once supplied carpets for the Taj Mahal and Houses of Parliament and now houses the Bavarian-owned West brewery (p. 192). In 1888 James Templeton was granted permission to build his factory on the green, provided he erect a structure befitting the prestigious surroundings. So, he modeled the facade on the Doges' Palace in Venice. It collapsed during construction, killing 29 women in the adjacent weaving sheds; the statue atop the highest pinnacle of a woman holding flowers is a memorial to the victims. **St Andrew's on the Green,** on the green's northern edge, was the first Episcopal church in Scotland but is most famous for its distinction as the "Whistlin' Kirk," for the raspy sounds emitted from the first organ to be installed in a church in Glasgow, in 1775.

Just a bit farther to the north of the green is the junction of the four main streets of the medieval city at the **Glasgow Cross.** The seven-story **Tolbooth Steeple** to one side of the Cross once towered above a long-since-demolished jail that stood at the base of the steeple through the 17th and 18th centuries. Witches, thieves, and murderers were often hung from a platform attached to the tower, and those considered to be especially villainous were further humiliated by having their severed heads impaled on spikes. The last Glaswegian to be hung in a public spectacle was Dr. Edward Pritchard, who in 1865 was found guilty of poisoning his wife and mother-in-law—his execution drew a jeering crowd of 80,000 onlookers. Inmates of the attached debtors' prison languished in relative comfort, benefiting from a provision that upon release it was mandatory to treat fellow prisoners to an alcoholic libation of their choice. The square in front of the Tolbooth was a gathering spot for wealthy merchants and traders, who paraded in their finery. As a further display of wealth they erected what still might be the finest church in all of Scotland, stately **St Andrew's in the Square,** once surrounded by the city's most fashionable homes. Despite the exclusiveness of the address, the hoi polloi gathered in the churchyard on November 23, 1765, to watch Italian daredevil Vincenzo Lunardi make Scotland's first flight, an ascent in a hot-air balloon.

Glasgow Cathedral ★★★ CATHEDRAL   Glasgow's oldest structure and Scotland's only complete medieval cathedral was consecrated in 1197 and dedicated to St Mungo, the city's patron. The 6th-century missionary, also known as Kentigern, spent 13 years converting Glaswegians. These efforts, along with the deprivations of a life of fasting and prayer in a rock cell, wore the poor fellow out to such an extent that he was forced to wear a bandage to support his chin. Mungo lies amid a forest of pillars in a vaulted crypt beneath

Glasgow Attractions

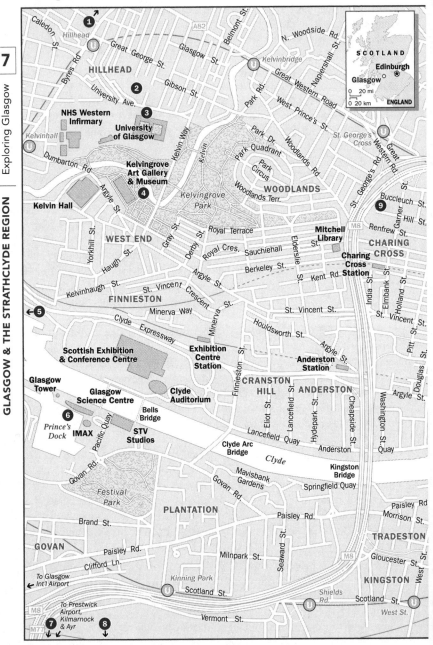

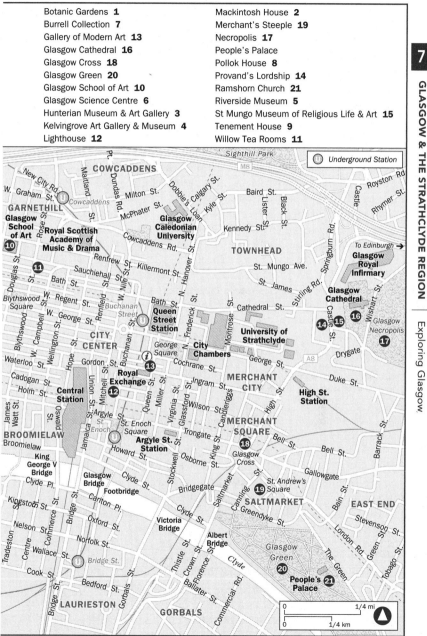

Botanic Gardens **1**
Burrell Collection **7**
Gallery of Modern Art **13**
Glasgow Cathedral **16**
Glasgow Cross **18**
Glasgow Green **20**
Glasgow School of Art **10**
Glasgow Science Centre **6**
Hunterian Museum & Art Gallery **3**
Kelvingrove Art Gallery & Museum **4**
Lighthouse **12**

Mackintosh House **2**
Merchant's Steeple **19**
Necropolis **17**
People's Palace
Pollok House **8**
Provand's Lordship **14**
Ramshorn Church **21**
Riverside Museum **5**
St Mungo Museum of Religious Life & Art **15**
Tenement House **9**
Willow Tea Rooms **11**

the church. The fact he has lain here peacefully through the centuries, and that the church's beautiful nave and timbered roof are intact, is due, in part, to the courageous intervention of the faithful. During the destruction of churches during the 16th century Reformation, congregants linked arms around the cathedral to prevent mobs from smashing the place to bits.

7

Cathedral Square. www.glasgowcathedral.org.uk. ℂ **0141/552-6891.** Free. Apr–Sept Mon–Sat 9:30am–6pm, Sun 1–5:30pm; Oct–Mar Mon–Sat 9:30am–4pm, Sun 1–4pm.

People's Palace ★★ HISTORIC SITE   It's only fitting that this red sandstone pavilion built in 1898 as a cultural center for the enlightenment of slum dwellers in the East End should now trace the history of Glaswegians from 1750 through the present day. Photographs of tenements show how grim life has been for many, and provide some fascinating glimpses in such everyday realities as going to the "steamie," or communal laundry. Glasgow-trained artist Ken Currie's evocative mural of the Canton Weaver's Massacre in 1787 captures Scotland's first major labor dispute that came to a bloody end when troops fired on strikers in a village just outside Glasgow, killing six. Plenty of joyous moments are captured, too, including dances at the Barrowland Ballroom and outings aboard steamers down the Firth of Clyde. In the adjoining Winter Gardens, you can enjoy a cup of coffee amid a jungle of tropical plants, and in the forecourt of the palace is the magnificent Doulton Fountain. Sir Henry Doulton, founder of the famous tableware firm, presented what is still the world's largest terracotta fountain to Glasgow in 1887 to commemorate Queen Elizabeth's Golden Jubilee.

Glasgow Green. www.glasgowlife.org.uk. ℂ **0141/276-1625.** Free. Tues–Thurs and Sat 10am–5pm; Fri and Sun 11am–5pm.

St Mungo Museum of Religious Life & Art ★ MUSEUM   Glasgow's patron saint is nicely honored with a wide-ranging look at world religions, housed in a medieval-looking reconstruction of a Scottish fortress on the site of the former Bishop's Palace. The Hindu snake demon Naga Rassa and dancing skeletons from Mexico's Day of the Dead celebrations share space with crosses, stained glass, menorahs, monk's habits, Turkish prayer rugs, and other religious artifacts. What comes through are the themes—birth, death, renewal—and the message of hope that lie at the core of all religions, something to contemplate as you stroll through the tranquil Zen Garden.

2 Castle St. www.glasgowlife.org.uk. ℂ **0141/276-1625.** Free. Mon–Thurs and Sat 10am–5pm; Fri and Sun 11am–5pm.

City Center & Merchant City

It seems that anybody who's anybody in Scotland sooner or later ends up in stone effigy in vast **George Square,** laid out in 1781 and by most calculations the city center. Novelist and poet Sir Walter Scott (1771–1832) surveys the scene from atop a 24m (80-ft.) column in the center of the square and around him is a statuary Who's Who of Scottish achievement: poet and favorite son Robert Burns (1759–96), inventor of the steam engine James Watt

THE LOVE LETTERS murder case

Among the elite interred in the overgrown churchyard of Ramshorn Church is the man who might be Glasgow's most beloved murder victim, Pierre Emile L'Angelier (died 1857). The apprentice nurseryman had the misfortune of entering into an affair with socialite Madeline Smith (1835–1928). When Smith became engaged to a more suitable match, she demanded that L'Angelier return her passionate love letters. He refused, and she likely poisoned him. Despite overwhelming evidence, including Smith's revealing letters found in L'Angelier's lodgings and proof that she had purchased a bottle of arsenic, the case was resolved as "not proven." This uniquely Scottish verdict means there's not enough evidence to find the accused guilty or not guilty. Smith left Scotland under a cloud of scandal and eventually settled in New York City, where she died at the ripe old age of 93. Director David Lean told the story in his 1950 film *Madeline*, starring his wife, Ann Todd.

(1736–1819), and chemist Thomas Graham (1805–69), to name but a few. King George III (1738–1820) is here, as are Queen Victorian and her beloved prince consort Albert (the pair are astride horses, as if they've just trotted out for a bit of air). Fine weather can bring hundreds of workers from the surrounding offices out to the greens to soak up the sun. The sight of armies of shirtless, pasty-skinned accountants may well send you into the dark depths of the nearest pub—or into the **City Chambers** for a look at the mosaics, grand marble staircases, and other excesses of Victorian splendor; free guided tours are conducted daily at 10:30am and 2:30pm.

Several blocks to the south and east rises an icon of Glasgow's turn-of-the 20th-century prosperity, the **Lighthouse,** at 11 Mitchell Lane, completed in 1895 for the *Glasgow Herald* newspaper to designs by the great Glaswegian architect Charles Rennie Mackintosh. A spiral staircase ascends the namesake tower, while the floors below, enriched with terracotta tile work and other Art Nouveau detailing, house the Centre for Design and Architecture, with changing exhibitions, and the Mackintosh Interpretation Center, with drawings, furnishings, and other material chronicling the life and work of Mackintosh and his wife, designer Margaret Macdonald. The Lighthouse (www.thelighthouse.co.uk; ✆ **0141/276-5365**) is open Monday through Saturday 10:30am to 5pm and Sunday noon to 5:30pm; admission is free, as are Saturday tours at 1pm.

From the 17th through mid-19th centuries, Glasgow's tobacco lords, traders who made their fortunes importing and exporting tobacco, as well as spices, sugar, and slaves, lived in mansions near their warehouses just south of the Square, in the blocks now known as Merchant City. **Merchant's Steeple,** completed near the River Clyde on Bridgegate in 1665, wasn't just a show of might but also served as a lookout to watch the comings and goings of ships laden with cargo from the Far East and New World. The merchants would descend from their perch into the since-demolished Guildhall, where they

Throughout the City Center, almost two dozen bright, color-saturated murals enliven storefronts, billboards, and the sides of buildings. One of the most refreshing scenes is the riverside "Swimmer," under the Kingston Bridge, done by Australian artist Smug to commemorate Glasgow's 2014 Commonwealth Games. Smug also did what might be the most beloved mural, a painting of a modern-day, stocking-capped version of city patron St Mungo, holding the robin that, according to legend, the hermit, when still a boy, brought back to life after his mates killed the little creature with a stone. For more about the murals and a walking tour map, pick up the "City Centre Mural Trail" leaflet in the Glasgow Information Centre (see above) or go to www.citycentremuraltrail.co.uk for a downloadable version.

would do their trading and sort out the city's commercial interests. Here they agreed to join the Crown to help crush the rebellious American colonists, who threatened their lucrative tobacco trade, and they repeatedly raised funds to deepen the Clyde and make the river more navigable. These dredging schemes signaled the neighborhood's decline, as the shipping and shipbuilding that made Glasgow into one of the great centers of the Industrial Revolution shifted to the riverbanks alongside deeper stretches of the Clyde to the west. Many of the tobacco lords are spending eternity in the churchyard of nearby **Ramshorn Church,** on Ingram Street, the city's oldest burial ground, once rather optimistically known as "Paradise."

Gallery of Modern Art ★ GALLERY   In 1778, tobacco lord William Cunninghame had this ridiculously pompous townhouse designed to resemble a grand public building. In its current guise, the neoclassical edifice is a showcase for changing exhibitions of some of Scotland's top contemporary artists, among them Glaswegians Douglas Gordon, best known for his eerily altered photographs and video projections, and Ken Currie, whose paintings explore the dark depths of illness, aging, and social inequities. They take their place alongside David Hockney and other internationally acclaimed artists. Out front is a much-beloved statue of the Duke of Wellington, wearing a plastic traffic cone on his head as a symbol of Glaswegian defiance of authority. The police have long since stopped removing the irreverent millinery, because every time they do so it reappears.

Royal Exchange Sq. www.glasgowlife.org.uk. ℂ **0141/287-3005.** Free. Mon–Wed and Sat 10am–5pm; Thurs 10am–8pm; Fri and Sun 11am–5pm.

Glasgow School of Art ★★★ HISTORIC STRUCTURE   Charles Rennie Mackintosh is Glasgow's local boy made good. He was born in Glasgow in 1868, studied at the Glasgow School of Art, and designed some of the city's most distinctive landmarks. His masterpiece is the school's main building, completed in 1907. The striking design leans toward the Art Nouveau, with a sparse stone facade of huge windows to light the north-facing studios, with subtle hints of turrets, arches, and ironwork to suggest a Scottish castle. A fire ripped through the structure in May 2014, destroying studios and the piece de la resistance, the galleried library. Restoration was underway with an indefinite date for completion when an even more destructive fire broke out again in June 2018. In the meantime, students escort you up the light-filled staircases of the new Reid Building across the street to a gallery filled with Mackintosh furniture. The master's straight-backed chairs are easy on the eye, but it might be torture to sit in one, though that's certainly not allowed. The center also leads 2-hour architectural walking tours (£19.50 adults, £16 seniors, £9.75 children 5–17) throughout the year.

167 Renfrew St. www.gsa.ac.uk. © **0141/353-4500.** £10 adults, £5.75 seniors, £3.50 children 5–17. Tours daily 10:30am, 11am, 11:30am, 2:30pm, and 3:30pm, plus noon and 1:30pm Apr–Sept.

Tenement House ★★ HISTORIC HOME   A voyeuristic look into the home life of shorthand typist Agnes Toward says a lot about early-20th-century domesticity in Glasgow. In local parlance, tenements aren't the squalid fleapits of American industrial cities, but small apartments like this that went up across the city to house the growing and upwardly mobile population. Folks like Miss Toward lived in relative comfort in cramped but well-furnished rooms, with coal fires, indoor plumbing, and gas lighting. Fortunately for us, Miss Toward was a bit of a packrat, and many of the scraps she saved, including wartime leaflets, are on view in her ground floor flat. You'll also learn the ins and outs of tenement life so you'll never again have to wonder what a "hurly" is.

145 Buccleuch St. www.nts.org.uk. © **0844/493-2197.** £7.50 adults, £5.50 seniors and children, £12.50 families of one adult, £18.50 families of two adults. Apr–June and Sept–Oct daily 1–5pm, July–Aug Mon–Sat 11am–5pm, Sun 1–5pm.

The West End

By the 19th century, Glasgow was caught up in the full-thrust of the industrial revolution, and the City Center was becoming unbearably crowded and sooty. Those who could afford to do so began resettling in mansions and terrace houses in the West End, where **Kelvingrove Park** was laid out along the banks of the River Kelvin. **Glasgow University** followed suit in 1870, moving from High Street to settle into a faux-Gothic campus that looks like an Oxfordian dreamscape, or Hogwarts. The park is named for **William Thomson, aka Lord Kelvin** (1824–1907), the son of a professor, one of the university's most illustrious graduates, and later a world-renowned professor himself. He gave us the Kelvin Absolute temperature scale and numerous inventions, and lent his name to the Kelvinator, one of the first refrigerators for home use. His statue commands a place of honor near the river that also bears his name, as it flows through the lord's namesake park. Nearby is a statue of another Glasgow innovator, **Sir Joseph Lister** (1827–1912), a pioneer of antiseptic surgery who all these years later commands a place on the bathroom shelf in the form of Listerine.

The West End is still *the* place to live, preferably in a red sandstone townhouse surrounded by flowery gardens. The **Kelvingrove** and **Hunterian** museums supply a heady dose of culture, while 25,000 students infuse the pretty streets with a bohemian vibe. Shop-lined Breyers Road cuts a swath through the West End, easily reached from the City Center on the Underground to Hillhead, Kelvinbridge, or Kelvinhall stations.

Hunterian Museum & Art Gallery ★★★ MUSEUM   The oldest museum in Scotland (opened in 1803) is a wondrous, sometimes oddball, treasure-trove divided into several buildings. It was founded by William Hunter (1718–83), a physician and anatomist, who seems to have had an interest in just about everything. On display in the Victorian era, high-vaulted timber-roofed galleries are (among other fab items): a 2,000 year-old coin that bears a portrait of Cleopatra; a 17th-century map of the world that a Jesuit missionary prepared for Chinese Emperor Kangxi; dinosaur fossils; Viking plunder; and a 350-million-year-old shark. Despite the shiny displays and high-tech lighting, you'll feel as though you're exploring a fusty old curiosity cabinet. Across the avenue is the Hunterian Art Gallery, which holds the world's largest collection of works by Scottish-American painter James McNeill Whistler (1834–1903). The main gallery also displays 17th century paintings (Rembrandt to Rubens) and 19th century art by the Scottish Colourists and so-called "Glasgow Boys," such as Hunter, Cadell, and Fergusson. Temporary exhibits, culled from Scotland's largest collection of prints, are in the second floor print gallery. A final lure: the home of architect Charles Rennie Mackintosh and his wife, Margaret, has been painstakingly recreated. Tours of these sparse, pleasing, and surprisingly contemporary rooms are by timed ticket only.

University of Glasgow, University Ave. www.hunterian.gla.ac.uk. *©* **0141/330-4221.** Museum and Art Gallery free, Mackintosh House £6 adults, £3 seniors and children. Tues–Sat 10am–5pm, Sun 11am–4pm. Subway: Hillhead.

Kelvingrove Art Gallery & Museum ★★★ MUSEUM   The Hunterian may be the oldest museum in Scotland, but the Kelvingrove is the country's most visited, its attendance numbers the greatest in the U.K., outside of London's museums. A magnificent, faux Spanish baroque palace, built for the 1901 Glasgow International Exhibition, houses a collection that spans from 17th century Dutch and Flemish masters through the French Impressionists and colorful works by the so-called Glasgow Boys (local painters who began to gain fame at the same time as Renoir and his fellow Impressionists) and beyond. Among the Kelvingrove's "Mona Lisas" are Rembrandt's 1655 painting *Man in Armor,* in which a pensive young man seems to be contemplating his mortality in light of an upcoming battle; and Salvador Dali's *Christ of St. John of the Cross,* in which Christ floats across a darkened sky. Elsewhere along the balconies and in the high-ceilinged spaces delightful touches of whimsy abound. Where else can you see a RAF Mark 21 Supermarine Spitfire suspended above an Asian elephant named Sir William? Wandering through

Get ready to meet internationally celebrated artist, architect, and designer Charles Rennie Mackintosh (1868–1928). Not only are the houses and buildings he designed some of Glasgow's favorite landmarks, but you probably won't get out of town without a Mackintosh teacup or dish towel in your baggage. Mackintosh achieved considerable success early in his career and was already a noted architect by age 21. He gentlemanly claimed that his wife, the glass and textile designer Margaret Macdonald, "has genius, I only have talent." Mackintosh abandoned architecture in 1914, eventually moved to France to paint, and died in London at age 60. The **Charles Rennie Mackintosh Society** (www.crmsociety.com) has info on

Mackintosh-related properties around the city. The master is still changing the face of the city: **House for an Art Lover** (www.houseforanartlover.co.uk; ✆ **0141/353-4770**), built from plans Mackintosh and Macdonald submitted for a competition in 1901, was completed in the 1990s. Several rooms show off Mackintosh's designs and Macdonald's screens and other decorative elements. Hours vary, but the house, located on the Southside in Bellahouston Park, is generally open Wednesday through Saturday and Monday, 10am to 4pm, and Sunday 10am to 12:30pm, and admission is £6. You can reach the house via underground to Ibrox Station and a short walk from there.

the sumptuously tiled halls you'll come upon a working hive of bees, a leather satchel worn by a medieval monk, and a complete set of armor for a man and horse. The latter is a nice counterpoint to the famed Rembrandt painting; making comparisons like this is one of the pleasures of spending an afternoon here. This remarkable collection is refreshingly manageable, so you can peruse it in an hour or two, with luck as the Kelvingrove organ belts out some music (at 1pm Mon–Sat and 3pm Sun).

Argyle St. www.glasgowlife.org.uk. ✆ **0141/276-9599.** Free. Mon–Sat 10am–5pm and Sun 11am–5pm. Subway: Kelvinhall.

Along the Clyde

According to a popular saying, the Clyde made Glasgow and Glasgow made the Clyde. The river made the city into a great medieval trading power and later a shipbuilding center—the *QE2* was launched here in 1967, and the Clyde would be just another trickle if Glasgow hadn't put it on the map. Though most of the riverside industry has died out, both banks of the Clyde are coming back into their own, with shiny new riverside apartment and office buildings, the **SSE Hydro** exhibition center and **SEC Armadillo** auditorium (both by acclaimed British architect Sir Norman Foster and the latter so-called for its shape), and two flashy museums, the **Glasgow Science Centre** and the **Riverside Museum.** One of the most impressive riverside sights is the out-of-commission **Finnieston Crane,** a giant, 53m-tall (174-ft.) cantilever crane dating back to the 1920s that was once used to load steam locomotives and heavy cargo onto ships. Its hulking presence on the northern banks near the

Glasgow's other great architect, whose legacy is often eclipsed by the work of Charles Renee Mackintosh, is Alexander "Greek" Thomson (1817–75). In his work Thomson combined Greek elements with Egyptian, Assyrian, and other Eastern-influenced motifs and, as many architectural critics have noted, not only defined a distinctive style for Victorian-era Glasgow but also had a profound effect on the work of American Frank Lloyd Wright. A number of Thomson's works in Glasgow have been lost to the wrecker's ball, but those remaining include terraced houses in Moray Place (where he lived on the city's Southside) and Eton Terrace in the West End, near Glasgow University campus; St Vincent Street Church and the Grecian Buildings at 336–356 Sauchiehall Street, both on the west side of the City Center; and Holmwood, a villa about 4 miles outside the central city in the southern suburb of Cathcart, at 63–65 Netherlee Rd. (www.nts.org.uk). The house is open March through late October, Friday through Monday, noon to 5pm, and admission is £7.50; Holmwood can be reached via suburban rail from Glasgow Central Station to Cathcart and a short walk.

strikingly modern exhibition center and auditorium speaks volumes about the city's transformation from its industrial past.

Glasgow Science Centre ★★★ MUSEUM/PLANETARIUM   This gleaming titanium-clad, crescent- shaped landmark resembles the hull of a ship, a reference to the adjacent basin where ships were once brought to have barnacles scraped off their hulls. You can learn all about marine invertebrates inside the Science Mall, as well as ship engineering, and just about anything else having to do with science and technology. Sections on health and the human body are especially enlightening. The adjacent Planetarium and IMAX put on spectacular shows, but the biggest thrill is a trip up the 100m (328-ft.) tall Glasgow Tower. The entire tower turns, making it the tallest rotating structure in the world. Ironically, given the center's devotion to cutting-edge technology, the tower is often closed for repairs.

50 Pacific Quay. www.gsc.org.uk. (℗ **0141/540-5000.** £11.50 adults, £9.50 seniors and children 5–15, Planetarium £3 extra, IMAX £2.50 extra, Tower £3.50 extra; Planetarium only £5.50, Tower only £6.50. Late-Mar to Oct daily 10am–5pm, Nov to late-Mar Wed–Fri 10am–3pm, Sat–Sun 10am–5pm. Bus 90 from Union St.

Riverside Museum ★★★ MUSEUM   The zigzag roof of this landmark by the late star architect Zaha Hadid represents waves on the River Clyde, while its long, linear shape is supposed to evoke a tunnel that connects the city and the river. The lime green interior seems a bit less inspirational, more like a trolley barn—which, come to think of it, is the ideal setting for the trolleys, buses, cars, planes, even skateboards and wheelchairs that entertainingly celebrate the glories of transport, the subject of the museum. Stepping aboard vintage 1930s buses and looking into old house trailers (called caravans here) means pleasantly indulging in some nostalgia, and the experience is made all the richer by enlightening taped commentary. A Pakistani talks about arriving in Glasgow in the 1950s, getting a job as a bus driver, and encountering his first-ever first snowfall. Several Glaswegian ladies of a certain age recall their evenings at dance halls and rushing to catch the last homeward-bound street-cars of the night. The three-masted tall ship *Glenlee,* launched in Glasgow in 1896, is berthed outside. Onboard you'll encounter what might be the most haunting story of all: One of the ship's hands sailed around Cape Horn three times, survived multiple typhoons and hurricanes at sea, took up flying, and was with Amelia Earhart when her plane disappeared over the Pacific in 1937.

100 Pointhouse Pl. www.glasgowlife.org.uk. © **0141/2872720.** Free. Museum: Mon–Thurs, Sat 10am–5pm, Fri and Sun 11am–5pm. SV *Glenlee:* thetallship.com. © **0141/357-3699.** Free. Feb–Oct daily 10am–5pm, Nov–Jan daily 10am–4pm. Subway: Patrick Station or Bus 100 from the north side of George Sq.

Southside

You have less incentive to venture across the Clyde into the largely residential Southside these days now that the **Burrell Collection,** a mind-boggling treasure trove of decorative objects from medieval doorways to French painting, is closed for long overdue repairs and rebuilding (reports suggested the roof was in danger of collapsing). The Burrell is slated to reopen in 2020.

Pollok House ★★ HISTORIC HOME/GALLERY The Maxwell clan lived at the Pollok Estate for 700 years, and since 1752 they resided in this handsome country house designed by William Adam, the most famous architect of his day. End-of-the-line Dame Anne Maxwell donated the mansion to the city of Glasgow in 1966, giving the rest of us a chance to vicariously enjoy a posh lifestyle. Time in the lavish interiors seems to have stood still since the 1930s, not a bad place to be stuck amid glamorous drawing rooms, a 7,000-book library, and plush bedrooms. The Maxwells had a taste for Spanish painting, and their Goyas and El Grecos are part of one of the best collections of Spanish art in the U.K. The vast Edwardian kitchen is now an atmospheric tea room. As you nibble on a home-baked scone think about the times when a staff of 48 toiled down here in service to a household of three. The estate is now 146-hectare (361-acre) Pollok Country Park. A well-manicured section is planted in the house's formal gardens, famous for their rhododendrons, while the rest of the acreage is given over to woods and meadows where a herd of Highland cattle graze.

Pollok Country Park, 2060 Pollokshaws Rd. www.nts.org.uk. © **0844/493-2202.** House £7.50 adults, £5.50 seniors/children, £12.50–£18.50 families. Daily 10am–5pm. 3 miles south of the city center. First buses 45, 48, or 57.

Tours

City Sightseeing Glasgow (www.citysightseeingglasgow.co.uk; © **0141/204-0444**) operates frequent open-top bus tours around the city throughout the year. A complete circuit takes about 1 hour and 15 minutes, but you're free to hop off and on at any of the 21 stops along the way. This is an easy way to get to the sights around far-flung Glasgow, and you'll be enlightened by a

As Glaswegians began to move west in the 19th century, city fathers had the foresight to create two tranquil green spaces in the West End. The **Botanic Gardens,** at 732 Great Western Rd., were laid out in 1841 to supply the University of Glasgow with plant material for research, though the glass-dome Kibble Palace greenhouse seems more like a pleasure palace than a laboratory. The city bought the parcel in 1981 and opened it to the public. Greenhouses filled with exotic plants and tropical rainforests are surrounded by lawns and gardens, and pleasant tearooms occupy the former curator's house. Nearby **Kelvingrove Park,** an 85-acre strip of greenery straddling both banks of the River Kelvin, opened in 1852. The lawns and shaded groves were meant to entertain the middle classes moving to the West End and also to provide a bit of relief to those remaining behind in the crowded city center. The Botanic Gardens (www.glasgowbotanicgardens. com; ✆ **0141/276-1614**) are open daily 7am to dusk, greenhouses from 10am to 6pm (to 4:15pm in winter), tearooms from 10am to 6pm (to 4pm in winter). Entry is free.

history-rich recorded commentary narrated by a smooth-talking Scot. Buses depart from stop no. 1 at George Square from 9:30am until 4:30pm and run every 15 minutes from April to October and every half-hour November to March. Tickets can be bought from the driver and cost £14 for adults for 1 day, £15 for 2 days; £7 for children 5 to 15 for 1 day, £8 for 2 days; or £31 for families for 1 day, £33 for 2 days. Given the small difference in price, the two-day ticket is a better investment, allowing more time to see the sights and enjoy the surrounding neighborhoods; at a breakdown of £7.50 a day for a 2-day adult ticket, you won't be spending much more for transport than you would on buses and the subway.

Walking Tours in Glasgow (www.walkingtoursin.com) leads informative and highly entertaining tours of the City Center and East End. Walks leave from George Square, last about 2½ hours, and cover quite a bit of ground, east to the cathedral and south to Glasgow Green, so they may not be suitable for those with limited mobility. From June through September, tours depart daily at 10:30am and 2pm, and from October through May, on Saturdays at 10:30am and 2pm; cost is £10. £8 seniors, and £5 children under 16.

The **Charles Rennie Mackintosh Society** (www.crmsociety.com) has three downloadable walking tours on its website that are excellent introductions to the city's Victorian and Edwardian-era architecture, focusing on the City Center and the West End.

WHERE TO STAY

In Glasgow, your best lodging options come down to the choice of two neighborhoods: the City Center and the West End. The many excellent hotels and guest houses in both put you within easy reach of the sights and amid everything that's good about life in this vibrant city.

City Center & Merchant City

EXPENSIVE

Blythswood Square ★ This row of elegant Georgian-era townhouses long served as the headquarters of the old Royal Scottish Automobile Club, and even lots of contemporary style doesn't detract from an old world clubby atmosphere of grand staircases, pillars, and Art Deco flourishes. The huge, high-ceilinged guest rooms in the old houses are especially bright and airy, despite their relentless purple and gray color schemes and black-fabric chandeliers—front-facing views into the colorful gardens in the square are a real perk. Smaller rooms in a new wing in the rear have less character but are stylishly luxurious. There's a lively restaurant and bar, and the spa has steam rooms, saunas, and two small pools, though it's complimentary to guests only at off hours.

11 Blythswood Sq. www.phcompany.com. ℂ **0141/138-486.** 88 units. Doubles £165–£285, most rates include breakfast. **Amenities:** Restaurant; bar; 2 pools (indoor); health club and spa; room service; free Wi-Fi.

Grand Central Hotel ★★ Everything about these grand Edwardian-era spaces and comfy guest rooms exudes a hint of glamor and the romance of the bygone age of travel—including what must be the longest hotel corridors in the world (along with the world's second-largest crystal chandelier cascading down a grand staircase). Vintage railway scenes decorate the contemporarily styled bedrooms, some of which overlook the tracks of adjacent Central Station through heavily soundproofed windows. Photos of Frank Sinatra and other globe-trotting guests hang in the darkly welcoming lobby, and a marble floored Champagne Bar overlooks the station concourse. For one more bit of historic provenance, consider that in 1927, John Logie Baird transmitted the first television pictures from London to a receiver in the hotel.

99 Gordon St. www.phcompany.com. ℂ **0141/139-717.** 186 units. Doubles £100–£165, most rates include breakfast. **Amenities:** Restaurant; 2 bars; room service; free Wi-Fi.

MODERATE

Citizen M ★ Go ahead—you won't be the first guest who's said "Beam me up, Scotty" when stepping into the futuristic-looking lobby where black clad "ambassadors" walk you through the self-check-in process. If you've ever wondered what sleeping quarters on the *Starship Enterprise* might be like, you'll find out upstairs, where all the compact, cubical-like guest rooms are exactly the same (no anxiety about an upgrade here). A bedside tablet controls the blinds, temperature, lamps, free movies, and some very romantic mood lighting, but you're probably better off experiencing this *Jetsons*-worthy lodging on your own. Floor space is limited; square beds are exactly the width of the room, demanding that one half of a twosome sleep on the inside; and you put on an X-rated floor show when you step into the glassed-in, room-facing shower pod. For a bit of space, the sprawling lounge-restaurant-bar downstairs is artfully furnished with couches and worktables.

60 Renfrew St. www.citizenm.com. ℂ **0203/519-1111.** 198 units. Doubles £90–£120, some rates include breakfast. **Amenities:** Restaurant; bar; room service; free Wi-Fi.

Glasgow Hotels & Restaurants

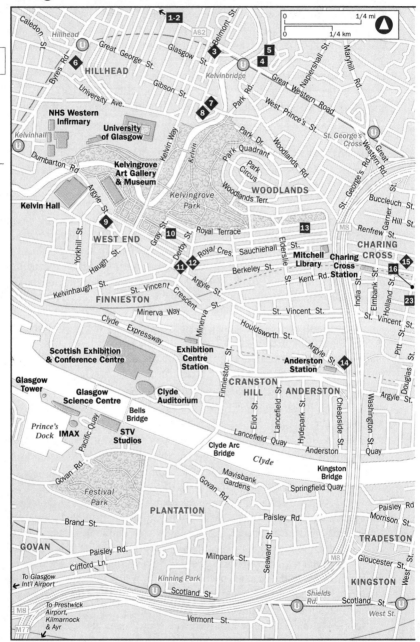

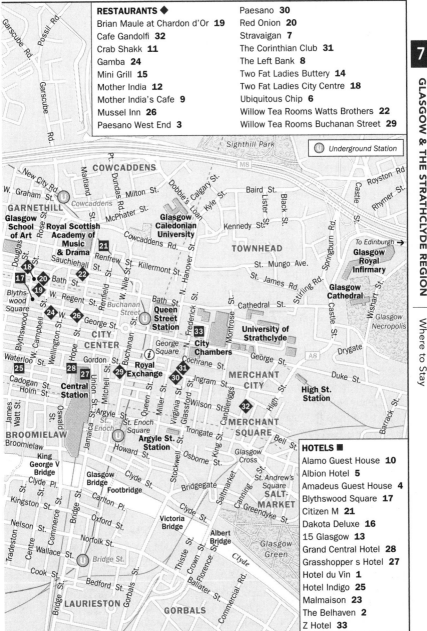

RESTAURANTS ◆

Brian Maule at Chardon d'Or **19**
Cafe Gandolfi **32**
Crab Shakk **11**
Gamba **24**
Mini Grill **15**
Mother India **12**
Mother India's Cafe **9**
Mussel Inn **26**
Paesano West End **3**

Paesano **30**
Red Onion **20**
Stravaigan **7**
The Corinthian Club **31**
The Left Bank **8**
Two Fat Ladies Buttery **14**
Two Fat Ladies City Centre **18**
Ubiquitous Chip **6**
Willow Tea Rooms Watts Brothers **22**
Willow Tea Rooms Buchanan Street **29**

Ⓤ *Underground Station*

HOTELS ■

Alamo Guest House **10**
Albion Hotel **5**
Amadeus Guest House **4**
Blythswood Square **17**
Citizen M **21**
Dakota Deluxe **16**
15 Glasgow **13**
Grand Central Hotel **28**
Grasshopper s Hotel **27**
Hotel du Vin **1**
Hotel Indigo **25**
Malmaison **23**
The Belhaven **2**
Z Hotel **33**

Dakota Deluxe ★★★ Urbane elegance is on conspicuous display throughout this stunning redo of an 1950s office building—deep chairs and couches, walls lined with art and books, discreet lighting—all providing a soothing retreat from city life. Stylish yet comfortable rooms and suites make guests feel right at home, though few probably live in such design-perfect surroundings, lit by huge, loft-like windows shaded with wooden slats and done up with walls of framed musical scores and other artful touches, handsome wood and leather furnishings, and crisply tiled baths with spa-worthy showers. A bar, lounges, and in-house grill restaurant are likewise sophisticated and relaxing.

179 W. Regent St. http://glasgow.dakotahotels.co.uk. ℂ **0141/404-3680.** 83 units. Doubles from £90, most rates include breakfast. **Amenities:** Restaurant; bar; room service; free Wi-Fi.

Grasshoppers Hotel ★★★ The worn entryway and stark elevator don't prepare you for the pleasure of stepping into this welcoming and stylish sixth-floor lair high above Central Station. Soothing rooms are geared to tasteful, pared-down luxury. Handmade Scandinavian furnishings are clean-lined, Italian lighting is warm and efficient, and handmade mattresses are topped with Egyptian cotton sheets and feather-down pillows. Breakfast and weeknight dinners are served family-style in a kitchen-dining room that's as warm and inviting as everything else about this place.

87 Union St. www.grasshoppersglasgow.com. ℂ **0141/222-2666.** 30 units. Doubles £80–£120, includes breakfast. **Amenities:** Restaurant; bar; free Wi-Fi.

Hotel Indigo ★★ Employees who once toiled in these early 20th-century sandstone headquarters of a city electricity provider wouldn't recognize their old digs now, converted into high-ceilinged guest quarters where bold hues and plush fabrics create a playful yet comfortable ambience. Most welcome of the many amenities is free use of a mobile phone for local and international calling, plus data for handy navigating around town, and complimentary beer, wine, and soft drinks in the minibars. Downstairs is a popular and flashy steakhouse and grill, and just outside the door, a conveniently placed stop for the airport bus.

75 Waterloo St. http://indigo-glasgow.hotel-rn.com. ℂ U.S.: **888/697-3791;** U.K.: **0808/145-3715.** 94 units. Doubles from £79, most rates include breakfast. **Amenities:** Restaurant; bar; room service; free Wi-Fi.

Malmaison ★★ A former Greek Orthodox church has been revamped to be both hip and cozy, with a dramatic, double-height atrium bar and welcoming, stylish guest rooms thoughtfully done up with contemporary furnishings, bold plaid carpets for a touch of tradition, and soothing murals. Crisp, white-tile bathrooms are equipped with powerful showers and, in many, deep bathtubs, while large windows throughout are double paned to keep out street noise, a concession to the convenient, edge-of-the-center location. A chic, brasserie-like cellar lair serves a generous cooked breakfast as well as modern French fare for lunch and dinner.

278 W. George St. www.malmaison.com. ℗ **0141/378-0384.** 72 units. Doubles from £85, some rates include breakfast. **Amenities:** Restaurant; bar; room service; free Wi-Fi.

INEXPENSIVE

Z Hotel ★★   Industrial chic dominates in these tiny but welcoming quarters in an old printing house. Guest rooms, many without windows, surround a ceramic-tiled courtyard displaying old presses and other equipment, and clever design turns the limited spaces into luxurious little retreats, with soft lighting, supremely comfortable mattresses, with storage tucked beneath, and chic glass-walled shower rooms. A few choice "Queen Rooms" are a bit larger than the others and some have city-view windows. A brick-walled cafe downstairs serves as reception and breakfast room, while outside the door is a surfeit of shopping and entertainment.

42 N. Frederick St. www.thezhotels.com/glasgow. ℗ **0141/212-4550.** 104 units. Doubles from £35, some rates include breakfast. **Amenities:** Cafe; free Wi-Fi.

West End

EXPENSIVE

Hotel du Vin ★★★   Devonshire Gardens has always been one of Glasgow's most posh addresses, and these five connected, beautifully decorated townhouses do justice to the neighborhood. A warren of corridors and wooden staircases lead off a series of soothing, clubby lounges to similarly welcoming rooms and suites. Bold, deep colors and wall coverings offset acres of Victorian-era woodwork, fireplaces, and large bay windows, and handsome classic furnishings hit just the right tone of chic and comfort. Plenty of nice flourishes include deep bathtubs and walk-in monsoon showers. Some of the grander suites have their own conservatories and saunas, but any room here sets you up in style.

1 Devonshire Gardens. www.hotelduvin.com. ℗ **0030/016-0390.** 49 units. Doubles £105–£275, includes breakfast. **Amenities:** 2 restaurants; bar; exercise room; free Wi-Fi.

MODERATE

15 Glasgow ★★   An exquisitely redone Georgian townhouse shows off a tiled and pillared entry, gracious grand staircase geared to make any one feel like nobility (or at least a merchant prince, for whom the house was built), and other beautiful period details, enhanced by a soothing and starkly contemporary aesthetic and many luxurious overtones. Stylish and tastefully done as it all is, design doesn't trump comfort in quiet, oversize bedrooms equipped with plush headboards and fine linens, with large, exquisitely outfitted bathrooms, some with deep soaking tubs. A communal drawing room overlooking the green gardens out front is furnished with big couches around the fireplace to invite lazy lingering. Breakfast is delivered on a tray to your room, a nice way to start a day of sightseeing—easy to do from this spot just off Sauchiehall Street at the far eastern edge of the West End, so Kelvingrove Park, museums and restaurants, and the City Center are all an easy walk away.

15 Woodside Pl. www.15glasgow.com. © **0141/332-1263.** 5 units. Doubles £99–£215, includes breakfast. **Amenities:** Free parking in a few spots; free Wi-Fi.

Alamo Guest House ★★   Remember the Alamo, because intimate Glasgow lodgings don't get much more welcoming than this rambling inn on two floors of a Victorian house on a quiet cul-de-sac at the edge of Kelvingrove Park. The fireplaces, elaborate moldings and big bay windows are homily atmospheric, and nice iron bedsteads, four posters, and other antiques are scattered among the comfortable, beautifully decorated guest rooms. Quarters vary considerably in size and price, but many show off 14-foot ceilings, acres of ornate woodwork, and from a choice few, airy views over Kelvingrove Park through huge windows; the five rooms with shared facilities are especially good value, and are just a step or two away from beautifully done and well-maintained bathrooms. The surrounding greenery is soothing, and big city attractions, including the West End museums and restaurants, are just around the corner.

46 Gray St., G3 7SE. www.alamoguesthouse.com. © **0141/339-2395.** 12 units, 7 with private bathrooms. Doubles £80–£130, includes breakfast. **Amenities:** Free Wi-Fi.

INEXPENSIVE

Albion Hotel ★★   The stereotype of Scottish efficiency and economy come to the fore in these bright, tidy rooms scattered across two interconnecting Victorian houses on a quiet cul-de-sac above Kelvingrove Park. Crisp, pleasant decor is contemporary and no frills, with good beds and sparkling, shower-only bathrooms, without a single nod toward quaint tradition or high style. What is traditional is the warm welcome and expert, friendly service, and the hearty Scottish breakfast served in a front parlor. Kelvingrove underground station is at the end of the street.

405–407 N. Woodside Rd. www.albion-hotel.net. © **0141/339-8620.** 21 units. Doubles from £30, includes breakfast. **Amenities:** Free Wi-Fi.

Amadeus Guest House ★★   A Victorian townhouse on a ridge overlooking parkland along the River Kelvin is still the welcoming home it was built to be, with bright, individually decorated and cozily stylish guest rooms tucked onto the upper floors, with some under the eaves and another opening off a landing. Some are set up for families and all are nicely maintained. A buffet breakfast is served by candlelight in the former parlor that doubles as an inviting lounge at other times. The Kelvinbridge underground station is just down the street, making this a handy base for sightseeing.

411 N. Woodside Rd., G20 6NN. www.amadeusguesthouse.co.uk. © **0141/339-8257.** 9 units. £48–£58 double, includes breakfast. Enter "Frommers" as the promo code for a 10% discount. **Amenities:** Free Wi-Fi.

The Belhaven ★   A commodious and gracious Victorian terrace house lends itself well to these spacious guest quarters, with soothing earth tone color schemes and clean-lined, contemporary furnishings nicely set amid ornate woodwork and other decorative flourishes, all adding up to a pleasant, style-meets-function ambience. To one side of the massive staircase, a welcoming bar and breakfast room warmed by a tiled hearth serves evening snacks and drinks, while guest rooms upstairs are large and high-ceilinged, and those facing the tree-lined parkway out front through huge windows are especially nice; a massive family room houses a group in style, filling the enormous former parlor with beds and plush couches. The Botanic Gardens are across the street, West End museums and restaurants are a short walk away, and the nearby Hillhead underground station puts the rest of the city within easy reach.

15 Belhaven Terrace. www.belhavenhotel.com. © **0141/339-3222.** 16 units. £75–£95 double, includes breakfast. **Amenities:** Bar/cafe; free Wi-Fi.

WHERE TO EAT

Many Glasgow restaurants offer good-value menus for lunch and early dinner, so if you're willing to forgo a later evening repast you can dine well at a very good price while enjoying some of the city's top restaurants. It's also noteworthy that Glasgow restaurants often keep long hours and rather than taking a break between lunch and dinner often serve throughout the day.

Glasgow's longtime standby for a quick bite is **Peckham's** ★ (www.peckhams.co.uk) at two locations in the West End: 124-126 Byres Rd. (© **0141/357-1454**) and 139 Hyndland Rd. (© **0141/357-0398**); the shops serve sandwiches and other light fare throughout into the evening, until 9pm on Byers Road and 10pm on Hyndland Road. **Riverhill Coffee Bar** ★, next to Central Station at 24 Gordon St. (www.riverhillcafe.com; © **0141/204-4762**), has worked its way into the hearts of Glaswegians with excellent city-roasted Deer Green coffee and a short eat-in/eat out menu, with cheese-topped scones, chorizo bagels, and crayfish sandwiches; it's open Monday to Friday 7am to 5pm, Saturday 8am to 5pm, and Sunday 10am to 5pm.

City Center

Brian Maule at Chardon d'Or ★★★ FRENCH/SCOTTISH   It would be hard to find more splurge-worthy surroundings than these discreetly elegant rooms on the grand, high-ceilinged parlor floor of a Georgian townhouse, where abstract artworks hang above polished floorboards, crystal glistens atop crisp white linens, and a smartly turned out staff exudes professional flare. The scene-stealers here, though, are the creations of namesake chef Brian Maule, who's from nearby Ayr and earned acclaim in London, and now close to home turns Scottish staples into works of art. Such standard fare as the humble cod, oven roasted, is elevated with squid ink pasta and tempura of squid, while the tarte tatin or sorbet alone ensure a return visit.

176 W. Regent St. www.brianmaule.com. © **0141/248-3801.** Main courses £24–£28. Mon–Fri noon–2:30pm, Mon–Thurs 5–10pm.

Gamba ★★★ SEAFOOD   Glaswegians love seafood, and the place to splash out when fish and chips just won't do is this discreet, soothing earth-toned cellar space off Blythswood Square. Tasteful, piscine-themed art works line the walls, setting the stage for a meal that should open with the acclaimed fish soup with prawn dumplings and can move onto mussels from nearby sea lochs, grilled langoustine from the Isle of Skye, peat-smoked haddock from the island of Gigha, or, for carnivores, filet of Scotch beef. You can enjoy a feast of local bounty on a special market menu or one of the other good-value menus, most including a glass of wine.

225A W. George St. www.gamba.co.uk. ⓒ **0141/572-0899.** Lunch 2 courses £17, 3 courses £20; dinner main courses £14–£22. Mon–Sat noon–2:30pm and 5–10:30pm.

Mini Grill ★★ STEAKHOUSE   Stepping down into this small cellar room, with candlelight softening the stone walls and bare wood floors, is a bit like being invited into a friend's basement lair, and the casual buzz and friendly service seem right in keeping. This is the perfect setting for the car-nivorous feasts that come off the grill—steaks mostly, as well as venison and a superb burger, with a few nods to vegetarians with a sophisticated mac and cheese and Asian stir fry, accompanied by a well-curated selection of beers and wines.

244A Bath St. www.minigrillglasgow.co.uk. ⓒ **0141/332-2732.** Mains £15–£30. Mon–Thurs noon–10, Fri–Sat noon–11:30pm, Sun noon–9pm.

Mussel Inn ★ SEAFOOD   You can almost smell the sea air in this breezy two-level room operated by shellfish harvesters in western Scotland. That translates to the freshest oysters in town—like the mussels (sold by the kilo or half kilo in a choice of preparations), they're cultivated in plankton-rich sea lochs. Equally fresh are the chowders, fish stew, and especially admirable seafood pasta. They grill a good burger here, too, but really, that would be a desecration to the sea gods. Lunch specials are a remarkably good deal.

157 Hope St. www.mussel-inn.com. ⓒ **0141/572-1405.** Mains £7–£23. Mon–Fri noon–2:30pm and 5–10pm, Sat noon–10pm, Sun 12:30–10pm.

Paesano ★ PIZZA   No one's ever going to confuse Glasgow with Naples, and the white-tiled walls and industrial lighting seem decidedly northern. But Glaswegians, who are wild about pizza, crowd onto the trestle-table benches to be appreciatively transported by creations from the wood-fired ovens, accompanied by a small selection of Italian wine and beer. A West End branch is likewise popular and keeps the same long hours.

94 Miller St. www.paesanopizza.co.uk. ⓒ **0141/258-5565.** Pizzas from £5. Daily noon–11pm (until midnight Fri–Sat). West End: 471 Great Western Rd. ⓒ **0141/370-0534.**

Red Onion ★★ MODERN SCOTTISH/ECLECTIC   Booths, mirrors, and plain wooden tables and chairs might bring to mind an American diner, while double height windows and an overhanging mezzanine suggest something a little grander and a bit more dramatic, all adding up to a decidedly cheerful and comfortable ambience. The eclectic menu also hovers between down to earth and exotic—deep fried haggis, finnan haddie (smoked haddock) fish-cakes, and dry-aged sirloin are solidly classic Scottish, but they can be creatively paired with French onion soup, Thai-spied fish, creamy Italian risotto, and other slightly more adventurous choices, served a la carte or well represented on a choice of good-value set menus.

257 W. Campbell St. http://red-onion.co.uk. ⓒ **0141/221-6000.** Mains £13–£25. Daily noon–9pm.

Willow Tea Rooms ★ TEAROOM   Glasgow's most famous spot for tea was for decades several levels of rooms at 217 Sauchiehall St. The architect Charles Rennie Mackintosh and his wife, Margaret Macdonald, redesigned the four floors for proprietor Kate Cranston in 1901, taking control of every detail right down to the last teaspoon. The willow-motifs that abound aren't arbitrary; look at the address: Sauchiehall is a combo of two old Scots words for *saugh,* willow, and *haugh,* meadow. These premises have gone out of the tea-dispensing business and are being preserved as the Willow Tearooms Trust, a learning and conference center, opening to the public by 2019. You can still sip tea while getting a taste for the couple's design at two nearby offshoots of the original, in the Watts Brothers department store east on Sauchiehall Street and on Buchanan Street, with interiors inspired by Macintosh-Macdonald designs and infused with hints of rose, purple, and silver. Light and basic Scottish fare is served all day and includes scrambled eggs with smoked salmon and better-than-it-sounds cullen skink (a thick, creamy soup of smoked haddock, potatoes, and onions). At afternoon tea, your three-tiered cake stand will be laden with sandwiches, scones, and pastries.

Original: 217 Sauchiehall St. www.willowtearoomstrust.org. Watts Brothers, 119 Sauchiehall St. and 97 Buchanan St. www.willowtearooms.co.uk. Watts Brothers: ⓒ **0141/332-8446.** Mon–Sat 9:30am–5pm, Sun 11:30am–4pm. Buchanan Street: ⓒ **0141/ 204-5242.** Mon–Sat 9am–6:30pm, Sun 10:30am–5pm. Light mains £5–£9.

Merchant City

Cafe Gandolfi ★★★ SCOTTISH/FRENCH   Many Glaswegians can recall some of their happiest meals out at this ever-popular cross between a gastro pub and family-friendly cafe, founded almost 40 years ago and still providing a comforting refuge with rustic wood floors, tables and chairs fashioned from driftwood, and white-tiled walls and stained glass windows. The menu is as welcoming as the surroundings, and food is locally sourced—smoked salmon and venison from nearby seas and forests, and even the macaroni and cheese is made with cheddar from Mull; this might be the place to introduce yourself to cullen skink (a creamy fish soup, not for the lactose-challenged) or haggis. Upstairs, Bar Gandolfi serves the same fare, along with pizza, in cozy, attic-like surroundings beneath eaves and skylights, and Gandolfi Fish, in a sleek, black-accent space down the street, highlights sustainably sourced Scottish seafood, while next-door Fish to Go is a praiseworthy fish and chipper.

64 Albion St. www.cafegandolfi.com. ⓒ **0141/552-6813.** Main courses £7.50–£16. Daily 9am–11:30pm.

The Corinthian Club ★ INTERNATIONAL   One of Glasgow's most opulent venues is a five-story Victorian extravaganza from 1842, once the Glasgow Ship Bank and now restored to all its glory—crystal chandeliers, rococo friezes, a forest of pillars, all crowned with a 7.5m (25-ft.) illuminated glass dome. Decor trumps the overpriced and generally underwhelming cuisine, so it's best to luxuriate amid the visual splendor while sticking to straightforward choices, like a burger or club sandwich, or come for coffee; afternoon tea, served daily from 2:30pm until 5pm; or, as most of Glasgow's young professional crowd seems to do, a cocktail.

191 Ingram St. www.thecorinthianclub.co.uk. ℂ **0141/552-1101.** Main courses £10–£24. Afternoon tea £15–£22. Sun–Thurs 10am–2am, Fri–Sat 10am–3am.

West End

Crab Shakk ★★★ SEAFOOD   The age old rule with fish and seafood is to keep it simple, and that's what they do at the few tables and long counter in a cramped but chicly turned out space that bears no resemblance whatsoever to a shack. Instead, rough-hewn wood and some sleek glass and metal touches evoke the same thoughtful simplicity that comes across in deftly done preparations of grilled langoustines, lightly seared scallops, or any of the other bounty from nearby seas and lochs. Even the most casual fare—crab cakes, the fish sandwich, fish and chips—is done with the care that makes this a mandatory stop for piscivores trolling for a memorable meal.

114 Argyle St. www.crabshakk.com. ℂ **0141/334-6127.** Mains £7–£14. Daily noon–midnight.

The Left Bank ★ MODERN SCOTTISH   This split-level space seems to capture all the upscale-yet-still-bohemian vibe of the West End. So does the eclectic menu that dips into some South Asian exoticism while also sticking to the basics—take your pick, depending on your mood, Goan chicken with curry leaf sauce or beer-battered North Sea haddock. Brick walls, neutral tones, and worn wood floors are welcoming in an easygoing way, so much so that the neighborhood folks sitting at tables with kids or laptops, or both, seem to be in no hurry to move on. A daily brunch and an all-day menu of salads, burgers, and noodle dishes are good enough reasons to linger in the bright, sunlit spaces. A few more substantial fish and meat dishes are added in the evenings, when excellent cocktails are served from a concrete-sculpted bar.

33–35 Gibson St. www.theleftbank.co.uk. ℂ **0141/339-5969.** Mains £8–£16. Mon–Fri noon–midnight, Sat–Sun 10am–midnight.

Mother India's Cafe ★ INDIAN   In a laid-back, intimate, photo-lined space opposite the Kelvingrove Museum, an appreciative crowd of West End locals and other regulars are treated to a wide range of fresh and exotic dishes on an extensive tapas menu, with 50-some choices in all, from fish *pakoras* to butter chicken topped with almonds and lamb cooked with coconut cream. The staff is admirably adept at handling crowds while juggling multiple dishes and making recommendations, and a bring-your-own wine policy (with a corkage fee) keeps the reasonable tab even more so. The mother ship, the original Mother India, is around the corner and delivers a more traditional experience on three floors of dark, atmospheric rooms.

1355 Argyle St. www.motherindiascafeglasgow.co.uk. © **0141/339-9145.** Tapas £3–£10. Daily noon–10pm. Mother India: 28 Westminster Terrace. © **0141/334-3815.** Wed 11:30am–2:30pm and 5–10pm, Thurs–Fri 11:30am–10pm, Sat–Sun 12:30–10pm.

Stravaigin ★★ SEAFOOD Haggis—you have to try it sooner or later, and no better place to do so than this attractive, straightforward room with plain wood tables and straight-backed chairs where the menu focuses on all things Scottish, with some exotic global flourishes thrown in. A small plate of haggis, neeps and tatties—that's lamb's heart, liver, and lungs, minced with onion, spices, and a few other ingredients and served with turnips and potatoes—washed down with a wee draught of single malt should satisfy your curiosity. Thus fortified, you might want to backpedal into something as conventional as lamb livers simmered in Madeira or even beer-battered fish and chips. A similarly intriguing, Scots-oriented menu is available in the casual cafe upstairs.

28 Gibson St. www.stravaigin.co.uk. © **0141/572-0899.** Mains £14–£22. Mon–Sat noon–2:30pm and 5–10:30pm.

Two Fat Ladies West End ★★ MODERN SCOTTISH/SEAFOOD Glaswegians are adamant about their picks for best seafood in town, and this intimate space often comes out on top. The name has nothing to do with the proprietors' physique but is a reference to the slang term for the bingo number that happens to be the same as the address of this charmingly ornate Fat Ladies original. (This branch was undergoing renovation at press time, but there are several Fat Ladies in Glasgow.) Many of the ingredients are straight from Scottish waters, and cooked to perfection. Hand-picked scallops, halibut or other local fish prove that "fresh" is the element that really matters when it comes to what the establishment calls "seriously fishy" dishes. If that's *too* fishy for your landlubber taste, excellent locally sourced beef and pork dishes are also offered. Two Fat Ladies at the Buttery, in the Finnieston neighborhood, is all rich paneling and tartan-plaid upholstery, well suited to business lunches or romantic evenings, while the City Center branch serves the same crowd and achieves a similarly atmospheric effect in a handsome, woody room adorned with playful art.

88 Dumbarton Rd. www.twofatladiesrestaurant.com. © **0141/339-1944.** Fixed-price lunch/pre-theatre £16–£21. Mon–Sat noon–3pm and 5:30–10:30pm, Sun 1–9pm. Buttery: 652–654 Argyle St. © **0141/221-8188.** City Center: 118a Blythswood St. © **0141/847-0088.**

Ubiquitous Chip ★★★ SCOTTISH The plant-filled, stonewalled nooks and crannies of a former undertaker's stables give off an easygoing vibe that seems to suggest "we're so solidly good we don't have to put on airs." That's true, and since 1971 this fab place, as much a mandatory Glasgow stop as the nearby Kelvingrove and Hunterian museums, has celebrated local produce and Scottish cuisine that, as they claim, is inspired by "aunties, grannies and even folklore." Perhaps the venison haggis might be a bit too folkloric, but Aberdeen beef and Orkney salmon are surefire hits. The bar serves generous cocktails and snacks, but they don't include the fries (chips here) that inspired the name, a snide reference to what at one time passed as haute cuisine in Glasgow.

12 Ashton Lane, off Byres Rd. www.ubiquitouschip.co.uk. ℂ **0141/334-5007.** Mains £16–£27. Mon–Sat noon–2:30pm, Sun 12:30–3pm; daily 5–11pm.

SHOPPING

By the look of things, Glaswegians are consummate consumers. In the U.K., only London and—a matter of some debate—Manchester have more shops. Most of this trade transpires along pedestrian streets and malls in the City Center and Merchant City. The main shopping venues are Buchanan Street, a long pedestrian thoroughfare that runs north to south through the City Center; Argyle Street, stretching east from Central Station; Sauchiehall Street, rather refreshingly lowbrow with bargain shops and outdoor vendors, running east–west through the north end of the City Center; and **Ingram Street,** which leads east from Royal Exchange Square through Merchant City to High Street. Shopping malls include Buchanan Galleries, off Buchanan Street, with an enormous branch of the **John Lewis** department store; **Princes Square,** with many designer shops behind an early 19th-century blonde sandstone facade, also off Buchanan Street; and **St Enoch Shopping Centre** under the biggest glass roof in Europe, off Argyle Street, to the east of Central Station.

The **Argyll Arcade** at 30 Buchanan St. was built in 1827 and is Europe's oldest shopping covered arcade. Note the spelling: The namesake dukes of Argyll use the double "L," but the same-named Glasgow street has been listed as "Argyle" ever since an 1830s city address directory misspelled the name. The largest group of retail **jewelers** in Scotland is clustered beneath the vaulted glass roof, making this the place to shop for high- quality diamond jewelry, watches, and wedding rings. The **Italian Centre,** a small complex off Ingram Street in Merchant City, is nicknamed "mini-Milan" for its designer outlets.

Elsewhere in the city, independent, quirky shops are located along or close to Byres Road and Great Western Road in the West End. **De Courcy's Arcade** on Cresswell Lane is heaven for vintage clothing.

For a real slice of Glaswegian market life, stop by **The Barras**

> ### Bring Your Passport!
>
> Visitors from outside the European Union should take along their passports when they go shopping, in case they make a purchase that entitles them to a **VAT (value-added tax)** refund. See "Taxes" on p. 457.

(www.theglasgowbarras.com; Sat–Sun 10am–5pm), on a large patch of ground between London Road and Gallowgate in the East End. This legendary market has been operating for nearly a century, with hundreds of traders who ply everything from clothes to collectibles.

Art & Crafts

Compass Gallery ★   The curators of this refreshing gallery concentrate on new local young artists. Prices are reasonable and you can find something special for as little as £25, depending on the exhibition. 178 W. Regent St., City Center. www.compassgallery.co.uk. ℰ **0141/221-6370.**

Cyril Gerber Fine Art ★★   One of Glasgow's most respected art galleries veers away from the avant-garde, specializing in British paintings, sculptures, and ceramics crafted between 1880 and the present day, as well as the work of Scottish artists. Cyril Gerber is a respected art authority with lots of contacts in art circles throughout Britain and has supplied work to many major galleries. Pieces begin at around £200. 148 W. Regent St., City Center. www.gerberfineart.co.uk. ℰ **0141/221-3095.**

Glasgow Print Studio ★   This contemporary studio is part of the wider **Trongate 103** center for arts and creativity, and sells and exhibits a diverse selection of original work by local print artists. Knowledgeable staff can advise on framing requirements for each piece at this very accessible new gallery. Trongate 103, King St., Merchant City. www.gpsart.co.uk. ℰ **0141/552-0704.**

Glasgow School of Art Shop ★★★   Products inspired by the work of Charles Rennie Mackintosh include books, cards, stationery, coffee and beer mugs, glassware, and sterling-and-enamel jewelry all created from original designs. Although the shop doesn't sell furniture, the staff will refer you to **Bruce Hamilton, Furnituremaker,** based in the Lindwood district (www.brucehamilton.co.uk; ℰ **01505/322-550**), a craftsman whose work they recommend and who produces high-quality reproductions of Mackintosh-designed furniture. Reid Building, 164 Renfrew St., City Center. www.gsa.ac.uk. ℰ **0141/353-4526.**

Books

Caledonian Books ★★   Scottish history is a specialty in this jam-packed West End second-hand shop, but you can pick your way through stacks of out-of-print literature and volumes on just about everything else. 483 Great Western Rd. www.caledoniabooks.co.uk. ℰ **0141/334-9663.**

Food

I.J. Mellis Cheesemonger ★★   If you're a cheese lover, this tiny shop with an outstanding selection of British and Irish cheeses is a mandatory stop. 492 Great Western Rd., West End. www.mellischeese.net. ℰ **0141/339-8998.**

Roots, Fruits and Flowers ★   The West End "nuts and berries" crowd gathers for carefully curated fruits, veggies, and organic foodstuffs, as well as

7

It hardly seems right to come to Glasgow without paying homage to the national beverage at several in-town and near-town whisky distilleries. All offer tours and tastings that elevate the distilling process to sacred science, and after a few drams you'll tend to agree that there is indeed something wondrous about the results.

Clydeside, The Old Pump House, Queen's Dock, 100 Stobcross Rd. (www.theclydeside.com) is open daily, with hourly tours and tastings Monday through Thursday, half hourly Friday through Sunday, from 10am to 4pm (until 4:30pm in July and Aug), £15. The distillery is a 20-minute walk from the Partick Underground station, a 10-minute walk from Exhibition Train Station, and is a stop on the City Sightseeing circuit (see p. 173).

Auchentoshan, in the suburbs 10 miles outside the city off the Great Western Rd. in Clydebank (www.auchentoshan.com; ☎ **01389/878561**) is open daily 10am to 5pm and tours and tastings last 1 to 2 hours and cost from £10 to £55. The distillery is a 10-minute walk from the last stop of the number 66 bus from the city center. **Glengoyne,** 14 miles north of the city in Dumgoyne, in the hills

around Loch Lomond (www.glengoyne.com; ☎ **01360/550-254**) is open daily, with tours on the hour March through November between 10am and 5pm and December through February between 10am and 4pm, lasting 45 mines. to 1½ hours and costing from £10.50 to £28. The number 10 bus from Buchanan Street Station stops at the distillery gates.

You can buy fine whiskies from throughout Scotland and the rest of the world at **Robert Graham,** 111 West George St., City Center (www.robertgraham1874.com; ☎ **0141/248-7283**) and **The Good Spirits,** 23 Bath St., City Center (www.thegoodspiritsco.com; ☎ **0141/258 8427**).

And then there's beer. For many Glaswegians, a pint is a fine accompaniment to a dram, and it's no accident that many Glasgow pubs are called "half 'n' halfs." The local brew on tap is usually **Tennent's,** the output of the East End's Wellpark Brewery, 161 Duke St. (www.tennentcaledonian.com; ☎ **0141/552-6552**), on a site where beer has been brewed for the past 475 years or so. Tours with tastings are on the hour, Monday through Saturday, from 11am to 6pm, and Sunday, from noon to 4pm, and cost £10.

wholesome scones, soups, coffee, and other cafe offerings, dispensed in pretty surroundings brightened with the city's largest selection of fresh flowers. 451–457 Great Western Rd., West End. www.rootsfruitsandflowers.com. ☎ **0141/334-3530.**

Kilts, Tartans & Woolens

Hector Russell ★★   Founded in 1881, Scotland's oldest and most prestigious kiltmakers sell more than skirt-like male attire. Crystal and gift items can be picked up here, but the real heart and soul of the store is the selection of impeccably crafted and reasonably priced tweed jackets, tartan-patterned trousers, waistcoats, and sweaters made from top-quality wool for both men and women. Hand-stitched kilts for men, women, and children are also for sale and an experienced sales staff is on hand to help you choose. 110 Buchanan St., City Center. www.hector-russell.com. ☎ **0141/221-0217.**

House of Cashmere ★★ Sweaters, scarves, and other fine, made-or-woven-in-Scotland woolens are the stock in trade. 34 Gordon St., City Center. www.houseofcashmere.co.uk. ☎ **0141/249-9857.**

House of Fraser ★ This U.K.-wide department store got its start in Glasgow as a drapery shop back in 1849 and is still a city institution, selling lots of tweeds and tartans amid the high fashion and high-design home furnishings and accessories. An ascent up the grand staircase amid tiers of balconies beneath a glass arcade sets the mood for a memorable shopping experience even if you're buying nothing more glamorous than a toothbrush. 45 Buchanan St., City Center. www.houseoffraser.co.uk. ☎ **0344/800-3728.**

Toys

The Sentry Box ★ This local institution tucked off Byres Road is an Aladdin's cave of traditional handcrafted toys, supplying a fascinating old-fashioned shopping experience for children and adults wanting a quick trip down memory lane. 175 Great George St., West End. www.sentryboxtoys.co.uk. ☎ **344/800-3728.**

SPECIAL EVENTS & FESTIVALS

Following Glasgow's **Hogmanay** celebrations—which sees thousands of revelers gather in George Square to cheer in the new year—**Celtic Connections** (www.celticconnections.com; ☎ 0141/353-8000), the city's annual festival of contemporary and traditional Celtic music, lights up venues and stages around Glasgow during the latter part of January and early February.

The **Glasgow Film Festival** (www.glasgowfilm.org; ☎ 0141/332-6535) takes over the city's cinemas in late February and early March, about the same time as the **Aye Write!** (www.ayewrite.com; ☎ 0141/287-2999) book festival, usually followed, in March, by the **Glasgow International Comedy Festival** (www.glasgowcomedyfestival.com; ☎ 0141/552-2070).

Glasgow International (www.glasgowinternational.org; ☎ 0141/276-8383), Scotland's largest showing of contemporary art, is mounted in late April and early May, and in June the **Glasgow International Jazz Festival** (www.jazzfest.co.uk; ☎ 0141/552-3552) attracts top names to venues around the city. Also in June, the **West End Festival** (www.westendfestival.co.uk; ☎ 0141/341-0844) kicks off with a large opening parade and features all kinds of music, theatre, and family-friendly events.

In August, **Merchant City** celebrates with a program of theater, music, comedy, and dance events (www.merchantcityfestival.com), and huge crowds gather on Glasgow Green for the **World Pipe Band Championships** (www.theworlds.co.uk; ☎ 0141/353-8000).

In December, the **Glasgow Loves Christmas** (www.glasgowloveschristmas.com) celebrations take to the streets, transforming George Square into an outdoor ice skating rink and hosting a program of family events, including a Santa Dash.

ENTERTAINMENT & NIGHTLIFE

Glasgow is one of the most happening cities in the U.K. For detailed info on all entertainment options around the city, check **www.list.co.uk**.

The Performing Arts

Kings Theatre, 297 Bath St., City Center (www.kingstheatreglasgow.net; ℂ **0844/871-7648**) stages plays, musicals, and comedies and in winter an annual pantomime in opulent surroundings from 1904. The **Theatre Royal,** 282 Hope St., City Center (www.glasgowtheatreroyal.org.uk; ℂ **0844/871-7647**), resplendent with Victorian Italian Renaissance plasterwork and glittering chandeliers, is home to the Scottish Opera and regularly hosts the Scottish Ballet, as well as touring productions by national theatre companies from across the U.K. Glasgow's beloved Victorian-era **Citizens Theatre,** 119 Gorbals St., Southside (www.citz.co.uk; ℂ **0141/429-0022**) stages its own productions and hosts touring companies, favoring emerging theatre companies. The ornate **Pavilion Theatre,** 121 Renfield St., City Center (www.pavilion theatre.co.uk; ℂ **0141/332-1846**), specializes in mainstream music concerts and comedy.

The **Tron Theatre,** 63 Trongate, Merchant City (www.tron.co.uk; ℂ **0141/552-4267**), occupies the former Tron Church, with its famous dome by architect Robert Adam and presents contemporary drama, dance, and music events. For a real slice of bygone Glasgow nightlife, catch a show at the **Britannia Panopticon,** 113-117 Trongate, Merchant City (www.britannia panopticon.org; ℂ **0141/553-0840**), the oldest surviving music hall in the U.K., where Stan Laurel first trod the boards in 1906. Even though the building is in need of restoration, it still plays host to a number of cabaret, comedy, music, and film events—be warned that this old charmer has no heating so bundle up for winter performances.

The **Theatre Royal** (see above) hosts performances by **Scottish Opera** (www.scottishopera.org.uk; ℂ **0141/248-4567**), while **Scottish Ballet** (www. scottishballet.co.uk; ℂ **0141/331-2931**) is based at the **Tramway** on the Southside, although most of its Glasgow performances are held at the **Theatre Royal.** The **Glasgow Royal Concert Hall,** 2 Sauchiehall St., City Center (www.glasgowconcerthalls.com) is home to the **Royal Scottish National Orchestra** (www.rsno.org.uk; ℂ **0141/226-3868**), and alongside its performances you can catch folk, world, country, and rock and pop concerts in its 2,475-seat auditorium. **City Halls,** Candleriggs, East End (www.glasgowcon certhalls.com) is home to the **BBC Scottish Symphony Orchestra** (www. bbc.co.uk/bbcsso; ℂ **0141/552-0909**); the **Scottish Chamber Orchestra** (www.sco.org.uk; ℂ **0131/557-6800**) also regularly performs at this elegant Victorian venue. Adjacent to City Halls on Candleriggs is the **Old Fruitmarket** (www.glasgowconcerthalls.com) where jazz, pop, and world music gigs regularly rock the roof.

The Club & Music Scene

Barrowland ★★, Gallowgate, East End (www.glasgow-barrowland.com; ✆ **0141/552-4601**) is a legendary holdover from the 1930s Golden Age of dance halls and is now the city's most celebrated pop concert hall, filling its 1,900 seats with big names as well as emerging talent. Cover charges run £12 to £30. There's someone onstage every night at **King Tut's Wah-Wah Hut** ★, 272-ASt Vincent St., City Center (www.kingtuts.co.uk; ✆ **0141/221-5279**), a 300-seat venue that hosted Blur, Travis, Radiohead, and other legends before they became legends. Cover £5 to £18.

Other musical watering holes include **Nice 'n' Sleazy** ★, 421 Sauchiehall St., City Center (www.nicensleazy.com; ✆ **0141/333-0900**), the unpretentious fave of students at nearby Glasgow School of Art, with reasonable cover charges, inexpensive beer, and Japanese food to accompany the alt music and open mic events. Cover from £3. **Sub Club** ★, 22 Jamaica St., City Center (www.subclub.co.uk; ✆ **0141/248-4600**), is an underground venue near Central Station where the top DJs and a stellar sound system guarantee the best dance nights. Cover £3 to£10.

Òran Mór ★★, Byres Rd., West End (www.oran-mor.co.uk; ✆ **0141/357-6200**), stages theater and music events beneath the glorious ceiling mural of a repurposed Victorian church. A standout is A Play, A Pie and A Pint, a 45-minute-long lunchtime treat that features new talent and includes a pint and a pie. Cover free to £6.

The Stand, 333 Woodlands, West End (www.thestand.co.uk; ✆ **0141/212-3389**), is Glasgow's premiere comedy club. In March, the Glasgow International Comedy Festival (www.glasgowcomedyfestival.com; ✆**0141/552-2070**) blazes across many city venues.

Favorite Pubs & Bars

Pub hours are generally Monday to Saturday, noon to midnight, and Sunday, noon to 11pm.

Ben Nevis ★   Even the trendy decor, fashioned from stone and recycled wood, can't dispel an older-timer aura, enhanced by the dozens of single malts and beers on offer and much appreciated by a crowd of neighborhood regulars. 1147 Argyle St., West End. ✆ **0141/576-5204.**

Bon Accord ★★   A large selection of malts from across Scotland and live music will help you pass happy hours at this amiable institution. There's no better place to sip a pint of hand-pumped real ale. The knowledgeable bar men claim to dispense 900 different kinds of beer a year. 53 North St., West End. www.bonaccordweb.co.uk. ✆ **0141/248-4427.**

Curler's Rest ★   The West End's favorite local invites you to sink back into one its deep sofas and enjoy one of the five ales, 19 specialty beers, and three ciders on tap. The fish and chips are first rate. 256–260 Byres Rd., West End. www.thecurlersrestglasgow.co.uk. ✆ **0141/341-0737.**

Delmonicas ★   This stylish Merchant City gay bar and pre-club stop is jam-packed most evenings and hosts quiz and DJ nights and karaoke. 68 Virginia St. www.delmonicas.co.uk. ✆ **0141/552-4803.**

Drygate ★★   A former factory just down the hill from the cathedral is now a micro-brewery, beer hall, and restaurant, where you can sample the "experimental" brews and enjoy a burger while watching the brew masters at work. 85 Drygate, East End. www.drygate.com. ✆ **0141/212-8815.**

The Horse Shoe ★   The crowd of regulars who gather round the longest bar in Scotland (the namesake shape snakes through the Victorian room) have a musical bent—seven-nights-a-week karaoke is serious business here. 17 Drury St., City Center. ✆ **0141/248-6368.**

Islay Inn ★★   All good things come together in this West End favorite: choice whisky and beer, good food, and live music 5 nights a week. 1256 Argyle St. www.islayinn.com. ✆ **0141/334-7774.**

The Pot Still ★★★   Glasgow's most famous whisky pub claims to have 483 varieties on hand, served in convivial surroundings. 154 Hope St., City Center. www.thepotstill.co.uk. ✆ **0141/333-0980.**

The Scotia Bar ★   One of Glasgow's old timers, established in 1762 as a gathering spot for sailors in port, is a woody, low-ceilinged place that will make your feel at right at home. Lots of writers, actors, and singers do, and many of them take the stage for some of the city's best low-key entertainment. 12-114 Stockwell St., East End. ✆ **0141/552-8681.**

Waterloo Bar ★★   The oldest gay bar in town attracts a crowd that seems to have been there from the beginning. Each night of the week celebrates the music of a different decade. 306 Argyle St., City Center. ✆ **0141/248-7216.**

West ★★   The former wool-winding room of Glasgow's iconic Templeton Carpet Factory is now in the hand of a respected brewer, and you can sample the output as you sit in a Bavaria-worthy beer hall and look down into the brew house below. German/Scottish dishes accompany a fine selection of premium beers brewed according to German purity laws of 1516. Glasgow Green, East End. www.westbeer.com. ✆ **0141/550-0135.** Beer hall and restaurant daily 11am–9pm; bar daily 11am–11pm, Fri–Sat to midnight.

Spectator Sports & Outdoor Activities

FOOTBALL (SOCCER)   Glasgow has two main football teams: **Rangers** and **Celtic.** Rangers home ground is Ibrox Stadium (www.rangers.co.uk; ✆ **0871/702-1972**) and Celtic's home ground is Celtic Park (www.celticfc.net; ✆ **0871/226-1888**).

GOLF   **Glasgow Life** (www.glasgowlife.org.uk; ✆ **0141/287-4350**) manage six golf courses around the city and charge £12.60 for a round of 18 holes, £7.60 for 9 holes. Courses include **Lethamhill,** 1240 Cumbernauld Rd. (✆ **0141/276-0810**), which is set in mature parkland and is 3 miles northeast of the city center; and **Linn Park,** Simshill Road (℡ **0141/276-0702**), which boasts wide views of the city alongside good facilities. Two 9-hole courses are **Alexandra Park,** Alexandra Parade (℡ **0141/276-0600**), and **Knightswood,** Lincoln Avenue (℡ **0141/276-0700**). Visitors are advised to call 24 hours in advance to arrange tee times. Open daily from 10am to 5pm in winter, daily from 7am to 8pm in summer.

WATERSPORTS & ICE-SKATING   The **Lagoon Leisure Centre,** Mill Street, Paisley (www.renfrewshireleisure.com; ℡ **0141/889-4000**), offers indoor facilities that include a free-form pool with a wave machine and flume. You'll also find sauna suites with sun beds, Jacuzzis, and a Finnish steam room. The center is open Monday through Friday from 7am to 10pm and Saturday and Sunday from 9:30am to 5pm. A session in the pool costs £4 adults, £2 children 16 and under. There are frequent trains throughout the day from Glasgow Central Station to Paisley. **Braehead Arena,** King's Inch Rd. (www.braehead-arena.co.uk; ℡ **0141/886-8300**), 6 miles west of the center of Glasgow, converts to an Olympic-size ice skating rink during the winter. A peak-time session costs £7 for adults, £6 off-peak, and £6 for children 15 and under, £5 off-peak, and skate rental is £1. It's advisable to check in advance before heading out because this venue converts back to an arena when large concerts are scheduled.

SIDE TRIPS FROM GLASGOW

When Glaswegians want a quick fix of sea air, they head 35 miles or so west to the rugged Ayrshire coast. That also happens to be the place to pay homage to national poet **Robert Burns,** at his birthplace in Alloway.

Northwest of Glasgow

Ever since the 19th century, Glaswegians in need of a breath of fresh sea air have boarded trains for the 24-mile journey to Helensburgh, facing a broad stretch of the Firth of Clyde. The city's wealthy elite once built beautiful sea-facing villas here, and the one that will bring you to town these days is Hill House, by Charles Rennie Mackintosh. ScotRail trains leave from Glasgow Queen Street about every half hour, and the trip takes about an hour. From the station, it's about a mile walk to the house. Taxis are available.

Hill House ★★★ HISTORIC HOME   When Glasgow publisher Walter Blackie decided to build a house in Helensburgh in 1904, he turned to the architectural star of the day, Charles Rennie Mackintosh. The young architect and his wife, designer Margaret Macdonald, set to work, designing everything from the soothing, vaguely traditional exterior to all aspects of the Art Nouveau and Art Deco inspired interiors, right down to rose motifs on the fabrics and wall stencils, ladder back chairs, and fireplaces. The couple spent many hours with the Blackie family to determine how they preferred to live, and the effort shows through in the light-filled hallway, library, drawing room, and master bedroom, where sparse, white spaces contrast with handsome paneling and colored glass. Mackintosh earned a reputation for insisting upon complete control over a project, often to his clients' chagrin, but wandering through these beautiful, transporting rooms it's hard to imagine why anyone would want it any other way.

Upper Colquhoun St., Helensburgh. www.nts.org.uk. © **0844/493-2208**. £10.50 adults, £7.50 seniors and children 5–17, £24.50 families of 2 adults and 4 children, £18 families of 1 adult and 4 children. Daily 11:30am–5:30pm.

South of Glasgow

Two intriguing sights are just beyond the spread of Glasgow's southern suburbs and easy to reach by train and bus.

National Museum of Rural Life ★ MUSEUM Nothing about this well-done assemblage of displays, and a working farm, is coy or nostalgia-laden. Tractors, threshers, and other equipment in a huge barn-like pavilion show the move to mechanized farming and its effect on what was once an agricultural society. A 1950s-era farm captures a time when machines like these were starting to replace manpower and horsepower; cows, pigs, chickens, and sheep are reared as they would have been in ways that, even half a century ago, required considerably more labor—as you might realize when you milk one of the cows.

11 miles south of Glasgow. Wester Kittochside, Philipshill Rd., East Kilbride. www.nms. ac.uk. © **0300/123-6789**. £7 adults, £6 seniors, £4 children, £19 families of 2 adults and 2 children. Daily 10am–5pm. First bus no. 31.

New Lanark ★★★ HISTORIC SITE In 1799, Welsh social reformer Robert Owen took control of cotton mills powered by falls in the Clyde and established a community that would greatly improve workplace conditions. He did away with child labor and cruelly long work weeks, improved safety, and provided healthcare, education, and housing. Profits soared, though most of Owen's innovations would not be legislated into common practice for at least another century. Working machinery, a school, the company store, and the homes of Owen and a worker show what life was like in this enlightened place.

25 miles southeast of Glasgow, New Lanark Rd., off the A73. www.newlanark.org. © **01555/661345**. £12.50 adults, £10.50 seniors, £9 children 3–15, £38 families of 2 adults and up to 3 children. Apr–Sept daily 10am–5pm, Oct–Mar daily 11am–5pm. Train from Glasgow Central to Lanark station, connected by bus with New Lanark.

Northwest of Glasgow

Dumbarton Castle ★ CASTLE From the 5th century until 1018, Dumbarton was the center of the ancient kingdom of Strathclyde, and its castle was the kingdom's mighty fortress. This historic building hangs on a

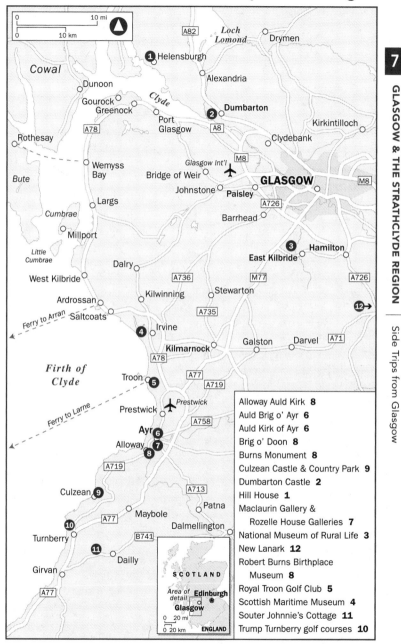

Alloway Auld Kirk **8**
Auld Brig o' Ayr **6**
Auld Kirk of Ayr **6**
Brig o' Doon **8**
Burns Monument **8**
Culzean Castle & Country Park **9**
Dumbarton Castle **2**
Hill House **1**
Maclaurin Gallery &
   Rozelle House Galleries **7**
National Museum of Rural Life **3**
New Lanark **12**
Robert Burns Birthplace
   Museum **8**
Royal Troon Golf Club **5**
Scottish Maritime Museum **4**
Souter Johnnie's Cottage **11**
Trump Turnberry golf courses **10**

volcanic rock perched beside the Firth of Clyde and offers stunning views and, surprisingly for a building whose history stretches back 1,500 years, fine examples of Georgian military architecture. The castle's Dark Age history is never far away and legends of Merlin and Viking raids run deep. Mary Queen of Scots also sought royal refuge at this dramatic site in 1548 while waiting to be whisked to safety in France.

Off the A814 at Dumbarton. www.historicenvironment.scot. © **01389/732-167.** Admission £5 adults, £4 seniors, £3 children 5–15. Apr–Sept daily 9:30am–5:30pm; Oct daily 9:30am–4:30pm; Nov–Mar Sat–Wed 10am–4pm. 20 miles northwest of Glasgow. A regular train service links Glasgow Queen Street with Dumbarton East.

Ayr ★

35 miles southwest of Glasgow

The largest and most popular resort on Scotland's west coast braces itself against the breezy Firth of Clyde at its confluence with the River Ayr. **ScotRail** trains from Glasgow's Central Station (www.scotrail.co.uk; © 0845/601-5929) whisk you to Ayr in 50 minutes. Ayr's **Tourist Information Centre** is at 22 Sandgate (www.ayrshire-arran.com; © 0845/225-5121). It's open year-round from 9am to 5 or 6pm Monday to Saturday, and Sunday from 10 or 11am to 5pm.

First order of business is to stroll along the town's noted seaside mile, past Georgian and Victorian houses that have seen some better days. Another walk, this one along the River Ayr, will introduce you to the local reverence for Scotland's unofficial national poet Robert Burns (1759–96). He was baptized in the **Auld Kirk of Ayr.** Looking out at the river from the gloomy old churchyard, you can see the setting for Burns' poem "Twa Brigs," in which the 13th-century **Auld Brig o' Ayr,** just north of the church, argues with the new bridge (completed in 1788) downstream, calling him a "conceited gawk."

EXPLORING THE TOWN

Ayr claims two main draws: its bracing seaside and Burns associations. The Scots always claimed that their mile differed in length to the English mile, and even after the Union of the Crowns in 1701 they continued to measure their own miles in their own way until the end of the 18th century. Ayr seafront still upholds the historic "lang Scots mile," partly in honor of Burns, who pays reference to it in his famous poem *Tam o' Shanter.* You can blow away the cobwebs and stroll the Scots mile, which leads south along the coast and measures about 5,952 feet.

In the town itself riverside walks lead past the **Auld Brig o' Ayr** and the **Auld Kirk of Ayr** (www.auldkirk.org), where Burns's father William served as an Elder. In the center of town on the High Street, the **Wallace Tower** rises 34m (112 ft.) and was constructed in 1828 on the site where the Scottish hero's father is thought to have lived.

Located about 1½ miles south of Ayr, on Monument Road in Rozelle Park, the **Rozelle House Galleries** (www.south-ayrshire.gov.uk/galleries; ✆ **01292/443-708**) exhibits a significant amount of work by Scottish artist Alexander Goudie alongside a major collection of contemporary art in the adjacent **Maclaurin Gallery.** Goudie (1933–2004) was born in nearby Paisley, attended Glasgow School of Art, and became one of Scotland's leading 20th century painters. His colorful 60-painting cycle illustrating Burns's narrative poem *Tam o' Shanter* hangs throughout Rozelle House and includes some terrifying images of dancing witches and warlocks. The surrounding 37 hectares (90 acres) of woodland are laced with nature trails and feature a craft shop and tearooms. The park leads off the B7024 (Monument Road) to Alloway and is open Monday through Saturday from 10am to 5pm and Sunday noon to 5pm. Admission is free.

The **Ayr Racecourse** (www.ayr-racecourse.co.uk; ✆ **01292/264-179**), about 1½ miles north of the town center (follow signs on the A77), is open year-round. Races are usually held Friday, Saturday, and Monday, generally at 2:15pm. Peak racing season is May to October, with jumping events held in November, January, and April. The Scottish Grand National is held mid-April.

Three golf courses are nearby; the best is the municipal **Belleisle Golf Course,** Doonfoot Rd., Alloway (www.ayrbelleislegolfclub.com; ✆ **01292/616-255**), and there are some three dozen courses in the surrounding area.

Alloway ★

2 miles south of Ayr

A Burns pilgrimage hits high gear in the pretty village where the poet was born in 1757. From Ayr, follow the A77 south, or take Stagecoach bus 57 (www.stagecoachbus.com; ✆ **01292/613-500**) from the seafront. A pleasant, well-marked route leads around the village to such spots as the tiny thatch-roofed gardener's cottage—the "auld clay biggin"—where the poet entered the world and lived until he was seven. The cottage and five other Burns sights in the village are part of the **Robert Burns Birthplace Museum ★** (www.burnsmuseum.org.uk; ✆ **0844/493-2601**). A handsome stone and timber gallery near the cottage houses the world's largest collection of Burns memorabilia, including a cast of his skull, his desk and spectacles, and some 500 manuscripts. The admission price includes a ride in the electric carts that run along the paths between the sights. The gallery is open daily 10am to 5pm daily, and the birthplace cottage is open daily 11am to 5pm. Admission is adults £10.50, seniors and children 5–17, £7.50, family of 2 adults and 2 children £24.50, family of 1 adult and 2 children £18.50.

Burns set part of his famous *Tam o' Shanter* in the ruins of **Alloway Auld Kirk,** where you can pause to read the poem, chiseled on the gravestone of the poet's father, William. The **Burns Monument** is the grandest building in town, a pillared Grecian-style pavilion from 1823 that houses a statue of the poet—one of many around the world, and they're plotted on a map with the boast that there are more statues to Burns on the planet than to any other writer. From gardens surrounding the monument you can see the River Doon slipping beneath the **Brig o' Doon,** the romantic-looking 13th-century stone span you may have just seen mentioned in your graveyard reading of *Tam o' Shanter.*

Troon ★

6¾ miles N of Ayr and 31 miles SW of Glasgow

The lively little windswept resort town has a huge sailing marina, six golf courses, and 1¾ miles of sandy beaches that stretch along both sides of the harbor. Troon takes its name from the curiously shaped promontory on which it sits, once called Trwyn, the Cymric word for "nose," which later became Trone, and finally Troon.

The **Royal Troon Golf Club** on Craigends Road (www.royaltroon.co.uk; ✆ **01292/311-555**) is one of the world's finest championship courses, founded in 1878 and nine-time host of the British Open. The 7,175-yard, par-71 **Old Course** is the more famous, while the 6,289-yard, par-71 **Portland** is, by some estimates, even more challenging. Visitors can play between mid-April and mid-October, on Monday, Tuesday, and Thursday; greens fees are £250 for the Old Course and £85 for Portland (Portland is £40 if played in conjunction with the Old Course). Mind what you wear: Shirts must have collars and be tucked into tailored trousers or shorts.

ScotRail trains from Glasgow's Central Station (www.scotrail.co.uk; ✆ **0845/601-5929**) bound for Ayr stop at Troon en route. The journey from Glasgow takes around 40 minutes.

Scottish Maritime Museum ★ MUSEUM Irvine harbor, 6 miles north of Troon, was once a major port and is now a major stop for maritime history buffs. A shipyard worker's tenement is restored to its 1920s state, and a collection of machinery, ships models, lifeboats, and other paraphernalia are stashed in a glorious glass-roofed Victorian shed. In the harbor are moored the SY *Carola,* built on the Clyde in 1898 and the oldest seagoing steam yacht in Great Britain, and the MV *Kyles,* a steam-engine cargo coaster launched in 1872, making it the oldest Clyde-built vessel still afloat. If you're feeling energetic, you can walk between Troon and Irvine on a well-marked coastal path.

Linthouse Building, Harbour Rd., Irvine. www.scottishmaritimemuseum.org. ✆ **01294/278-283.** £7.50 adults, £5.50 seniors and students, up to 3 children 16 and under free with holder of adult or senior ticket. Daily 10am–5pm. From Troon, follow A78 north. Trains from Glasgow Central bound for Ayr and Troon stop at Irvine train station.

WHERE TO EAT

The Highgrove ★ TRADITIONAL SCOTTISH Traditional Scottish taste merges with contemporary design on a hillside north of Troon. Diners can chose between a decor rich with tartan carpets and wood paneling or a glass pavilion, while feasting on terrific sea views and Scottish cuisine that's drawn from land and sea, with an especially lengthy menu of the freshest fish and seafood.

Old Loan's Rd., Troon. www.highgrovehouse.co.uk. © **01292/312-511.** Main courses £10–£17. Daily coffee shop menu served 9am–5pm, lunch noon–2:30pm, dinner 6–9:30pm. Drive 1¾ miles north of Troon on A78.

Turnberry ★

This small town has a big name, and some recent notoriety, for its **Trump Turnberry golf courses** (www.turnberry.co.uk; © **01655/331-000).** The 7,217-yard, par-70 Ailsa is one of the most exacting courses yet devised, with the added challenge of buffeting winds. The par-72 King Robert the Bruce frames glorious views of the coastline. Greens fees start at £200 on Ailsa and £90 on King Robert the Bruce. If you're exploring the coast by car, you might want to head 10 miles south of Turnberry past the little town of Girvan to the forlorn seaside ruins of **Carleton Castle.** According to local legend, laird of the castle Sir John Cathcart married and murdered seven women in order to get his hands on their money. He was foiled when his eighth wife, May, realized what he was up to and pushed him off the cliff to his death. It's said that Cathcart's desperate screams can still be heard; the tale is the inspiration for "The Ballad of May Colvin."

Culzean Castle & Country Park ★★★ CASTLE One of Scotland's finest stately homes may also be its most romantic. In the late 18th century, the Kennedy clan asked fashionable Scottish architect Robert Adam to revamp a medieval seaside castle and told him to go to town. Adams' formal designs are almost playful. The house seems to teeter on the edge of the cliff, the effect enhanced by a viaduct that crosses a precipice to the entrance. Inside, the two main spaces are circular, a sweeping grand staircase that ascends in graceful double arcs and a vast oval salon. Engaging as the interiors are, the surrounding 228-hectare (563-acre) park is just as magical, with ponds, pagodas, an orangery, beaches, woodlands, and an enchanting walled garden. Then-general Dwight D. Eisenhower stayed at Culzean during World War II.

4 miles north of Turnberry and 12 miles south of Ayr, off A719 near Maybole. www.nts. org.uk. © **0844/493-2149.** £16.50 adults, £12.25 seniors and children 5–15, £30–£41 families; country park only £11.50 adults, £8.25 seniors and children 5–15, £26.25 families with 2 adults and £19.50 families with 1 adult. Castle open Apr–Oct daily 10:30am–5pm; park open year-round daily 9:30am–sunset. Bus no. 57 from Turnberry or Ayr.

Souter Johnnie's Cottage ★ HISTORIC HOME This was the 18th-century home of the village cobbler, John Davidson (Souter Johnnie), who, with his friend Douglas Graham of Shanter Farm, was immortalized by Burns in *Tam o' Shanter*. Burns met the men, whom you'll encounter in the form of life-size sandstone statues, when he spent a summer in the village. Burns described "scenes of swaggering riot and roaring dissipation," but Davidson remained sober enough to use the tools on display and amass the fine furniture in the cottage rooms.

Main Road, in Kirkoswald, 3 miles west of Turnberry via A77. www.nts.org.uk. ⓒ **0844/493-2147.** Free admission. Apr–Sept Fri–Tues 11:30am–5pm.

WHERE TO EAT & STAY

Glenapp Castle ★★ This superbly restored and sumptuously decorated Scottish baronial castle from 1870 stands 14½ hectares (36 acres) of stunning gardens and woodlands riddled with walks and wildlife, high above a tiny village overlooking the Irish Sea around 20 miles southwest of Turnberry. Elegant lounges and dining rooms await you inside this vast Victorian mansion along with 17 spacious and individually furnished bedrooms and suites. Antiques and oil paintings spread through every room and high Victorian windows allow the sun to stream through. Some of the finest wine cellars complement a gourmet experience for which the kitchen makes full use of produce grown in its own gardens. Glenapp is also very family friendly and lays on books, games, and DVDs for its young visitors.

Ballantrae, Ayrshire on the A77. www.glenappcastle.com. ⓒ **01465/831-212.** 17 units. £380–£525 double. Rates include all meals. **Amenities:** Restaurant; bar; tennis court; croquet lawn; room service; free Wi-Fi.

Malin Court Hotel ★ Views over one of the most beautiful strips of the Ayrshire coast, the Firth of Clyde, and the Turnberry golf courses are the main features of these modern, medium-sized guest rooms that provide an especially good-value getaway given the surrounding scenery. Cotters restaurant augments the stunning location with relaxed service and traditional Scottish fare from the finest local ingredients. In addition to golf, the staff can also arrange hunting, fishing, riding, and sailing.

Off the A719 between Turnberry and Middens. www.malincourt.co.uk. ⓒ **01655/331-457.** 18 units. £105 double. Rates include breakfast. **Amenities:** Restaurant; bar; room service; free Wi-Fi.

Trump Turnberry Resort ★★ This remarkable and opulent seaside Edwardian property, built in 1908, has long been a legendary Ayrshire landmark, and, for better or worse, has become even more so now that the wide white facade, red-tile roof, and dozens of gables are all part of the empire of one of the world's better-known real estate moguls. As befits the namesake's extravagant taste, public areas are awash with Waterford crystal chandeliers, ionic columns, molded ceilings, and oak paneling. Classically styled guest rooms are only a little less glitzy, with marble-sheathed bathrooms, and views of the lawns, forests, and (in the best) the Scottish coastline. Many guests gravitate here to make full use of the resort's championship golf courses, but other leisure facilities such as its large sea-facing indoor pool and serene spa are equally first class.

Maidens Rd., Turnberry. www.turnberry.co.uk. © **01655/331-000.** 221 units. £145–£450 double. 50 miles south of Glasgow off the A77. **Amenities:** 3 restaurants; 3 bars; pool (indoor); 2 tennis courts; health club and spa; bike rental; concierge; room service; babysitting; free Wi-Fi.

ARGYLL & THE SOUTHERN HEBRIDES

By Stephen Brewer

8

The lands of Argyll comprise much of the west of Scotland, a generous sweep of forests, mountains, and lochs. In the far southern reaches is Kintyre, the long narrow peninsula that stretches from southwest Scotland toward Ireland, and in the seas around this long, scenic sliver of mainland are a cluster of beautiful islands. A certain enchantment takes hold here in the west. Golden eagles sore over Arran's craggy mountains, seals and otters swim along the shores of sea lochs and bays around Inveraray, deer and wild sheep scramble across moors and glens on Jura. Add the peaty single malt whiskies of Islay, and top it all off with the freshest seafood you'll ever taste and you begin to understand the great allure of these mountains, forests, moors, and coasts.

Don't Leave Argyll & the Southern Hebrides Without . . .

Enjoying the view of Inveraray from the shores of Loch Fyne. The collection of tidy white houses looks almost picture perfect, just as the duke of Argyll intended when he had the whole town rebuilt in the 18th century to match his castle.

Ambling down the Kintyre Peninsula. As if the moors, forests, and rocky coastlines weren't scenic enough, all this beauty hits a high note at land's end, where you might agree with Sir Paul McCartney, "My desire is always to be here, Oh Mull of Kintyre."

Make the rounds on Arran. An endless panorama of moors, mountains, and rocky coastlines come into view on a 60-mile circuit around this enchanting island, making it easy to see where the moniker "Scotland in Miniature" comes from.

Argyll & the Southern Hebrides

Getting a taste of the tropics at Arduaine Gardens. It's an intoxicating mixture: A setting on the southern slopes of the Arduaine Peninsula next to the Sound of Jura and a colorful display of Tibetan poppies and Himalayan lilies that thrive here in a microclimate next to the sea.

Sipping whisky on Islay. Aficionados from around the world come to sample smoky single malts at eight distilleries, while taking time out to gaze at sea cliffs and bask in the tiny island's many other natural wonders.

INVERARAY ★★

57 miles NW of Glasgow

Splendidly poised on the upper shores of Loch Fyne, Inveraray, seat of the dukes of Argyll, is especially lovely when seen from the east. As you approach from Glasgow, the town begins to take shape as a trim collection of white houses arranged tidily on a finger of land jutting out into the loch. The little resort town does not offer a lot to see and do, and that's just fine. Sitting on a bench and looking across the sparkling waters of the loch can fill a few happy hours.

Essentials

GETTING THERE   The CityLink-926 Service (www.citylink.co.uk; ℭ 08712/663-333) operates **buses** out of Glasgow to Inveraray. The journey takes about 2 hours. If you're **driving** from Glasgow, follow the A82 north and east to its junction with A83 for the final leg east to Inveraray.

VISITOR INFORMATION   The **Tourist Information Centre** is on Front Street (www.inveraray-argyll.com; ℭ **01499/302-063**). It's open from June to mid-September, daily 9am to 6pm; with reduced hours the rest of the year.

Exploring the Area

When the Duke of Argyll revamped his castle in the 18th century, he went all out and redid the whole town as well. That explains the remarkably orderly arrangement of white houses with black trim and black-slate roofs. The duke built cottages for workers, a woolen mill, and a pier to boost the export of herring pulled from the loch (herring appear on the town coat of arms, and the town motto translates as "May a herring always hang to thee.") Another town symbol is a **Celtic burial cross** imported from the Hebrides island of Iona that now stands next to the lakefront in the center of town. A nice place to take it all the surrounding natural beauty is the **Ardkinglas Woodland Garden ★** (www.ardkinglas.com; ℭ **01499/600-261**), where conifers and rhododendrons thrive on a 4,800-hectare (12,000-acre) estate at the head of Loch Fyne 4 miles east of town. Admission is £5 for adults, £15 for families; it's open daily from 9am to 5pm. At **Crarae Garden ★** (www.nts.org.uk; ℭ **0844/493-2210**), 8 miles southwest of Inveraray, cliffs, a gorge, and a rippling stream on a wooded hillside along Loch Fyne are planted with rare Asian species and in a scene reminiscent of a Himalayan woodland valley. Admission is £7.50 adults, £5.50 seniors and children 5 to 16, £12.50 families of one adult, 18.50 families of 2 adults. The gardens are open year-round daily 9:30am to sunset.

Inveraray Castle ★★ CASTLE   The dukes of Argyll, chiefs of the Clan Campbell, have occupied their hereditary seat since the early 15th century. But their gray-green stone castle, all crenulations and pointy-roofed turrets, is a wildly romantic 18th-century Gothic Revival version of what the fifth duke thought an ancestral seat should look like. The Victorian Room pays homage to Princess Louise, the daughter of Queen Victoria and Prince Albert, who married the 9th duke in 1871. While salons and staterooms are appointed with some excellent art works and dainty 18th-century French furniture and old porcelain, the standout is the remarkable, 1,300-piece collection of arms, from battle axes to muskets. It's on display in the Armory Hall beneath a 21m (69-ft.) ceiling, the highest in Scotland. The castle has a shop and a tea room. Fans of *Downton Abbey* might recognize the castle and grounds—they stood in for Duneagle Castle, home of the Marquess and Marchioness of Flintshire, whom the Grantham/Crawley clan travels north to visit.

Main St., Inveraray. www.inveraray-castle.com. © **01499/302-381.** £11 adults, £10 seniors, £8 children 5–16, families of 2 adults and 2 or more children, £32. Apr–Oct daily 10am–5:45pm.

Inveraray Jail ★★ MUSEUM Ever wonder what it was like to be locked up in a small cell with a lunatic or strapped to a whipping table? Well, you'll learn more than you ever wanted to know about the ins and outs of the British penal system in an exhaustive tour of recreated cells, torture chambers, and a Victorian-era courtroom. The setting is realistic enough, a formidable complex of 3-foot-thick stone walls that served as Inveraray's prison from 1820 to 1889. Sound effects (jangling keys, screams, the sound of footfalls) accompany your visit, as do taped commentary of prisoners' stories and extracts from 19th-century trials. You'll leave on a bright note, with a visit to a modern cell that seems like the Ritz compared to the accommodations of yore.

Church Sq., Inveraray. www.inverarayjail.co.uk. © **01499/302-203.** £11.95 adults, £10.75 seniors, £8.95 students, £7.25 children. Apr–Oct daily 9:30am–6pm; Nov–Mar daily 10am–5pm.

Around Inveraray

ARGYLL FOREST PARK ★★★

Some of Scotland's most dramatic scenery, from lush forests to bleak moorlands and mountains, spreads west from Loch Fyne to the coast, where fjord-like sea lochs cut deeply into forested hillsides. In all, Argyll Forest Park covers an area of 24,000 hectares (59,000 acres), extending north into the so-called Arrochar Alps, where Ben Arthur reaches a height of 877m (2,877 ft.). In the early spring and summer, the forest trails are at their most beautiful—woodland birds sing out their territorial rights, and the forest is filled with violets, wood anemones, primroses, and bluebells. Sometimes the wildflowers are as thick as carpets. Ferns and mosses also grow in abundance in the rainy climate. More challenging trails lead up the loftier peaks, and the sea lochs are habitats for sea otters and gray seals. An easy gateway to the park is Dunoon, 38 miles south of Inveraray on the Cowal Peninsula; follow the A83 to the A815 for the scenic, hour-long drive. Dunoon has been a holiday resort since 1790, created for the merchant princes of Glasgow, and later, with steamer service along the River Clyde, was a place for working-class

Glaswegians to spend a holiday "doon the watter." To pick up info about the park and a trail map, stop in at the Dunoon Tourist Centre, 7 Alexandra Parade (www.visitcowal.co.uk; ℂ **01369/703-785;** Apr–Sept Mon–Fri 9am–5:30pm and Sat–Sun 10am–5pm, Oct–Mar daily 9am–5pm, 4pm only Sun).

AROUND THE CRINAN CANAL ★★

The Crinan Canal starts at Ardrishaig on Loch Fyne and ends 9 miles away at the village of Crinan on the Sound of Jura. Ardrishaig is 27 miles south of Inveraray, via the A83, which scenically follows the eastern shores of the loch for much of the way. The canal was completed in 1801 to provide a quick link between the Clyde Estuary and the west coast and islands, avoiding the long voyage around the Kintyre Peninsula. Commercial sailing vessels once plied the waters, though today sailors and yachters navigate the canal purely for recreation. Even staying on dry land along the towpath is a picturesque outing that leads past 15 locks, seven bridges, two lighthouses, and numerous lock-keepers' cottages.

The varied landscapes of Knapdale spread south from the canal, and part of the flat lands are covered by Knapdale Forest. To explore these varied landscapes by land, follow the canal along the B841 west from Ardrishaig toward Crinan. At Bellanoch, about 7 miles west of Ardrishaig, is **Moine Mhor,** or "Great Moss" (www.nature.scot; ℂ **01546/603-611**), a water world of pools and bogs that are home to hen harriers and ospreys in the summer, and geese and swans in winter. Trails into Moine Mhor lead off the towpath outside Bellanoch. Just east of Crinan, a turn onto the B8025 toward the village of Taynish leads south about 8 miles to the **Taynish National Nature Reserve** (www.nature.scot; ℂ **01546/603-611**), a breeding ground for up to 20 species of butterflies and on the migratory routes of many rare birds.

Kilmartin Glen, north of the canal and 10 miles north of Ardrishaig via the A83 and A816, was 1,500 years ago a center of the vast Kingdom of Dalriada, spreading across Northern Ireland into this part of Western Scotland. In the mid-9th century, Dalriada king Kenneth I brought warring Pict and Scoti peoples together to form the kingdom of Scotland. More than 800 ancient sites and monuments, including standing stones, burial tombs, and forts, litter the grassy glen. At the **Kilmartin House Museum** (www.kilmartin.org; ℂ **01546/510-278**), you can see archaeological finds and get maps and information to help you locate the most important monuments. The museum is open March to October daily from 10am to 5:30pm, November to December daily from 11am to 4pm; closed from Christmas to the end of February. Admission is £5 for adults, £4 for seniors, and £2 for children,

From Kilmartin, the A816 leads 10 miles north onto the **Arduaine Peninsula,** wedged between the Sound of Jura to the south and Loch Melfort to the north. These coastal landscapes comprise something of a promised land, since here in chilly Scotland they're blessed with the North Atlantic Drift, ensuring a relatively fair amount of sun and warmth.

Arduaine Gardens ★★ PARK/GARDENS As if the setting on the southern slopes of the Arduaine Peninsula next to the Sound of Jura weren't spectacular enough, these 8 hectares (20 acres) are laced with a colorful display of Tibetan poppies, Himalayan lilies, and other species that thrive in temperate zones around the world, especially eastern Asia and South America. The gardens were planted around the turn of the century as part of the Arduaine House estate, now the adjacent Loch Melfort Hotel (see below). Horticulturalist brothers Edmund and Harry Wright nurtured them back to robust health in the 1970s and 80s. Barriers of hearty evergreens protect the gardens from sea gales, allowing many different species of rhododendrons to thrive among ferns, mosses, and tender plants that carpet slopes besides ponds and streams. Well-maintained paths weave through the gardens and end at a breezy bluff above the sea.

Arduaine, 15 miles north of the Crinan Canal on A816. www.arduainegarden.org. ℗ **01852/200-366.** £6.50 adults, £5 seniors and children 5–16, £12–£16.50 families of 2 adults, £11.50 families of 1 adult. Daily 9:30am–sunset.

Where to Stay & Eat

Crinan Hotel ★★★ Frances Macdonald—one of the operators of this 1930s lodge perched at the point where the Crinan Canal flows into Loch Crinan—is a well-known landscape artist, and it's easy to see where she gets her inspiration. Sparkling blue water and achingly green hillsides fill every window, and views extend out to the Hebrides. Being in the light, airy bedrooms is a lot like floating across the loch on a boat, and a top floor lounge is filled with dizzying crow's nest outlooks. Downstairs are comfy sitting rooms and a cozy pub room where fishermen and yachters gather to chat over meals of local seafood. The village is a good starting point for walks along the Crinan Canal Towpath.

Crinan. www.crinanhotel.com. ℗ **01546/830-261.** 20 units. Double from £100, includes breakfast. **Amenities:** 2 restaurants; bar; free Wi-Fi.

Loch Fyne ★★ The Loch Fyne chain of popular restaurants operates around the U.K., but none can compare to the fresh-from-the-source experience in this attractive room of white stone walls. Oysters, mussels, and much of the other seafood on the menu has just been hauled out of the loch a few steps away. Even breakfast can be a feast of Loch Fyne kippers and house-smoked salmon. A shop sells Loch Fyne's famous smoked fish.

Clachan, 8 miles east of Inveraray. www.lochfyne.com. ℗ **01499/600-264.** Mains £11–£28. Mon–Thurs 9am–5:30pm, Fri–Sun 9am–7:30pm (9am–4pm in winter).

Loch Melfort Hotel ★★ When diamond and tea merchant James Arthur Campbell designed his house in 1898, he wanted to take advantage of views far across Asknish Bay to the islands off the west coast. Next to the mansion he planted what have become some of the finest seaside gardens in Scotland (see Arduaine Gardens, above). Five character-filled rooms are in the old house, while the rest are in an atmospheric motor-lodge-like extension. Just about all take advantage of the views from terraces and balconies. Dinner in a large sea-facing room begins and ends with drinks in the gracious lounges, making you feel like you're a guest at a private Scottish retreat.

Arduaine, 15 miles north of the Crinan Canal on A816. www.lochmelfort.co.uk. © **01852/200-233.** 25 units. Doubles £140–£204, includes breakfast (dinner, bed, and breakfast rates available). **Amenities:** 2 restaurants; bar; beach; free Wi-Fi.

LOCH AWE & LOCH ETIVE ★

17 miles NW of Inveraray, 68 miles NW of Glasgow

Only 1 mile wide in most places and 22 miles long, Loch Awe is the longest lake in Scotland and once served as a freshwater moat protecting the Campbells of Inveraray from their enemies to the north. For good measure the Campbells added all those now-ruined fortifications you'll see along the banks. To the north, the waters flow into Loch Etive, which itself flows into the Atlantic at the west coast village of Connel. Wild countryside rises from the banks of both lochs, with the bulk of **Ben Cruachan** rising to 1,119m (3,671 ft.) at the north end of Loch Awe to loom above the surrounding, craggy peaks.

From Inveraray, the A819 heads north for 14 miles to the ruins of **Kilchurn Castle,** at the northern tip of Loch Awe. One of the most photogenic of all Scottish castles seems to rise from the water, with stark hillsides looming behind a tall tower and the remains of a massive barracks that could house 200 troops. From here the A85 continues west through the Pass of Brander to meet Loch Etive as it flows toward the sea.

Where to Eat & Stay

Hotel Ardanaiseig ★★   This gray-stone manor house is set amid some of the most spectacular scenery in Scotland, with Loch Awe in the foreground and Ben Cruachan forming a backdrop. Enhancing all this natural beauty are rare trees planted when the house was built in 1834. As wild as the surroundings are, the house is sophisticated in a shabby chic sort of way, with a hodgepodge of quirky antiques set against deep colors and a flamboyant decor that manages to be welcoming and relaxed. The in-house restaurant is worth a trip in itself, and a good thing, too, as dining options are few and far between here in the remote uplands.

Kilchrenan by Taynuilt, about 30 miles north of Inveraray via A819 to A85 and B845. www.ardanaiseig.com. © **01866/833-333.** 16 units. From £185 double. Closed Jan to mid-Feb. **Amenities:** Restaurant; tennis court; free Wi-Fi.

THE ISLE OF ARRAN ★★

So many glens, moors, lochs, sandy bays, and stretches of rocky coast are packed onto this small island near the mouth of the Firth of Clyde that the overused moniker "Scotland in Miniature" could not ring truer. A single day on this speck of scenic beauty, only 25 miles long and 10 miles wide, might make you want to stay forever.

The Isle of Arran & the Kintyre Peninsula

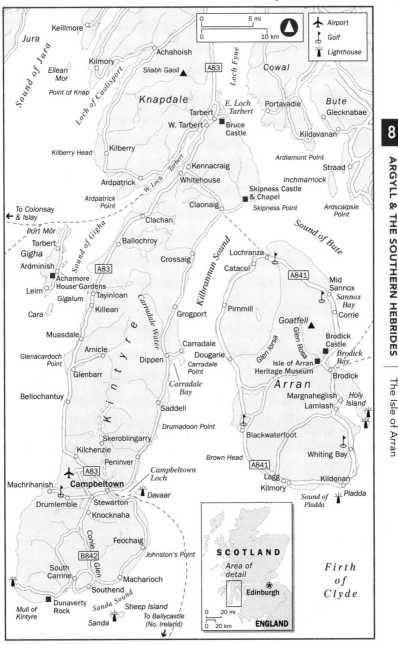

Legend:
- ✈ Airport
- ⛳ Golf
- 🗼 Lighthouse

Scale: 0 — 5 mi / 0 — 10 km

Jura
Keillmore
Kilmory
Eilean Mor
Achahoish
Sliabh Gaoil ▲
A83
Loch Fyne
Cowal
Point of Knap
Loch of Caolisport
Knapdale
E. Loch Tarbert
Tarbert
W. Tarbert
Bruce Castle
Portavadie
Bute
Glecknabae
Kildavanan
Sound of Jura
Kilberry Head
Kilberry
W. Loch Tarbert
Kennacraig
Whitehouse
Ardlamont Point
Inchmarnock
Straad
Ardpatrick
Ardpatrick Point
Claonaig
Skipness Castle & Chapel
Skipness Point
Ardscalpsie Point
To Colonsay & Islay ←
Clachan
Sound of Bute
Port Mór
Tarbert
Gigha
Ardminish
Ballochroy
Crossaig
Lochranza
Catacol
A841
Mid Sannox
Sannox Bay
Sound of Gigha
Achamore House Gardens
A83
Leim
Gigalum
Tayinloan
Killean
Grogport
Pirnmill
Goatfell ▲
Corrie
Cara
Kilbrannan Sound
Glen Iorsa
Glen Rosa
Brodick Castle
Muasdale
Arnicle
Dippen
Carradale
Dougarie
Carradale Point
Isle of Arran Heritage Museum
Brodick Bay
Glenacardoch Point
Carradale Water
Carradale Bay
Arran
Brodick
Glenbarr
Kintyre
Margnaheglish
Holy Island
Bellochantuy
Saddell
Lamlash
Drumadoon Point
Blackwaterfoot
Skeroblingarry
Kilchenzie
Peninver
Whiting Bay
Machrihanish
A83
Campbeltown
Campbeltown Loch
Brown Head
A841
Lagg
Kildonan
Drumlemble
Stewarton
Davaar
Kilmory
Sound of Pladda
Pladda
Knocknaha
Conie Glen
Feochaig
Johnston's Point
Firth of Clyde
B842
South Carrine
Macharioch
Southend
Mull of Kintyre
Dunaverty Rock
Sanda Sound
Sheep Island
To Ballycastle (No. Ireland) ↓
Sanda

SCOTLAND
Area of detail
Edinburgh ✶
ENGLAND
0 — 20 mi
0 — 20 km

Essentials

GETTING THERE   Express **trains** (www.nationalrail.co.uk; ✆ **08475/484-950**) operate from Glasgow Central direct to Ardrossan Harbour, taking 1 hour. If you're **driving** from Glasgow, follow A737 to Ardrossan, 33 miles southwest.

From Ardrossan, you'll make a 45-minute ferry crossing to Brodick, Arran's main town, on the east coast. **Caledonian MacBrayne** (www.calmac.co.uk; ✆ **0800/066-5000**) operates up to six boats daily. If you're bringing a car onboard, the company requires you arrive no later than 30 minutes before departure—they enforce this policy with rigor.

VISITOR INFORMATION   The **Tourist Information Centre (TIC)** is at the Pier, Brodick (www.ayrshire-arran.com; ✆ **01770/303-774;** Mon–Sat 9am–5pm, Sun July–Oct only 10am–5pm). If you plan on hiking, look for one of two detailed guides at the tourist office—*Seventy Walks in Arran* and *My Walks in Arran*—and ask about guided walks.

Exploring the Island

You'll encounter some splendid mountain scenery almost as soon as you step off the ferry in the pleasant little settlement of Brodick. Nearby, the conical peak of **Goatfell** (called the "mountain of the winds") reaches a height of 869m (2,851 ft.). The mountainous north is also laced with some beautiful glens, none more transporting than **Glen Sannox** and **Glen Rosa,** just north of Brodick.

As you drive around the island (the full 60-mile circuit should take about 3 hours) you'll pass long stretches of pebbly shoreline and several small settlements. **Lochranza,** in the north, opens onto a bay of pebbles and sand. The ruined castle nearby was reputedly the hunting seat of Robert the Bruce (1274–1329). Little **Lamlash,** on a pretty bay along the southeast coast, is where the Viking fleet prepared for the 1263 Battle of Largs. The village is now the jumping off point for Holy Island (six daily ferries make the crossing in season), where Scotland's own 6th-century Saint Molaise returned from a pilgrimage to Rome and took up residence in a cave at the base of 303m (994-ft.) Mullach Mor. A Buddhist community now owns the islet, though visitors are welcome to hike alongside the goats and wild ponies roaming the rough terrain.

About 6 miles south of Lamlash, a well-marked path leads from the highway for a mile or so through fern-carpeted woodlands to **Glenashdale,** a double waterfall that plunges 130-feet into a forest gorge.

Arran Distillery ★★ SHOP/TOUR   The telltale copper roofs at the edge of Lochranza, and often the presence of golden eagles floating overhead, signals the presence of Arran's prestigious distillery, founded in 1995. The operation carries on a long island tradition from the early 19th century when more than 50 Arran distillers were producing what many connoisseurs consider to be among the best of Scottish single malts. The malts are said to acquire their taste from the pure waters of Loch na Davie and the combo of sea breezes, mountain air, and the warm flow of the Gulf Stream. Judge the quality of the output with a draught or two, offered in a tasting room/shop and at the end of an engaging tour.

Lochranza. www.arranwhisky.com. ⓒ **01770/830-264.** £8 and £15, based on tastings. Mar–Nov daily 10am–5:30pm. Winter hours vary.

Brodick Castle ★★ CASTLE   If the historic home of the dukes of Hamilton looks familiar, it's because you've seen it on the back of 20-pound notes issued by the Bank of Scotland. Aristocracy has lived here at the base of Goatfell Mountain since the Dalriada Irish, a Celtic tribe, founded their kingdom in the 5th century. The red-sandstone castle dates from the 13th century, though a 19th-century redo is in the style of a grand Victorian hunting lodge. The sitting rooms and bedrooms seem almost homey once you get past the 87 sets of stag horns in the main hall and grand staircase. The ghost of one of the dungeon inmates, a woman locked away to starve to death as she succumbed to the plague, still haunts the paneled hallways. The specter of a white stag is said to roam the beautiful gardens, laced with streams and waterfalls and overlooking Brodick Bay. His presence supposedly foretells the death of a chief of the Hamiltons; the castle has long since passed out of their hands, which may explain the presence of so many deer in the fern-carpeted woodlands.

1½ miles north of the Brodick pier head. www.nts.org.uk. ⓒ **0844/493-2152.** Castle and gardens £14 adults, £10 seniors, students, and children ages 6–16, £24 families of 1 adults and 2 children, £31 families of 1 adults and 3 children. Gardens £7.50 adults, £19 families of 2 adults and 3 children, £15 families of 1 adult and 3 children. Castle: Apr–Oct daily 11am–4pm (until 3pm in Oct); gardens and park: year round, daily 9:30am–sunset.

Isle of Arran Heritage Museum ★ MUSEUM   A snuggly furnished cottage, blacksmith shop, and 1920s schoolroom recall island life over the centuries. The well-done archaeology room reaches into the far distant past to tell the story of 5,000-year-old Clachaig Man, whose remains were unearthed on the island, and delves into the significance of the Machrie Stone Circle and other remnants of early Arran inhabitants. Geology exhibits explain what brings rock hounds from around the world to Arran to scour the terrain for some incredibly rare igneous specimens.

Rosaburn, 1½ miles north of the Brodick ferry piers. www.arranmuseum.co.uk. ⓒ **01770/302-636.** £4 adults, £3 seniors, £2 children, £9 families. Apr–Oct daily 10:30am–4:30pm.

Where to Stay & Eat

Auchrannie House Hotel ★★   The dowager duchess of Hamilton would probably be pleased to see what's become of her Victorian mansion. She and just about everyone else should certainly be impressed with the two large indoor swimming pools, saunas, and other resort amenities that are a lot fancier than anyone might expect to find on the little island. Rooms in the old manor house are especially atmospheric, while new outbuildings on the estate house bright, spacious, and handsomely styled rooms, along with 30 two- and three-bedroom "lodges" with kitchens and woody, cabin-like couple's retreats with wood-fired hot tubs. Three dining rooms include a delightful conservatory where diners enjoy nice views of swaying palm trees through the glass panes.

Auchrannie Rd., Brodick. www.auchrannie.co.uk. © **01770/302-234.** 70 units. Doubles from £120, includes breakfast. **Amenities:** 3 restaurants; bar; 2 pools (indoor); gym; spa; sauna; free Wi-Fi.

Brodick Bar and Brasserie ★ SEAFOOD/SCOTTISH Don't let the plain, tartan-themed decor deceive you: This is one of the best places on the island for a good meal, and in the unlikely event you're tired of fresh seafood you're in luck. Specialties include Arran lamb and beef, along with hand-dived scallops, local shellfish, and just-caught fish.

Alma Rd., Brodick. www.brodickbar.co.uk. © **01770/302-169.** Mains £9–£24. Mon–Sat noon–2:30pm and 5:30–9pm (until 10:30pm on Fri and Sat); bar until midnight.

The Douglas ★★ This stunning Victorian landmark is the first manmade beauty to catch your notice as you step off the ferry, while views from the lounges and enormous guest rooms are of the island's natural spectacle of glimmering sea and jagged mountains. You can enjoy these outlooks from the plump armchairs next to high windows in your own quarters, but the sophisticated bar and bistro downstairs are also inviting, and menus show off island mussels and scallops alongside lamb and game. The fireside lounges are very well suited to enjoying a dram from the island's own distillery.

Shore Rd., Brodick. www.thedouglashotel.co.uk. © **01770/302-968.** Doubles from £149, includes breakfast. **Amenities:** Restaurant; bar; free Wi-Fi.

Shopping

Arran Aromatics (© **01770/302-595**), in an old dairy farm near Brodick Castle, sells high-end toiletries and cosmetics made on Arran, including some fragrances for the home that will make your visit last long after you leave the island. The **Old Byre Showroom,** Auchencar Farm (www.oldbyre.co.uk; © **01770/840-227**), 5 miles north of Blackwaterfoot along the coastal road in Machrie, is a good source for sheepskin, leather, and tweeds, but its biggest draw is the large selection of locally produced woolen sweaters.

THE KINTYRE PENINSULA ★★

The longest peninsula in Scotland seems like an island, surrounded by water except for a wee slip of land, often approached by ferry, and seemingly lost in a sleepy world of its own. Kintyre drops 30 miles south from the old fishing village of Tarbert. The southern end of the peninsula looks toward Ireland across 12 choppy miles of the Mull of Kintyre, immortalized by local resident Paul McCartney, and the east coast faces the island of Arran. This scenic sliver of land is wonderfully isolated, and its quiet glens and woodlands rise and fall above pebbly shorelines that are largely unspoiled.

Essentials

GETTING THERE & GETTING AROUND **Loganair** (www.flybe.com; ℂ **0871/700-2000**) makes two scheduled 45-minute **flights** a day from Glasgow Airport to Campbeltown, the chief town of Kintyre. From Glasgow, the trip by **Scottish CityLink buses** (www.citylink.co.uk; ℂ **08705/505-050**) to Tarbert, Campbeltown, and other towns along the peninsula takes about 4 to 5 hours (schedules vary seasonally).

The most efficient way to travel to and around Kintyre is by **car.** Though Tarbert, at the northern end of the peninsula, is due west of Glasgow, the drive takes you a bit out of your way, but scenically so, quite a way north along the scenic shores of Loch Lomond then back south along Loch Fyne. From Glasgow, take the A82 up to Loch Lomond and cut across to Arrochar and over the "Rest and Be Thankful" route to Inveraray (the A83). Then drive down along Loch Fyne to Lochgilphead and continue on the A83 south to Tarbert, which is the gateway to the peninsula. Allow about 2½ hours for the trip. The two-lane A83 follows the western coast of the peninsula to Campbeltown, while the scenic but much slower single-track B842 drops down the eastern shore (take your time along this road, yield to sheep, and use the turnouts to accommodate oncoming traffic).

Tarbert ★

103 miles W of Glasgow

The name of this sheltered harbor derives from a Gaelic word meaning isthmus, because this is where the Vikings used to drag their boats from Loch Fyne across the mile-wide neck of land that connects the Kintyre Peninsula to the rest of Scotland. Some of the fishermen who live in the pretty village houses beneath the ruined castle of Robert the Bruce still haul herring and shellfish out of the waters of Loch Fyne (see Inveraray, p. 204), but these days the docks are mostly crowded with pleasure craft.

Campbeltown ★

37 miles S of Tarbert, 140 miles SW of Glasgow

This fishing port at the southern tip of the Kintyre Peninsula is charmingly old fashioned. So much so that the way locals refer to it simply as the "wee toon" makes perfect sense. The 14th-century Celtic **Campbeltown Cross** ★ stands picturesquely next to quays that are crowded with fishing boats and yachts. Similar scenes are captured in a decent collection of paintings by Scottish artists in the **Campbeltown Museum** (www.museumsgalleriesscotland.org.uk; ℂ **01586/559-017**), in the center of town on St John's Street. Among them is a seascape by William McTaggart, who was born in Campbeltown in 1835 and went on to become one of Scotland's best-known landscape painters. He returned to Campbeltown continually, drawn by the light and scenery, and it's been said that being in Kintyre is like stepping into his paintings. (You'll also see them at the National Galleries of Scotland and other museums.)

The **Kintyre Way** ★★ is one of Scotland's most scenic long-distance walks. It stretches for 89 miles, beginning at Tarbert in the north of the peninsula and rambling all the way down to the village of Southend. Hikers generally complete the route in 4 to 7 days. Some of the miles that traverse hill terrain can be difficult, although nothing to challenge the serious hiker. Most of the walk is a gentle ramble through low-lying terrain along the rugged coastline, taking in castles, woodlands, and wildlife along the way. Pep Cars taxi service (www.pepcars.co.uk; ✆ **01880/730-369**) will transport luggage from point to point along the route. Pick up a map of the trail at any local tourist office or visit www.kintyreway.com.

Cambeltown's **Wee Picture House,** 20 Hall St. (www.campbeltownpicturehouse.co.uk; ✆ 07938/713-900) occupies an Art Deco building from 1913 and is believed to be the oldest surviving purpose-built cinema in Scotland.

The **Tourist Information Centre** is at MacKinnon House, The Pier (www.visitscottishheartlands.com; ✆ **01586/552-056**). Hours vary, with longer summer hours, but you can mostly count on it being open 10am to 5pm Monday to Saturday and 11am to 4 or 5pm on Sundays.

Some of southern Scotland's finest golf courses are near Campbeltown. About 5 miles east are the historic **Machrihanish Golf Club** (www.machgolf.com; ✆ **01586/810-277**) and **Machrihanish Dunes** (www.machrihanishdunes.com; ✆ **01586/810-000**). The 18-hole **Dunaverty Golf Course** (www.dunavertygolfclub.com; ✆ **01586/830-677**) is outside Southend.

Southend & the Mull of Kintyre ★★

Southend is 10 miles S of Campbeltown

Land's end on Kintyre is near the village of Southend. A debate has been raging for centuries about the origins of the footprint-shaped indentations on a rock near the town's old chapel. Some claim the prints mark the spot where St Columba first set foot on Scottish soil. Others suggest that they mark the spot where ancient kings were crowned. Just about everyone agrees that some of the most savagely beautiful seascapes in Scotland surround the lighthouse south of town on the Mull of Kintyre. Let Paul McCartney's lyrics inspire you as you make the trip out to the desolate point along a single track road: "Mull of Kintyre, oh mist rolling in from the sea/My desire is always to be here/Oh Mull of Kintyre."

WHERE TO STAY & EAT

Two places for live music are next door to each other on Cross St. in Campbeltown. **The Feathers Inn** (www.thefeathersinn.co.uk; ✆ **01586/554-604**) hosts groups on Thursday and Friday nights, while the **Commercial Inn** (✆ **01586/553-703**) has live music on Fridays and alternate Saturdays. They're open from noon to 1am.

Torrisdale Castle Estate ★★★   The romantic 19th-century castle that Niall and Emma Macalister Hall and their family call home is perched in meadows and woodlands above the eastern shore, and they share these colorful surroundings with guests in a castle apartment and four lodges and cottages on extensive grounds. The apartment in the former servant's quarter is especially comfortable, with three bedrooms and sitting rooms (as well as a secret chamber) occupying the former kitchens, wine cellar, and store rooms. A wood-fired hot tub and sauna next to a gurgling stream are unexpected luxuries. A tannery in the former laundry building uses centuries-old natural methods to produce sheepskin and deer-hide rugs and cat mats that are great souvenirs, while another estate building houses Kintyre's first gin distillery.

Torrisdale, off B842 13 miles north of Campbeltown, 20 miles south of Tarbert. www.torrisdalecastle.com. ✆ **01583/431233.** 5 units. Doubles from £340 a week; shorter stays available. **Amenities:** Beach; watersports; sauna and hot tub; free Wi-Fi.

Ugadale Hotel ★★   Once upon a time, well-to-do Glaswegians arrived by steamer to spend summer months at this grand hotel overlooking the sea. After some decades of neglect and weather-induced battering, the sea-facing resort has been redone top to bottom and is looking better than ever. Large rooms are smartly done in wood, brass, and plaids to provide lodging for golfers on two superb courses, the Machrihanish Golf Club and Machrihanish Dunes, and they are the most comfortable base for miles around for anyone else exploring the southern peninsula. Even if you're not golfing or staying elsewhere, the Old Clubhouse, the hotel's casual restaurant, is tops for a pub lunch.

Machrihanish, 5 miles east of Campbeltown. www.machrihanishdunes.com. ✆ **01586/810-001.** 22 units. Doubles from £149, includes breakfast. Golf and meal packages available. **Amenities:** 2 restaurant; 2 bars; golf; spa; free Wi-Fi.

THE ISLE OF GIGHA ★

3 miles W of Kintyre's western coast

It's easy to get the feeling that the world has passed this 6-mile-long islet by. The Vikings stored their loot here after plundering the west coast of Scotland, and cairns, ruins, and legends speak of times when the island might have been a little busier than it is now. The **Ogham Stone** is one of only two standing stones in the Hebrides that bears an Ogham inscription, a form of script used in the 6th-century Scottish kingdom of Dalriada, and the ruins of the **Church of Kilchattan** date back to the 13th century. Quiet is how the 100 or so islanders like it. To keep things that way, in 2002 they formed the Isle of Gigha Heritage Trust (www.gigha.org.uk) and bought Gigha in its entirety for £4 million. Islanders now celebrate March 15, when the purchase was completed, as "Independence Day."

Walking is what brings most visitors to Gigha, along with the island's glorious garden. **Ferries** link Gigha with Tayinloan, halfway up the west coast of Kintyre on the A83. Sailings are daily on the hour during the summer, and take about 20 minutes; boats arrive at **Ardminish,** Gigha's main hamlet. For ferry schedules, contact Caledonian McBrayne, www.calmac.co.uk; © **0800/066-5000**). Gigha has no tourist office, but you'll find a wealth of information at www.gigha.org.uk, and the islanders will gladly tell you what you need to know about exploring their little patch of turf.

Achamore House Gardens ★★ PARK/GARDEN   These 20 hectares (49 acres) are the creation of the late Sir James Horlick. Aside from being an astute businessman who made a fortune from the soothing malted bedtime drink that bears his name, he was also one of the world's great horticultural-ists. He bought Achamore House, along with rest of Gigha, in 1944, because he was interested in growing exotic plants in the island's favorable microcli-mate. He surrounded Achamore House with roses, hydrangeas, rhododen-drons, and azaleas, as well as pines from Central America, conifers from Australia, and other rare specimens. A largely volunteer staff toils to restore and maintain this enchanting parcel. Paths wind through the plantings into woodlands and up ridges overlooking the mountains and sea, and a 2-acre walled garden is often ablaze with color.

1 mile outside Ardminish. www.gigha.org.uk. © **01583/505-400.** £5. Daily–dusk.

Where to Stay & Eat

Gigha Hotel ★   Gigha's only hotel and pub occupies an 18th-century farmhouse near the ferry landing. The small rooms are plain and cozy, as befits the island's down-to-earth lifestyle, and their best assets are the lovely views of the sea and the rugged countryside. Even if you're not overnighting on the island, you should stop in for a pub lunch or a drink, both of which come with a chance to talk with the islanders, many of whom have chosen to relocate to this tranquil place from elsewhere. A shop next door sells a nice selection of handmade crafts, woolens, and souvenir mugs and plates deco-rated with the Gigha tartan.

Isle of Gigha. www.gigha.org.uk. © **01583/505-254.** 13 units. Doubles £80–£120, includes breakfast. **Amenities:** Restaurant; bar; free Wi-Fi.

THE ISLE OF ISLAY ★★

16 miles W of the Kintyre Peninsula

This windswept island is a serene and unspoiled place of moors, salmon-filled lochs, sandy bays, and rocky cliffs. Small and out of the way as the island is, Islay (the name is pronounced "*Eye*-la") is famous around the world for its whisky. The tiny island, only 20 miles at its widest point and 25 miles long, is home to eight distinguished distilleries, offering the chance to drink some of the world's finest single malts at the source. Islay would be intoxicating even without its smoky malts: While the stark beauty doesn't reach the standards of some of the other Hebrides, that's not saying Islay is anything less than lovely.

Essentials

GETTING THERE Caledonian MacBrayne (www.calmac.co.uk; ℭ **08705/650-000**) provides a daily **ferry** service from Kennacraig on the Kintyre peninsula to Port Askaig, on the northeastern coast of Islay. In the summer there are up to four ferries a day. The journey takes about 2 hours. By **air,** Flybe makes the short hop from Glasgow to Islay's little airport between Port Ellen and Bowmore (www.flybe.com).

VISITOR INFORMATION The Islay Tourist Information Centre is on The Square, Bowmore (www.islayinfo.com; ℭ **01496/810-254**). Opening hours are: April to June, Monday to Saturday 10am to 5pm, Sunday 2 to 5pm; July and August, Monday to Saturday 9:30am to 5:30pm, Sunday 2 to 5pm; September and October, Monday to Saturday 10am to 5pm.

Port Ellen ★

Islay's principal port, on the south coast, is most visited for the string of three distilleries—Ardbeg, Lagavulin and Laphroaig—along the stretch of coast known as the Golden Mile just north of town. A nice time out from the whisky circuit is a visit to the **Kildalton churchyard** in lovely countryside about 7½ miles to the northeast. The 8th century **Kildalton Cross ★**, is one of Scotland's finest early works; the hard stone is richly carved with biblical scenes that are still a vivid work of pictorial story telling: the Virgin cradles the child, Abraham is poised to sacrifice Abel, and David fights a lion. At the **Oa Nature Reserve,** 8 miles south of Port Ellen, spectacular, windswept headlands overlook the Mull of Oa.

The Oa Nature Reserve ★★★ PARK/GARDEN The 1,931-hectare Oa Peninsula, where impoverished tenant farmers once worked the scrappy land and illicit whisky smugglers hid their stashes in sea caves, is now designated a Special Protected Area. Sheer cliffs are home to golden eagles and other rare sea birds, while Highland cattle and longhorn sheep graze on the rippling grasslands and moors. At the edge of the bluffs stands a forlorn stone tower, the **American Monument,** commemorating lives lost at sea in two incidents. On February 5, 1918, 9 months before the end of World War I, a German U-boat sunk the *Tuscania,* a luxury liner converted to a troop ship, with the loss of 230 lives. Eight months later, on October 6, another 400 lives were lost when the troop ship HMS *Ontario* collided with the steamship HMS *Kashmire.*

Oa peninsula, 8 miles south of Port Ellen. www.rspb.org.uk. ℭ **01496/300-118.** Always open.

Bowmore ★

Islay's pint-sized capital is unusually orderly, built in 1770 along wide, grid-like streets on orders of Daniel Campbell the Younger, overlord of the island. If the tidy streets seem to inspire good behavior, the town's Round Church

whisky ISLAND

A drive across Islay, past emerald-green fields, along roads often clogged with sheep, makes it clear that even in this mecca for drinkers of single malts, for most residents whisky distilling comes second to farming. Even so, locals will tell you that there are eight good reasons to come to their island, and that happens to be the number of major working distilleries. They also like to say that their little island was created only to produce whisky. For many visitors, that certainly seems to be the case, and especially so the last weekend in May, when Islay celebrates the Festival of Malt and Music. Just about any islander can point to the distinctive qualities of the local output. Whiskies from the north of the island, for instance, are especially smoky and peaty, with the taste imparted by the barley and water, with just a hint of the sea. And little wonder: Distilleries have been part of island life since Bowmore went into operation in 1779 and soon had as many as two dozen competitors. Carrying on the tradition, three new distilleries are opening or are slated to open soon, so stay tuned.

does so in spades, providing no corners where the devil can hide. All this righteousness doesn't put a damper on whisky-making, big business at the town's Bowmore Distillery.

Loch Gruinart ★, 8 miles north of Bowmore, is the winter home for wild geese and also haven for many rare sea birds, otters, common and grey seals, hares, red and roe deer. The 1,215 hectares (3,000 acres) of moors and farmland around the loch are protected as the **Loch Gruinart Nature Reserve** (www. rspb.org.uk; ✆ **01496/850-505**); the visitor center is open daily, 10am to 5pm.

Finlaggan (www.finlaggan.com), 7 miles northwest of Bowmore off A846, is a pretty but godforsaken-looking place with a storied and important past. The stone ruins clustered on an islet in a little loch were at one time home to the lord of Clan Donald, who ruled the islands and large sections of the West Coast; walking around the overgrown ruins might remind you of "Ozymandias," Shelley's poem about long-vanquished power, depending on how many distillery stops you've made. A visitor center is open April through September Monday through Saturday 10:30am to 4:30pm and Sunday 1:30pm to 4:30pm, with reduced hours October through March.

Port Charlotte ★

Much of southern Islay curves around Loch Indaal, with trim, proud little Bowmore holding court on the eastern shore and Port Charlotte lying directly across the waters on the western shore. The picturesque port town is the place to bone up on island history, at the **Museum of Islay Life ★** (www.islaymuseum.org; ✆ **01496/850-358;** £3 adults, £2 seniors, and £1 kids 5–16) in an old church. Among a predictable showing of whisky stills and ships' figureheads are a charmingly random mishmash of Victorian bedroom sets, photos of shipwrecks, and fossils. From Easter to October, the museum is open Monday through Saturday 10am to 4pm.

Visiting the Distilleries ★★

Islay's peat-flavored single malts made by the antiquated pot-still method put the island on the world map. Boatloads of aficionados come ashore to visit the Islay's eight working distilleries, all of which offer tastings and tours and sell their products onsite. At all expect to pay about £6 for a tour, and £15 for a basic tasting, with prices increasing for lengthier tours and more extensive tastings. Most offer a draught to visitors for free. Distilleries are open daily, usually from 9am to 5pm, sometimes with shorter hours on Sundays and in winter. You can get more info from the distillery sites:

- **Ardbeg,** Port Ellen, www.ardbeg.com
- **Bowmore,** Bowmore, www.bowmore.com, ℂ **01496/810-441**
- **Bruichladdich,** Bruichladdich, www.bruichladdich.com, ℂ **01496/850-190**
- **Bunnahabhain,** Port Askaig, www.bunnahabhain.com, ℂ **01496/840-557**
- **Caol Ila,** Port Askaig, www.malts.com
- **Kilchoman,** Bruichladdich, www.kilchomandistillery.com, ℂ **01496/850-011**
- **Lagavulin,** Port Ellen, www.malts.com
- **Laphroaig,** Port Ellen, www.laphroaig.com, ℂ **01496/302-418**

Remember, whether you visit one distillery or all eight, Scotland has strict laws against driving while intoxicated. Most distilleries will give you a takeaway sampler in lieu of a tasting.

Shopping

The **Islay Woollen Mill** ★, Bridgend (www.islaywoollenmill.co.uk; ℂ **01496/810-563;** Mon–Sat 9am–5pm) has been making country tweeds and accessories for more than a century. The mill shop sells items fashioned with tweeds created for Mel Gibson's *Braveheart* as well as smart Shetland wool ties, Jacob mufflers and ties, flat caps, travel rugs, and scarves. **Islay House Square,** next to Islay House in Bridgend, occupies what were once servants' quarters and workshops for the manor house; it now houses a brewery, photography galleries, a marmalade shop, and other distinctive businesses.

Where to Stay & Eat on Islay

Harbour Inn ★ SEAFOOD/PUB FOOD   Workers from nearby Bowmore Distillery gather at this old-fashioned, white-washed pub/inn that's been carefully refurbished to make the most of its historic provenance, with stone walls, a fireplace, and wooden floors. The selection of single malts is, not surprisingly, extensive, and they are accompanied by sure-handed and inventive preparations of fresh-from-the-docks seafood. Accommodation is in several comfortable guest rooms and four surrounding cottages, all tastefully done in contemporary Scottish style, with lots of wood and plaids, and the occasional fireplace.

Main St., Bowmore. www.bowmore.com/harbour-inn. ℂ **01496/810-330.** Mains £17–£26. Daily noon–2:30pm and 6–9:30pm. Bar until 1am. Rooms from £105, includes breakfast. **Amenities:** Restaurant; bar; free Wi-Fi.

Islay Hotel ★   You couldn't find a better base for touring Islay's famous trio of distilleries just outside Port Ellen. Quite conveniently, a path from the hotel leads right to them. The large, bright rooms just beyond the ferry landing are also well poised for exploring the rest of the island, and are nicely done in sporty pine furnishings, and light colors and fabrics. The excellent restaurant downstairs spills out onto a terrace in good weather; it's not unusual to come upon an impromptu music session in the adjoining whisky bar/pub, where more than 100 singe malts are on offer.

Charlotte St. www.theislayhotel.com. ℭ **01496/300109.** 13 units. Doubles from £120, includes breakfast. **Amenities:** Restaurant; bar; free Wi-Fi.

Islay House ★★   One of Scotland's finest manor houses, once the home of the Campbell clan, puts a sophisticated spin on the notion of a bed and breakfast. The large and gracious old bedrooms are beautifully redone with period furnishings and retain original architectural details. All overlook the sea and the wooded grounds, where a 2-acre walled garden is not only a horticultural masterpiece but also feeds the island with fresh produce. You could not outdo the Peat Cutter bar for grand surroundings in which to sample a dram or two of island whiskies.

Bridgend. www.islayhouse.co.uk. ℭ **01496/810-702.** 11 units. Doubles from £195, includes breakfast. **Amenities:** Bar; free Wi-Fi.

Lochindaal Hotel ★★   Saying this welcoming old place is "family owned and operated" means more here than that phrase often does, since MacLellans have been running the show for more than 100 years. Their pub rooms are a favorite of distillery workers, who gather around the peat fires to discourse on the virtues of single malts (many of which are on offer), and they are often joined by musicians. The seafood on offer is from the waters across the road. Confortable, unfussy guest rooms are in the rear and in a nearby annex, and a two-bedroom apartment is available as well.

Main St., Port Charlotte. www.lochindaalhotel.co.uk. ℭ **01496/850-202.** 5 units. Doubles from £75, includes breakfast. **Amenities:** Restaurant; bar; free Wi-Fi.

THE ISLE OF JURA ★

⅔ mile E of Islay

The red deer on Jura—Scotland's largest animals, at around 1.2m (4 ft.) in height—outnumber human islanders by about 25 to 1 on Jura. As it should be, since the name comes from the Norse *jura* for "deer." Only about 250 hearty souls live on the 27-mile-long island, and they're surrounded by a dramatic landscape of mountains, soaring cliffs, and moors.

Jura's only road, the A846, begins at Feolin (little more than the anchoring place for the ferry from Islay) and runs up the east coast of the island as far as the village of Lussagiven. Most walkers head for the so-called **Paps of Jura,** the three steep conical mountains of quartzite on the uninhabited western side of the island. The highest, Beinn-an-Òir (or "mountain of gold" in Gaelic),

Orwell on Jura

Novelist and critic George Orwell (1903–50) spent much of 1946 and 1947 in a remote island cottage on Jura, and the landscapes appear to have inspired him in a strange way: Rather than observing simple, old-fashioned Hebridean life and natural beauty, Orwell completed his dystopian novel *1984* while on Jura. Perhaps the overpowering presence of the Paps of Jura and the ever-present howl of winter winds found their way into Orwell's evocation of Big Brother and omnipresent government surveillance. He died of tuberculosis shortly after the novel was published to widespread acclaim.

reaches 786m (2,575 ft.). The island's hamlet capital, **Craighouse,** has Jura's only shop, church, and hotel/pub, along with a whisky distillery (www. isleofjura.com; ✆ **01496/820-385**). Guided distillery tours are offered April to September, Monday through Friday at 11am and 2pm. Advance booking is required.

From Port Askaig, on Islay, **ferries** make the 5-minute trip across the Sound of Islay to Feolin at the southern tip of Jura about every half-hour during the summer. Boats are operated by **ASP Ship Management Ltd** (www.islayinfo. com/jura-ferry.html; ✆ **01496/840-681**).

FIFE & THE CENTRAL HIGHLANDS

By Lucy Gillmore

The Kingdom of Fife is a hoity-toity name for what is, in fact, a pint-sized peninsula of picturesque fishing villages fringed by golden sandy beaches between the Firths of Forth and Tay. This ancient region is adorned with all the romance and pageantry of the early Stuart kings, and its gently rolling landscape is sprinkled with royal palaces and evocatively crumbling ruins. In the Central Highlands, the landscape takes a more dramatic turn. The raw, rugged peaks and glassy lochs of the Trossachs have been described as the Highlands in miniature. Its history is the stuff of legend (and popular with the odd Hollywood filmmaker) from William Wallace to Robert the Bruce to Rob Roy. Whether you take the high road or the low road in the Fife, make sure to wend your way to Loch Lomond's bonnie, bonnie banks.

The medieval city of St **Andrews** is the hallowed home of golf, and players from around the world make a pilgrimage to its famous **Old Course.** History seeps out of the stonework of the clifftop castle and ruined cathedral, once the resting place of St Andrew, Scotland's patron saint. **Stirling,** with its magnificent castle and towering **Wallace Monument,** forms the lynch pin; meanwhile, between the Highlands and Lowlands and this is where pivotal battles were fought in Scotland's rip-roaring history.

Legendary **Loch Lomond** is Scotland's largest loch. Its southern edge forms a lowland landscape of gentle hills and islands, but as its waters cross the Highland Boundary Fault to the north, the loch takes on a more dramatic character, edged with craggy peaks. Part of the same National Park, the **Trossachs** is the wild, loch-strewn Highlands east of Loch Lomond, home to some of Scotland's finest scenery, immortalized by the romantic writings of Sir Walter Scott.

One of Scotland's best-kept secrets, the picturesque fishing villages strung along the East Neuk of Fife are linked together by a

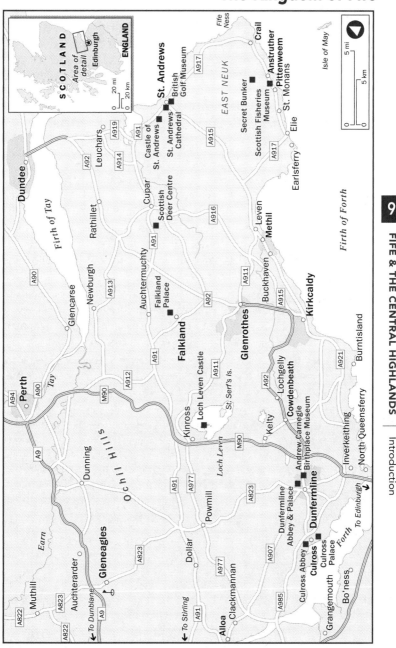

SCOTLAND

Area of detail

Edinburgh

ENGLAND

0   20 mi
0   20 km

Fife Ness

Crail

Anstruther
Pittenweem

EAST NEUK

Secret Bunker

St. Andrews
British
Golf Museum

Scottish Fisheries
Museum

St. Monans

Isle of May

5 mi

5 km

A917

Castle of
St. Andrews

St. Andrews
Cathedral

A919   A91

Leuchars

A914

A92

A915

Elie

Earlsferry

A916

Dundee

Firth of Tay

Rathillet

Newburgh

Glencarse

A90

A913

Cupar

Scottish
Deer Centre

A91

Auchtermuchty

Falkland
Palace

Falkland

Firth of Forth

Leven

Methil

Buckhaven

A911

A915

Kirkcaldy

Glenrothes

Burntisland

A92

A912

A91

Loch Leven Castle

St. Serf's Is.

A911

Lochgelly

Cowdenbeath

A92

Kelty

A921

Perth

A94

A90

Tay

A9

Dunning

Ochil Hills

M90

Kinross

Loch Leven

M90

Andrew Carnegie
Birthplace Museum

Inverkeithing

North Queensferry

To Edinburgh

Earn

Auchterarder

Gleneagles

A823

Muthill

A822

A823

Dollar

Powmill

A91   A977

A823

A977

Dunfermline
Abbey & Palace

Dunfermline

Culross Abbey

Culross

Culross
Palace

Forth

Grangemouth

Bo'ness

A907

A985

To Dunblane

To Stirling

A9   A91

A822

Alloa

Clackmannan

A9

9

long-distance walking trail, the **Fife Coastal Path.** The villages are peppered with cafes and galleries, artists drawn here inspired by the region's landscape and light.

Fife's coastal villages are famous for their seafood, smokehouses and working harbors, and clutch of seafood restaurants—not forgetting the best fish and chip shop in the U.K. The rivers and lochs of the **Central Highlands** also leap with salmon and trout, while the moorland and hills provide wild venison, the woods foraged mushrooms.

Don't Leave Fife & the Central Highlands Without . . .

Standing on the battlements of Stirling Castle. One of the most imposing and impressive castles in Scotland, Stirling is both a military fort and royal Renaissance palace. Take in sweeping views of the surrounding countryside where some of the pivotal battles in Scotland's history were fought.

Taking the high road in the Trossachs through the Duke's Pass. This legendary road trip in the heart of Rob Roy Country dishes up the most spectacular Highland scenery, a medley of majestic mountains, steely lochs, and dense forest.

Surveying the 18th hole of St Andrews' historic Old Course from the Royal and Ancient clubhouse. Follow in the footsteps of the world's most famous golfers to this iconic course where many claim the game was born. If you're good enough, and lucky enough, you might even snag a round.

Taking a boat trip on Loch Lomond. Cruise across Scotland's largest loch, chugging past some of its many picturesque islands, and view the famous fault line that divides Scotland's lowlands and highlands.

Hiking the Fife Coastal Path. This bucolic trail links picturesque fishing villages, ruined clifftop castles, nature reserves, long sandy beaches, and a medieval university town.

DUNFERMLINE & ITS ANCIENT ABBEY ★

14 miles NW of Edinburgh; 39 miles NE of Glasgow; 52 miles SW of Dundee

The ancient town of Dunfermline is a heritage hotspot and pit stop for history buffs. Robert the Bruce is buried here, Andrew Carnegie was born here, and this "auld grey toun" was once Scotland's capital until the Union of the Crowns in 1603, when the royal court skedaddled down to London. The main attraction is the magnificent **Abbey** and the ruins of its royal palace in the heart of Dunfermline's Heritage Quarter. Once the center of Scottish linen making, specializing in damask, Dunfermline's most famous son, steel magnate and philanthropist Andrew Carnegie, was born in one of its tiny weaver's cottages. Today, it makes an easy day-trip from Edinburgh or a history-laced detour on your way to Fife's prettier parts. If you want to stay this side of the **Forth Bridges,** base yourself in the little waterfront village of **North Queensferry**—accommodation and restaurant options in Dunfermline itself aren't that inspiring.

Essentials

GETTING THERE A regular **ScotRail** service (www.scotrail.co.uk; ✆ **0344/811-0141**) links Edinburgh's Waverley and Haymarket train stations with Dunfermline. The journey takes around 35 minutes and a same-day round-trip fare is £6.70. **Scottish CityLink** (www.citylink.co.uk; ✆ **0871//266-3333**) operates a regular route between Edinburgh's bus station and Dunfermline. It's a 45-minute journey, and a same-day round-trip fare is £12.20.

If you're driving from Edinburgh, join the A90 to the west of the city, travel north across the Queensferry Crossing, and merge into the M90.

VISITOR INFORMATION The VisitScotland tourist information center has 14 digital kiosks across Fife; the closest to Dunfermline is at Deep Sea world in North Queensferry (www.visitdunfermline.com).

Exploring Dunfermline

Dunfermline, with its elevated position and views out over the Firth of Forth, can easily be done in a day. All the main attractions are within its **Heritage Quarter** and **Pittencrieff Park,** which dominates the west side of town. Also called "the Glen," this large, leafy park, 76 acres in total and famous for its peacocks, was gifted to the town by its most famous son, Andrew Carnegie, in 1903. It's also home to 17th-century **Pittencrieff House**, now a small museum, an aviary and glasshouse and miles of pleasant pathways and trails to meander. The park butts up against Dunfermline's Heritage Quarter, where you'll find the **Abbey** and ruined palace and the **Andrew Carnegie Birthplace Museum.** Also worth checking out is the **Fire Station Creative,** Carnegie Drive (www.firestationcreative.co.uk; ✆ **01383/721-564;** open Wed and Thurs 10am–5pm, Fri and Sat 10am–4pm and 5pm–11pm, Sun 11am–4pm). This building was once the home of the Fire and Rescue Service, built in 1934 and designed by James Shearer. It lay empty for years but has now been converted into a vibrant cultural hub, home to artists' studios, a gallery, and cafe, with cocktails and live music on weekends.

Andrew Carnegie Birthplace Museum ★ HISTORIC HOME In 1835, American industrialist and philanthropist Andrew Carnegie was born in a tiny weaver's cottage in the shadow of Dunfermline Abbey. This little gem of a museum celebrates his early life in the 19th-century cottage (complete with weaver's loom), and follows his story after he emigrated to the United States and became one of the world's richest men. From the fortune he made in steel came a legacy of libraries: Carnegie gave away more than £244 million before his death in 1919, and Dunfermline received the first of the 2,811 free libraries he provided throughout Britain and the U.S. *Sesame Street* was produced with a grant from the Carnegie Corporation, and children should look out for Bert and Ernie in the memorial hall.

Moodie St. www.carnegiebirthplace.com. © **01383/724-302.** Free. Mar–June and Sept–June Mon–Sat 10am–5pm, Sun 1–4pm, July–Aug daily 10am–5pm, Nov 10am–4pm, Sun 1–4pm. Closed Dec–Mar.

Dunfermline Abbey & Palace ★ ABBEY   There has been a church on this site since C.E. 800. Robert the Bruce is buried here beneath the church pulpit—although his heart was taken on Crusade and finally laid to rest at Melrose Abbey in the Scottish Borders (p. 121). In fact, the place is full of tombs of Scottish monarchs, including Queen Margaret, later made a saint and the mother of three kings of Scotland, who founded a priory here in the 11th century on the spot where she'd married Malcolm III. It was their son, David I, who turned the priory into a grand abbey. Today, only its striking Romanesque nave survives. Edward I of England inflicted severe damage on the abbey in 1303 and it was Robert the Bruce who bankrolled its magnificent rebuilding in a symbolic display of Scottish resilience. In 1600 the palace witnessed the birth of Charles I, the last monarch to be born in Scotland. Even in ruins, the long and lofty monks' refectory is spectacular.

St. Margaret's St. www.historicenvironment.scot. © **01383/739-026.** £5 adults, £4 seniors, £3 children 5–15. Apr–Sept daily 9:30am–5:30pm; Oct–Mar Sat–Wed 10am–4pm.

North Queensferry

This little village on the waterfront huddles beneath a medley of Forth Bridges and is a good base for exploring.

WHERE TO EAT & STAY

Doubletree by Hilton ★   If it's a room with a view you're after, they don't come much more spectacular than floor-to-ceiling windows overlooking the Queensferry Crossing. This modern hotel sits between the Forth Road Bridge and the new cable-stayed bridge in 10 acres of peaceful parkland on the edge of the historic village of North Queensferry. The smart, contemporary rooms feature a soothingly neutral color palette and the chain's signature Sweet Dreams beds. The restaurant, The Shore Grill and Fish House, with its sleekly contoured interiors and ceiling of whimsical wooden waves, comes with window booths boasting panoramic views over the River Forth along with a menu packed with fresh local seafood and sizzling steaks. The Scottish East Coast Fish Pie is crammed with cod, Pollock, haddock, and salmon and topped with creamy mash. Or grab a stool at the marble-topped bar and check out the carefully curated cocktail list. The "Juniper" is a Shore favorite, a heady blend of Caorunn gin, Belvedere citron, lemon, cloudy apple juice, almond syrup, and kiwi fruit topped with lemon foam.

St Margaret's Head. www.doubletree-queensferry.co.uk. © **01383/410-000.** 145 units. Doubles £79–£260, suites £124–£280. **Amenities:** Restaurant; bar; gym; free Wi-Fi.

The Wee Restaurant ★ MODERN SCOTTISH   Good things come in small packages or so the saying goes. That certainly holds true for Craig and Vikki Wood's relaxed little eatery (capacity 40), tucked beneath the Forth Rail Bridge, which has been notching up the awards since it opened in 2006. The philosophy is simple: to showcase the region's best seasonal ingredients. The restaurant is cozy, contemporary and candlelit, while dishes such as roast rump of Perthshire lamb with risotto of petits pois and wild garlic with red wine jus and olive oil pearls are packed full of flavor. They also run a little sister restaurant in Edinburgh's New Town (61 Frederick St.; ✆ **0131/225-7983**).

17 Main St., North Queensferry, 6 ½ miles south of Dunfermline. www.theweerestaurant.co.uk. ✆ **01383/616-263.** 2-course dinner £29, 3-course £36, 2-course lunch £16 3-course £20. Tues–Sat noon–2pm and 6:30–9pm, Sun noon–3pm.

Culross ★★

The 17th-century conservation village of **Culross ★★**, 6 miles west of Dunfermline, is picture-postcard pretty and has been painstakingly restored by the National Trust for Scotland. Strolling its medieval cobbled streets lined with white harled houses (traditional limed weather-proofing) and quaint cottages, it's easy to believe you've stepped back in time. It's not surprising that it's in high demand as a TV and film location and has had a starring role in a clutch of historical dramas, including *Outlander*.

The ochre-hued **Culross Palace ★★** (www.nts.org.uk; ✆ **0844/493-2189**) is set in tranquil lavender-lined gardens at the center of the village. The palace was built between 1597 and 1611 for prosperous merchant George Bruce. More of a grand hall in fact, this imposing, turmeric-tinged building features magnificent painted ceilings, antique furniture, and gives a tangible sense of life in the late 16th century. It's open daily April to June and September to October 11am to 4pm; July to August daily 11am to 5pm; closed November to March. Admission is £10.50 adults, £7.50 seniors, and £18–£24.50 for families.

At **Culross Pottery & Gallery** (www.culrosspottery.com; ✆ **01383/882-176**), you can watch resident potter, Camilla Garrett-Jones creating her distinctive hand-thrown pieces before browsing the gallery upstairs and tucking into gooey handmade cakes and locally roasted coffee in the rustic **Biscuit Café**. Alternatively, head to the **Red Lion pub,** next to the village post office (www.redlionculross.co.uk; ✆ **01383/880-225**), for hearty pub grub such as steak and haggis pie.

The other major attraction here is **Culross Abbey,** a Cistercian monastery founded by Malcolm, Earl of Fife, in 1217. Some of the building is in ruins, but part of it still serves as a parish church.

The Stagecoach no. 8 bus operates between Dunfermline bus station and Culross; the round-trip fare is £5.80.

9

FIFE & THE CENTRAL HIGHLANDS

Dunfermline & Its Ancient Abbey

LOCH LEVEN & FALKLAND ★

Loch Leven ★ is a National Nature Reserve on the western outskirts of **Kinross,** 13 miles north of Dunfermline and 27 miles north of Edinburgh. The loch is peppered with seven islands, and from Kinross you can catch a small ferry to one of the largest, Castle Island (signposted from the center of town), to wander among the evocative ruins of **Loch Leven Castle** (www.historicenvironment.scot; ✆ **01577/862-670**). "Those never got luck who came to Loch Leven"—this saying sums up the history of the island's Douglas fortress, which dates back to the late 14th century. Mary Queen of Scots was the most famous of its ill-fated prisoners, and it was inside its forbidding walls that she was forced to sign her abdication on July 24, 1567. Mary eventually escaped on May 2, 1568, fleeing to England and the protection of her cousin Elizabeth I. Around half the original castle still remains, and visitors can explore the ruins of a 14th-century tower house and 16th-century curtain wall. It's open April to September daily from 10am to 4:15pm, in October from 10am to 3:15pm and is closed from November until the end of March. Admission includes the boat ride from Kinross to Castle Island (booking in advance is recommended as there is limited capacity): £7.50 adults, £6 seniors, and £4.50 for children 5 to 15.

Curling on Loch Leven dates back to the 17th century, and large curling "bonspiels" used to take place in winter on its thick frozen waters. You can learn more about the history of the loch via the 13-mile **Heritage Trail** (www. lochlevenheritagetrail.co.uk), which skirts its banks. The trail has been divided into five manageable chunks and you can download leaflets detailing points of interest and prime wildlife-watching spots for each of these walks from the website. From Burleigh Sands to Pow Burn for instance, the route starts among towering Scots Pines before heading down to the water's edge, running beside fields where you will be able to hear skylarks in summer and meadow pipits along with reed warblers in the rushes. The southern shore of the loch is an **RSPB** reserve (www.rspb.org.uk; ✆ **01577/862-355**) and important wetland site: osprey fish here during the summer, and up to 20,000 pink-footed geese flock here in spring and autumn. Loch Leven is also famous for its brown trout fly-fishing. Anglers should contact **Loch Leven Fisheries** (www.fishlochleven.co.uk; ✆ **01577/863-407**).

The historic village of **Falkland** (12 miles northeast of Kinross) butts up against the eastern slopes of the Lomond Hills, whose forests were once an ancient hunting ground. Falkland's 17th- and 18th-century streets, lined with small gift shops and pubs, gather around its famous palace, today managed by the National Trust for Scotland. **Falkland Palace** ★ (www.nts.org.uk; ✆ **01337/857-397**) dominates the village and is an impressive Renaissance royal hunting lodge once favored by the Stuarts. Highlights of the Palace's lavishly furnished interior include 17th-century Flemish tapestries and royal portraits, and the magnificent gardens feature a large orchard and the oldest royal tennis court in Britain, built in 1539 for James V. The palace is open

March to October Monday through Saturday 11am to 5pm, Sunday noon to 5pm; admission costs £13 adults, £9 children and seniors, and £30 families.

Exploring the Area

Scottish Deer Centre ★ ZOO There's more to this family-friendly attraction than deer. The park covers 55 acres and is home to an array of wildlife, including 13 species of deer, wildcats, wolves, brown bears, otters and birds of prey. Ranger-led tours run throughout the day and a good time to visit is 3pm—the Carnivore Feed Walk and Talk, when it's feeding time for the wildcats and wolf pack. There are both indoor and outdoor children's play areas, a kart track and woodland walks. The center also has a cafe and a picnic area.

Off the A91, 3 miles west of Cupar. www.tsdc.co.uk; ✆ **01337/810-391.** £9 adults, £6 children, £7.50 seniors, £28 families. July–Aug daily 10am–5:30pm; Sept–June daily 10am–4:30pm.

Where to Eat

Ostlers Close ★★ MODERN SCOTTISH For more than three decades, Amanda and Jimmy Graham have been celebrating the Fife's bountiful natural larder in their award-winning restaurant down a little lane off Cupar's busy high street. Sourcing fresh local ingredients from neighboring producers (lamb from Balhelvie Farm and lobster, crab and prawns from the East Neuk for a start), Jimmy also grows his own organic vegetables, herbs, salad and fruit such as apples, plums, damsons and rhubarb, and forages for wild mushrooms in nearby woodland. The regularly changing menu includes starters such as roast filet of wild Scottish hake with Pittenweem prawns and samphire on a prawn bisque sauce and beetroot tarte tatin with celeriac remoulade and goats cheese honey ice-cream. Mains include roast roe venison with red cabbage, skirlie (fried, seasoned oats), and roast vegetables on a game sauce with a selection of Scottish cheeses, homemade biscuits, and wild plum paste to finish.

25 Bonnygate, Cupar. www.ostlersclose.co.uk. ✆ **01334/655-574.** Reservations recommended. Main courses £24–£28. Tues–Sat 6:30–11pm.

EAST NEUK'S SCENIC FISHING VILLAGES ★★

"Neuk" is the Scottish word for corner. This peninsula in the southeast of Fife is fringed by the Firth of Forth and North Sea. Just half an hour's drive from St Andrews to the north and easily reachable by car from Edinburgh, the string of fishing villages lining this rugged coastline are some of loveliest in Scotland and a honeypot for local artists. Fishing boats still chug out of small harbors and the catch is dished up in the area's gourmet seafood restaurants.

One of the best ways to explore is on foot, and you can tramp this stretch of coastline along the **Fife Coastal Path** (www.fifecoastalpath.co.uk) which runs from North Queensferry in the south to Newport-on-Tay in the north.

You can't reach East Neuk by rail; the nearest stations are Ladybank, Cupar, and Leuchars, on the ScotRail Edinburgh to Dundee line serving northeast Fife. Buses from St Andrews connect the villages, but you really need to have your own car here.

Elie ★

With its step-gabled houses and little harbor, Elie, 13 miles south of St Andrews, is a popular village along this coast and a good starting point from which to explore the East Neuk. Elie and its close neighbor, Earlsferry, overlook a crescent of golden sand and are popular with weekenders from Edinburgh during the summer (the city is just a 25-minute drive away). The name Elie is believed to come from the *ailie* (island) of Ardross, which now forms part of the harbor and is joined to the mainland by a road. A large stone building, a former granary, at the harbor is a reminder of the days when Elie was a busy trading port.

Earlsferry, to the west, got its name from an ancient ferry crossing, which Macduff, the thane of Fife, is supposed to have used in his escape from Macbeth. East of the harbor there's a stone structure known as the **Lady's Tower,** once used by Lady Jane Anstruther, a famous 18th-century beauty (and naturist), as a bathing house.

WHERE TO EAT & STAY

Catchpenny Safari Lodges ★★　Fall asleep to the sound of waves lapping gently on the shore. Train your binoculars on the sea and spot a pod of dolphins from your tent's terrace. Toast marshmallows over the fire-pit and watch the sun rise over the water. Are you sold? With so much in the way of old-fashioned, tired accommodation in Fife, life under canvas is a chic and appealing option. We're talking glamping, of course, not camping. These canvas lodges, between Elie and St Monans, sleep six and have chunky wooden beds (a king, a twin, and a romantic wooden box bed), wood-burning stoves and hot showers. Each is named after the local wildlife, from yellow hammer to bumblebee, and they're off-grid. The power comes from solar and wind and is stored in batteries beneath the tents. There's also a gas stove for cooking and you can buy supplies at the Ardross Farm Shop (www.ardross farm.co.uk; ✆ **01333/331-400**) nearby.

Broomlees Farmhouse, Elie. www.catchpennyelie.co.uk. ✆ **01333/330-594.** 8 units. 4-night breaks £420–£485. **Amenities:** Fire pit; 4G mobile reception (depending on your internet service provider).

Ship Inn ★★★　If you're looking for seaside chic this is the only place to stay in Fife. Overlooking Elie's golden sands, the Ship Inn is a cracking local pub, dating back to 1778, which was snapped up by Graham and Rachel Bucknall (owners of the award-winning Bridge Inn in Ratho, near Edinburgh; see p. 85) and converted into a bucket and spade gourmet bolthole. Just a flip-flop from the shore, there are six individually designed rooms (four with sea views), all sea-green tongue and groove, white shutters and window seats, roll-top baths, monsoon showers and a maritime theme.

One of the best ways to explore this bucolic part of the Kingdom of Fife, just a pebble's throw from Edinburgh, is on foot, meandering along the Fife Coastal Path (www.fifecoastalpath.co.uk). This 117-mile waymarked trail (follow the brown signs) curves around the clifftops and sweeps along the shoreline, passing romantic ruins, fertile farmland, dune-backed wildlife reserves, and quaint fishing villages. It starts at the Firth of Forth in the south and winds its way to the Firth of Tay in the north. You can do the whole route over a period of days depending on your pace and pit stops (the website divides it into eight sections), or just dip in and out and do a bitesize chunk. Elie to Cambo Sands is a good 16-mile stretch and should take about 5 to 6 hours. From Elie Lighthouse you pass the crumbling ruins of Ardross and Newark castles and 14th-century St Monans church. Also in St Monans check out the restored windmill once used to pump seawater into the adjacent saltpans. The next village on the route is Pittenweem, with its working fishing harbor and the cave used by St Fillan in the 7th century. Continue on to Anstruther with its bustling marina (a good spot for fish and chips and an ice cream) before heading on again toward Crail and its 17th-century harbor and finally Cambo Sands.

Downstairs in the remodeled bar (old glass buoys, oars hung on the walls and seafaring prints) there's a roaring log fire in winter. In summer, you can grab a seat in the beer garden on the edge of the sands and watch a game of beach cricket. The inn touts itself as the only pub in the U.K. to have a cricket pitch on the sand. In the airy upstairs dining room, with its rustic decor and cozy woodburner, you can tuck into gastropub fare such as Scottish clams steamed with red curry or apple cider, or paella with langoustine, clams, salmon, chorizo, peas, broad beans, and lemon. On the grill are Scottish dry-aged steaks from Henderson's butchery. The Bucknalls also bagged **The 19th Hole** (www.19thhole.scot; ☎ **01333/330-610**), a rustic-chic sports bar just down the road overlooking Elie golf course.

The Toft, Elie. www.shipinn.scot. ☎ **01333/330-246.** 6 units. Doubles £120–£185; includes breakfast. **Amenities:** Restaurant; bar; beer garden; free Wi-Fi.

St Monans ★

The village of St Monans was named after a 6th-century Irish bishop and is 2½ miles to the east of Elie. The old kirk on the water's edge dates back to 1362 and is one of the oldest in Scotland. There are stone steps beneath the graveyard leading down to the shore, while further east along the coastal path you'll find Fife's last remaining windmill, a testament to the region's salt producing industry.

The village is also a surprising gourmet hotspot: the bright blue (you can't miss it) **East Pier Smokehouse ★★** (www.eastpier.co.uk; ☎ **01333/405-030**) is a rustic little place that packs a gastronomic punch. The food is dished up in cardboard boxes, and you eat at the open-air rooftop tables or inside beside the woodburner—and it's sublime. Think hot smoked sea bass with apple,

9

FIFE & THE CENTRAL HIGHLANDS | East Neuk's Scenic Fishing Villages caramelized onion, pink peppercorn chutney with salad and chips for £14.50. Or how about pan-fried sardines in smoky garlic butter with pickled rhubarb? Local crabcakes are dished up with tarragon mayonnaise, the alder-smoked prawn tempura with Asian dipping sauces. And then there's the local crab, langoustine, and lobster. It's more than a cut above your average seafood shack.

Pittenweem ★

A mile farther along the coast is the last of Fife's fishing villages, where you can still see the jaunty trawlers chugging out of to sea each day and returning with their catch to be sold at the bustling fish market on the harbor. Its picturesque waterfront is filled with lobster pots, fishing boats, and ice cream shops, the village's narrow streets sprawling uphill and peppered with artists' galleries and cozy cafes. If you're feeling peckish, make a beeline for the **Pittenweem Chocolate Company and Cocoa Tree Café** (www.pittenweemchocolate.co.uk; ✆ **01333/311-495**) which is as wickedly indulgent as it sounds. Sip a signature hot chocolate, served with a dash of chili, and tuck into a slab of tempting homemade chocolate cake. Before you go, stock up on the handmade artisan chocolates.

In August, a lively **Arts Festival** (www.pittenweemartsfestival.co.uk) transforms the village and local artists open up their studios as exhibition spaces.

The *weem* in the village's name means "cave," a reference to **St Fillan's Cave** (✆ **01333/311-495**) at Cove Wynd just off the harbor. This cave contains the shrine of St Fillan, an early Christian missionary from the 7th century who's said to have lived here as a hermit, writing sermons by the light of his luminous left arm. Admission to the cave is £1 for adults and free for children, and you get the key from the **Cocoa Tree Café.**

Anstruther ★★

The largest of East Neuk's fishing communities, Anstruther was once an important herring-fishing port. Today this bustling village is famous for its picturesque harbor and its award-winning fish and chips. The nearest **Tourist Information Centre** is in Crail.

The **Scottish Fisheries Museum ★**, St Ayles, Harbourhead (www.scotfishmuseum.org; ✆ **01333/310-628**), at the eastern end of the harbor, is housed in a cluster of 16th- to 19th-century buildings around a cobbled courtyard, scattered with old fishing nets and boats. Inside, the history of East Neuk's fishing industry is brought vividly to life. Allow a couple of hours to explore this fascinating little museum, which charts the development of seafaring craft from primitive boats made from skins and bark to the introduction of steam and diesel, and includes a covered boatyard, a fisherman's cottage, and the last remaining 24m (78-ft.) Zulu fishing boat, once the backbone of the herring industry. Built in Banff in 1903, her last fishing trip was to Shetland in 1968. The museum is open April to September Monday through Saturday 10am to

5:30pm, Sunday 11am to 5pm; and October to March Monday through Saturday 10am to 4:30pm, Sunday noon to 4:30pm. Admission is £9 adults, £7 seniors, and free for children under 16.

Around 5 miles offshore, the **Isle of May** ★★ (www.nature.scot) is a national nature reserve, its cliffs crammed with a cacophony of 250,000 nesting seabirds in early summer (guillemots, razorbills and shags), its choppy waters bobbing with a colony of Atlantic grey seals which breed here each autumn. It's a magical medley of wildlife, whales sighted off the coast in July and August and thousands of comical puffins waddling its craggy shores (the best time to see them is April to mid-August). There's a bird observatory (Scotland's oldest, established in 1934) and a field station, along with the ruins of a 12th-century monastery and the oldest lighthouse in Scotland dating back to 1636.

A jaunty little passenger boat, the **May Princess** (www.isleofmayferry.com; ✆ **07957/585-200**) departs for the Isle of May from Anstruther harbor once a day every day, weather permitting, between April and September. You can buy tickets from a kiosk 1½ hours before departure, or in advance by phone or email. The trip costs £26 for adults, £23 for seniors and students, and £13 for children 3 to 16; departure times vary with the tide. The trip lasts around 4 to 5 hours and includes 2 to 3 hours on the island. Adrenaline-junkies should book the fast, bouncy crossing on the RIB Osprey through the sister company Isle of May Boat Trips (www.isleofmayboattrips.co.uk; ✆ **07473/631-671**). Bird-watchers can arrange to stay in the island's observatory for up to a week from mid-March to early November. Visitors are expected to carry out observatory duties, filling out a daily migration log and recording wildlife sightings (see www.isleofmaybirdobs.org for details).

If you're looking for outdoor activities check out **East Neuk Outdoors,** Cellardyke Park (www.eastneukoutdoors.co.uk; ✆ **01333/310-370**), which organizes everything from kayaking and canoeing to bushcraft (wilderness survival skills), bouldering, and raft-building.

WHERE TO EAT & STAY

Anstruther Fish Bar ★★ SEAFOOD   Do you want your haddock in breadcrumbs or batter (the recipe's a tightly guarded secret)? Red sauce or brown? With chips—that goes without saying. This award-winning "chippie" on the harbor has been named best fish and chip shop in the U.K. on countless occasions. There are plenty of tables inside, but for a really authentic experience, you need to order a takeaway and tuck into a "fish supper" (battered haddock, chips, and mushy peas) perched on the harbor wall or a bench on the waterfront, ducking and diving as the seagulls swoop. Deep-fried is the way to go, from haddock to the Pittenweem prawns, hake and lemon sole, but you can also order dressed Scottish crab, caught by local fishermen in their creels (traditional cages), and hot smoked salmon salad from the smokehouse in St Monans. Sustainability is also a key part of the picture at this legendary seafood joint—the haddock is bought from local fishermen on the quayside and the oil used to fry the fish is recycled into biodiesel. And for dessert? They also make artisan ice cream in-house. There's a choice of 70 different flavors with 18 available each day. The best-seller? Still vanilla . . .

42–44 Shore St., Anstruther. www.anstrutherfishbar.co.uk. © **01333/310-518.** Main courses £5.60–£11.25. Sun–Thurs 11:30am–9:30pm, Fri–Sat 11:30am–10pm.

The Cellar ★★ MODERN SCOTTISH   Billy Boyt dishes up Michelin-starred magic in this cozy restaurant. Once a cooperage producing barrels for salting the local herrings, then a smokehouse and a fishermen's store, this low-slung restaurant with its exposed stone walls, original beams, and a roaring fire is the low-key backdrop for a spellbindingly innovative tasting menu. Instagram-perfect dishes include aged beef tartare, onion mayo, smoked cod roe mousse, Anster cheese, and gherkin followed by hogget (1- to 2-year-old sheep), white cabbage, wild leeks, mint, and lemon balm relish.

24 E. Green, Anstruther. www.thecellaranstruther.co.uk. © **01333/310-378.** Reservations required. 7-course tasting menu £60, wine pairing an extra £50, 5-course lunch menu £35, wine pairing an extra £28. Wed 6–9pm, Thurs–Sun noon–9pm.

The Waterfront ★   This harborside restaurant with rooms has the location, but design-wise is nothing to shout about. The 10 simple rooms are plain and comfortable, some clustering around a small courtyard garden, others with views of the marina. The restaurant dishes up fresh Scottish seafood, from locally caught spiced potted crab to scallops, sea bass, and steamed Shetland mussels and, of course, fish and chips. For breakfast, you can stick with the seafood theme and tuck into a plate of kippers or smoked Scottish haddock and scrambled eggs.

18–20 Shore Rd., Anstruther. www.anstruther-waterfront.co.uk. © **01333/312-200.** 10 units. £80–£120 double; £100–£150 family room includes breakfast; £120–£175 family suite. **Amenities:** Restaurant; free Wi-Fi.

Crail ★★

Crail is yet another gem, a picture-perfect fishing village tumbling down to the harbor where fishermen still land lobster and crab. Check out the rustic little **Lobster Store** on Shoregate (© **01333/450-476**) where you can buy freshly cooked lobster to go. The village dates back to the 12th century (although the harbor was built by the Dutch in the 16th century) and is a favorite with local artists. Which is hardly surprising. Meander among the old fishing cottages and lobster creels that cluster around the medieval Shoregate, then dip into the **Crail Harbour Gallery and Tearoom** on Shoregate (www. crailharbourgallery.co.uk; © **01333/451-896**), a quaint 17th-century fisherman's cottage, now a gallery showcasing the work of local artist DS Mackie and a cozy harbor-facing tearoom complete with outdoor patio looking out towards the Isle of May.

From Shoregate follow **Castle Walk** for panoramic views of the harbor and shoreline, which leads to the upper part of the village. At the west end of Marketgate, a tree-lined street flanked by small two- and three-story houses, stands Crail's **tolbooth** dating from 1598 and formerly the town jail. The **Crail Museum & Heritage Centre,** 62 Marketgate (www.crailmuseum.org.uk; ✆ **01333/450-869**), is adjacent to the tolbooth and its collections provide an insight into the fishing industry and former trading links of these tiny villages. It's open during the Easter school holidays daily Monday to Saturday 11am to 4pm and Sunday 1:30pm to 4pm; in May it's open at weekends, from June to October it's open daily; admission is free.

Crail Pottery (www.crailpottery.com; ✆ **01333/451-212**) on Netherbow is another popular haunt. Set in a tranquil courtyard, this long-established pottery shop sells handcrafted earthenware and ceramics. To catch a sample of local folk music, check out the **Crail Folk Club** (www.crailfolkclub.org.uk), whose regular live music nights take place at the **Crail Town Hall** on Marketgate. Check the Folk Club's website for dates and times.

EXPLORING THE AREA

Secret Bunker ★★ HISTORIC SITE Dubbed Scotland's best-kept secret, this amazing labyrinth, built 30m (100 ft.) below the ground and encased in 4.5m (15 ft.) of reinforced concrete was, for 40 years during the Cold War, where government and military officials would have run the country if the U.K. had been involved in a nuclear conflict. Its entrance was designed to look like a traditional Scottish farmhouse. You can visit the BBC studio, where emergency broadcasts would have been made, and the switchboard room, set up to handle 2,800 phone lines. At least 300 people would have been able to live, work, and sleep in safety here while coordinating war efforts. There are two cinemas showing Cold War films, an audiovisual theatre, a cafe, and a gift shop.

Crown Buildings, Troywood, 3 miles west of Crail, off the B940. www.secretbunker.co.uk. ✆ **01333/310-301.** £13 adults, £12 seniors, £8.50 children 5–16, £34 families. Easter–Oct 10am–5pm.

ST ANDREWS ★★★

14 miles SE of Dundee; 51 miles NE of Edinburgh

There's more to St Andrews than golf. As sacrilegious as that might sound to those who've travelled halfway round the world to visit the medieval royal burgh where golf was first played in the 1400s, St Andrews is also home to the oldest and most prestigious university in Scotland—the place where the Duke and Duchess of Cambridge (William and Kate) first met. Add a magnificent ruined cathedral and a clifftop castle, a cluster of cobbled streets and a clutch of gorgeous beaches—and there are plenty of other reasons to swing by.

Essentials

GETTING THERE **Trains** from Edinburgh to Leuchars run every half-hour and take about an hour. From there a connecting bus takes you on the 8-mile, 11-minute journey to St Andrews. A one-way fare with **ScotRail** (www.scotrail.co.uk; ✆ **0344/811-0141**) is £14.70 and a round-trip fare is

£21.10. The journey by **car** also takes an hour. Head northwest along the A90 and cross the Queensferry Crossing bridge. Continue north exiting at junction 8 and follow the A91 west to St Andrews.

VISITOR INFORMATION A **Tourist Information Centre** is located on 70 Market St. (www.visitstandrews.com; ✆ **01334/472-021**) and opens April to July Monday to Saturday 9:15am to 5pm, Sunday 10am to 5pm. July to September it closes at 6pm, and 5pm on Sundays. From September to April it opens Monday to Saturday 9:30am to 5pm.

Exploring St Andrews

From meandering the medieval streets, clambering over a ruined castle or going for a wild, wind-whipped walk along West Sands: St Andrews is easy to explore on foot. The 2-mile, seemingly endless stretch of **West Sands** is backed by grassy dunes and bordered by one of the most famous golfing greens in the world. This is where the opening scenes of the iconic movie *Chariots of Fire* were filmed. **East Sands,** by the old harbor behind the cathedral, is smaller, more family-friendly and a good place to join the **Fife Coastal Path** (www.fifecoastalpath.co.uk). On a Sunday one of the university's oldest traditions takes place along the harbor wall: the red-gowned students' post-chapel pier walk.

Known as Scotland's "Oxbridge," the **University of St Andrews** was founded in 1410 and is the third oldest in Britain. It dominates the town and its ancient stone buildings and quadrangles dot the streets: landmarks such as the tower and church of **St Salvator's College** (1450) and the courtyard of **St Mary's College,** which dates back to 1538. The three main thoroughfares, North Street, South Street, and Market Street in the middle, are threaded together by tiny cobbled alleys and run parallel to each other, meeting at the ruined cathedral. Golf aficionados head to the other end of town for the hallowed **Old Course ★★** along with the iconic **Royal and Ancient** clubhouse and, on Bruce Embankment, the recently revamped **British Golf Museum ★** (www.britishgolfmuseum.co.uk; ✆ **01334/460-046**) which romps through 500 years of golfing history.

St Andrews Castle ★ CASTLE This atmospheric 13th-century ruin teeters on the cliff-edge as the waves crash far below. At one time a bishop's palace and later a prison, its bottle dungeon (only accessible through a hole in the top) carved 7m (23 ft.) down into the rock, was said to be the worst in Scotland. The castle was the scene of the trial and burning at the stake of religious reformer George Wishart in 1546, watched by Cardinal Beaton. A group of vengeful reformers murdered Beaton 3 months later and took control of the castle for almost a year. Both attacking Catholic forces and the holed-up reformers dug underground passages to attack each other, a perfect example of medieval siege warfare.

The Scores. www.historicenvironment.scot. ✆ **01334/477-196.** Castle only £6 adults, £3.60 children 5–15, seniors £3.60. With cathedral £9 adults, £5.40 children 5–15, seniors £7. Apr–Sept daily 9:30am–5:30pm; Oct–Mar daily 10am–4pm.

St Andrews Cathedral ★ CATHEDRAL   Poised on the edge of the coast by the old harbor, the evocative ruins of what was once Scotland's most important cathedral are among the most significant in the country. The cathedral was founded in 1160 and consecrated in 1318 in the presence of Robert the Bruce. The relics of St Andrew, Scotland's patron saint, were once enshrined in its high altar. Today, the ruins strike a dramatic pose against the North Sea, and highlights include climbing to the top of 12th-century St Rules Tower for spectacular views of the coastline and the cathedral museum.

Off Pends Rd. www.historicenvironment.scot. ℭ **01334/472-563.** Cathedral only £5 adults, £3 children, seniors £4. With castle £9 adults, £5.40 children 5–15, seniors £7. Apr–Sept daily 9:30am–5:30pm; Oct–Mar daily 10am–5pm.

Hitting the St Andrews Links

St Andrews Links is made up of seven public courses, most famously the **Old Course,** established in 1552 and the oldest golf course in the world. The other courses are young whipper-snapper, the **New Course,** which opened in 1895; the **Jubilee Course,** opened in 1897, in honor of Queen Victoria's Diamond Jubilee; the **Eden,** opened in 1914; the **Strathtyrum,** the most far-flung, opened in 1993; **Balgove,** a 9-hole course ideal for children, families, and beginners and the newest addition, the **Castle Course** which opened in 2008. There's no handicap limit on any of the courses, except the Old Course—max 24 men, 36 ladies, and a handicap certificate is required to play. All courses are maintained by the **St Andrews Link Trust** (www.standrews.com; ℭ **01334/466-728**), and the website outlines the procedure you need to follow to book a round.

The **Royal and Ancient** ★ (www.randa.org; ℭ **01334/460-000**), the world's most prestigious golf club, founded in St Andrews in 1754 by a group of noblemen, professors, and landowners, and which to this day governs the rules of golf everywhere except the U.S, was for almost 3 centuries an "old boys' club" but in 2014 it finally opened its doors to women. The Links Clubhouse is far less stuffy and set 400 yards from the first tee of the Old Course. It's open year-round to golfers and non-golfers and offers lockers, showers, and changing facilities. There's also a bar and restaurant on site.

Where to Stay

With a world-famous golf course, historic university, and postcard setting, it's not surprising that there's no shortage of accommodation options, from upmarket resort hotels to streets lined with traditional B&Bs for the steady stream of year-round visitors. What is surprising is that they're so uninspiring. The B&Bs are generally dated and old-fashioned, most of the hotels lackluster. There is a clutch of cute little self-catering options in Fife but even these are few and far between. Check out **21 Shoregate** in Crail (www.21shoregate.com; ℭ **07879/480-529**) which offers 4-night breaks from £350. **Rose Cottage** near Kingsbarns is pretty as a picture (www.rosecottage-standrews.com; ℭ **07909/970-150**) with 3-night breaks from £270, while **Shoreleave** in St

Monans, a luxury harbor-front house and **Bell Cottage** in Pittenweem a seaside chic gem, are available through Homeaway (www.homeaway.com).

EXPENSIVE

Eden Mansion ★★ For sumptuous old-world luxury, look no further than this opulent historic B&B just a couple of miles outside St Andrews. Rooms are swathed in decadent fabrics and decked out with fine antiques. There are ancestral paintings on the walls and wooden floors are strewn with Persian rugs. The 1st Earl Haig room oozes boudoir-chic, with a rich red color scheme—even the walls are clad in red and gold wallpaper, while the romantic Duchess of Cambridge bedroom is a vision of gentle navy and cream.

Cupar Rd. www.edenmansion.com. ℂ **01334/614-400.** 6 units. Doubles £139–£599, includes breakfast. **Amenities:** Free Wi-Fi.

Fairmont St Andrews Bay Golf Resort & Spa ★★ This swanky, all-singing, all-dancing 520-acre luxury resort is perched on a cliff overlooking the North Sea and is home to two championship golf courses: the Torrance (7,230-yard, par-72) designed by Rider Cup captain Sam Torrance and the Kittocks (7,192-yard par-72) by Bruce Devlin and Gene Sarazen. This is where Prince William famously first fell for Kate Middleton when she took part in a fashion show here. Bedrooms are spacious and comfy with the odd splash of tartan, and have views of the sea or golf course. The spa has 10 stylish treatment rooms, there's an indoor pool, sauna, steam room, and Jacuzzi, and five dining options. from the Italian restaurant **La Cucina** to the relaxed **Rock and Spindle** sports bar. Essentially it does what is says on the box: It's a big luxury golf resort.

St. Andrews Bay. www.fairmont.com. ℂ **800/257-7544** in the U.S., or 01334/837-000. 211 units. £179–£339 double; £229–£649 suite includes breakfast. **Amenities:** 5 restaurants; 2 bars; pool (indoor); health club and spa; children's programs; concierge; room service; babysitting; free shuttle bus to St Andrews; free Wi-Fi.

Old Course Hotel ★★ This is St Andrews' original honey-hued golf and spa resort, looming out of the landscape as you approach the town along the A91. The hotel might soar over the 17th fairway of the Old Course, but, in fact, they're not connected—the resort's championship course is The Duke's nearby, the area's only heath-land course (which has been described as a cross between English links and American parkland with sandy soil and moorland-like vegetation). When you're not teeing off, there's a luxurious spa, pool and a clutch of dining options including the gourmet **Road Hole** and relaxed **Jigger Inn** a St Andrews' stalwart dating back to 1850. Rooms are traditional in design, some boasting balconies overlooking the Old Course to the sea and a dramatic color palette of rich reds and black and white stripes.

Old Station Rd. www.oldcoursehotel.co.uk. ℂ **01334/474-371.** 144 units. Doubles £230–£399, suites £600–£1,180 includes breakfast. **Amenities:** 4 restaurants; 4 bars; pool (indoor); spa w/Jacuzzi; children's activities; concierge; babysitting; free Wi-Fi.

The Peat Inn ★ This Michelin-starred restaurant with rooms is in a pretty, rural setting, the village of Peat Inn, 6 miles outside St Andrews. The village took its name, in fact, from the 18th-century coaching inn—I know it's confusing. The restaurant here is the star attraction, Geoffrey Smeddle's six-course tasting menu dished up in an intimate series of small dining rooms looking out over picturesque gardens. The restaurant and reception lounge have the wow factor in terms of fresh, contemporary design (think pale painted wooden walls, exposed stonework, an open fire, and turquoise velvet banquettes). They could do with drafting the designer back in to give the bedrooms the same treatment, as they're a bit tired and old-fashioned and not worth the hefty price tag.

Peat Inn. www.thepeatinn.co.uk. ℂ **01334/840-206.** 8 units. Suites £205–£225, includes breakfast. **Amenities:** Restaurant; bar; room service; free Wi-Fi.

MODERATE

Hotel du Vin ★★ Leather sleigh beds are certainly a statement. The accommodation scene in St Andrews is so staid that when this wine-themed boutique hotel chain breezed into town in 2014, there were more than a few corks popping. The hotel looks out over the heart-stopping golden sweep of West Sands beach. There's a Gallic-infused bistro dishing up escargots a la Bourguignonne and moules frites, and a bar where you can check out whether the hotel lives up to its name, while downstairs in the basement is another bar, the old revamped student haunt, Ma Bells. Rooms range from standard to sea-view suites and along with the custom-made beds, come with fabulous bathrooms with monsoon showers or roll-top tubs.

40 The Scores. www.hotelduvin.com. ℂ **01334/845-313.** 36 units. Doubles £129–£309, suites £209–£409. **Amenities:** Restaurant; 2 bars; free Wi-Fi.

INEXPENSIVE

Cambo Country House and Estate ★★ This heavenly spot, just a 10-minute drive from St Andrews, is famous for its annual snowdrop festival. The estate dates back to the 12th century when one John de Cambo first put down roots here. There is a whole range of accommodation options from B&B in four-poster splendor, the walls hung with ancestral portraits, the bathrooms boasting romantic roll-top tubs (the Blue Room and Yellow Room) to antique-peppered apartments or holiday cottages in the grounds. From May to October you can also snuggle up in the two yurt-like bell tents in a woodland glade close to the beach. Each has a real bed, fire-pit, and fairy lights (2-night breaks from £178).

Cambo House, Kingsbarns. www.camboestate.com. ℂ **01333/450-313.** 5 units. Doubles £129–£189, includes breakfast. **Amenities:** Children's play area; tennis court; woodland and gardens; barbecue; free Wi-Fi.

Where to Eat

The streets are crammed with cafes and pubs and a clutch of gourmet food shops such as Italian deli **Rocca** (33 Bell St.; ℂ **01334/473-130**) and

Mitchell's (110-112 Market St.; www.mitchellsdeli.co.uk; ✆ **01334/441-396**) which also has a buzzing shabby chic cafe, two great cheese shops: **The Old Cheese Shop** (141 South St.; www.oldcheeseshop.co.uk; ✆ **01334/477-355**) and **I.J. Mellis** (149 South St.; www.mellischeese.net; ✆ **01334/471-410**) along with old favorites such as **Fisher and Donaldson** (13 Church St.; www.fisheranddonaldson.com; ✆ **01334 472-201**) famous for its fudge donuts, and **Jannetta's Gelateria** at 31 South St. (www.jannettas.co.uk; ✆ **01334/473-285**), which has more than 50 flavors of ice cream including Tablet (vanilla mixed with grainy, deliciously addictive Tablet or Scottish fudge)—so there's no excuse not to picnic on the beach. For high-class fish and chips head to **Cromars** (1 Union St.; www.cromars.co.uk; ✆ **01334/475-555**), named the Best Fish and Chip Shop in Scotland in 2018. The fish is locally caught, the fishcakes homemade, the ales to wash it all down from a local craft brewery.

Balgove Larder ★★★ FARM SHOP/CAFE As posh farm shops go, this is a humdinger. A cluster of old stone farm buildings on the edge of St Andrews has been converted into a gorgeous rustic deli and light, bright cafe brimming with fresh fruit and veg straight from the fields. There's a traditional butcher selling free-range beef, pork, and game from the estate. (When the animals are not grazing the grass they're eating pulses and grains also grown on the farm.) The deli also stocks a range of local produce including artisan cheeses, oatcakes, and delicacies such as haggis Scotch eggs. In the cafe you can breakfast on homemade granola drizzled with honey and piled high with seasonal fruit or tuck into the Balgove Breakfast, a traditional fry up with the estate's homemade pork sausages, black pudding, back bacon and free range eggs. For lunch, how about a steaming bowl of St Monans' smoked haddock chowder made with leeks and potatoes from the farm? In the summer you can dine in the relaxed steak barn in the old sawmill. The walls are made from potato boxes, the tables rough-hewn from wind-blown beech off the estate and on the menu, steak, of course: their own, dry-aged beef hung for 28 days and sausages and burgers made on-site and grilled on the barbecue—washed down with local beer.

Balgove Farmhouse, Strathyrum Estate. www.balgove.com. ✆ **01334/898-145.** Farm shop and cafe Mon–Sun 9am–5pm, Steak Barn Wed–Sun noon–9pm.

The Seafood Ristorante ★★ SEAFOOD "We serve seafood on the seashore" quips the blurb, a pun on the traditional tongue-twister. And it's seafood with an Italian twist. The setting of this smart seaside restaurant is sublime and architecturally it has real wow factor: a glass box suspended over the cliff looking out towards West Sands beach. In terms of food it's also sublime, think raviolo of Scottish lobster to start with baby spinach, caviar and shellfish bisque or seafood and squid ink risotto with scallops, baby squid, clams, mussels and spring greens. Follow with John Dory with west coast langoustines, wild garlic, gnocchi and sprouting broccoli or a whole salt-baked sea bream for two with an anchovy salad. The restaurant has an equally transparent sustainable seafood policy: serving fish in season, proud of its provenance and fishing methods.

Bruce Embankment. www.theseafoodrestaurant.com. © **01334/479-475.** Mains £25–£42. Fixed-price lunch £20 for 2 courses, £25 for 3 courses; Daily noon–2:30pm; 6–9:30pm.

Shopping

St Andrews is small, so this is no shopping Mecca, but in addition to a handful of gourmet food stores there are a few independent boutiques, plus the usual rash of high street chains around South and Market streets. (Golfers should head to the west end of town near the Old Course.) Boutiques to browse include **Sam Brown** (www.sambrownboutique.co.uk; © **01334/461-517**) on Market Street which stocks brands such as Avoca Anthology. Another St Andrews stalwart is **J&G Innes** (www.jg-innes.co.uk; © **01334/472-174**) on South Street, an independent bookstore, art and stationery supplier with an ornately carved facade.

Entertainment & Nightlife

For a one-stop cultural hub head to the **Byre Theatre,** Abbey Street (www.byre theatre.com; © **01334/475-000**), which mixes it up with a varied program of theatre, music, comedy, film and dance, while the **New Picture House** on North Street (www.nphcinema.co.uk; © **01334/474-902**) is an independent cinema dating back to the 1930s with three cinema screens showing mainly mainstream films. Tickets cost £8 to £9 for adults and £5.50 for children 12 and under.

St. Andrews is a university town, and there's a vibrant student scene with a young crowd dominating many of the pubs and bars. Old stalwarts include **"The Vic"** or the **Victoria Café and Bar,** 1 St Mary's Place (www.vicstan drews.co.uk; © **01334/476-964**); which dubs itself a pub, kitchen and social club with a chilled out vibe, drinks in jam jars and live music at night. **The Criterion** is another legendary drinking hole and family-run pub at 99 South St. (www.vicstandrews.co.uk; © **01334/474-543**) with over 160 whiskies and 30 Scottish gins along with a fair few cask ales. **The Central Bar** on Market Street manages to mix town and gown: it's popular with both locals and students (www.centralbar-standrews.co.uk; © **01334/478-296**). **St Andrews Brewing Co.** (www.standrewsbrewingcompany.com; © **01334/471-111**), founded in a garage in 2012, was named Best Scottish Pub in 2017. This is craft beer central, with 18 beers and ciders on tap, 30 rare malt whiskies and 30 craft gins. Design-wise think barrels as tables and a beer hall vibe upstairs with long table and benches. They also do great gastropub grub: from a steaming bowl of creamy Cullen skink (a traditional Scottish smoked haddock soup), or pan-seared saddle of roe deer with juniper berry jus and fresh brambles.

The Dunvegan Hotel's tartan-trimmed Golfer's Corner bar on Pilmour Place (www.dunvegan-hotel.com; © **01334/473-105**), is a traditional favorite with the golfers, a mere 112 yards from the Old Course. The bar's walls are lined with memorabilia from the many past masters who have enjoyed a dram or sunk a pint of ale or two here.

STIRLING ★

35 miles NW of Edinburgh; 28 miles NE of Glasgow

You can't miss Stirling Castle. This all-guns-blazing fortress perched on a 76m (250-ft.) hunk of basalt rock dominates the town crouched in its shadow. This ancient settlement stands on the main east–west route across Scotland and is sometimes described as "the broach which clasps the Highlands and Lowlands together." Its central location ensured Stirling's strategic importance for anyone wanting to rule Scotland, and the city's history is bloody and turbulent. Two pivotal battles in the fight for Scotland's independence from the English were fought here—Stirling Bridge in 1297, when freedom fighter William Wallace spurred on Scottish troops, and Bannockburn in 1314 when Robert the Bruce took command—both resulting in decisive victories over England.

Stirling flourished from the 15th to the 17th centuries when it was in favor with Stuart monarchs. Today, it has a small Scottish town feel and in terms of accommodation options and restaurants, doesn't hold up well when compared to Edinburgh and Glasgow just down the road. It's easily accessible by rail and road to both and it's tempting to just do its historical sites as a daytrip or on the way to explore the Trossachs.

Essentials

GETTING THERE   Frequent trains run between Glasgow and Stirling (a 40-min. trip) and Edinburgh and Stirling (a 50-min. trip). A 1-day round-trip ticket from Edinburgh is £9.70 and from Glasgow £8.40. For schedules, contact National Rail Enquiries ✆ **03457/484-950** or visit **ScotRail's** website at www.scotrail.co.uk.

Hourly buses run to Stirling from Glasgow (a 45-min. trip) and Edinburgh (a 1-hr. 20-min. trip). An off-peak 1-day round-trip ticket from Glasgow costs £8.50 and from Edinburgh £11.60. Check with **Scottish CityLink** (www.citylink.co.uk; ✆ **0871//266-3333**) for details.

If you're driving from Glasgow, head northeast along the A80 to the M80, and then continue north. From Edinburgh, head northwest along the M9.

VISITOR INFORMATION   The **Tourist Information Centre** is in the grounds of the Old Town Jail on St John St. close to the castle (www.visitscotland.com; ✆ **01786/475-019**). It's open daily year round.

Exploring Stirling

The Old Town, the city's ancient center, straddles a steep rocky outcrop crowned with the magnificent castle. This area has a handful of historic attractions, some are in ruins and many are closed during the winter. Highlights include the **Old Town Jail** (www.oldtownjail.co.uk; ✆ **01786/464-640**), Stirling's Victorian prison on St John Street, where the harsh squalor of 19th-century justice is revealed in all its grim glory. There are 14 performance tours each day (guides dress as characters from the past) during the summer (it's

Stirling, Loch Lomond & the Trossachs

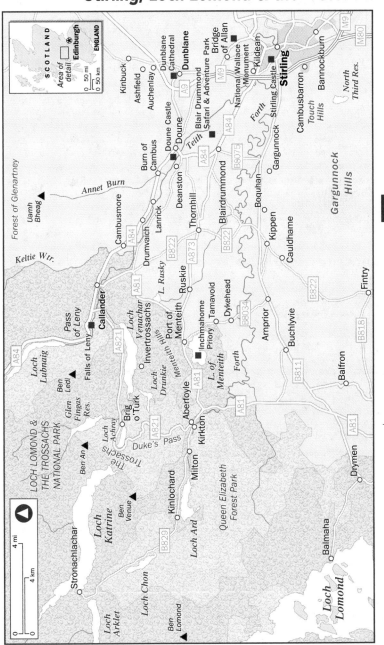

STIRLING battles

To find out more about the pivotal battles and the famous figures in Scottish history associated with Stirling, you need to head out of the city. It was at **Bannockburn,** 2 miles south of Stirling, that Robert the Bruce and his army defeated the far larger forces of Edward II in June 1314. The National Trust for Scotland runs a state-of-the-art, immersive 3D visitor center, the **Battle of Bannockburn Experience,** where you can take command of a virtual battlefield learning all about medieval combat before heading out onto the site itself to see where Robert the Bruce raised his royal standard (flag). The site is on Glasgow Road (www.nts.org.uk; *©* **01786/812-664;** off the M80/M9 at Junction 9) and is open daily year-round until dusk, while the visitor center and exhibition are open November to February daily 10am to 5pm and March to October daily 10am to 5:30pm. There are regular buses from the bus station in Stirling (numbers 24, X39 and 54). Admission costs £11.50 for adults, £8.50 for seniors and children, and £30.50 per family.

Seventeen years before Bannockburn, William Wallace also defeated English forces in this area at the Battle of Stirling Bridge on September 11, 1297. The actual battlefield is thought to be a number of miles upstream from the site of the present-day Stirling Bridge, and the place to find out more about this battle and Wallace himself is the **Wallace Monument** (www.nationalwallacemonument. com; *©* **01786/472-140**), which stands on Abbey Craig 1½ miles north of Stirling. Known to many through Mel Gibson's cheesy, gory, and not altogether historically accurate film *Braveheart,* freedom fighter William Wallace is a Scottish national hero and exhibits include his mighty sword. The Monument is open daily November to February 10am to 4pm, March 10am to 5pm, April to June and September to October 9:30am to 5pm, and July and August 9:30am to 6pm. Admission is £10.50 for adults, £6.50 for children 16 and under, seniors £8.50 and £27.50 per family.

only open during July and August) and the views from the top of the tower are spectacular. Also on St John Street, the **Church of the Holy Rood ★** (www. holyrude.org; *©* **01786/475-275**), which was founded in the 12th century, is a must-see for its original oak roof beams and elaborate 19th-century stained glass. It's also the only church still in use in the U.K., apart from Westminster Abbey in London, to have hosted a coronation: James VI of Scotland (later James I of England) was crowned here in 1567.

Other sites of historical interest are marked with plaques, and to get a real feel for the history of this area stroll along the **Back Walk,** which leads along the 16th-century city walls from the castle, past an old watchtower, and down into the modern town center.

Here head along Dumbarton Road to the **Stirling Smith Art Gallery & Museum** (www.smithartgalleryandmuseum.co.uk; *©* **01786/471-917**), whose exhibits include *The Stirling Story,* a journey through the city's history, and changing displays of the work of Scottish artists.

Stirling Castle ★★★ CASTLE   One of Scotland's most dramatic historical sites, perched on top of a steep volcanic crag, Stirling Castle dates back to the Middle Ages. Stand beside the larger-than-life statue of Robert the Bruce on the castle forecourt and survey the surrounding countryside, the setting of some of the most important battles in Scottish history. Stirling's impregnable castle was an important seat for Scotland's late medieval monarchs and home of Mary Queen of Scots for the early years of her life. The **Royal Palace ★★** forms the castle's centerpiece and was built in the 16th century by James V. James married the French Mary of Guise, and masons and craftsmen were brought from France to transform their palace into a royal home of European standing. It remains one of the finest examples of Renaissance architecture in Britain. A massive restoration project recently transformed it back to its 16th-century glory. Costumed guides are on hand to explain the details of royal life 500 years ago. Also, don't miss the **Stirling Heads**—16th-century meter-wide oak medallions, carved by local master craftsmen and detailing the faces of Scottish royalty and Roman emperors and the **Hunt of the Unicorn** tapestries, which adorn the royal chambers. They took years to weave as part of the restoration project and cost £2 million.

The regimental **Museum of the Argyll and Sutherland Highlanders** is also housed inside the castle, and admission includes a tour of **Argyll's Lodging** at the top of Castle Wynd, Scotland's best example of a complete 17th-century Renaissance townhouse.

Upper Castle Hill. www.stirlingcastle.scot. ℭ **01786/450-000.** £15 adults, £12 seniors, £9 children 5–15, free for children 4 and under. Apr–Sept daily 9:30am–6pm; Oct–Mar daily 9:30am–5pm.

Exploring the Area

Bridge of Allan is a small Victorian spa town 3 miles north of Stirling. Authors Robert Louis Stevenson and Charles Dickens were once regular visitors. Today, there's not much to keep you here, but it's a pleasant place to meander. Its main street (Henderson Street) lined with shops and cafes, leads towards Allan Water, a large tributary of the River Forth that surges through the west side of town. While you're here swing by the **Bridge of Allan Brewery** for a behind the scenes tour, and sample a pint of locally brewed ale at Queens Lane (www.allanwaterbrewhouse.co.uk; ℭ **01786/834-555**). A frequent train service runs between Stirling and the Bridge of Allan (£3 round-trip) or catch the no. 54 bus from Murray Place in Stirling town center (£4 round-trip).

Doune Castle ★★ CASTLE   For fans of historical romp *Outlander* this is Castle Leoch. In fact, it's had a few starring roles over the years. In the pilot for *Game of Thrones* it doubled as Winterfell and it was one of the locations in the 1975 cult classic *Monty Python and the Holy Grail*. Doune Castle was a medieval stronghold built around 1400. Much of the castle is still intact, and it's easy to get a sense of both domestic and royal life at the time as you wander around the labyrinth of royal apartments, the great hall, kitchens, and cellars all built around a defended courtyard. Make sure you pick up an audio tour (included in the admission charge) narrated by Monty Python's Terry

Jones, which brings to life both the castle's history and the making of the Holy Grail movie. Combine a visit here with a trip to Inchmahome Priory (p. 252), 8½ miles west of Doune, for a history-soaked day out.

Doune. www.historicenvironment.scot. © **01786/841-742.** £6 adults, £3.60 children, £4.80 seniors. Apr–Sept daily 9:30am–5:30pm; Oct–March 10am–4pm.

Dunblane Cathedral ★ CATHEDRAL   Dunblane has been a place of worship since around C.E. 602 when St Blane first established a Christian site here. The cathedral, (where, incidentally, tennis star Andy Murray and Kim Sears married) is one of the few surviving medieval churches in Scotland and dates back to the 12th century. Most of the glorious Gothic architecture still intact today was built in the 13th century and restored in the 19th and 20th centuries. Highlights include a magnificent wooden barrel-vaulted roof with colorful armorials and the Barty windows, two stained-glass windows created by artist Louis Davis in the early 20th century featuring scenes from the Song of Simeon. Housed in the 1624 Dean's House opposite the cathedral, there is a **Cathedral Museum** (www.dunblanemuseum.org.uk; © **01786/825-691**), It's free and displays artifacts, photographs, and papers detailing Dunblane's history. It's open from Easter to mid-October, Monday to Saturday from 10:30am to 4:30pm.

Cathedral Close. www.dunblanecathedral.org.uk. © **01786/823-388.** Free; donation requested. Apr–Sept Mon–Sat 9:30am–5:30pm, Sun 2–5:30pm; Oct–Mar Mon–Sat 10am–4pm, Sun 2–4pm.

Where to Stay & Eat

The accommodation options and restaurants in Stirling itself are not very exciting. There are the usual disappointing, old-fashioned B&Bs and a few historic hotels that have been uninspiringly modernized. The best options can be found in the surrounding countryside, including one of Scotland's most luxurious country house hotels and some lovely farmhouse and heritage B&Bs.

EXPENSIVE

Cromlix ★★★   Tennis superstars spend a lot of the time in five-star hotels. So it should come as no surprise when they decide they've learned enough about what makes them tick to open one. In 2014 Andy Murray launched Cromlix, 3 miles outside his hometown of Dunblane. This Victorian mansion set in 34 acres of secluded grounds and woodland was built for the local laird in 1880 and converted into a country house hotel in 1981. It was the setting for many of the Murray family celebrations during his childhood and where his brother Jamie got married in the tiny private chapel. So when it came up for sale Andy snapped it up.

The day to day running is down to Inverlochy Castle Management, which has a portfolio of properties across Scotland, but Murray was involved in many of the design decisions. He wanted to keep the Highland look but lighten things up a little, mixing antiques with a more contemporary feel. The hotel is swathed in opulent fabrics, there are ancestral portraits on the wood-paneled walls and no fewer than nine log fires. There's a grand games room, a whisky room and a sleek, contemporary conservatory restaurant overseen by the celebrity chef Albert Roux. (Don't miss the legendary signature twice-baked cheese soufflé.)

The 10 rooms and 5 suites are all named after famous Scots, past and present, from Wallace to Fleming. Rooms are sumptuous, some with four-posters and free-standing bath tubs. You can borrow fishing rods to try your hand at catching the brown trout in the private loch and there's also clay pigeon shooting, archery, and falconry. As well as the a la carte menu in the restaurant there is a set three-course lunch for £37 and three-course dinner each day for £40.

Kinbuck. www.cromlix.com. *©* **01786/822-125.** 16 units. Doubles £235–£392, suites £410–£625 includes breakfast. **Amenities:** Restaurant; bar; tennis court; fishing; clay pigeon shooting; archery; games room; free Wi-Fi.

MODERATE

Stirling Highland Hotel ★   This old Victorian school (the bar was once two French classrooms) is now an ordinary modern hotel. It's within strolling distance of the castle and still features a working observatory on the top floor. The new wing and tower were added between 1886 and 1890, and the observatory was paid for by a local MP, Henry Campbell-Bannerman, who later became Prime Minister. Bedrooms are plain and more than a little dated. The Scholars Bar and Restaurant offers three-course dinners for £25 or two courses for £22, and there's also a health club and pool.

Spittal St. www.thecairncollection.co.uk. *©* **01786/272-727.** 96 units. Doubles £95–£200. **Amenities:** Restaurant; pool (indoor); health club; fitness suite; sauna; steam room; free Wi-Fi.

INEXPENSIVE

Cardross ★★   If you want to live like a laird, check into this stately B&B. There are just three charming rooms, each beautifully decorated with antiques and thick floral drapes and boasting views out over the gardens to the parkland beyond. Staying here feels more like visiting well-to-do friends than checking into a B&B. There's a double room with an en suite, a twin bedroom with a private bathroom across the corridor, and a tower room with a private bathroom. The dining room is wood-paneled; the elegant drawing room features a woodburning stove. There are also a handful of self-catering cottages on the estate.

Port of Menteith. www.cardrossestate.com. *©* **01877/385-223.** 3 units. Doubles £110–£120, includes breakfast. **Amenities:** Free Wi-Fi.

The Inn at Kippen ★   A pretty 16th-century coaching inn and gastropub to boot, in a small village just 20 minutes from Stirling, this is a good base for exploring the area. Tuck into a Farmer's Market Sharing platter in the rustic-chic bar: honey grain mustard sausages, oat-rolled Scotch egg, apple and black pudding sausage roll and whisky mayo and apple puree, washed down with a pint from one of the local breweries (Houston, Fallen, and Loch Lomond) before stumbling upstairs to bed in one of the four cozy rooms.

Splash out on the double deluxe (cheap at the price) for rustic-chic style with a rough-hewn wooden bed and emerald metal side lamps.

Fore Rd., Kippen. www.theinnatkippen.co.uk. ℰ **01786/870-500.** 4 units. Doubles £65–£130, includes breakfast. **Amenities:** Free Wi-Fi.

Powis House ★ Old-world charm seeps out of the stonework of this Georgian gem. The 18th-century mansion is in the shadow of the Ochil Hills, just four miles to the northeast of Stirling, and surrounded by gracious grounds. The three bedrooms, Thistle, Heather and Hazel (two doubles and a twin) have old-style elegance with traditional wrought iron or carved wooden beds, original features such as 19th-century fireplaces, polished wooden floors and handmade Harris Tweed curtains and throws. Breakfast is served in the grand dining rooms with fresh Scottish produce and eggs from their hens. (Just a couple of fields away you'll also find the Blairmains Farm Shop and Coffee Bothy: www.blairmains.com; ℰ **01259/762-266.**)

Stirling. Off the A91, just past the Manor Powis roundabout, 4 miles northeast of Stirling. www.powishouse.co.uk. ℰ **01786/460-231.** 3 units. Doubles £110 includes breakfast. Open Mar–Nov. **Amenities:** Free Wi-Fi.

West Plean House ★ This elegant farmhouse B&B is just 3 miles outside Stirling in rolling countryside. The house dates back to 1803 and is set to the side of the working farm, surrounded by sweeping lawns, a lovely walled garden and woodland walks, which are a sea of daffodils in the spring. For breakfast there are free-range eggs and, when you arrive, homemade shortbread and tea. In the drawing room you can browse books in front of the fire or play one of the board games. Rooms are old-school traditional and comfortable, with tranquil views and a smattering of original features.

Denny Rd., 3¾ miles south of Stirling on the A872. www.westpleanhouse.com. ℰ **01786/812-208.** 4 units. Doubles £100, family room £150 includes breakfast. **Amenities:** Free Wi-Fi.

THE TROSSACHS ★★

16 miles NW of Stirling; 43 miles N of Glasgow; 52 miles NW of Edinburgh; 42 miles W of Perth

There's heart-stirring scenery on a loop in the Trossachs, one of Scotland's most jaw-droppingly gorgeous pockets, with glassy lochs fringed by pebbled shores and mirroring majestic mountain peaks. It's sometimes dubbed the Highlands in miniature. Highlights include the **Falls of Leny,** cascades of frothing water crashing through narrow rocks in woodland near the village of Kilmahog and **Glen Finglas,** part of the **Great Trossachs Forest National Nature Reserve,** an area of scenic superlatives, heather clad uplands, and bosky glens.

This is prime road trip country, the 7-mile stretch through the **Dukes Pass** from Kilmahog to Aberfoyle is one of those bucket list drives, originally built by the Duke of Montrose to improve access to his estate and later upgraded

The Trossachs is often referred to as "Rob Roy Country," because the Scottish folk hero and outlaw Rob Roy MacGregor lived and died in this area. Dubbed the Robin Hood of Scotland, Rob Roy was born in 1671 at Glengyle at the head of Loch Katrine and has been immortalized through the works of Sir Walter Scott and the 1995 Hollywood blockbuster starring Liam Neeson. He died in 1734 and is buried at **Balquhidder Church ★**, 13 miles northwest of Callander off the A84 at the eastern tip of **Loch Voil.** You can walk through the churchyard where he is buried up to Kirkton Glen, continuing along through grasslands to a little lake. This footpath leads to the next valley, called Glen Dochart, before it links up once again with A84. Alternatively head west along the banks of this loch to the **Braes o' Balquhidder** where you'll find some of the most bucolic countryside walks in the Trossachs.

for the Victorian tourists flocking here after Sir Walter Scott let the cat out of the bag about local beauty spot **Loch Katrine** in his poem *The Lady of the Lake.* It's also **Rob Roy Country.** Hero or hoodlum? From the Highlands to Hollywood, this highwayman, blackmailer, and Scottish Robin Hood has been immortalized, and his escapades have led to the creation of a 77-mile long distance walking route from Drymen north of Glasgow to Pitlochry.

The Trossachs is part of **Loch Lomond and the Trossachs National Park,** the first national park to be founded in Scotland in 2002. It encompasses 720 acres of spectacular mountain scenery and is prime outdoor activity terrain, from mountain biking to munro-bagging, hiking, fishing, kayaking, you name it—it's one big outdoor adventure playground out there. Within its boundaries there are over 20 munros (mountains over 3000-ft: Ben Lui, Beinn Challuim, Ben Lomond and Ben Vorlich for a start), 19 corbetts (slightly lower than a munro), and over 50 areas designated "special nature conservation sites."

Essentials

GETTING THERE   Stirling (p. 242) is the nearest train station. From here you can catch the C59 bus to Callander, a 45-minute journey (www.firstgroup.com; ✆ **0141/420-7600**). Driving from Stirling, head north along the M9 to junction 10 and then cut northwest along the A84.

Callander

Callander is the gateway to the Trossachs and has been pulling in the tourists since the end of the 19th century. This little town, littered with the usual gift shops, woolen mills, and a peppering of artisan eateries is one of the most obvious bases for exploring the Trossachs. The **VisitScotland iCentre** (www.visitscotland.com; ✆ **01877/330-342**) is located at 52-54 Main Street and is open April to the end of October daily 9:30am to 5pm, November to the end of March daily from 9:30am to 4pm and has information on local walks, cycling and mountain biking trails, and places to visit.

This is a great center for outdoor activities and there are a handful of walks from the center of town and trails nearby such as a 4-mile hike to **Bracklinn Falls.** Or head deeper into the Trossachs to the village of **Brig o' Turk,** 6¾ miles from Callander, which lies between lochs Achray and Venachar, at the foot of **Glen Finglas,** for treks through stunning forests studded with lochs.

Where to Eat & Stay

Harbour Café ★ SCOTTISH Location, location, location. This little lochside cafe is perched right on the water's edge 4 miles north of Callander on Loch Venachar. From the picnic tables and benches scattered with vibrant cushion and rugs on the wooden decking, and through the floor-to-ceiling windows of the restaurant, you can gaze over to the wooded shores on the opposite bank. Tuck into starters showcasing local, seasonal ingredients such as McQueen's of Callander Gin and citrus cured salmon with a beetroot scone, Katy Rodgers crème fraiche, fresh horseradish, pickled cucumber, and beetroot foam. Or how about foraged mushroom and chestnut pate with pear and shallot chutney, toasted nut dukkha, confit tomato, and carrot bread? For mains, there is trout from the loch, and you can also arrange boat rental and fishing at the cafe.

Loch Venachar. www.venachar-lochside.com. ☏ **01877/330-011.** Main courses £13– £18. Daily from 10am, lunch noon-4pm.

Monachyle Mhor ★★ The entrepreneurial Lewis family have a portfolio of innovative accommodations and artisan eateries (Mhor Fish and Mhor Bread) in Callander and Balquhidder glen. The family farm, Monachyle Mhor, is now a gourmet boutique hotel with a choice of Feature, Farmhouse and Courtyard rooms. The four rooms in the original farmhouse are quirky and cozy, all white wood paneling, antlers on the wall and splashes of vibrant color. The six Feature rooms (Granary, Sawmill, Midnight, Coach House, Sprocket and Suite 16) are decadent and striking, decked out with an eclectic mix of antique furniture and contemporary designer pieces. Midnight has twin slipper baths while Sprocket has a raised bed and views over the glen. There's also a cabin on the grounds, the old waiting room from the Port Appin to the Isle of Lismore ferry was converted into a funky place to bed down, complete with cozy woodburner. The family also took on the tired old Kingshouse Hotel, a former coaching inn, just off the A84 at the end of the glen, converting it into a cool motel with 11 quirky rooms and a holiday cottage (www. mhor84.net; ☏ **01877/384-646**).

Balquhidder. www.monachylemhor.net. ☏ **01877/384-622.** 16 units. Doubles £195– £285 includes breakfast. **Amenities:** Restaurant; bar; free Wi-Fi

Roman Camp Hotel ★ Pretty in pink: This turreted confection was once a 17th-century hunting lodge, built for the Dukes of Perth in 1625 on the site of an old Roman camp. It's surrounded by 20 acres of gardens, paraded by preening peacocks and tumbling down to the wild brown trout-, sea trout- and salmon-stocked River Teith. (The hotel has its own fishing beat, the term for private area of riverbank where guests can fish for free.) The property has been a hotel for almost a hundred years, famous for its afternoon tea (£23 per person), within the silk-paneled walls of the drawing room, its wood-paneled library (and hidden chapel) and the Whyte bar with its grand piano and collection of malt whiskies. The cozy bedrooms are eclectically furnished with a smattering of antiques and William Morris wallpaper. Dining in the restaurant is a formal, white linen affair with mains from £29 to £33. Some of the produce is grown in the hotel's own gardens.

Main St., Callander. www.romancamphotel.co.uk. *C* **01877/330-003.** 15 units. Doubles £160–£260; suite £290 includes breakfast. **Amenities:** Restaurant; bar; free fishing; free Wi-Fi.

ABERFOYLE ★

56 miles NW of Edinburgh; 26 miles N of Glasgow

This pretty little village has had some high-profile fans over the centuries. Sir Walter Scott fell for this spot at the beginning of the 19th-century and his evocative verses even lured Wordsworth and Coleridge away from their beloved Lake District. Wordsworth was so inspired he wrote *To a Highland Girl*. Fast forward a few decades and Queen Victoria was so enchanted by the beauty of the region that she had a holiday home built on nearby Loch Katrine.

Essentials

GETTING THERE The Loch Lomond and Trossachs National Park has a section dedicated to getting to the park on the website at www.lochlomond-trossachs.org highlighting public transport options, although these are sketchy at best and to really explore the area, you need a car. From Stirling, take the A84 west until you reach the junction of the A873 and continue west to Aberfoyle. **First** (www.firstgroup.com; *C* **01324/602-200**) operates the C11 bus from Stirling to Aberfoyle and the journey takes about an hour.

VISITOR INFORMATION The **Aberfoyle iCentre** is on Main Street (*C* **01877/381-221**). It's open April to November daily 10am to 5pm; November to March daily 10am to 4pm.

Exploring the Area

The **Queen Elizabeth Forest Park ★★** stretches from the eastern shore of Loch Lomond to the rugged peaks of Strathyre in the Trossachs and encompasses 50,000 acres of spectacular terrain from mountain to moorland, pungent pine forest and bosky woodland, burbling rivers, and steely lochs. Within its boundaries is the impressive **Lodge Forest Visitor Centre** (*C* **0300/067-6615**) around a mile north of Aberfoyle in Achray Forest. It was gifted to the Forestry Commission in 1960 by the Carnegie Trust, and along with a smart, contemporary cafe, information center, and magnificent views, offers live wildlife viewing via CCTV cameras of osprey, peregrines, red squirrel, and

A loch AND A LAKE ★

Loch Katrine is a freshwater loch, 8 miles long, whose beauty once inspired flowery verse. Its name is a little more prosaic and comes from the Gaelic for Highland thief—Rob Roy was born on its northern shores. Sir Walter Scott put pen to paper in 1810 after being captivated by its bucolic good looks, drafting the *Lady of the Lake* after his visit and sparking a 19th-century tourist boom. Queen Victoria then sailed its waters in 1869 and was so taken with the setting she built a holiday home here. Today you can still clamber onboard the small steamer, the *Sir Walter Scott*, which first set sail in 1899 or ply its waters on the more modern boat, the *Lady of the Lake* (www.lochkatrine.com; ✆ **01877/376-315**). Regular sailings depart from Easter to late October, between Trossachs Pier and Stronachlachar; a 2-hour round-trip fare on the *Sir Walter Scott* costs £17 for adults, £15.50 for seniors and students, and £9 for children 15 and under and £42 for a family.

And if you're equally enamored with the location you can bed down here too, in one of the eight quaint Hobbit-like eco-houses huddled beneath the trees. The lodges are named after local lochs: Arklet, Venachar, Achray and Katrine. Katrine sleeps two and has a king-size bed and full glass front, giving views over the loch to Ben Venue. Arklet sleeps two and has a ramp for disabled access and Achray and Venachar sleep four. They cost from £80 per night.

The Lake of Menteith, 4 miles east of Aberfoyle, is famous for being Scotland's only lake that's actually called a lake and not a loch. Loch is the Scots word for lake, although you can also get sea lochs, which are sea inlets—are you with us so far? Regardless of nomenclature, this pretty lake is dotted with a handful of small islands, one of which is home to **Inchmahome Priory** ★ a ruined Augustinian monastery dating back to 1238. Robert the Bruce is known to have sought solace here and it was once a refuge for Mary Queen of Scots. You can visit the island, a peaceful rural haven home to three Spanish chestnut trees; fish the waters, which are brimming with rainbow and brown trout; or picnic on the banks.

The small boat from the Port of Menteith holds 12 people, and the crossing takes just 7 minutes. Boats run daily April to September from 10am with the last sailing at 4:15pm, and daily throughout October from 10am with the last sailing at 3:15pm. The ticket price includes the crossing and is £7.50 for adults, £6 for seniors, and £4.50 for children 5 to 15. For information call ✆ **01877/385-294,** or see www.historicenvironment.scot.

badgers. There are numerous walking and cycling trails snaking through the park. From the lodge, the 1.75-mile **Oak Coppice Trail** takes you through ancient woodland strung with velvety lichen, while the 4-mile **Lime Craig Trail** climbs through the forest for magnificent views over the Carse of Stirling and along part of the geological fault that separates the Highlands from the Lowlands.

Around Loch Ard nearby, two of the best walks for families are the **Lochan Spling Trail** (2 miles) an area teeming with wildlife and the **Loch Ard Sculpture Trail** (3½ miles). In the lodge's grounds you will also find **Go Ape** (www.goape.co.uk; ✆ **0845/094-9032**) for budding Tarzans, a treetop adventure course strung with rope ladders, bridges, swings, and zip wires through the forest canopy. Booking is essential during the summer; it costs £28 for gorillas (adults) and £22 for baboons (children ages 10–15). The Lodge is open daily July and August from 10am to 6pm, May to June and September from 10am to 5pm, March to April and October to December 10am to 4pm and January and February 10am to 3pm.

Where to Eat & Stay

Lake of Menteith ★ At the heart of this lovely lakeside hotel is an 18th-century manse (the Gothic-style church is still next door). The hotel that grew up around it dates back to 1854, when it was known as the Port of Menteith Inn. Today, it is a charming country retreat with spectacular views from the waterfront restaurant. Rooms are decorated in a New England Bostonian style—think soothing cream tones and the odd half-tester bed. Try to bag one of the elegant lakeview rooms. The restaurant focuses on showcasing seasonal Scottish ingredients—some with almost no carbon footprint or food miles at all (pan-seared Lake of Menteith trout). Then there's Perthshire venison loin with truffled wild mushroom risotto or Prosciutto-wrapped local pheasant breast on chestnut bubble and squeak with balsamic jus. And if you fancy a nightcap, the hotel also has a malt whisky tasting room where you can splash out on a 36-year-old cask strength Isle of Jura, or how about a 40 year-old Glengoyne? Distilled in 1968 and one of only 250 bottles in the world available by the glass, it has crème brûlée and red apples on the nose and ripe bananas and spiced plums in the mouth. On the wallet it's an eye-watering £450 for the opening nip, £220 if you fancy another.

Port of Menteith. www.lake-hotel.com. *C* **01877/385-258.** 16 units. Doubles £138–£255 includes breakfast. **Amenities:** Restaurant; bar; free Wi-Fi.

Macdonald Forest Hills Hotel & Spa ★ This elegant loch-side resort hotel, set on Loch Ard in 25 acres of landscaped grounds, had a smart revamp in 2017. There are 55 charming rooms—with a touch of tartan (throws, drapes, and armchairs) in the house itself, some with sweeping views and balconies overlooking the gardens and loch to the mountains beyond. There are roaring fires to curl up besides—and a dreamy Elemis spa and leisure center with a good gym, indoor pool, and steam room. The resort also has a number of loch-facing lodges, ideal for families, which come with one to three bedrooms, private balcony or patio, fully equipped kitchen—and a private sauna. Dining options include the Garden Restaurant (try free-range confit chicken and rabbit terrine followed by seared fillet of wild cod with truffle pomme puree and wild mushrooms) and the relaxed Rafters Bar & Bistro.

Kinlochard, Aberfoyle. www.macdonaldhotels.co.uk. *C* **0344/879-9057.** 120 units. Doubles £80–£479, suites £219–£882. **Amenities:** 2 restaurants; bar; pool (indoor); health club and spa; kids club; room service; free Wi-Fi.

THE BONNIE, BONNIE BANKS OF LOCH LOMOND ★

The largest of Scotland's lochs packs a wallop of scenic splendor. The river-fed loch stretches for 24 miles between forested heights, none more imposing than Ben Lomond on the eastern shore, rising to 968m (3,176 ft.). Surrounding the lakes are woodland glens, braes (hills), and smaller lochs, all making up the 720-square-mile **Loch Lomond and the Trossachs National Park** (www.lochlomond-trossachs.org). A commonwealth of "elfs, fawns, and fairies" is how one 18th-century observer described this region of shimmering waters, moors, and woodlands.

This region was once dominated by the powerful Lennox clan, but their ancient lands were divided following the execution of the Earl of Lennox in 1425, and much of them possessed by the branch of the Stewart (Stuart) family that spawned Lord Darnley, Mary Queen of Scots' ill-fated second husband. The ruins of **Lennox Castle** stand on Inchmurrin, one of the loch's 30 islands, also famous for its yew trees, planted by Robert the Bruce to ensure a suitable supply of wood for the bows of his archers.

The famous song "Loch Lomond" was supposedly composed by one of Bonnie Prince Charlie's followers on the eve of his execution in Carlisle Jail. The "low road" of the song is the path through the underworld that his spirit will follow to his native land after death, more quickly than his friends can travel to Scotland by the ordinary "high road."

ESSENTIALS

GETTING THERE A regular train operated by **ScotRail** (www.scotrail.co.uk; ☏ **0344/811-0141**) runs between Glasgow Queen Street and Balloch stations. The journey takes around 45 minutes. **Scottish CityLink** (www.citylink.co.uk; ☏ **0871/266-3333**) and **First** (www.firstgroup.com; ☏ **0871/200-2233**) run several buses a day to Balloch from Glasgow; the trip takes 45 minutes.

VISITOR INFORMATION The **VisitScotland iCentre** is located in the old station building in the town center on Balloch Road (www.visitscotland.com; ☏ **01389/753-533**). It's open daily from 9:30am in summer and 10am in winter until 6pm except November to March when it closes at 5pm. However, one of the best places to find out more about the region is the flagship **National Park Centre** off the B837 at Balmaha (www.lochlomond-trossachs.org; ☏ **01389/722-100**), on the banks of Loch Lomond which opens daily Easter to October 9:30am to 4pm and weekends-only the rest of the year.

EXPLORING THE AREA

While you can reach some places in the national park by bus, a car makes touring much easier.

BALLOCH   You'll probably catch your first glimpse of Loch Lomond at Balloch. On a sunny day it will probably seem like the entire population of Glasgow has had the same idea and decamped to the loch, but you can soon get out onto the water and leave the crowds behind. **Sweeney's Cruisers** (www.sweeneyscruiseco.com; ℂ **01389/752-376**), depart from Sweeney's Shipyard off Balloch Road. The 1-hour circular cruise around the loch's southern basin takes in a number of stately homes along the shore. Keep an eye out for the ruins of **Lennox Castle** on Inchmurrin, one of the loch's 33 islands, where Robert the Bruce sheltered in the 14th century. The cruise costs £10.50 for adults, £7 for children under 12, £8.50 for children between 12 and 15, under 5's go free. A family of two adults and two children costs £30, two adults and three children costs £35. **Loch Lomond Shores** (www.lochlomondshores.com; ℂ **01389/751-035**), an unabashedly touristic enclave on the eastern edge of town off Ben Lomond Way, is also the departure point for cruises; you can rent bikes, kayaks, and canoes as well.

Along the nearby shores, the 81-hectare (200-acre) **Balloch Castle Country Park** ★ surrounds **Balloch Castle** (www.west-dunbarton.gov.uk; ℂ **01389/752-977**; 8am–dusk daily; free), built in 1808 in the Gothic style. The landscape is a mix of ornamental woodland, open parkland, meadows, and walled gardens, and there's an impressive display of rhododendrons and azaleas in late May and early June. The park is about 1 mile east of town.

DRYMEN ★   This lakeshore village 5 miles northeast of Balloch was at one time known for the famous visitors to **Buchanan Castle** ★★, the ancient fortress of the Duke of Montrose. Hitler's deputy, Rudolf Hess, was imprisoned here in 1941 after he flew solo to Scotland to negotiate a peace agreement with Britain. Other illustrious guests have included the Shah of Iran and King Victor Emmanuel of Italy. The roof was removed in 1955 to avoid paying tax, and the castle fell into the romantic ruin you see today.

BALMAHA ★   Things quiet down a bit on the eastern shore 4 miles west of Drymen. Excellent walking trails lead into the surrounding countryside from the **National Park Visitor Centre** (ℂ **01389/722-100**). The Balmaha

---

You Take the High Road & I'll Take the Low Road

One of the great long distance walks in Scotland, the **West Highland Way** (www.westhighlandway.org) runs along the eastern side of Loch Lomond. The trail starts at Milngavie, outside Glasgow, and ends 96 miles later at Fort William and the foot of Ben Nevis. Serious walkers often hike the whole route, but you can just tackle sections of it.

The website breaks it down into bitesize chunks and day hikes. Most people trek south to north as the southern section is easier going and gives you time to build up your stamina for the harder slogs. However much of the trail you do, it will take you through some of Scotland's most iconic and breathtaking scenery.

Millennium Forest Trail follows a circular route via the oak-lined shore before climbing up to Craigie Fort for a magnificent view over the loch. You can board a vintage wooden ferry for a loch cruise at the **Balmaha Boatyard** (www.balmahaboatyard.co.uk; *C* **01360/870-214**) or for the short hop over to Inchcailloch Island, a 52-hectare nature reserve cobwebbed with walking trails through oak woods carpeted with bluebells in spring.

LUSS ★★ This storybook collection of picturesque sandstone and slate cottages, now a conservation village, is essentially an 18th-century town improvement scheme. There has been a settlement here, on the western shores of Loch Lomond, 8⅔ miles north of Balloch off the A82, since the 7th century, however, and in the churchyard you can still see gravestones from the Dark Ages. The **Luss Visitor Centre** (*C* **01436/860-229**) is open daily from 10am until 7pm in summer and from 10am until 4pm in winter.

WHERE TO EAT & STAY

Balloch House This traditional inn (low-beamed ceilings, flagstone floors) by the river in the center of the village has been given a funky revamp and has a handful of contemporary bedrooms. The bar has a roaring fire and mismatched tables and chairs in vintage fabrics or rich red leather and scattered with vibrantly colored cushions. It's cozy and quirky. The large dining area is a family-friendly spot for either lunch or dinner; the outside decking is great in summer.

Balloch Rd., Balloch. www.vintageinn.co.uk. *C* **08451/551-551.** 12 units. Doubles £72–£99. **Amenities:** Restaurant; bar; free Wi-Fi.

Loch Lomond Arms Hotel ★★ This former coaching inn dates back to the 17th century and is by far the loveliest place to stay on Loch Lomond. Rooms are named after Scottish clans, some under the eaves, others in the coach house, and have been gorgeously renovated, all tongue and groove, freestanding slipper baths, and a soft color palette of dove greys, dusky pinks, periwinkle blues, and cream. Colquhoun has loch views; Lomond a romantic four-poster and views over the village; while the two-floor Riversedge suite is a short walk away on the banks of Luss Water. All individually designed, they are peppered with antiques, woolen throws, a smattering of tasteful tweed and tartan, and vintage prints.

Main Rd., Luss. www.lochlomondarmshotel.com. *C* **01436/860-420.** Doubles £180–£210, suite £250. **Amenities:** Restaurant; bar; free Wi-Fi.

The Lodge on Loch Lomond Hotel ★ Do you want to bed down in a classic Graham, a deluxe Corbett, or an executive Munro? (Munros are mountains over 3,000 ft., Corbetts between 2,500 ft. and 3,000 ft., Grahams between 2,000 ft. and 2,500 ft.). This modern loch-front hotel surrounded by mountains and woodland has it all when it comes to location, and rooms classified like lofty peaks (although the Carter suite was named after the ex-American president, Jimmy Carter, who liked to bed down here), some with views of the beach and loch, others with private saunas. The hotel has its own jetty and can organize a range of watersports for you to enjoy just a pebble's throw away from stand-up paddle-boarding to speedboat rides and canoe safaris. And after you've worked up an appetite you can tuck into the best that Scotland's natural larder can dish up on the outside decking or in front of the picture windows looking out over the loch in Colquhoun's restaurant.

Luss. www.loch-lomond.co.uk. © **01436/860-201.** 46 units. Doubles £144–£215; £214–£275 suite. **Amenities:** Watersports; restaurant; bar; free Wi-Fi.

ABERDEEN, THE GRAMPIANS & TAYSIDE

By Lucy Gillmore

Draw a line roughly north to south from the Moray Firth to Perth and the Firth of Tay: To the east is a rugged mountainous region bordered by the North Sea, crammed with castles and whisky distilleries. Tayside is named after the longest river in Scotland, the Tay, which flows down from the Highlands through the cities of Perth and Dundee and offers some of Europe's best salmon and trout fishing. The Grampians boasts granite Aberdeen, Scotland's third city, as well as Braemar, home to one of the most famous Highland Gatherings, attended by the Queen and royal family.

CITIES **Aberdeen,** the Granite City, might boast an ancient university, but for years has been synonymous with the offshore oil industry. Farther south, down-at-heel **Dundee** has been dusting itself off and is now more famous for design than its marmalade and past as a whaling port. Designated a UNESCO City of Design, 2018 saw the launch of a glittering new museum, the V&A Dundee. Inland, genteel **Perth** is a sleepy town on the River Tay, but was once the capital of Scotland. On its outskirts is Scone Palace, where Scottish kings were once crowned.

COUNTRYSIDE **Perthshire** is "hunting, shooting, fishing" territory, famous for its salmon fishing, shooting estates, and golf courses. The rolling hills of **Speyside** attract whisky buffs tippling from distillery to distillery on the bucolic Malt Whisky Trail. **Aberdeenshire** is Castle Country, with a clutch of turreted confections such as Fyvie Castle and the Queen's Highland holiday home, Balmoral.

EATING & DRINKING The larder is stocked with Aberdeen Angus beef from the north-east's lush, green farmland, wild venison from the Highland estates and smoked salmon. If you get the

The Tayside & Grampian Regions

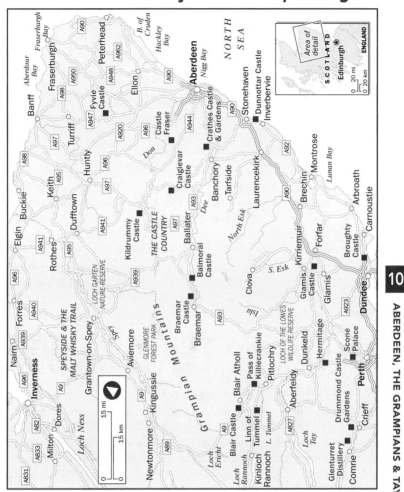

chance, try an **"Arbroath smokie,"** or splash out on the gourmet tasting menu at Andrew Fairlie's at **Gleneagles,** Scotland's only two-Michelin-starred restaurant. Then curl up with a dram. Speyside is home to a host of distilleries and the rural **Malt Whisky Trail.**

COAST   There's more to this stretch of coast than sand and sea. Golfers arrive in droves at the seaside resort of **Carnoustie** for its championship links courses. Farther north, **Dunnottar Castle** teeters on the clifftop above the bleak North Sea. Aberdeen's **Maritime Museum** fills in the backstory to the region's remarkable seafaring history, from the herring industry to oil drilling.

Don't Leave Aberdeen, Tayside & the Grampians Without . . .

Marveling at the V&A Dundee. The regenerated waterfront in this UNESCO City of Design is the location for the only V&A museum anywhere in the world outside London. It's an architectural showstopper celebrating Scotland's design heritage and future. See p. 290.

Meandering the postcard-perfect streets of Dunkeld. One of the prettiest villages in Scotland, most of the buildings were painstakingly restored by the National Trust. See p. 281.

Shopping for Scottish cashmere in Elgin. With its medieval center, magnificent ruined cathedral, and elegant townhouses, Elgin oozes history. At Johnstons of Elgin's cashmere emporium, café, and homewares store, you can tour the old mill before stocking up on luxury woolens. See p. 304.

Winding through Speyside's bucolic countryside on the Malt Whisky Trail. Follow this well-trodden tourist route, taking in a handful of distilleries along the way, from The Glenlivet to Glenfiddich and historic Dallas Dhu. At the Speyside Cooperage watch the barrels being charred. See p. 299.

Following in royal footsteps at Glamis Castle. The late Queen Mother's childhood home and the castle where Princess Margaret was born is a turreted beauty. It's also steeped in literary connections, featuring in Shakespeare's play *Macbeth*. See p. 293.

ABERDEEN & CASTLE COUNTRY
★★

130 miles NE of Edinburgh; 67 miles N of Dundee

Fringed with wide, sandy beaches and lapped by the North Sea, Aberdeen's coastal location has influenced its economy throughout its history. In the 18th century, the harbor bobbed with small boats fishing for herring or "silver darlings." At the beginning of the 19th century, whaling had taken over; by the end of the century, fleets of trawlers would land their catch here. Today, the fishing trawlers have been replaced with vessels servicing the offshore oil industry. Although, that too, is changing, the city's fortunes suffering as a result of the global slump in oil prices.

The Granite City does have other strings to its bow including a clutch of cultural attractions and an ancient university. The cobbled streets of **Old Aberdeen** are home to the **University of Aberdeen,** where you can wander round the ancient buildings of King's College as well as the **Cathedral of St Machar** and the **Cruickshank Botanic Garden.**

The city is also a good base for exploring the castles in the vicinity, fishing the salmon-rich River Dee, and playing golf at one of the many courses in the area.

Aberdeen

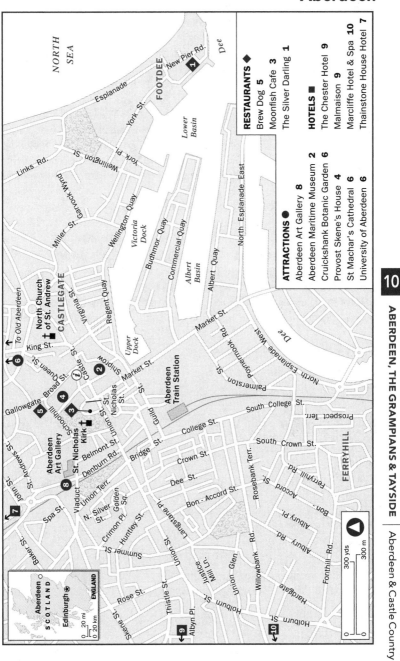

RESTAURANTS ◆
Brew Dog **5**
Moonfish Cafe **3**
The Silver Darling **1**

HOTELS ■
The Chester Hotel **9**
Malmaison **9**
Marcliffe Hotel & Spa **10**
Thainstone House Hotel **7**

ATTRACTIONS ●
Aberdeen Art Gallery **8**
Aberdeen Maritime Museum **2**
Cruickshank Botanic Garden **6**
Provost Skene's House **4**
St Machar's Cathedral **6**
University of Aberdeen **6**

Essentials

GETTING THERE   Aberdeen is served by a number of airlines, including British Airways, Flybe, easyJet, Ryanair, Aer Lingus, SAS and KLM. For flight information, contact Aberdeen **Airport** (www.aberdeenairport.com; ✆ **0344/481-6666**), which is situated about 6¾ miles from the city center and connected by a bus service. Dyce train station is just 2 miles from the airport and on the Inverness to Aberdeen line and easily reached by taxi.

Aberdeen has direct rail links to Britain's major cities. For fares and schedules, check out **ScotRail** (www.scotrail.co.uk; ✆ **0344/811-0141**). The journey from Edinburgh takes about 2½ hours, from Glasgow around 3 hours.

Several bus companies have express routes serving Aberdeen including **CityLink** (www.citylink.co.uk; ✆ **0871/266-3333**). Frequent buses arrive from both Glasgow and Edinburgh, and the journey time from both is around 3 hours. There are also frequent arrivals from Inverness. For bus schedules in Aberdeen, call **Stagecoach** at ✆ **01224/212-266.**

If you're heading to the northeast by car from Edinburgh head over the Queensferry Crossing and Tay bridges, and take the coastal road.

VISITOR INFORMATION   The **VisitScotland iCentre** is in the center of the city at 23 Union St. (www.visitabdn.com; ✆ **01224/269-180**). During the summer it's open Monday through Saturday 9am to 6:30pm, Wednesday from 9:30am and Sunday 10am to 4pm. From September through December it's open Monday through Saturday 9:30am to 5pm, Wednesday from 10am and Sunday 11am to 4pm. From January through March it's open Monday through Saturday 9:30am to 5pm.

Exploring Aberdeen

Aberdeen is known as the Granite City and can feel slightly dour and forbidding, its grand, grey architecture veering toward the severe. It was originally two distinct quarters, Old Aberdeen and New Aberdeen. Today, Old Aberdeen, where you'll find its ancient university and St Machar's Cathedral, is a hidden gem with its cobbled streets and tranquil atmosphere, yet just a half-hour walk or short drive from the bustling center of town.

The **University of Aberdeen** (www.abdn.ac.uk; ✆ **01224/272-000**) is the third-oldest university in Scotland and the fifth-oldest in the U.K. In fact, **King's College,** along University Road, is the oldest school of medicine in the U.K., founded by William Elphinstone, Bishop of Aberdeen and Chancellor of Scotland in 1495 to train doctors, teachers and clergy. The college is particularly renowned for its chapel (dating from around 1500), its pre-Reformation carved woodwork is the finest of its kind in Scotland; it's open daily 9am to 4:30pm, is free to visit, and you can download a self-guided tour and map from the website.

In the center of town on Broad Street, don't miss the spectacular exterior of **Marischal College,** founded in 1593 by Earl Marischal—it's the second-largest granite structure in the world (after El Escorial, outside Madrid). In

1860, the two colleges joined together to form the nucleus of the University of Aberdeen, however, the building is no longer used for teaching and is leased to Aberdeen Council.

Also part of the University of Aberdeen, the **Cruickshank Botanic Garden,** St Machar Drive (www.abdn.ac.uk/botanic-garden; ✆ **01224/272-704**), is a peaceful 11-acre haven founded in 1898 and featuring an arboretum, rock and water gardens and fine collections of alpines, shrubs, and herbaceous plants. It's free to visit and open daily April to September from 9am to 7pm; October to March, it's open daily 9am to 4:30pm. It's closed from 24 December to 5 January.

The **Cathedral of St Machar,** The Chanonry (www.stmachar.com; ✆ **01224/485-988**) was founded in 1131, but the present structure dates from the 15th century. Its splendid heraldic ceiling contains three rows of shields. Look out for the magnificent modern stained-glass windows by Douglas Strachan and the pre-Reformation woodwork. The cathedral is open daily April to October 9:30am to 4:30pm; November to March 10am to 4pm.

Aberdeen Art Gallery ★ GALLERY   Built in 1884 to neoclassical designs by A. Marshall MacKenzie, Aberdeen Art Gallery closed its doors in 2015 for a ground-breaking £30 million redevelopment, reopening in 2019. Also comprising Cowdray Hall (a concert venue) and Remembrance Hall, the glittering new cultural complex will contain twice as many galleries to showcase what is one of the most important art collections in Great Britain. It includes 18th-century portraits by Raeburn, Hogarth, Ramsay, and Reynolds, as well as acclaimed 20th-century works by Paul Nash, Ben Nicholson, and Francis Bacon. In addition there are paintings by Monet, Pissarro, Sisley, and Bonnard, as well as a collection of Scottish domestic silver.

Schoolhill. www.aagm.co.uk. ✆ **01224/523-700.** Free admission. Daily 10am–5pm.

Aberdeen Maritime Museum ★ MUSEUM   This eclectic collection of model ships, historic oil paintings and artifacts and films gives a fascinating overview of the city's long relationship with the sea from herring fishing during the 18th-century to the discovery of oil in the North Sea. A major display on the offshore oil industry features a model of the Murchison oil platform and an in-depth film outlining life on a rig. The complex is on four floors, incorporating the 1593 Provost Ross House linked by a modern glass structure to the granite Trinity Church. Windows open onto panoramic views of the harbor.

Shiprow. www.aagm.co.uk. ✆ **01224/337-700.** Free admission. Mon–Sat 10am–5pm; Sun noon–3pm.

Provost Skene's House HISTORIC HOME   Check out the exterior of this impressive historic building, named after a rich merchant who was Lord Provost of Aberdeen from 1676 to 1685, now cradled by the new development of Marischal Square. Originally housing a small museum with displays of artifacts relating to domestic life, it was closed during the square's redevelopment. Its new format, charting the achievements of local figures over the centuries, will be revealed during 2019.

5 Guestrow, off Broad St. www.aagm.co.uk. ℗ **01224/641-086.**

Where to Stay & Eat

Travellers have been held to ransom for years by Aberdeen hoteliers because of the high demand for accommodation from the offshore oil industry. Room rates were racked up to ridiculous levels for largely uninspiring business hotels because the oil companies, one way or another, were picking up the tab. The city is blanketed with all the usual chains from Mercure to Marriott, Hilton to Ibis, Travelodge and Premier Inn. With the downturn that left many floundering. Now there is more availability and prices are no longer astronomical, but the city still lags behind cities such as Edinburgh in the style stakes.

EXPENSIVE

The Chester Hotel ★   Practically next door to the Malmaison, in Aberdeen's fashionable West End, this is another hotel formed from two traditional granite townhouses. Design-wise the interiors are contemporary in a muted palette of espresso, cappuccino, and latte (yep, shades of brown). The IX restaurant dishes up mains such as Mossie's farm pork belly, aromatic glazed cheek, sweet potato, cashew nuts, and sherry jus along with loin and shoulder of Dornoch lamb, peas, Jersey royals, tomato, goats curd, and lamb jus with prices ranging from £18 to £30.

59 Queens Rd. www.chester-hotel.com. ℗ **01224/327-777.** 50 units. £104–£231 double, £192–£251, includes breakfast. **Amenities:** Restaurant; bar; gym; free Wi-Fi.

Malmaison ★★   The Malmaison is in a smart residential district about half an hour's walk from the city center, the broad leafy streets lined with elegant mansions housing schools, bank headquarters and wealth management companies. The grand, granite building is set back from the street, in front of the entrance are a smattering of tables and chairs for al fresco aperitifs. Inside the music is pumping and the trademark dramatic decor takes over, all dark wood and giant tartan chairs in reception. The cozy bar boasts an enclosed glass whisky room displaying over 100 malts while the Chez Mal Brasserie is cavernous with tasteful tartan and tweed (softs greens and greys) and ox-blood leather chairs, banquettes, and booths. The double height ceilings strung with the signature industrial piping and antlers and boars' heads mounted on the walls. The menu includes prime cuts of aged Aberdeen Angus beef, steaks cooked on the Josper Grill charcoal oven (450g prime rib £34 to T-bone £36). However, there is also a vegan menu featuring dishes such as squash and red onion tagine, coriander and apricot couscous (£13.50) and caramel roasted pineapple with sorbet and almonds (£6.50).

Bedrooms and suites feature the same dramatic decoration, dark wood furniture, tasteful tartan carpets, over-sized padded headboards and heavy taffeta-style drapes. The beds are some of the dreamiest around, downy feather pillows, marshmallow soft and topped with crisp white linen.

49–53 Queen's Rd. www.malmaison.com. ℂ **01224/507-097.** 79 units. £104–£183 double; £214–£373 suite, includes breakfast. Free parking. **Amenities:** Restaurant; bar; spa; free Wi-Fi.

Marcliffe Hotel & Spa ★★ On the city's western edge, just a couple of miles from the center, and less than half an hour from the airport, the Marcliffe has long been regarded as Aberdeen's best hotel. The elegant white Victorian house, dating back to 1852, is set in 3.2 hectares (8 acres) of beautifully landscaped gardens. It was opened (bizarrely) by former Soviet president Mikhail Gorbachev in 1993, and famous guests have included Prince Charles, Tony Blair, Rod Stewart, Charlton Heston, and golfer Tom Watson. It is a family-owned property and the drawing room, bar and lounge, decorated with paintings by Scottish artists, are peppered with items collected by the Spence family over the years (including a collection of 140 cheese dishes). There's a log fire to cozy up beside with a dram (the bar has over a hundred malt whiskies) and also a baby grand piano. Bedrooms are on the traditional side, with muted colors and reproduction antique furniture, while the Conservatory restaurant focuses on regional produce such as lemon sole and monkfish from Peterhead, Aberdeen Angus beef and venison from the Auchmacoy estate. Main courses cost between £19 and £45. The spa offers a range of decadent treatments from hot stone to aromatherapy and Swedish massage.

N. Deeside Rd., Pitfodels. www.marcliffe.com. ℂ **01224/861-000.** 40 units. £150–£190 double; £250–£350 suite, includes breakfast. Free parking. **Amenities:** Restaurant; bar; spa; free Wi-Fi.

Moonfish Cafe ★★ MODERN BRITISH This cool little joint in the medieval merchants' quarter looks out onto the 12th-century kirk of St Nicholas. With an unfussy French bistro style (think wooden floors, bistro chairs, and pale grey wood paneling), it's a relaxed restaurant dishing up a mouth-wateringly inventive menu (dishes look like culinary works of art) focused firmly on fresh, seasonal produce. Small plates include cured haddock, cabbage, carrot, shrimp and whipped feta with beetroot, cucumber, and toast. "Large" dishes of pork belly, artichoke, broccoli or grilled onion, gnocchi, ricotta, almond are equally tempting.

9 Correction Wynd. www.moonfishcafe.co.uk. ℂ **01224/644-166.** Lunch main courses £9.95–£10.95. Two-course lunch menu £17; Dinner 2 courses £30, 3 courses £36, 4 courses £44. Tues–Fri noon–2pm and 6–9pm, Sat noon–2:30pm and 6–9pm.

The Silver Darling ★ MODERN SCOTTISH Silver Darling is the local nickname for herring, and this popular restaurant down on the cobbled quayside in the old customs house sits at the mouth of the harbor. From the upstairs restaurant, dramatic floor-to-ceiling windows give panoramic views over Aberdeen's long sweep of sand and the historic fishing village, Footdee, known locally as "Fittie," along with occasional sighting of dolphins and seals in the bay. The menu, unsurprisingly, features plenty of fish, but there is also a hefty helping of turf to go with the surf. Start with a warming bowl of creamy Cullen Skink (smoked haddock and potato soup) or hot smoked salmon roulade with pickled cucumber and horseradish panna cotta. For carnivores, there's black pudding and haggis croquettes with red onion marmalade, saffron and grain mustard aioli. Mains are divided into two sections: From the Sea and From the Land. Try monk cheek and pancetta linguine with spicy red pepper and paprika sauce (£19) or seared lamb chump with roasted shallots, pea and mint risotto, and fire-roasted pepper dressing.

Pocra Quay, Footdee. www.thesilverdarling.co.uk. © **01224/576-229.** Main courses £13–£36. Mon–Thurs noon–2pm, Fri noon–3pm, Mon–Fri 5:30–9:30pm, Sat noon–9:30pm, Sun noon–8pm.

Thainstone House Hotel ★★   On the outskirts of Aberdeen, you can bed down in an elegant Palladian mansion surrounded by 16 hectares (40 acres) of landscaped grounds. The opulent interiors feature high ceilings, columns, neoclassical plaster reliefs, and cornices and bear testimony to architect, Archibald Simpson's Italian travels. Think dark claret paintwork, ornate wallpaper, roaring fires, grand ancestral portraits, deep velvet sofas to sink into in the drawing room, a smattering of tasteful tartan and a grand billiards room. The sumptuous bedrooms are characterful and individually decorated, one with a decadent freestanding copper bathtub.

There's a choice of dining options, from the more formal Green Lady restaurant with its Wedgewood green walls and picture windows looking out over rolling parkland to the more relaxed Stockman's Bar (Thursday is steak night: Aberdeen Angus sizzling from the grill for £17). The six-course tasting menu (£33) in the Green Lady focuses on fresh local produce with dishes such as fillet of North Sea halibut with truffle mashed potatoes, bourguignon sauce, and sea vegetables.

Inverurie. www.crerarhotels.com. © **01467/621-643.** 48 units. £81–£180 double; £175–£225 suite, includes breakfast. Free parking. **Amenities:** Restaurant; bar; pool (indoor); sauna, steam room and spa; free Wi-Fi.

Shopping

Aberdeen's center has a liberal sprinkling of shopping malls containing the usual high-street chains around **George** and **Union streets.** Union Street has been dubbed the very grand sounding Granite Mile, but these days has a slightly scruffy, down-at-heel air and is nothing to write home about in terms of stores of note. Veering off the main drags you can find little pockets of specialty shops and boutiques around **St Nicholas Kirkyard** on **Back Wynd** and **Schoolhill** and on **Chapel** and **Thistle streets.**

Antique hunters should head to **Colin Wood Antiques,** 25 Rose St. (www.colinwoodantiques.com; © **01224/643-019**), which stocks antique and vintage furniture and crystal, but whose specialty is rare maps from the Elizabethan to the Victorian eras and 17th- to early-20th-century prints of northern Scotland. Also browse through the eclectic mix of bric-a-brac and antiques at

Aberdeenshire has around 165 miles of glorious coastline, much of it backed by towering dunes—and sprinkled with some of the country's most challenging and picturesque golf courses. Within Aberdeen itself there is the championship course, the **Royal Aberdeen** (www.royalaberdeengolf.com; ☎ **01224/702-571**), created in 1780, its "Royal" designation courtesy of Edward VII in 1903 and the host of the Scottish Open in 2014. There's also the **Murcar Links** Golf Club (www.murcarlinks.com; ☎ **01224/704-354**) just 10 minutes north of the city center and designed by Archie Simpson in 1909, which has a par of 71 and 6,156-yard course. Along the coast is Aberdeenshire's newest (and controversial) course, the **Trump International Golf Links** (www.trumpgolf scotland.com; ☎ **01358/743-300**) cradled by the magnificent Balmedie dunes and an impressive 72-par links course.

Elizabeth Watt Restoration Studio, 69 Thistle St. (www.elizabethwattrestoration.co.uk; ☎ **01224/647-232**), from glass and brass to antique jewelry and silver. The shop is also a china and glass restoration studio.

To trace your Scottish ancestry, go to the **Aberdeen Family History Shop,** 164 King St. (www.anesfhs.org.uk; ☎ **01224/646-323**), where membership to the Aberdeen and North East Family History Society costs £21. Once you join, you can access a vast range of publications to help you trace your family history. And then, if you'd like to have a kilt made up in your tartan, head to kiltmakers, **Alex Scott & Co.,** 43 Schoolhill (www.kiltmakers.co.uk; ☎ **01224/674-874**), founded in 1925.

Entertainment & Nightlife

The 19th-century **Music Hall,** on Union Street (www.aberdeenperformingarts.com; ☎ **01224/641-122**), is one of the many historic buildings that closed for restoration and renovation over the last few years and is the flagship for the regeneration of Union Street. Work began in 2016 for the grand reopening in 2019. This A-listed building, once known as the Assembly Halls, holds a special place in the city's heart, ornately gilded—with pillars, gilding, and plush seats—and renowned for its acoustics. Conductor Sir John Barbirolli said of it: "nowhere is there a hall which has perfect acoustics such as this." In 1858 and in 1866, novelist Charles Dickens gave a series of celebrated readings here. The theatre stages concerts by the Scottish National Orchestra, the Scottish Chamber Orchestra and visiting international orchestras.

His Majesty's Theatre, Rosemount Viaduct (www.aberdeenperformingarts.com; ☎ **01224/641-122**) is an ornate gem designed entirely of granite by Frank Matcham in 1906. The Victorian interiors are so opulent that comedian Billy Connolly described performing here as "like playing a gig inside a wedding cake!" The 1,491-seat auditorium hosts opera, dance, musicals, classical concerts, and comedy shows year-round.

10

ABERDEEN, THE GRAMPIANS & TAYSIDE

Aberdeen & Castle Country

Pick up a map of *Scotland's Castle Trail* from one of VisitScotland's tourist information centers and hit the road. The only signposted route of its kind in Scotland, the brown and white signs guide motorists around rural Aberdeenshire, while the accompanying leaflet highlights 19 of the region's finest properties, from fairy-tale castles to imposing stately homes, magnificent ruins and spectacular gardens and parkland.

Pinpointed properties include the ruins of 13th-century Kildrummy Castle, the elegant five-towered Fyvie Castle, and two grand examples of 18th-century architect William Adam—Duff House and Haddo House—and Balmoral of course, the Queen's Highland holiday home. You can also download the leaflet online (although it is an older version and only includes 14 castles) at www.aberdeen grampian.com/pdf/Castle-Trail.pdf.

The **Aberdeen Arts Centre,** King Street (www.aberdeenartscentre.com; ℡ **01224/641-122**), has a 350-seat theatre and art-house cinema and an eclectic program of poetry readings, plays, musicals, opera, and comedy. There is also a cinema screening art-house films, gallery space for temporary exhibitions, and a relaxed cafe/bar.

The **Lemon Tree** (5 W. North St.; ℡ **01224/641-122**) is a more intimate venue with an experimental and alternative artistic program. Its 150-seat theatre stages dance recitals, theatrical productions, and stand-up comedy. Downstairs, the 500-seat cafe-theatre hosts folk, rock, blues, jazz, and comedy acts.

Haddo House (www.nts.org.uk; ℡ **01651/851-440**) about 20 miles from Aberdeen, is a grand, stately home near Tarves, designed by William Adam in the Palladian style, which, for over 70 years, has been home to the Haddo House Choral and Operatic Society (www.hhcos.org.uk). The house hosts operas, concerts, and events throughout the year in a purpose-built hall on the estate. An early-20th-century hall built of pitch pine, it's based on the Canadian town halls that Lord Aberdeen saw on his travels abroad. The hall was built for the people of the surrounding area on Aberdeen family land. Also check out the Haddo Arts website (www.haddoarts.com), for more information on the annual program of events including the Haddo Arts Festival each October, a mix of music, theatre and art.

Admission to the stately home itself costs £11 for adults, £9.50 for seniors and children, and £27 for a family ticket. The house is open only for guided tours from April to the end of October which take place Monday to Friday at noon and 2pm and Saturday and Sunday hourly from 11:30am to 3:30pm. The house is closed from November until the end of March.

PUBS BrewDog ★, 5-9 Union Street (www.brewdog.com; ℡ **01224/586-650**), is one of the rash of bars springing up all over the U.K. from this Aberdeenshire craft brewery, which has had a stratospheric trajectory over the past few years. Its hometown hub is a rustic-chic bar in the center of town with 16

10

ABERDEEN, THE GRAMPIANS & TAYSIDE | Aberdeen & Castle Country craft beers to sup and sharing platters and hot dogs to tuck into. It's open 11am to midnight Monday to Thursday, 11am to 1am Friday, 10am to 1am Saturday and 10am to midnight on Sunday.

Side Trips from Aberdeen: Castle Country

Aberdeen is the center of "castle country"—40 inhabited castles lie within a 40-mile radius. In fact, Aberdeenshire is home to no fewer than 263 castles. There are more castles per acre here than anywhere else in the U.K.

Castle Fraser ★★ CASTLE   One of the most impressive of the fortified tower houses in Scotland, Castle Fraser is surrounded by 10 hectares (25 acres) of sweeping parkland. The sixth laird, Michael Fraser, started to construct the castle in 1575, and his son completed it in 1636. Home to the Fraser family for more than four centuries, it is crammed with family portraits and mementos along with hidden trapdoors, secret staircases and spy holes. Visitors can view the spectacular Great Hall and grand apartments, and wander around the grounds, which include an 18th-century walled garden.

Sauchen, Inverurie. www.nts.org.uk. ℂ **01330/833-463.** £11 adults, £9.50 seniors, students, and children 5–15; £27 families. Castle Apr–June Wed–Sun 10am–4pm; July–Aug daily 10am–4pm; Sep–Oct Wed–Sun 10am–4pm. Gardens daily 10am–4pm.

Craigievar Castle ★★ CASTLE   This pink-hued confection of turrets, cupolas, crow-step gables, and gargoyles is straight out of a fairytale. In fact, it's said to be the inspiration for Walt Disney's *Cinderella*. Pretty much unchanged since its completion in 1626, Craigievar Castle is an impossibly romantic Scottish baronial tower house bedded into a picturesque hillside. A family home until the 1960s, when it came under the care of the National Trust for Scotland, it still feels quirkily informal and homey despite the ornate 17th-century plaster ceilings and grand portraits.

Around 3¾ miles south of the castle, clearly signposted on a small road leading off the A980, near Lumphanan, is **Macbeth's Cairn,** where the historical Macbeth is believed to have fought his last battle. Originally built of timber in a "motte and bailey" layout, it's now nothing more than a steep-sided hillock marked with a sign and a flag.

On the A980, 6 miles south of Alford. www.nts.org.uk. ℂ **01339/883-635.** £13 adults, £9.50 seniors and children 5–16, £30 families. Castle by guided tour. Apr–June Fri–Tues 10:30am–5pm; July–Sept daily 10:30am–5pm. Closed Oct–Mar. Gardens daily dawn–dusk.

Crathes Castle & Gardens ★★ CASTLE   Just east of Banchory, and 15 miles west of Aberdeen, Crathes' royal associations date back to 1323, when the Burnett family was granted the land by King Robert the Bruce. The castle itself was built in the 16th century and is set against a bucolic backdrop of rolling hills. A turreted tower house in the traditional style, it features stunning late-16th-century painted ceilings and medley of family portraits and antique furniture. The glorious walled garden is divided into eight sections

ABERDEEN, THE GRAMPIANS & TAYSIDE

Aberdeen & Castle Country

and features carefully sculpted topiary and towering yew hedges dating from 1702. The estate was once part of the Royal Forest of Drum, and there are six waymarked trails through the grounds. Keep your eyes open for roe deer, red squirrels, and woodpeckers.

Banchory. www.nts.org.uk. © **01330/844-525.** £13 adults, £9.50 seniors and children 5–16, £30 families. Nov–Mar Sat–Sun 11am–4pm; Apr–Oct daily 10:30am–5pm.

Dunnottar Castle ★★ RUINS As movie locations go, these ruins, which include a square tower and chapel built in 1292, are a knockout. Dunnottar Castle is perched on a rocky promontory towering 49m (160 ft.) above a surging sea and in 1991, it was the setting for Zeffirelli's film of *Hamlet,* starring Mel Gibson. This impregnable fortress was home to the Earls Marischal. William Wallace stormed the castle in 1297, but failed to take it. The best way to get there is a dramatic 30-minute walk from Stonehaven along the cliffs. Trains run about every half-hour from Aberdeen to Stonehaven, and the journey time is about 20 minutes.

Stonehaven. www.dunnottarcastle.co.uk. © **01569/766-320.** £7 adults, £3 children 15 and under, £17 families. Apr–Sept daily 9am–5:30pm; Oct–Mar 10am–dusk.

Fyvie Castle ★★ CASTLE/ARCHITECTURE This magnificent fortress will make you stop in your tracks. It's probably the finest example of Scottish baronial architecture in the country today, its history stretching back over 800 years. Over the course of 5 centuries, five successive families lived here, each adding a tower and the result is a glorious pink confection. Originally built in a royal hunting forest, Fyvie means "deer hill" in Gaelic. The interior, created by the first Lord Leith of Fyvie, reflects the opulence of the Edwardian era. His collections contain arms and armor, 16th-century tapestries, and important artworks by Raeburn, Gainsborough, and Romney. In the grounds the grandeur continues with a pretty loch, a walled garden and a glass-roofed racquets court dating back to 1903. The castle also has its share of ghosts, curses, and legends to explore . . .

Turriff. www.nts.org.uk. © **01651/891-266.** £13 adults, £9.50 seniors and children 5–16, £30 families. Castle Apr–May and Sept–Oct Sat–Wed 11am–5pm; June–Aug daily 11am–5pm (last entry 4:15pm). Gardens daily 9am–dusk. 23 miles northwest of Aberdeen.

PERTH ★: GATEWAY TO THE HIGHLANDS

44 miles N of Edinburgh; 22 miles SW of Dundee; 64 miles NE of Glasgow

Known as the Fair City, genteel Perth on the bosky banks of the River Tay was the capital of Scotland until the mid-15th century, and it's here that the Highlands meet the Lowlands. Perth itself has an attractive historic center and handful of fascinating museums and galleries to wander around. Its main draw, **Scone Palace,** lies on the outskirts, surrounded by lush, rolling countryside.

Essentials

GETTING THERE   ScotRail (www.scotrail.co.uk; ✆ 0344/811-0141) runs a regular service between Edinburgh and Perth, the journey takes about 90 minutes. There are also plenty of buses. **CityLink** (www.citylink.co.uk; ✆ **0871/266-3333**) operates a regular service, as does **Megabus** (www.uk.megabus.com; ✆ **0141/352-4444**) with a journey time of around 1 hour.

To reach Perth from Edinburgh by car, take the A90 northwest and cross the Queensferry Crossing, continuing north along the M90. Again the journey will take about 90 minutes.

VISITOR INFORMATION   The **VisitScotland iCentre** is on the pedestrianized shopping strip, 45 High St., (www.visitscotland.com; ✆ **01738/450-600**). It's open from April to June and September to October, Monday to Saturday 9:30am to 5pm, Sunday 11am to 4pm, July to August until 5:30pm Monday to Saturday and Sunday 10am to 4:30pm, November to March it shuts at 4:30pm Monday to Saturday, Sunday 11am to 4pm.

Exploring the Area

For a bird's-eye view of the city, head a mile east of Perth to **Kinnoull Hill,** which rises to a height of 240m (787 ft.). It's an easy climb, and from the top you can make out the geological Highland Line dividing the Highlands from the Lowlands. Kinnoull Hill is one of five hills, in fact, in the Kinnoull Hill Woodland Park and was Scotland's first woodland park, launched in 1991. There are marked nature trails through woodlands woven with Scots Pine, larch, oak, birch, and Norwegian spruce, and red squirrel and roe deer can sometimes be seen. From the top, panoramic views of the River Tay and Perthshire countryside unfold and you can see a romantic 19th-century folly, the **Kinnoull Watch Tower,** and its counterpart, 1 mile to the east, **Binn Hill,** both said to be based on castles along the Rhine.

Perth itself is peppered with parkland and has a picturesque setting beside the river. Just to the northeast of the city center is **North Inch,** a 41-hectare (100-acre) park lounging along the west bank of the Tay. It is here that a bloody battle is supposed to have been fought between two warring clans in 1396. Clan Combat took place between 30 champions from the clans Kay and Chattan, in front of King Robert III and his queen and was later immortalized by Sir Walter Scott in *The Fair Maid of Perth.* To the south of the city center is another park, unsurprisingly called **South Inch.** Both parks were originally granted to the city by King Robert III in 1377.

North of Perth is one of Scotland's famous golf courses. **Blairgowrie Golf Club,** Golf Course Road, Rosemont, Blairgowrie (www.theblairgowriegolf club.co.uk; ✆ **01250/872-622**), has two courses, the Rosemount and the Lansdowne, a challenging championship course that undulates through a wild landscape of pine, birch, and fir; you might even spot a deer or two grazing on the course.

This annual 10-day musical shindig has been taking place each May since 1972. In fact, the **Perth Festival of the Arts** is one of the longest-running arts festivals in Scotland. It began as an opera and classical music festival but now also features jazz and contemporary bands and attracts international orchestras and chamber music societies from around the world. Big names that have appeared over recent years include Dame Kiri Te Kanawa, Nigel Kennedy, Lesley Garrett along with Jools Holland, Van Morrison, and Joan Armatrading. Concerts are held in churches, theatres and concert halls, and even Scone Palace. For information, call ℂ **01739/621-031,** or visit www.perthfestival.co.uk.

Balhousie Castle ★ CASTLE   In the 16th century, this turreted pile was the home of the earls of Kinnoull, but today it houses the Black Watch Museum, with hundreds of weapons, medals, and documents of the Black Watch Regiment from the 18th century to the present day. The regiment was raised in 1739 by General George Wade to help the government pacify rebellious Highlanders, and became famous all over the United Kingdom for its black tartans, which contrasted with the red of government troops.

Hay St. www.theblackwatch.co.uk. ℂ **01738/638-152.** £8 adults, £6.50 seniors and students, £3.50 children ages 5–16, £19 families. Apr–Oct daily 9:30am–4:30pm; Nov–Mar daily 10am–4pm.

Branklyn Garden ★ GARDEN   This lovely 2-acre hillside garden was created in the 1920s by John and Dorothy Renton after they had built their Arts and Crafts–inspired house on Kinnoull Hill overlooking Perth. They were keen to include rare and unusual plants and so used seeds collected by intrepid plant hunters such as Frank Ludlow and George Forrest. Today, Branklyn belongs to the National Trust for Scotland, and along with its outstanding collection of rhododendrons, alpines, and peat-garden plants from around the world, is home to the National Collection of Meconopsis and Cassiope. Check out the stunning magnolias and purple Japanese maple in the summer.

116 Dundee Rd. (A85), in Branklyn. www.nts.org.uk. ℂ **01738/625-535.** £6.50 adults, £5 students, seniors, and children ages 5–15, £16.50 families. Apr–Oct daily 10am–5pm. Closed in winter.

Fergusson Gallery ★ GALLERY   John Duncan Fergusson (1874–1961) was one of the four painters known collectively as the Scottish Colourists. He was born in Edinburgh and spent much of his career in France, but had ancestral links with Perth. The Fergusson Gallery displays around 6,000 of his artworks. The Scottish Colourists were renowned for their vivid use of color and vibrant brushwork, which reveal the influence of Fauvism. The work of his partner, the dancer Margaret Morris (1891–1980), is also displayed in the gallery. She was also a talented artist, and there is a collection of photographs of dancers performing her choreography.

Marshall Place. www.culturepk.org.uk. *C* **01738/783-425.** Free. Tues–Sat 10am–5pm, Apr–Oct Sun 12:30–4:30pm.

Kirk of St John the Baptist ★ CHURCH   The first reference to a church dedicated to St John the Baptist is in a grant by King David I in the early 12th century, but it's believed that the original foundation on this site dates back a century earlier. During the 15th century Perth grew in importance and wealth, and the present choir dates from around 1448 and the nave from 1490. On 11 May 1559, the kirk was the location of a pivotal event in Scottish history. John Knox preached his famous sermon attacking idolatry here, inflaming the congregation to strip the church of its ornamentation and to rampage through the city and causing a turbulent wave of iconoclasm to sweep across the land. In its wake, religious artifacts, stained glass, and organs were destroyed all over Scotland. The church was restored as a World War I memorial in the mid-1920s. Today, music plays a central part in the life of the kirk, which hosts regular ensembles, organ recitals and concerts.

31 St John Place. www.st-johns-kirk.co.uk. *C* **01738/633-192.** Free (donations suggested). Daily 7am–7pm.

Perth Museum and Art Gallery ★ MUSEUM   During the Victorian era, the museum received many important bequests of paintings. Among the most notable artworks are three paintings by Pre-Raphaelite John Everett Millais (1829–96) who had important links to the city. You can view portraits of his wife Effie and daughter Mary in *Waking,* and his last portrait of Sir Robert Pullar. The museum also houses a large collection of Scottish landscape paintings. Horatio McCulloch (1805–67) was known as a specialist of Highland scenes, and one of his finest works, *Loch Katrine* (1866), is on display, as is a series of paintings illustrating the town's history, as well as numerous archaeological artifacts and galleries crammed with natural history exhibits such as a replica of Miss Ballantine's Salmon. Caught in the River Tay by Miss Georgina Ballantine in 1922, fishing with her father and ghillie, at 64 pounds it was the heaviest rod-caught salmon ever landed.

78 George St. www.culturepk.org.uk. *C* **01738/632-488.** Free. Apr–Oct Tues–Sun 10am–5pm. Closed Sun Nov–Mar.

Scone Palace ★★ PALACE   This is one of Scotland's most popular tourist attractions and the place where Robert the Bruce was crowned. Old Scone, 1¾ miles from the city center on the River Tay, was the ancient capital of the Picts. The early Scottish monarchs were crowned here on a slab of sandstone known as the "Stone of Destiny." In 1296, however, King Edward I of England, the "Hammer of the Scots," moved the stone to Westminster Abbey, and for hundreds of years it remained there. It was finally returned to Scotland in 1996, and can now be viewed in Edinburgh Castle.

ABERDEEN, THE GRAMPIANS & TAYSIDE

Perth

Scone Palace is the seat of the earls of Mansfield and the birthplace of David Douglas (of fir-tree fame). The palace you see today was largely rebuilt in 1802, incorporating the old 16th-century building. Inside you can view the impressive collection of French furniture, china, ivories, and 16th-century needlework, including bed hangings made by Mary Queen of Scots. On the grounds, wander among the giant redwoods and noble firs in the Pinetum. Rhododendrons and azaleas grow profusely in the gardens and woodlands around the palace.

Scone. www.scone-palace.co.uk. ℂ **01738/552-300.** £12 adults, £10.50 seniors and students, £8.50 children ages 5–16, £40 families. May–Sept daily 9:30am–5pm; Apr & Oct daily 10am–4pm.

Where to Eat

63 Tay Street ★★ MODERN SCOTTISH   Local, honest, simple is chef-owner Graeme Pallister's mantra. This smart, sunny city restaurant across the road from the river in historic Perth is a gourmet gem and has been notching up the awards for over a decade. An advocate of the Slow Food movement, he also hosts regular Slow Food suppers at the restaurant. Starters include cured pigeon, walnut and brie salad with raisin vinaigrette or red mullet, ginger noodle tea and lemon puree while for mains, there's roast quail, butterbean and herb stew with pancetta, or cod fillet, mussel pie with winter greens. To finish, the desserts are equally mouth-watering: dark chocolate cremeux, caraway and beetroot ice cream or blood orange panna cotta with smoked curd and walnut granola. You can also opt for a 5-course tasting menu which showcases Pallister's passion for local, seasonal ingredients.

63 Tay St. www.63taystreet.com. ℂ **01738/441-451.** Lunch main courses £13.50; dinner, 4-course tasting menu £22, dinner mains £19, 5-course tasting menu £45. Tues–Sat noon–1:45pm, Tues–Fri 5:45–8:45pm, Sat 6:30–8:45pm.

Deans Restaurant ★ MODERN SCOTTISH   This family-owned restaurant is an advocate of those buzzwords: fresh, seasonal and locally sourced. Willie and Jamie Dean (who spent a number of years in Andrew Fairlie's two-Michelin-starred restaurant at Gleneagles) have a passion for foraging as well as growing many of the vegetables themselves. The restaurant, in an old theatre dating back to 1822, is cozy with a log-burning stove and comfy sofas. On the menu you have Shetland scallops with hot-smoked salmon, potato and leek broth to start, followed by pink roast rump of lamb with asparagus, pea and broad bean fricassee, tarragon gnocchi, and glazed sweetbreads.

77–79 Kinnoull St. www.letseatperth.co.uk. ℂ **01738/643-377.** Lunch main courses £13–£19; dinner main courses £16–£28. Wed–Sat noon–2:30pm and 6–8:30pm, Sat noon–6pm.

The Roost ★★ BRITISH/INTERNATIONAL   Tim Dover worked all around the world for chefs such as Daniel Boulud in New York before heading to rural Perthshire to open his own restaurant in what was once a little village

Perth Farmers Market was the first in Scotland, and it's all thanks to a local shepherd—who happens to be the brother of the only chef in Scotland to have been awarded two Michelin stars: Andrew Fairlie. Jim Fairlie was travelling around France and was so inspired by the local markets there that he decided to set one up at home. The farmers market takes place on the first Saturday of every month from 9am until 2pm at King Edward Street and St John's Place. There are around 40 stallholders under the jaunty blue and white striped canvas awnings, including Hubertus Game (wild venison), Puddledub Pork (home-reared pork and bacon), Dunkeld Smoked Salmon, Scarlett's honey, Summer Harvest cold-pressed rapeseed oil and the St Andrews Cheese Company. Many farmers markets have gradually morphed into country fairs, but Perth has stayed true to its origins and is predominantly produce-led. It's a popular monthly event packed with appreciative crowds gathered round the cookery demos and grazing their way round the stalls. For more information call **01738/582-159**, or visit www.perth farmersmarket.co.uk.

café. It's the perfect backdrop for his foraging forays and innovative menus, featuring starters such as duck pastrami with nasturtium and watercress or ash-smoked beets with yoghurt, cucumber and dill. For mains, you can tuck into cod fillet with purple-sprouting broccoli, chili and chimichurri or a Porterhouse steak from the charcoal oven. To finish, how about sea buckthorn posset with almond and chocolate crumb or stem ginger, white chocolate and honeycomb cheesecake with poached rhubarb.

Forgandenny Rd., Kintillo, Bridge of Earn. www.theroostrestaurant.co.uk. ©**01738/812-111**. Reservations recommended. Sunday lunch 2-courses £26, 3-courses £30; dinner main courses £14.50–£27. Wed–Sat 12:30–8pm, Sun noon–4pm.

Shopping

Perth's High Street has gone the way of many around the country, with increasing numbers shopping online or in large malls. In parts it feels a bit unloved with boarded up shopfronts. McEwan's of Perth, the department store that was a local institution since 1868, finally closed its doors in 2016, although the following year Beales, an independent department store chain from England took over the space, opening their first branch in Scotland. There are still a couple of independent shops to browse. Two brothers, Alexander and George Cairncross founded a jewelry shop, **Cairncross of Perth,** 18–20 St John's St., in 1869 (www.cairncrossofperth.co.uk; © **01738/624-367**). Today, it is still a family business, their specialty Scottish freshwater pearls. They are one of only two shops in the U.K. to have a license to sell natural Scottish river pearls. Also on St John's St, at number 25 is **Timothy Hardie** (www.timothyhardie.co.uk; © **01738/633-127**), which sells a range of antique jewelry.

Entertainment & Nightlife

The historic **Perth Theatre,** 185 High St. (www.horsecross.co.uk; ℭ **01738/621-031**) reopened at the end of 2017 after a £16.6-million transformation. The Edwardian auditorium was restored to its former glory and a new 200-seat studio theatre was created. From the end of May to early June, it's also one of the venues for the Perth Festival of the Arts. The box office is open Monday through Saturday from 10am to 6pm. Next door is the contemporary **Perth Concert Hall** (contact details the same as for the theatre) which hosts a wide range of events, from classical music to comedy.

Where to Stay

Leonardo Boutique Hotel Huntingtower Perth ★ Once upon a time this Victorian country house hotel was simply called the Huntingtower Hotel. Now it's a bit of a mouthful. You can't help wondering who thought a never-ending name was a good idea. The hotel is just 3 miles from the center of the city and set in 2.5 hectares (6 acres) of lovely landscaped grounds. Style-wise it's a Scottish hotel of a certain ilk (tartan carpets, leather sofas, bucket chairs in the bar and wood-paneling in the dining room). As well as the rooms in the old house, a new wing has been added.

Crieff Rd, Perth. www.leonardo-hotels.com. ℭ **01738/583-771.** 34 units. £84–£224 double, includes breakfast. Free parking. **Amenities:** Restaurant; bar; room service; free Wi-Fi.

Murrayshall Country House Hotel & Golf Club ★ The tree-lined driveway, leading up to the hotel from the hedgerow-fringed lane, has golfing greens to one side and a driving range on the other. At the end is one of the prettiest country house hotels around, all warm sandstone and mullioned windows, set in 147 hectares (365 acres) of glorious parkland. The old mansion dates back to 1664. It was built by Sir Andrew Murray and remained in the same family for around three centuries. It was converted into a country house hotel in the 1970s and a golf course added, designed by J. Hamilton Stutt. In fact, there are two 18-hole golf courses: the Murrayshall and the Lynedoch. There's no denying that it's a magnet for golfers, but unlike some golfing hotels, the golf course doesn't overwhelm the property. There are also plenty of other activities on offer from cycling to horse-riding, quadbiking, and the full range of country pursuits: hunting, shooting, and fishing. If you want a day out on a local shoot or to try your hand at fishing for trout with a ghillie, the hotel can arrange it.

The hotel's bedrooms are traditional in style, some in the old house, others in a nearby building: the one to bag the Miller Suite with its four-poster bed and sweeping views of the surrounding countryside. You can eat either in the smart new Lynedoch Brasserie (re-opened in 2018 after a complete refurbishment): mains from £14, or the slightly old-fashioned Stutts Bar and Restaurant.

Murrayshall Rd. Scone, Perthshire. www.murrayshall.co.uk. ℭ **01738/551-171.** 40 units. £69–£179 double; £99–£249 suite, includes breakfast. **Amenities:** 2 restaurants; bar; 2 golf courses; bike rentals; free Wi-Fi.

Parklands Hotel ★ This classic Georgian townhouse was once home to the city's Lord Provost from 1867 to 1873. Today, it is a boutique hotel overlooking South Inch Park with a Victorian conservatory for afternoon tea. One of its main draws is its food. (The executive chef is none other than award-winning Graeme Pallister of 63 Tay Street.) The relaxed No.1 The Bank Bistro is contemporary brasserie in style, with marble tabletops and views over the gardens. It prides itself on using local Perthshire produce and the beef from the grill comes from a local butcher and can be traced right back to the farm. The more formal 63@Parklands Restaurant takes things up a notch with its four-, five- or seven-course tasting menu (from £30 for four courses).

2 St Leonard's Bank. www.theparklandshotel.com. © **01738/622-451.** 14 units. £109–£179 double, includes breakfast. **Amenities:** 2 restaurants; bar; free Wi-Fi.

The Townhouse ★★ Scottish-born David Henderson and Laurent Moller from France spent 26 years living the high life in the Caribbean (managing luxury hotels and running a coffee-roasting business on St. Barts) before heading to Perth and setting up a luxurious boutique B&B in 2012. The elegant Georgian townhouse overlooks South Inch Park and has five bedrooms with original features peppered with fine antiques and boasting oversize upholstered headboards. There's a smattering of tasteful tartan (drapes and cushions) and the rooms at the front have tranquil park views through large sash windows.

17 Marshall Place. www.thetownhouseperth.co.uk. © **01738/446-179.** 5 units. £70–£145 double includes breakfast. **Amenities:** Free Wi-Fi.

GLENEAGLES ★

53 miles NE of Glasgow Airport; 42 miles NW of Edinburgh Airport

Gleneagles has become synonymous with golf and one of the most famous golf resorts in the world, but it was first and foremost a glen through the Ochil Hills. The name, in fact, has nothing to do with eagles but is thought to come from the Gaelic *Gleann-an-Eaglais,* meaning "glen of the church," referring to a chapel dedicated to St Mungo.

Essentials

GETTING THERE The train ride from Perth takes 15 minutes. The direct train takes 1 hour from Edinburgh but most journeys require a change and the trip on average takes 1 hour and 25 minutes. For information, call © **0344/811-0141** or visit www.scotrail.co.uk.

The only direct bus service departs from Glasgow. The trip takes 1 hour and 15 minutes. For information and schedules, call © **0871/266-3333,** or visit www.citylink.co.uk.

Gleneagles is situated just off the A9, about halfway between Perth and Stirling, a short distance from the village of Auchterarder. It lies 44 miles from Edinburgh and 45 miles from Glasgow.

Where to Eat & Stay

The Gleneagles Hotel ★★★ Even if you're not a golfer or a fan of large resorts, this grand hotel will woo you. There's just something about it—despite its rather austere facade. It was built in isolated grandeur in 1924 and is surrounded by its own 344-hectare (850-acre) estate. It has three championship courses (and hosted the 2014 Ryder Cup), but it also offers a whole range of outdoor pursuits including shooting, fishing, horse-riding, cycling, tennis, archery and falconry, and there are two off-road driving courses. It's also one of the most luxurious hotels in Scotland and has a gloriously decadent spa. Public areas are designed in grand classic style, with pilasters and fine cornicing. Bedrooms ooze understated luxury and pure class. The color palette is subtle and subdued, the effect low-key yet somehow sumptuous. For all-out luxury you can't beat the Royal Lochnagar Suite with its opulent decoration, four-poster bed and uninterrupted views of the Ochil Hills. This is Scotland's premier resort hotel, all others, frankly, pale in comparison. And then there's the food.

Scotland has just one two-Michelin-starred restaurant and it's here. The tasting menu at **Andrew Fairlie's** restaurant lives up to the hype and is a gastronomic extravaganza, the signature dish, smoked lobster—smoked over old whisky barrels for 12 hours.

Auchterarder. www.gleneagles.com. ℂ **866/881-9525** in the U.S. 01764/662-231. 232 units. £285–£665 double; £780–£2,995 suite, includes breakfast. Free parking. **Amenities:** 3 restaurants; 4 bars; pool (indoor); 4 golf courses; tennis courts (lit); health club & spa; bike rental; concierge; hair salon; nail bar; free Wi-Fi.

CRIEFF & DRUMMOND CASTLE GARDENS ★

18 miles W of Perth; 60 miles NW of Edinburgh; 50 miles NE of Glasgow

Crieff is a little market town on the edge of the Perthshire Highlands. This small burgh was the seat of the court of the earls of Strathearn until 1747. The gallows in its marketplace were once used to execute Highland cattle rustlers. From here you can explore **Strathearn,** the valley of the River Earn, where craggy Highland mountains meet gentler Lowland slopes, and heather-pricked moorland mingles with rich, green pastures. North of Crieff, the road to Aberfeldy passes through the narrow pass of the **Sma' Glen,** a breathtaking route, with hills rising steeply on either side to 600m (1,970 ft.).

Essentials

GETTING THERE You'll need a car to explore the area. There's no direct train service. The nearest rail stations are at Gleneagles, 8⅔ miles away, and at Perth, 18 miles away.

VISITOR INFORMATION **The Crieff Visitor Centre** on Muthill Road is garden center, café art gallery and antique shop and Caithness Glass studio in one. There so much to do here you might forgot what you came in to ask (www.crieff.co.uk; ✆ **01764/654-014**). There's also a Highland Drovers Exhibition. It's open daily 9am to 5pm.

Exploring the Area

Drummond Castle Gardens ★★ GARDEN   A little girl was once overheard asking her mother if this was Alice in Wonderland's garden, and it's easy to see why as you meander the paths between neatly trimmed topiary and box hedges. The gardens of Drummond Castle, first laid out in the early 17th century by John Drummond, second earl of Perth, are among the finest formal gardens in Europe. Queen Victoria visited the castle with Prince Albert in 1842 and remarked that they "walked in the garden which is really very fine, with terraces, like an old French garden." A stunning panorama unfolds from the upper terrace, overlooking the early Victorian parterre in the form of St Andrew's Cross, while the multifaceted sundial by John Mylne, master mason to Charles I, has been the centerpiece since 1630. Unfortunately, the castle itself isn't open to the public.

Muthill, Crieff. www.drummondcastlegardens.co.uk. ✆ **01764/681-433**. £6.50 adults, £5.50 seniors, £2 children 5–15, family £14. May, Sept–Oct daily 1–6pm June–Aug daily 11am–6pm, Easter weekend 1–6pm. Closed Nov–Apr.

Glenturret Distillery ★ DISTILLERY   Scotland's oldest distillery, Glenturret was established in 1775 on the banks of the River Turret. That's the year, they point out, before America declared independence and when the Scottish bard, Robert Burns was still a teenager. Since 2002 it has been home to the Famous Grouse Experience, a highly rated interactive visitor attraction. Visitors can view the milling of malt, mashing, fermentation, distillation, and cask filling, followed by a couple of tastings at the end of the tour. There's also an interesting video, *The Water of Life,* and a small museum on the whisky trade. Real connoisseurs can also book a blending experience which includes an in-depth tour, a guided nosing and tasting and the opportunity to try your hand at blending your own malt. It lasts 2 hours and costs £75.

The Hosh, Glenturret. www.thefamousgrouse.com. ✆ **01764/656-565**. Guided tours £10 adults, £9 seniors and children 8–17, free for children ages 7 and under. Apr–Oct daily 10am–6pm, Nov–Mar daily 10am–5pm.

Innerpeffray Library ★★ LIBRARY   This extraordinary Georgian library is improbably situated on open farmland down an unpromising farm lane just 4 miles to the south of Crieff. Founded in around 1680 by the local landowner, Lord Madertie, who donated his collection of precious leather-bound volumes, it provided a book-lending service to the local population. He also founded a school nearby, and the fruits of his educational zeal can be seen in the borrowers' ledger, where farm workers, students, and artisans of all kinds signed out books in their own, sometimes shaky, hands. Indeed, the Scottish Enlightenment in general saw to it that literacy rates were far higher in Scotland than England up until about 1750.

In the 1760s, the library was provided with a purpose-built home, adjoining the old chapel next door (which is also worth a look). As you enter the library (on the first level), you're greeted by a librarian who's happy to give you a guided tour and will provide you with white gloves to leaf through some of the old tomes (which include atlases and books on gardening, natural history, biography, and a host of other subjects). If you find a particularly good read, you can settle into an old armchair and spend the afternoon there. As you leave, a short diversion farther down the road by which you came brings you to the ruins of Lord Madertie's stone castle.

Innerpeffray, Crieff. www.innerpeffraylibrary.co.uk. ℂ **01764/652-819.** £7.50 adults, under-15s free. Mar–Oct Wed–Sat 10am–5pm, Sun 2–5pm; Nov–Feb closed.

Where to Eat & Stay

Barley Bree ★★   Fabrice and Alison Bouteloup turned this picturesque old coaching inn into a gourmet restaurant with a clutch of lovely boutique hotel-style rooms in the pretty conservation village of Muthill. (Bree is the Scottish word for soup, so the inn's name is a play on words: barley-bree means whisky). Design-wise the inn is rustic-chic, with rough-hewn wooden floors, exposed stone walls, beamed ceilings and cozy wood-burning stoves with antlers and old fishing nets strung from the walls.

Fabrice is from northwest France and his menus combine traditional French cooking style with the best seasonal Scottish produce. Everything is made fresh in his state-of-the-art kitchen and his crusty bread is legendary—as is the Tarte Tatin, his signature dessert. For starters you can tuck into game and black truffle pithivier (a French puff pastry pie), carrot puree, pickled vegetables and salad leaves or salted Arbroath smokie and smoked salmon with Avruga caviar, kombu seaweed and soy dressing. Mains include Perthshire saddle of venison, crispy baby kale, pancetta, chestnut, baby parsnip, potato and cost £24. Stay here. Eat here. This is what a restaurant with rooms should be.

6 Willoughby St., Muthill, Crieff. www.barleybree.com. ℂ **01764/681-451.** 6 units. £99–£160 double, includes breakfast. Free parking. **Amenities:** Restaurant; bar; free Wi-Fi.

Knock Castle Hotel ★   This 19th-century Scottish baronial, turreted, country house hotel was once the home of Scottish shipping magnate, Lady MacBrayne. Bedrooms are split between the castle and the (more basic) lodge in the gardens, some boasting four-posters, others romantic sleigh beds while the Glenalmond suite has a sunken bath with views out over the grounds. There's a spa and pool in a large glasshouse surrounded by the lush, wooded gardens, with a sauna, steam room and range of organic spa treatments.

The Rooftop Restaurant has panoramic views of the Strathearn Valley, and offers a six-course tasting menu (try duck liver and apple pâté coated in pistachio butter with poached pear dressing and toasted brioche) for £70 per person. Mains from the a la carte menu cost from £25 to £38.

Drummond Terrace. www.knockcastle.com. ℂ **01764/650-088.** 30 units. £149–£199 double, £239–£259 suite, includes breakfast. Free parking. **Amenities:** Restaurant; bar; pool; spa; gym; free Wi-Fi.

DUNKELD ★★

58 miles N of Edinburgh; 14 miles N of Perth; 98 miles SW of Aberdeen

Dunkeld is one of the most picturesque villages in Scotland. It is postcard-pretty, many of its pastel-painted houses restored by the National Trust for Scotland. It's setting is equally heavenly, in a thickly wooded valley on the banks of the Tay River at the edge of the Perthshire Highlands. Once an important ecclesiastical center, Christianity gained a foothold here in the 7th century when Columba came over from Iona and in the 9th century, Kenneth MacAlpin, the King of the Scots, made Dunkeld the head of the Celtic Church.

The surrounding countryside is stunningly beautiful, and there are trails on both sides of the River Tay around Dunkeld and Birnam. In all, 36 miles of paths have been linked to create a network of 8 circular routes varying from 3 to 7 miles in length. Pick up maps and detailed descriptions from the tourist office and set out on an adventure, armed with a picnic.

Essentials

GETTING THERE Trains to Dunkeld Birnam from Edinburgh take just under 2 hours, trains from Glasgow 1½ hours (www.scotrail.co.uk; ℭ **0344/811-0141**). **Stagecoach** (www.stagecoachbus.com; ℭ **01738/629-339**) operates Aberfeldy- or Pitlochry-bound buses leaving from Perth with a stopover in Dunkeld (journey time: 50 min.). If you are driving from Perth, head north on the A9.

VISITOR INFORMATION There's a **VisitScotland iCentre** at The Cross (www.visitscotland.com; ℭ **01350/727-688**). It's open April to June, Monday to Saturday 10:30am to 4:30pm and Sunday 11am to 4pm; July to August, Monday to Saturday 10am to 5pm and Sunday 11am to 4pm; September to October, Monday to Saturday 10am to 4:30pm and Sunday 11am to 4pm; November to December, weekends only, Friday to Sunday 11am to 4pm (closed Jan–Mar).

Exploring the Area

Founded in c.e. 815, **Dunkeld Cathedral** ★ (www.dunkeldcathedral.org.uk) has a breathtakingly lovely setting, fringed by trees on the banks of the River Tay. It was converted from a church to a cathedral in 1325, growing in wealth and power until it was destroyed during the Reformation in the 16th century. The cathedral was partly restored in 1815, and traces of the medieval structure (the 14th-century choir) remain today although the 15th-century nave is roofless. Admission is free, and the cathedral is open April to September daily 10am to 5:30pm; October to March, daily 10am to 4pm.

In 1689, much of the town burnt to the ground during the violent Battle of Dunkeld between the Jacobites (followers of Bonnie Prince Charlie) and Cameronians who supported William of Orange. Dunkeld was rebuilt and became a bustling market town and the point where the cattle-droving roads

ABERDEEN, THE GRAMPIANS & TAYSIDE

Dunkeld

met. The National Trust for Scotland has restored many of the old houses and shops around the marketplace and cathedral and also owns 20 houses on **High Street** and **Cathedral Street**. The National Trust runs the **Ell Shop,** The Cross (named after the "ell," a unit used by weavers to measure cloth), which specializes in Scottish crafts (*C* **01350/728-641**). It's open April to October daily from 10am to 5:30pm and November until December 24, daily 10am to 4:30pm. It's closed from Christmas until the end of March.

Shakespeare fans will want to seek out the oak and sycamore in front of the destroyed **Birnam House,** 1 mile south. This was believed to be a remnant of the Birnam Wood in *Macbeth;* the famous line, "Macbeth shall never vanquished be until great Birnam Wood to high Dunsinane Hill shall come against him."

There's another wonderful woodland spot off the A9 about 1¾ miles west of Dunkeld. **The Hermitage** is a picturesque folly above the wooded gorge of the River Braan, built in 1758 as part of the pleasure grounds designed for the Dukes of Atholl (who lived nearby in the long-since demolished Dunkeld House). Ossian's Hall was built in honor of a legendary 3rd century blind bard of the same name, and is decorated with mirrors and sliding panels. From here you can look down over the Black Linn Falls as the water tumbles frothing into the pool below and wander through the giant Douglas Firs, some of the tallest trees in Scotland, looking out for red squirrels—and totem poles hidden amongst them.

Another place of great natural beauty near Dunkeld is the **Loch of the Lowes Wildlife Reserve** ★ (www.scottishwildlifetrust.org.uk; *C* **01350/727-337**), about 2 miles from the center of town, along the A923 heading northeast. You can also walk here from Dunkeld along the Fungarth Path. On the south shore of the loch there's a visitor center and two bird hides. The 98-hectare (245-acre) reserve is famous for its ospreys, which were once threatened with extinction and are still rarer than golden eagles in Britain. The birds migrate from Africa every summer to breed and bird-watchers can see them on their nests between April and August via a closed-circuit television camera. Telescopes and binoculars are also available to borrow in the hides. The ospreys might be the star attractions, but the wildlife reserve is also home to red squirrels, wildfowl, deer and beavers. The reserve is open March to October from 10am to 5pm and November to February from 10:30am to 4pm. Admission is £4 for adults, £3.50 for seniors, and £0.50 for children. A family ticket costs £7.50.

For golfers, the **Dunkeld & Birnam Golf Club** at Dunkeld (www.dunkeld andbirnamgolfclub.co.uk; *C* **01350/727-524**) has been a historic draw. The legendary Old Tom Morris designed the original course in 1892, but the current course, opened by the Duchess of Atholl on a heath-blanketed hillside above Dunkeld, dates back to 1922. It's widely regarded as one of the most picturesque golf courses in the Highlands.

Where to Eat & Stay

Hotels in Dunkeld are on the staid and traditional side, historic 19th-century coaching inns offering basic but comfortable accommodation. There are a handful of stylish self-catering options springing up nearby, however, such as the exquisite **Pheasant Cottage** (www.pheasantcottage.co.uk) in Dalguise (think a soft grey and white palette, hand-built Shaker kitchen, range cooker, and wood-burning stove) converted into a sleek rural retreat in 2017, and it sleeps six. In terms of eateries, there are a clutch of cute cafes and bistros, but one of the best places in town is the **Scottish Deli** (www.scottish-deli.com; *✆* **01350/728-028**) a rustic place with a mismatched cluster of cafe tables and chairs which turns into a wine bar and tapas restaurant at night.

Dunkeld House Hotel ★   This gracious whitewashed country house hotel on the banks of the River Tay (prime salmon fishing territory), has a beautiful setting, surrounded by its own 113-hectare (280-acre) estate. The hotel's extensive parkland and woodland is threaded with walking trails and cycling routes and the perfect backdrop for the other outdoor activities from archery to clay pigeon shooting and tennis. There's also a spa to soothe aching muscles at the end of the day. Rooms and suites are split between the main house and General Wade's Lodge and are a mix of traditional (the odd four-poster bed and sumptuous drapes) and contemporary (bold striped carpets and a smattering of tartan).

The chefs source fresh, seasonal produce from local artisan producers as well as gathering herbs from the kitchen garden, smoked salmon from the hotel's own smokery and wild venison from the estate. Try the starter of venison carpaccio with sweet juniper berry cured loin, pickled mushrooms, parsley oil and garlic crumb.

Dunkeld. www.dunkeldhousehotel.co.uk. *✆* **01350/727-771.** 96 units. £119–£259 double, £189–£284 suite, includes breakfast. Free parking. **Amenities:** Restaurant; bar; pool (indoor); 2 tennis courts, spa; free Wi-Fi.

PITLOCHRY ★★

71 miles NW of Edinburgh; 27 miles NW of Perth; 15 miles N of Dunkeld

Pitlochry is a perennially popular Highland resort—ever since Queen Victoria declared it one of the finest resorts in Europe, visitors have flocked here every summer. It's a good base for touring the **Valley of the Tummel,** but has plenty of attractions in its own right to keep you close by. It's home to the renowned **Pitlochry Festival Theatre,** Scotland's theatre in the hills, two whisky distilleries, a famous **Explorers Garden** and a ground-breaking dam and fish ladder, while the main high street is perfect for whiling away an hour or so browsing around the little boutiques, gourmet stores and cute cafes. Nearby beauty spots include **Loch Rannoch** and the **Pass of Killiecrankie,** while at Blair Atholl is the grand, turreted **Blair Castle.**

Essentials

GETTING THERE   Direct trains from Edinburgh and Glasgow take under 2 hours, from Perth the journey time is just 30 minutes (www.scotrail.co.uk; ℘ **08457/484-950**). There are regular buses from Inverness, Edinburgh, Glasgow and Perth to Pitlochry; contact **CityLink** (www.citylink.co.uk; ℘ **0871/266-3333**) for schedules.

If you're **driving** Pitlochry is just off the main A9. From Edinburgh allow about 1 hr. 40 mins. From Perth it takes about 45 mins.

VISITOR INFORMATION   The **VisitScotland iCentre** is at 22 Atholl Rd. (www.pitlochry.org; ℘ **01796/472-215**) and is open year-round. From July through August, it's open Monday to Saturday 9am to 6pm, Sunday 9:30am to 5pm; September and October, it's open Monday to Saturday 9:30am to 5:30pm and Sunday 10am to 4pm; and November to April, hours are Monday to Saturday 10am to 4pm.

Exploring the Area

Who would have thought that a giant hydro-electric plant could become a fascinating tourist attraction? **Pitlochry Dam** and power station took 4 years to build and began generating electricity in the early 1950s. By building the dam, the engineers created an artificial loch—Loch Faskally. They also constructed a **salmon ladder** to help the fish swim upstream on their annual journey to their breeding grounds and for years, tourists have flocked to a viewing chamber where an underwater section of the ladder can be seen through the glass (it's estimated that 250,000 salmon have used the ladder since 1952). In 2017, the innovative new **Pitlochry Dam Visitor Centre** was unveiled (www.pitlochrydam.com; ℘ **01796/484-111**), its unique design making it appear to hover above the dam, river, and loch. Its interactive exhibitions explore the history of hydro-electric power, the visionaries who spearheaded the project and the engineering feats of the men who risked their lives in the process, as well as explains the life cycle of the salmon. There is also a sleekly designed cafe with floor-to-ceiling windows and balcony above the River Tummel from where you can see the salmon leaping from April to September. Admission is free and it's open daily from 9:30am to 5:30pm.

A short walk away, hunkered into the hillside above the Pitlochry Festival Theatre, is the spectacular 6-acre **Explorers Garden** (www.explorersgarden. com; ℘ **01796/484-286**). Divided into six sections, this woodland oasis is brimming with plants brought back by intrepid Scottish plant hunters from all corners of the globe. Magnificent views of the surrounding mountains can be glimpsed through gaps in the trees. It's open daily during the summer from April, from 10am to 5pm and costs £4 for adults, £3.50 seniors, £1 for children ages 5 to 16, £9 families.

The **Linn of Tummel** is good walking country with several signposted trails beside the river and into the forest to the north of the town center. If you've got a car, drive north to the stunning **Pass of Killiecrankie ★**. The

National Trust established the **Killiecrankie Visitor Centre** (www.nts.org.uk; ℱ **01796/473-233**) here, open April to October daily from 10am to 5pm. Admission is free and the exhibition inside tells of the story of the famous battle that took place here during the 1689 Jacobite rebellion. John Graham of Cleverhouse (1649–89) rallied the mainly Highlander Jacobite army to meet government troops. It was one of the goriest battles in Jacobite history. Graham was killed, and the quest for Scottish independence soon fizzled out. From Soldier's Leap you can see where a Redcoat soldier leapt 18ft. across the raging River Garry to escape the Jacobites.

The B8019 leads to **Loch Rannoch,** almost 10 miles long and ¾ mile wide. The setting so impressed Robert Louis Stevenson that he wrote about it in *Kidnapped* (1886): "Much of it was red with heather, much of the rest broken up with bogs and hags and peaty pools." It is a desolate but stunningly beautiful spot.

For those hankering after a round of golf, the **Pitlochry Golf Course** (www.pitlochrygolf.co.uk; ℱ **01796/472-334**) is a challenging 18-hole, par-69 course set in a spectacular undulating landscape and boasting stunning views of the Tummel Valley.

Where to Eat & Stay

You can't move without stumbling over a B&B or guesthouse in this buzzing tourist hotspot. There's also no shortage of places to eat from pub grub to fish and chips and quaint cafes. The **Port-na-Craig Inn** (www.portnacraig.com; ℱ **01796/472-777**) on the banks of the River Tummel just below the Pitlochry Festival Theatre has one of the most bucolic settings, a clutch of cute rooms and serves delicious food, while **Torrdarach House** (www.torrdarach.co.uk; ℱ **01796/472-136**) is a luxury B&B, its rooms all named after famous golf courses. **Victoria's** (www.victorias-pitlochry.co.uk; ℱ **01796/472-670**) is a local institution, a low-key, unpretentious place, dishing up everything from smashed avo on toast to homebaked cakes.

Craigmhor Lodge ★★ In 2018 Craigmhor Lodge was crowned the best guesthouse in Scotland. That's a lot to live up to. Hidden away from Pitlochry's hurley burley in a peaceful woodland setting, there's one room in the original Victorian lodge (high ceilings and views over the valley) and 12 in the contemporary courtyard building with balconies or terraces looking out over the grounds. Breakfast is a highlight here from the full Scottish (Ayrshire bacon, local butcher's sausages, sautéed mushrooms, grilled tomatoes, Stornoway black pudding, and potato scones with free-range Perthshire eggs) to peat-smoked Buckie haddock cooked in milk and topped with a free-range egg. Or maybe you'd like a warming bowl of creamy porridge topped with a dram of whisky? Packed lunches and supper hampers can also be made up on request.

27 West Moulin Rd. www.craigmhorlodge.co.uk. ℱ **01796/472-123**. 13 units. £99–£180 double, includes breakfast. **Amenities:** Lounge; free Wi-Fi.

Head uphill towards Braemar and you'll stumble upon the **Edradour Distillery** (www.edradour.co.uk; © **01796/472-095**), touted as Scotland's smallest, and possibly prettiest, distillery where whisky is still made in the old farm buildings. This whitewashed distillery, with its jaunty red paintwork, dates to 1825 and prides itself on its artisan approach and small-scale production.

The distillery is open for 1-hour guided tours and tastings in the old Malt Barn, April to October, Monday through Saturday 10am to 5pm; November to March, Monday to Friday 10am to 4:30pm. Tickets cost £10 for adults, £5 for children 12-17. You can stock up on your favorite in the shop, which stocks 25 Expressions of Edradour single malt whisky.

East Haugh House ★★   This family-run country hotel is warm and welcoming and just a stone's throw from Pitlochry. The pretty, turreted stone house was built in the 17th century by the Duke of Atholl for one of his tenant farmers and was converted into a hotel by the McGown family in 1989. The contemporary bedrooms (fish-themed wallpaper anyone?) are individually decorated, one with an antique four-poster bed, tartan carpets and Jacuzzi, another with a roaring log fire and vampish red decor, another with a "movie room" attached (49-inch TV, DVD player, and movie library).

Salmon fishing breaks are a specialty: The hotel has its own fishing beat (a private stretch of riverbank and the exclusive rights to fish it) and resident fly fishing instructor and can also organize day rods and a ghillie for the Tay and Tummel rivers as well as shooting and stalking activities.

The hotel is also renowned for its restaurant (owner Neil McGowan is an award-winning chef) and was recommended in the 2018 Michelin guide. Think slow-braised shoulder of lamb with dauphinoise potatoes, buttered spinach, and rosemary jus or pan-seared venison liver with Stornoway black pudding, bubble and squeak, and red onion thyme gravy. The restaurant is open for dinner daily from 5:30 to 9pm and mains cost £13 to £27.

Old Perth Rd., East Haugh. www.easthaugh.co.uk. © **01796/473-121.** 13 units. £120–£210 double, £210 suite includes breakfast. **Amenities:** Restaurant; bar; fishing beat; free Wi-Fi.

Killiecrankie Hotel ★   This is your quintessential small Scottish country house hotel. It's an impossibly pretty, whitewashed house, looking out over the Pass of Killiecrankie and built in 1840 for the local church minister. It's surrounded by 4 acres of lush lawns, gardens brimming with flowers and shady woodland. The bedrooms are all quirkily quaint and individual, there's a cozy wood-paneled bar stocked with around 25 single malts and snug sitting room with a log fire for chillier nights. During the summer you can sit out on the patio during the long evenings and enjoy the heady scent of the rose garden. The tartan-trimmed restaurant is all crisp white tablecloths and a focus on fresh, seasonal meat, fish, and game, while for a more relaxed meal you can eat in the conservatory.

Killiecrankie. www.killiecrankiehotel.co.uk. ✆ **01796/473-220.** 10 units. £280–£335 double. Rates include half-board. Free parking. **Amenities:** Restaurant; bar; free Wi-Fi.

Entertainment & Nightlife

The **Pitlochry Festival Theatre** (www.pitlochryfestivaltheatre.com; ✆ **01796/484-626**) is one of the town's main attractions (a 10-minute walk from the center over a bridge across the river) and the only theater in the U.K. to put on a different play every day. Founded in 1951 (in a tent in a field nearby), the founding stone of its present site, at pretty Port-na-Craig on the banks of the River Tummel, was laid in 1979. This contemporary theatre, surrounded by trees with sweeping lawns sloping down to the water's edge, next to the **Pitlochry Dam,** draws people from all over the world for its program of plays, musicals, concerts, and art exhibits, from May to December. Each season there's also a series of popular backstage tours and talks outlining the theater's approach to stage production.

BLAIR ATHOLL ★★

The village of Blair Atholl is charmingly idyllic, the houses all a uniform grey stone huddled outside the gates of its gobsmacking castle. This is the headquarters of **Atholl Estates** (www.atholl-estates.co.uk; ✆ **01796/481-355**), which covers 145,000 acres of the Highlands and offers a host of ranger-led outdoor activities, Land Rover safaris, and pony trekking, as well as a 40-mile network of hiking and cycling trails. In the center of the village you can take a tour of the **Blair Atholl Watermill** (www.blairathollwatermill.co.uk; ✆ **01796/481-321**), a restored working mill dating back to the 16th century and today, producing stoneground oatmeal and flour once more. It is also an artisan bakery famous for its bagels (made the traditional way, boiled before baking). In the rustic-chic tearoom and shop (on the original kiln-drying floor) buy a bag of bagels to go or grab a seat and tuck into a smoked salmon and salad bagel for lunch.

Just outside Blair Atholl, beside the A9 is the **House of Bruar** (www. houseofbruar.com; ✆ **01796/483-236**), a sprawling luxury Scottish shopping emporium and gourmet food hall and one of the best pitstops for travellers heading north or south.

Blair Castle ★★ CASTLE   The seat for centuries of the Dukes of Atholl, this is one of Scotland's great castles. Dating from 1269, it wouldn't look out of place in a Disney fairytale. It might date back to medieval times but the current white turreted vision was created after a spot of Victorian remodeling. Inside you can marvel at the palace's sumptuous interior crammed with antique furniture and paintings, along with a treasure trove of arms, armor, and porcelain. Then stroll through the Victorian walled garden and out into the parkland. The castle also offers a range of self-catering accommodation. As well as a campsite, there are a number of luxury lodges scattered across the Atholl Estate and, in a secluded meadow setting, a group of contemporary woodland lodges (from £280 for a 3-night short break for a lodge sleeping two) with waymarked trails on the doorstep and ranger-led activities.

Blair Atholl. www.blair-castle.co.uk. ✆ **01796/481-207.** £12 adults, £10.30 seniors and students, £7.70 children 5–16, £35 families. Apr–Oct daily 9:30am–5:30pm (last admission to Castle Tour 4:30pm).

DUNDEE, UNESCO CITY OF DESIGN ★★

63 miles N of Edinburgh; 67 miles SW of Aberdeen; 22 miles NE of Perth; 83 miles NE of Glasgow

Dundee, on the north shore of the Firth of Tay, is reveling in a vibrant cultural and artistic renaissance and has been designated a UNESCO City of Design. For years the city languished, down-at-heel, its industries on the economic scrap heap, but now its waterfront is a hive of activity with a host of new hotels springing up to cater to the thousands of tourists flocking here to visit the new **V&A Dundee** museum, the only offshoot of London's renowned V&A in the world, which opened in the autumn of 2018.

Added to that, you have **Dundee Contemporary Arts** (www.dca.org.uk; ✆ **01382/909-900**) a world-class center for the development and exhibition of contemporary art and culture, which houses two contemporary art galleries, a print studio, visual research center, cinema, and cafe.

Historically, Dundee was once a bustling port and shipbuilding was one of its main industries from the 1860s until World War I. Many of the ships built here were for the whaling industry. The city was also renowned for jute and flax production and mills, while its other claim to fame is culinary: The city is famous for its rich Dundee fruitcakes, marmalades, and jams.

The city is also a good base from which to visit Glamis Castle (one of the most famous in Scotland) and the little town of Kirriemuir, which Sir James M. Barrie, author of *Peter Pan,* disguised in fiction as Thrums. One of Scotland's most famous golf courses, Carnoustie, is also nearby.

Essentials

GETTING THERE   There are frequent trains from Perth and Aberdeen to Dundee's smart new railway station (part of the revamped waterfront). The journey from Perth takes around 20 mins. Check out **ScotRail** (www.scotrail. co.uk) or phone ✆ **08457/484-950** for schedules.

CityLink buses offer frequent services from Edinburgh and Glasgow. Contact ✆ **0871/266-3333,** or log on to www.citylink.co.uk.

If you are driving from the north or south the quickest route to Dundee is to head for Perth along the A9, and link up with the A972 going east.

10

Dundee

ABERDEEN, THE GRAMPIANS & TAYSIDE

The **Tourist Information Centre** is in City Square beside Caird Hall (www.dundee.com; ✆ **01382/527-527**). It is open Monday to Saturday 9:30am to 5pm, Sunday 10am to 4pm; October to March, Monday to Saturday 9am to 5pm.

Exploring the Area

For a panoramic view of Dundee, the Tay Bridge across to Fife, and the mountains to the north, go to **Dundee Law,** a 174m (571-ft.) hill, 1 mile north of the city. The hill is an ancient volcanic plug with an observation point at the summit. There was once an Iron Age hillfort here and graves dating back to 1500 B.C.E. have been discovered as well as Roman pottery from the 1st century C.E.

Spanning the Firth of Tay is the **Tay Railway Bridge,** opened in 1888 after the original rail bridge collapsed in a terrible storm in 1879. There was a train crossing at the time and all those onboard, around 75 people, were killed. Constructed over the tidal estuary, the bridge is 1¾ miles long and one of the longest in Europe. A road bridge 1¼ miles long, with a walkway in the center, offers spectacular views of the city and over to the Kingdom of Fife (www.tayroadbridge.co.uk).

Broughty Castle ★ CASTLE   This 15th-century coastal fort is 4 miles east of the city center at Broughty Ferry, a historic fishing village where ferries crossing the Firth of Tay would dock before the bridges were built. It was constructed at a strategic point on the Tay in 1490 to defend the country against a gathering English navy. Besieged by the English again in the 16th century and attacked by Cromwell's army under General Monk in the 17th century, the castle was restored in 1861 as part of Britain's coastal defenses in response to the threat from France. It now houses a museum with displays on local history, arms and armor, wildlife, and Dundee's past as a whaling port. From the top of the castle there are wonderful views of the Tay estuary and northeast Fife.

Castle Green, Broughty Ferry. www.historicenvironment.scot. ✆ **01382/436-916.** Free. Apr–Sept Mon–Sat 10am–4pm, Sun 12:30–4pm, Oct–Mar Tues–Sat 10am–4pm, Sun 12:30–4pm.

HMS *Unicorn* ★ HISTORIC SITE   This 46-gun ship of war, commissioned in 1824 by the Royal Navy, is now the oldest intact war ship in the world and one of the 6 oldest ships. It has been restored and visitors can explore all four decks: the quarterdeck, with its 32-lb. carronades; the gun deck, with its battery of 18-lb. cannons and captain's quarters; the berth deck, with its officers' cabins and crew's hammocks; and the orlop deck and hold. Various displays portraying life in the navy and the history of the *Unicorn* make this a great day out.

Victoria Dock. www.frigateunicorn.org. ✆ **01382/200-900.** £6.50 adults, £5 seniors, £2.50 children 5–15 £9–£15.50 families. Apr–Oct daily 10am–5pm; Nov–Mar Thurs–Sun noon–4pm.

RRS Discovery ★★★ HISTORIC SITE The RRS *Discovery* is the wooden three-masted sailing ship built in Dundee for Captain Scott's Antarctic expedition of 1901 to 1904. This award-winning visitor attraction is a must-see, with its fascinating exhibition rooms and emotive and inspiring films documenting the intricate preparations for this incredible journey and the Polar explorers' personal stories. You learn about the unique design features of the ship, which was built to withstand being frozen in the ice and the harsh polar environment. The propeller and rudder could be raised to prevent ice damage and the hull was formed from layers of different woods including greenheart from South America, known for its strength. The vessel was, indeed, frozen in the ice for 2 years and relief ships had to be sent with supplies, before the sailors managed to blast themselves clear. Boarding the ship, which now nudges up to the V&A Dundee, you can wander the upper decks before descending into the bowels of the ship to explore the engine room, bosun's store, crew quarters, galley, and sick bay.

Discovery Point, Discovery Quay. www.rrsdiscovery.com. ℂ **01382/309-060.** £11.25 adults, £8.75 seniors, £6.25 children 5–15, £30 families. Combined ticket with Verdant Works £18.25 adults, £15.50 seniors, £10.25 children 5–15, £46 families. Apr–Oct Mon–Sat 10am–6pm, Sun from 11am; Nov–Mar Mon–Sat 10am–5pm, Sun from 11am.

V&A Dundee ★★★ MUSEUM Scotland's first dedicated design museum—and the only other V&A museum in the world apart from London—opened in September 2018. The museum was designed by renowned Japanese architects Kengo Kuma & Associates after an international competition and the extraordinary state-of-the-art building has been created from curved concrete walls clad with 2,500 rough stone panels to resemble a Scottish cliff-face. The museum is part of an ambitious £1-billion waterfront redevelopment and showcases Scotland's design heritage—its past, present, and future. The Scottish Design Galleries feature displays from architecture to engineering and furniture to fashion alongside a dynamic program of temporary exhibitions. The innovative space has a café at its center and upstairs a restaurant with floor-to-ceiling windows and spectacular views of the RRS *Discovery* and the River Tay. The shop is a cut above your average museum store showcasing designers found in the Scottish Design Galleries.

1 Riverside Esplanade. www.vam.ac.uk. ℂ **01382/305-665.** Free; fee for some temporary exhibitions; daily 10am–5pm.

Verdant Works ★★ MUSEUM This old jute mill is a 15-minute walk from the waterfront and its sister attraction the RRS Discovery, and is one of the city's most fascinating sights. It's a sprawling complex (they give you a map) and is dedicated to the history of an industry that sustained Dundee through most of the 19th and 20th centuries. On the ground floor you wander through the old lodge keeper and works office to a display showing how raw jute from Bangladesh was processed. In the machine hall the scale of the operations, from fiber to fabric, is evident, with the old machines in situ and an explanatory film rolling on the screen at one end. The vast space housing the old Boulton & Watt steam engine and mechanics workshop is also worth exploring. On the first floor you can learn more about the city's social history through exhibitions on health and housing, women and work, children and leisure, and the jute barons of 19th-century Dundee.

West Henderson's Wynd. www.verdantworks.com. ✆ **01382/309-060.** £11.25 adults, £8.75 seniors, £6.25 children 5–15, £30 families. Combined ticket with RRS *Discovery* £18.25 adults, £15.50 seniors, £10.25 children 5–15, £46 families. Apr–Oct Mon–Sat 10am–6pm, Sun from 11am; Nov–Mar Mon–Sat 10am–5pm, Sun from 11am.

Where to Stay & Eat

The ambitious regeneration of Dundee's waterfront includes a swathe of new design-led hotels. For the past few years this area has resembled a building site, in fact. First off the blocks was the **Apex City Quay Hotel & Spa** (www.apexhotels.co.uk; ✆ **01382/202-404**), which along with smartly contemporary bedrooms comes with a pool, sauna, steam room and Yu Spa. The **Malmaison** swaggered into town in 2014, converting one of the city's historic buildings on the southern edge of the Central Conservation Area into a bold design hotel, while above the sleek new train station is **Sleeperz** (www.sleeperz.com; ✆ **01382/725-888**), a funky budget option. **Hotel Indigo** (www.ihg.com; ✆ **0330/331-1750**) converted one of the city's old jute mills on Constable Street into a 102-room boutique hotel, opening in the summer of 2018, retaining the exposed brickwork and commissioning throws made from jute for the beds. Opposite the V&A Dundee, meanwhile, **Marriott** nabbed a prime site for a luxury 150-room hotel.

The food and drink scene also received a much-needed shot of adrenalin. Head to the popular **Jute cafe bar** (www.jutecafebar.co.uk; ✆ **01382/909-246**) in the Dundee Contemporary Arts center during the day for a lunch platter of East Coast cured meats, Scottish cheddar, olives, toasted bread, and pickle platter or **Tailend** (www.thetailend.co.uk; ✆ **01382/229-990**), a cool little joint and restaurant, takeaway, fishmonger, and deli in one. This family-run business, G&A Spink from Arbroath up the coast has been in the industry for four generations, smoking and filleting fish from Kinlochbervie, Fraserburgh, and Lerwick. This is the sister venture to their fish and chip shop in St Andrews. Then there's **Collinsons** (www.collinsonsrestaurant.com; ✆ **01382/776-000**) in Broughty Ferry or **Castlehill** in town (see below).

Castlehill ★ MODERN SCOTTISH Graham Campbell was the youngest Scottish chef to be awarded a Michelin star in 2009, when he was just 25 years old and working near Fort William at Ballachulish House. He became head chef at Castlehill in Dundee in 2015 where he focuses on Scotland's overflowing natural larder. A keen forager, from the woodlands around Dundee he sources wild garlic, sorrel, ground elder, pink purslane and sweet cicely. Signature dishes include ballotine of foie gras, wild halibut and scallop tortellini in a vanilla velouté with black olive crushed potatoes.

22 Exchange St. www.castlehillrestaurant.co.uk. ✆ **01382/220-008.** Lunch 2 courses £18, 3 courses £22. Dinner 2 courses £32, 3 courses £38, 6-course tasting menu £55. Wed–Sat 5:30–10pm, Fri–Sat noon–2:30pm.

Doubletree by Hilton Hotel Dundee ★ If you'd rather bed down outside the city center, this restored Victorian mansion, built in 1870, is now a Doubletree by Hilton and surrounded by 2.4 hectares (6 acres) of landscaped grounds, including a listed maze and a walled garden, on the outskirts of Dundee. You get a chocolate chip cookie at check-in, bedrooms are sleek and contemporary in a soft, neutral palette, and the Maze restaurant is housed in a glasshouse-style conservatory and has an all-day dining menu featuring mains such as roast breast of guinea fowl and beer-battered North Sea haddock and chips from £11 to £18.

Kingsway West. www.doubletree3.hilton.com. ℰ **01382/641-122.** 95 units. £93–£156 double; £158 suite, includes breakfast. Free parking. **Amenities:** Restaurant; bar; pool (indoor); health club and spa; free Wi-Fi.

Malmaison ★★ This forward-thinking boutique hotel chain got wind that the tide was turning in Scotland's sunniest city and careered into town in 2014. It managed to acquire one of the historic buildings at the southern edge of the central conservation zone and converted it into a funky design hotel. Bedrooms peppered over six floors are dark and decadent with purple velvet wrap-around headboards, furry throws and images of cartoon character Dennis the Menace on the walls (Dundee is home to DC Thomson which published the Beano comics). Some rooms also feature romantic freestanding bathtubs and come with panoramic river views.

The trademark Chez Mal Brasserie dishes up classic bistro fare in an opulent setting. There are views of the waterfront from the windows, the V&A visible in the distance, and velvet button-back chairs in mustard and mushroom tones, the boudoir-chic tempered by an industrial vibe. Exposed piping snakes across the ceiling. The indoor charcoal oven's flames give the New York strip steaks a wonderfully smoky flavor, while starters such as tuna tartare with pickled ginger and wasabi are light and fresh. Mains cost from £15 to £19. The wine list is helpfully broken down into price points, going up in £5 increments.

44 Whitehall Crescent. www.malmaison.com. ℰ **01382/339-715.** 91 units. £49–£199 double; £179–£289 suite. **Amenities:** Restaurant; bar; free Wi-Fi.

Entertainment & Nightlife

The **Dundee Rep Theatre,** Tay Square (www.dundeerep.co.uk; ℰ **01382/223-530**), puts on an eclectic program of productions each season with opera, comedy, plays, and ballet. Founded in 1939, the building is a center of creative energy and also home to the Scottish Dance Theatre. The box office is open Monday through Saturday from 9:30am until the start of each performance. There is also a popular bar and brasserie on-site, the **Rep Restaurant** (www.dundeereprestaurant.co.uk; ℰ **01382/206-699**).

Duke's Corner, 13 Brown Street (www.dukescorner.co.uk; ℰ **01382/205-052**), is a lively late-night haunt offering bands, beer, and BBQ—the gastropub grub is cooked on a charcoal grill, the music is live, the beers from craft breweries.

FROM lost boys TO ROCK GODS

The little town of **Kirriemuir** in Angus is 4 miles north of Glamis Castle or 16 miles north of Dundee via the A929 and the A928. Thousands of visitors each year come here to pay their respects to J. M. Barrie (1860–1937), the author of *Peter Pan* who was born here and, more recently, to Bon Scott (1946–1980), the lead singer of AC/DC who is the town's other famous son.

The little town of red-sandstone houses and narrow crooked streets, in the heart of Scotland's raspberry country, was the birthplace of James Barrie in 1860. His father was employed as a hand-loom weaver of linen. **Barrie's birthplace** still stands at 9 Brechin Rd. (www.nts.org.uk; ✆ **01575/572-646**) and is owned by the National Trust for Scotland. The small cottage contains some of the writer's manuscripts and mementos as well as the writing desk from his apartment in London where he penned *Peter Pan*. The family lived crowded into 2 tiny upstairs rooms while his father's workshop was on the ground floor. From April to June and September to October, the house is open Saturday to Monday 11am to 4pm; in July and August, it's open Thursday to Monday 11am to 4pm. Admission is £6.50 for adults; £5.50 for seniors, students, and children 5 to 15; £17 for a family ticket.

Barrie first became known for his sometimes-cynical tales of Kirriemuir, disguised as Thrums, in works such as *Auld Licht Idylls* (1888) and *A Window in Thrums* (1889). He then turned to the theatre and in time became known for bringing supernatural and sentimental stories to the stage. It's said that talking to a group of children while walking his dog gave him the idea for the stories about Peter Pan. The character first appeared in a book, *The Little White Bird*, in 1902 and then in a play in 1904.

He went on to write more dramas, including *Alice Sit-by-the-Fire* (1905), *What Every Woman Knows* (1908), *The Will* (1913), and *Mary Rose* (1920)—the latter a popular play in its day. But, besides Barrie scholars, who remembers these works now? Peter Pan, meanwhile, has become a legendary figure, known by almost every child in the Western world through films, plays, musicals, as well as the original book.

Although he spent most of his working life in London, Barrie is buried in Kirriemuir Cemetery. To reach **Barrie's grave,** turn left off Brechin Road and follow the cemetery road upward. The path is clearly marked, taking you to the grave pavilion. A camera obscura in the **Barrie Pavilion** on Kirriemuir Hill gives views over Strathmore to Dundee and north to the Highlands.

Bon Scott was born in Kirriemuir in 1946 and lived here with his family for the first six years of his life before moving to Australia. The lead singer of rock band AC/DC, he died at the age of 33. A life-size bronze statue of the singer was crowdfunded by fans and unveiled in 2016 in the Braes car park during the annual BonFest held each year in his honor.

A Side Trip to Glamis Castle ★★

Glamis Castle (www.glamis-castle.co.uk; ✆ **01307/840-393**), pronounced *Glarms*, was the late Queen Mother's childhood home and the place where Princess Margaret was born, the first royal princess to be born in Scotland in 3 centuries. Its royal connections go back much further—as does its literary claim to fame. William Shakespeare visited Glamis with King James VI, and it's thought he gained inspiration here for his play *Macbeth*, written at the beginning of the 17th century. The play is loosely based on the 11th-century Scottish king, Macbeth, but bears little resemblance to real events. In Glamis Castle one of the rooms has been dubbed Duncan's Hall, which the Victorians claimed was where Macbeth murdered King Duncan, but in Shakespeare's play the murder takes place at Macbeth's castle, Cawdor, near Inverness. The real Macbeth did kill King Duncan, but on the battlefield near Elgin. (Incidentally, Shakespeare was wrong in naming Macbeth Thane of Glamis; Glamis wasn't made a thaneship—a sphere of influence in medieval Scotland—until years after the action in the play took place.)

The present Glamis Castle, a turreted confection at the end of an elegant driveway, dates from the early 15th century, but there are records of a hunting lodge here in the 11th century and it has been in the Lyon family since 1372.

The castle is open to the public, with guided tours of the Royal Apartments, as well as the landscaped grounds, the walled Italian garden and pine plantation that features a Macbeth trail (peppered with wooden sculptures of characters from the play). It is open from April to October, daily 10am to 5:30pm (last tour 4:30pm). Admission to the castle and gardens costs £12.50 for adults, £10.50 for seniors, £9 for children 5 to 15, and £40 for a family ticket. Tickets for entry to the grounds only are: £7.50 for adults, £6.50 for seniors, and £6 for children. Glamis Castle is 12 miles north of Dundee along the A90. The journey takes around 20 minutes.

BALLATER ★ & BALMORAL CASTLE ★

111 miles N of Edinburgh; 41 miles W of Aberdeen; 67 miles NE of Perth; 70 miles SE of Inverness

Ballater is the kind of place that lifts your spirits, with its picturesque setting on the River Dee, cradled by the tree-clad Grampian Mountains in the heart of Royal Deeside. With its wide, well-to-do streets lined with cafes, ice cream parlors and gift shops, it feels every inch the charming Victorian holiday resort. For most visitors it is also, of course, the stepping-stone for visiting Balmoral Castle, the Scottish home of the Windsors. The town still centers on its Station Square, where the royal family was once photographed as they arrived to spend their holidays in the Highlands. (The railway is now closed.) From Ballater, you can drive west to view the spectacular scenery of Glen Muick and Lochnagar, where herds of wild red deer wander the moors. The drive between Ballater and Braemar (see "Braemar," below) is also incredibly scenic.

Essentials

GETTING THERE   You can take the train to Aberdeen and continue the rest of the way by connecting bus. For rail schedules and information, call ℂ **08457/484-950** or check www.scotrail.co.uk.

Buses run hourly from Aberdeen to Ballater and the journey takes just under 3 hours. The bus and train stations in Aberdeen are next to each other on Guild Street (www.stagecoachbus.com; © **01224/212-266**). The bus continues on to Braemar from Ballater (trip time: 30 min.).

It is easier to explore the area by car. The A93 from Blairgowrie through Glen Shee to Braemar and Ballater is one of Scotland's great drives (a favorite with motorcyclists) through stunning Highland scenery.

VISITOR INFORMATION The **Tourist Information Centre** is in the historic railway station on Station Square (www.visitballater.com; © **01339/755-306**). March to December daily 10am to 5pm. Closed January to February.

Balmoral Castle ★

"This dear paradise" is how Queen Victoria described Balmoral Castle, rebuilt in the Scottish baronial style by her beloved Albert. And Balmoral was the setting for the story of Victoria and her faithful servant, John Brown, as depicted in the film *Mrs. Brown.* Today, Balmoral is still the royal family's private residence. Albert, Victoria's prince consort, leased the property in 1848 and bought it in 1852. As the original castle proved too small, the present edifice was built and completed in 1855. Its principal feature is a 30m (98-ft.) tower. Only the ballroom is actually open to the public with pictures, porcelain, and other artworks on display. There's also an exhibition in the Carriage Hall outside and visitors are free to explore the grounds.

Balmoral, Ballater. www.balmoralcastle.com. © **01339/742-534.** £11.50 adults, £10.50 seniors, £6 children 5–16, free for children 4 and under, £32 families. Apr–July daily 10am–5pm. Closed Aug–Mar.

Where to Stay & Eat

One of the stalwarts of Royal Deeside, the **Darroch Learg Hotel,** Braemar Rd. (www.darrochlearg.co.uk), an elegant country house dating back to 1888, was devastated by a fire in 2015, but its extensive restoration and refurbishment was completed for the 2018 reopening. It stands in 2 hectares (5 acres) of lush woodlands opening onto views of the Dee Valley and the Grampian Mountains beyond. On the outskirts of Ballater there's an all-singing, all-dancing Hilton resort, the long-winded **Hilton Grand Vacations at Craigendarroch Suites** (www3.hilton.com; © **01339/755-858**). A number of villas are scattered through the estate around a historic mansion that once belonged to marmalade barons, the Keiller family. The resort has a pool, tennis and squash courts, and a spa. One of the most stunning properties, however, is a 20-minute drive from Ballater toward Aboyne. **Douneside House** (www.dounesidehouse.co.uk; © **01339/881-230**) on the MacRobert Estate is a gorgeous historic house with 14 exquisite rooms, with fetching freestanding bathtubs, button-back chairs, rich drapes, and a softly muted color palette, epitomizing classic understated elegance (and double rooms from £153).

In 2018 a tiny new glamping spot opened near Ballater. **Howe of Torbeg** (www.howeoftorbeg.co.uk; ✆ **01339/756-262**) has just four cute wooden glamping pods and two tent pitches in 1 acre of land in Glen Gairn surrounded by birch woods and farmland. Each comes with a Kadai fire bowl for BBQs under the stars, a small deck area and a picnic table and costs from £55 per night.

Ballater is dotted with little cafes and food stores, traditional butchers, coffee roasters (www.roaringstagcoffee.com; ✆ **01339/756-200**), and an ice cream parlor. **Rock Salt & Snails** (✆ **07834/452-583**) on Bridge St. is a funky little eatery, with wooden floors, pale grey painted tongue-and-groove walls and metal chairs and wooden banquettes, and is a great place for a cappuccino and homebaked scones. **Shorty's Ice Cream Parlour** (www.shortysicecream parlour.co.uk; ✆ **01339/756-215**), meanwhile, is legendary. All the ice cream is made on site with flavors from lemon meringue pie to wild cherry, and it also has a good range of gluten-free cakes. It's open daily July and August from noon to 8pm, March to June and September to October it's open Tuesday to Sunday noon to 8pm; November to February Tuesday to Sunday 2pm until 7pm.

Deeside Inn ★   With its roaring log fires, wood-paneling, beamed ceilings, and wooden floors strewn with Persian rugs, this traditional inn in the center of Ballater oozes character, Scottish hospitality and hominess. It's also famous for its traditional live music. Check into one of the recently refurbished rooms in the Victoria Wing, which boast a soft mustard and grey color palette with a smattering of tongue and groove woodwork and floral fabrics. The dining room with its mismatched antique tables and windows overlooking the village green and Glenmuick Church dishes up fish fresh from the River Dee, beef from the hotel's own grass-fed herd and wild venison from nearby Highland estates. The comforting all-day menu features hearty soups such as Scotch broth packed with pearl barley, heritage carrots, and pressed lamb shoulder £7 and steaks supplied by John Davidson of Inverurie, aged for a minimum of 40 days in Scotland's only Himalayan Salt ageing cellar (£19–£27).

13-15 Victoria Rd. www.crerarhotels.com. ✆ **01339/755-413.** 56 units. £90–£184 double, includes breakfast. **Amenities:** Restaurant; bar; lounge; free Wi-Fi.

BRAEMAR ★

85 miles N of Edinburgh; 58 miles W of Aberdeen; 51 miles N of Perth

The picturesque village of Braemar sits in the heart of some of Grampians' most spectacular scenery. It's famous for its Highland Games and romantic castle. The village is set against a backdrop of hills, blanketed with vibrant purple heather in summer, where Clunie Water joins the River Dee. The mountain of **Cairn Toul** which towers over Braemar, is a munro and the fourth highest mountain in Scotland soaring to a height of 1,287m (4,222 ft.).

Essentials

GETTING THERE Take the train to Aberdeen, and then continue the rest of the way (60 miles/100km) by bus. For information and schedules, call ✆ **08457/484-950** or check www.scotrail.co.uk. Buses run hourly from Aberdeen and the journey takes around 2 hours 15 mins (www.stagecoachbus.com; ✆ **01224/212-266**).

It is easier to explore the area by car. The A93 from Blairgowrie through Glen Shee to Braemar is one of Scotland's most scenic routes (a favorite with motorcyclists) through stunning Highland scenery.

VISITOR INFORMATION The year-round **VisitScotland Braemar iCentre** is in The Mews, Mar Road (www.braemarscotland.co.uk; ✆ **01339/741-600**). From May to October, it's open daily 9:30am to 5pm; from November to April it's open daily 10am to 5pm.

SPECIAL EVENTS The spectacular **Royal Highland Gathering** (www.braemargathering.org; ✆ **01339/741-098**) takes place each year on the first Saturday in September in the Princess Royal and Duke of Fife Memorial Park. The Queen and members of the royal family usually attend the event. It's thought that these ancient games were conceived by King Malcolm Canmore, a chieftain who ruled much of Scotland at the time of the Norman conquest of England. He selected his hardiest warriors from all the clans for a "keen and fair contest." Today, it's a great day out featuring everything from field sports, to marching bands, traditional Scottish dancing, tossing the caber and tug o' war.

Braemar is overrun with visitors during the gathering—you need to book tickets well in advance via the website and as well as accommodation.

Exploring the Area

You might spot members of the royal family, even the Queen herself, at **Crathie Church,** 8⅔ miles east of Braemar on the A93 (www.braemarandcrathie parish.org.uk; ✆ **01339/742-208**), where they attend Sunday services when in residence. Services are at 11:30am; otherwise, the church is open April to October, Monday to Saturday 10am to 4pm and on Sunday 12:45pm to 4pm. It was Queen Victoria who laid the foundation stone in 1893 and the kirk was opened in 1895.

About 4 miles west of Braemar is the **Mar Lodge Estate** (www.nts.org.uk; ✆ **01339/741-276**), owned and managed by the National Trust for Scotland and encompassing 29,000 hectares of ancient forest, rugged glen and wild rivers. Nature lovers can also explore Glen Muick, Loch Muick, and Lochnagar.

Braemar Golf Club (www.braemargolfclub.co.uk; ✆ **01339/741-618**) founded in 1902 is the highest golf course in the country. The 2nd-hole green is 380m (1,250 ft.) above sea level—this is the trickiest hole on the course. Pro golf commentator Peter Alliss deemed it "the hardest par 4 in all of Scotland." Set on a plateau, the hole is bordered on the right by the River Clunie and on the left by rough.

ABERDEEN, THE GRAMPIANS & TAYSIDE

Braemar

Braemar Castle ★ CASTLE   This romantic 17th-century castle is the only one in Scotland to be run by the local community, who share vivid tales of its colorful history through the last 4 centuries as they show visitors around. Originally built as a hunting lodge for the Earl of Mar in 1628, it has strong Jacobite connections and was used as a garrison for Hanoverian troops after the Battle of Culloden to help to control wayward Highlanders. For the last 200 years it has been the private residence of the Chief of the Clan Farquharson. The castle has barrel-vaulted ceilings and an underground prison (where sheep and rustlers were once imprisoned) and is known for its remarkable star-shaped defensive curtain wall. Queen Victoria once took tea in the drawing room.

Braemar. www.braemarcastle.co.uk. ✆ **01339/741-219.** £8 adults, £7 seniors and students, £4 children 5–15, free for children 4 and under. Apr–June and Sept–Oct Wed–Sun 10am–5pm; daily July and Aug 10am–5pm. Closed Nov–Easter.

Where to Eat & Stay

One of the most exciting developments on the accommodation scene, and most eagerly anticipated openings in the Highlands, has been the major refurbishment and redesign of one of Braemar's oldest hotels, **The Fife Arms** (www.thefifearms.com; ✆ **07876-327-603**). This important landmark in the heart of the village has been sensitively restored to its former splendor by owners Iwan and Manuela Wirth, presidents of renowned art gallery, Hauser & Wirth. In line with their dedication to contemporary art, the Fife Arms will feature works by internationally renowned artists and host a program of cultural events. The sympathetic remodeling has been orchestrated by Crathie-based Scottish architects Moxon for the re-launch at the end of 2018—but hasn't shied away from creating a wow-factor, for instance a heather-topped courtyard roof. The revamped hotel has 46 sleek bedrooms and restaurant focusing on local Highland produce.

Braemar Lodge Hotel ★   In Victorian times this was a hunting lodge, today it's popular with skiers tramping to the nearby slopes at Glen Shee. It's just a couple of minutes' stroll from the center of Braemar, and has a picturesque setting at the head of Glen Clunie, close to the cottage where Robert Louis Stevenson wrote *Treasure Island.* On cool evenings, there are log fires blazing away and you can sip a warming dram in the wooden-paneled Malt Room (there are over 200 whiskies to choose from) decked out with old hunting trophies. Bedrooms are steadfastly traditional—tartan carpets, tartan blankets, solid wood furniture—while the restaurant serves hearty comfort food. There are also nine log cabins in the grounds sleeping up to six, and a bunkhouse for budget beds.

6 Glenshee Rd. www.braemarlodge.co.uk. ✆ **01339/741-627.** 7 units. £120–£150 double, includes breakfast; £385–£560 weekly cabin rental (Sat–Sat). Free parking. **Amenities:** Restaurant; bar; free Wi-Fi.

SPEYSIDE ★ & THE MALT WHISKY TRAIL ★

Much of the Speyside region is in the Moray district, on the southern shore of the Moray Firth, a large inlet cutting into the northeastern coast of Scotland. The district stretches in a triangular shape south from the coast to the wild heart of the Cairngorm Mountains near Aviemore. It's a land steeped in history, as its many castles, battle sites, and ancient monuments testify.

The valley of the second-largest river in Scotland, Strathspey, as it's also known, runs north and south of Aviemore, and is an area of great natural beauty. The Spey's source is in the Highlands above Loch Laggan, which lies 40 miles south of Inverness. Little more than a creek here, it gains in force, fed by the many "burns" that drain water from the surrounding hills. It's one of Scotland's great rivers for salmon fishing and its main center is Grantown-on-Spey.

To reach Speyside from Aberdeen take the A96 northwest, towards Elgin. If you're traveling north on the A9 from Perth and Pitlochry, you can stop at Dalwhinnie, which at 575m (1,886 ft.) has the highest whisky distillery in the world. It's not in the Spey Valley, but at the northeastern end of Loch Ericht, with fine views of forests and hills.

Keith ★

Keith, 11 miles northwest of Huntly, on the banks of the River Isla, grew up because of its location, straddling the main road and rail routes between Inverness and Aberdeen. It has an ancient history, but owes its present layout to late 18th and early 19th centuries town planning. Today it's a good stopover on the **Malt Whisky Trail.**

The oldest working distillery in the Scottish Highlands, the **Strathisla Distillery,** on Seafield Avenue (www.chivas.com; ✆ **01542/783-044**), was established in 1786. It's open from April to October, daily 9:30am to 6pm; admission costs £15 for adults, free for children 8 to 18 (children 7 and under not admitted), which includes a tour and tutored tasting of four whiskies.

Dufftown ★

James Duff, the fourth Earl of Fife, founded Dufftown in 1817. This picturesque little market town, its four main streets converging at the **clock tower,** is the area's malt whisky capital. On the banks of the rivers Fiddich and Dullan and at the foot of the Conval hills, Dufftown is surrounded by no fewer than seven distilleries.

The biggest of the bunch, family-owned **Glenfiddich** is ⅔ mile to the north (www.glenfiddich.com/uk; ✆ **01340/820-373**). It's open daily year-round from 10am to 4pm. The most basic Explorers tour (£10 per person) starts with a film about the family (five generations and counting involved in the distillery's history) before a tour of the property and explanation of the distilling process. At the end there's a tutored nosing and tasting.

Other sights include **Balvenie Castle** (www.historicenvironment.scot: ℂ **01340/820-121**), the ruins of a moated 14th-century stronghold that lie on the south side of the Glenfiddich Distillery. During her northern campaign against the Earl of Huntly, Mary Queen of Scots spent 2 nights here. It's open from April to September, daily from 9:30am to 5:30pm, closed for lunch from 12:30pm to 1:30pm. Admission is £5 for adults, £4 for seniors, and £3 for children 5 to 15.

Grantown-on-Spey ★

Founded on a heather-covered moor in 1765 by Sir James Grant, Grantown-on-Spey became the seat of Grant's ancient family. The town went on to develop into a 19th century Highland resort. Today, this grey, granite town, in a wooded valley surrounded by the Cairngorm mountains, 34 miles southeast of Inverness, is still a popular base for winter sports and the first-rate salmon fishing on the Spey. From here, you can explore the valleys of the Don and Dee, the Cairngorms, and Culloden Moor, scene of the historic battle in 1746 when Bonnie Prince Charlie and his army were defeated. A **Tourist Information Centre** can be found on High Street (www.visitgrantown.co.uk; ℂ **01479/872-242**). It's open from April to October only, Monday through Saturday 10am to 5pm.

WHERE TO STAY

Culdearn House Hotel ★ Sometimes you just want a bit of chintz and a room wreathed in floral fabrics or striped wallpaper. Culdearn House is a real find. One of 5 houses built by Lord Seafield in 1860 for his daughters and surrounded by sprawling grounds, it has retained plenty of its period features. The 6 luxurious rooms are all individually decorated in rich fabrics and smattered with antique furniture. Craigevar is a roomy luxury king with windows looking out over the Hills of Cromdale and a champagne and claret color palette, Castle Fraser a twin in soft buttercup and dove grey, the walls striped, the bedspread floral, Balmoral and Inveraray boast blowsy blooms, Dunnottar delicate powder blue wallpaper.

The daily changing four-course menu (£48 per person) focuses on the best produce from Scotland's natural larder: hill-grazed lamb, fish from the Moray coast, free-range eggs and vegetables grown locally. Think chef's game terrine with homemade onion marmalade to start followed by breast of guinea fowl stuffed with pistachio nuts and lemon. On your doorstep are Speyside's distilleries to explore (the hotel stocks 60 for you to sample) fishing in the Spey and Aviemore with all its outdoor activities.

Grantown-on-Spey. www.culdearn.com. ℂ **01479/872-106.** 6 units. £160–£180 double, includes breakfast. Craigevar only available half-board £340. **Amenities:** Restaurant; lounge; free Wi-Fi.

Speyside & the Malt Whisky Trail

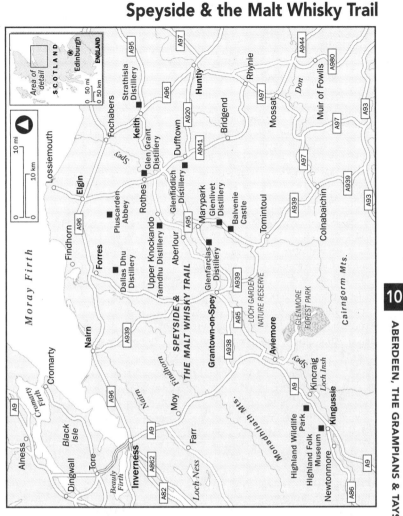

Glenlivet ★

The **Glenlivet Distillery** (www.theglenlivet.com; © **01340/821-720**) is in a remote glen, 10 miles north of the nearest village, Tomintoul. Near the River Livet, a Spey tributary, this distillery is one of the most famous in Scotland. It's open March to October, daily 9:30am to 6pm and tours start from £10 per person.

Glenfarclas at Ballindalloch (www.glenfarclas.com; © **01807/500-345**), is another that should be on your itinerary as one of the few malt whisky distilleries that's still independent of the giants. Since 1865 Glenfarclas has been

Follow the road signs for the **Malt Whisky Trail** ★★ (www.maltwhisky trail.com), a bucolic tourist route linking eight distilleries and one cooperage from the Moray coast through the rolling hills of Speyside. There are more than 50 distilleries sprinkled through this picture-perfect sweep of lush, rolling countryside. The ones on the trail include Benromach, a friendly little distillery on the coast near Forres, the historic distillery Dallas Dhu, Cardhu, Glenfiddich, Glen Grant, Strathisla and Glen Moray. At **The Glenlivet** (www. theglenlivet.com; ℭ **01340/821-720**) you can take an exclusive Spirit of the Malt tour and tasting or fill your own bottle straight from the cask, cork, cap and label it. At the **Speyside**

Cooperage, meanwhile, you can watch the fiery barrel-making process. A good place to spend the night is the pretty little village of Aberlour on the banks of the River Spey, the fastest-flowing river in Britain. The long distance walking route, the **Speyside Way,** meanders along its banks. Aberlour is the home of Walkers Shortbread and the **Aberlour** distillery. **The Mash Tun** (www.mashtun-aberlour.com; ℭ **01340/881-771**) is a quirky little stone pub with five rooms named after local distilleries. In May each year the **Spirit of Speyside Whisky Festival** (www.spiritofspeyside.com) features a host of whisky-themed events, and many distilleries normally closed to the public fling open their doors.

owned and managed by the Grant family. The 90-minute tour of the distillery takes visitors from grain to glass and costs £7.50 per person, finishing with a couple of drams in the Ship's Room. There's also a special connoisseur's tour and tasting, which begins at 2pm on Fridays between April and October; tickets cost £40; advance booking advisable. The distillery is open Monday to Friday year-round with tours October to March, 10:30am, noon, 1:15pm and 2:30pm; April to September Monday to Friday, 10:30am, noon, 2pm and 3:30pm; and on Saturdays from July to September.

Kincraig ★

Kincraig, at the northern end of Loch Insh, overlooking the Spey Valley to the west and the Cairngorm Mountains to the east is where you'll find polar bears. The 105-hectare (260 acres) **Highland Wildlife Park** ★ (www.highlandwild lifepark.org.uk; ℭ **01540/651-270**), is the home of Hamish, the first polar bear cub to be born in the U.K. in 25 years in 2018 (and his parents). There are also herds of European bison, red deer, shaggy Highland cattle, reindeer, camels and St Kilda Soay sheep. In enclosures you can see wolves, polecats, wildcats, beavers, badgers, and pine martens. You can observe protected birds, such as golden eagles and several species of grouse—of special interest is the *caper-caillie* ("horse of the woods"), a large Eurasian grouse that's native to Scotland's pine forests. There's a visitor center with a gift shop, a cafe, and exhibition areas. Ample parking and picnic sites are also available.

The park is open every day (except 25 December) from 10am. From April to October, it closes at 5pm (the last entrance is at 4pm), in July and August it closes at 6pm (last entrance at 5pm). From November to March, last entrance is at 3pm and the park closes at 4pm. Admission costs £17 for adults, £14.50 for seniors and students, and £9.95 for children 3 to 15; children ages 2 and under go free.

Kingussie ★

117 miles NW of Edinburgh; 41 miles S of Inverness; 11 miles SW of Aviemore

The little town of Kingussie (pronounced "King-*you*-see") is just off the A9. It's the capital of Badenoch, a district known as "the drowned land" because the Spey can flood the valley when the snows of a severe winter melt in the spring.

The **Highland Folk Museum ★**, Aultlarie Croft, Kingussie Rd in nearby Newtonmore (www.highlifehighland.com; ℰ **01540/673-551**), was the first folk museum established in Scotland (1934) and Britain's first open-air museum. The site stretches for over a mile and features over 30 historical buildings. Visitors can see how Highlanders lived and worked from the 1700s until the 1950s through the domestic, agricultural, and industrial exhibits. There's a turf kailyard (kitchen garden), a Lewis "black house," and old vehicles and carts. Events, such as spinning demonstrations, music-making, and handicraft fairs, are held throughout the summer. Admission is free. The museum is open daily, April to August, from 10:30am to 5:30pm, and in September and October, from 11am to 4:30pm.

Where to Eat & Stay

The Cross ★ SCOTTISH   This little restaurant with rooms has an idyllic setting in 1.6 hectares (4 acres) of gardens, with the Gynack Burn tumbling through the grounds. The building was once an old tweed mill and has a beamed ceiling and French doors leading out onto a terrace, over the water's edge, where dinners are served during the summer. You can choose between a three-course menu or the signature six-course tasting menu. Think loin of local venison, creamed cabbage, braised oxtail, pickled beets, celeriac, and red wine jus. After dinner you can stumble upstairs to one of the eight tranquil bedrooms (one with a balcony overlooking the mill pond).

Tweedmill Brae, Ardbroilach Rd. www.thecross.co.uk. ℰ **01540/661-166.** 8 units. £110–£200 includes breakfast. Fixed-price 3-course dinner £55; 6-course tasting menu £65 with wine pairing an extra £30. Closed Dec–Feb.

Elgin ★

38 miles E of Inverness; 68 miles NW of Aberdeen

This ancient royal burgh, the cathedral city of Elgin, sits on the banks of the Lossie River. The city's medieval plan has been retained, with "wynds" and "pends" connecting the main artery with other streets. The castle, as was customary in medieval town layouts, stood at one end of the main thorough-fare, with the cathedral—now a magnificent ruin—at the other. Nothing remains of the castle, but the site is a lovely place for a stroll. Samuel Johnson and James Boswell came this way on their Highland tour and reported a "vile dinner" at the Red Lion Inn in 1773.

On King Street you'll find the ruins of the **Elgin Cathedral** ★ (www.his toricenvironment.scot; ℂ **01343/547-171**). It was founded in 1224 but destroyed in 1390 by the "wolf of Badenoch," the natural son of Robert II. After its destruction, the citizens of Elgin rebuilt their beloved cathedral and turned it into one of the most attractive and graceful buildings in Scotland. However, when the central tower collapsed in 1711, the cathedral was allowed to fall into decay. It's open April to September, daily 9:30am to 5:30pm; there's late night opening in July on Tuesday and Saturday until 8pm, October to March daily, 10am to 4pm. Admission is £7.50 for adults, £6 for seniors, and £4.50 for children 5 to 15.

One of the town's main attractions is **Johnstons of Elgin Cashmere Heri-tage Centre** (www.johnstonsofelgin.com; ℂ **01343/554-099**), a picturesque shopping emporium where you can stock up on luxurious woolens. There's also a stylish homeware store and cute café, as well as mill tours where you can learn about the production process. The shop is open 9:30am to 5:30pm daily. Mill tours take place hourly Monday to Thursday from 10am to 3pm and on Fridays from 10am to noon and are free.

After exploring Elgin, you can drive 6 miles southwest to **Pluscarden Abbey** (www.pluscardenabbey.org). This is one of the most beautiful drives in the area, through the bucolic Black Burn Valley, where a priory was founded in 1230 by Alexander II. After centuries of decline, a new order of Benedictines arrived in 1974 and reestablished monastic life. You can visit the restored transepts, monastic buildings, and the church choir. Admission is free to the home of this active religious community; it's open daily from 8:30am to 4:30pm.

Another historic ruin is **Spynie Palace** (www.historicenvironment.scot; ℂ **01343/546-358**) the 15th-century residence of the bishops of Moray, used as a guesthouse by royals passing through. This is another great place for country walks, and from the top of a tower are magnificent vistas over the Laigh of Moray. It's open April to September daily from 9:30am to 5:30pm; and closed from October to March. Admission is £5 for adults, £4 for students and seniors, and £3for children 5 to 15 (under-4s free).

WHERE TO STAY

Mansion House Hotel ★ Built in the 19th-century baronial style, this grand, grey stone hotel is located beside the River Lossie, set within lovely grounds yet within a short stroll of the historic heart of Elgin. Bedrooms are furnished in an old-fashioned country-house style, some with sleigh beds, others with four-posters. The hotel's fine dining restaurant is open for lunch and dinner daily (main courses £15–£24), while the more relaxed bistro is only open in the evenings (from 6pm).

The Haugh. www.mansionhousehotel.co.uk. © **01343/548-811.** 23 units. £79–£129 double, includes breakfast. Free parking. **Amenities:** 2 restaurants; bar; billiards room; health club w/Jacuzzi, pool (indoor) and sauna; free Wi-Fi.

11 INVERNESS & THE HIGHLANDS

By Lucy Gillmore

Mist-shrouded mountains, glowering glens, boggy peat moors sprung with heather and hills blanketed with Narnia-like pine forest: this vast, ancient landscape has a breathtaking grandeur. Magnificent stags graze only yards from the road, golden eagles wheel high above, rushing rivers leap with wild salmon, while a mythical monster lurks in Scotland's most famous loch. Add gnarled castles, desolate, windswept battlefields, the shadow of Macbeth and the ghost of Bonnie Prince Charlie and you've got all the ingredients for a jam-packed, history-soaked road trip.

The capital of the Highlands—and the only town of any great size—is **Inverness.** This royal burgh sits on the banks of the Ness River at the northeast end of the Great Glen. From here you can visit the romantic ruins of **Urquhart Castle** and the wind-whipped battlefield of Culloden, where Bonnie Prince Charlie suffered his final, devastating defeat.

The landscape is vast and varied. This is where you'll find **Ben Nevis,** the highest mountain in Britain, but also **Loch Ness,** the deepest and most mysterious loch. The slopes around **Aviemore** provide Britain's best skiing, while the crags around **Knockan** form a natural geological playground. And once you come down from the heights, there's the Flow Country of **Caithness** and **Sutherland**—the seemingly endless heather-sprung flatlands of Europe's largest peat bog.

For many visitors schlepping up to the Highlands, the goal is **John o' Groats,** traditionally seen as the northernmost tip of the British mainland. Along the way are the family-friendly, sandy beaches around **Nairn,** a pretty Victorian seaside resort, and boat trips to watch dolphins frolicking in the **Moray Firth.** On the west coast you can explore the uninhabited Summer Isles and endless sweeps of sand lapped by a turquoise sea (dune-backed Sandwood Bay is only accessible on foot), while the north coast, around Dunnet Bay, is prime surfing territory.

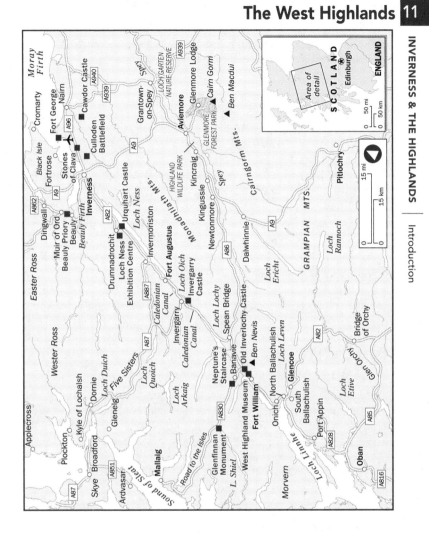

The Highlands' natural larder is well-stocked. For breakfast tuck into organic porridge from the Golspie Mill in Sutherland drizzled with heather honey, for lunch oatcakes and artisan smoked salmon. Highland estates such as Rothiemurchus in the Cairngorms provide wild venison and Angus beef, while the West Coast's waters are laced with scallops and the Kyle of Tongue, in the far north, produces oysters. To wash it all down, not only are there craft breweries and artisan gin producers at every turn, but Speyside is peppered with whisky distilleries.

11

INVERNESS & THE HIGHLANDS

Don't Leave the Inverness & the Highlands Without . . .

Driving the North Coast 500. Pegged as Scotland's Route 66, this 500-mile coastal road trip takes you careering up the east coast from Inverness, up over the top of Scotland and down the ruggedly ragged west (or the other way round). See p. 319.

Dining in style at Inverlochy Castle. This historic hotel has been serving grand dinners since the days of Queen Victoria. Today, celebrity chef Albert Roux has upped its gourmet credentials. See p. 348.

Hiking up Britain's highest mountain. Ben Nevis looms over the town of Fort William. In good weather, walkers ascend along the well-constructed path on the south side; climbers, however, take the more challenging routes up sheer cliff faces. See p. 346.

Riding the Cairngorms funicular railway. While skiers and snowboarders slalom downhill, you can sit back and relax as this mountain railway creaks its way up to a visitor center, restaurant, and panoramic views. See p. 328.

Playing a round at the Royal Dornoch Golf Club. The immaculate turf of the northernmost first-class course in the world is fringed by dunes and backed by an endless sweep of sand: the perfect setting for a game of golf. See p. 310.

INVERNESS ★

156 miles NW of Edinburgh; 134 miles W of Aberdeen

Inverness is the capital of the Highlands. That makes it sound rather grand. However, it's essentially a provincial capital with a small-town feel. At the end of the **Great Glen,** which slices diagonally across Scotland from the southwest coast at Fort William to Inverness in the northeast, this royal burgh has a pretty historic center and is built on the banks of the River Ness. From here you can explore **Loch Ness, Culloden Battlefield,** and **Cawdor Castle.**

Essentials

GETTING THERE Inverness Airport (www.invernessairport.co.uk; ☏ **01667/464-000**) is about 15 minutes' drive east along the A96 from the city center. The tiny airport (although it has doubled in size in recent years) is mainly a domestic hub—there are flights to Amsterdam. You can fly direct to Inverness from three London airports: Heathrow, Luton and Gatwick. The flight time from Gatwick is 1½ hours. **Trains** arrive at Inverness station in the city center (Station Square, off Academy St.) from London, Glasgow, Edinburgh and Aberdeen and from the north and west coasts. The train from Edinburgh and Glasgow takes 3½ hours from either city.

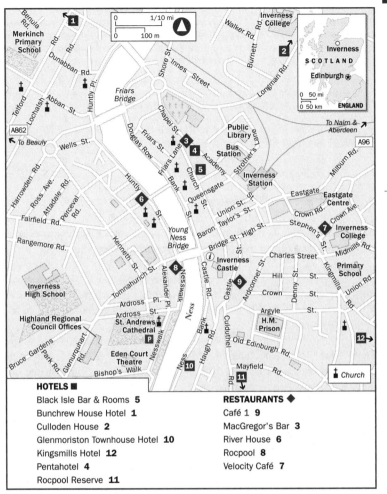

HOTELS ■

Black Isle Bar & Rooms **5**
Bunchrew House Hotel **1**
Culloden House **2**
Glenmoriston Townhouse Hotel **10**
Kingsmills Hotel **12**
Pentahotel **4**
Rocpool Reserve **11**

RESTAURANTS ◆

Café 1 **9**
MacGregor's Bar **3**
River House **6**
Rocpool **8**
Velocity Café **7**

Scottish CityLink (www.citylink.co.uk; ℰ **0871/266-3333**) has daily **bus** services from Edinburgh and Glasgow (around a 4-hr. trip each way). The bus station is near the train station at Farraline Park, off Academy Street.

It's a 3½ hour **drive** from Edinburgh, along the M9 north to Perth, and then the A9 to Inverness—one of the most notorious roads in Scotland and an accident hotspot. This is the main route north so traffic is heavy. Add trucks with a lower speed limit into the mix and as the road veers back and forth from single lane to dual carriageway, drivers stuck behind the trucks get frustrated which can lead to dangerous overtaking—if you're driving take care. The good news is that the route is finally being dualled. Short term that means more roadworks, but by 2025 the work is due to be completed. For now average speed cameras have helped ease congestion and frustration.

VISITOR INFORMATION The comprehensive VisitScotland tourist information center is half way along the pedestrianized High Street at number 36 (www.visitscotland.com; *C* **01463/252-401**); check the website for the ridiculously complicated and variable opening times. Generally speaking it's open daily from 9 or 10am until 5 or 6pm—except when it's not. Confirm opening times on the site to avoid a wasted effort.

SPECIAL EVENTS The July **Highland Games,** founded in 1822, feature traditional sporting events such as tossing the caber (traditionally a trimmed tree trunk) along with Highland dancing and piping bands (www.invernesshigh landgames.com; *C* **01463/785-006**).

Exploring Inverness

Inverness is a bustling little town straddling the River Ness, with a pretty center and picturesque riverfront. There's not much to see in the town itself, but it's a handy jumping off point for nearby attractions. This is one of the oldest inhabited areas in Scotland, with a handful of key archaeological sites. On **Craig Phadrig** the remains of a vitrified fort are believed to date from the 4th century B.C.E. while one of the most important prehistoric monuments in the north, the **Stones of Clava,** Bronze Age cairns and standing stones, are 6¼ miles to the east.

King David I built the first stone castle in Inverness around 1141, but the **Clock Tower** is all that remains of the fort later erected on the site by Cromwell's army between 1652 and 1657. The rebellious Scots blew up the old castle in 1746 to keep it from falling to government troops, and the present Victorian **castle** houses local government offices. Pick up a City Center Trail map from the tourist, which outlines a walking tour around a number of historic buildings including 16th-century **Abertarff House** on Church Street and the **Old Mercat Cross,** with its Stone of the Tubs, said to be the stone on which women rested their washtubs as they ascended from the river. Known as "Clachnacudainn," the lozenge-shaped stone was the spot where early local kings were crowned.

St Andrew's Cathedral (1866–69) is a neo-Gothic twin-towered building, framed by trees beside the river. Inside, you can see a painting depicting the original design of the cathedral (the spires were never added) and magnificent oak choir stalls. The cathedral is open daily from 9:30am to 6pm (www.mor ayepiscopalchurch.scot; *C* **01463/225-553**).

If you're looking for a round, you can hit the links at the renowned **Royal Dornoch Golf Club** (www.royaldornoch.com; *C* **01862/810-219**), located 40 miles to the north of Inverness. Closer to town is the **Castle Stuart Golf Links** (www.castlestuartgolf.com; *C* **01463/796-111**) overlooking the Moray Firth and **Torvean Golf Course,** Glen Q Road (www.torveangolfclub.co.uk;

(C) 01463/225-651), an 18-hole, par-69 course set in 400 acres of parkland looking out over the Great Glen and the Caledonian Canal.

Culloden Battlefield ★★★ HISTORIC SITE   Make sure this powerful and moving site is on your itinerary. The stark, state-of-the-art visitor center brings this bloody and brutal battle vividly to life. At Culloden, Bonnie Prince Charlie and the Jacobite army suffered their final defeat on April 16, 1746. Walking along a timeline corridor, visitors listen to atmospheric accounts from characters caught up in the historic events, before entering a room where a 4-minute long battle immersion film plunges you into the chaos, the 360 degree film projected on all four walls. A guide then takes you out onto eerie, windswept Culloden Moor, weaving tales as you trudge through the Field of the English, where 52 men of the Duke of Cumberland's forces who died during the battle are supposedly buried. Check out the **Graves of the Clans,** communal burial places with simple stones bearing individual clan names; the great **memorial cairn,** erected in 1881; the **Well of the Dead;** and the huge **Cumberland Stone,** from which the victorious "Butcher" Cumberland is said to have reviewed the scene. The battle lasted only 40 minutes; the prince's army lost some 1,200 men out of 5,000, and the Duke's army 300 of 9,000.

Culloden Moor, 6¼ miles SE of Inverness. www.nts.org.uk/culloden. (C) **01463/796-090.** Battlefield free; visitor center £11 adults, £9.50 seniors and children 5–15, £27 families. Battlefield open daily year-round; visitor center daily Nov–Feb, 10am–4pm, Mar–May, Sept–Oct 9am–6pm; June–Aug 9am–7pm.

Fort George ★★ MUSEUM   Follow a visit to Culloden Battlefield with Fort George for an atmospheric historical overview: this 18th century fortress was constructed after the defeat of the Jacobites as a safe base for King George II's army. Fort George is a great day out. It is still an active army barracks and soldiers wander past as you meander this sprawling coastal complex, checking out the recreated barrack rooms with their tableaux of soldiers' lives in centuries past. From canon-lined battlements you may be lucky enough to spot dolphins leaping in the waves of the Moray Firth far below. Don't miss the Robert Adam-designed garrison chapel and the Queen's Own Highlanders Regimental Museum, with objects from 1778 to the present.

Ardersier, 11 miles northeast of Inverness. www.historicenvironment.scot. (C) **01667/460-232.** £9 adults, £7.20 seniors £5.40 children. Apr–Sept daily 9:30am–5:30pm; Oct–Mar daily 10am–4pm.

Inverness Museum & Art Gallery ★ MUSEUM   Hidden up Castle Wynd in frankly one of the ugliest modern buildings in town, you might be tempted to give this odd little museum a miss. That would be a mistake as it has a real old-school charm and plenty of interesting exhibits to while away an hour or so. It's also free which is not to be sniffed at. Check out the stuffed Scottish wild animal tableaux and exhibits focusing on the social and natural history, archaeology, art, and culture of the Scottish Highlands.

Castle Wynd, off Bridge St. www.highlifehighland.com. (C) **01463/237-114.** Free. Apr–Oct Tues–Sat 10am–5pm; Nov–Mar Thurs–Sat 10am–5pm.

West of the River Ness rises the wooded hill of Tomnahurich, known as the "hill of the fairies." Now a cemetery, it's the best place to go for a country walk in the vicinity of Inverness for panoramic views. The boat-shaped hillock is immediately to the southwest of the city center. From the hill's vantage point you can see wooded islands in the Ness that have been turned into parks and are now linked to Inverness by suspension bridges.

Where to Stay

The accommodation scene in Inverness is frustratingly old-fashioned. It lags about 30 years behind the rest of the U.K. in terms of style—but has no problem catapulting itself into the 21st century when it comes to the room rates. In fact, that is the problem in a nutshell: the standard does not match the astronomical price tag. It's fair to charge high rack rates for a sleek design or sumptuous traditional hotel, but expecting guests to pay the same prices demanded by top hotels in Edinburgh or London is a joke (we're talking around £500 a night in July and August). Hoteliers get away with it because this is the "capital" of the Highlands, and most tourists wash up here at some stage of their trip and need somewhere to stay.

If you don't care that the design is dated and just want somewhere to crash at the end of the day it might not worry you, but it's still galling having to pay through the nose for a mediocre B&B or lackluster hotel. The only real reason, however, to stay here is if you want a night out and don't want to drive. So if you're willing to think outside the box—think outside Inverness.

Head west along the loch for a few miles for a luxurious B&B, **Loch Ness Lodge** (see p. 321) or rustic-chic inn, the **Loch Ness Inn** (see p. 321). Just half an hour's drive west towards Glen Affric is a stunning collection of real log cabins (built with whole tree trunks, not chalet-style). **Eagle Brae** (www.eaglebrae.co.uk; ✆ **01463/761-301**) is rustic luxury on a Highland estate. Veer east towards Nairn for a gourmet restaurant with rooms, **Boath House** (see p. 324), and tasteful self-catering on another Highland estate, **Cawdor Cottages** (see p 325). For one of the most exclusive and stylish tweed-trimmed luxury hotels, **Links House** (see p. 334) in Dornoch is just an hour north.

EXPENSIVE

Culloden House ★★ This stately Grade A–listed Georgian mansion has architectural wow factor with its glorious ivy-draped Adam facade. Bonnie Prince Charlie also once slept here, if you need an added incentive. On 15 April 1746, Charles Edward Stuart, who was leading the Jacobite rebellion, spent the night here before the Battle of Culloden. Today, it is a relaxed and charming country house hotel surrounded by 40 acres of sweeping lawns, bluebell woods and parkland, with a croquet lawn, tennis court and a restored walled garden. Bedrooms are a comfortable throwback to another era, wreathed in flouncy florals and chintz with original marble fireplaces and chandeliers. Relax in the library bar with a dram or in front of the fire in the elegant drawing room. The fine dining restaurant focuses on the best local ingredients.

Culloden. www.cullodenhouse.co.uk. ℰ **01463/790-461.** 28 units. Doubles £295–£350, suites £425–£475, includes breakfast. **Amenities:** Restaurant; bar; tennis court; croquet lawn; room service; free Wi-Fi.

Rocpool Reserve ★   From the outside, this 19th-century buttercup and cream villa in a quiet residential neighborhood is all pastel-painted prettiness. Inside it jumps into the 20th century—and stays there, somewhere around 1990. This is Inverness's attempt at a modern design hotel, but feels unfathomably retro. The color scheme in the public areas is dramatic black, white and red, in the rooms (divided into Hip, Chic, Decadent and Extra Decadent) the palette plunges into murkier realms: espresso to cappuccino via a flat white. Two rooms have outdoor hot tubs, some have double showers and freestanding baths, but overall the feeling (shiny fabrics and leather headboards anyone?) is very dated—and doesn't warrant the hefty room rates. The restaurant (not to be confused with the **Rocpool**, p. 314) is a Chez Roux (as in famous French chef, Albert Roux). The food is sublime, the atmosphere much less-so. Main courses cost between £18 and £27.

Culduthel Rd. www.rocpool.com. ℰ **01463/240-089.** 11 units. Doubles £230–£465 includes breakfast. **Amenities:** Restaurant; bar; room service; free Wi-Fi.

MODERATE

Bunchrew House Hotel ★   Pretty in pink: This glorious turreted 17th-century Scottish mansion sits on the pebbled shore of the Beauly Firth. Once the ancestral home of the Fraser and the McKenzie clans, today it is a traditional country house hotel at the end of a stately tree-lined drive, set in 8 hectares (20 acres) of landscaped gardens. Inside, history seeps out of the wood-paneling in the drawing room where you can curl up in front of a roaring log fire or sip a dram in the cozy bar. The old-fashioned bedrooms have names not numbers, are all decorated in period style (some with four-poster beds), but could do with updating.

Bunchrew, Inverness (on the A862). www.bunchrewhousehotel.com. ℰ **01463/234-917.** 16 units. Doubles £176–£545, includes breakfast. **Amenities:** Restaurant; bar; room service; free Wi-Fi.

Glenmoriston Townhouse Hotel ★   Originally a Victorian merchant's house built in 1895, on the tree-fringed banks of the River Ness, this townhouse hotel is just a short amble into the center of town. It also boasts the largest whisky collection in Inverness—260 malts—in its Italian marble-trimmed Whisky and Piano Bar, as well as 40 gins from around the world (try the gin-themed afternoon tea). The buzzing brasserie, **Contrast,** showcases the finest Scottish produce, the prime beef from their own dry-ager. Bedrooms are "modern" but dated, with leather bucket chairs and a red-and-beige color palette.

20 Ness Bank, www.glenmoristontownhouse.com. ℰ **01463/223-777.** 30 units. Doubles £79–£550, includes breakfast. **Amenities:** Restaurant; bar; room service; free Wi-Fi.

Kingsmills Hotel ★ Once upon a time, the Kingsmills Hotel was an 18th-century mansion on the edge of Inverness. The Scottish bard, "Rabbie" Burns, dined here in 1786. Today, it's an attractive, cream-clad but rather bland, middle-of-the-road resort hotel set in 1.6 hectares (4 acres) of parkland beside an 18-hole golf course. Rooms are comfortable but uninspiring, there's a whisky bar, various dining options and a "leisure club" with spa, gym, and indoor swimming pool. There's a huge free car park—parking comes at a premium in Inverness—although it's a bit of a schlep if you want to walk into town.

Culcabock Rd. www.kingsmillshotel.com. ⓒ **01463/257-100.** 147 units. Doubles £97–£305, suites £142–£355, includes breakfast. **Amenities:** Restaurant; bar; pool (indoor); health club w/sauna; room service; free Wi-Fi.

INEXPENSIVE

Black Isle Bar & Rooms ★ If all you want is a place to lay your head, you could do far worse than check into the simple rooms above the hip Black Isle Bar. Think pale wooden bunk beds, crisp white linen and en-suite shower rooms. That's it. Rooms are clearly geared towards those more interested in the Black Isle Brewery's beer than beds. There are 14 rooms above the bar, the rest in the hostel opened on Academy Street in 2018, with a mix of four-bed, six-bed and eight-bed dormitories with shared facilities, and private en-suite single, twin, double and family rooms.

47-49 Academy St. www.blackislebar.com. ⓒ **01463/233-933.** 24 units. Single £55, twin £70, double £80–£100. **Amenities:** Bar; free Wi-Fi.

Pentahotel ★★ The bar doubles as reception at this long overdue funky budget option in Inverness. Why not order a cocktail with your key? Pentahotel is slap bang in the center of town, has a relaxed vibe, billiards table, bare brick walls, comfy sofas, books to read in the bar and a smattering of kitsch. Food-wise it's simple, hearty fare. There's a burger bar, pizza, and pasta to tuck into. Bedrooms are simple and sleek—with free movies and premium sports channels. On Sundays and Bank Holidays you can enjoy a free late check out until 3pm. The concept is a breath of fresh air in this time-warped town—although even here there's a sharp price hike in summer.

63 Academy St. www.pentahotels.com. ⓒ **01463/228-850.** 90 units, Doubles £89–£436 (prices vary widely depending on season). **Amenities:** Restaurant; bar; fitness room; room service; free Wi-Fi.

Where to Eat

EXPENSIVE

Rocpool ★★★ MODERN SCOTTISH There's no denying that the Rocpool is the best restaurant in town. Book as early as you can to bag a table at Steven Devlin's buzzing riverside brasserie, as this is no hidden gem or best-kept secret. The food is consistently good and the atmosphere electric. It all starts with the best Highland produce: they are passionate about provenance, from Speyside venison to hot-smoked salmon from Mallaig on the

West Coast, crab from Orkney and razor clams from Fortrose. Think starters such as Scotch beef carpaccio with crisp fried artichokes, fresh greens and shaved Manchego cheese with gremolata followed by roast fillet of Shetland halibut with griddled new season Wye Valley asparagus, watercress and soft boiled egg salad with crisp polenta and steamed surf clams with capers. Check out the great lunch and early evening menu deals too.

1 Ness Walk. www.rocpoolrestaurant.com. ℂ **01463/717-274.** Mains £14–£40; lunch menu £17 for 2 courses; early evening menu (5:45–6:45pm) £20 for 2 courses. Mon–Sat noon–2:30pm and 5:45–10pm.

MODERATE

Café 1 ★ MODERN SCOTTISH   This farm-to-fork eatery is an Inverness stalwart. The farm is the owner's croft, Holly House, where they breed Hebridean sheep and Highland cattle for signature dishes such as the Holly House Highlander Burger in a brioche bun with red onion marmalade, melted gruyere cheese, maple-cured bacon, tomato mayo, and hand-cut chips (£14).

75 Castle St. www.cafe1.net. ℂ **01463/226-200.** Lunch special £15 for 2 courses, £20 for 3 courses; dinner mains £12–£28; Mon–Fri noon–2:30pm, Sat noon–3pm, Mon–Fri 5–9:30pm, Sat 6–9:30pm.

River House ★★ FISH   Alfie Little's quaint little fish restaurant on the riverside dishes up the Highlands and Islands' best seafood and shellfish: from oysters to crab, langoustine, mussels, clams and halibut. Provenance is key—the fish fresh off the boats in Scrabster on the north coast and Shetland, the beef from an organic farm in Caithness. There's a smattering of turf to go with the surf, but fish is the main event. Starters include pan-seared Shetland scallops with a shellfish bisque risotto and crispy kale, and pan roasted octopus with chorizo, potatoes, and caper berries in a tomato and Rioja sauce. You can have your mussels four ways: traditional marinière with white wine, garlic, shallots, and cream, Perry with pear cider, cream and sliced pears, Islay with cream and a splash of malt and Thai with sweet chili, lemongrass, coconut and cream. The oyster options are equally inventive: the Pearl of the Sea Martini is Harris Gin, martini, samphire and an oyster. There's even an oyster "happy hour" from 5:30pm: £1 a shuck.

1 Greig St. www.riverhouseinverness.co.uk. ℂ **01463/222-033.** Mains £20–£29; Tues–Sat 3–9:45pm.

INEXPENSIVE

Black Isle Bar ★★ GASTROPUB   The quirky Black Isle microbrewery is just over the Kessock Bridge. This cool, industrial-chic bar with its huge columns, rough wooden floors and mismatched tables and chairs naturally has its own beers on tap. Each comes with tasting notes and the option to order ⅓ pint as well as half-pints and pints for a DIY tasting session or beer flight. Yellowhammer is a straw-colored pale ale with flinty grapefruit aromas and a citrus hops hit, while Red Kite has a biscuity backbone. To eat? Sizzling pizzas emerge from the wood-fired oven with inventive toppings: venison salami with passata, mozzarella, smoked Orkney cheddar, and Portobello mushrooms along with organic Hebridean lamb meatballs and spring onions. There is also a range of daily specials and many of the ingredients are grown bio-dynamically on their farm beside the brewery.

68 Church St. www.blackislebar.com. ✆ **01463/229-920**. Mains £10–£12. Daily 11am–1am.

MacGregor's Bar ★★ GASTROPUB   Craft beer, burgers, and good craic. This modern, rustic Scottish bar has attitude and atmosphere. The walls are clad in wood, the bar stools in Harris Tweed, there's a piano in the corner, a cozy wood-burning stove and a beer garden for sunny days. The beer tasting menus introduce you to local craft beers from Orkney ales to Speyside pilsners, while if you're peckish the menu focuses on hearty gastropub fare from fish and chips to venison on mustard crushed baby potatoes with green asparagus and a redcurrant and raspberry jus. On Thursdays the homemade burgers (Ardgay venison, Angus beef or grilled Halloumi and honey) served with their own coleslaw, hand-cut chips, and a brioche bun are buy one get one free.

113 Academy St. www.macgregorsbars.com. ✆ **01463/719-629**. Mains £12–£19.50. Daily 11am–1am.

Velocity Café ★ VEGAN CAFE   This vegan cafe and bicycle repair shop is one of the coziest spots in town. Its jaunty blue exterior is matched by bright blue painted floorboards. It's a homey place to chill out with a cappuccino—or a *bicy*latte—and munch on a slice of homemade carrot cake. For lunch you can slurp a steaming bowl of homemade soup such as earthy eggplant and mushroom with a chunk of sunflower bread or gluten-free oatcakes.

1 Crown Ave. www.velocitylove.co.uk. ✆ **01463/419-956**. Mains £3.95–£6.90. Mon-Wed and Fri 8am–5pm, Thurs 8am–9pm, Sat 9am–5pm, Sun 10am–5pm.

Shopping

Inverness, like many small Scottish towns, is marred by a modern shopping mall. The **Eastgate Shopping Centre** is an uninspiring place in the center of town with the usual chain stores, while the **Victorian Market** (constructed in 1870) on Academy Street, could be a quaint tourist attraction but feels unloved, peppered with boarded up shopfronts. One place to check out inside, however, is **Boarstone Tartans,** 14-16 Victorian Market (www.boarstone-tartans.co.uk; ✆ **01463/239-793**) a Highland dress specialist selling kilts, jackets, tartan trousers, shooting coats, and deerstalker hats. The hunting, shooting, and fishing fraternity, meanwhile, makes a beeline for **Grahams** at 37-39 Castle St. (www.grahamsonline.co.uk; ✆ **01463/233-178**). This Inverness stalwart, established in 1857, is the place to come for everything from fishing tackle and permits to waders, Barbour jackets and Dubarry boots.

Another highlight is **Leakey's Bookshop,** Scotland's largest secondhand bookstore, in an old 18th-century church, complete with stained glass windows, on Church Street (✆ **01463/239-947**). Filled to the rafters with old books, this cavernous space is fabulous for rummaging. You could lose hours among the shelves jam-packed with musty paperbacks and rare leather-bound tomes, old maps and prints. There's a wood-burning stove and sofas to curl up on as you flick through the pages—in fact you might hole up here and never leave. Other places worth checking out are **WoodWinters Wines & Whiskies** just opposite at 74 Church Street (www.woodwinters.com; ✆ **01463/225-656**) which stocks a good range of organic and even orange wines and the **Inverness Coffee Roasting Co** at 15 Chapel Street (www.invernesscoffee roasting.co.uk; ✆ **01463/242-555**). The coffee is roasted on their farm just outside Inverness.

Entertainment & Nightlife

Inverness is rowdy and riotous on the weekends. If you want to let your hair down, this is the place to be. Be warned, restaurants are often fully booked. You need to reserve a table for dinner, sometimes weeks in advance.

When it comes to pubs and bars there really is something for everyone, from sleek hipster hangouts to hole-in the-wall whisky bars and traditional Highland pubs. **Hootananny** means an "informal gathering with folk music" and that's exactly what you get at this popular old-school haunt on Church Street (www.hootanannyinverness.co.uk; ✆ **01463/233-651**), three packed floors of bars, pubs, and live music from traditional Scottish to local bands. A much smaller venue but a legendary part of the Inverness scene is the **Market Bar,** 32 Church St. (✆ **01463/220-203**) down a narrow alley and up some backstairs. This tiny dive is standing room only for the local musicians who play in the scruffy, friendly little bar. Just next door is **The Malt Room** at 34 Church St. (www.themaltroom.co.uk; ✆ **01463/221-888**) a tiny backstreet gem. What's a surprise is that it took until 2017 for Inverness to get its first dedicated whisky bar. It was worth the wait: This intimate little place with its backlit bar, polished concrete floors and sleek design is a great place for a late-night dram or a whisky flight paired with chocolate.

The Black Isle Bar at 68 Church St. (www.blackislebar.com; ✆ **01463/229-920**) is a hip hotspot, the off-shoot of the microbrewery over the Kessock Bridge, where you can sup a pint or taste a few of their brews on a beer flight in the industrial-styled bar or secret beer garden, while at **MacGregor's Bar** at 109-113 Academy St. (www.macgregorsbars.com; ✆ **01463/719-629**) you can also experiment with a beer tasting menu. If you're in town at the weekend, check out their lively Sunday sessions of traditional Scottish music.

The **Gellions Pub,** 8-14 Bridge St. (www.gellions.co.uk; ✆ **01463/233-648**) is also legendary and has been pulling pints since 1841. It has nightly live music and a ceilidh on Saturday, while the **Castle Tavern,** 1 View Place (www.castletavern.pub; ✆ **01463/718-178**) perched on top of the hill near the castle, has great views and an outdoor beer garden.

The cultural hub of Inverness is **Eden Court** (www.eden-court.co.uk; ✆ **01463/234-234**), Bishops Road, next to the cathedral. This contemporary theatre complex also has a cinema, cafe, bar, and restaurant.

Side Trips from Inverness
MUIR OF ORD

This small town, 10 miles west of Inverness, is a good stopping off point if you're doing the **North Coast 500** road trip. It also has a distillery, a great little café, the **Bad Girl Bakery,** serving the best cupcakes north of Hadrian's Wall, and one of Scotland's largest agricultural shows.

Where to Eat & Stay

Bad Girl Bakery ★ CAFE   There's just one thing you need to know about the Bad Girl Bakery: they do a mean Gin and Tonic cupcake topped with a slice of lime. Of course there are other fabulous flavors too: from white chocolate and vanilla to chocolate raspberry and salted caramel. And then there are the traybakes and "naked" cakes without the wanton wickedness of buttercream and icing. They're so good in fact that the bakery's muffins are now served for breakfast on the Caledonian Sleeper. The coffee's not bad either.

7, Great North Road, Muir of Ord. ✆ **01463/872-734.** Mon–Fri 8am–5pm; Sat 9am–5pm, Sun 10am–4pm.

The Dower House ★   This pretty, 18th-century cottage is surrounded by equally picturesque gardens. Once the farmhouse on a Highland Estate, it's now a charming B&B, with antiques, wing back armchairs around a cozy wood-burning stove, shelves crammed full of books, board games, and vases of fresh flowers from the grounds. There's also a baby grand piano to while away the hours. The country-chic bedrooms have peaceful views over the gardens and either a shower or romantic roll-top bathtubs.

Muir of Ord. www.thedowerhouse.co.uk. ✆ **01463/870-090.** 4 units. Doubles £145; suite £165, includes breakfast. Drive 1 mile north of the A862. **Amenities:** Free Wi-Fi.

BEAULY ★

Beauly, 12 miles west of Inverness on the A862, is a pretty little village garlanded with flowers during the summer months, with the picturesque ruins of a monastery at one end. French monks first settled here in the 13th century and gave the town its name: literally, "beautiful place."

Dating back to around 1230, ruined **Beauly Priory ★** (www.historicenvironment.scot; ✆ **01463/782-309**) is one of three priories built for the Valliscaulian order left, an austere body that drew its rules from the Cistercians and Carthusians. Some of the intricate windows and arcades remain intact.

Beauly is a lovely place to wander around, with its antiques shop, art galleries, and boutiques. **Iain Marr Antiques** is a treasure trove of antique glass and silverware (www.iain-marr-antiques.com; ✆ **01463/782-372**), while **Campbell's of Beauly** (www.campbellsofbeauly.com; ✆ **01463/782-239**) is an institution, run by the same family from 1858 until 2015. The young new young owners have maintained its sense of tradition, its excellence in tweed tailoring, and the unique atmosphere of this fabulously old-fashioned store, while gently adding a few contemporary touches such as hand-knitted cashmere socks and gloves.

You've got to take your hat off to the bright spark who came up with the concept of the **North Coast 500**—"Scotland's Route 66" (www.northcoast500.com). Ingenious. And controversial. It's as much a successful marketing initiative as a road trip. The road was always there, snaking quietly north from Inverness around Scotland's coastline, up the west coast, along the top and down the east coast (or the other way around). And, some would argue, it was a far more pleasant drive before the tourist boards and marketing depart- ments gave it a name. In its early days NC500, as it now calls itself, had a few teething problems: As the hordes hit this "new" tourist trail, they quickly realized there weren't enough beds. Sports cars, campervans, motorbikes, and sheep on the stretches of single-track road also caused a few interesting scenarios. It all seems to have settled down now, the website can help you to plan an itinerary—for a price. It is easy enough to opt instead for the DIY option. It's not rocket science. But make sure you book ahead. It gets busy.

If you're here in early August, the **Black Isle Show** (www.blackisleshow.com; ⓒ **01463/870-870**), one of the largest agricultural shows in Scotland, is held annually on the showground between Beauly and Muir of Ord. It's a great day out featuring everything from show-jumping to gun-dog displays, and you can wander among pens of rare-breed sheep, shaggy Highland "coos" and marquees squawking with chickens.

Where to Eat

Corner on the Square ★★   This cracking little deli and cafe is a local institution. The counter is crammed with artisan cheeses and homemade pâtés, the shelves with oatcakes, homemade marmalades, chutneys, and organic chocolate. There's also a good wine, whisky, and gin section. If you're eating in—or outside at the smattering of tables on the pavement—the fish chowder is always popular, or tuck into the daily changing quiche and salad specials or pungent Stilton and Guinness pate and oatcakes.

1 High St. www.corneronthesquare.co.uk. ⓒ **01463/783-000.** Mon–Fri 8am–5:30pm; Sat 8am–5pm, Sun 9am–5pm.

AROUND LOCH NESS ★★

It's not the deepest loch (that's Morar), nor the longest (that title goes to Loch Lomond), but Loch Ness contains the largest volume of water of any Scottish loch, more, in fact, than all the lakes in England and Wales put together. It's also the most famous. The Loch Ness Monster, or "Nessie," is one of Scotland's most enduring myths and biggest tourist attractions. Since the 1930s visitors have been traipsing to this mysterious loch 23 miles long and 600 feet deep in search of that elusive monster.

Though the legend dates back to the 6th century, things kicked off in earnest in 1933 after a local man, George Spicer, told newspapers he'd seen a prehistoric beast crossing the road and disappearing into the water. Renowned naturalist Sir Peter Scott even gave the monster a fancy Latin name, *Nessitera rhombopteryx,* although sceptics later pointed out that it was an anagram for "monster hoax by Sir Peter S." And there have been many hoaxes over the years, but still the sightings continue, with their blurred film footage and photographs.

In the summer, you can take boat cruises down Loch Ness from both Fort Augustus and Inverness. In Fort Augustus, **Cruise Loch Ness** (www.cruise lochness.com; ℂ **01320/366-277**) offers both traditional boat trips and fast RIB rides (rigid-hulled inflatable boat) for adrenaline junkies—narrated with fascinating facts about Nessie and the loch.

If you're driving, the A82 snakes along the northern side of the loch between Fort Augustus and Inverness (with plenty of scenic photo ops) and in high season is clogged with traffic. It is possible to do a circuit of the loch. It's around 67 miles and there are plenty of points of interest to tick off along the way. From Fort Augustus you will not be on the water's edge until you dip back down at Foyers, where there's a waterfall and farm shop and café, but the pay off on this quieter rural southern side (and at times narrow, single-track route) is spectacular views of rolling moorland and mountains grazed by herds of red deer as you weave your way through tiny villages between large Highland Estates. At the picturesque **Dores Inn,** you can also walk along the pebbled beach right on the loch.

Drumnadrochit ★

The bucolic village of Drumnadrochit is the home of the **Loch Ness Centre and Exhibition** (see below), a pretty village green, a local farm shop and a buzzing whitewashed inn, **Fiddler's** (www.fiddledrum.co.uk; ℂ **01456/450/678**) with tables spilling out onto the terrace in summer. Dishing up good hearty pub food, think wild venison and bacon chili, Highland platters piled high with chicken liver and whisky pate, home-smoked duck breast and Great Glen wild venison served with crusty bread and homemade chutneys and an encyclopedic selection of whiskies.

Loch Ness Centre & Exhibition ★ MUSEUM The Nessie mystery continues to fascinate and pull in the tourists. Is it all an elaborate hoax? What is the scientific evidence? This attraction could so easily be cheesy but is, actually, far more interesting than you might imagine, taking visitors on a geological journey from C.E. 565 to the present day with the help of grainy photographs, audio, and archive film footage, exploring the myths and folklore around the "monster" and listening to firsthand accounts. The accounts of all the scientific expeditions on the loch and old newspaper cuttings are particularly fascinating. Of course, there is a gift shop piled high with Nessie toys and memorabilia, but that's the only kitsch part of this great little museum.

Drumnadrochit. www.lochness.com. ℂ **01456/450-573.** £7.95 adults, £6.75 students and seniors, £5 children ages 6–15, under 6 free, £23 families. Easter–Oct daily 9:30am–5pm (July–Aug to 6pm); Nov–Easter daily 10am–3:30pm.

Urquhart Castle ★★★ RUINS Pronounced "urkut," a short 8-minute film whisks you through 1,000 years of turbulent Scottish history, then the curtains part and there, perched on a promontory overlooking Loch Ness, are the ruins of largest medieval castle in the Highlands. That it has the "wow" factor goes without saying. Coach-loads of summer tourists agree, so get there early or you might not get in at all. The modern visitor center with its cafe, gift shop and theatre is excellent. You can wander at will using the interpretation boards, but it's well worth taking the free half-hour guided tour. You'll learn how Clan Grant was given the castle by the Scottish king in return for keeping the unruly Macdonalds in check. With the Jacobite uprisings and the castle in ruins by the end of the 17th century, they cut their losses and headed back to Speyside.

Drumnadrochit, Loch Ness. www.historicenvironment.scot. *(C)* **01456/450-551.** £9 adults, £7.20 seniors, £5.40 children 5–15. Apr–May and Sept daily 9:30am–6pm; June–Aug 9:30am–8pm, Oct daily 9:30am–5pm; Nov–Mar daily 9:30am–4:30pm.

WHERE TO EAT & STAY

Loch Ness Inn ★ This pretty cream inn dating back to 1838 is within ambling distance of the center of Drumnadrochit and Urquhart Castle, and just a 25-minute drive from Inverness if you'd rather base yourself outside town. Inside, the rustic-chic design features stone-flagged floors, exposed stonewalls, a cozy woodburning stove, eclectic mismatched wooden tables and chairs and a smattering of local artworks. Outside there's a large beer garden. In the kitchen they take pride in the provenance of the fresh produce with fish from Mallaig on the west coast, venison from Invergarry, game from Pitlochry and pork from Invercannich farm just down the road. In the bar you can sip a dram or sup a pint from the local Loch Ness Brewery—before clambering upstairs to bed. The inn also has a handful of charming contemporary rooms—and the slap-up breakfast features a "Full Highland" fry up, smoked haddock with a poached egg, or a stack of Highland pancakes with maple syrup.

Lewiston, Drumnadrochit. www.staylochness.co.uk. *(C)* **01456/450-991.** 12 units. Doubles £112–£150, includes breakfast. **Amenities:** Free Wi-Fi.

Loch Ness Lodge ★★ If you're looking for a luxurious B&B, this is a far better option than Inverness. Teetering above the loch, this contemporary, baronial-style lodge, bedded into the hillside and set in lovely grounds, is just a 20-minute drive into town. The bedrooms all have gorgeous views and are named after Scottish lochs and glens. Coruisk is sumptuous, swathed in tweeds, silks, and velvets inspired by the Scottish thistle, while Affric has a huge sleigh bed, Jacuzzi, and turret. In Assynt there's a modern four-poster dressed with oyster silk and a romantic roll-top bath. Complimentary afternoon tea in front of the blazing fire in the drawing room is a relaxed country-house affair. There's also a hot tub and sauna, and a therapy room where you can indulge in a range of treatments.

Brachla, Loch Ness-side. www.loch-ness-lodge.com. *(C)* **01456/459-469.** 9 units. Doubles £150–£375, includes breakfast. **Amenities:** Spa; free Wi-Fi.

Fort Augustus ★

There's no longer a fort here, and this pretty village at the other end of the loch from Inverness, 36 meandering miles along the A82, is now more famous for its staircase of locks. General George Wade, of road- and bridge-building fame, made his headquarters here in 1724, and in 1729 the government constructed a fort on the banks of the loch, naming it Augustus after William Augustus, the Duke of Cumberland and son of King George II. The Jacobites seized the fort in 1745 and controlled it until their defeat at Culloden. Long since destroyed, Wade's fort was turned into the Fort Augustus Abbey. A Benedictine order was installed in 1867, and the monks ran a Catholic secondary school on the site for years—later at the center of an infamous child abuse scandal.

Fort Augustus is one of the best places to see the locks of the **Caledonian Canal ★★**, an engineering marvel designed by Thomas Telford, in action. In the heart of the village, the locks are a popular attraction when boats pass through. Built between 1803 and 1822, the canal runs right across the Highlands, almost in a straight line, from Inverness on the northeast coast, to Corpach, near Fort William on the west coast. The canal is 60 miles long, with 22 man-made miles and the rest natural lochs.

To tackle the locks yourself, hire a boat from **Caley Cruisers,** Canal Road, Inverness (www.caleycruisers.com; © **01463/236-328**) for a week or 3-day break. Cabin cruisers for two to six people are available from March to October—you don't need to have much marine experience and are given a full briefing. The waters of Loch Ness can be a little choppy, but the canal is calm and doesn't pose any of the dangers of cruising on the open sea. A week's rental ranges from £663 to £2,774; fuel, taxes, and insurance are extra.

For something a little more fast-paced, book a RIB ride with **Cruise Loch Ness** (www.cruiselochness.com; © **01320/366-277**), one of the most thrilling ways to explore this mysterious stretch of water. There are three options to choose from including a 90-minute Urquhart Castle experience and a 60-minute jaunt focused on finding Nessie, whipping across the waves at high speed then drifting quietly as the skipper weaves tales of underwater explorations and captivating Kelpie sagas. (Water kelpies are mythical creatures believed to inhabit lochs and pools.) The Finding Nessie cruise costs £20 for adults, £15 for children, or £60 for a family of two adults and two children.

Foyers, Inverfarigaig & Dores ★

The southern side of Loch Ness is more rural than the traffic-choked northern section, and part of the route is along single-track roads with passing places. A circuit of the loch makes a perfect day out: you can tick off a ruined castle, a mythical monster, an engineering marvel (the Caledonian Canal), a famous waterfall and you might even see a magnificent herd of red deer. From Fort Augustus to Foyers, the road weaves across moorland and through forestry and small Highland villages, eventually veering back down to the water's edge. "Rabbie" Burns wrote a poem about the famous **Falls of Foyers** in 1787: "Among the heathy hills and ragged woods/the roaring Foyers pours his mossy floods." The waterfall is worth a pit stop. The steep path down through the woods brings you to two viewpoints where you can see the water plummeting 140ft into the gorge. Near the top is **Cameron's Tea Room & Farm Shop** (www.lochnesscottage.com; ✆ **01456/486-572**). At **Inverfarigaig** there are some lovely waymarked walks through Narnia-like forestry with panoramic views over Loch Ness, while in the little village of **Dores** you can stop for a well-earned pint at the picturesque **Dores Inn** on the shore of the loch.

WHERE TO EAT

The Dores Inn ★ GASTROPUB Wooden picnic tables spill from the lawn onto the beach outside the picture-postcard-pretty Dores Inn. This low-slung whitewashed pub dishes up traditional pub classics including fish and chips: sustainable Fraserburgh haddock in a light beer batter with chips and peas, and Haggis, neeps and tatties (Scotland's traditional dish: neeps are turnips, tatties are potatoes) with whisky sauce. The cozy bar has impromptu music sessions some evenings and opens into two rustic-chic dining rooms with a wood-burning stove.

Dores. www.thedoresinn.co.uk. ✆ **01463/751-203.** Mains £10–£30. Daily 10am–9pm.

NAIRN & CAWDOR CASTLE ★

172 miles N of Edinburgh; 91 miles NW of Aberdeen; 16 miles E of Inverness

A favorite family seaside resort on the sheltered Moray Firth, Nairn (from the Gaelic for "Water of Alders") is a royal burgh at the mouth of the Nairn River. Its fishing harbor dates back to 1820 and was constructed by Thomas Telford, while golf has been played here since 1672.

Essentials

GETTING THERE Nairn can be reached by **train** from the south, changing at either Aberdeen or Inverness. For train times and fares check **National Rail Enquiries** (www.nationalrail.co.uk; ✆ **03457/484-950**). If you're driving from Inverness, take the A96 east to Nairn.

VISITOR INFORMATION The **Tourist Information Centre** is in the community centre at 62 King St. (www.nairncc.co.uk; ✆ **01667/453-476**) and is open all year Monday to Thursday 8:30am to 10pm, Friday to Saturday 8:30am to 5pm, Sunday 9am to 9pm.

Exploring Nairn

Nairn is a little seaside town, with a beautiful sandy beach and promenade. The harbor area is also worth exploring, as is **"Fishertown"** just to the south, with its narrow streets of fishermen's cottages.

Nairn is also a famous golfing destination, with two 18-hole championship golf courses. The **Nairn Golf Club,** Seabank Road (www.nairngolfclub. co.uk; ✆ **01667/453-208**), was established in 1887 and is one of the finest traditional links courses in the world. The **Nairn Dunbar Golf Club,** Lochloy Road (www.nairndunbar.com; *C* **01667/452-741**), is a whipper-snapper in comparison, only able to trace its history back to 1899.

Cawdor Castle ★★ CASTLE   Shakespeare scholars and anyone with even a passing interest in the bard's "Scottish play" will shiver at the name Cawdor. This romantic pile has been home to the thanes of Cawdor since the early 14th century. Although the castle was constructed two centuries after his time, it has been linked to Shakespeare's character *Macbeth,* also the thane of Cawdor. The castle has all the architectural ingredients you'd expect: a draw-bridge, an ancient tower, and fortified walls. Its severity is softened by pretty gardens and rolling lawns. Inside, grand rooms are decked out with paintings by Sir Joshua Reynolds, antique furniture, and historical artifacts. The grounds include five woodland nature trails, a 9-hole golf course, a putting green, a picnic area, and a restaurant.

Off the A96, Cawdor. www.cawdorcastle.com. *C* **01667/404-401.** £11.50 adults, £10.50 seniors and students, £7.20 children, free for children 4 and under. May–Sept daily 10am–5:30pm.

Where to Stay

Boath House ★★★   A Regency gem dating back to 1825 on the Moray Coast, the Boath House was painstakingly restored by owners Don and Wendy Matheson in the early 1990s. They turned the Georgian mansion, set in 22 acres of glorious parkland, walled gardens, and an ornamental lake swimming with trout into a gourmet restaurant with rooms. All individually designed, they are an exquisite blend of past and present with roll-top baths, opulent fabrics and a peppering of elegant antiques. The original master bed-room, room 3, has twin slipper baths as well as a walk-in shower; room 5 has a freestanding copper and zinc bath; and room 4 a four-poster bed. Room 9 or Apple Cottage is a gorgeous 400-year-old stone bothy decked out in soft contemporary dove greys and cream. You can also indulge in an Ayurvedic spa treatment.

Auldearn, Nairn. www.boath-house.com. *C* **01667/454-896.** 9 units. Doubles £295–£365, includes breakfast. **Amenities:** Restaurant; spa treatments; free Wi-Fi.

In the Footsteps of Macbeth

The area around Nairn is great walking country. Ask at the tourist office about hikes along the banks of the River Nairn. There are also five marked **Cawdor Castle Nature Trails,** sign-posted from the castle's grounds. They vary in length from around one to 5 miles and weave through the Big Wood along some of the loveliest and most diverse (Birch, Aspen, Rowan, Wych Elm, Holly, Scots Pine, Oak and Beech) wooded areas in the Highlands. The wood is also home to 131 species of lichen and you might be lucky enough to spot red deer, red squirrels, herons, and capercaillies.

Cawdor Cottages ★★ To get a feel for life on an ancient Highland estate, book one of these gorgeous boltholes sprinkled across the high moorlands and tree-fringed meadows. Each has been stylishly converted by Lady Isabella Cawdor, who was once a magazine stylist working for publications such as Elle and Vogue. Her creative flair is evident, from the opulent 19th-century Drynachan Lodge to the tastefully renovated crofters' cottages. These are some of the best self-catering options in the Highlands. Achneim, was once a gamekeeper's cottage, and is now a bijoux hideaway sleeping two in a brass bed with sweeping views over the Moray Firth. Periwinkle blue Lochanshelloch Cottage is surrounded by woodland close to Cawdor village, has a log fire and sleeps six. They all come with a welcome basket.

Cawdor. www.cawdor.com. ⓒ **01667/404-666.** From £534 for a 3-night break.

Denson Villa ★ The guesthouse scene in the Highlands can be depressingly old-fashioned even today. Denson Villa is a breath of salty seaside air. Helen and Alex Williamson took on a dilapidated Victorian house that had lain empty for 2 years and converted it into funky boutique B&B with a retro-chic vibe at the end of 2017. The two rooms, Forres and Nairn, have old wooden floors, original fireplaces, and views of the coast and golf course. Forres has emerald green-painted woodwork, Nairn is deep indigo with splashes of ochre. Guests are given a bag of homemade cookies when they leave.

Lochloy Rd. Nairn. www.densonvilla.co.uk. ⓒ **07843/383-747.** 2 units. Doubles £50–£80, includes breakfast. **Amenities:** Free Wi-Fi.

Where to Eat

The Boath House ★★ CONTEMPORARY SCOTTISH In 2017 the owners of Boath House (see above) controversially asked to be stripped of the Michelin star they'd held for over a decade. They explained that it put a small family business under an enormous financial strain and customers wanted a more relaxed dining experience. That's not to say that dining here is no longer a gourmet experience. Advocates of the Slow Food movement, they grow much of the produce themselves from the organic vegetables to herbs and fruit in the walled kitchen garden. They source meat from a nearby organic farm and use locally foraged wild mushrooms and fish from the West Coast. You can also indulge in a gourmet afternoon tea.

Boath House, Auldearn. www.boath-house.com. ⓒ **01667/454-896.** 2-course lunch £24, 3-course lunch £30; fixed-price 3-course dinner £45. Daily 12:15–1:45pm and 7–8:30pm.

Cawdor Tavern ★ MODERN SCOTTISH In the summer months diners spill out onto the patio of this old pub—once the carpenter's shop—in the pretty conservation village close to Cawdor Castle. When the weather's "dreich," you can tuck into braised pigs cheeks with apple caramel, celeriac remoulade, and pea shoots, followed by venison meatballs with rosemary and garlic crushed potatoes, root vegetable casserole, and crispy onions in front of

INVERNESS & THE HIGHLANDS | Nairn & Cawdor Castle

Follow the road signs for the **Malt Whisky Trail** ★★ (www.maltwhiskytrail.com) a bucolic tourist route linking eight distilleries and one cooperage from the Moray coast through the rolling hills of Speyside. There are more than 50 distilleries sprinkled through this picture-perfect sweep of lush, rolling countryside. The ones on the trail include Benromach, a friendly little distillery on the coast near Forres, the historic distillery Dallas Dhu, Cardhu, Glenfiddich, Glen Grant, Strathisla, and Glen Moray. At **The Glenlivet** (www.theglenlivet.com; ℗ 01340/821-720) you can take an exclusive Spirit of the Malt tour and tasting or fill your own bottle straight from the cask, cork, cap and label it. At the **Speyside Cooperage** you can watch the fiery barrel-making process. A good place to spend the night is the pretty little village of Aberlour on the banks of the River Spey, the fastest-flowing river in Britain. The long distance walking route, the **Speyside Way,** meanders along its banks. Aberlour is the home of Walkers Shortbread and the **Aberlour** distillery. **The Mash Tun** (www.mashtun-aberlour.com; ℗ 01340/881-771) is a quirky little stone pub with five rooms named after local distilleries. In May each year the **Spirit of Speyside Whisky Festival** (www.spiritofspeyside.com) features a host of whisky themed events, and many distilleries normally closed to the public fling open their doors.

an open fire in the cozy restaurant. Or just sink a pint of ale or a single-malt whisky in the oak-paneled bar

Cawdor. www.cawdortavern.co.uk. ℗ **01667/404-777.** Lunch mains £11.50–£22; dinner mains £13.50–£25. Lunch Mon–Sat noon–5pm, Sun 12:30pm–5pm; dinner daily 5–9pm.

Shopping

Nairn has a pleasant town centre lined with cafes, delis, antique shops and the independent **Nairn Bookshop** at 97 High St. (www.nairnbookshop.co.uk; ℗ **01667/455-528**). Just outside Nairn, in the village of Auldearn is a rambling antiques emporium in an old church which is always worth a rummage, **Auldearn Antiques,** Dalmore Manse (www.auldearnantiques.co.uk; ℗ **01667/453-087**).

Also east of Nairn on the A96 is **Brodie Countryfare** in Brodie (www.brodiecountryfare.com; ℗ **01309/641-555**). This shopping complex and cafe stocks everything from Scottish knitwear to jams and chutneys. It's well worth continuing along the A96 to Elgin (22 miles east of Nairn), where Scottish cashmere producer since 1797, **Johnstons of Elgin,** Newmill (www.johnstonsofelgin.com; ℗ **01343/554-000**), has a lovely visitor centre: mill, cafe, and luxury shopping complex.

Entertainment & Nightlife

Nairn has its own theatre, **The Little Theatre**, King Street (www.nairndrama.org.uk; ℗ **01667/455-899**), which stages productions throughout the year. In September the town hosts the **Nairn Book & Arts Festival** (www.nairnfestival.co.uk; ℗ **07825/415-887**), with author events, films, exhibitions, plays, and music.

AVIEMORE ★

129 miles N of Edinburgh; 29 miles SE of Inverness; 85 miles N of Perth

Outdoor activity center Aviemore, located on the River Spey in the heart of the **Cairngorms National Park ★★★**, was established as a year-round resort in 1966. Although the center of Aviemore is often lambasted as ugly, it's no worse than many French ski resorts, and it's a bustling little place with outdoor sports shops and buzzing cafes. Visitors make a beeline here to ski in winter and hike in summer—or to bag a Munro. Munros are Scottish mountains over 914m (3,000 ft.) and Munro-bagging (climbing and ticking off the 282 summits) is a national sport.

The Cairngorms is the largest national park in Britain, covering 4,500 sq. km (1,467 sq. miles)—almost 10% of Scotland in fact. An Area of Outstanding Natural Beauty, it's home to 55 summits over 900m, including five of the U.K.'s six highest peaks and 43 Munros. Here you'll find a quarter of Scotland's native woodland and 25% of its threatened species. The park encompasses wild mountain tundra, heathered moorland and on the lower slopes, the ancient Caledonian pinewoods. This is the home of Britain's largest mammal, the red deer and its most majestic bird of prey, the golden eagle. Rushing rivers, icy lochs, and dense pine forests are dotted with farms and small hamlets. It's an open-air adventure playground, networked with cycling and walking trails and offering kayaking, canoeing, wildlife-watching, horse-riding, and fishing. For maps, advice on walks, and other information, contact **Cairngorms National Park Authority,** 14 The Square, Grantown-on-Spey (www.cairngorms.co.uk; ✆ **01479/873-535**).

Essentials

GETTING THERE   Aviemore is on the main Inverness–Edinburgh **railway** line. It's a half-hour journey from Inverness, 3 hours from Edinburgh and Glasgow. For train information, contact Scot Rail (www.scotrail.co.uk; ✆ **0344/811-0141**).

Aviemore is also on the main Inverness–Edinburgh **bus** route. The trip from Edinburgh takes about 3 hours. Frequent buses also arrive throughout the day from Inverness (trip time: 40 min.). For schedules, call ✆ **0871/266-3333**, or visit www.citylink.co.uk.

If you're **driving** from Edinburgh, after the Queensferry Crossing road bridge, take the M90 to Perth, and then continue along the A9 to Aviemore.

VISITOR INFORMATION   The **VisitScotland Tourist Information Centre** is on Grampian Road (www.visitaviemore.com; ✆ **01479/810-930**). It's open year-round but with messily variable times, so check the website: Generally it's 9am to 5pm but on Wednesdays it opens at 10am and on Sundays at 9:30am. In June it remains open until 6pm, but 5pm on Sundays, in July and August 6:30pm but 6pm Sundays. From mid-September to March it shuts at 4pm on Sundays.

Exploring the Area

Climb on board a vintage steam train with the **Strathspey Railway ★**, Dalfaber Road (www.strathspeyrailway.co.uk; ☏ **01479/810-725**), and chug along the valley of the River Spey between Boat of Garten and Aviemore. The round-trip takes about an hour. Trains run between April and October but check the website for the schedule.

You can also travel to the top of Cairngorm Mountain on the highest funicular railway in the U.K. The **Cairngorm Funicular Railway ★** (www.cairngormmountain.org; ☏ **01479/861-261**) cranks up to the top where there's a visitor center, viewpoint and the highest restaurant (over 3,500 ft.) in the country. From there you can take a guided walk. A day ticket costs adult £13.90, senior £12.70 and child £9.30 (ages 6–16).

One of the most charming attractions in the area is the **Cairngorm Reindeer Centre ★**, Reindeer House, in Glenmore (www.cairngormreindeer.co.uk; ☏ **01479/861-228**). While visiting the area in 1952, Swedish reindeer herder Mikel Utsi realized how similar it was to the reindeer's natural habitat in Lapland, and that it also had a plentiful supply of lichen, their native food. Utsi brought over a handful of Swedish reindeer and the rest is history. Alan and Tilly Smith now own the Cairngorm Reindeer Herd, and today the herd of around 150 roams across the mountains. You can hike up the mountain slopes with a herder and feed the reindeer each morning at 11am. Visits last around one and a half hours. From May to September there is also a trek up at 2:30pm, and in July and August another at 3:30pm Monday to Friday only. It costs adult £15, senior £12, child £9 (ages 6–16). To visit the reindeer at the center in the paddock costs £3.50 for adults, senior £ 3 and child £ 2.50. At Christmas the reindeer go on the road, making guest appearances around the country, but a few stay in the paddock, and there's a wonderfully old-fashioned feeling to the grotto here.

Where to Eat

The Druie Restaurant Café ★★ SCOTTISH   The owners of the Rothiemurchus estate are a switched-on, forward-thinking, far-sighted bunch who have created a great tourist experience on the edge of Aviemore's urban sprawl. You can eat, sleep, and romp on this picturesque and pristine Highland estate. The rustic-chic cafe has a cozy wood-burning stove and is in the same old stone building as the gourmet farm shop where you can pick up wild venison and beef from the estate along with fresh or smoked trout, artisan cheeses and chutneys and their homemade "ready meals"—perfect if you're staying in their pretty woodland campsite or cute cottages. Check out this little beauty, **Forest Cottage** (www.forest-cottage.co.uk; ☏ **07984/791-623**). The also stock **Inshriach Gin** (www.inshriachgin.com), distilled just down the road. In the cafe you can tuck into a steaming bowl of homemade soup and crusty bread for lunch or gooey coffee-and-walnut cake and coffee after a hike.

Rothiemurchus Center. www.rothiemurchus.net. ☏ **01479/810-005.** Daily 9:30am–5pm.

Mountain Cafe ★ CAFE   This iconic cafe above the ubiquitous outdoor clothing and equipment store is popular and always packed, so prepare to wait for a table. Inside it's all rustic wood, tongue and groove and a balcony for warmer summer months and dishes up everything from hearty homemade soups to traditional fried breakfasts, pancakes, and yummy homemade cakes and scones.

111 Grampian Rd. www.mountaincafe-aviemore.co.uk. ℂ **01479/812-473.** Mon–Fri 8:30am–5pm, Sat–Sun 8:30am–5:30pm.

Old Bridge Inn ★★ SCOTTISH   Singer-songwriters and folk musicians perform each week in this friendly, low-slung whitewashed pub on the banks the river Spey. The food's good too. Think gourmet gastropub grub in front of a roaring fire in a rustic setting, all charred wooden walls, strung with reindeer skins and a Scandinavian meets retro-chic vibe. On the menu there's twice-cooked pigs cheeks with borlotti bean, chorizo, and smoked tomato stew with braised shallots and Loch Etive seatrout with smoked haddock and herb risotto, broccoli, asparagus, and saffron aioli. They also have a bunkhouse next door and gorgeous little self-catering place nearby, **Railway Cottage** (www.lovecairngorms.com; ℂ **01479/811-181**).

23 Dalfaber Rd. www.oldbridgeinn.co.uk. ℂ **01479/811-137.** Lunch mains £4–£10. Dinner mains £12–£20. Sun–Thurs noon–midnight, Fri–Sat noon–1am, Lunch served noon–2:30pm, dinner Fri–Sat 5:30–9pm, Sun–Thurs 6–9pm.

Where to Stay

Hilton Coylumbridge Aviemore ★   It's a sprawling 26-hectare (65-acre) modern resort, but it's family friendly, with a whole host of activities to keep you occupied. Strap on a hard hat and scale the climbing wall, careen down the dry ski slope or round the skating rink, jump on a skateboard or hire a bike and head off-campus to explore the trails around Aviemore. For young children there's a Fun House, for sybarites a Thai Lodge Spa. As well as a traditional restaurant and bistro, there's a funky log cabin–style Woodshed Bar with a roaring log fire for chilly days, and outside decking for the summer sun, and a fun 1950s-style American diner with free jukebox for the kids.

Coylumbridge. www.hiltonaviemore.com. ℂ **01479/810-661.** 88 units. Doubles £119–£264, suites £211–£316, includes breakfast. **Amenities:** 3 restaurants; 2 bars; babysitting; 2 pools (indoor); hydrotherapy pool, sauna, tennis courts, gym; spa; room service; free Wi-Fi.

Lazy Duck ★★   This feathered family is industrious rather than lazy, and just keeps growing. Once upon a time this 6-acre family outfit was just a cozy eight-bed hostel. Then the owners hand-built a tiny log cabin. Properly. From scratch. The Woodman's Hut, a cute eco-retreat sleeping two, has a wood-burning stove, an outdoor shower, and the chicest compost toilet you've ever seen hidden among the trees. The Duck's Nest was the next to hatch, a wooden cabin beside the duck pond with a skylight for stargazing, an outdoor hot tub—and Wi-Fi. The latest young'un to join the brood is the Lambing

Bothy, an off-grid hideaway with and outdoor chiminea stove, cozy Hebridean box-bed, and frolicking heritage breed Soay lambs in the field.

Nethy Bridge. www.lazyduck.co.uk. © **01479/821-092.** 4 units. Doubles £105–£125. **Amenities:** Sauna; wood-fired hot tub; free Wi-Fi.

THE BLACK ISLE PENINSULA ★

Cromarty: 23 miles NW of Inverness (via Kessock Bridge)

Despite its name, the Black Isle isn't an island—or black. Just over the Kessock Bridge from Inverness, it's a lush, wooded peninsula with a rugged coastline, pretty villages and family-friendly beaches—and a great little craft brewery that offers tours and tastings: **Black Isle Brewery** (www.blackisle brewery.com; © **01463/811-871**). They also organize a mini festival each September: Jocktoberfest. The name, the Black Isle, is thought to come from the fact that, as snow usually doesn't settle here in winter, the promontory looks black while the surrounding countryside is white. In summer, however, the land is green and fertile, with fields of broom and whin, bordered by salt mudflats and scattered coastal villages. The peninsula has been inhabited for 7,000 years, as the 60-odd prehistoric sites testify, and Pictish kings, whose thrones passed down through the female line, once ruled the land. Later it was the Vikings who held sway, and the existence of many gallows hills testifies to their harsh justice.

Essentials

GETTING THERE   The nearest **train** station is Inverness. **Stagecoach** (© **01463/233-371,** or visit www.stagecoachbus.com) runs a **bus** service from Inverness (nos. 26, 26A) bus station stopping at North Kessock, Munlochy, Avoch, Fortrose, Rosemarkie, and Cromarty.

If you're **driving,** take the A9 north from Inverness over the Kessock Bridge and follow signs for Munlochy and Fortrose. It's about 23 miles from Inverness to Cromarty (on the western tip of the Black Isle).

VISITOR INFORMATION   Ask at the **Inverness Tourist Information Centre** (p. 310) for details on the Black Isle, because the peninsula is often included on a day tour from the city.

Fortrose ★ & Rosemarkie ★

In the sleepy village of Fortrose you can wander around the ruins of **Fortrose Cathedral ★.** Founded in the 13th century, the cathedral was dedicated to Sts Peter and Boniface and you can still see fine detailing in the 14th-century remains. If the stones scattered about don't seem adequate to fill in the gaps, it's because Cromwell's men took many of them to help build a fort in Inverness. There are no formal hours; you can wander through the ruins at any time.

Fortrose adjoins **Rosemarkie,** the next village along. The two villages share the **Fortrose & Rosemarkie Golf Club** (www.fortrosegolfclub.co.uk;

© 01381/620-529) established in 1888. Set on the Chanonry Ness, the course juts out into the Moray Firth with fabulous views across to **Fort George** on the other side. The golf course is the site of the **Chanonry Point Lighthouse** at the 4th hole, which was designed by Alan Stevenson (the uncle of writer Robert Louis Stevenson) and began operating 1846. This is also a good place for dolphin spotting.

The charming village of Rosemarkie has been inhabited since the Bronze Age. A center of Pictish culture, the town saw the arrival of the first Christian missionaries, and it's reported that St Moluag founded a monastery here in the 6th century. The **Groam House Museum** ★ on the High Street (www.groam house.org.uk; © 01381/620-961) tells the story of the region from prehistoric times. The museum's prize exhibits are 15 carved Pictish stones, some dating back to the 8th century C.E. The pride of the collection is the **Rosemarkie cross-slab** ★, decorated with enigmatic Pictish symbols. Visitors can also learn about the legendary prophet Brahan Seer, who was buried alive at Chanonry Point. The museum is open daily April to October Monday to Friday 11am to 4:30pm, Saturday and Sunday 2 to 4:30pm. Admission is free.

Rosemarkie is not just of historical interest, however, it's a lovely little seaside spot with a good beach, popular with families and dog-walkers, a bistro on the shore and a gourmet deli in the village.

WHERE TO EAT & STAY

The Anderson ★   It's not far to stumble up to bed after a few drams and a mouthwatering meal in this quirky restaurant with rooms strung with jaunty flower-filled hanging baskets on the corner of Cathedral Square in Fortrose. History seeps out of the woodwork in this little joint dating back to 1840: the wine cellar is said to be another 200 years old. The nine charming, characterful—and compact—rooms come with four-posters, sleigh beds and roll-top baths. Downstairs is the whisky bar and restaurant where you can chill out in front of the fire before tucking into a bowl of Viking Fish soup or "skagen" packed with salmon, crayfish, and prawns (£6) for all those fed up with Cullen Skink, followed by slow-cooked ox cheeks served with star anise gravy and bone marrow toast (£15).

Union St. www.theanderson.co.uk. © **01381/620-236.** 9 units. Doubles £109–£119, includes breakfast. **Amenities:** Restaurant; bar; free Wi-Fi.

Black Isle Yurts ★   Go glamping. Who needs a tired hotel or old-fashioned guesthouse when you can bed down in a hand-built yurt-with-a-view on a working farm? Around a third of Jenny and Kenneth's land is part of the protected coastal Site of Special Scientific Interest that runs from Rosemarkie to Shandwick. There are cliff paths down to a secluded sandy beach where you can spot bottlenose dolphins playing in the bay. Or help to feed the animals: Hebridean sheep, Highland cows, pigs and chickens. Choose between Juniper, Aspen, Rowan, Willow, Cherry, Hazel and Holly, all off-grid yurts with solar hand-powered lighting units, wooden floors, wood-burning stoves and double beds, sleeping between two and five people. They also have a two-hob gas cooker/grill and utensils for cooking. Toilets and showers are at the Hub a sleek wooden barn with panoramic views.

Easter Hillockhead Farm, Eathie Hill, Rosemarkie. www.blackisleyurts.co.uk. © **01381/620-634.** 7 units. 2 nights from £155–£235. **Amenities:** Free Wi-Fi.

Crofters Bistro ★   They bake their own bread, cure the bacon, smoke the meat, fish, and cheese, and grow their own vegetables and herbs in this relaxed bistro on the seafront in Rosemarkie. They don't brew the beer—that's down to their friends at **Cromarty Brewery**—but they do infuse their own vodkas. Dishing up great brasserie-style food in a buzzing atmosphere, try the Indian spiced prawns with green chutney and rotti and crispy fried whitebait with tartar sauce.

11 Marine Terrace, Rosemarkie. www.croftersbistro.co.uk. © **01381/620-844.** Mains £12–£18. Wed–Sun 11am–2:30pm, Wed 5–8pm; Thurs–Sun 5–8:30pm.

Cromarty ★

Cromarty is a picturesque village at the tip of the peninsula, where the North and South Sutors (the high rocky outcrops) guard the entrance to the Cromarty Firth, the second-deepest inland-waterway estuary in Europe. The village, with its lanes of cottages that seem to hunch against the north winds, was once a flourishing port, and the clutch of larger 18th-century merchants' houses are testament to this. In more recent times, the coast was home to a large facility for the manufacture and maintenance of North Sea oil platforms. The remnants of this industry can still be seen in the waters of Cromarty Firth, on the northern side of the town. In fact, on a boat trip with **Eco Ventures ★**, Victoria Place (www.ecoventures.co.uk; © **01381/600-323**) you can get up close to the giant legs of one of the old platforms. The 2-hour wildlife-watching trips are one of Cromarty's highlights, the dolphins leaping around the boat a truly magical experience (Adults £30; children 5–12 £23).

Cromarty is also the birthplace of Hugh Miller, fossil hunter, folklorist and geologist. One of the 19th century's great Scots, Miller was born in 1802 in a little thatched cottage and worked as a stonemason as a young man, but became an expert in the field of geology, as well as a powerful man of letters. **Hugh Miller's Cottage ★**, Church Street (www.nts.org.uk; © **01381/600-245**) contains many of his personal belongings and collections of geological specimens. From mid-March to October, it's open daily from 1pm to 5pm; £6.50 for adults, £5.50 for students and seniors, and £16.50 per family.

WHERE TO EAT

Sutor Creek ★   This cozy little restaurant on the harbor dishes up delicious seafood (Cromarty langoustines, crab and lobster are landed on the doorstep) and gourmet, artisan wood-fired pizzas (they also do gluten-free pizzas). Tear apart a "Sutor" with artichoke hearts, spinach, olive, garlic and Parma ham or a "Black Isler" with local haggis, black pudding, bacon, egg and mushrooms. The Black Isle is prime agricultural land and meat is sourced from local farms along with foraged mushrooms and edible flowers. It's a popular place so make sure you book. **Coupers Creek** on Church Street is its sister cafe and ice-cream parlour with wooden floors, woodburning stove, and jaunty striped tables (www.couperscreek.co.uk; ℂ **01381/600-729**) open daily from 10am to 5pm.

21 Bank St. www.sutorcreek.co.uk. ℂ **01381/600-855.** Mains £8–£18. Daily noon–9pm

SUTHERLAND & THE FAR NORTH ★

Sutherland is off-the-beaten-track—and off many tourists' radars. This is the far-flung northern Highlands, although ironically the name is derived from "southlands," the Vikings' term for all the country under Caithness. The joke is that there are more sheep here than people—with a population of around 13,000 in an area of 2,300 square miles, that's probably true.

Bordered to the north and west by the Atlantic and to the east by the North Sea, it's a land of heather-swept moorland, bleak mountains, and mysterious lochs. The area isn't overloaded with attractions, although there are one or two castles to visit. What there is is a vast empty landscape to explore. This is perfect road trip territory.

Sutherland bore the brunt of the notorious 19th-century Highland Clearances, when many residents were driven out of their ancestral crofts. Some made their way to the New World. In remote glens, you can still see the ruins of the crofting villages they left behind.

Dornoch ★

63 miles NW of Inverness and 219 miles NW of Edinburgh

Motoring north on the A9, one of the most picturesque settlements along the way is Dornoch, famous for its ancient cathedral and golf club. This tiny town on the coast is also known for its sandy beaches backed by wild dunes and perfect for windswept walks.

The **Tourist Information Centre** is in the Carnegie Courthouse on Castle Street (www.visitdornoch.com; ℂ **01862/810-594**). It's open year-round Monday to Friday 12:30pm to 4:30pm and Saturday and Sunday 11am to 3pm. From Inverness bus station Stagecoach (www.stagecoachbus.com; ℂ **01463/233-371**) and Scottish CityLink run **buses** to Dornoch: The journey takes 60 to 90 minutes.

EXPLORING DORNOCH

The Royal Burgh of Dornoch is famous for its golf club on the sheltered shores of Dornoch Firth. The **Royal Dornoch Golf Club ★**, Golf Road (www.royaldornoch.com; ℂ **01862/810-219**), was founded in 1877 with a royal charter granted by Edward VII in 1906. Golf was first played here, in fact, by monks in 1614.

Dornoch Cathedral ★, Castle Street, was built in the 13th century and partially destroyed by fire in 1570. Its fine 13th-century stonework remains intact. The cathedral is famous for its modern stained-glass windows—three are in memory of Andrew Carnegie, the American steel magnate—and more recently for the fact that Madonna had Rocco, her son with Guy Ritchie, christened here. The cathedral is open daily from 9am to dusk.

In the cathedral's cemetery, where the marketplace used to be, is the **Plaiden Ell,** a medieval measure for cloth. In one of the gardens is the 1722 **witch's stone,** marking the spot where the last burning of a condemned witch to take place in Scotland.

Poking around shops such as the **Dornoch Bookshop** and the **Jail on Castle Street** (www.jail-dornoch.com; ✆ **01862/810-555**) opposite the cathedral whiles away an hour or so. Housed in a converted jail, this craft centre sells jewelry and pottery, along with knitwear, tartans and tweeds. On the other side of the Dornoch Firth you have **Anta**'s charming Highland showroom in Tain (www.anta.co.uk; ✆ **01862/832-477**)—think contemporary tartan rugs, pottery, blankets and homeware. It also has a lovely little cafe.

At **Embo ★**, about 3 miles north of the beaches of Dornoch, are the remains of two funereal vaults believed to date from around 2000 B.C.E. Another 1¼ miles north of Embo are the shores of lovely **Loch Fleet,** where there's a meager ruin of **Skelbo Castle** on a lonely grassy mound. At one time, in the 14th century, Skelbo was a powerful fortification.

WHERE TO EAT & STAY

Dornoch Castle Hotel ★　There aren't many hotel rooms these days that boast a real log fire. Splurge on the Old Courtroom with its wood-paneling and exposed stonewalls and you can curl up in a hand-carved four-poster bed and watch the flames flicker. The 24 rooms in this rambling hotel have bags of character and are split between the original building, once the residence of the bishops of Caithness and dating back to the 15th century, and an extension looking out over the gardens. It's had a checkered history over the centuries, once set alight during clan feuding and turned into a school, jail, court house, and hunting lodge before being converted into a hotel.

Castle St. www.dornochcastlehotel.com. ✆ **01862/810-216.** 24 units. Doubles £135–£260, includes breakfast. **Amenities:** Restaurant; bar; free Wi-Fi.

Links House ★★★　If you've been dreaming about a luxurious Scottish country house hotel, smattered with exquisite antiques and wreathed in tasteful tweeds, this is it. There's no tired tartan or faded grandeur here. This honey-hued hotel drips with class and oozes elegance, and it's within putting distance of the Royal Dornoch golf course. American businessman Todd Warnock restored the dilapidated manse and turned it into a hotel with 15 opulent bedrooms, all named after Scottish salmon rivers, spread between three buildings. Each is decorated with antiques and artworks reflecting the local landscape or Scottish field sports, while bathrooms are clad in decadent Italian marble. The golf course is on the doorstep, and the Activities Manager can arrange salmon and trout fishing, deer-stalking, grouse-shooting, hill-walking, and tours of the Highlands' castles and historic sites. After a day exploring,

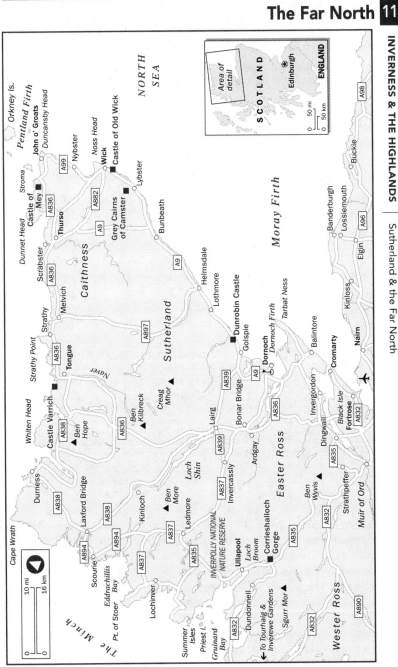

you can curl up in front of a log fire in the library with a dram. Gourmet dinners are served in the contemporary dining room with its antler chandelier. Then how about a cigar from the humidor, smoked under the stars beside the open-air fireplace?

Golf Rd. www.linkshousedornoch.com. ℭ **01862/811-279.** 15 units. Doubles £270–£375, suites £360–£780 includes breakfast. **Amenities:** Library bar; restaurant; free Wi-Fi.

Golspie ★

Just north of Dornoch, Golspie has a crescent-shaped sandy beach but its main attraction is the magnificent Dunrobin Castle.

EXPLORING GOLSPIE

Dunrobin Castle ★★ CASTLE This glorious castle, all turrets and spires, looks like it's jumped straight out of the pages of a fairytale. Home of the earls and dukes of Sutherland, Dunrobin is the largest of the great houses in the northern Highlands, dating in part from the early 13th century. Some of the castle's 189 rooms are open to the public—the ornately furnished dining room, a billiard room, and the room with the gilded four-poster bed where Queen Victoria slept when she visited in 1872. The formal gardens were laid out in the manner of Versailles. There's a museum in the grounds, which contains many relics from the Sutherland family and falconry displays most days at 11:30am and 2pm.

Golspie. www.dunrobincastle.co.uk. ℭ **01408/633-177.** £11.50 adults, £9.50 students and seniors, and £7 children 5–16, £34 families. Apr–May and Oct daily 10:30am–4:30pm, June–Sept daily 10am–5pm. Last entrance 30 min. before closing.

Tongue ★

257 miles NW of Edinburgh and 101 miles NW of Inverness

Leaving the coast and slicing diagonally up to the far north of Scotland along the A836, you sweep through a vast empty landscape of bleak moorland crouching beneath brooding mountain peaks, to Tongue. The rugged north coast is wild and untamed. It's here you'll find the tallest cliffs on the mainland and the highest waterfall. The mighty cliffs of **Clo Mor** soar 920 ft. (281m) near Cape Wrath (known for its large colonies of puffins) while the **Eas-Coul-Aulin** waterfall plummets 650 ft. (200m). At the **Falls of Shin,** you can watch salmon leap, while towering peaks to climb include **Ben Loyal,** a Corbett at 2,506 ft. (one down from a Munro, mountains over 3,000 ft.), nicknamed the Queen of Scottish mountains.

West of Tongue, on a promontory, stands the ruin of **Castle Varrich,** said to have been built by the Vikings. Possibly dating from at least the 14th century, this castle was once the stronghold of the MacKays.

For a dramatic hike head from Tongue towards the **Kyle of Tongue,** a shallow sea loch crossed by a narrow causeway. Protected from the wild and raging sea nearby, this is a long, shallow inlet. At low tide, wearing a pair of boots, you can wade out to Rabbit Island. You pass towering cliffs, sandy bays, odd rock formations, and deserted rocky islets.

WHERE TO EAT & STAY

Ben Loyal Hotel ★   There's slim pickings this far north in terms of good accommodation but this small inn, known affectionately as The Ben, has panoramic views over the Kyle of Tongue to Ben Loyal and its own trawler, so the seafood on the menu comes straight off the boat. Its place in local history is also well-established: The cellar was once the village bakery where they used peat to bake the bread, while the bar was the village shop and staff quarters the old post office.

Main St. www.benloyal.co.uk. ⓒ **01847/611-216.** 11 units. Doubles £70–£110, includes breakfast. **Amenities:** Restaurant; bar; free Wi-Fi

Tongue Hotel ★   Built in the middle of the 19th century as a sporting lodge for the Duke of Sutherland, this traditional stalwart on the road to Durness on the blustery north coast has the whole Highland works: tartan carpets, period features, roaring fires, wood-paneling and a slew of antiques. It oozes old-world charm—especially after a sherry or two from the complimentary decanter.

Tongue. www.tonguehotel.co.uk. ⓒ **01847/611-206.** 19 units. Doubles £135–£160, includes breakfast. **Amenities:** Restaurant; 2 bars; free Wi-Fi.

Durness ★

John Lennon spent his summers in Durness as a teenager and today there's a memorial garden in his honor. The far north of Scotland might not sound like a traditional summer holiday hotspot, but the beaches here, such as **Balnakeil,** are drop-dead gorgeous, sheltered coves of honey-hued sand and turquoise water. **Sandwood Bay** is a mile-long golden sweep, reputed to be haunted and with no road access, you have to hike in. (The closest access point is 4 miles away at Blairmore.) Durness is also the jumping off point for trips to the most northwesterly point in Scotland, **Cape Wrath,** only accessible by ferry and minibus during the summer, and the Clo Mor cliffs between the Kyle of Durness and Cape Wrath.

Scotland's first **Geopark,** an austere rock-hewn landscape covering 772 square miles, stretches from Durness down to Achiltibuie in the south. It's wonderful walking country, bare and rugged. The rocks littering the shoreline are 3 billion years old. In limestone caves under the mountains of Beinn an Fhuarain, the bones of reindeer, lynx, arctic fox, wolves and bears have been found, some 47,000 years old.

Just outside Durness in Balnakeil craft village is **Cocoa Mountain** (www.cocoamountain.co.uk; ⓒ **01971/511-233**) a cute cafe and chocolatier where you can indulge in a warming hot chocolate and pick up some handmade truffles, of course.

WHERE TO EAT & STAY

Mackay's ★   Fiona and Robbie Mackay are a ring-out-the-bells godsend to this remote northwest corner of coastal Scotland with their burgeoning portfolio of accommodation. Mackay's is a quirky boutique B&B with seven eclectic rooms smattered with retro touches and tweed trim. There's a cozy lounge with an open fire and a daily changing breakfast menu to boot. There's no restaurant, but they can provide you with a delicious picnic lunch. They also have a bunkhouse, cabin, cottage and sleek high-end eco-retreat, **Croft 103 ★★** made up of two state-of-the-art buildings, visions of glass and stone bedded into the landscape, with real architectural wow-factor as well as a price tag that might also make you gasp. A week's rental starts from £1,680.

Durness. www.visitdurness.com. ℂ **01971/511-202.** 7 units. Doubles £129–£149, includes breakfast. Closed Nov–May. **Amenities:** Free Wi-Fi.

Lochinver ★

This attractive little fishing village on the west coast sits in the shadow of soaring Suilven is a good stop-off along the North Coast 500. It's also famed for its pies from the **Lochinver Larder** and a gourmet hotspot.

WHERE TO EAT & STAY

The Albannach ★★   For 8 years, this tall, whitewashed hotel was the home of the most northerly Michelin-starred restaurant in Scotland. At the end of 2017, however, Colin Craig and Lesley Crosfield untied their aprons at The Albannach and wandered down the road to their next venture, the **Caberfeidh** (www.thecaberfeidh.co.uk; ℂ **01571/844-321**), a rustic dining pub. They still run the Albannach as a luxury B&B with its five individually designed rooms and suites. Check out the Byre in a separate cottage, all grey tweeds, slate, and an outdoor hot tub.

Baddidarroch. www.thealbannach.co.uk. ℂ **01571/844-407.** 5 units. Doubles £170, suites £235–£250, includes breakfast. **Amenities:** Restaurant; free Wi-Fi.

CAITHNESS ★

If you're travelling the length of Britain, Land's End (in Cornwall) to John O'Groats is the traditional route: a journey of 876 miles (1,407km). This is the end of the road, the most northerly point on the British mainland—only it isn't, of course. **Dunnet Head** is, in fact, a few miles further north. To the west of Thurso, Dunnet Head is a far more atmospheric spot with a bright, white lighthouse and unspoiled panoramas over the waves to the Orkney Islands. If you're schlepping this far north, however, you probably want to tick off John O' Groats.

While Caithness doesn't have the grandeur prevalent in much of the Highlands, this northernmost county of mainland Scotland is a rolling, ancient landscape. There are Stone Age relics—most notably the enigmatic **Grey Cairns of Camster,** which date from 4000 B.C.E. The county is dotted with cairns, mysterious stone rows and circles, and standing stones. The Vikings once occupied the region with its natural harbors, craggy cliffs and quiet coves. Many of the place names derive from Old Norse. Caithness also has churches from the Middle Ages, as well as the odd clifftop castle. The late Queen Mother's home, the **Castle of Mey**, which dates from 1570, is situated between John O' Groats and Thurso and is a must-see. Add rich animal and birdlife, lochs full of trout and rivers brimming with salmon and the reasons to visit soon add up.

This is also, incidentally, where you catch a ferry to the Orkney Islands. The main car-and-passenger services leave from the harbor at Scrabster.

Wick ★

287 miles NW of Edinburgh and 126 miles NW of Inverness

Wick, on the eastern Caithness coastline, was once a famous herring port. Today, a sleepy nostalgia hangs over the town. There's daily **bus** and **rail** service from Inverness, and **Wick Airport** (www.hial.co.uk) is served by flights from Aberdeen and Edinburgh.

The **Wick Heritage Museum ★**, 18-27 Bank Row (www.wickheritage. org; ℭ **01955/605-393**), is packed with exhibits relating to Wick's herring-fishing industry. From Easter to October, it's open Monday to Saturday 10am to 5pm; last entrance is at 3:45pm. Admission is £4 for adults and 50p for children 5 to 16.

Wick also produces its own whisky. The **Old Pulteney Distillery ★**, Huddart Street (www.oldpulteney.com; ℭ **01955/602-371**), has been in operation since 1826. Book a distillery tour, which explains the history and art of whisky making. The one-hour tour and tasting take place at 11am and 2pm Monday to Friday and costs £10. For real enthusiasts, the Pulteney Tour with Additional Expressions (that's a sampling of four drams at the end) costs £25. These tours must be booked in advance.

The most visited sites in the area are the two megalithic **Grey Cairns of Camster ★**, 6¼ miles north of Lybster on the Watten Road off the A9. The ruins of the **Castle of Old Wick ★** are also worth exploring. The castle is located just off the A9, 1½ miles south of Wick. Once known as Castle Oliphant, the ruined structure dates back to the 14th century. You can still see three floors of the old castle rising up on a rocky promontory.

WHERE TO STAY & EAT

Ackergill Tower ★★★ This is no drafty bare-bones castle. Ackergill Tower might date back to the 1400s, but the luxury is pure 21st century, the appeal timeless. Its setting is spectacular. The ancient fortress is within a pebble's throw of the 7-mile beach, surrounded by 3,000 acres of grounds, a walled garden and a private fishing loch. There's a magnificent wood-paneled Great Hall, a pub (the Smuggler's Inn), and the rooms are dripping with antiques, period features, and four-poster or wrought iron beds. You can drift off to sleep to the sound of waves crashing on the shore and wake to the gentle sound of (thankfully) distant bagpipes. There are also a handful of self-catering properties on the grounds sleeping from 4 to 12 people and a glamorous Treehouse suite.

Ackergill. www.ackergilltower.com. © **01955/603-556.** 35 units. Doubles £119–£350, includes breakfast. **Amenities:** Bar; restaurant; fishing; clay-pigeon shooting; croquet lawn; parking; billiards; mountain bikes; archery; games room; library; free Wi-Fi.

John O'Groats ★

17 miles N of Wick

For decades John O'Groats was down-at-heel, a tacky tourist spot, its old hotel unloved and boarded up. Visitors would swing by, tick it off, and get out of there as fast as possible. Now all that has changed thanks to the vision of Natural Retreats. The company breathed new life into this far-flung spot, revamping the old inn into a stylish hotel and apartments.

John O'Groats was named after Dutch ferryman Jan de Groot, and you can still see his tombstone at Canisbay Church. From here you can hike along the coast to **Duncansby Head ★**, 1¾ miles east—one of the most dramatic coastlines in Scotland, the jagged cliffs the precarious home of seabirds such as puffins. A road leads out to a lighthouse perched on the cliffs; from where you can gaze out over the churning Pentland Firth to the Orkney Islands. These turbulent waters have claimed the lives of countless mariners, with around 400 wrecks in the past century and a half alone.

John O'Groats has its own **ferry terminal** (www.jogferry.co.uk; © **01955/611-353**), from where a passenger-only ferry service operates to Orkney every day from May to September. The journey takes 40 minutes, costs £19 one way for adults and £9.50 for children and the ferry company also offers tour packages that include bus trips around the Orkneys once you're there.

The late Queen Mother's legacy to Scotland is the restored **Castle of Mey ★★**, 6 miles west of John O'Groats on the A836 (www.castleofmey.org.uk; © **01847/851-473**). The Queen Mother first saw the castle in 1952 when she was mourning the death of her husband, King George VI. Hearing that it was to be abandoned, she set out to restore both the castle and its gardens. She returned every summer for the rest of her life, and Prince Charles now follows in her footsteps.

Looking out over the Pentland Firth towards the Orkney Islands, the castle was constructed on a Z-plan between 1566 and 1572, with jutting towers and corbeled turrets. The castle is furnished just as it was when the Queen Mother departed from it. You can even see her rain boots beside the dog bowl and her blue coat hanging on the back of a chair. The guides in each room will regale you with personal anecdotes of her life there. The walled kitchen garden in July is one of the most beautiful private gardens in Scotland. The castle and gardens are open for Easter and then from May to October (closed for the last week in July and first week in August; check the website for exact dates) from 10:20am to last entry at 4pm daily. Admission is £11.75 for adults, £9.75 for seniors, and £6.50 for children 5 to 16, £32 for families. Tickets for the gardens and grounds cost £6.50 for all adults, £3 for children. Allow at least 1½ hours for a visit.

WHERE TO EAT & STAY

The Inn at John O'Groats ★★★ Incredible design at a reasonable price. See, it's not so difficult. The north coast was a wasteland in terms of stylish accommodation until Natural Retreats blew in and got to work rescuing this iconic site. After a multi-million pound regeneration project—and Norse-style brightly daubed extension—the inn was transformed into a series of high-spec lodges, luxury penthouses, apartments and sleek bedrooms. Interiors have a Scandinavian vibe, all clean lines, blonde wood, dove grey tongue-and-groove, antler chandeliers, wood-burning stoves and copper bathtubs along with lights made from lobster pots and rope. There's plenty to keep you busy while you're here. You can visit **Dunnet Bay Distillery** the home of **Rock Rose** gin, hire bikes, take a day-trip to Orkney, or walk along the headland for wildlife-spotting. There's also a spa and The Storehouse restaurant.

John O'Groats. www.naturalretreats.co.uk. ✆ **01625/810-724.** 37 units. Doubles from £92. **Amenities:** Restaurant; bar; spa; free Wi-Fi.

Scrabster ★

Scrabster is a giant fishing harbor, ferry port, and the location of one of the best seafood restaurants in Scotland.

WHERE TO EAT

The Captain's Galley ★★ Jim Cowie is a self-taught, multi-award-winning chef with a passion for sustainability. He and his wife, Mary, renovated a 19th-century icehouse and salmon bothy on the harbor in Scrabster and turned it into one of the hottest little rustic restaurants on the north coast. He's up early to go to the fish market in the morning and dishes up only what's in season. Starters include mussels with lemongrass, ginger, chili, and coconut juice; for mains, pan-roasted cod with celeriac and smoked oxtail might be on the menu.

Scrabster. www.captainsgalley.co.uk. ✆ **01847/894-999.** 3-course menu with amuse bouche £53.50 with matching wines £77, 4-course menu £60 Thurs–Sat 6:30–9pm.

WESTER ROSS ★

Ullapool ★

59 miles NW of Inverness and 238 miles N of Glasgow

Ullapool is a tourist hotspot, a bustling harborside village in Wester Ross, built by the British Fishery Society in 1788 as a port for herring fishers—chunks of it still look much the same as it did in the 18th century. Ullapool is the departure point for travelers crossing the Minch, a treacherous stretch of the North Atlantic separating Scotland from the Outer Hebrides. You can catch a ferry from here for Stornoway on the Isle of Lewis.

Ullapool has a picturesque location on the shore of **Loch Broom,** surrounded by rugged mountains. If you fancy bagging a Munro (mountains over 3,000 ft.), the peaks of An Teallach to the south or Beinn Dearg to the east are nearby.

The craggy coastline around here is perfect road trip territory, one of the most scenic stretches is from Ullapool to the village of Lochinver (a 40-mile run north along the A835). After the hamlet of Armair on Loch Kanaird, you'll come to **Inverpolly** ★, part of the Assynt Estate. As well as lochs and lochans (many with tiny islands), you can also see the peaks of Cul Mor (849m/2,785 ft.), Cul Beag (769m/2,523 ft.), and Stac Pollaidh (612m/2,008 ft.). It's good country for spotting golden eagles and peregrine falcons during the breeding season.

Knockan Crag ★ (www.nnr.scot), 13 miles north of Ullapool, is a National Nature Reserve where you can explore the landscape that first led geologists in the 19th century to theorize about plate tectonics. Here you can follow signposted nature trail and see "the Moine Thrust," which runs through the crag; geologists observed that the schists at the top of the crag were older than the limestone lower down. The colliding of the great plates of the earth's crust had caused the planes of rock to buckle, creating a fault where older rocks became exposed.

Much of the countryside north of Knockan has now been designated the North West Highlands Geopark (www.nwhgeopark.com) by UNESCO due to its special scientific interest. To explore farther, continue north on the A835 and at the Ledmore junction, take the A837 to the left, passing along **Loch Awe,** with the mountain peaks of Canisp (847m/2,779 ft.) and Ben More Assynt (984m/3,228 ft.) forming a backdrop. Eventually, you'll reach the spectacular 6¼-mile-long **Loch Assynt** ★.

From Ullapool, you can explore **Corrieshalloch Gorge** ★ (www.nts.org. uk) another national nature reserve, 12 miles to the southeast. Corrieshalloch means "ugly hollow" in Gaelic but this spot is anything but. This slot-gorge was carved by glacial meltwater up to 2.6 million years ago. Today the River Droma thunders through it via a series of waterfalls, one of which, the Falls of Measach is 45m (148-ft.) high. The tree-threaded gorge is networked with paths; there's a Victorian suspension bridge over the chasm and a spectacular viewing platform.

Another popular excursion is to **Inverewe Gardens** ★ (www.nts.org.uk; ⓒ **0844/493-2225**). The garden blooms with over 2,500 species of exotic plants from the South Pacific, the Himalayas, and South America—despite being further north than Moscow, due to the warming effect of the North Atlantic Drift. The gardens are along the A832, 6¼ miles northeast of Gairloch. Opening times are daily, April and September 9:30am to 5pm, May to 5:30pm, June to August to 6pm, and October to 4pm; £11 for adults, £9.50 for seniors, £27 per family. From November to March, the visitor center is closed, but the gardens can still be visited from 10am to 4pm daily; during this period, admission is by donation.

From either Ullapool or Achiltibuie, you can take excursions in season to the **Summer Isles ★★**, a beautiful group of almost uninhabited islands off the coast. They get their name because sheep are transported here in summer for grazing; the islands are a mecca for bird-watchers. The lovely **Summer Isles Hotel** (www.summerisleshotel.com; ℂ **01854/622-282**) is a perennially popular summer retreat. Boat schedules vary, depending on weather conditions. Information is available from the **Tourist Information Centre** at 6 Argyle St. (ℂ **01854/612-486**).

WHERE TO EAT & STAY

The Ceilidh Place ★   Forget restaurants with rooms—this is a bookshop with rooms—and a music venue, bar and buzzing bistro. A quirky and creative hangout in a string of whitewashed cottages near the harbor, this Ullapool institution is a cultural hub and *the* place to stay in the village. The warren of rooms, all different shapes and sizes, are charmingly shabby-chic and cozy, with books and retro radios rather than TVs. There's an upstairs lounge where you can relax with a book, a small kitchen where you can help yourself to tea and coffee, and an honesty bar for a night cap.

12-14 Argyle St. www.theceilidhplace.com. ℂ **01854/612-103.** 13 units. Doubles £155–£170. **Amenities:** Restaurant; bar; lounge; bookshop; free Wi-Fi.

Applecross ★

On the approach to the Bealach na Ba pass, one of the highest in the U.K., a road sign warns: ROAD NORMALLY IMPASSABLE IN WINTRY CONDITIONS. This is the vertiginous route snaking up, over and down to the remote Applecross Peninsula in Wester Ross. (Luckily there is also a coastal road in for when severe snowstorms hit.) The single-track lane with passing places weaves down to a sprinkling of little cottages and a cozy inn on the waterfront. **The Applecross Inn** (www.applecross.uk.com/inn; ℂ **01520/744-262**) is famous for its fresh seafood, live music and buzzing atmosphere, tables spilling down onto the water's edge. The inn also has seven simple rooms if you can't bring yourself to move on, although it's a popular spot so it's best to book (£140 B&B). **The Potting Shed** (www.applecrossgarden.co.uk; ℂ **01520/744-440**) an award-winning farm-to-table restaurant is also worth a punt. The vegetables and herbs come from the restored walled kitchen garden, the venison off the estate, and the fish from a pebble's throw away.

Plockton ★

Palm trees fringe the waterfront of pretty Plockton. Designated a conservation village by the National Trust for Scotland, the little fishing hamlet dates back to the 19th century. NTS rangers lead regular guided walks of historic Plockton, taking in the old pier and pontoons. Its famously mild climate is thanks to the warming effect of the Gulf Stream and its sheltered position on the east-facing shore of Loch Carron. Tourists flock here to browse the little galleries and tuck into fresh seafood in little pubs, or take a boat trip. Plockton is one of the best places to learn to kayak because of its calm bay. Alison French (www.seakayakplockton.co.uk; ℂ **01599/544-422**) organizes trips and courses for families, beginners and intermediates, paddling out to remote coral beaches or along the coastline around Strome and Kishorn islands. One of the coziest—and most creative—places to stay is **The Plockton Gallery ★** (www.plocktongallery.com; ℂ **01599/544-442**) an art gallery–cum–bed-and-breakfast. Artist Miriam Drysdale hosts exhibitions in this rambling old manse and offers tuition. The four charming bedrooms are eclectically decorated with bags of character and cost from £90 including breakfast. Just opposite is the buzzing **Plockton Inn** (www.plocktoninn.co.uk; ℂ **01599/544-222**) famed for its seafood (Kenny the owner has a smokehouse and Martin the barman catches the prawns) and traditional live music every Thursday night throughout the year and on Tuesdays too during the summer. The 14 simple rooms won't win any design awards but some come with sea views and cost from £124 per night including breakfast.

Dornie

Dornie is a little village you hardly notice as you're so busy gazing in the other direction at the star attraction.

Eilean Donan Castle ★★★ CASTLE   Anyone who saw the Hollywood blockbuster *Highlander* will remember Christopher Lambert running, kilt-flying, across a stone causeway to a tiny castle in the middle of a loch. This is it. Eilean Donan was built in 1214 as a defense against the Danes. It was destroyed by clan fighting and lay in ruins for around 200 years until it was restored and rebuilt by Colonel MacRae of Clan MacRae at the beginning of the 20th century. It is now a clan war memorial and museum. You can clamber around the ramparts and poke around the dimly lit nooks and crannies of this mini-fortress. After immersing yourself in Highland history, peruse the shop or grab lunch in the cafe of the contemporary visitor center. They also have a lovely self-catering cottage and swanky new holiday apartments (think tasteful tartan and tweed) in a building which blends seamlessly into the loch-side setting and which don't cost the earth: from £120 per night for an apartment sleeping two (www.eileandonanapartments.com; ℂ **01599/555-728**).

Dornie. www.eileandonancastle.com. ℂ **01599/555-202.** £7.50 adults, £6.50 seniors, £4 children 5–15, £20 families. Apr–Oct daily 10am–6pm; Nov–Mar daily 10am–4pm.

THE WEST HIGHLANDS ★

Fort William: Gateway to Ben Nevis

133 miles NW of Edinburgh; 68 miles S of Inverness; 104 miles N of Glasgow

There's no escaping it: Fort William is an eyesore. What the town planners were thinking is anyone's guess. Fort William is on most unsuspecting tourists' itineraries of the Highlands because it's the jumping off point for **Ben Nevis ★★**, Scotland's highest mountain, at the southern end of the **Great Glen.** The setting is picturesque, on the shores of Loch Linnhe, but as is often

The **Great Glen** is in fact a series of glens along a geological fault that slices diagonally through Scotland coast to coast, from Fort William in the southwest to Inverness and the Moray coastline in the northeast. **The Caledonian Canal,** designed by Thomas Telford at the beginning of the 19th century, took advantage of the series of lochs (Dochfour, Ness, Oich, and Lochy) lying along this fault and linked them with canals to create a watery highway connecting the Atlantic Ocean with the North Sea. The chain of freshwater inland lochs and manmade stretches of canal is 60 miles (96.5km) in length: 22 of these are manmade. There are 29 locks and 10 swing bridges along the way. **The Great Glen Way** is a long distance walking trail that follows the Great Glen. You can hike the route or sail along it. **Caledonian Discovery** (www.caledonian-discovery. co.uk; ℭ **01397/772-167**) operates two old Belgian barges, Fingal of Caledonia and Ros Crana, floating activity centers that ply the route each week in summer between Inverness and Fort William. Their activity holidays include hiking the Great Glen Way using the boat as a floating hotel.

the case in Scotland, the natural landscape is spectacular, the manmade, not quite so much.

Historically, Fort William stands on the site of a fort built by General Monk in 1655 in case of rebellion by the Highlanders. The town was later named after Prince William, Duke of Cumberland, who oversaw the crushing of the Jacobite Rebellion at the Battle of Culloden in 1746. After several reconstructions, the fort itself was finally torn down in 1864 to make way for the railroad.

ESSENTIALS

GETTING THERE   Fort William is one of the main stops on the scenic West Highland **rail** line from Queen Street Station in Glasgow to Mallaig, on the west coast. You can travel the leg of the West Highland line between Fort William and Mallaig on The Jacobite steam train. This scenic route is popular with Harry Potter fans because of the Glenfinnan Viaduct featured in the films. Services operate between April and the end of October from Monday to Friday, and also on weekends from June through September; visit www. westcoastrailways.co.uk.

The **bus** from Glasgow to Fort William, takes approximately 3 hours. Contact **Scottish CityLink** coaches (www.citylink.co.uk; ℭ **0871/266-3333**) for schedules. If you're **driving** from Glasgow, head north along the A82, but this route is often clogged with motor homes in the summer.

VISITOR INFORMATION   The **Tourist Information Centre** is at 15 High Street (www.visitscotland.com; ℭ **01397/701-801**). Opening times vary considerably so check the website—generally speaking it's open year-round from Monday to Saturday 9am to 5pm and on Sunday 10am to 3pm, except in the summer, when it stays open until 6:30pm from Monday to Saturday, and until 6pm on Sundays.

EXPLORING THE AREA

Old Inverlochy Castle ★ You can clamber around the ruins and pick your way through the walled courtyard of this 13th-century castle, 1¾ miles north of Fort William on the A82. The castle looms large in the pages of Scottish history as it was the scene of two famous battles. The first was in 1431, when clansmen of Alexander MacDonald defeated the larger army of King James I of Scotland. In the second battle, in 1645, the Royalist forces of the Marquess of Montrose won an important victory against the Covenanter army of the Marquess of Argyll. In all, 1,500 men were killed that day.

Neptune's Staircase ★, 3 miles northwest of Fort William, off the A830 at Banavie, is a series of nine locks constructed as part of the Caledonian Canal, which connected the eastern seaboard at Inverness with the west coast at Fort William. This shortened the distance that goods had to be transported from the North Sea to the Atlantic Ocean, avoiding the treacherous storms of Scotland's northern coast. This "staircase" of locks is one of the most prominent engineering triumphs in Scotland in the mid-19th century, raising boats up 19m (62 ft.) in total.

Fort William itself is relatively flat, and therefore a good place for cycling. You can hire bikes at **Off Beat Bikes,** 117 High St. (www.offbeatbikes.co.uk; ✆ **01397/704-008**). If you feel more adventurous, there are numerous mountain bike trails in the countryside around town (visit www.ridefortwilliam. co.uk). There are routes for all abilities, culminating in the white-knuckle Off Beat Downhill Track (graded Orange Extreme) at the Nevis Range resort, 7 miles north of Fort William on the mountain of Aonach Mor. The gondola takes you and your bike to the top, while gravity does the rest. The downhill track is open only in the summer, from May to September; bikes and protective gear are available for hire. In the winter season the resort offers skiing and snowboarding instead. See www.nevisrange.co.uk for details.

Ben Nevis ★★★ or The Ben, is the highest mountain in the British Isles, the summit soaring 1,344m (4,408 ft.) above sea level. It's one of the most straightforward Munros to bag, most of the trail up a well-constructed path—although the last part of the climb is a rocky scramble. More than 125,000 people make it to the top each year, another 100,000 part of the way up. But this is not a walk in the park and you need to make sure you are properly equipped. Each year climbers get into trouble, sometimes with tragic consequences, setting off, for instance, in shorts and sneakers on a sunny summer's day, unaware of how quickly the weather can change on the slope. Hurricane strength winds, blizzards and fog can all roll in and disorient climbers. For more information, swing by the Glen Nevis Visitor Center, open daily from 9am to 3pm in winter and 9am until 5pm in spring and autumn and 8:30am until 6pm in summer (www.ben-nevis.com; ✆ **01397/705-922**). After your climb, the **Ben Nevis Inn and Bunkhouse** (www.ben-nevis-inn.co.uk; ✆ **01397/701-227**) at the bottom of the mountain is a welcome sight, an old stone barn with a cozy wood-burning stove and beer on tap it's open 7 days a week in summer from noon until 11pm and serving food until 9pm.

Glenfinnan Monument ★ MONUMENT A lone Highlander stands on the top of an 18-meter-high column at the head Loch Shiel, at Glenfinnan. The monument, designed by James Gillespie Graham, a Scottish architect, marks the spot where Bonnie Prince Charlie unfurled his proud red-and-white silk banner on August 19, 1745, in his ill-fated attempt to restore the Stuarts to the British throne. At the visitor center, learn about the prince's campaign, which ended in his defeat at Culloden.

About 14 miles west of Fort William, on the A830, toward Mallaig. www.nts.org.uk. ℂ **01397/722-250.** Site free (open year-round). Visitor center £3.50 adults, £2.50 seniors and children, £9 families. Mar–May and Sept–Oct daily 9am–6pm; June–Aug daily 9am–7pm Nov–Feb 10am–4pm.

West Highland Museum ★ MUSEUM Fans of *Outlander* are making a beeline for the Jacobite collections in this quirky little museum in the center of town, to learn more about the world of Claire and Jamie Fraser. The museum has even created an interesting leaflet to explain the relevant exhibits. Founded in 1922 to preserve and showcase artifacts of historical significance from the West Highlands, it's packed with interesting items including the gifts Queen Victoria gave to her beloved personal servant, John Brown, and memorabilia relating to the history of mountaineering.

Cameron Square. www.westhighlandmuseum.org.uk. ℂ **01397/702-169.** Free. Oct–Apr Mon–Sat 10am–4pm; May–Sept 10am–5pm, July & Aug Sun 11am–3pm.

WHERE TO STAY

There are far more attractive places to stay in the Highlands than Fort William. Try to organize your itinerary so that you can just swing by or stop off briefly. The traditional luxury option, Inverlochy Castle is, thankfully, 3 miles outside town.

Expensive

Inverlochy Castle ★★★ In the 19th century this sumptuous baronial mansion at the foot of Ben Nevis basked in royal approval. Queen Victoria stayed here in 1873, meandering the grounds and sketching the dramatic landscape. A private home until 1969, when it was converted into a hotel, today it's one of the most luxurious places to bed down in the Highlands—with a price tag to match—and the epitome of historic elegance. Decorated with fine antiques and traditional oil paintings, past guests include Charlie Chaplin, Robert Redford, and Sean Connery. A Relais & Châteaux property, it oozes old-world pomp, with 17 opulent rooms and suites and four-poster beds wreathed in chintz fabrics, frills, and flounces.

Torlundy. www.inverlochycastlehotel.com. ℂ **01397/702-177.** 17 units. Doubles £490–£625; suites £650–£725, includes breakfast. **Amenities:** Restaurant; tennis court; snooker room; room service; babysitting; free Wi-Fi.

Moderate

The Lime Tree ★ If you are set on staying in Fort William, this is the place to choose: a stylish boutique-hotel-cum-art-gallery and an award-winning restaurant in a pretty 19th-century manse. The rooms are split between the old house and a more recent extension. Think wooden floors, beds in the eaves, the odd four-poster and loch views. In the lounge there's a roaring log fire while the gallery shows the work of contemporary Scottish painters and puts on two exhibitions each year.

The Old Manse, Achintore Rd. www.limetreefortwilliam.co.uk. (C) **01397/701-806.** 9 units. Doubles £100–£150, includes breakfast. **Amenities:** Restaurant; art gallery; lounge; bike storage; free Wi-Fi.

WHERE TO EAT

Crannog Seafood Restaurant ★ SEAFOOD Finlay Finlayson's iconic red-roofed restaurant on the harbor, looking out over Loch Linnhe, has had many reincarnations, from a Second World War lookout point to a fisherman's bait shed. Today, it's a no-brainer for anyone wanting a slap-up seafood meal, the fish straight from the owner's boats and smokehouse. Starters include crab, leek and gruyere tart, and creamy Cullen Skink, along with West Coast mussels and Loch Creran oysters. Also check out the daily specials board and set three-course lunch for £19.

Town Pier. www.crannog.net. (C) **01397/705-589.** Mains £16–£24. Daily noon–2:30pm and 6–10pm.

Inverlochy Castle ★★ BRITISH Celebrity chefs Albert and Michel Roux Jr.'s tasting menu is a gastronomic extravaganza. And you're requested to dress for the occasion. Gentlemen have to wear a jacket and tie and no mobile phones are allowed. The menu might be 21st-century gourmet—with the likes of seared scallop with smoked bone marrow and beef consommé, along with home cured halibut with celeriac, lemon, and pear—but the dining room, decorated with period furniture gifted to the hotel by the king of Norway, and the experience are lavishly old-world.

Torlundy. www.inverlochycastlehotel.com. (C) **01397/702-177.** Fixed-price lunch, 2-courses £28, 3 courses £38; fixed-price dinner £67. Daily 12:30–1:30pm and 7–9pm. Closed Jan–Feb.

SHOPPING

The pedestrianized High Street, which runs parallel to the shoreline, has slim pickings but there is a branch of the single malt specialist, **The Whisky Shop** at 93 High St. (www.whiskyshop.com; (C) **01397/706-164**) and the fragrant **Highland Soap Company,** 48 High St. (www.highlandsoaps.com; (C) **01397/710-980**), its lush products handmade in the Scottish Highlands using natural ingredients.

Glencoe ★★★

Bare, brooding grandeur: Glencoe's haunting history stays etched on your memory long after you've left the most famous glen in Scotland. This is where one of the Highland's most brutal massacres took place in 1692. The drive through Glencoe, which snakes across wild and windswept Rannoch Moor to

Loch Leven, winding between bleak crags and over boggy moorland, is also one of the most iconic. It's easy to imagine a fierce battle between Highlanders knee-deep in springy heather. It's also easy to understand why this barren place was the perfect film set for blockbusters such as *Harry Potter and the Prisoner of Azkaban.*

Known as the "Glen of Weeping," on February 11, 1692, the Campbells massacred the MacDonalds—men, women, and children—who'd been their hosts for 12 days. Mass killings weren't uncommon in those times, but this one shocked even the Highlanders because it was a breach of hospitality. The **Monument to the Massacre of Glencoe,** at Carnoch, was erected by the chief of the MacDonald clan. After the incident, the crime of "murder under trust" was introduced into Scottish law as an aggravated form of murder that carried the same penalty as treason.

The eye-catching, state-of-the-art **Glencoe Visitor Centre ★** (www.nts. org.uk; ✆ **01855/811-307**) is 1 mile to the south of Glencoe village, just off the A82. There's a moving film of the massacre, plus exhibitions on geology, mountaineering, and conservation in the Highlands, as well as information for walkers. The center has a bright cafe and picnic tables outside and is open from March to October daily 9:30am to 5:30pm, and from November to March 10am to 4pm, closed from 18 to 26 December. Admission is £6.50 for adults and £5 for seniors, students, and children 16 and under and £16.50 for families.

The village of Glencoe is a pretty backwater where you can dip into the **Glencoe Folk Museum ★** (www.glencoemuseum.com; ✆ **01855/811-664**) crammed with everything from Victorian dolls to weapons from the Battle of Culloden. It's open April until the end of October, Monday to Saturday 10am to 4:30pm and costs £3 adults £2 seniors, children under 16 free.

Today, Glencoe is also a vast open-air adventure playground. In the winter it's a skiing and snowboarding hotspot; in the summer, hill-walking, mountain-biking, and Munro-bagging take over. Check out **Glencoe Mountain** resort (www.glencoemountain.co.uk; ✆ **01855/851-226**) for more information. There's a cozy cafe serving hearty breakfasts and hot food such as homemade soup and local venison burgers. Swing up to the top of Creag Dhubh for breathtaking views over Glen Etive from the viewpoints. The ride takes 12 minutes and the lift operates all year. It costs £12 for adults, £6 for children, and £30 for families.

There are a handful of low-level walks around the valley floor as well as lung-busting climbs. The ramble around picturesque Lochan (a manmade lake surrounded by trees) is just above the village. Follow the red arrows for a 40-minute circuit of the lake weaving through the rhododendrons. To bag a Munro, tick off two in one on a classic Scottish ridge walk: Meall Dearg and Sgorr nam Fiannaidh are two Munros separated by a narrow, rocky ridge known as the Aonach Eagagh.

WHERE TO EAT & STAY

The Clachaig Inn ★   Take off your muddy boots, pull up a pew, and sink a pint or two of beer or nurse a warming dram. This legendary whitewashed inn is a beacon of Highland hospitality in the heart of Glencoe's bleak, brooding grandeur. Decked out with mountaineering memorabilia, there's not one but three bars to choose from—and, in fact, you don't have to take off your hiking boots in the "Boots Bar." There's a pool table, weekly live folk music, a roaring fire and rustic wooden benches. In the restaurant you can tuck into Stornoway black pudding with locally smoked sweet bacon with apple and plum chutney, or haddock fried in breadcrumbs, oatmeal, crushed pink peppercorns, parsley, and lemon zest with pea and potato mash. The 23 contemporary rooms are split between the original building (Ossian wing), the newer Bidean Wing, and The Lodge. The Clachaig also has self-catering cottages around the glen.

Glencoe. www.clachaig.com. ✆ **01855/811-252.** 23 units. Doubles £102–£118, includes breakfast. **Amenities:** Restaurant; 3 bars; free Wi-Fi.

THE HEBRIDES

By Stephen Brewer

The ruggedly beautiful west coast of Scotland is a perfect set up for the even more alluring islands scattered along offshore. A spirit of adventure takes hold the moment you step onto the breezy deck of an outbound ferry (or for that matter, even zip across the road bridge that connects the Isle of Skye with the mainland). Once ashore on any of the dozen or so main isles, and dozens of other smaller islands, you're transported as sights and experiences unfold, one after another, all of them heightened with a sense of remoteness. The shortlist of what to expect includes some of Europe's best beaches (though beach-going out in the Hebrides is usually a chilly undertaking); soaring mountains; an abundance of wildlife that flourishes in undisturbed habitats here at the western edge of Europe, and a palpable sense of history that, in the case of standing stones and cairns, goes back four millennia or so. Seafood that seems to jump right out of the sea onto your plate and locally distilled, peaty whiskies, best enjoyed in front of a welcoming fire, also add a lot to the pleasure of island hopping.

Getting around the Hebrides

Footloose and fancy free as you may feel at the prospect of exploring the Hebrides, navigating ferry timetables and bus schedules will soon bring you back to earth. You're going to have to do a little advance planning because boats to the islands operate on somewhat limited schedules, with service to many sailing only once a day, or even less frequently. The first port of call in your planning should be the website of **Caledonian MacBrayne,** www.calmac.co.uk, the ferry operator that, aside from a very few independent operators, lords it over boat travel in the islands. The company operates ferries out of **Oban** to ports on Mull (and from there to Iona), Coll & Tiree, and Barra (with connections from there via ferry and road through the Outer Hebrides to South & North Uist and Harris & Lewis). From **Mallaig,** ferries sail to Eigg, Muck, Rum, Skye (with connections from there to North Uist and Harris), and South Uist.

From **Ullapool,** ferries make the crossing to and from Lewis. Ferries sail within the Outer Hebrides to connect a road route between Barra, South & North Uist, and Lewis & Harris. Getting between the mainland ports of Oban, Mallaig, and Ullapool can be time-consuming, especially on Sundays, and often involve a bus and train journey through the western Highlands with at least one transfer along the way. **Traveline Scotland** (www.travelinescotland. com) is a great help in putting together these ferry, bus, and boat connections.

Don't Leave the Hebrides Without . . .

Being mesmerized at the entrance to Fingal's Cave. The sound and spectacle of this natural phenomenon inspired the *Fingal's Cave Overture* by Mendelssohn, verse by Keats, and appreciative awe in legions of other travelers.

Walking out to Neat Point on the Isle Of Skye. What may be the most scenic Hebridean Island of all is overloaded with natural wonders, but for an exhilarating, windswept thrill it's hard to top the short trek across this wave-battered, green headland flecked with sheep grazing on salt-tinged grasses to a lonely lighthouse at the edge of the world.

Savoring a seafood feast next to the sea. The stand-up Seafood Hut on the wharf in Oban introduces you to the pleasures of the sea even before you step onto a ferry, and the scallops, mussels, crabs, and fish only seem to get fresher as you wind your way through the islands.

Stopping to smell the roses, or rhododendrons, at Colonsay House. Of all the transporting gardens in Scotland, the acres of plantings and shady woodlands at an aristocratic retreat on the little Isle of Colonsay might be the most exotic, blooming amid so much remote beauty.

Standing beneath the Callanish Stones on Lewis. The most august of the islands' castles and other historic monuments were erected for reasons unknown but sill inspire awe, as they no doubt did for onlookers three millennia ago.

Watching an eagle soar over the flanks of Ben More on Mull. Majestic mountains, rugged coastlines, and water-soaked lowlands are the settings for an unfolding spectacle of wildlife in the Hebrides, where porpoise, otters, and seals swim in the seas and puffins and other seabirds thrive on untrammeled shorelines and in the cloud-shrouded heights.

OBAN

85 miles NW of Glasgow

The bustling port of Oban is the gateway to a cluster of Hebridean islands. Most visitors come to town to ship out, often to the nearby Isle of Mull, and there's a tinge of excitement and adventure along the lively seafront backed by Victorian landmarks from the days when Oban was itself a resort. Oban has

The Hebrides

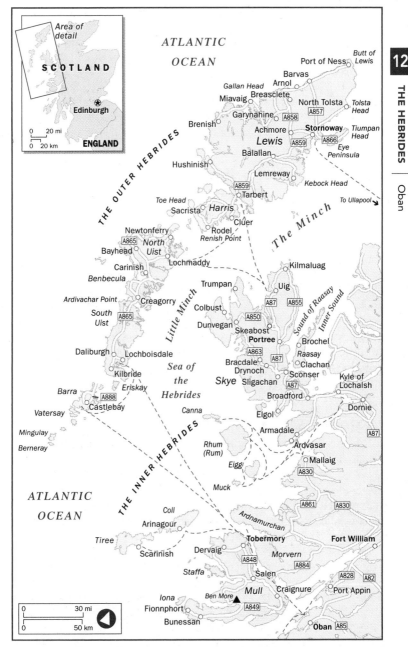

been a busy fishing port since the 18th century and is considered the seafood capital of Scotland, so reason enough to linger before hopping onto an island-bound ferry is to tuck into a heaping seafood platter, or at least some fish and chips.

Essentials

GETTING THERE From Glasgow, the West Highland train lines run directly to Oban, with departures from Glasgow's Queen Street Station (www.scotrail.co.uk; ☏ **0344/811-0141**). The trip is one of Scotland's most scenic rail journeys, following the north bank of the Clyde before climbing through the mountains past Loch Lomond and several other bodies of water glimmering in the folds of mountains.

Frequent coaches (www.citylink.co.uk; ☏ **0871/266-3333**) depart from Buchanan Station in Glasgow, taking about the same time as the train.

If you're driving from Glasgow, head northwest along the A82 through the mountains until you reach Tyndrum, and then drop west along the A85 down to Oban.

VISITOR INFORMATION The **Tourist Information Centre** is on Argyll Square (www.oban.org.uk; ☏ **01631/563-122**). The office leads amusing and insightful walking tours of Oban on a varying schedule; cost is £11. Opening times are April to mid-June and mid-September to October, Monday through Friday 9am to 5pm and Saturday and Sunday 10am to 4pm; mid-June to mid-September, Monday through Saturday 9am to 8pm and Sunday 9am to 7pm; and November to March, Monday through Saturday 9:30am to 5pm and Sunday noon to 4pm.

SPECIAL EVENTS The **Oban Highland Games** are held in August, with massed pipe bands marching through the streets. The **Oban Pipe Band** regularly parades on the main street during summer.

Exploring Oban

Adding a touch of exoticism to the town is **McCaig's Tower,** the hulking granite shell of an unfinished amphitheater atop Battery Hill. Local businessman John Stuart McCaig begin this immodest monument to himself and his family (their larger-than-life statues were never installed as planned) in 1897 and modeled the tower on the Roman Coliseum, McCaig died before much more than the shell was completed, though he provided a fine lookout from the grounds all the way out to the Isle of Mull.

Oban has been linked to the sea since cave dwellers fished here 5,000 years ago, and the position on Scotland's western sea lanes was a mixed blessing, as the coastline was rife for plunder and attack by rival clans and Vikings. A walk of about 1 mile north along Oban's horseshoe-shaped harbor leads to the ruins of the 13th-century **Dunollie Castle** (☏ **01631/570-550**). This imposing stone fortress seems to grow out of the rock on which it is perched and for 900 years has been the seat of the Clan McDougall, the lords of Lorn, who once owned a third of Scotland. From Dunollie the lords could keep an eye on anyone sailing in and out of the bay, and their aerie was pretty much unassailable. Just for good measure, the Great Hall was reached by a wooden staircase that could be dismantled quickly in case of a breach in the massive walls. The ruins and a museum in the 1775 Laird's House are open April through October, Monday through Saturday 10am to 5pm and Sun, noon to 5pm; admission is £6 adults, £3 children 5 to 15, £16 families of two adults and two children.

About 2 miles up the coast path another rocky outcropping is topped with the ruins of **Dunstaffnage Castle** ★ (www.historicenvironment.scot; ✆ **01631/562-465**), square and massive, taking shape among the trees above the Firth of Lorn as a sheer wall of stone. The forbidding fortress is best known as the short-term prison in 1746 of Flora MacDonald, a wildly romantic figure from the Hebrides who helped Bonnie Prince Charlie, or Charles Edward Stewart, escape after he led an unsuccessful rebellion to claim the British throne. Flora was transferred from Dunstaffnage to the Tower of London, was later pardoned, and emigrated for a time to North Carolina. The castle is open April to September daily from 9:30am to 5:30pm, and from November to March Saturday through Wednesday from 9:30am to 4:30pm. Admission is £6 adults, £4.80 for seniors and students, and £3.60 for children ages 5 to 16. You can take a bus from the railway station in Oban to Dunbeg, but it's still a 1½-mile walk to the castle.

Next to the castle is the **Ocean Explorer Centre** (www.oceanexplorercentre.org; ✆ **01631/559-123**), part of Scotland's oldest oceanographic institute where exhibits explore marine life in the Firth of Lorne and farther afield. The center is open April through late December, Monday to Friday 10am to 4pm; January, Monday to Friday noon to 2pm; and February through March Monday to Friday 11am to 3pm Admission is free.

Where to Stay in Oban

Glenburnie Hotel ★★ A prominent Victorian-era doctor built this rambling, granite-block house on the Esplanade, and the old place still instills the respect due to such a man of standing. Guest rooms are nattily done up with plaids and deep colors. Rooms 4 and 9 are the largest and best in the house, just as they were meant to be as private chambers for the doctor and his guests, overlooking the bay through huge windows with comfy armchairs placed before them. Room 3 has its own view-filled sitting room.

The Esplanade. www.glenburnie.co.uk. ✆ **01631/562-089.** 13 units. Doubles £100–£150, includes breakfast. Closed mid-Nov to Easter. **Amenities:** Free Wi-Fi.

Glenview Guest House ★ It's a 10-minute walk from the ferry docks out to this humble little B&B at the southeastern edge of town, where the comfortable rooms are basic but snug and nicely equipped with updated bathrooms and come with an enormous Scottish breakfast, served in a sunny parlor. Free parking and easy access to the main car routes along the western coast makes this a good stop for road trippers.

Soroba Rd. www.glenviewguesthouse.com. ℃ **01631/562-267.** 10 units. Doubles £60, includes breakfast. Free parking. **Amenities:** Free Wi-Fi.

Isle of Eriska Hotel ★★★   The turn-of-the-20th-century estate of a Glasgow industrialist has changed very little since the days of lavish house parties and is still a privileged retreat, set in 121 hectares (300 acres) on a forested island at the mouth of Loch Linnhe. A paneled hall, drawing room, and intimate library make any guest feel like the laird or lady of the manor, and baronial bedrooms and cottages spread across the lush grounds do nothing to dispel the illusion. Lazing around the beautiful pool and taking walks through woodlands provide an idyllic easygoing country retreat, but dinner is a formal affair as befits the acclaimed cuisine.

Ledaig, 12 miles north of Oban. www.eriska-hotel.co.uk. ℃ **01631/720-371.** 34 units. Doubles £295–£880, includes breakfast. **Amenities:** Restaurant; bar; 6-hole golf course; tennis court; health club & spa; room service; free Wi-Fi.

Manor House Hotel ★★   The dukes of Argyll used to set their aging relations up in style in this handsome 1780 stone manor house overlooking Oban Bay. The gardens and terrace provide an eagle's eye perch from which to watch the isles-bound ferries slip in and out of the harbor below, while plenty of winged-back chairs and fireside sofas lend a country-house ambience ideal for sipping a single malt. A couple of the cozy, traditionally furnished bedrooms overlook the harbor, and the one on the ground floor is handy for guests who want to avoid a trip up the grand staircase to sleep. Dinner in the formal dining room is a pretty grand show, and open to non-guests.

Gallanach Rd., on bluff just west of harbor. www.manorhouseoban.com. ℃ **01631/562-087.** 11 units. Doubles £115–£215, includes breakfast. No children under 12. **Amenities:** Restaurant; bar; room service; free Wi-Fi.

Perle Oban Hotel ★★   Waiting to ship out can be stylishly fun at this to cellar-to-attic redo of a proud Victorian landmark on the harbor. The high-ceilinged guest rooms come in all sorts of shapes and sizes, with some tucked into towers and many facing the sea through enormous bay windows. Colors schemes incorporate lots of deep-blue hues to bring the big expanses of sea and sky indoors. A bar and cafe are popular gathering spots, and Baab Meze Grill gets into the spirit of a port to serve seafood and other local fare with exotic Middle Eastern flavorings and flair.

Station Square. www.perleoban.com. ℃ **01631/700-301.** 59 units. Doubles £110–£170, includes breakfast. **Amenities:** Restaurant; bar; room service; free Wi-Fi.

Where to Eat in Oban

The place to stop for a Guinness, single malt, or music is **O'Donnells,** an Irish pub on Breadalbane Street (℃ **01631/566-159**). Music is on tap from

Thursday to Saturday, in the form of a live band or a DJ. It's open daily from 3pm to 1am.

Cuan-Mor ★ SEAFOOD   If you find yourself docked in Oban and don't like fish, step into this woody and friendly pub on the waterfront. Burgers are big and juicy, as are the steaks, and they're accompanied by house-brewed beers and dozens of whiskies.

60 George St. www.cuanmor.co.uk. © **01631/565-078.** Main courses £10–£20. Daily noon–9:30pm (bar open later).

Ee-Usk ★★ SEAFOOD   The name is Gaelic for "fish," and this ever-crowded, brightly lit room at the end of a pier claims to be the "seafood capital of Oban," which is quite a big boast, since Oban calls itself the seafood capital of Scotland. Tile floors and utilitarian furnishings suggest that the emphasis here is more on taste and freshness than on style, and the crabs mussels, scallops, langoustines, and sole, appearing grilled, steamed, baked, and in fish cakes, never disappoint.

North Pier. www.eeusk.com. © **01631/565-666.** Main courses £12–£30. Daily noon–3pm and 5:45–9:30pm.

Oban Fish and Chips ★★ SEAFOOD   Some Glaswegians don't think twice about driving over to Oban just for a heaping platter of what regulars consider to be the best fish and chips in Scotland. While this simple takeaway and attractively plain room may not inspire such awe and devotion in everyone, just about anyone who stops in agrees the fish is fresh and expertly prepared, and the many choices often include lobster tails, monkfish, and other specials. The alcohol policy is BYOB, with no corkage fee.

116 George St. www.obanfishandchipshop.co.uk. © **01631/567-000.** Main courses £8–£20. Daily 11am–11pm.

The Seafood Hut ★★★ BRITISH   You may never feel the need to sit down to eat a seafood meal again, because unless you're lucky and grab a seat at the one table here (and outdoors, at that), you'll probably devour your crab sandwich, scallops, or langoustines while standing, and the maritime snack will be nothing less than transporting. Fisherman/owner John Ogden honed his skills while cooking for his crews at sea, and what's good enough for those savvy seafaring gourmands is surely good enough for appreciative landlubbers, who would have to sail to the ends of the earth to find a seafood feast as fresh, good, and fairly priced than this one

Calmac Pier. © **7881/418565.** Main courses £4–£25. Daily 9am–6pm.

Tours from Oban

Caledonian MacBrayne, the ferry operator that connects the Hebrides, operates day tours from Oban that are an extremely convenient way to explore the nearby islands. The day-long **Mull and Iona Day Adventure** (£38) shows off a bit of Mull by bus then makes the crossing to the holy island of Iona. **Three Isles Day Adventure** (£65) adds in a trip to Staffa. Even if you can't squeeze a lengthy Hebrides island-hop into your plans, it's well worth coming to Oban for an overnight to ship out on one of these tours to get a small taste of the islands. For information, go to calmac.co.uk. Cycle paths follow the coast around Oban, and you can explore them with a rental from **Oban Cycles,** Barr Bheag, Taynuilt (www.rcscycles.co.uk; *©* **01866/822-736**).

ISLE OF MULL ★★

11 miles W of Oban

The third-largest island in the Hebrides (after Lewis & Harris and the Isle of Skye) is said to be a land of ghosts, fairies, and the wee folk, but what draws most visitors is rugged beauty: wild upland moors, craggy mountains, and shimmering sea lochs. The island's highest peak, **Ben More,** soars to 961m (3,153 ft.), and the climb, on well-marked paths, three hours up and two down, is on the checklist of every serious Scottish hill walker. All across the island, roe deer, polecats, and feral goats roam the moors and woodlands, and sea eagles soar overhead as osprey patrol the rugged coastlines. Little wonder that many islanders and their appreciative, nature-loving visitors consider Mull to be the most beautiful of all the Hebrides; it's one of the wettest, too, so bring a raincoat.

Essentials

GETTING THERE & GETTING AROUND   Caledonian MacBrayne (www.calmac.co.uk; *©* **0800/066-5400**) makes the 45-minute crossing from and to Oban five or six times per day. **West Coast Motors** coaches (www.westcoastmotors.co.uk; *©* **01586/552-319**) connect with the Craignure ferry at least three times a day and will take you to Fionnphort and Tobermory.

VISITOR INFORMATION   The **Harbour Visitor Centre** in Tobermory provides information and will help with booking accommodation and boat trips (www.tobermory.co.uk; *©* **01688/302-875**). It's open from Easter to October, Monday through Friday from 9am to 6pm, though hours vary.

Exploring Mull

Deer far outnumber the human population of Mull, and the island's scattered settlements are often called "sleeping villages," because the aging residents tend to retire early. Bus service is limited, and the only way to get around the island with any ease is by car, and even that is slow going on single-track roads.

CRAIGNURE & THE SOUTH

The island's main ferry port is only a 45-minute ferry crossing away from Oban, but the short voyage lands you in such remote-seeming surroundings that you might feel you've sailed across an entire ocean or engaged in some time travel. Sailing into **Craignure** harbor can be a bit of a thrill, with lonely Duart Castle rising above the sea and moors and the island's untamed landscapes spreading away in every direction.

Duart Castle became part of the fiefdom of the Macleans in 1367, when the clan chief found an expeditious way to expand his fortunes and landholdings, including all of Mull—he decided to marry the daughter of the Lord of the Isles, so he had her kidnapped. A later chief showed even less gallantry when, around 1520, he became annoyed that his wife, a member of the powerful Clan Campbell, had not produced a male her and had her stranded on Lady's Rock, within sight of the castle, where the incoming tides would drown her. Sure enough, the lady was no longer on the rock with the break of the next dawn.

The Campbells invited the grieving widower to a banquet a few months later and, to his surprise, his wife, who had been rescued by fishermen, was seated next to him. Her brother capped off the event by stabbing him to death. The Macleans did not mellow with the passing years, and when a later chief did not approve of the fellow his widowed mother chose to marry, he crashed the wedding party, killed 18 guests, and imprisoned and tortured his new stepfather. The current Macleans, who still occupy Duart Castle, are a bit more subdued these days.

From Craignure, a signal track leads southwest for 35 miles to **Fionnphort,** a tiny little place clustered around a dock from which boats depart for the 1-mile crossing to the Isle of Iona and to Staffa. Scattered across the moors are little lochs, in the middle of which are manmade islets, not much more than a raft-sized patch of dry land. These were built as a refuge of last resort during the clan warfare that often erupted on the island. It's said with a wink that Mull was never the scene of a great clash against invaders, so islanders had to make up for it by fighting among themselves. The patches of forests you pass as the road skirts the flanks of 3,000-foot-tall **Ben More** are from recent plantings for commercial purposes. As much as 85% of the island was once forested, though the trees long ago disappeared as everyone from ancient peoples to the Vikings cut them for fuel and boat building. Mussels are another Mull export, and they're cultivated in **Loch Spelve,** where farms yield up to 500 tons a year. A century ago islanders also harvested kelp, a backbreaking, chilling enterprise in which entire families would wade in the sea for hours on end to collect the plants, then dry and burn them to produce sodium carbonate, a component in glass-making. Long-haired Highland cattle graze in the pastures, and islanders like to say that these days the shaggy beasts are producing a new revenue source as their long, orange-hued hair is exported to America to craft wigs for a certain prominent politician.

Duart Castle ★ CASTLE For several turbulent centuries, the fiery Maclean Clan kept an eye on the busy west coast sea lanes from their fortified fief on a rocky promontory outside Craignure harbor. In 1791 the dukes of Argyll sacked the castle, and walls and towers lay in ruin until 1911. That's when Sir Fitzroy, the 26th chief of the Macleans and grandfather of the present occupant, began restoring what was essentially a pile of stones. He must have been a romantic, as the silhouette of turrets, ramparts and gables seem to leap right out of medieval legend. You might run into one of the Macleans, who reside at the castle on and off, as you walk through the Great Hall, kitchens, and bedrooms.

On the eastern point of Mull 3 miles east of Craignure. www.duartcastle.com. *℃* **01680/812-309.** £6 adults, £5 seniors and students, £3 children, £14 families. Apr Sun–Thurs 11am–4pm; May to mid-Oct; daily 10:30am–5pm.

TOBERMORY & THE NORTH

The unofficial capital of Mull, and the island's largest village, is **Tobermory ★**, 21 miles northwest of Craignure. The pretty port is not much more than a row of brightly painted houses facing a flotilla of boats bobbing in a sheltered harbor. Adding to the romance of this setting is the alleged presence, somewhere on the seabed, of the *Florencia,* a galleon in the Spanish Armada which, after sheltering in the bay in 1588 while fleeing the British fleet, went down laden with gold bullion and other treasure.

The little **Mull Museum ★** (www.mullmuseum.org.uk; *℃* **01688/301-100**) in an old bakery on Main Street, is the place to bone up on island history. Among the fascinating bits crammed into the display cases are fragments of the cockpit and nose section of a Dakota transport plane that crashed into the 2,500-foot-high summit of Mull's Beinn Talaidh in bad weather in 1945 after a transatlantic crossing from Canada to Prestwick airfield, near Glasgow. One of the crew managed to climb down the mountain in deep snow to summon help at a cottage, and islanders mounted a dramatic rescue that saved four others stranded on the mountainside. Admission is free, and the museum is open Easter to mid-October, Monday to Friday from 10am to 4pm, and sometimes on Sundays in the summer. Tobermory's other cultural institution is the **Mull Little Theatre,** proclaimed as the "smallest professional theater in the world" when the actors performed in an old cowshed outside nearby Dervaig and earned quite a bit of fame for their productions. The **Tobermory Malt Whisky Distillery** (*℃* **01688/302-645**), gives tours by appointment only.

Dervaig, 8 miles west of Tobermory, is a single street of white-washed houses tucked amid gardens and little copses above Loch a' Chuilinn. The soft greenery is a welcome contrast to the stark surrounding moorlands, and it's easy to see how the name translates from the Gaelic to "little grove." The **Old Byre Heritage Centre ★** (www.old-byre.co.uk; *℃* **01688/400-229**) houses 25 charming scale models, painstakingly made by a local historian, that illustrate the history of Mull from the first settlers to the Highland Clearances. Admission is £3 for adults, £2 for seniors and students, and children 5 to 12. It's open from April to October, Wednesday through Sunday from 10:30am to 6:30pm.

From Dervaig, the B8073 follows the west coast through seascapes that seem all the more spectacular with the heights of Ben More, often wrapped in clouds, looming in the near distance. **Calgary,** 5 miles west of Dervaig, is a perfect slip of starched white sand backed by meadows. The name in old Gaelic roughly means "beach of the meadow," and time was that shepherds would ship their sheep to and from the beach to the Treshnish Isles to graze in the summer, letting them snack in these grasslands behind the sands before herding them onto boats. Pretty as the setting is, sands and sea are often shrouded in mists and can be chilly even on a fine day. This remote little strand gave its name to the Canadian city, after an officer in the Mounties came for a visit and took fond memories home with him.

The relatively easy, 7-mile trek around the **Treshnish Headland,** at the island's western edge, leads past sea cliffs and caves etched into the shoreline, and comes with the company of deer and sheep. The only reminders of civilization in this remote place are Crakaig and Clac Gugairigh, twin villages that were abandoned more than a hundred years ago. Just offshore are the Treshnish Isles, a haven for seabirds and seals; the most distinctly shaped of these geological formations is known for good reason as Dutchman's Cap.

Where to Stay & Eat on Mull

Café Fish ★★ SEAFOOD   This simple little seaside place claims that "the only thing frozen is the fisherman," and it's true: Much of the fish and seafood come off the restaurant's own boat, and other staples are from boats bobbing alongside theirs in the harbor and from nearby cottage gardens. You can savor the straight-from-the-sea freshness in a cold shellfish platter, hearty seafood stews, rich seafood bisques, and simply grilled fish. Plain as the surroundings are, this is no mere fishermen's shack: The easygoing banter is likely to be German, French, and Aussie-accented English, so it's best to reserve well in advance.

The Pier. Tobermory. www.thecafefish.com. ℭ **01688/301-253.** Main courses £12–£22. Mid-Mar to Oct daily noon–3pm and 5:30–10:30pm.

Glenforsa Hotel ★★   The woodsy side of Mull comes to the fore in this log, seaside lodge on the east coast. Glenforsa is Norse for "swiftly flowing water" and a rushing river enhances the wilderness setting. Pine-paneled rooms (every board and timber was imported from Norway in the 1960s) are done with crisp white linens and draperies and are rustically elegant, as are the lounges looking beyond tall evergreens to the Sound of Mull. Many guests fly their own planes onto the hotel's grass airstrip to fish for salmon, and the lovely grounds and panoramic upstairs sitting room are prime spots for bird watching and observing otters and seals on the shore.

Salen, by Aros. www.glenforsa.co.uk. ℭ **01680/300-377.** 15 units. Doubles £100, includes breakfast. **Amenities:** Restaurant; bar; room service; free Wi-Fi.

Glengorm Castle ★★   You'd be surprised at just how easy it is to feel at home in the Great Hall of a castle, sitting next to a roaring fire, sipping a single malt (complimentary), and looking over the Sound of Mull. That's the point at this 1860 castle/county house, home to the Nelson family and welcomingly furnished with an eclectic mix of their heirlooms and comfy couches and armchairs. Bedrooms range in size from large to enormous and are appointed with period pieces, handsome wall coverings, and paintings and have huge bathrooms equipped with deep tubs and baronial old-fashioned sinks. The views from most rooms seem to extend forever. A turn-of-the-century stone pool next to the shore provides a dip that's only a little less bone-chilling than a swim in the sea.

On the B8073, 5 miles south of Tobermory. www.glengormcastle.co.uk. *℗* **01688/302-321.** 5 units. Doubles £165–£210, includes breakfast. A £30 discount applies after the first night. **Amenities:** Bar; pool, library; coffee shop; free Wi-Fi (in Great Hall only).

The Ninth Wave ★★★ SEAFOOD   Your waiter may be John Lamont, who often wears a kilt for the evening but spends part of the day in his little fishing boat landing the catch that appears on your table. The set menu includes the thoughtful creations of John and his wife, Carla, and might include their wildly imaginative innovations like smoked crab cheesecake and soups made with dandelion leaves and nettles from the cottage garden. The name is from mythology, and you'll indeed feel otherworldly in this handsomely decorated cottage that transports diners to other realms.

Bruach Mhor, Fionnphort. www.ninthwaverestaurant.co.uk. *℗* **01681/700757.** Fixed-price menus only: 3, 4, or 5 courses £48, £56, £68. Wed–Sun 6–9pm.

Sheiling Holidays ★   You won't be living in luxury, but these tents are carpeted, have firm beds, and are framed with extra thick canvas to keep out the wet and chill. A communal toilet block is sparkling clean, as are the shared cooking facilities. A seat at the campfire comes with views over the Sound of Mull, Loch Linnhe, and the Firth of Lorne.

Outside Craignure. www.shielingholidays.co.uk. From £40 a night, minimum 2 nights. **Amenities:** Communal kitchen; free Wi-Fi (in some areas only).

Tours on Mull

Sea Life Surveys (www.sealifesurveys.com; *℗* **01688/302-916**) will take you out on all-day or 4-hour whale-watching cruises or 2-hour seal-watching trips. Departures are from Tobermory. Day cruises operate April through October, Tuesday, Thursday, and Friday with departures at 9:30am, and cost £80 for adults, £40 children, and £205 families. The 4-hour whale watch operates April through October, Monday, Wednesday, and Saturday, with departures at 9:30am, and costs £60 for adults, £30 children, and £155 families. Seal and porpoise-watching trips operate May through October daily at 1:45pm and cost £25 for adults, £12.50 for children, and £65 for families.

From the Ulva Ferry Piers, on the west side of Mull, you can cruise to the lonely **Treshnish Isles,** a sanctuary for puffins, guillemots, and seals. The *Turus Mara* (www.turusmara.com; *℗* **01688/302-916**) makes half-day visits from April to early-August, with a stop in Staffa, departing at 11:40am. The cost is £65 adults, £32.50 children, £170 families. The Treshnish Isles are murky, muddy, and boggy, so bring dry clothes, boots, and a sense of humor.

Discover Mull Wildlife Tours (www.discovermull.co.uk; *℗* **01688/400-415**) show off the island's glorious flora and fauna, along with glens, mountains, and coastlines. Typical sightings are golden eagles, otters, grey seals, porpoises, and basking sharks. The 7-hour tours run from May into October, Sunday through Friday, and depart from Dervaig at 9am and Tobermory at 9:30am. The £40 fee includes a packed lunch and coffee.

Outdoor Activities on Mull

At the isolated 9-hole **Craignure Golf Course** (www.craignuregolfclub. co.uk), 22 miles west of Tobermory, you're requested to deposit £15 greens fees into an honesty box. **Tobermory Golf Club** (www.tobermorygolfclub. com; ✆ **01688/302-741**) is a 9-hole course with hilly terrain, and wind that poses a challenge offset by what must be some of the best views from any course in the world. Islanders will tell you that both these courses are really 18-holes, because you can play them twice; you won't find club rentals or many other amenities at either course. Mull is a playground for **hikers,** and you can find a good selection of walks at www.isle-of-mull.net.

IONA ★★

⅛ mile west of Mull

This tiny piece of meadow-clad rock, only 1-mile wide and 3½ miles long, sheltered the first Christian settlement in Scotland, founded by Irish monk St Columba in 563. Columba and his disciples spread Christianity throughout the Western Isles and mainland Scotland, while the monastic community and scriptorium they founded on Iona preserved learning throughout the Dark Ages. It's believed, with some weight to the theory, that the Book of Kells, the beautiful illuminated manuscript that is the pride of Trinity College in Dublin, was produced here around 800, then carried off to Ireland with Iona's monks fleeing Viking raids. Iona is still a spiritual place. The green meadows, white beaches, and restored abbey are a lure for day trippers who, following in the footsteps of countless pilgrims, step off ferries running between Fionnphort, on Mull, and quaint Baille Mor, Iona's only village, nestled amid trees and garden plots on the eastern shore.

Essentials

GETTING THERE Caledonian MacBrayne (www.calmac.co.uk; ✆ **0800/066-5400**) passenger ferries run hourly and with even more frequency between Fionnphort on Mull and Iona; the crossing takes only 10 minutes.

Exploring Iona

Heavily restored **Iona Abbey** commands a green seaside knoll just beyond the village, and in its shadow is the much-more evocative **St Oran's Chapel,** from around 1150. Surrounding the mossy old walls is a relic from St Columba's time, the **Relig Odhráin** graveyard. Eternal residents include 48 Scottish kings, as well as 8 Norwegian and 4 Irish kings. Amid them is Odhráin, a companion of Columba who, according to legend, was a hard man to keep down. One story has it that Odhráin gamely stepped to the plate when Columba learned that the walls of the chapel he was building would collapse unless someone was buried alive within them. So, Odhráin was interred and the chapel built atop him, until one day he chose to stick his head out of the ground to announce, "There is no Hell as you suppose, or Heaven that people talk about." Columba quickly had the body reburied, lest the news muddy the message he was preaching. Another story claims that Odhráin died peacefully and was laid to rest, but Columba missed his friend so much that he had him exhumed for one more look. Odhráin was so pleased to see the light of day again that he tried to climb out of his grave, but Columba quickly piled dirt upon him again so his soul would not be tainted by the world and sin.

A stone cross rising near the graveyard along the so-called **Street of the Dead** is one of hundreds such markers that once stood on the island. Seeing these old relics, set amid emerald green seaside pastures flecked with sheep, it's easy to agree with essayist Samuel Johnson, who visited in 1774 and said, "The man is little to be envied . . . whose piety would not grow warmer among the ruins of Iona." Similarly moving is a beautiful, and beautifully named, beach on the western coast, **Bay at the Back of the Ocean,** a short trek of about 1 mile across the island.

Iona Abbey ★★ CHURCH/RELIGIOUS SITE   A shrine to St Columba from the 9th or 10th century still brings pilgrims to this much-restored abbey, as it has for centuries. The shrine remained intact through the centuries as the abbey was expanded continuously from the 12th through 15th centuries to accommodate the growing throngs of the faithful from throughout the British Isles and Ireland. Abandoned in the 16th century, the church was a derelict ruin when, in 1874, the 8th Duke of Argyll began restorations that continued well into the 20th century. Just beyond the lovely cloisters is a collection of early tombstones and other artifacts that include a stone pillow allegedly used by Columba himself. The abbey is run by Historic Scotland (www.historic-scotland.gov.uk), which leads tours and runs a coffee shop.

Iona. £7 adults, £6 students and seniors, £4 children 5 to 15. Daily 9:30am–4:30pm in winter, 9:30am–5:30pm in summer.

Staying on Iona

In the past, the **Iona Community** (www.iona.org.uk; ✆ **01681/700-404**) has led weeklong seminars in Iona abbey, though the guest quarters were closed in 2018 for extensive refurbishment. Check the website for updates.

STAFFA ★★

6¼ miles north of Iona

This tiny island was once home to a few hearty shepherds and farmers, but what's really just a grass-covered outcropping was never very hospitable and has long since been abandoned. These days the island is in the care of the National Trust for Scotland (www.nts.org.uk) and visitors come ashore for an hour or so to see **Fingal's Cave** ★★, known in Gaelic as *An Uaimh Bhinn,* or "musical cave," as well as to perch on the grassy bluffs and observe a colony of enchanting puffins who, from April through August, breed and nest on the sea ledges.

Essentials

GETTING THERE Staffa is accessible by tour boat from Fionnphort, timed to allow about an hour on the island before the return trip. For details, contact www.staffatours.com and see "Tours from Oban," p. 357.

Exploring Staffa

The island's famous cave, carved out of the basalt by crashing waves and swirling waters, emits an eerily harmonious sound that could pass for a symphony, with heavy use of drums and bass, of course, and the phenomenon has brought legions of visitors to the out-of-the-way island. The sounds inspired Mendelssohn to write the *Fingal's Cave Overture*, while Turner painted the cavern and Keats, Wordsworth, and Tennyson all praised it in their poetry, and even Queen Victoria came to witness and listen to the spectacle. They could walk deep into the cave, though storms have damaged the walkway and today's visitors settle for a look from a ledge next to the entrance and from the sea on one of the boats coming and going from the island.

Remarkable rock formations around the entrance and along the nearby shoreline are shaped into hexagonal pillars and perfectly squared-off blocks that look like they've been crafted by stonemasons. (The name of the island is from the Old Norse for "pillar.") Molten rock being spewed from undersea volcanoes formed into these shapes as they cooled in the seawater, but far more enticing is the legend that these are the very stones that Irish warrior Finn MacCool (Fingal) laid across the Irish Sea, with the similarly shaped basalt columns at Giant's Causeway on the coast of Northern Ireland forming the other end of his passage.

COLONSAY ★★

15 miles S of the Isle of Mull, 37 miles S of Oban

The western shores of this 20-square-mile island floating south of Mull face nothing but the open Atlantic—only a lighthouse stands between Colonsay and Canada. Joining the 130 or so islanders are sheep and wild goats with elegant horns and long shaggy hair, who staked a claim on the mountainsides after they swam ashore from a 16th-century Spanish shipwreck. Colonsay is as remote, quiet, and wild as it gets, and for most visitors, that's the appeal.

Essentials

A ferry operated by **Caledonian MacBrayne** (www.calmac.co.uk; ⓒ **0800/066-5400**) sails once daily between Oban and Colonsay. The crossing takes 2½ hours, and since the boat makes a quick turnaround, it's necessary to spend at least a night on the island.

Exploring Colonsay

A single-lane track connects **Scalasaig,** the island's only town, with a few other spots, but the only way to see much of the island is on two feet along some well-marked paths. Wherever you wander, you may encounter golden eagles, falcons, and bees—the island is a haven for the protected British black bee. Otters and seals cavort at **Ardskenish,** a lonely, 1/2-mile-long beach in the southwest, and **Kilhoran Bay,** a long stretch of white sand in the north. The island's outpost of civilization is the 1701 **Colonsay House** (www.colonsay.org.uk), once home to the MacNeill clan and, in the early 20th century, to Donald Smith, Baron Strathcona and Mount Royal (1820–1914). Smith built the Canadian Pacific Railroad, served as Canadian high commissioner to the United Kingdom and as governor of the Hudson's Bay Company, and he racked up a lengthy roster of other stellar accomplishments. Looking for a quiet place to retire, Smith bought Colonsay House, along with the rest of the island, in 1905 and put his energies to work directing a legion of gardeners to create an exotic Edwardian bower of rhododendrons, myrtles, magnolias, eucalyptus, and even palm trees. Less formal are the adjacent woodland gardens, where paths lead through fuchsias and ferns. The gardens are a bit overgrown, and though his lordship might raise an eyebrow, the lack of perfection and informality are part of the appeal. From April to October, the gardens are open on Wednesday from noon until 5pm, and on Friday from 2 to 5pm (admission £3). The adjacent woodland gardens are open 7 days a week all year round. **The Strand,** a mile-long sandy isthmus, connects Colonsay with the islet of **Oronsay,** where St Odhráin, a 6th-century disciple of St Columba (see Iona, above) is said to have established a beachhead of Christianity. The sparse ruins of a 14th-century priory poke up from the sandy soil, but don't spend too much investigating them, since the Strand is only passable within 2 hours of low tide.

Where to Eat & Stay on Colonsay

Isle of Colonsay Hotel ★   It's only fitting that remote and enchanting Colonsay should have a place like this stay, a mid-18th-century inn with gables and chimneys rising above herb and vegetable gardens next to the harbor. Fires burn in the welcoming downstairs lounges, while upstairs the bedrooms are small and simply furnished, with good beds and fine linens. A few share immaculate communal bathrooms, and some have views out to sea. The relaxed pub is the island's social center and serves just-landed seafood and local produce. The hotel also operates 16 self-catering cottages scattered across the island.

Scalasaig, Isle of Colonsay. www.colonsayholidays.co.uk. ⓒ **01951/200-316.** 12 units, 9 w/private bathroom. Double £70–£145, includes breakfast. **Amenities:** Restaurant; bar; library; bike and scooter rental; free Wi-Fi (in public rooms only).

COLL & TIREE ★

Coll: 50 miles W of Oban; Tiree: 68 miles W of Oban

Stark and tranquil, tiny Coll and Tiree are exposed to the open Atlantic, a position that comes with many pluses for outdoor enthusiasts. Prevailing winds push the clouds right over the minute land masses, and the islands get more sunshine than anywhere else in Britain. The windy islands, where every breeze carries the scent of sea and grass, are also havens for Arctic skuas, razorbills, and 150 other bird species, common and gray seals have breeding colonies along the rocky shorelines, and dolphins and porpoises swim in the surrounding waters.

Essentials

Loganair (www.loganair.co.uk) flies directly to Tiree from Glasgow. **Caledonian MacBrayne** (www.calmac.co.uk; ✆ **0800/066-5400**) sails daily from Oban to Coll (a 3-hr. trip) and Tiree (an extra 45 min.).

Exploring Coll & Tiree

Low-lying **Coll,** home to 190 hearty souls, stretches for some 13 miles along beach-lined coasts backed by tall sand dunes. **Breacachad Castle,** rising grimly above a chilly-looking seaside loch in the southeast, is a formidable looking tower house combined with the adjacent "New" Castle, added in 1750 and embellished with pepper-pot turrets and parapets. You won't be able to get inside unless you happen to be invited by one of the residents, who have included the Macleans, the island's lairds. In 1773 they took in British men of letters Samuel Johnson and James Boswell when they were stranded on the island for 10 days because of storms at sea. Johnson, impressed with the views of the sea, was an appreciative guest at first, calling the castle "a neat, new-built gentleman's house." As the days passed and Johnson became bored and cranky, he revised his opinion, saying "there is nothing becoming about it . . . a mere tradesmen's box" and, for that matter, time on the island was "a waste of life." Coll's most august landmarks are two standing stones, in the west near the settlement of Totronald. The **Na Sgeulachan ("Teller of Tales")** are believed to have been part of a temple complex from as early as the third century B.C.E. and were perhaps used for astronomical observations.

Fertile, flat **Tiree,** so low-lying it's known as the "land below the waves," is a bustling metropolis in comparison to Coll and many of its other neighbors. Most of the 800 residents are farmers and live in and around **Scarinish,** with its little stone harbor. They're faring better than their forbearers, who lived in the thatch-roofed cottages that still appear among the fields. Ordered off the land in the late 1880s, they were sent, destitute, to Canada and other far-off lands. The island's 36 miles of coastline are etched with coves that are a magnet for gulls, shags, guillemots, Arctic terns, skuas, and gannets, along with bird watchers who come to observe them. The **Ringing Stone,** on the northern coast near Vaul, balances precariously upon smaller stones and emits a metallic ring when struck. Islanders warn that it's best not to strike with too much force, since legend has it that if the stone ever topples over Tiree will sink into the sea.

Where to Stay & Eat on Coll & Tiree

Coll Hotel ★   Samuel Johnson and James Boswell rejected Coll's only inn as an inappropriate place to spend the night during their 18th-century tour of Scotland. (The pair eventually succeeded in securing lodgings with the laird of Coll at Breacachad Castle, see above.) That dubious honor aside, the nicely redone rooms present little to complain about these days, and downstairs, the island's only pub serves freshly caught fish and seafood.

Arinagour, Coll. www.collhotel.com. ℰ **01879/230-334.** 6 units. Doubles £95–£120, includes breakfast. **Amenities:** Restaurant; bar; free Wi-Fi.

Scarinish Hotel ★   Islanders gather here for a pint in front of the fire in the Lean To bar and for meals in the Old Harbour dining room, by far Tiree's best, albeit one of its only, restaurants, noted for local lamb and lobster. Homey bedrooms, likewise the best lodgings the island has to offer, are immaculate and share an airy lounge overlooking the harbor. Only six have private bathrooms, so specify when booking if that's a priority (two have nonconnecting private bathrooms across the hall).

Scarinish, Tiree. www.tireescarinishhotel.com. ℰ **01879/220-308.** 10 units, 6 with private bathroom. Doubles £70–£80, includes breakfast. **Amenities:** Restaurant; bar; free Wi-Fi.

RUM ★

8⅔ miles SW of the Isle of Skye

George Bullough, heir to an industrial fortune, who owned this storm-tossed volcanic outcropping in the early 20th century, must have been a bit of a snob. He added an "H" to the name, as he did not like being called "The Laird of Rum," lest he might be thought to be a vulgarian. Whether or not the "H" made any sort of difference in social circles is of little matter, because this square chunk of mountainous terrain, only about 8 miles wide and 8 miles long, seems far removed from any signs of civilization. Whether you spell it Rhum, or Rum, the island is remote, wild, beautiful, and wet, with more than 229cm (90 in.) of rainfall recorded annually. And since 1991, the official name is once again "Rum."

Essentials

A **Caledonian MacBrayne** (www.calmac.co.uk; ℰ **0800/066-5400**) passenger **ferry** sails between Mallaig, on the western coast of Scotland, and Rum about five times a week. Crossings are from April to October only. **Arisaig Marine** (www.arisaig.co.uk; ℰ **01687/450-224**) sails from Arisaig to Rum

May through September on Tuesdays and Thursdays; there are also crossings on Saturdays during June, July, and August. It takes about 2 hours to reach Rum from these ports.

Exploring Rum

Since the mid-1950s, Rum has been owned by the Edinburgh-based Nature Conservancy Council, an ecological conservation group, and the 22 islanders are all connected with the council in one way or the other. Red deer, feral goats, and wild ponies roam terrain that was once known as the "kingdom of the wild forest," while massive sea eagles, reintroduced in 1980s, sometimes soar among the heights. The Island of Rum Community Trust, www.isleo-frum.com, operates a visitor center near the pier (open daily in summer) as well a teashop and other services on the island. Scottish Natural Heritage manages much of the island and can provide a wealth of information at www.nature.scot.

Kinloch Castle ★ HISTORIC SIGHT   Sir George Bullough, a playboy and heir to an enormous textile fortune, spared no expense when he commissioned this huge and elaborate hunting lodge in 1897. A force of 300 stone masons, carpenters, and other craftsmen completed the house at a cost of $15 million. Included was a hydro plant that gave Kinloch the distinction of being the first residence in Scotland to be electrified, and, a bit more frivolously, an Orchestrion, an electric organ built for Queen Victoria, who died before it could be installed in Balmoral Castle. World War I and its economic aftermaths put an end to shooting parties, armies of servants and gardeners, and lavish balls, but much of the Edwardian grandeur remains, though decidedly faded and, given leaky roofs and missing window panes, a bit weather-worn. Even so, fascinating tours show off the ballroom, drawing rooms, bedrooms, and other musty corners, still filled with paintings and animal heads.

Rum, 20-minute walk from ferry terminal. www.isleofrum.com. ℗ **01687/462-026.** Guided tours £9 adults, £8 seniors and students, £4.50 children 6–12. Apr–Oct, tours on Mon at 1:15pm, Tues, Wed, and Sun at 2pm, Thurs at 2:15pm, Fri at 2:30pm.

EIGG & MUCK ★

Eigg: 4 miles SE of Rhum; Muck: 6¾ miles SW of Eigg

These tiny islands aren't near the top of most European itineraries, but they deliver remoteness, a sense of stepping back into the 19th century, if not an earlier time, and the company of golden eagles and seals.

Essentials

GETTING THERE **Caledonian MacBrayne** (www.calmac.co.uk; ℗ **0800/066-5400**) sails from Mallaig to Eigg three times a week. From Arisaig, south of Mallaig, **Arisaig Marine** (℗ **01687/450-224**) sails to Muck May through September on Mondays, Wednesdays, and Fridays; there are also crossings on Sundays during June, July, and August.

Exploring Eigg & Muck

The 70 or so farmers, shepherds, and fishermen who live on **Eigg** raised the US$2.4 million to buy their island in 1997. Included in that price tag was a famous natural landmark, the **Sgurr of Eigg,** a tall column of lava that soars to 394m (1,300-ft.). A fairly steep but well-worn path mounts the summit, where it's said that the last of the pterodactyls roosted on the Sgurr—and it's easy to imagine them sharing the aerie with you. On the shores below, a long white beach follows **Laig Bay** and faces the mountains of Rum, while the beach of the **Singing Sands** takes its name from the melodic squeaks the quartz pebbles emit when trod upon.

All of **Muck,** 6¾ miles southwest of Eigg, is a farm (www.isleofmuck.com) owned by two brothers, the Laird of Muck, Lawrence MacEwan, and Ewen MacEwan. The name of this 2½-square-mile island was originally a Gaelic word, *muic,* meaning "island of the sow," though Eigg is these days home to sheep and cows, as well as to large colonies of nesting seabirds in May and June. When the 30 or so islanders yearn for a view of the wider world, they need only climb **Ben Airean,** at 137m (450 ft.), the highest hill, for a panoramic view across the waters to neighboring Rum and Eigg.

THE ISLE OF SKYE ★★★

83 miles W of Inverness; 176 miles NW of Edinburgh; 146 miles NW of Glasgow

Crossing the Sound of Sleat onto Scotland's second-largest island has the transformative effect of the wave of a magician's wand. Few places on earth are as transporting as this near-mystical land of heather-carpeted moors, weird rock formations, mossy glens, green headlands, boulder-strewn beaches, craggy saw-toothed mountains, and transformative seascapes. Oh yes, and frolicking lambs, nesting puffins, cavorting seals, bubbling brooks and gushing cascades, ever-changing skies, white-sand beaches, brooding lochs . . . well, suffice it to say this chunk of rock some 50 miles long, from 3 to 25 miles wide, and shaped like a butterfly or, to some, a lobster, is appealing in many, many ways (not the least of which is a convenient link to the mainland via a road bridge).

Skye can be crowded, especially in July and August, but it's always possible to find a lonely place to sit and contemplate a velvety hillside or silvery sea. It's harder in this busy season to find a place to stay, so book well in advance. The weather is notoriously *dreich*—it's not by accident that Skye is from the Old Norse for "Cloud Island"—but at some point on the long summer days the sun, and a rainbow or two, are likely to appear, enhancing the magic all that much more.

Essentials

GETTING THERE By **car,** from Kyle of Lochalsh, 82 miles southwest of Inverness and 125 miles north of Oban, drive west along the ½ mile Skye Road Bridge over the Strait of Sleat to Kyleakin. Another popular approach to

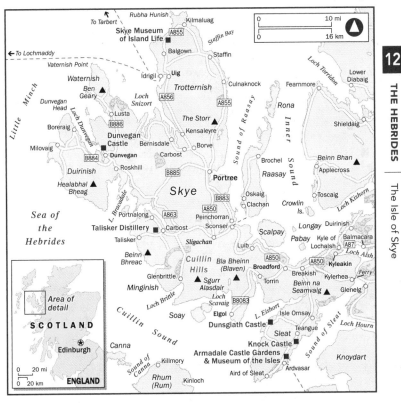

Skye is via **ferry** between the mainland town of Mallaig, 104 miles southwest of Inverness, and the port of Armadale, with as many eight 30-minute crossings a day. This is not a good option if you're traveling by public transport, since bus service onward to the rest of the island from Armadale is very limited. For ferry information, contact **Caledonian MacBrayne** (www.calmac.co.uk; ✆ **0800/066-5400**). **CityLink buses** (www.citylink.co.uk) make runs to and from Port William through Kyle of Lochash on the mainland and from there across the Skye Bridge, with service to and from Kyleaikin, Portree, and Uig.

GETTING AROUND   For all its popularity, Skye has limited public transportation and getting around without a car can be a real challenge. **CityLink** (www.citylink.co.uk) buses connect Kyleakin, Portree, and Uig. Service operates several times a day, so you can use the buses to get to some of the main towns on Skye, but venturing off this main corridor can be difficult and time-consuming. **Stagecoach** (www.stagecoachbus.com) operates local bus services, with routes into the west of the island and around the north end, but

371

many of these runs are geared to school schedules, with most service in the early morning and late afternoon. If you plan on getting around without a car, you'll be better off staying in Portree, a good choice because of its central location, or another town that's on one of the main bus routes. A good way to see a lot of the island is to sign on to one of the many **day tours** that operate out of Portree and make stops at the major sights. **Go Skye** (www.go-skye.co.uk; ✆ **01470/532-264**) and **Real Scottish Journeys** (www.realscottishjourneys.com; ✆ **01470/532-428**) Skye Bus tours are among many that make stops at the Fairy Pools, Nest Point, Fairy Glen, Old Man of Storr, and other top spots, and the journey across the scenic countryside is accompanied by commentary enriched with a lot of Scottish smooth talk.

VISITOR INFORMATION The Tourist Information Centre is at Bayfield House, Bayfield Road in Portree (www.isleofskye.com; ✆ **01478/612-992**). It's open Monday to Saturday 9am to 5pm (6pm in the summer) and Sunday 10am to 4pm.

Exploring the Isle of Skye

A slow-paced road trip along Skye's single tracks through heart-stopping scenery is easily one of Scotland's best experiences. Allow at least three days to get a taste of Skye, with one day seeing the Fairy Pools, the Quiraing, and other top scenic sights, another sailing across Loch Scavaig into the Cuillin mountains, and a third taking in Dunvegan Castle or some other outpost of iconic Skye civilization, with timeout to sit on a grassy seaside at Nest Point or another scenery-saturated spot and soak in the views.

Kyleakin & the South of Skye ★★

On its southern flanks, Skye stretches along the Strait of Sleat. The landscapes are a little gentler and greener than they are on the rest of the island, but as you drive north from Kyleakin, at the end of the Skye Bridge, the landscapes become bleaker and lonelier. Heather-carpeted moors stretch toward the Cuillins (pronounced *Cool*-lins), the saw-toothed mountains that rise in a horseshoe-shape in the middle of the island with a dozen of the 17 peaks topping 3,000 feet.

Armadale Castle, Gardens & Museum of the Isles ★ MUSEUM   If you're arriving by ferry from Mallaig, you can immediately fall under the island's spell just down the road from the pier in these lush gardens surrounding the romantic ruins of Armadale Castle, onetime home of Clan MacDonald and seat of a 20,000-acre estate. The house was destroyed by fire in the 19th century, rebuilt with an abundance of Gothic bravado, and abandoned in 1925 and left to molder, windows and doorways agape. The baronial stables house an excellent café, but before sitting down for some refreshment take time to step through the Museum of the Isles for a head-spinning journey through 1,500 years of Highlands and island history, from clan warfare, cattle raids, and the Clearances, when families were forced off the land to make way for sheep, who turned a better profit. On a charmingly light note, homage is paid to Greyfriars Bobby, the little Skye terrier who for 14 years loyally sat upon the grave of his master, an Edinburgh policeman, until passing away himself in 1872.

Armadale. www.armadalecastle.com. © **01471/844-305.** £8.50 adults, £6.95 seniors and children aged 5–15. Apr–Oct daily 9:30am–5:30pm (last entry at 5pm).

Bright Water Visitor Centre ★ MUSEUM/NATURE RESERVE
Author and naturalist Gavin Maxwell lived in an old lighthouse keeper's cottage on Eilean Ban from 1968 until his death 1969. He was by then a celebrity with the success of his book *Ring of Bright Water*, and the island is still a place of pilgrimage for fans. The visitor center, on the pier in Kyleakin across the straits on Skye, celebrates the author's life and work, while a statue on the quayside out front honors Teko, one of his otter companions. Maxwell, aristocratic and well-educated, was a complex and romantic figure who loved adventure and fast cars and was a gifted writer and passionate conservationist. The book that would become a bestseller began to take shape when Maxwell returned from Iraq in the 1950s with a pet otter cub, Mijbil. Guided tours of the island show off the elegant, comfortable Long Room where Maxwell relaxed and wrote, and though the Skye Bridge looms overhead and the cottage and gardens are a lot noisier than they were in Maxwell's day, they manage to evoke the natural beauty and allure of the coastal setting and why the world traveler said, "I felt drawn to Kyleakin as I had to few places in my life. I felt as if I were coming home."

The Pier, Kyleakin. www.eileanban.org. © **01599/530-040.** Center: Free. Guided tours: £8 adults, £7 seniors and children, £22 families. Access to the island is via a wooden gate on the Skye Bridge. Apr–Oct Mon–Fri 10am–4pm, tours at 2pm.

Elgol ★★★ This straggling little fishing village, 22 miles southwest of Kyleakin, has a huge star attraction: a spectacular outlook across moody Loch Scavaig into the craggy Cuillins. On a clear day, the jaw-dropping views across the wind-whipped waters figuratively pull you into the heart of the savage mountains, and you can get there literally on a boat trip (see Outdoor Activities, below) across the loch and from there by foot into the flanks of the steep slopes. Boats will ferry you across the water to a pier at the head of the loch, from where a fairly easy path follows the Scavaig River through the bleak landscape to freshwater Loch Coruisk. The chilly waters are reputedly the home of an elusive seahorse that chooses to make an appearance from time to time. Also evasive are views of the enclosing mountains, of which, as Alfred, Lord Tennyson, observed, "only the extremist tiptoes" might be visible, "all else being thick wool-white fog." Novelist Sir Walter Scott waxed poetically, with a bit of his typical purplish hyperbole, "Rarely human eye has known a scene so stern as that dread lake with its dark ledge of barren stone."

Eliean Ban ★ Most travelers crossing the Skye Bridge may not even be aware that they're zooming over 2.5-hectare (6-acre) Eliean Ban. Floating in the straits between Kyle of Lochalsh on the mainland and Kyleakin on Skye, the little island is a stepping stone in the two-part bridge—a low-level crossing connects the mainland with Eilean Ban, where a busy road continues onto a gracefully arched span toward Skye. Eilean Ban has always been a place between: Drovers used to swim their cattle from grazing lands on Skye to Eilean Ban and from there across the straits to markets in mainland towns. Legend has it that "Saucy Mary," a 10th-century Norse princess, made a fortune when she strung chains to Skye from one side of Eilean Ban and to the mainland from the other side and extracted tolls from passing boats. The island enjoys some fame as the onetime home of author and naturalist Gavin Maxwell (1914–1969). Maxwell's 1960 classic *Ring of Bright Water,* about life on the coast with pet otters, was made into a popular film and is one of the best-selling nature books of all time, still an inspiration to wildlife enthusiasts around the world. See the Bright Water Visitor Centre, above.

The Fairy Pools ★★★   The chilly River Brittle flows out of the Cuillins near the village of Glenbrittle, 35 miles west of Kyleakin, through a series of enchanting falls and pools, creating a magical landscape and one of Scotland's most popular natural attractions. A well-worn path fords the bubbling stream via boulders at a couple of spots and leads across heather-clad moors to the crystal-clear pools. The bone-chilling waters don't deter enthusiasts who can't resist a swim, or at least a toe dip, in some of the world's most beautiful swimming holes. You can make the mile-long-walk from the car park up to the pools and back in about an hour, though you might be so enchanted that you'll want to linger by the side of a pool for a bit and count the moss-covered stones at the bottom.

Portree & the North ★★★

Skye goes for broke in the north, where weird rock formations, towering sea cliffs, and supernatural landscapes build up to a scenic crescendo on the spectacular Trotternish Peninsula, the island's northernmost point of land. Set amid all this natural splendor is Portree, 33 miles northwest Kyleakin and the island's largest and prettiest town, with a quaintly Victorian square set above a snug harbor lined with a row of brightly painted houses. Most folks linger in Uig, 15 miles northwest of Portree, only long enough to hop on or off one of the ferries to and from Uist and Harris, in the Outer Hebrides. If you happen to be passing through in the evening, you may be treated to some of the island's most spectacular sunsets from this west-facing port. A drive north along the coast from Portree, then across the Trotternish Peninsula to Uig, plunges you into some of the island's most stunning scenery.

Fairy Glen ★★   It's pretty well accepted fact that fairies created this magical landscape as their own enchanted domain, where they can dance and cavort amid the cone-shaped hills, craggy spires, and little lochs. It's said you can hear them playing the pipes at night, though naysayers say that's just the wind rustling through Castle Ewan, a tall outcropping that looks like the ruins of some laird's domain. Whatever the truth might be, it's best not to try to join the fairies in their nightly frolics. The story goes that an unfortunate fellow named Alistair once ventured into the glen at night to play the pipes with the wee folk and returned home to find that, fairy time being quite a bit different from that of humans, a hundred years had passed and his wife, children, and friends were long gone. Even if fairy music doesn't guide you, the reward for a scramble to the top of Castle Ewan is a fine view over the grassy glen. Fairy Glen is down a small road east of Uig, from a well-marked turning at the Uig Hotel.

Kilmuir ★   This village on the northwest coast of the Trotternish Peninsula, 6 miles north of Uig, is tiny but plays large in the history of Skye. In 1746, Prince Charles Edward Stuart, aka Bonnie Prince Charlie, born in exile in Rome and having little knowledge of Scotland or even a mastery of English, managed to raise an army of Highlanders and enlist the aid of the French in his ill-fated attempts to claim the British throne. After a final defeat at Culloden, and with a stiff bounty on his head, he managed to escape to the Hebrides. In hiding on South Uist, he met Fiona MacDonald, who was smitten with the handsome young prince and smuggled him to Skye disguised as her Irish maidservant. The couple was betrayed by a loose-lipped boatman while living at Mactintosh House outside Kilmuir. Charles was exiled to France, and after a life of dissipation and drunkenness, died in Rome in 1788. Fiona was sent to the Tower of London, released after a year, and in 1774 emigrated to America. She returned to Scotland and is buried in Kilmuir churchyard.

Kilt Rock ★★   About 15 miles north of Portree, a viewpoint overlooks an imposing sea cliff laced with basalt pillars that resemble the pleats of the eponymous garment. From the heights of the cliffs, Mealt Waterfall tumbles more than 200 feet into the sea.

Old Man of Storr ★★   This jagged volcanic outcrop is the highest of many oddly shaped rock pinnacles in the Storr section of the Trotternish Ridge, formed by a massive landslide in ancient times. The resemblance to an old man not only gives one of Scotland's most iconic natural wonders its name but, on this island so steeped in myth, has fostered more than a few tales about the pinnacles' origins. It's said the rock and a smaller one nearby are the work of fairies who turned to stone an elderly couple who wished to never be apart. It's also believed that the rock is the thumb of a giant buried deep in the earth. You can contemplate these matters as you walk across the pinnacle-littered terrain or make the not-too-challenging climb of about 160 feet to the top of the Old Man; it's about 45 minutes through the magical landscape to the top from the car park, 7 miles north of Portree.

The Quiraing ★★★   Just when you think this island could not deliver another scenic punch, the northeast coast explodes into a remarkable landscape where rocky peaks and bluffs rise above hidden gullies and plateaus. The name, from the Norse, means "round fold," and the natural formations once provided a place to hide cattle from invading Vikings. You can get a glimpse of the Quiraing from a car park about 9 miles northeast of Uig off the

Uig–Staffin road, from where a path loops for about 4 miles through the surreal landscape.

Skye Museum of Island Life ★ MUSEUM/HISTORIC PLACE Seven thatch-roofed cottages transport you back in time to life in the Hebrides as it was a century ago. An aromatic peat fire and snug box beds evoke domestic coziness, but the looms, grinding stones, and other primitive tools show just how hardscrabble life in the islands was at a time when flour was ground, butter was churned, and yarn was spun.

Kilmuir. www.skyemuseum.co.uk. ⓒ **01470/552-206.** £3 adults, 50p children 5–16. Easter–Oct, Mon–Sat, 9:30am–5pm.

Dunvegan & the West ★★

In Dunvegan, 21 miles west of Portree at the head of Loch Dunvegan, you may encounter cows wandering down to the harbor to take a plunge in the River Osdale where it flows into the loch. Rural as the small village is, Dunvegan is an important place, the seat of Clan MacLeod for the past 800 years. Just about the only man who could argue that the MacLeod's aren't the biggest wigs around is Angus MacAskill (1825–1863), who stood 7 feet 8 inches tall and weighed 425 pounds. He still holds the record as Scotland's tallest man, and the little, thatch-roofed **Giant Angus MacAskill Museum** ★ (ⓒ **01470/521-296**) in the village center chronicles Angus' exploits, which included lifting a horse over a fence and his appearance in traveling shows alongside Tom Thumb, the shortest man of the time. The museum is open Easter through October daily, 9:30am to 6pm; admission is £2.

The big show in town, though, is wildly romantic looking **Dunvegan Castle,** the moated MacLeod domain on the loch about 1 miles east of Dunvegan. The MacLeods have also appropriated nearby **Healabhal Mhòr,** so-called the "MacLeod Table" because it's said the lairds would hold banquets atop the flat-topped mastiff, with clansmen standing around the table holding torches. Legend has it that a MacLeod chieftain once visited Edinburgh Castle, where he was made to feel like a country bumpkin as he dined beneath the frescoed ceilings. So, he invited a royal party to Dunvegan, led a procession up Healabhal Mhòr to enjoy a feast, and during the meal pointed to the star-filled sky and announced that the spectacle far outshone any painted firmament.

Coral Beach, 3 miles north of Dunvegan outside the tiny hamlet of Claigan, might transport you to the tropics—at least on a sunny day, when white crystalized seaweed on the seabed can cause the water to glisten a startling shade of blue. The isolated strand is about a 25-minute walk along a well-marked farm track.

Dunvegan Castle ★ CASTLE/HISORIC HOME The chiefs of Clan MacLeod have occupied their ancestral seat for the past 800 years, making this formidable redoubt commanding a rocky promontory above Loch Dunvegan Britain's oldest continually inhabited castle. Once upon a time, the

A Dunvegan Fairy Tale

As the story goes, a handsome MacLeod chieftain married a fairy princess, though it was agreed that the couple would share the earthly realm for only a year to spare the pretty maiden the sadness of watching the prince grow old while she, like all fairies, remained eternally youthful. At the end of that time, the princess departed for the fairy world, leaving her bereft husband and a baby behind. The princess requested that the baby never be allowed to cry, as she could not bear the sound. But on the night of a ball the nursemaids crept down the hall to watch the merriment, and in their absence the baby began to wail. When the nurses returned they found the infant swaddled in silk and the sounds of a beautiful lullaby filling the room. Only the infant could see his mother, who left the cloth behind, and for good measure she imbued it with magic powers. A wave of the so-called Fairy Flag is said to protect the clan from harm, but this talisman can only be used three times. Once the MacLeods used the power to repel an attack by the rival MacDonalds, who vastly outnumbered them, and a second time they waved the flag to revive their cattle herds when the beasts were stricken by an epidemic. Dame Flora MacLeod vowed to wave the flag over the White Cliffs of Dover in the event of a German invasion during World War II, but she never had need to do so. This means the MacLeods have one protective wave left.

castle was only accessible via a steep stone stairway cut into the rock and through a sea gate, but these days a gracious drive crosses the grassy moat to the front portico, and acres of appealing lawns and gardens fall away from the landward side of the somber stone walls. Many of these refinements, including fake battlements and pepper-pot towers, came with a 19th-century restoration that brought centuries' worth of scattered towers and halls together in a then-popular style known as "baronization" to create a romantically magical kingdom to befit a lord. Ornately decorated staterooms show off family heirlooms and a menagerie of stuffed hunting trophies, but most treasured of all is a battered bit of brown silk known as the Fairy Flag, reputed to bring the clan good luck (see box above). Rory Mor's Drinking Horn is kept on hand for the inauguration of a new clan chief, who's known as the MacLeod of MacLeod and must drink the entire contents, almost two bottles of wine, in one gulp. The castle makes an especially imposing appearance from the loch, and castle boatmen escort visitors across the waters for the view, along with a close-up look at seals and herons.

Dunvegan. www.dunvegancastle.com. © **01470/521-206.** The castle is open daily: Apr to mid-Oct daily 10am–5:30pm. £14 adults; £11 seniors; £9 children 5–15; £34 families of 2 adults and 4 children. Gardens only: £12 adults, £9 seniors, £7 children. 25-minute boat trips operate Apr–Sept daily, 10am–5:30pm; £7.50 adults with castle or garden ticket; £6.50 seniors; £5.50 children.

Neist Point ★★★ The most westerly spur of Skye, 11 miles west of Dunvegan, is a magical seascape of cliffs and high bluffs carpeted in emerald green, flecked white here and there with grazing sheep. At the end of the long, meadow-topped headland is a now-disused and highly photogenic lighthouse, a lonely sentry looking out toward the North Atlantic (with some of the Outer Hebrides floating on the near horizon). The waters below the point are the domain of whales and basking sharks, while gannets, guillemots, and other seabirds nest on the cliffs. The walk out to the lighthouse and back is along a well-maintained path, steep in places and stepped in others, and takes about an hour, with some strenuous uphill exertion on the trip back up. If the weather's fine, you'll want to meander off the path to find a view-filled perch on the edge of the cliffs, but heed the well-posted advice to use caution.

Where to Stay & Eat on Skye

Big news around Britain every summer is that police are turning motorists away from crossing the Skye Bridge. That's an exaggeration, though police have on occasion warned incoming travelers that unless they have booked in advance they're unlikely to find a place to stay on the island. Rumors also abound that islanders are making small fortunes renting out tents in their yards or charging hefty fees to park a trailer in their drives. While some of this is hyperbole, suffice it to say that space is tight on Skye in the busy months of July and August, and you'd be wise to heed the advice not to venture onto the island without a reservation. At any time, you might want to include Airbnb (www.airbnb.com) listings in your accommodation search, since many home-owners on Skye rent out cottages or one or two rooms in their homes.

KYLEAKIN & THE SOUTH

Café Sia ★★ No trip across the island is complete without a stop at this lively little cafe in central Broadford, where a terrace faces the Cuillin mountains. What just about anyone agrees are the island's best pizzas come out of the wood-fired ovens, and for a full meal these can be paired with seafood specials, salads, or sandwiches and washed down with cocktails and wines. The in-house Skye Roastery provides what is claimed to be "the best cup of coffee on the Isle of Skye."

Broadford. www.cafesia.co.uk. ℂ **01471/822-616.** Main courses from £7. Daily 9:30am–9:30pm.

Hotel Eilean Iarmain ★★ The former home of Gaelic scholar Sir Ian Noble overlooks the Isle of Ornsay Lighthouse and makes no pretense to being smart or stylish, and is about as comfortably traditional as you'd expect. In the homey lounges, saggy sofas and slipcovered armchairs surround the logs fires, and the bedrooms are decidedly lived-in, though charmingly done with old-fashioned tongue-and-groove paneling and chintz; they're divided between the main house and a cottage, while 4 suites are in the converted stable block. Musicians sometimes perform in the paneled bar, and a charmingly formal dining room is the setting for excellent candlelight suppers.

Isle of Ornsay, Sleat. www.eileaniarmain.co.uk. ℂ **01471/833-332.** 16 units. Doubles £120–£190, includes breakfast. **Amenities:** Restaurant; bar; room service; free Wi-Fi.

Kinloch Lodge ★★   The 16th-century home of the MacDonald Clan on the Sound of Sleat has earned great acclaim in recent decades as a hotel, restaurant, and cooking school overseen by Lady Claire MacDonald, a renowned cookbook author and wife of the clan chief. Their daughter, Isabella, now oversees the elegant hotel and renowned restaurant, and stepping into lounges filled with family heirlooms and paintings, or strolling in the beautiful grounds is, as always, a memorable experience, as is a meal in the tartan-swathed restaurant under the watchful eyes of the MacDonald ancestors on the walls. Spacious guests rooms are in the old house and a tasteful new wing and combine traditional chintzes and plaids with some contemporary touches, and many are filled with sea views.

Isle of Ornsay, Sleat. www.kinloch-lodge.co.uk. ℗ **01471/833-333.** 19 units. Doubles £220–£350, includes breakfast. Tasting menus from £70. **Amenities:** Restaurant; bar; free Wi-Fi.

Sligachan Hotel ★   One of the island's oldest coaching inns, a fixture on the main road between Portree and Kyleakin since 1830, is in the shadow of the darkly dramatic Cuillin hills and has been a popular base for walkers and climbers for almost two centuries (and even has its own mountaineering museum). Guests can enjoy fishing in the sea loch that washes against the grounds, angle for salmon in on the Sligachan River, rent a boat or fish for trout in the Storr Lochs, or set off on hiking expeditions, well mapped out by resident experts. With so much to do outdoors, guests don't seem to mind that their quarters are more comfortable and functional than luxurious, and the restaurant, two bars, and a microbrewery are especially handy since there's nowhere else to go in tiny Sligachan village in the evening.

Sligachan. www.sligachan.co.uk. ℗ **01478/650-204.** 21 units. Doubles £100–£160, includes breakfast. **Amenities:** Restaurant; 2 bars; room service; free Wi-Fi.

PORTREE & THE NORTH

The Cuillin Hills Hotel ★   Another island retreat of the MacDonald Clan was built in 1820 and lends itself well to its current guise as an unfussy country hotel, set on 15 acres but just outside Portree and overlooking the bay and the Cuillin hills. Sofa-filled lounges are welcoming, all the more so when you're perched in front of a fire with one of many single malts on offer, and guest rooms are large and some have views out to the sea and mountains; a choice few enjoy the outlook from sitting areas tucked into bay windows. Dinner in the restaurant or bar is an appealing option when even the short walk into town seems like just too much of an effort.

Portree. www.cuillinhills-hotel-skye.co.uk. ℗ **01478/612-003.** 27 units. Doubles £210–£310, includes breakfast. **Amenities:** 2 restaurants; bar; room service; free Wi-Fi.

The Isle of Skye Baking Company ★★ CAFE/BAKERY   An old woolen mill on the edge of Portree houses this excellent bakery (with delicious filled lunch breads) and a homey cafe that's a favorite spot to while away an hour or two (or longer, when the weather turns wet). The Skyeworks gallery upstairs shows off some handsome island crafts and works by some of the island's more accomplished painters.

The Old Woolen Mill, Dunvegan Rd., Portree. www.isleofskyebakingco.co.uk. ℂ **01478/612-669.** Mon–Sat 9am–5pm, Sun 10am–4pm.

The Pink Guesthouse ★ It's hard to miss this colorful fixture on Portree's harbor, where guest rooms ramble through a couple of attached houses. Accommodations are pleasantly functional and nicely equipped, with firm, low-slung beds, and a choice few have water views. A friendly staff serves an excellent made-to-order breakfast, and a welcome perk is free parking on the wharf out front, handy for sightseeing.

1 Quay St., Portree. www.pinkguesthouse.co.uk. ℂ **01478/612-263.** 11 units. Doubles £85–£120, includes breakfast. **Amenities:** Free Wi-Fi.

Viewfield House ★★★ In this fine old house overlooking Portree Bay, fire-warmed sitting rooms show off antiques and curios, wooden floors are strewn with Persian rugs, and gilt framed oil paintings hang on the walls alongside antlers. The old-fashioned Scottish house party atmosphere is the real McCoy, or in this case, MacDonalds, who have lived here for more than 200 years. They host their guests in enormous bedrooms with brass beds and lots of polished pieces, along with fireplaces and freestanding bathtubs. All have views over the 8 hectares (20 acres) of woodlands and gardens, and the few in front look out to sea. The center of Portree is just a 10-minute walk away.

Portree. www.viewfieldhouse.com. ℂ **01478/612-217.** 11 units. Doubles £120–£150, includes breakfast. **Amenities:** Restaurant; free Wi-Fi.

DUNVEGAN & THE WEST

Roshkill House ★ No country house atmosphere here—this plain white cottage was once the village post office, and a utilitarian, rustic charm still prevails in the stone-walled sitting room and comfortable bedrooms, done in neutral tones with handsome oak furniture. The location in the bucolic northwest corner of the island is a real plus, putting Nest Point and Dunvegan Castle a short drive away, and Portree is within easy reach when bright lights beckon.

Roshkill by Dunvegan. www.roskhillhouse.co.uk. ℂ **01470/521-317.** 6 units. Doubles £85, includes breakfast. **Amenities:** Lounge; free Wi-Fi.

Skeabost Hotel ★★ The Clan MacDonald built up this estate as a hunting lodge in 1851, and the lawns and gardens on the shores of Loch Snizort are still a privileged retreat, all the more so now that they surround a private 9-hole golf course and fishing rights along 8 miles of the River Snizort. A paneled drawing room and billiard room deliver on the country house ambience, and a beautifully carved staircase leads to comfortable, traditionally done bedrooms in a variety of shapes and sizes, while smaller rooms in a garden cottage are contemporary and open to large decks. Just down the road is an ancient island cemetery where you can see the graves of four Crusaders.

Skeabost Bridge. www.skeabosthotel.com. ℂ **01470/532-202.** 14 units. Doubles £90–£170, includes breakfast. **Amenities:** 2 restaurants; 2 bars; 9-hole golf course; room service; free Wi-Fi.

Stein Inn ★   The island's oldest inn, from 1790, wears its age well, serving solid bar food and whiskies in snug paneled rooms and on a sunny terrace overlooking Loch Bay. The kitchen serves up big platters of Skye mussels and scallops, with a good selection of steaks and chops from local butchers. Upstairs are five homey bedrooms.

Waternish. www.stein-inn.co.uk. *ⓒ* **01470/592-362.** 6 units. Doubles £85–£195, includes breakfast. Main courses £10–£18. Mon–Sat noon–4pm and 6–9:30pm, Sun 12:30–4pm and 6:30–9pm.

Three Chimneys Restaurant and the House Over-By ★★★

SCOTTISH   An old cottage is chicly cozy, with low-slung ceilings and roaring fires and acclaimed cuisine that is as carefully staged as the surroundings. This temple of gastronomy in such a far-flung spot has achieved much fame and many awards over the past 3 decades and continues to emphasize local produce and of course, freshly caught fish and seafood and even wild game from Skye's mountains. Such dishes as mussels with cauliflower and scallops with artichokes are all sourced from patches of land and sea within sight of the kitchen door and are served on set tasting menus, including the Skye Showcase. Six suites, done up with soothingly spare Scandinavian flair, are in a cottage across the road and offer such luxuries as separate sitting areas (many are split level) and views of Loch Dunvegan.

Colbost. www.threechimneys.co.uk. *ⓒ* **01470/511-258.** 6 units Double £345, includes breakfast. Fixed-price dinner £60 for 3 courses, £90 for 8 courses; lunch £37 for 3 courses. Dinner daily 6:15–9:45pm; lunch mid-Mar to mid-Nov Mon–Sat 12:15–1:45pm.

Outdoor Activities on Skye

BIKING   **Island Cycles ★★,** Portree (www.islandcycles-skye.co.uk; *ⓒ* **01478/613-121**) charges £10 to £18 a day and dispenses a load of advice on routes. The shop is open Monday through Saturday from 9am to 5pm.

BOATING   **Bella Jane Boat Trips ★★★,** The Harbourfront, Elgol (www. bellajane.co.uk; *ⓒ* **01471/866-244**) provides one of the island's most scenic outings, from Elgol across Loch Scavaig into the craggy Cuillins. You're left at the base of the hills to wander for 90 minutes then returned over water to Elgol. The trip lasts 3 hours and costs £28 per person, £16 for children 4 to 12 (children under 4 go free). If you're up for more hiking, you can extend the experience to a full day. One option is to take the boat trip (one-way only) from Elgol into the Cuillins then follow the brown-and-white signs across an undulating, rock-strewn landscape for about 10 miles to the Sligachan Hotel (see above).

GOLF   The island's best course is the 9-hole **Isle of Skye Golf Club ★** (www.isleofskyegolfclub.co.uk; *ⓒ* **01478/650-414**) in the hamlet of Sconser, on the southeast coast. Maintained by the local municipality, it has a simple snack bar and pub, and an on-again, off-again employee who cuts the grass when necessary.

HIKING Any branch of Skye's **Tourist Information Centre** will offer advice on the many hikes available through the heather and glens of the island. An excellent online resource is the "Walks" section of www.isleofskye.com.

Shopping on Skye

Craft Encounters ★★ At this artists' showplace you'll find pewter jewelry, stained-glass light catchers, salt-dough bric-a-brac, folk and landscape paintings, tartan ties, and handmade jumpers (sweaters). Celtic patterns show up on glassware, tableware, linens, and pieces of marquetry. The island's musical talent is represented in a selection of traditional Scottish music CDs. Old Post Office building, Broadford. ✆ **01471/822-754.**

Edinbane Pottery ★★ Artists here produce wood-fired stoneware and salt-glazed pottery, and they can fill custom orders in a wide range of finishes. On the A850, 8 miles east of Dunvegan. www.edinbane-pottery.co.uk. ✆ **01470/582-234.**

Ragamuffin ★★ Quality Scottish, Irish, and British hand-knits for the whole family include beautiful sweaters, along with such accessories as hats, gloves, and scarves. On the pier in Armadale. ✆ **01471/844-217.**

Skye Batik ★ Wall hangings and cotton, tweed, wool, and linen clothing are hand-printed with Celtic designs from the 6th to the 8th centuries. The Green, Portree. www.skyebatiks.com. ✆ **01478/613-331.**

Skye Original Prints at Portree ★ Artist Tom Mackenzie's etchings, prints, aquatints, and greeting cards are all inspired by the scenery and day-to-day life of the island. 1 Wentworth St. Portree. ✆ **01478/612-544.**

Skye Silver ★★ This decades-old studio designs and produces silver and gold jewelry, ceramic tiles, chessboards, platters, and clocks, all featuring intricate Celtic patterns. Old School, Glendale Rd. 6¾ miles west of Dunvegan. www.skyesilver.com. ✆ **01470/511-263.**

BARRA ★★

60 miles W of the Isle of Skye, 93 miles NW of Oban

Extraordinary-looking Kismul Castle, or the Rock in the Bay, guards the entrance to 19th-century Castlebay, Barra's capital and ferry terminus. At the northern end of the island, planes land on the white sands of Cockle Strand, one of the few airports in the world inundated by the tides. These distinctive ports of entry aside, the island is also one of the most beautiful in the Hebrides, with heather-clad meadows, beaches, sandy grasslands, peaks, rocky bays, and headlands ranging beneath **Ben Heaval,** Barra's highest mountain at 379 meters (1,243 ft.).

Barra is the southernmost of the Outer Hebrides, also known as the Western Isles. These isolated islands lie about 40 miles off the mainland, floating at the far the western edge of Europe, and the bare, often austere landscapes are a haven for birds and other wildlife that flourish in many places largely untouched by human intervention. Many of the people who live on these islands are as likely to speak Scottish Gaelic as they are English. From Barra the Outer Hebrides stretch for 130 miles north through Lewis, and via a network of causeways and short ferry hops you can drive the length of the chain.

Essentials

GETTING THERE At the northern end of Barra is **Cockle Strand,** the airport. A long and wide beach of white sand, it's the only runway in Britain that's washed twice daily by sea tides. The Scottish airline **Loganair** (www. loganair.co.uk) flies here from Glasgow.

Barra can be reached from Oban on the mainland and from Eriskay on South Uist by **Caledonian MacBrayne** car ferries (www.calmac.co.uk; *©* **0800/066-5400**). The 5-hour crossings from and to Oban operates once a day in each direction.

VISITOR INFORMATION The **Castlebay Tourist Information Centre** (*©* **01871/810-336**) is near the pier where the ferry docks. From Easter to mid-October, it's open Monday to Saturday 9am to 5pm, and Sunday 1 to 4pm. The staff can help you locate a room should you arrive on Barra without a reservation.

Exploring Barra

A 10-mile circular road circumnavigates the island, measuring only 4 by 8 miles, and passes snug bays and long strands of sand and pebbles that are more popular with seals than with two-legged beachgoers. Roads end in the south is a headland ringed by a magnificent stretch of sand, Vatersay. Along the route, shared with wandering sheep, are the stony remains of some of the island's oldest inhabitants: standing stones at **Borve** and **Dun Bharpa** and the scant remains of 3,000-year-old round house at **Tigh Talamhanta** are all the more evocative since they litter fields often ablaze with wildflowers, of which islanders claim there are some 1,000 varieties on Barra. At Eoligarr, **St Barr's Church,** is named after St Findbarr of Cork (C.E. 550–623), who, it's said, converted the islanders to Christianity after finding many of them practicing cannibalism when he arrived. The island may be named after the saint as well, a combination from Barr and the old Norse "ey" for island—and bestowed, it's said with more concern for local color than for fact, by Omund the Wooden Leg, the first Viking to arrive on Barra, in the early 9th century.

Kisimul Castle ★ HISTORIC SIGHT The Clan MacNeil of Barra were known for piracy and lawlessness, so it was probably in their best interest to build their fortified tower house, begun in the early 1400s, on a rocky islet in the middle of what's come to be known as Castlebay. Generations of successive MacNeils left their marks on the water-girded fortress, adding a Great Hall, a chapel, and kitchens. The clan abandoned the castle when defense was no longer their primary concern, and over the years the interiors were gutted by fire and the stones purloined to be used as ballast in the island's fishing fleet. After an American architect, Robert MacNeil, was recognized as the

45th clan chief of the MacNeils, he arrived on Barra in 1937 to begin rebuilding the ancestral home, now an intriguing warren of walkways, courtyards, and towers. Near the main gate, walls surround what looks like a tiny harbor but was actually a handy trap in which fish would become beached at low tide, providing the kitchens with fresh food. The castle closed in 2018 for conservation works but is expected to open in the near future and is quite spectacular when viewed from the water.

Castlebay. www.historic-scotland.gov.uk. Weather permitting, a boatman can take you over to the castle, and back again, between April and September, daily from 9:30am to 5:30pm, £5 for adults, £4 for seniors, and £3 for children 5–15, including the boat ride.

Where to Eat & Stay on Barra

Castlebay Hotel ★   A harborside perch provides this gabled inn from around 1890 with knockout views of the bay and Kisimul Castle. Guest rooms are fairly snug (as in small) but cozily done up, and, especially the four superior rooms with sea views, are about as deluxe as lodging on the island gets. The adjacent Castlebay Bar is the island's most popular gathering spot and offers live music some evenings.

Castlebay, Barra. www.castlebay-hotel.co.uk. ✆ **01871/810-223.** 14 units. Doubles £80–£150 double. **Amenities:** Restaurant; 2 bars; free Wi-Fi.

Isle of Barra Hotel ★   The remote Outer Hebrides aren't known for their beach hotels, but that's just what this rambling seashore inn next to the white sands of Tangasdale Beach on the island's western coast is. Overlooking Halaman Bay, "the most westerly hotel in Britain" also lays claim to housing the most westerly pub in Scotland and serves the "last dram before America." Bedrooms are basic but bright, with a decidedly casual beachcomber aura and knockout sea views that compensate for the lack of space and any attempt at luxury.

Tangasdale, Barra. www.isleofbarrahotel.co.uk. ✆ **01871/810-383.** 39 units. Doubles £75–£140, includes breakfast. Closed Oct 18–Mar 20. **Amenities:** Restaurant; bar; free Wi-Fi.

SOUTH & NORTH UIST ★

South Uist is 14 miles N of Barra

It would be easy to write off these two long, narrow stretches of land floating in the Atlantic well west of the much-more-civilized Isle of Skye as nothing more than remote outposts in the Outer Hebrides. Which they are, and that's part of the draw. The relative inaccessibility, empty landscapes and vast expanses of sky lend the islands a sense of being at the edge of the world. They reward the effort of reaching them with long stretches of white sand, expanses of *machair* (grassy dunes) that reflect the wide skies, and silvery inland lochs that shelter an astonishing variety of birdlife. Aside from these natural riches, the islands are also liberally littered with standing stones and chambered cairns that bear testimony to some of Scotland's earliest peoples.

Essentials

GETTING THERE Loganair flies daily from Glasgow to **Benbecula,** an island between South and North Uist and linked to the two by causeways. Ferries run between Uig, on the Isle of Skye, to Lochmaddy, North Uist, and between Barra and Eriskay, connected to South Uist via a causeway. For information, contact **Caledonian MacBrayne** (www.calmac.co.uk; ℰ **01876/500-337**). In addition, a small private ferry runs from Newton Ferry, north of Lochmaddy, to Leverburgh, on Harris.

VISITOR INFORMATION The **Tourist Information Centre** at the pier in Lochmaddy, on North Uist (www.visithebrides.com; ℰ **01876/500-321**), is open Monday through Friday 9am to 5pm; Saturday 9:30am to 1pm and 2 to 5:30pm; and Monday, Wednesday, and Friday 7:30 to 8:30pm.

Exploring South & North Uist

The islands are linked by causeways and a road that crosses Benbecula, a much smaller island wedged between them. This means you can drive the length of the Uist archipelago, a total length of about 55 miles. It's slow going on single-track roads, with lots of tempting diversions down the tracks going off in various directions. These islands aren't geared to packed agendas, but wanderings can bring encounters with plovers and eagles, the discovery of a millennia-old stone circle in a wind-swept meadow, and long, long stretches of isolated coasts.

South Uist is 20 miles long and 6¼ miles wide at its broadest, and most of the 2,000 residents live in **Lochboisdale,** at the head of a deep-sea loch on the southeastern part of the island. The island's earliest history comes to the fore about 6 miles south on the southernmost shore, where the **Pollachar Standing Stone,** a jagged dolmen erected about 2000 B.C.E, rises a few paces from the water. Possibly the monument was a marker for ancient mariners, steering them to a landing place among the reefs and rocks. About 4 miles to the north near Daliburgh, off the main north-south road, is the circular **Klipheder Wheelhouse,** dating to C.E. 200. What seems like a hollow in the sandy earth is what remains of a fairly elaborate residence, with ten rooms arranged in a circle around a central hearth. Just beyond, at Airidh Mhuilinn, is the **Flora MacDonald memorial,** a cairn atop a little hill that marks the rebel's birthplace in 1722. MacDonald is revered in these parts for helping Charles Edward Stuart, aka Bonnie Prince Charlie, escape from forces of King George II after he ill-advisedly attempted to claim the British throne. The pretender fled from the Highlands to South Uist, where he met the lovely MacDonald, who became enamored of him, and the couple moved on to a hideaway on the Isle of Skye (see p. 379). You'll learn more about them at the **Kildonan Museum** (www.kildonanmuseum.co.uk; ℰ **01878/710-343**) just up the road, but the main attraction is the Clan Ranald Stone, carved to honor the clan chieftain in the 1500s. The museum has a cafe and a shop selling crafts produced by islanders and is open from April to October Monday through Saturday 10am to 5pm, and on Sundays from 2pm to 5pm.

A little farther north, the A865 passes the **Loch Druidibeg National Nature Reserve,** where *machair* and brackish lochs are a breeding ground for greylag geese. The northern end of the island is nearly bisected by **Loch Bee,** inhabited by mute swans, and on the flank of Reuval Hill stands **Our Lady of the Isles,** a 9m (30-ft.) statue of the Virgin and Child. The largest religious statue in Britain makes a statement, letting anyone venturing south from the protestant north that South Uist is staunchly Roman Catholic.

Much of **North Uist,** about 12 miles wide by 35 miles long, is covered in water that flows through brackish lochs and bogland. Deep sea lochs indent much of the coast, so the landscape seems more blue than green, and the light is soft and otherworldly. A single lane road with passing places connects the rest of the island with **Lochmaddy,** the main village about midway up the east coast and not much more than a shop, post office, and ferry landing. The untamed eastern shores are dotted with trout-filled lochs, set against a backdrop of rolling heather-clad hills. On the western side of the island, an almost unbroken, 20-mile-long stretch of white beaches is backed by meadows filled with wildflowers. Nothing stands between here and the Americas, and the sea can roll in with dramatic force. The **Balranald Nature Reserve** (www.rspb. org.uk), 16 miles west of Lochmaddy, is the winter home of large numbers of Barnacle geese and in summer to elusive corncrakes, one of Britain's rarest birds. You can walk through the reserve at any time at no charge, and guided tours (£5) are given at 2pm on most Mondays during the summer.

Trinity Temple (*Teampull na Trionad* in Gaelic), 8 miles southwest of Lochmaddy near Corunna, is a ruined monastery and early center of learning, sometimes considered to be Scotland's first university. Beathag, the first prioress of the convent in Iona, founded the monastery in the 13th century. She was the daughter of Somerland, an Irish mercenary who established the MacDonald Clan. In front of the ruins is the so-called Ditch of Blood, proof that perhaps education did not have the taming effect Beathag may have envisioned: The MacDonald's ambushed the rival MacCleods here and butchered them with swords, bows, and arrows. Local lore has it that the **Three Standing Stones of the False Men,** known in Gaelic as *Na Fir Bhreige,* were actual men, all wife deserters from Skye turned into stone by a witch. You'll encounter them about 3 miles northwest of Lochmaddy. A smattering of other prehistoric sites includes **Pobull Fhinn,** 7 miles southwest of Lochmaddy, a stone circle thought to be at least 3,000 years old, on a hillside above Loch Langais.

Where to Stay & Eat on South & North Uist

Borrodale Hotel ★ The friendly proprietors of this little gabled house, set amid lochs and moors in the center of South Uist about 3 miles west of the ferry terminal at Lochboisdale, go out of their way to provide guests with a friendly island refuge. Aside from the pleasant rooms, guests have use of a stone-walled lounge, along with a sunny conservatory where meals are served. The cozy bar offers live music. Daliburgh is tiny but central, and well-poised for exploring the Uists and, via causeway and ferry, Barra to the south.

Daliburgh, South Uist. www.isleshotelgroup.co.uk. ✆ **01878/700-444.** 14 units. £90–£105 double, includes breakfast. **Amenities:** Restaurant; bar; free Wi-Fi.

Langass Lodge ★ An old hunting lodge from 1876 with a new wing stands out in the windswept, barren countryside. Some of the island's few trees, and stately sycamores at that, tower over the grounds, and the level of unfussy comfort is a bit unexpected in these far reaches of the remote landscapes. Smartly furnished guest rooms overlook Loch Eport and Ben Eaval, as do the lounges and adjoining bar and restaurant downstairs. Excellent meals and lighter fare are on tap, and a good thing, too, because restaurants are thin on the ground in these parts.

Locheport, North Uist, about 7 miles southwest of ferry terminal at Lochmaddy. www.langasslodge.co.uk. ✆ **01876/580-285.** 12 units. Doubles £95–£115, includes breakfast. Closed Feb. **Amenities:** Restaurant; bar; free Wi-Fi.

Lochmaddy Hotel ★ This white gabled landmark, a few steps from the ferry terminal, is an oasis of civilization on North Uist and popular with anglers (who can buy permits here) and sightseers, since the locale makes it easy to tour the Uists as well as Harris & Lewis, an easy drive and short ferry crossing away. About half the functional guest rooms look across Lochmaddy Bay to Skye, and one of the island's best, and very few, restaurants serves fish and seafood right from these waters.

Lochmaddy, North Uist. www.lochmaddyhotel.co.uk. ✆ **01876/500-331.** 15 units. Doubles £100–£135, includes breakfast. **Amenities:** Restaurant; 2 bars; free Wi-Fi.

HARRIS & LEWIS ★

10 miles NE of North Uist; 56 miles NW of Mallaig

These two islands are not two islands at all but one long skinny land mass, divided by a land boundary, not water. Even so, residents of either Harris or Lewis would be quick to point out the difference between the two. Harris is mountainous in parts, etched by fjord like bays in other parts, and ringed with sandy beaches in others. Lewis, to the north, is flatter and marshier, with heather-covered moors that seamlessly merge into sea lochs. Harris has the dramatic scenery, Lewis is blessed with some stunning prehistoric monuments, and they both have tweed—it might be called Harris Tweed, but the beautiful woolens are woven on both islands.

Essentials

GETTING THERE You can reach Lewis & Harris by several routes. Ferries sail between Tarbert, capital of Harris, and Uig on the Isle of Skye, and between Stornoway, capital of Lewis, and Ullapool, on the mainland. You can also sail between Berneray, on North Uist, and Leverburgh, in the south of Harris. All these crossings are operated by **Caledonian MacBrayne** (www.calmac.co.uk; ✆ **0800/066-5400**).

Buses run from Leverburgh to Tarbert and from Tarbert to Stornoway. The A859 cuts a south–north path across the islands and connects the capitals of each, Tarbert on Harris and Stornoway on Lewis.

VISITOR INFORMATION   A **Tourist Information Centre** operates from the port at Tarbert (www.visitscotland.com; 𝄐 **01859/502-011**). April to October, it's open Monday through Saturday 9am to 5pm; November to March, it's open Monday and Friday 11am to 1pm, and Tuesday, Thursday, and Saturday 11am to 2pm. The **Western Isles Tourist Board** is at 26 Cromwell St., Stornoway (www.visitscotland.com; 𝄐 **01851/703-088**). It's open April to October Monday through Friday from 9am to 6pm and Saturday 9am to 5pm and 8 to 9pm; and October to April Monday through Friday from 9am to 5pm.

Exploring Harris & Lewis

Why far-flung **Harris** is known at all has less to do with the place itself than with the hand-woven tweeds the islanders have been producing for centuries. These rich woolens are inspired by the landscapes and tinted by natural dyes garnered from lichen, seaweed, nettle, and other wild plants that stubbornly take root in the island's sandy soil. You'll notice the same hues as you meander south from **Tarbert,** the one-street little capital wedged between two sea lochs.

The so-called **Golden Road** ★★ follows the east coast through a rocky landscape of bays and rocky headlands. It would be easy to assume this route takes its name from the wealth of scenery along the way, but the reference is to the cost of building the road in 1897 through such inhospitable terrain. At the southernmost tip of the island the surroundings mellow into pastureland where green and brown land seems to blend seamlessly into blue and gray sea and sky. From these flatlands 17 miles south of Tarbert rises the tower of **St Clement's Church,** at Rodel, unexpectedly medieval and grand. Clan chief Alexander MacLeod built the monument around 1520, and he's still a presence. In stone effigy and clad in armor, he reclines on top of his elaborate tomb, carved with a pictorial record of the laird's earthly pursuits and passions: a hunting scene in which he stalks stags; the MacLeod castle at Dunvegan, on the isle of Skye; and a sailing galley on which the laird may have traveled between his island domains.

On the west coast, skirted in parts by the island's main north–south road, white sands stretch for miles backed by dunes and *machair,* the typical Hebridean dune grasslands. Along the beaches at **Scarista** ★★ and **Luskentyre** ★★, brilliant white sands are washed by azure waters that, were they 20 degrees, or maybe 30 degrees, warmer, would lure throngs of beachgoers. As is, you might not see another soul, save for sheep who wander along the sands to find a patch of grass. Just off the western coast is the Robinson Crusoe island of **Taransay,** at some 1,335 hectares (3,300 acres) one of the largest uninhabited islands in Scotland and the largest in private hands. Once home to a few struggling farmers, the island is now the domain of sheep, deer, and seals.

The main north–south road crosses a boggy, treeless landscape from Tarbert to **Stornoway** ★, the capital of **Lewis,** 30 miles north. Even the Ancient Roman geographer Ptolemy referred to Lewis as "marshy." It's said most of the island's trees fell to the axe of Norse raider Magnus the Barefoot, intent on building more ships to continue his western conquests, and from the 9th century Lewis was part of the Norse Kingdom of the Isles. Stornoway faces a sheltered harbor the Vikings called Steering Bay, and with gabled houses and somber stone and brick facades, the town still gives off a decidedly Nordic air. Surprisingly, given the sparsity of human habitation elsewhere in these islands, Stornoway has 6,000 residents and is by far the largest town in all the Hebrides. On a shopping day the little center can seem positively bustling— and would be even more so if the government ever decided to implement a far-fetched plan to connect the town with Ullapool, on the mainland, through a 40-mile-long tunnel. For the time being, ferries reliably steam between the two ports.

The star attraction on Lewis far predates the Vikings: at **Callanish** ★★, 16 miles west of Stornoway, 13 standing stones from about 1800 B.C.E. are laid out in a circle to depict a Celtic cross with a burial cairn at the center. They're approached from either north or south by a lane lined with another 40 or so stone pillars. An old Gaelic legend claims that when the giants, who were said to have once inhabited the island refused to convert to Christianity, St Kieran turned them to stone. It's unknown what the purpose of the carefully laid-out stones might have been, though some scholars suggest that Callanish was aligned in some way with the moon, stars, and distant hills and used for rituals. You can wander among the stones for free, day or night. The excellent **Stories of the Stones** exhibition in an adjacent visitor center (www.callanish-visitorcentre.co.uk; ✆ **01851/621-422**), provides background about the excavation of the stones in the 1980s and the island's early past. You'll learn a bit about the so-called **Lewis Chessman,** dug up in 1831. Carved from walrus tusks around C.E. 500, they're now in the British Museum in London. The center is open from April to September, Monday through Saturday 10am to 9pm, and from October to March Wednesday through Saturday 10am to 4pm, and has a nice cafe.

Dun Carloway Broch ★, about 20 miles northwest of Stornoway, is a rounded stone tower from the 1st century B.C.E. built into a hillside above Loch Roag. The *broch* must have been a fairly showy dwelling, commanding the heights with stables for animals on the ground floor and extensive family quarters on several wooden floors above, beneath a conical roof. The broch was still largely intact in the 1500s, when a clan took refuge inside to thwart the onslaughts of rivals but were eventually smoked out when their attackers threw burning heather through the few openings. The ruin is always accessible.

A later island dwelling is the **Blackhouse** ★ (www.historicenvironment. scot), in Arnol, 14 miles northwest of Stornoway. Crafted from stone and turf, with a thatched roof, the long, dark, windowless chamber housed animals and humans, the latter cooking and seeking warmth around a chimneyless peat fire. Primitive as the abode is, blackhouses like this were well suited to the harsh, damp island climate and efficient, too—smoke from the ever-present fire killed vermin and insects, and the thatch was removed every so often and used as fertilizer. A nearby "whitehouse" is from around 1900, and shows off such welcome modern amenities as windows and chimneys, along with a wall that separated man and beast. The Blackhouse is open April through September, daily 9:30am to 5:30pm, and October through March, Monday and Tuesday and Thursday to Saturday, 9:30am to 4pm. Admission is £5 adults, £4 seniors and students, £3 children 5 to 15.

Where to Eat & Stay on Harris & Lewis

Harris Hotel ★ This landmark from 1865 has housed many of the island's distinguished guests over the years, including *Peter Pan* creator J.M. Barrie. On Harris he found inspiration for his play *Mary Rose,* about a woman who vanishes while visiting a remote island. He even etched his initials on the dining room window. Pleasant guest rooms deliver old-fashioned comfort, and while Tarbert is more functional than charming, the lounges and garden are lovely places to relax, and the hotel is an excellent base for exploring Harris & Lewis. The pub and restaurant are popular island gathering spots.

Tarbert, Harris. www.harrishotel.com. ✆ **01859/502-154.** 23 units. Doubles £80–£150, includes breakfast. **Amenities:** Restaurant; bar; free Wi-Fi.

Park Guest House ★ A century-old stone house about a 10-minute walk north of the ferry terminal is the most character-filled lodging on Lewis, with large bedrooms done in an unfussy mix of old and new pieces. A downstairs restaurant is also one of Stornoway's best, and is conveniently open throughout the day and offers excellent dinners as early-bird specials.

30 James St., Stornoway, Lewis. www.the-parkguesthouse.com. ✆ **01851/702-485.** 7 units. Doubles £110, includes breakfast. **Amenities:** Restaurant; bar; free Wi-Fi.

Scarista House ★★★ A seaside Georgian manse is a remote and extraordinary retreat, with bright lounges and charmingly country-chic bedrooms facing the white sands of Scarista Beach, maybe the most exquisite stretch of sand in all the Hebrides, and taking in seemingly endless views of water, sky, and moors and fields. You might be tempted to brave a bracing dip, and if you do, a peat fire or soak in a deep tub awaits. Lewis kippers can start the day, packed lunches are provided for excursions, a cocktail in front of the fire and a four-course dinner of local shellfish and heather-fed lamb rounds out an evening. The restaurant is open to non-guests, and two self-catering cottages are on the property.

Scarista, Harris, 24km (15 miles) SW of Tarbert on the A859. www.scaristahouse.com. ✆ **01859/550-238.** 5 units. Doubles £190–£210, includes breakfast. **Amenities:** Restaurant; free Wi-Fi.

Shopping on Harris & Lewis

You can buy Harris Tweed at the source, at the **Tarbert Tweed Shop** (www. harristweedisleofharris.co.uk; ℗ **01859/502-040**), with a huge selection of fabric as well as jackets and other garments. Lewis also has a long weaving tradition, and these days outdoes Harris when it comes to woolens production—but who's ever heard of Lewis Tweed? You can see a selection of local craftsmanship at **Harris Tweed Hebrides,** 25 N. Beach, Stornoway (www. harristweedhebrides.com; ℗ **01851/700-046**). The **Isle of Harris Distillery** (www.harrisdistillery.com; ℗ **1859/502-212**), in Tarbert, produces peaty single malts and botanical gin. The operation is a big attraction in little Tarbert and can be visited Monday through Saturday, 10am to 5pm.

Tours on Harris & Lewis

The best way to see the plentiful birdlife and marine life around Harris & Lewis is on a boat trip. You can cruise with **Sea Trek,** 16 Uigen, Miavaig, Lewis (www.seatrek.co.uk; ℗ **01851/672-469**) on full- and half-day excursions that sometimes provide a close-up look at the seal colonies that thrive on some of the more remote, uninhabited nearby islands.

ORKNEY & SHETLAND

By Stephen Brewer

The top of Scotland trails off into these 170 wild and remote islands, only 34 of them inhabited, marooned between the North Sea and the Atlantic. Windswept, wave-battered, and largely treeless, the archipelagoes can work magic on visitors with their almost savage landscapes, miles of lonely coastlines inhabited by seals and seabirds, and mesmerizing northern light that lingers almost around the clock in summertime. Not that the islands are anything less than highly civilized—they had been inhabited for millennia by the time Vikings rowed their longboats into the surrounding seas, and Neolithic farmers, Pictish tribes, Norse clans, and generations of Celtic-influenced islanders have all left traces of their fascinating legacy around the islands.

Don't Leave Orkney & Shetland Without . . .

Climbing into some tombs. The farmers who lived on Orkney more than 5,000 years ago were sent off to the beyond in elaborate burial mounds and tombs that dot the islands, along with standing stones and entire settlements. Entrance to many sites requires donning a helmet, crawling through tunnels, or scaling ladders, so channel the Indiana Jones within you.

Becoming a World War I and II buff. Scapa Flow, on Mainland, Orkney, was the main base of the Royal Fleet and has witnessed explosions, sinkings, and the presence of everyone from Winston Churchill to Italian POWs—the latter left a beautifully painted chapel on the islet of Lamb Holm.

Peering at puffins. Hundreds of thousands of seabirds inhabit the islands, and some top places to observe them are Fair Isle, Sumburgh Head on Mainland, Shetland, the sea cliffs on Hoy, the Hermaness Reserve on Unst . . . hundreds of feathered species roost all over the islands, and even if you don't know a puffin from a petrel, you'll be enchanted. Among other charmers from the animal kingdom are seals, otters, and, of course, Shetland ponies.

The Orkney Islands

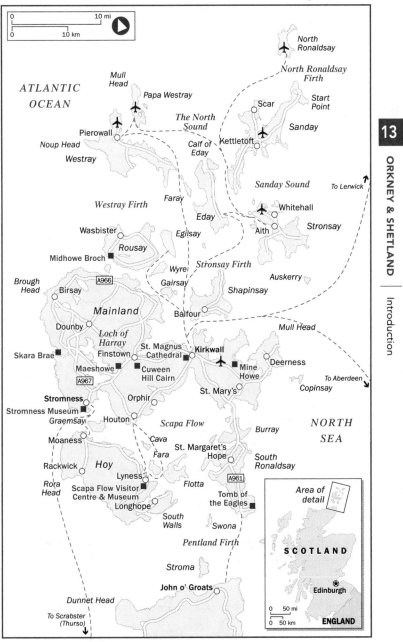

0 | 10 mi
0 | 10 km

ATLANTIC
OCEAN

Mull
Head

Papa Westray

North
Ronaldsay

North Ronaldsay
Firth

Scar

Start
Point

The North
Sound

Sanday

Pierowall

Kettletoft

Noup Head

Calf of
Eday

Westray

Sanday Sound

To Lerwick

Westray Firth

Faray

Whitehall

Eday

Aith

Stronsay

Wasbister

Egilsay

Rousay

Midhowe Broch

Wyre

Stronsay Firth

Auskerry

Brough
Head

Birsay

Gairsay

Shapinsay

A966

Mainland

Balfour

Dounby

Loch of
Harray

Mull Head

Skara Brae

Finstown

St. Magnus
Cathedral

Kirkwall

Maeshowe

Cuween
Hill Cairn

Mine
Howe

Deerness

A967

Stromness

Orphir

St. Mary's

To Aberdeen

Stromness Museum

Houton

Scapa Flow

Copinsay

Graemsay

Cava

Burray

NORTH
SEA

Moaness

Fara

St. Margaret's
Hope

Rackwick

Hoy

Lyness

Flotta

South
Ronaldsay

A961

Rora
Head

Scapa Flow Visitor
Centre & Museum

Longhope

Tomb of
the Eagles

Area of
detail

South
Walls

Swona

Pentland Firth

SCOTLAND

Stroma

John o' Groats

Edinburgh

Dunnet Head

0 | 50 mi
0 | 50 km

ENGLAND

To Scrabster
(Thurso)

Picking up some knitting needles. You might be inspired to do so when you see the beautiful knitwear that islanders have been turning out for centuries. Prime places to admire the output are in Lerwick, Shetland, in thoughtful displays at the Shetland Museum and the Böd of Gremista.

Putting on some Viking horns. They might inspire you on your explorations of the legacy these seafarers left behind at St Magnus Cathedral in Kirkwall, at Jarlshof on Mainland, Shetland, and elsewhere through the islands. Place names, the mid-winter Up Helly Aa festival in Lerwick, and blonde-haired, blue-eyed islanders reflect these Nordic roots.

13 ORKNEY ★★

6¼ miles N of Duncansby Head (mainland Scotland), across Pentland Firth; 280 miles N of Edinburgh

First things first: Orkney is not one single place, but an archipelago of 70 islands, 20 of them inhabited (though many by only a few hearty souls) that stretches 50 miles from the southernmost point, on South Ronaldsay, to the northern tip, on North Ronaldsay. To make matters a little more confusing, the main island is called Mainland, even though the turbulent waters of the Firth of Pentland lay between Mainland and what most of us consider to be the *real* mainland. Nomenclature aside, treeless, salt-tinged Orkney is spellbinding, set apart geographically and in sense of time, too. The green, fertile, mostly low-lying islands are liberally littered with the tombs, houses, and monuments of early peoples who farmed here 5,500 years ago. Nowhere else on earth is quite so evocative of these early Europeans. The Vikings came ashore sometime around the late 8th century, using the islands as a launch pad for their raids throughout the northern seas and leaving behind their port towns, place names, and a decidedly Nordic culture. During both world wars Orkney was an important base for the Royal Navy, and the surrounding seafloor is littered with sunken battleships. Human endeavors aside, the islands are a haven for sea birds, otters, seals, and other wildlife, whose boisterous clamor blends with the roar of the surf, about the only noises likely to disturb a walk along the sea cliffs that ring many of the windswept islands. And if should you wish to take that walk after dinner on a summer's evening, you're in luck, because the midsummer sun casts a glow until well past midnight.

Essentials

GETTING TO ORKNEY **Loganair** (www.loganair.co.uk; ✆ **0344/800-2855**) operates **flights** between Kirkwall Airport on Mainland (the largest Orkney island) and Aberdeen, Edinburgh, Glasgow, Inverness, and Lerwick on Shetland.

By car, the shortest ferry crossing is **Pentland Ferries'** (www.pentland ferries.co.uk; ✆ **01856/831-226**) route from Gill's Bay in Caithness to St. Margaret's Hope, a port on the island of South Ronaldsay that's connected to Mainland by road. **NorthLink** runs frequent sailings from Scrabster on

Scotland's north coast to Stromness on Mainland (www.northlinkferries.co.uk; ✆ **0845/600-0449**); the trip takes just over 2 hours. Three times a week (four in summer), the company's overnight Aberdeen–Shetland service also stops in at Kirkwall; the journey takes 6 hours.

John o' Groats Passenger Ferries (www.jogferry.co.uk; ✆ **01955/611-353**) operate to and from Burwick on Mainland, twice daily from May through December (trip time is 40 min.). A bus ticket, included in fare, makes the 40-minute trip between the ferry terminal and Kirkwall. From June through early September, the **Orkney Bus,** operated by the ferry company, travels between Inverness and Kirkwall and makes the sea crossing via John o' Groats. The twice-daily service takes about 5 hours.

GETTING AROUND **Loganair** (www.loganair.co.uk; ✆ **01856/872-494**) operates flights from Kirkwall Airport to Sanday, Stronsay, Westray, Eday, North Ronaldsay, and Papa Westray. **Orkney Ferries Ltd.** (www.orkney ferries.co.uk; ✆ **01856/872-044**) operates scheduled services between Kirkwall and Eday, North Ronaldsay, Papa Westray, Sanday, Shapinsay, Stronsay, and Westray. From Houton, on Mainland, there's a service to and from Flotta and Lyness (Hoy), and from Tingwall, on Mainland, to and from Egilsay, Rousay, and Wyre. There's also a passenger-only ferry from Stromness, on Mainland, to and from Graemsay and Moaness (Hoy).

TOURS You can get a quick overview of some of Orkney's most important archaeological sites on a half-day tour with **Tour Orkney** (www.tourorkney.co.uk), operating on Monday, Wednesday, and Friday, with stops at sites in the Heart of Neolithic Orkney.

Mainland ★★

Carpeted in verdant green farmland, Mainland is the largest of the Orkney islands and, home to three out of four Orcadians, the most populated. Which means things haven't changed too much over the millennia. Mainland was a thriving community some 5,500 years ago, and the many Neolithic tombs, ceremonial sites, and dwellings these early farmers built remain. The Picts, or the Painted Ones, also lived on Orkney, until this confederation of northern tribes was overrun by Vikings, who left yet other imprints on the island. Mainland is scattered with the remains of these other eras, and climbing around them, of course, is what brings many visitors to the island. While there, the present-day intrudes gently and often quite picturesquely in Kirkwall, Stromness, and other salty old port towns and along low sea cliffs teaming with birdlife. Mainland is well connected to other islands—by road to four of them, and by sea and air to others, making this central island the best base for your Orkney explorations.

Kirkwall ★

Tucked into a bay on a stretch of flat, green coastline in the middle of the Orkney archipelago, Kirkwall is the islands' capital and a bustling port, just as it has been since Nordic seafarers plied their well-traveled routes around the coasts of Scotland and the northern isles. The name comes from the old Norse "Kirkjuvagr," or "church bay," for an 11th-century church dedicated to Olaf Haraldsson, the Norwegian king who became a saint. Olaf's church no longer stands, but a magnificent cathedral dedicated to a later Norseman is still the town's centerpiece.

ESSENTIALS

GETTING THERE & AROUND   *See also "Getting to Orkney," above.* Kirkwall is a hub for flights to and from the mainland, but the only mainland ferries to call are the ones on NorthLink's overnight Shetland–Aberdeen runs. **Orkney Ferries Ltd.** (www.orkneyferries.co.uk; ℂ **01856/872-044**) operates scheduled service between Kirkwall and Eday, North Ronaldsay, Papa Westray, Sanday, Shapinsay Stronsay, and Westray. **Stagecoach** buses (www.stagecoachbus.com; ℂ **01856/878-014**) connect Kirkwall with Stromness, St Margaret's Hope, and other towns on Mainland, and will make stops along the routes. Buses are timed to link with ferries and flights. Stagecoach operates some handy routes geared to sightseers during the summer; travel centers at the main bus stop in Kirkwall and in the ferry terminal in Stromness dispense timetables. You can get a good rundown on island bus service at www.orkney.gov.uk. Two island rental car companies are **J.D. Peace Cars,** Junction Road, Kirkwall (www.orkneycarhire.co.uk; ℂ **01856/872-866**); or **W.R. Tullock,** Castle Street, Kirkwall (www.orkneycarrental.co.uk; ℂ **01856/875-500**), the only company with an office at the airport (and one in town, as well).

VISITOR INFORMATION   The **Tourist Information Centre** is at West Castle Street (www.visitorkney.com; ℂ **01856/872-856**). September through May it's open Monday through Friday 9am to 5pm and Saturday 10am to 4pm; during June, July, and August, it's open daily from 9am to 6pm. To find out what's going on during your visit, consult *The Orcadian,* a weekly newspaper published since 1854 and viewable online at www.orcadian.co.uk.

EXPLORING KIRKWALL

Narrow lanes lead off the quays and wind toward the town's centerpiece, St Magnus Cathedral. These atmospheric streets are lined with solid stone houses from the 17th through the 19th century that give the town a decidedly Nordic aura. The shop-lined main thoroughfare, off limits to car for much of its length, plunges into the heart of the old town from the harbor, changing its name from Bridge Street, to Albert Street, to Broad Street.

Bishop's Palace and Earl's Palace ★★ HISTORIC SITES   These two imposing ruins, testaments to the fleeting nature of temporal power and might, loom next to the cathedral and its tomb-strewn churchyard. The Bishop's Palace was built in the style of a Norwegian castle to accommodate the overseers of the cathedral, and King Haakon of Norway, following a failed attempt to invade Scotland in 1263, died in one of the stately chambers. Earl Robert Stewart, illegitimate son of James IV of Scotland and half-brother of Mary

Queen of Scots, took control of Orkney in the late 16th century and soon commissioned the adjacent Earl's Palace, with plans to incorporate the Bishop's Palace into the massive complex. His son, Patrick Stewart, had an even grander vision for a residence of great size and beauty. He used forced labor to quarry the stone and build his dream palace, though he was arrested and executed before work was completed. Enough remains of the broad stone staircases, pillared facades, massive fireplaces, and vaulted windows to suggest the grandeur of what a later observer, Sir Walter Scott, said evokes the "residence of feudal princes, the character of a palace and of a castle." Orkney storms have taken a toll on the soft limestone, making the weather-worn ruins even more gloomily atmospheric.

Watergate. www.historic-scotland.gov.uk. (C) **01856/871-918.** £5 adults, £4 seniors and students, £3 children. Apr–Oct daily, 9:30am–5:30pm.

Grain Earth House ★ HISTORIC SITE   You don't have to wander far on Orkney before stumbling upon an early dwelling. This earth house, in which a curving subterranean passage leads into an oval chamber supported by rough stone pillars, is now surrounded by warehouses on the west side Kirkwall Harbor. These underground spaces, part of a farm from around 400 B.C.E., would have been warm and dry and probably used for storage, possibly for grain that farmers traded with the Roman army, then stationed in northern Scotland.

Swordfish Rd., Hatston Industrial Estate, 1 west of town center. Free admission. Always open. If locked, obtain key at 25 Broad St.

Highland Park Distillery ★ HISTORIC SITE   By the late 18th century, Viking descendant and butcher-by-day, smuggler-by-night Magnus Eunson was doing a brisk business distilling whisky in a cottage on a hillside overlooking Kirkwall. The operation became official in 1798, and Magnus's methods remain in place at the distillery that made him an upright and wealthy citizen. Grain germinates on traditional malting floors and is smoked in century-old kilns over 4,000-year-old peat from nearby Hobbister Moor, imparting a smoky sweetness to the acclaimed whisky.

Holm Rd. www.highlandpark.co.uk. (C) **01856/874-619.** Hourly tours, with prices from £10. Apr–Oct, daily 10am–5pm, Nov–Mar, Mon–Fri 10am–5pm.

Orkney Museum/Tankerness House ★ MUSEUM   The one-time residence of cathedral officials, and later a prosperous merchant family, is packed to the rafters with artifacts of 6,000 or so years of island life. Showing for this long history are stone slabs from prehistoric tombs, simple household tools from a 19th-century *bothy* (a simple farm cottage), and paintings by artists who have come to the islands to capture the magical light. The showpieces are the contents of a Viking boat burial from around 900, found near the Sanday Island coastal village of Scar. Some 300 rusted iron rivets marked out the shape of a 6.5m-long (21-ft.) wooden boat. A 30-year-old man, an elderly woman, and a child of 10 or so, sex undetermined, were buried in the vessel,

Orcadians still wince at the memory of Sir Robert Stewart (1533–1593) and his son, Patrick Stewart (1566–1615). Robert took control of the islands as Earl of Orkney in 1581, and soon brought the islanders under his yoke, forcing them to work without pay, torturing and executing those who resisted, and collecting ruinous taxes. Patrick was even more of a despot, earning the name "Black Pattie" for his iron grip and, it's said, never going anywhere without a convoy of 50 musketeers. The earl allegedly also had a corps of trumpeters who announced each course of his elaborate meals with a fanfare. Scottish King James VI finally intervened and had Patrick imprisoned in Edinburgh Castle on charges of treason and usurping royal authority. Patrick was beheaded in 1615, though the execution was postponed to give the earl time to learn the Lord's Prayer so he could recite it before the blade was lowered—it was said that his unfamiliarity with this fundamental statement of Christian devotion was a testament to just how evil he was.

alongside a sword, a whalebone comb, a quiver with 8 arrows, and the Scar Dragon Plaque, a utensil fashioned from the rib of a whale and use to smooth linen.

Broad St., opposite cathedral. Free admission. Mon–Sat 10:30am–5pm.

Orkney Wireless Museum ★ MUSEUM   What might seem at first like the musty collection of local radio buffs tells the riveting story of Orkney during World Wars I and II. With the islands' strategic position between the North Atlantic and North Sea, radio communications with the many old sets and other paraphernalia on display were vital in monitoring enemy shipping. Photographs chronicle the construction of the so-called Churchill Barriers, causeways that stretch from Mainland to four smaller islands and protected the Royal Navy anchorage at Scapa Flow. Sir Winston Churchill, then minister of the admiralty, commissioned the project in 1939 after a German U-boat slipped between blockades and sunk the HMS *Royal Oak*, killing 833 of the 1,234 men on board.

Kiln Corner, Junction Rd. www.orkneywirelessmuseum.org.uk. ℂ **01856/871-400.** £3 adults, £1 seniors and children 5–15. Apr–Sept, Mon–Sat 10am–4:30pm, Sun 2:30–4:30pm.

St Magnus Cathedral ★★ CHURCH/HISORIC SITE   Among the many Viking seamen who sailed around the northern islands was Magnus Erlendsson, who stayed ashore long enough to become Earl of the Orkneys. Magnus soon found himself at odds with his cousin, Haakon, a favorite of King Magnus Barelegs. Haakon became enraged when, in 1116, cousin Magnus refused to engage in a raid along the Welsh coast and instead stayed on board his longboat and sang psalms. Haakon settled the familial differences by having Magnus axed in the head. Inexplicably, a green field sprouted in the rocky ground where Magnus was buried, and after a few miraculous healings, within 20 years the gentle and pious man had been named a saint and Kirkland's mighty cathedral was begun in his honor. The colorful assemblage of yellow and red sandstone, laid out in stripes and checkerboard patterns, rises high above the gabled houses. Magnus was interred inside one of the pillars that run in two rows down the length of the church, and he has plenty of company in his eternal rest. Gravestones line the walls of the stark, lofty edifice, and on them a legion of pious, stone-carved medieval figures beseech the almighty for entrance into the gates of heaven.

Broad St. www.stmagnus.org. ✆ **01856/878-326.** Free, donations welcome. Apr–Sept Mon–Sat 9am–6pm, Sun 1–6pm; Oct–Mar Mon–Sat 9am–1pm and 2–5pm. Tours, on Tues and Thurs at 11am and 2pm cost £8.35 and must be booked in advance by calling ✆ **01856/874-894.**

WHERE TO EAT & STAY IN KIRKWALL

Albert Hotel ★★ Unassuming from the outside, this stone guesthouse next to St Magnus cathedral is a world of calm luxury inside. Guest quarters come in many shapes and sizes, with some of the coziest dormered-bedrooms tucked under the eaves, and all are done up in a slightly retro modern look, with soothing pastels and gray and plum accents. Woodsy Bothy Bar and the Lounge Bar serve good pub grub and host local musicians some nights.

Mounthoolie Lane. www.alberthotel.co.uk. ✆ **01856/876-000.** 18 units. Doubles £128–£151, includes breakfast. Restaurant daily, noon–2pm and 5–9pm. Main courses £9–£18. **Amenities:** Restaurant; bar; free Wi-Fi.

Ayre Hotel ★ Orkney accommodations don't get too much more stylish than these handsomely decorated rooms, done in deep hues and contemporary furnishings, in a 200-year-old house near the waterfront at the edge of the town center. Some, of course, have sea views, and a few without are as snug as ship cabins. Nine similarly attractive apartments are in an annex across the road, and since a minimum stay is not required, these are well suited to traveling families in Kirkwall for even a short stint. A convivial bar-restaurant serves basic fare.

Ayre Rd. www.ayrehotel.co.uk. ✆ **01856/873-001.** 36 units. Doubles £100–£130, includes breakfast. **Amenities:** Restaurant; bar; free Wi-Fi.

Foveran Hotel ★★★ MODERN SCOTTISH Cathedral ceilings and expanses of plate glass overlooking Scapa Flow bring the island's beautiful vistas of green and blue indoors, a perfect setting for chef/owner Paul Doull's passionate preparations of scallops, lobsters, crabs, fish, and a bounty from the island's green pastures, from North Ronaldsay mutton with a unique flavor imparted by the seaweed the sheep graze upon, to locally grown fruits and vegetables. The sprawling, California-modern inn is billed as "a restaurant with rooms," but accommodations, all on the ground floor, aren't a second thought—they're done in crisp Scandinavian style with island woolens. Best of all, a stay means you can end a memorable meal with a nightcap in front of the fire and wake to that glorious view.

St. Ola, 3 miles south of Kirkwall. www.foveranhotel.co.uk. ✆ **01856/872-389.** Doubles £125, includes breakfast; £180 with dinner and breakfast for two. Restaurant daily, 6–8:30pm. Main courses £14–£28. **Amenities:** Restaurant; bar; free Wi-Fi.

Lynnfield Hotel ★★ You might think you're in the Highlands in this charmingly quirky country house on the southern edge of town, about a mile outside the center. Orkney's longest list of single malts, including many from Kirkwall's own Highland Park Distillery, enhance the effect, especially if you're enjoying one in front of the fire in the baronial lounge. Guest quarters are suitably atmospheric, full of swags and polished antique armoires, along with cushy armchairs and a collector's array of elaborately carved beds. Many of the large bathrooms are equipped with deep soaking tubs. The little garden is a delightful place to enjoy a drink on the long summer nights, and the excellent in-house restaurant, one of the best in town, serves a bounty of local fish and seafood.

Holms Rd., St. Ola. www.lynnfield.co.uk. ✆ **01856/872-505.** 10 units. Doubles £125–£150, includes breakfast. Restaurant daily, noon–2pm and 6–8:30pm. Main courses £16–£25. **Amenities:** Restaurant; bar; free Wi-Fi.

Shore Inn ★ These harborside quarters show off a simple island chic, with small but spruce contemporary-style rooms, some of which face the waterfront. A two-bedroom loft suite sleeps five, a good setup for families, and two snug rooms are geared to solo travelers. The dinner-only restaurant is one of Kirkwall's most popular evening spots, so reservations are recommended, especially in summer—and you may want to dine here a couple of times, to work through choices that include a memorable Orkney crab tarte, pan-fried monkfish, and a vegetarian haggis.

Shore St., Kirkwall, Orkney, KW15 1LG. www.theshore.co.uk. ✆ **01856/872-200.** 17 units. Doubles from £75–£90, includes breakfast. Restaurant daily, 6–9pm. Main courses £15–£25. **Amenities:** Restaurant; bar; free Wi-Fi.

Woodwick House ★ Throughout much of the summer, this rambling old house set on 5 wild hectares (12 acres) of woodlands running down to a beach is rented out in its entirety to families or groups. When the house isn't booked, though, four delightfully old-fashioned rooms, each with their own bathrooms, are available, and guests can enjoy a homey lounge and conservatory, along with an excellent breakfast. The main towns of Kirkwall and Stromness are each about a 30-minute drive away, and many of the island's sights are within easy reach.

Evie, Orkney, 15 miles northwest of Kirkwall. www.woodwickhouse.co.uk. ✆ **01856/751-330.** 4 units. Doubles £50, includes breakfast. **Amenities:** Free Wi-Fi.

ENTERTAINMENT & NIGHTLIFE IN KIRKWALL

The 4-day **Orkney Folk Festival** (www.orkneyfolkfestival.com), usually at the end of May, features ceilidhs, a fiddlers' rally, and traditional music performed by artists from all around the globe, staged at venues in Stromness, and some in Kirkwall. The **St Magnus Festival** (www.stmagnusfestival.com), in June, celebrates classical music and the dramatic arts at performances in St Magnus Cathedral and other venues around Kirkwall and Stromness. At Christmas and New Year, the streets of Kirkwall host chaotic matches of mass football, known as the **Ba'.** With no rules to speak of and most of the town's men and boys joining in, the game can look a little unruly to visitors, as it is—wooden barricades are put in front of shop doors and windows to prevent breakage. Kirkwall's main nightclub and music venue is **Fusion,** in a former fish-processing warehouse on waterfront Ayres Road (✆ **01856/873-359**). Orkney bands perform most nights.

SHOPPING IN KIRKWALL

Judith Glue ★★   Beautiful knitwear is the stock in trade at this enchanting shop, opposite the cathedral, along with pottery and jewelry. An excellent cafe serves coffee, snacks, and lunch. 25 Broad St. www.judithglue.com. ✆ **01856/874-225.**

Longship ★★   The showpieces at this 150-year-old shop are works from the studio of Ola Gorie, a Kirkwall native who is a star of Scotland's modern crafts movement. Many pieces are inspired by archaeological finds on the island. Fine wines and other crafts are for sale, too. 7–15 Broad St. www.thelongship.co.uk. ✆ **01856/888-790.**

Sheila Fleet ★★   The collections of another noted island jeweler reflect the colors of Orkney's landscape, as well as Orkney folklore and history. 30 Bridge St. www.sheilafleet.co.uk. ✆ **01856/876-900.**

OUTDOOR ACTIVITIES AROUND KIRKWALL

Orkney is a land of midnight sun, with enough light for golfers to play at midnight. The two 18-hole courses on Mainland are **Orkney Golf Club** at Kirkwall (www.orkneygolfclub.co.uk; ✆ **01856/872-457**), and **Stromness Golf Club** (www.stromnessgc.co.uk; ✆ **01856/850-772**); day fees at both are £25. The 9-hole **South Ronaldsay Golf Club** (www.southronaldsaygolf.com; ✆ **01856/831-395**) is in the village of St. Margaret's Hope; green fees are £15, £10 after 6pm. Mainland's flat terrain is conducive to cycling, and rentals are available from **Bobby's Cycle Centre,** Tankerness Lane, Kirkwall (✆ **01856/875-777**) and **Orkney Cycle Hire,** 52 Dundas St., Stromwell (www.orkneycyclehire.co.uk; ✆ **01856/850-255**).

Around Kirkwall

Mainland is covered with the material traces of the people who have been living on the island for the past 6,000 years. Remnants of a more recent past include **Click Mill** (www.historic-scotland.gov.uk; ✆ **01856/841-815**), 14 miles northwest of Kirkwall and 2½ miles northeast of Dounby. This 19th-century water mill is not only notable because the paddle wheel is still turning but because it does so horizontally, rather than vertically like most mill wheels; the mill is free to visit and always open. The ruins of **Orphir Church,** about 9 miles southwest of Kirkwall and ½ mile off the A964, are notably round. Scotland's only surviving circular medieval church was built in 1123 by crusaders inspired by the church of the Holy Sepulcher in Jerusalem. The site is always open and admission is free.

Broch of Gurness ★★ ARCHAELOGICAL SITE   One fine day in 1929, antiquities scholar Robert Rendall was sitting on a seaside knoll sketching when the legs of his stool sank into the earth. He looked down and noticed some stones, began digging, and unearthed a staircase leading down into this large broch, a large, round stone tower that subsequent research has determined was probably home to a clan chief. Surrounding the tower are as many as 40 stone houses, with central hearths, stone furnishings, and toilets. The settlement, encircled by defenses ditches and ramparts and entered via a "main street," was probably founded around 500 to 200 B.C.E.

Off A966, 16 miles north of Kirkwall, 9 miles north of Finstown. www.historicenvironment.scot. £6 adults, £4.80 seniors and students, £3.60 children. Apr–Sept daily, 9:30am–5:30pm, Oct daily, 10am–4pm. Free access to the site in the winter.

Brough of Birsay ★★ ARCHAELOGICAL SITE   This tiny island, off the northern tip of Mainland near Birsay, is only accessible for 2 hours on either side of low tide. So you should time your trip across the narrow causeway carefully, leaving plenty of time to ensure you're not stranded on the island until the next low tide, but the planning is worth the effort. You'll be transported by the spirit of this windswept, isolated, long-deserted place as soon as you begin to climb the entrance path up the rocky shore, knowing that for half a millennia residents dragged their boats up the slope in advance of approaching storms. From about the 7th century, the island was home to Picts, the northern tribes who inhabited much of Scotland up to the end of the first millennia, then to Norse settlers until the end of the 12th century. Whether these Vikings slew the Picts to take possession of the island or assimilated them into their culture is unknown, but most of the houses, of which only stone slab floors and some fallen stones remain, are Norse, as is the sauna and bathhouse. A church, of which a few standing walls remain, is from around 1100.

Birsay, 23½ northwest of Kirkwall. www.historicenvironment.scot. ℂ **01856/841-815.** £5 adults, £4 seniors and students, £3 children 5–15. Jun–Sept daily, 9:30am–5:30pm. Free access in winter.

Cuween Hill Cairn ★ ARCHAELOGICAL SITE   You'll feel like you're entering the underworld after climbing a dirt track up a hillside and crawling on your hands and knees into a burial chamber cut into solid bedrock around 3,000 B.C.E. The skulls of 8 adults were discovered here when the cairn was excavated in 1901, but most intriguing was the presence of 24 dog skulls. It's been suggested that dogs may have been totems for the peoples who used the tomb, or that they were left inside as guardians. A box near the entrance contains flashlights, and you'll need one in the pitch darkness.

6 miles west of Kirkwall, 1 mile southeast of Finstown. Free admission. Always open.

Mine Howe ★ ARCHAELOGICAL SITE This mysterious subterranean chamber has been "discovered" twice, once in 1946 and again in 1999. The abandonment of the first exploration led to some sensational news stories suggesting that diggers had fled in terror at the aura of evil. More likely they simply didn't know what to make of the unusual structure, sunk into a hillside and accessed via 29 almost vertical steps, at the bottom of which is a small chamber. From a landing about halfway down the steps two narrow galleries extend into the hillside. It's not known what the purpose of the structure may have been, though it was possibly used for religious or ritualistic purposes and may have been a place to communicate with earth spirits or to contemplate the entrance to the underworld. The discovery of the skull of a small dog, perhaps a guardian, has led to more speculation, adding to what one newspaper headline proclaimed as "The Mystery of the 29 Steps." A wide ditch surrounding the structure may have been intended to set the spiritual precinct apart. Bring a flashlight and make the descent carefully.

6 miles east of Kirkwall, near Tankerness. Free admission. Always open.

Wideford Hill Chambered Cairn ★★ ARCHAELOGICAL SITE Cairns, or burial mounds, are commonplace on Orkney, but the one at Wideford Hill is distinctive because the exterior stonework is exposed, forming 3 stepped, concentric rings. When the mound was constructed about 3000 B.C.E., these stonework foundations would have been covered, so the cairn would have appeared as a large earthen mound. No human remains or burial objects have been found in the cairn, suggesting it was abandoned at some time in the distant past. One intriguing element is a slotted, chimney-like structure in the roof that may have allowed light to enter the subterranean chambers during a solstice or at other times of the year, or may have been a means for the living to communicate with the spirits of the dead.

The adjacent **Rennibister Earth House** is later, from about 1000 B.C.E., and is accessed through the roof via a ladder dropping down from a hatch in a farmyard. Inside, four pillars support the stone roof and small alcoves open off the main chamber. The earth-house may have been used for grain storage, while the presence of human remains has never been explained—but the disjointed bones are arranged in such a way to suggest the 6 adults and 12 children were not originally buried here but deposited haphazardly at some point in the past.

3 miles west of Kirkwall. Free admission. Always open.

Stromness ★★

25 miles SW of Kirkwall

In Orkney's quaint and picturesque second port it's easy to imagine the tall masts of 19th-century clipper ships swaying above the slate rooftops of tall, gabled houses, or the longboats of Vikings floating in the sheltered anchorage of the town they knew as Hamnavoe ("haven bay"). At now-sealed **Login's Well,** near the southern end of the main street, Captain's Cook's *Discovery* took on fresh water for the long voyage to the New World in search of the Northwest Passage, and ships of the Hudson Bay Company filled their tanks from the source into the early 1900s. Sailors, meanwhile, have found their own watering holes at the adjacent Login Inn (now a private home), and at least a dozen other pubs, with names like Arctic Whalers Inn and the Jolly Sailor. Little Stromness is quieter than it was in the days when these rowdy patrons made the most of their rare days on shore, but the town is a charmer, wedged between the sea on one side and Brinkles Brae, a granite ridge, on the other.

ESSENTIALS

Stromness has a **Tourist Information Centre** in the ferry terminal building (© **01856/850-716**), open April, May, and September Monday through Friday 9:30am to 3:30pm and Saturday 8:30am to 2:30pm; in June, July, and August, it's open daily from 9am to 5pm. The **Pier Arts Centre,** Victoria Street (www.pierartscentre.com; © **01856/850-209**) puts on exhibitions of painting and photography throughout the year and has a shop as well. It's open Monday through Saturday from 10:30am to 5pm; admission is free.

EXPLORING STROMNESS

The main street of Mainland's second-largest town follows a sheltered harbor for about a mile. Little lanes lead off in either direction, some down to the harbor, where high-gabled houses open directly onto their own piers. Other lanes climb high ground toward Brinkles Brae ridge, with enough of an incline that one is known as Khyber Pass.

Stromness Museum ★★ MUSEUM   Some big moments loom large in this small collection. In 1670 the Hudson Bay Company began using Stromness as the first and last landfall for its ships, and the outbound riggers often left port with local men and boys on board. These Orcadians labored for years, even lifetimes, in the company's outposts in Canada, and they sent money and souvenirs home (accounting for the incongruous presence of snowshoes in the display cases) and often returned themselves to build the fine houses that line the harbor. Nearby Scapa Flow, a huge natural harbor stretching between Mainland and four other Orkney islands, has provided anchorage for Viking longships, the British naval fleet, and modern oil tankers. Some rather humble objects, such as candlesticks, china, and maritime flag recount a particularly dramatic event, on June 21, 1919. At the end of World War I, 73 German warships had been impounded in the bay. When peace negotiations at Versailles appeared to have stalled, the German admiral in command gave the orders to scuttle the fleet, and 53 ships went to the bottom. Nine German sailors shot during the operation became the last casualties of World War I. Other Orkney maritime disasters noted here include the loss, on June 5, 1916, of the HMS *Hampshire.* The warship was sailing to Russia when it struck a mine a German submarine had laid off the north coast of the island, taking 650 men down

Like many ports, Stromness inspires a wild tale or two, among them the stories of two Stromness women. **Isobel Gunn** (1780–1861), from the small Orkney Village of Orphir, disguised herself as boy to ship out of Stromness with the Hudson Bay Company to the Canadian wilds. Her wages, meager as they would have been, were more than an uneducated girl could have made in Orkney at the time, plus it's been suggested that Isobel was following a lover. The ruse worked, and Isobel labored for more than a year at Fort Albany, in northern Ontario, then traveled 1,600 miles by canoe to the remote outpost of Pembina, in present-day North Dakota. Not only did she keep her gender a secret, but also her pregnancy. In December 1807 she delivered a boy, the first European child to be born so far west. Isobel and her son

were returned to Ft. Albany and from there, in 1809, to Stromness, where Isobel worked as a seamstress until her death. **Eliza Fraser** (1798–1858) sailed from Stromness with her ship captain husband in 1835, but after many months at sea the party became shipwrecked on the Great Barrier Reef off Australia. The story became more colorful with Eliza's many retellings, and word soon circulated that the survivors had been captured and tortured by aboriginal peoples. Eliza claimed that after her husband's murder, she escaped and was rescued by an Irish convict. She married another sea captain and, after a brief return to England, settled in Melbourne, where she was killed in a carriage accident. Her story has been told in a 1976 film, *The Adventures of Eliza Fraser,* and Patrick White's 1976 novel, *A Fringe of Leaves.*

with her, including Minister of War Lord Kitchener. On July 9, 1917, the HMS *Vanguard* exploded off the little island of Flotta, southeast of Mainland, killing 843 men.

A much-treasured archaeological artifact is so-called "Buddo," a 5,000-year-old, roughly fashioned human figurine from Skara Brae (see below). The figure was unearthed in the 1860s, donated to the museum in the 1930s, and tucked away in a box and forgotten until a curator recently "rediscovered" it in the storerooms.

52 Alfred St. ℂ **01856/850-025.** £5 adults, £4 seniors and students, £1 children 5–15. Apr–Oct daily, 10am–5pm.

Unstan Cairn ★ ARCHAEOLOGICAL SITE Within an earthen mound on a little promontory jutting into Loch Stenness is this round burial chamber from about 2500 B.C.E., unique in that slabs of rock divide the space into cells. The chamber is now covered with a protective roof from the 1930s and illuminated with skylights, rendering the underground room a lot airier and brighter than it originally was, or than it was in 1884, when excavators crawled upon two skeletons crouching in a side chamber. Around them were shards of pottery with decorations below the rim that has also been found elsewhere on the island and has come to be known as Unstan Ware.

3 miles northeast of Stromness along the A965. Free admission. Always open.

WHERE TO EAT & STAY IN STROMNESS

Ferry Inn ★★   This stylish institution spreads around a slice of the harbor, with some accommodations on two floors above the town's most popular pub and restaurant, and others in three nearby houses, including the old Royal Hotel across the street. The sea is in sight from most of these simple perches, all of them bright and cheery, with a few tucked onto the ground floor for guests who don't want to challenge stairs. Meals are served throughout the day in the pub/restaurant, and everything comes from local suppliers, from fresh seafood to North Ronaldsay lamb to locally brewed Orkney ales and Highland whiskies. Traditional musicians often stop in to show off their skills.

10 John St., Stromness. www.ferryinn.com. ✆ **01856/850-280.** 30 units. Doubles from £90, includes breakfast. Restaurant daily, noon–2pm and 5–9pm. Main courses £15–£30. **Amenities:** Restaurant; pub; free Wi-Fi.

Mill of Eyrland ★★   This 19th-century watermill once ground bere, a type of barley, for local farmers, and over the past 40 years or so has been beautifully restored, with gears and millstones still atmospherically in place and gardens blooming in what were once work yards. The Stone Room, the guest lounge, shows off the original workings, with ropes and gear shafts setting off the cushy furnishings, while other rooms are more traditionally cozy and include the two-bedroom Hopper Suite.

Outside Stenness, 4 miles east of Stromness. www.millofeyrland.com. ✆ **01856/850-136.** 4 units. Doubles £60–£90, includes breakfast. **Amenities:** Free Wi-Fi.

OUTDOOR ACTIVITIES AROUND STROMNESS

The three battleships, three light cruisers, and a mine sweeper scuttled by the Germans in **Scapa Flow** at the end of World War I have created a major dive site. They are what remain of the 53 ships that went down, the rest having been salvaged over the years. Divers must be PADI-qualified to explore the wrecks, which vary in depth from 26 to 46m (85–151 ft.). During World War II other ships were sunk to block off the harbor and fortify the Churchill Barriers, and many of these block ships lie in shallow waters and are accessible to less experienced divers. You can read about the wrecks and the sea life that flourishes around them at www.scapaflowwrecks.com. **Scapa Scuba,** Stromness (www.scapascuba.co.uk; ✆ **01856/851-218**) leads guided dives, offers PADI instruction, and rents equipment.

Heart of Neolithic Orkney ★★★

Some 5,000 years ago, Neolithic inhabitants of Orkney had a bit of a building spree along the flat coasts around present-day Stromness and Stenness, 13 miles west of Kirkwall. The ruins of these monuments, tombs, and dwellings provide rich insights into their way of life, farming culture, domestic arrangements, spiritual beliefs, ceremonies, and craftsmanship and are protected as a UNESCO World Heritage Site, collectively known as the Heart of Neolithic Orkney. If you're visiting in July and August, you can watch ongoing work at yet another find, the recently excavated **Ness of Brodgar.** Dwellings and a temple, enclosed within a massive stone wall, were in use from 3500 to 2000 B.C.E., and tools, figurines, and inscribed slabs suggest the folks who made and used them were part of a highly sophisticated civilization. The site is covered outside the summer dig season.

Maeshowe ★★★ ARCHAELOGICAL SITE   A tall grassy mound rising near the shores of Loch Harray is an extensive chambered tomb, one of the largest and best-preserved such structures in Western Europe. A large central chamber is surrounded by three side chambers and reached via a long, low passage. Around the winter solstice, light penetrates the passage to illuminate the rear wall of the chamber, and the spectacle was perhaps designed to mark the end of the old year and the beginning of a new one, a sign that days were lengthening again. (You can view this phenomenon via a webcam at www. maeshowe.co.uk.) Massive stones near the entrance may have once been part of a stone circle, and an encircling ditch may have been filled with water, isolating this world of the dead from the world of the living. It's estimated that construction of the tomb required at least 100,000 man hours, and this effort, along with so much sophisticated complexity, suggests that Maeshowe was the resting place of powerful and elite members of the local tribes. Adding a human element to the somber surroundings are runes, or the symbols used in old Norse language, that Viking intruders left behind on the walls around 1150. Sagas suggest that a group of warriors became lost in a snowstorm, sought shelter in the tomb, and left behind these 30 carved inscriptions. Among them are "Tryggr carved these runes" and "These runes were carved by the man most skilled in runes in the western ocean"—that is, they're as touchingly banal as the graffiti of today.

Outside Stenness. www.historic-scotland.gov.uk. ✆ **01856/761-606.** Visit by guided tour only, leaving from Maeshowe Visitor Center in Stenness; coach service to Maeshowe included (no parking at Maeshowe). £6 adults, £4.80 seniors and students, £3.60 children 5–15. Hourly tours daily, 10am–4pm; June–Aug, also tours at 6, 7, and 8pm. You may buy tickets online at the Historic Scotland website, above (strongly advised in busy summer months).

Ring of Brodgar ★★ ARCHAELOGICAL SITE   The 27 stones still standing here were once part of an original circle of 60 stones, erected between 2500 and 2000 B.C.E. and forming a ring about 104 meters (340 feet) in diameter enclosed by a massive ditch. The surrounding hills create a cauldron in which the ring forms the centerpiece, though the scenic location on a narrow isthmus between Loch Harray and Loch Stenness was not part of the original design—Loch Stenness wasn't formed until the sea breached the land some 1,000 years after the stones were erected. The ring may have been part of a massive ceremonial site, along with the nearby Stones of Stenness, a mile to the southeast (see below), but perhaps the purpose is more mundane. It's also been suggested that this and other stone circles on Orkney were an ancient way to keep up with the Joneses and were erected by competing groups eager to outshine one another with these shows of prestige and power.

5 miles northeast of Stromness on the B9055. Free admission. Always open.

13

ORKNEY & SHETLAND | Orkney

Skara Brae ★★★ ARCHAELOGICAL SITE About 5,000 years ago, a community of some 50 farmers, hunters, and fishermen dwelled in these ten houses, connected by a low, covered passage. The houses, sunk partially into the ground for insulation and stability, were constructed of flat stones laid one upon the other without mortar and each consisted of a square room with a hearth in the center. They were equipped with stone-slab doors, stone beds, dressers, and chairs, and had crude toilets linked to a central drain that carried waste to the sea. This early community is so well preserved because shifting sands covered it about 4,000 years ago, and the outlines of a few of the houses emerged only after a fierce storm in the winter of 1850 swept some of the protective covering away. The site is often labeled as the "Scottish Pompeii," though a less academic analogy to Bedrock, home to cartoon character Fred Flintstone, is certainly allowable. A summertime visit includes admission to adjacent 17th-century Skaill House, Orkney's finest residence, and home to a bishop and 12 lairds. Among them was William Graham Watt, 7th Laird of Breckness, who unearthed Skara Brae in 1850. His many possessions on display include a dinner service that belonged to Captain James Cook, the explorer. A year after Cook was killed in Hawaii in 1779, the crews of his ships *Discovery* and *Resolution* pulled into Stromness Harbor. Overjoyed to be on land again, the 180 men sold off Cook's delicate china and his extensive collection of natural specimens to pay for what amounted to a drunken binge in port.

6 miles northwest of Stenness. www.historic-scotland.gov.uk. ℗ **01856/841-815.** Apr–Oct, includes admission to Skaill House, £7.50 adults, £6 seniors and students, £4.50 children 5–15. Nov–Mar, Skara Brae only, £6.50 adults, £5.20 seniors and students, £3.90 children 5–15. Apr–Sept daily, 9:30am–5:30pm, Oct–Mar daily, 10am–4pm.

Stones of Stenness Circle ★ ARCHAELOGICAL SITE These 4 stones arranged in a vague ellipsis, towering some 6 meters (19 feet) above the eastern shores of Loch Stenness, are what remains of what might have been a circle of 12 stones, erected 5,000 years ago. Even in the absence of their companion pieces the four enormous stones are imposing and suggestive of ancient mysteries, and it's easy to see why they were once known as the Temple of the Moon. That romantic notion has about as much credibility as the imaginative assertion by the popular novelist Sir Walter Scott, who visited in the 19th century, and surmised that the large slab in the center of the circle was an altar used for human sacrifice.

5 miles north east of Stromness on the B9055. www.historicenvironment.scot. Free admission. Always open.

Burray ★ & South Ronaldsay ★

From the southeast coast of Mainland, the Churchill Barriers causeway road drops south across the small islands of Lamb Holm and Glims Holm then onto Burray and finally South Ronaldsay. Total length of the crossing from Mainland onto South Ronaldsay is only about 5 miles, with the barriers comprising about 2 miles of the route.

The **Churchill Barriers** ★★ are an attraction in themselves, the work of 1,300 Italian prisoners of war captured in North Africa during World War II and engineered to close off the eastern entrances to Scapa Flow, the huge natural harbor where the British Navy's Grand Fleet was based. The barriers were officially inaugurated in their entirety on May 12, 1945, four days after the end of the war. Rock was quarried in the Orkneys, and concrete blocks were cast on the islands to top off stone pilings sunk in 70 feet of water, and they can be seen above the waterline. On the southernmost stretch of the barriers, between Burray and South Ronaldsay, sands have accumulated against the pilings to create what seems to be a natural isthmus.

About 550 of the workmen were housed on Lamb Holm, and they left behind more of their handiwork in the **Italian Chapel** ★★, two conjoined Nissen huts painted with dazzling biblical scenes and a transcendent Virgin and Child over the altar. Lonely, cold, and homesick, the men undertook the project with relish, using paints and brushes supplied by a local artist. One POW wrote that he and his fellow prisoners were determined "to show to oneself first, and to the world then, that in spite of being trapped in a barbed wire camp, down in spirit, physically and morally deprived of many things, one could still find something inside that could be set free." The camp has long since been dismantled, but the chapel remains because the demolition crew refused to destroy such a testament to spiritual freedom. The chapel is usually open and admission is free.

Continuing south across the final causeway, you reach **South Ronaldsay** and the picturesque village of **St Margaret's Hope** ★. Small as it is, quaint St Margaret's is the third-largest town in the Orkneys, and lobster pots on the beach and boats bobbing in the harbor are a reminder of days when residents made their living from the herring banks just offshore. The name of the town is, with a bit of a stretch in the absence of any solid historical evidence, linked to Margaret, Maid of Norway, who was the daughter of the king of Norway and became queen of Scotland in 1286 with the death of her grandfather, Scottish King Alexander III. At the age of 8, Margaret was betrothed to the 6-year-old boy who would become Edward II of England. The marriage would have united the crowns of Scotland and England 300 years before that came to pass, but Margaret became seasick on the journey from Bergen to Leith, near Edinburgh. She was brought ashore here in the Orkneys and soon died.

Tomb of the Eagles ★ ARCHAEOLOGICAL SITE What's officially listed as the Isbister Cairn, discovered by a farmer digging for flagstones in 1958, has assumed its more poetic name from the presence of the bones of at least 8 sea eagles. These were placed next to a spooky array of human skulls and some 16,000 bones that account for 342 individuals. It's not too much of a stretch to assume that the magnificent bird, with a wingspan of 2 meters (7 ft.) could have been a totem for the peoples buried here. It's also been suggested that the eagles were brought here to eat the flesh and viscera of the dead before they were placed in the tomb. Other bones found around the sight also raise questions and inspire theories—the bones of calves outside the tomb may indicate that animals were led here for ceremonial slaughter, while charred lamb bones inside suggest the chamber was used for ceremonies. To traverse through the low, narrow entrance passageway, you'll be asked to lie flat on a wheeled trolley—not advised for the claustrophobic.

Liddle. www.tomboftheeagles.co.uk. ℘ **01856/831-339.** £7.50 adults, £6.50 seniors and students, £3.50 children 13–17, £2.50 children 5–12. March daily, 10am–noon; Apr–Sept daily, 9:30am–5:30pm; Oct daily, 9:30am–12:30pm.

WHERE TO EAT & STAY ON BURRAY & SOUTH RONALDSAY

The Creel ★★   One of the many appealing reasons to foray across the Churchill Barriers to charming St Margaret's Hope on the island of South Ronaldsay is a stay in one of these large, airy rooms, nicely done up with light fabrics and lots of blonde wood, and a garden flat in owner David's house next door. Many villagers still know the Creel as a fine restaurant, and David honors the tradition by preparing delicious seafood meals for guest, on request. While the little village enjoys a nice edge-of-the-world atmosphere, Scapa Flow, the islands' many war sights, as well as the remarkable Neolithic remains, are all within easy reach.

Front Rd., St. Margaret's Hope. www.thecreel.co.uk. ℘ **01856/831-311.** Doubles £110, rates include breakfast. **Amenities:** Wi-Fi (free).

Sands Hotel Bar & Restaurant ★   No pretense about an aristocratic past here. This sturdy waterfront property along the Churchill Barriers was built as a herring station in 1860, with part of the premises used to make barrels, another part to pack and store salted fish ready for shipping, and the upstairs rooms housing workers. The downstairs storerooms were later filled with coal reserves. The waterside location now ensures sea views from guest rooms that include two extremely spacious two-floor suites, each with a fireplace and two bedrooms. The restaurant is a local favorite and serves filling meals that can stick to homey basics like lasagna or battered cod caught outside the kitchen door or range into expert preparations of local scallops and duck.

Burray Village, Burray. www.thesandshotel.co.uk. ℘ **01856/731-298.** 8 units. Doubles from £120, rates include breakfast. Restaurant daily, noon–2:30pm and 6–9pm. Main courses £10–£20. **Amenities:** Restaurant; bar; free Wi-Fi.

Hoy ★★

10 miles S of Mainland

The name, from the Norse for "High Island," says it all. Hoy lays claim to the highest point in the chain, the 479m (1,571 ft.) **Ward Hill,** as well as to Britain's highest vertical cliffs at **St. John's Head** (352m/1,154 ft.). Aside from this highland scenery, the most dramatic in the Orkneys, the island also shows off its big role in Britain's military past.

ESSENTIALS

GETTING THERE   Visitors without cars can take the passenger-only ferry (www.orkneyferries.co.uk; ℘ **01856/850-624**) from Stromness to **Moaness** at the northern end of the island. There are four crossings per day during the week (two at weekends) and the journey takes 30 minutes. Many passengers use this route as the start to a walk out to the Hoy Sea Cliffs and the Old Man of Hoy (see below). In summer, a minibus meets the boats for the trip to Rackwick, the start of the cliffs walking trail; otherwise, it's a 5½-mile walk from Moaness to Rackwick. The more frequent vehicle ferry (www.orkney ferries.co.uk; ✆ **01856/811-397**) leaves from Houton and arrives in **Lyness** at the southern end of the island about 35 minutes later.

EXPLORING HOY

Lyness, on coastal flats at the southern end of the island, was the location of a huge naval base during both world wars, serving the British fleet based in Scapa Flow. The **Scapa Flow Visitor Centre and Museum** ★ (www.scapa flow.co.uk; ✆ **01856/791-300**) tells the story of the base and houses the expected collection of guns and other military equipment, along with some charming mementoes, such as letters home from men stationed on the ships anchored offshore. The museum is closed for renovations until at least 2020. In the meantime, guides lead two-hour walks around the now-deserted Royal Navy Base, leaving from the Lyness ferry terminal at 11am on Tuesdays and Thursdays, from April through October. The cost is £5 a person and stops include the Royal Navy Cemetery. For information, call ✆ **01856/791-300.** On the B9047 road, about a mile northwest of Lyness, is an evocative reminder of the World War II years, a handsome Art Deco theater, now a private home, that once had a huge Nissen hut attached to the back, where films were shown and performers entertained the troops. Among the celebrities who dropped in were Prime Minister Winston Churchill and music-hall star Gracie Fields.

Hackness Martello Tower and Battery ★ HISTORIC SITE   This round tower is a relic of earlier wars, built in 1813 to protect British merchant ships sailing through Longhope Sound with a safe anchorage in Scapa Flow. The main threats were from French and American privateers, who found British ships to be fair game during the Napoleonic Wars and British-American War of 1812. Hostile shots were never fired from the tower, though the 4-meter (14-foot) thick walls and huge gun emplacements are certainly a show of military might. Tucked around the artillery are the living arrangements for the troops stationed here, with homey officer quarters and a barracks for enlisted men at the top of the tower under a domed roof.

Hackness, 8 miles south of Lyness. www.historic-scotland.gov.uk. ✆ **01856/701-727.** £5 adults, £4 seniors and students, £3 children 5–15. Apr–Oct daily, 9:30am–5:30pm.

THE HOY SEA CLIFFS ★★

The island's main road hugs the east coast, and a track crosses the bleak, boggy interior west to tiny **Rackwick** ★, about 12 miles northwest of Lyness and surrounded by some of Orkney's most dramatic scenery. Rackwick is 5½ miles southwest of the passenger ferry terminal at Moaness, on the northern end of the island. A well signposted path leads from the village to the **Old**

Man of Hoy ★, a 137m (449-ft.) sea stack that has been carved out of the sea cliffs. These cliffs extend down the coast for 2 miles to St. John's Head ★, a dramatic swath of red and yellow sandstone that rises to 352 meters (1,154 ft.). Among the many seabirds that nest along and around the cliffs are white-tailed sea eagles, slowly making a reappearance after they were hunted into extinction in the early 20th century.

About 3 miles east of Rackwick, a boardwalk leads across boggy ground to **Dwarfie Stane** ★, a huge chunk of limestone into which a burial chamber has been neatly hewn. The lonely setting, hemmed in by steep valleys in desolate moors, has given rise to many tales about the hollowed-out stone, said to be a hermit's cell or the house of a giant and his wife who, when imprisoned by another giant, gnawed the hole in the roof as a means of escape. Short, narrow shelves within the chamber were once believed to be the beds of wee folk. These stories aside, it's a work of magic in itself that 5,000 years ago someone managed to carve out the chamber using stone and antler tools, along with a great deal of muscle and persistence. The site is always open and admission is free.

WHERE TO EAT & STAY ON HOY

Stromabank Hotel ★   Views over the surrounding farmlands and sea seem endless from these breezy, simple rooms at the southern end of Hoy. Since the outlook takes in the entrance to Scapa Flow and ranges across the Firth of Pentland to mainland Scotland, they almost *are* endless, and include a few lighthouses as well. Dinners, open to non-guests as well, make use of everything Orkney, from South Ronaldsay lamb to Orkney beef and cheeses and of course, a bounty of fresh fish and shellfish, and are served in a view-filled conservatory.

Longhope, South Walls. www.stromabank.co.uk. ℂ **01856/701-611.** 4 units. Double £75, includes breakfast. Restaurant daily, 6–8pm. **Amenities:** Restaurant; bar; free Wi-Fi.

Rousay ★

4 miles N of Mainland

This small island off the northwest coast of Mainland is known as the "Egypt of the North" for the wealth of archaeological sites. Not that you'll see most of them. A treasure trove of 160 graves and dwellings are clustered along a 1-mile stretch of the west coast and have yet to be unearthed, and shovel-wielding international teams are usually hard at work. One of Scotland's great archaeological artifacts, the Westness Brooch, was found on Rousay in the 1970s, when a farmer dug a hole to bury a cow and exposed the grave of a Norse woman who died in childbirth around 850 and was buried alongside her infant. This exquisite piece of jewelry is now in the National Museum in Edinburgh (see p. 73). You can visit two of Orkney's most sophisticated early sites at Midhowe, and the hilly island is also rich in birdlife and, in spring and summer, carpeted in wildflowers. The rocky coast is a haven for seals and otters.

ESSENTIALS

GETTING THERE The ferry (www.orkneyferries.co.uk; *©* **01856/751-360**) leaves from Tingwall and takes about 20 minutes to reach Rousay.

EXPLORING ROUSAY

A 13-mile road runs around the island, but you don't need to go far before you can climb into tombs. Taversoe Tuick and Blackhammer Cairn are both an easy walk from the pier, and they are always open and admission is free. **Taversoe Tuick ★**, half a mile west of the ferry landing, was found in 1896, when landowner General Frederick Traill-Burroughs commissioned s shelter where he could sit and enjoy the sea views. Obviously, he wasn't the first to take advantage of the scenic setting, because workers soon dug into the upper chamber of this round, two-level tomb, built into a hillside. Lady Burroughs voiced a sentiment that many Orcadians must have felt over the years, "There we had sat during many happy summers, stretched on the purple heather, basking in the sunshine; laughing and talking with the carelessness of youth, little dreaming that barely eight feet below us sat these grim and ghastly skeletons."

The **Blackhammer Cairn ★**, just down the road, is entered through a hatch in the roof and a ladder. A 13m- (40 ft.-) long chamber, divided into sections with large vertical slabs, and the exterior is decorated with stones arranged in a triangular pattern. Only two men were found inside when the tomb was discovered in 1936, fueling speculation that this and other tombs were regularly cleared out to make room for a new generation of occupants.

You also don't need to go far from the ferry landing to encounter the island's birdlife, at RSPB **Trumland** just across the road. Golden plovers, snipe, curlews, great skuas, red grouse, red-throated divers, merlins, and hen harriers make a summertime home on 183 hectares (452 acres) of boggy moors. A path climbs to the top of Knitchen Hill to a lookout with good views of the surrounding islands.

Midhowe Chambered Cairn ★★ ARCHAEOLOGICAL SITE This chambered tomb, reached on a half-mile walk along a path from the road to the shore (with a steep uphill climb on the return), is enclosed within a huge stone barn to protect the vulnerable ruins from coastal erosion. Inside, raised walkways beneath a curved roof equipped with skylights provide a good view of 24 stalls, arranged along a 23m (75-ft.) corridor sectioned off into compartments with stone slabs. The modern enclosure might be necessary for long-term preservation but the warehouse-like atmosphere makes it difficult to get into the spirit of the mass grave, where, upon discovery in the 1930s, 25 men, women, and children were found laid upon stone benches or left crouching against the walls, as they'd been for the past 5,500 years or so. In size and shape, the tomb resembles an upturned boat and is known as the "Ship of the Dead."

Midhowe Broch ★, a round tower house, is just beyond the cairn, on the same path. The broch is much newer than the cairn—to put Orkney's long history of human habitation in daunting perspective, the entombed would have been resting in Midhowe Cairn for more than 3,000 years when the broch was occupied from 200 B.C.E. to C.E. 200. While ramparts and defensive ditches to protect against sea invasion suggest that life here at the edge of Eynhallow Sound might have been risky business, the broch was impressive, rising at least twice as high as its current 4m (13 ft.) height. Residents enjoyed some relative comforts, including a cistern fed by spring water, and several levels reached by staircases would have provided ample accommodation and storage.

Off the B9064, 5 miles northwest of the ferry pier. Free admission. Always open.

Eday ★

21 miles N of Mainland

What's essentially a narrow, 8-mile-long piece of sea-girt rock is only 500 meters (1,650 feet) wide at its cinched-waist center. A sweep of interior moorland drops to sandy beaches and rises to limestone headlands that were quarried to provide material for St Magnus Cathedral in Kirkwall (see p. 398). The island is more hospitable to birds and wildflowers than it is to human settlement, though early Orcadians left their mark here, and 100 or so islanders cluster along the green coastal stretches. Offshore currents, once the bane or mariners, are now being harnessed for a tidal energy industry that has brought little Eday some international acclaim in recent years.

ESSENTIALS

GETTING THERE   During the summer, two ferries run daily between Kirkwall and the island's port, Backaland (www.orkneyferries.co.uk; ℗ **01856/872-044**). The journey takes 75 minutes direct (or more than 2 hours if the ferry is going via Stronsay and Sanday). **Loganair** (www.loganair. co.uk; ℗ **01856/872-494**) flies between Kirkwall and the island's little London Airport every Wednesday.

EXPLORING EDAY

First stop on the island is the **Eday Heritage and Visitor Centre ★** (℗ **01857/622-288**), about 3½ miles north of the Backaland ferry terminal. The island ranger posts notices about wildlife, and displays introduce Eday's early history and settlement up to recent times. You can also pick up a pamphlet to guide you along the 5-mile **Eday Heritage Trail** at the northern end of the island. The center is staffed by volunteers and is generally open from early May through late September, Monday through Saturday, 9am to 5:30pm, and Sunday, 10am to 4pm. In other months, the center is open only on Sunday, 10am to 5pm.

The most distinctive of several tombs along the Heritage Trail is the **Vinquoy Chambered Cairn ★,** built from red sandstone, with four beehive-shaped cells surrounding a large central chamber. Views over the sea to the surrounding islands have changed little over the millennial. Standout along

Eday has its own pirate legend, the story of John Gow, who commandeered the frigate *Caroline* in 1724 as it was sailing from Santa Cruz, in the Canary Islands, to Genoa. According to accounts, ill-tempered Gow was discontent with the food and shipboard conditions, so he stabbed and shot the captain then had him thrown overboard. He renamed the ship *Revenge* and enjoyed a brief run as a swashbuckler on the high seas, attacking ships off the coasts of Spain and Portugal. Before long, though, he was running low on supplies and began to yearn for the Orkney Islands, where as a boy he had developed his yen to go to sea. So he changed the name of the vessel again, this time to the *George,* and tried to pass himself off on Mainland as a respectable tradesman. But he and some of his mates were recognized, and when Gow tried to flee, he ran around in the treacherous tidal currents off Eday—the tides that are now being harnessed for power (see above). He was captured, found guilty of murder and piracy, and hanged in London. His death was more sensational than his career as a buccaneer. Honoring Gow's request for a speedy death, the executioner pulled on his legs to tighten the knot, but the rope broke and Gow tumbled to the ground. He was hung a second time, and this attempt was successful. Gow's corpse was chained, tarred, and hung on the Thames riverbank as a warming to would-be pirates. Sir Walter Scott based the main character of his 1822 novel *The Pirate* on Gow (see p. 431).

the route, quite literally, is the **Setter Stone ★★,** standing 4.5m (15 ft.). A monument of such stature is bound to inspire a legend or two, and the one surrounding the Setter Stone claims that the monolith was erected, with great effort, by an ancient laird. He and his men laid the massive stone on a slope above a ditch, with the idea of tipping one end into the hole to stand it upright. When this didn't work, the laird ordered his obedient wife to stand on the end the stone and jump up and down, to nudge it into the ditch. The poor woman became a bit too enthusiastic, bounced into the deep hole, and the stone slid in on top of her—much to the delight of the laird, who was eager to dispense with her. Weather has eroded the stone into the shape of a human hand . . . or, as another story goes, the hand is superhuman, that of a giant. The walk continues to **Red Head ★,** the northernmost tip of the island where fulmars nest on the cliffs. The tiny island of the **Calf of Eday** floats just off the coast and is home to large, noisy colonies of puffins, kittiwakes, razorbills, and guillemots who often make the short flight over to the headland.

Sanday ★

28 miles N of Mainland

Aptly named "sand island" is so low-lying that countless ships have run aground on the shores, not realizing that land lay ahead until the seas around the bay-indented, rock-and-reef littered coastline became too shallow to navigate. For those who come safely ashore on the island—divided into two elongated halves with a narrow isthmus in the middle—the broad expanses of sand provide long beach walks. Like many of the neighboring Orkneys, Sanday is also scattered with ancient tombs. But beware: The ones here are said to be protected by *hogboons,* nasty little creatures who bring no end of trouble to anyone who disturbs the peace of the dead.

ESSENTIALS

GETTING THERE   During the summer, two ferries a day run between Kirkwall and Sanday, where the port is near the southernmost tip of the island, near Stove (www.orkneyferries.co.uk; ℂ **01856/872-044**). The journey takes 1 hour and 15 minutes direct (or nearly 2 hours if the ferry goes via Eday). **Loganair** (www.loganair.co.uk; ℂ **01856/872-494**) flies a daily service between Kirkwall and Sanday. A bus meets the ferries and provides a link to the main settlements, Lady and Kettletoft.

EXPLORING SANDAY

Sanday's many maritime misfortunes were actually a boon for islanders, for whom the wood of stricken vessels once provided the only source of fuel in the treeless landscape. In fact, it's said that the faithful gathered in **Lady Kirk** ★ to pray for a shipwreck to get them through the winter. The church is now a gloomy roofless ruin, surrounded by tombstones, between the main settlements of Lady and Kettletoft, each with about a dozen houses, and about a mile from each. The parishioners' ill will may account for the mysterious presence of the Devil's Clawmarks, a set of grooves in the stone staircase that once led to the north gallery.

Navigation around the island became slightly safer in 1806, when Robert Stevenson, grandfather of the famous adventure novelist Robert Louis Stevenson, erected Scotland's first revolving lighthouse at **Start Point** ★, at the far eastern tip of the island. Migratory birds often congregate on the surrounding sands, as if the lighthouse, painted in black-and-white vertical stripes, is a beacon for them. The island's best beach, **Doun Helzie** ★, is at the western end of the island, a 2-mile walk from the ferry terminal. The sands are backed by caves and short sandstone cliffs that winds have carved into elaborate patterns.

Sanday's rich farmland has attracted settlers for millennia, and it's estimated that hundreds of burial mounds lie untouched beneath fields and grasslands. Finds from a Viking boat burial, at Scar, in the north, are in the Orkney Museum in Kirkwall, while the well preserved **Quoyness Chambered Tomb** ★ is on the southern peninsula of Elsness, near Kettletoft. The main chamber reaches a height of some 4m (13 ft.) and was at the end of a very low, 9m (30 ft.) long tunnel. Most of the roof has collapsed so the passage is now open to the elements, but 3.5m (11 ft.) remains intact and can only be navigated via a muddy crawl on hands and knees, sure to evoke the spirit of the ancient tomb. The tomb is always open, with free admission.

WHERE TO EAT & STAY

The island doesn't offer much in lines of accommodation and dining, but the best choices are in the tiny town of Kettlecroft. Facing the harbor are two old hotels, the Belsair (✆ **01857/600-206**) and the Kettlecroft (✆ **01857/600-217**). Both offer basic accommodation in a total of 9 rooms between them, at rates of about £60 for a double with breakfast. They also have pubs and restaurants that are the social centers of the island.

Westray ★

26 miles N of Mainland

More than 3,000 cows live on Westray, along with at least that many sheep, and an estimated 100,000 seabirds nest on the sea cliffs. Two-legged residents, who currently number about 500, have left some notable traces around the island that go all the way back to early history. Westray is famous as one terminus of the Westray to Papa Westray flight, lasting two minutes, making the hop the shortest commercial flight in the world. That makes it easy to explore both islands, both of which surround their appealing blend of historical and natural attractions with easygoing, rural ambience.

ESSENTIALS

GETTING THERE   In the summer, there are two to three ferries a day between Kirkwall to Rapness, at the southern end of the island (www.orkney-ferries.co.uk; ✆ **01856/872-044**). The journey takes 90 minutes. **Loganair** (www.loganair.co.uk; ✆ **01856/872-494**) operates up to three flights a day to and from Kirkwall. It's just a 2-minute hop to Westray from neighboring Papa Westray. The daily-except-Saturday flight to Westray, covering less than 2 miles, is operated like other inter-island services by Loganair.

EXPLORING WESTRAY

In places, the sea cliffs that ring Westray rise to 250 feet, and they are especially high and picturesque at Noup Head, a long, narrow finger of land in the north. The **RSPB Noup Cliffs Nature Reserve ★** (www.rspb.org.uk) is called "Seabird City," for the enormous colonies that nest below a lighthouse poised in photo-readiness at the end of the point. **Castle o'Burrian ★**, a sea stack that rises off the southwest coast, is a nesting place for puffins. As many as 300 of the little black and white birds are in residence between May and August, to the delight of binocular-wielding observers who congregate on the grassy cliff edges separated from the sea stack by only narrow channel of choppy sea. Male puffins are unusually attentive, loyal mates who bond for life, help build the nest, and share incubation duties with the female. Farther west, along a coastal path, the sea cliffs give way to a white, sandy beach at the **Bay of Tafts ★**.

   Pierowall ★, a somber-yet-appealing port of gray stone, sits on a wide bay at midpoint on the island's east coast and has been a snug harbor since Viking times. Gray, sandstone **Noltland Castle** ★ (www.historicenvironment.scot), a romantic ruin on a grassy slope just outside town, was the mansion-fortress of Gilbert Balfour, 16th century Sheriff of Orkney. Balfour had a way of becoming involved in political intrigues and making enemies, so it was in his best interest to make the lower part of the castle and impregnable fortress, with 71 gun loops in the thick, otherwise windowless walls. Above were fairly luxurious living quarters, reached by a grand spiral staircase and serviced by vast kitchens. Balfour did not have too long to enjoy the castle before he was implicated in the murder of Lord Darnley, the second husband of Mary Queen of Scots, and forced to flee to Sweden in 1572. The roofless ruins of medieval **Lady Kirk** in town rise next to the sea. The **Cross Kirk,** 4 miles away in in Tuquoy, was built by Norse settler Haflidi Thorkelsson in the 1100s, and is simple yet stately even in its roofless, almost wall-less state. Both churches are surrounded by fields of mossy tombstones, and all these ruins are always open and admission is free.

Westray Heritage Centre ★★ MUSEUM   These modest surroundings house two internationally acclaimed treasures. The 5,000 year old **Orkney Venus** ★★★, also known as the Westray Wife, is the oldest known representation of the human form found in Scotland and was unearthed on the island in 2009. Carved out of sandstone, probably with a bone tool, the figurine is diminutive, only 41mm (1½ inches) tall, 31mm (1.2 inches wide), and 12mm (½ inch) thick. Two little eye holes are topped by scrapings that suggest brows, and two circles on the torso could be breasts, or fasteners for a costume of some sort. Small as the figure is, it's existence has important implications, suggesting that the earliest island residents had enough leisure time to carve the figure, possibly used as a symbol, or as a toy or pendant. Some current islanders have proved to be enterprising artisans, too, and sell shortbread fashioned in the shape of the figurine. The 5,000-year-old **Westray Stone** ★ is in two parts, measuring 1.35m (4-ft.) in total, and inscribed with spirals. Similar patterns have been found in tombs in the Boyne Valley, in Ireland. Workers unearthed part of the stone while digging on the waterfront in Pierowall, and it probably once decorated a long-vanished tomb.

Pierowall. www.westrayheritage.co.uk. ✆ **01857/677-414.** £3 adults, £2.50 seniors and students, 50p children under 16. May–Sept, Mon 11:30am–5pm, Tues–Sat 10am–noon and 2–5pm, Sun 1:30–5pm.

WHERE TO EAT & STAY

No. 1 Broughton ★★   A rambling Victorian house overlooking Pierowall Bay is now home to artist Jerry Wood and filled with his artwork. The four guestrooms are bright and comfortable, and the quarters also extend into an upstairs sitting room, a fire-warmed lounge, and a conservatory, all overlooking the bay; a sauna is usually available.

Pierowall, Westray, KW17 2DA. www.no1broughton.co.uk. ✆ **01857/677-726.** 4 units. Doubles £60, includes breakfast. **Amenities:** Sauna; free Wi-Fi.

Pierowall Hotel ★ Social life on Westray centers around this cozy and simple inn and pub that's in the island's main settlement and feels like a family home. Guests share a comfortable lounge, and join islanders for stews, soups, and other solid home cooking, a lot of it made with produce from the hotel garden.

Pierowall Village, Westray. www.pierowallhotel.co.uk. ✆ **01857/677-472.** 5 units, 4 with private bathroom. Doubles £65, includes breakfast. **Amenities:** Restaurant; bar; free Wi-Fi.

Papa Westray ★★

4 miles E of Westray

Papa Westray is the terminus, or departure point, of the world's shortest scheduled flight, linking the little airfield with the one on neighboring Westray in just 2 minutes. Those who stay on the island long enough discover some remarkable remnants of early islanders, and can also enjoy the easygoing ambience provided by 100 or so current residents, whose number are slowly increasing as the Papay Development Trust promotes tourism and settlement on the island.

ESSENTIALS

GETTING THERE Aside from the 2-minute hop between Westray and Papa Westray (daily except Sunday), **Loganair** (www.loganair.co.uk; ✆ **01856/872-494**) also operates daily flights to and from Kirkwall. A vehicle ferry (www.orkneyferries.co.uk; ✆ **01856/872-044**) runs from Kirkwall on Tuesday and Friday. Journey times differ according to the route taken. There's also a passenger ferry from Pierowall on Westray that runs between three and six times a day; the journey takes about 30 minutes.

EXPLORING PAPA WESTRAY

The island is small, just 4¼ miles from north to south, and you can easily amble from sight to sight. The northern end of the island is a wild, windswept maritime heath and protected as the **RSPB North Hill Nature Reserve ★★** (www.rspb.org.uk; ✆ **01856/850-176**). The rare Scottish primrose blooms on the heath, and the short sea cliffs are the summertime home to Europe's largest breeding colony of Arctic terns, along with significant numbers of guillemots, puffins, kittiwakes, and Arctic skuas. The reserve's ranger leads tours on Wednesdays and Saturdays from May through August.

Knap of Howar ★★ ARCHAEOLOGICAL SITE Two adjoining, stone-walled structures, a dwelling and a workshop, are the oldest standing buildings in Europe and were home to a farm family around 3,600 and for several centuries afterwards. The remote farmstead lay covered for unknown centuries until a gale in 1929 blew some of the earthen covering away, exposing enough stones to pique the curiosity of a farmer, who dug out the structures. The dwelling is large, 10 by 5 meters (35 by 18 feet), with low stone beds that would have had heather mattresses running along a wall, and a kitchen separated by a stone slab, with a central hearth and a stone for grinding barley. A passage though the stone adjoining wall leads into a workshop/storage area, separated by stone slabs three stalls. While the stone walls appear to be dug into the earth, they would have been freestanding, and the houses would have been farther from the shoreline than they are now, surrounded by a meadow.

On the west coast, near the airfield. Free admission. Always open.

St Boniface Church ★ HISTORIC SITE   Namesake St Boniface (675–754) spread Christianity throughout Germany and his influence reached as far as Orkney. News of his life and martyrdom were spreading across Northern Europe when a chapel was built on this site in the 8th century, establishing a beachhead for Christianity in Scotland. A Norse gravestone, called a "hog-back" tomb for its unusual, humped shaped, and early Christian cross-slabs are in the graveyard of the now restored church. Despite the efforts of early missionaries, Orkney wasn't fully Christianized until, according to Norse saga King of Norway Olaf Tryggvason summoned Sigurd the Stout, earl of Orkney, in 995 and commanded, "I order you and all your subjects to be baptized. If you refuse, I'll have you killed on the spot and I swear I will ravage every island with fire and steel." That appears to have done the trick once and for all. Papa Westray was also home to Papars, early monks who lived like hermits in Scandinavia and the northern islands. The Old Norse name for Papa Westray was Papay Meiri, meaning "Big Island of the Papars."

⅔ mile north of the Knap of Howar. Free admission. Always open.

St Tredwell's Chapel ★ HISTORIC SITE   The Loch of St Tredwell and this ruined little waterside chapel, not much more than a jumble of weed-choked stones, once attracted pilgrims from throughout Britain and Scandinavia. It was believed that the loch waters were medicinal and especially beneficial for ailments relating to the eyes. The chapel was dedicated to mir-acle-working St Triduana (Tredwell), an 8th-century nun who traveled throughout the north to convert the Picts to Christianity. Clearly, Triduana was not the type of girl who accepted compliments with grace. When a Pictish king, Nechtan, admired Triduana's lovely eyes, she is said to have become so angry that she plucked them out and sent them to him, impaled on a branch. The chapel's reputation as a cure-all gained considerable credence in the 13th century, when a bishop whose tongue and eyes had been cut out came to the "resting place of the holy Trollhaena" and regained his power of speech and sight on the spot.

About 1 mile NE of ferry terminal. Free admission. Always open.

TOURS OF PAPA WESTRAY

You can book a bike for a self-guided tour by contacting the island ranger at papayranger@gmail.com or leaving a message at ℂ **0793/123-5213** or on the Facebook page of the Papay Ranger; rates are £10 a day. **Papay Peedie Tours** (also arranged through the ranger) include a walk to the Knap of Howar and St Boniface Kirk, a big lunch, and an afternoon walk through the RSPB North

Hill Nature Reserve. Tours come with a nice dose of island hospitality, run from May through August, and cost £50 adults, £25 children. The *Dunter,* a little excursion boat operated by the Papay Development Trust, makes May through August runs out to the Holm of Papay, where a 5,000-year cambered tomb is tucked away amid the scrub. The islet and surrounding seas teem with wildlife. Outings on the *Dunter* cost £25 for adults, £10 for children, and family rates are available. For information and to reserve call ℂ **01857/644-224** or leave a message on the Papay Ranger Facebook page.

SHETLAND ★

60 miles NE of the Orkneys

These northernmost reaches of the British Isles are about 600 miles from London but only 220 miles from Bergen, Norway. This geography, along with many centuries of Norse rule, imparts a Scandinavian overlay to the atmosphere that's as distinctive as the phenomenon Shetlanders call "simmer dim"—almost continuous daylight in the summer months. This means winter days bring less than 6 hours of daylight, but one thing Shetlanders haven't seemed to inherit from their Viking ancestors is a propensity to gloominess. They relish the brief glimmerings of crystal-clear winter light, and they light up the long winter nights with Up Helly Aa, a riotous fire festival.

Shetland comprises 100-plus islands, of which only 15 are inhabited, and most of those only sparsely. No point in Shetland is more than 3 miles from the sea, and the wild and rugged coastline is battered by both the Atlantic Ocean and the North Sea. Waves have sculpted the rocks into weird and wonderful shapes, creating stacks, natural arches, blow-holes, caves, and tunnels. The treeless, windswept inland reaches of the islands aren't much tamer, but there's a stark, savage beauty to it all—especially, of course, when experienced during the simmer dim. The main island, Mainland, has the lion's share of sights and is where most visitors spend their time. It's easy enough to explore the rest of the archipelago, too, on the ferries that sail in and out of Mainland ports, and on inter-island flights.

Essentials

GETTING THERE **Loganair** (www.loganair.co.uk; ℂ **0344/800-2855**) operates several services a day from and to Aberdeen, Edinburgh, Glasgow, Inverness, and Kirkwall on Orkney to the islands' main airport at **Sumburgh,** on the southern tip of Mainland. Ferries leave Aberdeen every evening throughout the year to arrive in Shetland at 7:30am the next day. On-board facilities include a restaurant, cafeteria, bars, lounges, a movie theatre, gift shops, and sleeping accommodations in cabins and "sleeping pods," extremely comfortable reclining seats. For information, contact **NorthLink** (www. northlinkferries.co.uk; ℂ **0845/600-0449**). Three times a week (four in summer), these ferries also stop at Kirkwall in Orkney.

GETTING AROUND Airtask (www.airtask.com; 📞 **01595/840-246**) operates flights between the Shetland islands of Fair Isle, Papa Stour, and Foula and Tingwall, 6 miles northwest of Lerwick. Inter-island ferries are operated by **Shetland Islands Council** (www.shetland.gov.uk/ferries). Regular vehicle services operate to the islands of Unst, Yell, Whalsay, Fetlar, Skerries, and Bressay. Passenger-only services operate to Papa Stour, Foula, and Fair Isle. **Buses** travel around Mainland from the Viking Bus Station hub on Commercial Road in Lerwick to major places of interest and larger towns around Mainland, including ports that serve the other islands. To download a timetable, visit www.zettrans.org.uk.

Car-rental firms based in Lerwick include **Bolts Car Hire** at 26 North Rd. (www.boltscarhire.co.uk; 📞 **01595/693-636**); **Grantfield Garage,** North Road (www.grantfieldgarage.co.uk; 📞 **01595/692-709**); and **Star Rent A Car,** 22 Commercial Rd. (www.starrentacar.co.uk; 📞 **01595/692-075**), the agent for Alamo, Sixt, and Europcar.

TOURS A good way to see several of the Mainland sights in one go is with **Island Trails** day tours, with stops at Jarlshof, the Croft House, and other points of interest (www.island-trails.co.uk; 📞 **07880/950-228**). **Trips for Knitters** offers multiday knitting tours and weaving workshops on Shetland, with visits to mills, shops, and artisans (www.tripsforknitters.com; in the U.S., 📞 **301/766-4543**). From November through March, **Shetland Wildlife Tours** leads a day-long look at the wildfowl that winters on Mainland, as well as otters, seals, and other wildlife (www.shetlandwildlife.co.uk; 📞 **01950/460-939**).

Lerwick ★

The capital of Shetland, home to 6,000 Shetlanders, or about a fourth of all islanders, is maritime and decidedly northern, with sturdy stone houses surrounding the harbor on Bressay Sound. Lerwick's modern-day beginnings were decidedly unsavory. From around 1600, a Dutch fishing fleet used to sail into what the Norse knew as Leirvik, or Dirty Harbor, each summer in pursuit of herring, and the sailors set up huts along the beach for what was nothing less than a drunken free for all, or as one contemporary noted, "the great abomination and wickedness committed yearly by the Hollanders." In 1625, an island court ruled that Leirvik be demolished and burned to put an end to this lewdness. The order was never carried out, and the busy and industrious town that instead grew up around the harbor is the ferry port for connections to mainland Scotland and is well poised for exploring the many sights on the southern end of the island as well as the rugged north.

ESSENTIALS

VISITOR INFORMATION **VisitScotland's Lerwick Centre** is at Market Cross (www.visitscotland.com; 📞 **01595/693-434**). The helpful staff can arrange rooms and provide information on ferries, boat trips, car rentals, local events, and visitor attractions. It's open from April to October, Monday

The Shetland Islands

through Saturday from 9am to 5pm and Sunday 9am to 4pm; and November to March, Monday through Saturday from10am to 4pm. You can also find a lot of helpful information on the web at www.shetland.org.

EXPLORING LERWICK

Attractive, shop-lined Commercial Street winds through the center of Lerwick. Little alleyways run between gaps in the sturdy stone buildings to the *lodberries,* houses that face the seafront and, built by fish merchants, have their own piers onto which the catch was unloaded from boats, then salted and stored in sheds. The private water access made the houses popular with for smugglers as well. A district known as the Lanes climbs up a steep hillside above Commercial Street along lanes that are often flights of steps.

Böd of Gremista Museum ★ HISTORIC SIGHT/MUSEUM Two of Shetland's traditional industries come together in this former fishing station. The böd, from 1780, was the main house of an operation that salted and shipped fish. Boats were beached and salted fish laid out to dry in the sun on the waterfront in front, and salt and shipping barrels were stored in the somber-looking house. Arthur Anderson, son of the station master, was born here in 1792, and he went to sea and became one of the world's most famous Shetlanders when he founded the Peninsula and Oriental Steam Navigation Company, better known as the P&O. These days the böd shows off Shetland's long-standing textile industry, with a collection of knitwear and woven taatit rugs, along with the wheels and looms on which island wool was spun and woven. It's only fitting that, in 1837, Arthur Anderson presented Queen Victoria with a pair of knitted "fine lace" stockings like the ones now on display in his birthplace.

Waterfront, ½ mile north of the ferry terminal. www.shetlandtextilemuseum.com. © **01595/694-386.** Free admission. Tues–Sat noon–5pm.

Clickimin Broch ★ ARCHAEOLOGICAL SITE Shetland's ancient history makes itself known amid Lerwick's straggling outskirts. On an island at the end of a causeway in the Loch of Clickimin, this sturdy broch, a round stone tower that once stood as high as 15m (49 ft.), was home to a group of farmers 3,000 years ago. The little community grazed cattle in lochside pastures and grew barley that they ground in stone troughs. The islet was surrounded by a stone wall with a massive blockhouse in the single gate, though in successive, more peaceable times the broch was lowered and became a single dwelling, and simple farmsteads were established around it. At some point, residents added a baffling element to the assemblage, a slab embedded in the causeway with two footprints carved into it. Some scholars have suggested this might be the remnant of a royal visit, or perhaps something as mundane as a welcome mat.

About a mile southwest of the town center off the A970. www.historic-scotland.gov.uk. Free admission. Always open.

Fort Charlotte ★ HISTORIC SIGHT This formidable pentagon, facing the sea with a battery of 12 powerful cannons, was built in 1781 and named for the wife of the monarch, King George III. Britain was then at war with the American colonies, as well as France and Spain, so it was provident to protect these northern sea lanes. Shots were never fired, though the fortress would have put on a good show with its dampness-and-explosion proof powder magazine and massive barracks, with accommodation for a garrison of 270 men.

Harbour St. www.historic-scotland.gov.uk. Free admission. Daily 7am–8pm.

Shetland Museum & Archive ★★ MUSEUM   You might come away from this extensive homage to everything Shetland with some new words in your vocabulary—as in, you might be keeping your *hap* in your *kishie*. Translations are available in the Folklife section, where most of the gear relates to the task of keeping warm and feeding oneself on these self-sufficient islands at times when a *joopie* (hand-knitted undershirt) came in handy when heading out to the moors with a *tushkar* (peat spade) or setting out to sea in a *fourareen* (four-oared boat) to fish. A flotilla of colorful island sailing craft are the scene stealers and hang from the rafters and float in the harbor alongside the galleries. Everything from lichen (hundreds of species flourish here) to the island's distinctive handcrafted knitwear is impressively displayed and provides a fascinating look at Shetland life over the millennia.

Hay's Dock. www.shetland-museum.org.uk. ℂ **01595/695-057.** Free admission. Mon–Sat 10am–5pm, Sunday noon–5pm.

WHERE TO STAY & EAT IN LERWICK

Grand Hotel ★   This grand old Victorian building, with pointed turrets and solid stone walls, has been an institution on the town's main thoroughfare since opening as a hotel in 1887. It appears as if some of the frayed carpeting in the darkly painted halls and stairways hasn't been replaced since then, but many regular wouldn't want anything about this atmospheric old place to change—though a little brightening up might bring out the best of the fine old woodwork and grand public spaces. Guest quarters are decidedly old-fashioned but better maintained than other parts of the premises, and a spacious four-poster room is particularly atmospheric, with good views over the harbor. Drink might get the better of this place yet—19th-century city fathers worried about the fate of inebriates exiting the bar onto steep stairs, and these days an in-house club, Poseurs, can wreak havoc with a night's sleep. Ask for a room well away from the noise.

149 Commercial St. www.kgqhotels.co.uk. ℂ **01595/692-826.** 24 units. Double £65–£90, includes breakfast. Restaurant daily, noon–2pm and 6–9pm. Main courses £8–£16. **Amenities:** Restaurant; 2 bars; room service; free Wi-Fi.

Hay's Dock Cafe Restaurant ★★ SCOTTISH/SEAFOOD   Seabirds and seals cavort beyond the huge windows overlooking the harbor in this bright, airy space, part of the waterside Shetland Museum (see above). Coffee, snacks, and lunch are served during the day, and three evenings a week the handsome space is transformed into a romantic dining room serving inventive preparations of island lamb and seafood. Tables fill up quickly for these evening meals, so it's best to reserve.

Hay's Dock. www.haysdock.co.uk. ℂ **01595/741-569.** Main courses £14–£19. Mon–Wed 10am–4pm, Thurs–Sat 10am–3pm and 5–11pm, Sun noon–4pm.

Kveldsro ★★   In typical Shetland, no-frills style, this suburban villa on a quiet cul-de-sac in a residential neighborhood is probably Lerwick's finest lodging choice, with homey, comfortable rooms that overlook surrounding

All Creatures Great and Small

The human population of the entire Shetland archipelago totals just 22,000, but the islands host a staggering numbers of birds and other wildlife. Birds create quite a spectacle in such places as the Noup of Noss sea cliffs (see above), where 23,000 gannets, 24,000 guillemots, and 10,000 puffins might be seen roosting in the spring and summer. For some perverse reason, Shetlanders are especially fond of the great skua (or *bonxie*), a spirited meanie who dive bombs walkers along the coastal paths. Shetland has more otters than any other place in Europe, and shy as they are, they often make surprise appearances on remote shorelines.

Seals can be seen bobbing up and down in the sea or lounging about on the rocks and beaches. Earthbound favorites are the tiny Shetland ponies that roam freely among the hills and common grazing lands, as they have for at least 4,000 years. Aside from the attentions of clamoring children, for whom they're a preferred mount, the shaggy little beasts are more carefree now that they are no longer being shipped south to mainland Britain to work in the coal mines. Also short in stature but long on charm is the Shetland sheepdog, bred to keep sheep in line but fiercely loyal to human companions.

gardens toward the harbor. Rooms differ considerably in outlook, size, and decor, but the best are in an old wing and have high ceilings and bay windows. The name (pronounced *Kel*-dro) is Old Norse for "evening peace," and that's ensured out here at the edge of town. The clubby restaurant downstairs is one of Shetlanders' top choices for a night out and serves old-fashioned basics, including the island's best steak and excellent seafood, in clubby spaces overlooking the harbor.

Greenfield Pl. www.shetlandhotels.com. © **01595/692-195.** 17 units. Double from £150, includes breakfast. Restaurant daily, noon–2:30pm and 5:30–9:30pm. Main courses £14–£26. **Amenities:** Restaurant; bar; free Wi-Fi.

Queens Hotel ★★   You couldn't stay any closer to the sea than this early 19th-century landmark that rises out of the edge of the harbor. In a strong gale guests who don't close their windows might get a good, salty soaking, but otherwise they enjoy endless water views, especially from the upper floors, where some rooms are tucked under the eaves. These simple and comfortable accommodations lean more toward function than luxury, but they've been hosting Lerwick visitors since 1868, when the former office, warehouse, and residence were combined to create a "first-class hotel, the finest premises in Lerwick," where rooms came with horses to rent. Aside from the remarkable location, these historic surroundings offer plenty of character (but no lift), along with a restaurant and cafe/bar that serve salads, burgers, and other casual fare, along with local seafood.

24 Commercial St. www.kgqhotels.co.uk. © **01595/692-826.** 26 units. Doubles £90, includes breakfast. Restaurant daily, noon–2pm and 6–9pm. Main courses £8–£16. **Amenities:** Restaurant; bar; room service; free Wi-Fi.

ENTERTAINMENT & NIGHTLIFE IN LERWICK

During the **Up Helly Aa** (www.uphellyaa.org) on the last Tuesday in January each year, a thousand-strong horde of loud, bearded men dressed as Vikings carry flaming torches through the streets of Lerwick to the harbor, where they storm a 10m (33 ft.) replica of a Viking longboat and set it alight. The harbor blaze is followed by a long night of eating, drinking, playing music, and dancing; the name means "Up Holy Day," but the proceedings can be uninhibitedly unholy. The **Shetland Folk Festival** (www.shetlandfolkfestival.com; © **01595/694-757**) usually takes place on the last weekend in April. Young fiddlers and accordion players on the islands take part, and international artists fly in for 4 days of concerts, workshops, and informal jam sessions in venues around Lerwick and local halls throughout the islands.

Other music-based annual events include the **Fiddle Frenzy** (www.shetlandfiddlefrenzy.com), with concerts and workshops in August; the **Shetland Blues Festival** in September; and October's **Shetland Accordion and Fiddle Festival** (www.shetlandaccordionandfiddle.com).

If you want to know the best places to go to hear traditional music, pay a visit to **High Level Music** (© **01595/692-618**), up the steps close to Market Cross. The shop is run by Brian Nicholson, a mine of information.

SHOPPING ON MAINLAND

More than 30 workshops and studios across the islands are included on the Shetland Craft Trail (www.shetlandartsandcrafts.co.uk).

Jamieson & Smith ★★★   The islands' famous wool broker has a retail shop filled with yarns and beautiful knitwear. 90 North Rd., Lerwick. www.shetlandwoolbrokers.co.uk. © **01595/693-579.**

North Rock Gallery ★   Most of the artwork, prints, photography, sculpture, jewelry, and textiles are by Shetlanders. Commercial St., Lerwick. www.northrockgallery.co.uk. © **01595/694-644.**

Peerie Shop ★   A good selection of island knitwear is displayed alongside whimsical creations, as in puffin-shaped coffee mugs, that have a way of finding their way into your carry-on luggage. A bustling little cafe serves coffee and sandwiches. Esplanade, Lerwick. www.peerieshop.co.uk. © **01595/692-816.**

Shetland Jewellery ★★   Artisans at this fine studio, established in the 1950s, base their designs on ancient Celtic and Viking patterns. Soundside, near Weisdale, 11 miles northwest of Lerwick. www.shetlandjewellery.co.uk. © **01595/830-275.**

Weisdale Mill ★★★   This cheery island gathering spot in a stone barley mil from 1855 houses a cafe; a shop that sells high-quality knitwear and other crafts; and the Bonhoga Gallery, showcasing painting, photography, and textile arts, much of it by island artists. Off B9075, Weisdale, 13 miles northwest of Lerwick. www.shetlandarts.org. © **01595/745-750.**

OUTDOOR ACTIVITIES AROUND LERWICK

One of the best ways to encounter Shetland birdlife is a cruise beneath the **Noup of Noss sea cliffs ★★★** with Shetland Seabird Tours (www.

shetlandseabirdtours.com; ℡ **07767/872-260**); stars of the show are the 25,000 gannets that congregate around the mile-long stretch on an island across the harbor from Lerwick. A 12m (39-ft.) replica of a Viking longboat, *Dim Riv* (**"Morning Light"**) ★★, sails across Lerwick harbor on summer evenings; times depend on bookings and crew availability (www.dimriv.com). Three golf courses on the islands offer simple facilities and modest fees to match—and the chance to play almost all night in the simmer dim. The 18-hole **Shetland Golf Club** ★ (www.shetlandgolfclub.co.uk; ℡ **01595/840-369**) is about 3¾ miles west of Lerwick on the A970. The nine-hole **Asta Golf Club** ★ (www.astagolfcourse.com; ℡ **07936/832-971**) is 1¼ miles north of Scalloway. If playing every out-of-the way course is on your bucket list, take note of **Whalsay Golf Club** ★ (www.whalsaygolfclub.com; ℡ **07936/832-971**), the most northerly courses in the U.K. Getting to the remote course requires a trip on the car ferry from the Mainland port of Laxo to Symbister on the island of Whalsay, and a 5-mile drive north from there. **Grantfield Garage,** North Road, Lerwick (www.grantfieldgarage.co.uk; ℡ **01595/692-709**) rents bikes for £12.50 per day or £50 per week.

Scalloway ★★

6 miles W of Lerwick

The name of Shetland's second largest town comes from the Norse "Scola Voe," or huts on the shore, because Vikings used to draw their boats up on the beach and take shelter when attending parliament on the Loch of Tingwall, at the north end of an adjacent valley. White mansions, built by 19th-century fish merchants, and multicolored cottages surround the sheltered natural harbor, filled these days with fishing boats. Quiet little fishing village that Scalloway appears to be, the town was the headquarters of a daring World War II resistance operation that comes to life in the town museum.

ESSENTIALS
GETTING THERE Island bus number 4 (www.zettrans.org.uk; ℡ **01595/744-868**) connects Lerwick and Scalloway and runs about every hour. The trip takes 25 minutes.

EXPLORING SCALLOWAY
Scalloway Castle ★ HISTORIC SIGHT The castle of despot Patrick Stewart, Earl of Orkney, has lost some its might, now that it's in ruin and surrounded by warehouses on Scalloway's busy waterfront. Stewart, also known as Black Pattie (see p. 398) used forced labor to build the castle in 1600, symbol of his attempt to exert control over Shetland. Scalloway did not have to endure Stewart's tyranny for long, as he was executed in Edinburgh in 1615. Today, just a grand flight of wide stairs, a roofless massive hall, and a circular staircase that once led to quarters on upper floors show off the grandeur of Stewart's onetime Shetland power base.

Behind waterfront. www.historic-scotland.gov.uk. ℡ **01856/841-815.** Free admission. Key available from Scalloway Museum.

Scalloway Museum ★★★ MUSEUM   Stone axes and medieval molds used to form buttons from softened animal horns paint a picture of Scalloway's long history, but most riveting is the story of the Shetland Bus, a clandestine World War II maritime operation. In 1942, Scalloway became the headquarters for operatives who sent boats carrying arms and resistance fighters into Nazi-occupied Norway, returning with refugees. At first, a fleet of fishing boats carried out the missions, crossing the North Sea in the dark and often during storms, when the Germans would be least likely to mount an attack. After substantial losses, the boats were replaced with three U.S. made submarine chasers that, with their speed and munitions, were better able to elude German attack. All told, the Shetland bus made 215 missions, carrying 192 agents and 389 tons of weapons into Norway, and bringing 73 agents and 373 refugees out. The operation comes to life here with maps, artifacts, and portraits of the brave men and women who oversaw and made the daring forays.

Castle St. www.scallowaymuseum.org. ✆ **01595/880-734.** £3 adults, £1 children 6–16. Mid-Apr to Sept Mon–Sat, 11am–4pm, and Sun 2–4pm.

WHERE TO EAT & STAY IN SCALLOWAY

Scalloway Hotel ★★★   Local chef Colin Maclean has helped put Peter and Caroline McKenzie's welcoming waterfront inn on the map as the islands' top place to dine with his memorable renditions of island shellfish, fish, and lamb. His creations range from simply battered haddock to roasted ling (it's a Shetland fish favorite) in black risotto and are served in a friendly bar room or a slightly more formal dining room. Upstairs are some of the island's most pleasant rooms, simply but carefully done with some exquisite touches that include hand-fashioned, locally crafted furniture and island woolens and, from a few, views over the harbor.

Main St. www.scallowayhotel.com. ✆ **01595/880-444.** 23 units. Doubles from £100, includes breakfast. Restaurant Mon–Sat 5–9:30pm (bar food from noon–3pm), Sun noon–9pm. Main courses £12–£22. **Amenities:** Restaurant; bar; free Wi-Fi.

Exploring South Mainland

South of Lerwick and Scalloway, Mainland narrows into a thin, 25-mile-long peninsula, along which many of Shetland's most intriguing sites are located. The main A970 heads down the eastern side of this finger of land and ends at Sumburgh Head, along the way crossing the runway of the island's airport (lights flash and gates descend when planes are taking off and landing).

Broch of Mousa ★★ ARCHAEOLOGICAL SITE   This round stone tower on the little island of Mousa is one of an estimated 500 brochs in Scotland, but Mousa is the best preserved of them all, and tallest, having stood guard over Mousa Sound at a height of 13m (43 ft.) for more than 2,000 years. Constructed of local stones, the towers consists of two circular walls, one within the other, and a narrow staircase between them leads to an open parapet at the top, suggesting the broch may have been purpose-built as a lookout tower. Stone supports also suggest the presence, at different times, of wooden and stone dwellings within the tower. Norse saga tells us the broch once provide a handy refuge for a couple eloping from Norway to Iceland who became shipwrecked off the Shetland coast in a storm. The tower is also a popular roost for storm petrels, and thousands of breeding pairs live on the island, designated as a special protection area for the birds.

Isle of Mousa. www.historicenvironment.scot. Free admission. Always open. Reached by 15-minute ferry crossing to Mousa from Sandwick, 6¾ miles south of Lerwick. www. mousaboattrips.co.uk. ℰ **07901/872–339.** £16 adults, £7 children 5–16. Apr–Sept, Mon–Fri, departure 11:30am, return 2:30pm; Sun, departure 1:30pm, return 4:30pm.

Croft House Museum ★★ HISTORIC SIGHT A sense of just how hard life may have once been on Shetland emerges at this small farm from the 1870s. The family lived in two dark rooms at one end of the house, and animals were stalled in the byre at the other end. The few comforts included a peat fire and cupboard-like box beds, fashioned from driftwood with wooden walls to provide warmth and comfort. It's said a Shetlander was a farmer who fished, and men were often at sea. Grinding wheat, spinning wool, much of the farming, and of course, child rearing, were left to the women, whose hands really were never idle, since even rare moments of rest were passed with knitting.

South Voe, Boddam, Dunrossness, off the A970, 25 miles south of Lerwick. www.shet landheritageassociation.com. ℰ **01950/460-557.** Free admission. May–Sept, daily 10am–1pm and 2–4pm.

Jarlshof ★★★ ARCHAEOLOGICAL SITE In 1897, a violent storm washed away sections of low sea cliffs, revealing a few stones of what would become one of Europe's most remarkable archaeological discoveries. Shetlanders have lived in this coastal community for the past 4,500 years, leaving behind an astonishing record of everyday life in past eras—houses of farmers from as early as 2500 B.C.E. as well as a broch, a round stone tower, from those who settled 2,000 years later, a wheelhouse of the Picts and a Viking longhouse, and a ruined castle, the 16th and 17th century stronghold of Robert and Patrick Stewart, the despotic earls of Orkney (see p. 398). The ruins of so many overlapping civilizations are a fascinating jumble, with stone walls and subterranean passages of one era merging into those of another, and distinct features taking shape—cattle stalls from 2500 B.C.E., a Norse sauna, a roundhouse from 200 B.C.E. Well-designed plagues help make sense of the history unfolding along the walkways, as do the excellent exhibits in the visitors center. There's a lot to take in amid these ruins, so allow several hours to do so.

Near Sumburgh Airport, 24 miles south of Lerwick. www.historicenvironment.scot. ℰ **01950/460-112.** £6 adults, £4.80 seniors and students, £3.60 children 5–15. Apr–Sept daily, 9:30am–5:30pm; Oct–Mar, sometimes open, hours vary.

St Ninian's Isle ★ NATURAL SIGHT A *tombolo*, a narrow, crescent-shaped sandbar, creates a causeway beach that emerges from the sea in summer and during low tide in winter, making the little island accessible to walkers. The ruins of a 12th-century chapel yielded a treasure in 1958 when a Shetland schoolboy helping on an archaeological excavation dug up a wooden box filled with silver bowls, brooches, and jewelry. These possibly constituted the worldly wealth of a family who buried the box to keep the valuables out of reach of raiding Vikings sometime around 800, but did not survive to reclaim their precious possessions. The horde is now in the Museum of Scotland in Edinburgh.

Near Bigton, just off the B9122, 17 miles southeast of Lerwick.

Sumburgh Head ★★ NATURAL SIGHT   At its southernmost tip Mainland drops into the sea at this 100m (330-ft) rocky headland. The name comes from Old Norse, *Dunrøstar høfdi,* or "The Head onto the loud tide-race," for the sound of the crashing surf. Adding to the cacophony is the clamor of a large colony of seabirds, whose habitats here are protected as an RSPB nature reserve. The headland is topped with a lighthouse from 1821 that, like many others on the Scottish coast, was built by Robert Stevenson, grandfather of the adventure novelist Robert Louis Stevenson. On another literary note, Sir Walter Scott visited Sumburgh in 1814 and used the settings in his novel *The Pirate,* in which he also gave the name Jarlshof to the ruins on the nearby coast. The lighthouse station provides a fascinating peek at the engines that power the foghorn, the lighthouse tower, and the radar hut, where bicycle pedals powered equipment on the roof. On the night of April 8, 1940, operators here signaled warning of a massive German attack on the British fleet anchored in Scapa Flow in Orkney, averting a disaster that could have changed the course of World War II.

Sumburgh Head, 25 miles south of Lerwick. www.sumburghhead.com. ℂ **01950/461-966.** Visitor Centre and Lighthouse: £6 adults, £4 seniors and students, £2 children. Apr–Oct daily, 11am–5:30pm. Headland always open.

Exploring North Mainland

North of Lerwick, Mainland is rugged and shaggy, a landscape of rolling moorland, rocky knolls, and long sea lochs, or *voes,* that make big dents into the coastline. At **Mavis Grind,** 24 miles northwest of Lerwick, the island narrows into an isthmus, just 33m (108 ft.) wide, with the Atlantic Ocean to the west and the North Sea to the east. Vikings used to haul their ships across the isthmus rather than sail around Mainland's treacherous, surf-battered northwestern coast.

Eshaness ★★★ NATURAL SIGHT   Mainland's most spectacular coastal scenery unfolds along the Northmavine peninsula, in the northwestern corner of Mainland. The Northmavine is all but an island, connected to the rest of Mainland only by the narrow, Mavis Grind isthmus. The rough, forsaken landscape, little of which is arable, meets the sea along a stretch of black, formidable cliffs, broken here and there with natural arches and steep-sided clefts or *geos,* and erupting offshore in sea stacks. To see the best of the scenery, find your way by car to Hillswick, 34 miles north of Lerwick, then follow the single track to even smaller Stenness. From there, a lane leads to a light-house built by David and Charles Stevenson, from a long line of lighthouse designers and cousins of adventure novelist Robert Louis Stevenson. From there paths cross the tops of the cliffs of Eshaness. You won't walk too long before coming to Calder's Geo, a deep cleft in the cliffs that funnels the surf into a wild fury.

An oasis of civilization is **Tangwick Haa** ★ (www.tangwickhaa.org.uk; © **01806/503-389**), a 17th-century house built for the Cheynes, lairds of the region. The bright rooms show off farm tools, household kitchen staples, radios, a fishing boat, and other essentials of life in these remote parts up to the present day. The paneled Lairds Room provides a look at how the well-to-do lairds of this remote manor lived, surrounded by simple comforts rather than ostentatious luxury. The museum is open May to September daily from 11am to 5pm, and admission is free but donations are welcome.

39 miles northwest of Lerwick.

Staneydale Temple ★ ARCHAEOLOGICAL SITE A ½-mile walk across damp, moody moors brings you to a field of about 3 hectares (8 acres) enclosed by a stone wall, enough of which is still standing to suggest its effectiveness. Piles of stones are what remains of dwellings that were probably occupied from around 2000 to 500 B.C.E., while walls indicate the presence of a much larger, oval-shaped building that would have been covered by a timbered roof. On treeless Shetland, the wood would have been driftwood that washed ashore and probably originated in Scandinavia. Was this really a temple? It may just as likely have been a meeting hall or even the "palace" of a tribal chief.

4 miles east of Walls, 21 miles northeast of Lerwick. Free admission. Always open.

WHERE TO STAY & EAT AROUND MAINLAND

Busta House ★★ Shetland's oldest continuously inhabited house, from 1588, is splendidly isolated on the shores of Busta Voe on the west side of Mainland. The hearth-warmed lounges filled with oil paintings and antiques and the beautifully maintained old-fashioned bedrooms that ramble across the upper floors have inspired a story or two. None are sadder than that of Barbara Pitcairn, who, after falling in love with the eldest son of the house, was forbidden to see the boy she bore in 1748 and died of a broken heart. Actually, the fate of the young father is pretty sad, too, since he drowned in the voe (bay) with his three brothers. Barbara is said to still roam the hallways, and you might encounter her as well in the gardens, filled with artifacts that include gargoyles salvaged from the House of Commons after World War II air raids. The well-tended patches supply much of the produce and fresh herbs for the excellent dining room, aptly named the Pitcairn Room.

Busta, near Brae, 24 miles north of Lerwick. www.bustahouse.com. © **01806/522-506.** 22 units. Double £110–£120, includes breakfast. Bar/lounge noon–2:30pm, restaurant 6–9pm. Set price dinner £35. **Amenities:** Restaurant; bar; free Wi-Fi.

St Magnus Bay Hotel ★ This 110-year-old timber-clad building was brought over from Norway timber by timber for an exhibition in Glasgow in the late 19th century and has been an island landmark ever since. The poet W.H. Auden created quite a stir when he stayed here with his lover in the 1930s, but generations of guests have come and gone quietly, content to enjoy the simple wood-paneled guest quarters and rather grand dining hall and drawing room, while taking in the abundance of wildlife, even the orcas that sometimes appear in the bay below the grounds. Some rooms are in a slightly less atmospheric modern annex, but most enjoy magnificent views.

Hillswick, 34 miles north of Lerwick. www.stmagnusbayhotel.co.uk. ✆ **01806/503-372.** 27 units. Doubles £95–£145, includes breakfast. **Amenities:** Restaurant; bar; free Wi-Fi.

Sumburgh Hotel ★ A former laird's house is a bit stuffy and fussy in a floral carpet sort of way, especially given the surroundings, with the surf roaring into the nearby headlands and the savage end-of-Shetland scenery exploding all around. Old-fashioned and uninspired as the decor may be, you can take in this natural spectacle in from the high windows, and you'll drift off to the sound of surf and awaken to the cries of seabirds. Some of the island's best walks are just outside the door. Full meals, sandwiches, and salads are served in the bar and restaurant.

Sumburgh Head, Sumburgh, 26 miles south of Lerwick. www.sumburghhotel.com. ✆ **01950/460-201.** 32 units. Doubles £110–£130, includes breakfast. Restaurant daily noon–2pm and 6–9pm. Main courses £9–£18. **Amenities:** Restaurant; bar; free Wi-Fi.

Papa Stour ★

7 miles W of Mainland

The "great island of priests" welcomed 6th century Celtic missionaries, was a place of banishment for lepers in the 17th century, and sustained about 400 fishing folk in the 19th century. These days, hardscrabble life on this remote slab of rock seems to deter permanent residence, though about a dozen hearty souls stay on Papa year round to raise sheep. Visitors come to walk (in the absence of all but one short road, the only way to get around). Paths follow the spectacular coastline, riddled with sea caves like the collapsed one at **Kirstan's Hole,** and provide viewpoints for observing an abundance of birds and wildlife, including seals and porpoises who congregate offshore.

The interisland ferry (www.shetland.gov.uk) from West Burrafirth on Mainland (26 miles northwest of Lerwick) operates five days a week, making the crossing in 45 minutes. As the boat enters the harbor on Housa Voe it passes beneath Frau Stack, a pinnacle atop which a Norse laird built a stone house to keep his daughter out of reach of the fisherman with whom she had fallen in love (for all the laird's efforts, the couple eloped anyway). Returns are timed in such a way that day trips are possible only a couple of times a week, so check the timetables carefully and plan accordingly. You can also fly to Papa Stour from Mainland, from Tingwall Airport, 6 miles northwest of Lerwick (www.airtask.com; ✆ **01595/840-246).**

The islands have earned primetime fame as the settings for *Shetland,* a BBC television crime drama first broadcast in 2013. In episodes filled with beautiful scenery and a mounting body count, inspector detective Jimmy Perez (Douglas Henshall) investigates grisly murders that, fortunately, are far more common on TV Shetland than they are on the real-life islands. The series is based on the crime novels of Ann Cleeves, who claims she was inspired to write her fist bestseller, *Raven Black* (2006), while visiting Mainland and being struck by the sight of black-plumed ravens against the snowy shores of Loch Clickimin. Cleeves lived on Fair Isle for two years, and islanders no doubt watched with knowing understanding the two episodes, based on Cleeves' novel *Blue Lightning* (2010), in which foul weather strands Perez and co-detective Tosh on the island as they try to determine who stabbed a scientist at the famous Bird Observatory. As Cleeves has it, Detective Perez is a native of the island, and that might not be too much of a fictive stretch. Among the 100 or so shipwrecks on the surrounding seafloor is that of *El Gran Grifón,* a Spanish galleon that went down in 1588. It's been documented that some of the sailors made it ashore, and the heritage (and DNA) they left behind may not just be figments of a novelist's imagination.

Foula ★

20 miles W of Mainland

This little outcropping, just 4 square miles, is pleased to claim its place as, along with Fair Isle, one of the most remote inhabited islands in Britain, though the name, from the Norse for "Bird Island," is more to the point. Joining a fluctuating population of about 38 farmers and fishermen are dozens of Shetland ponies, hundreds of sheep and hundreds of thousands of seabirds. Arctic skuas, puffins, guillemots roost on wind-lashed ledges at Da Kame and other sea cliffs that soar to 370m (1,214 ft.)

Atlantic Ferries runs twice-weekly service from Walls, on Mainland, 25 miles northwest of Lerwick (www.atlanticferries.co.uk; ✆ **01595/743-9760**), though service depends on weather. Some islanders still remember the winter of 1955, when Foula was cut off from the rest of the world for 48 days. **Airtask** (www.airtask.com; ✆ **01595/840-246**) operates seven flights a week during summer between Foula and Tingwall Airport on Mainland.

Unst ★

30 miles NE of Mainland

U.K.'s most northerly inhabited island is as wild as it is remote, with sweeping grasslands that meet the sea along tall cliffs. Tranquil beaches are backed by ruins of the island's past—the stones of an old Norse longhouse poke through the sands at **Sandwick** and the weather-worn stone and graveyard of ruins Kirk of Lund rise next to **Lunda Wick.**

ESSENTIALS

GETTING THERE   Reaching Unst from Mainland requires two ferry crossings. The first is from Toft, 28 miles north of Lerwick, to Ulsta on Yell. The crossing takes about 20 minutes, with ferries leaving at half-hour intervals (☏ **01957/722-259**). From there it's another 17-mile drive north to Gutcher for another ferry to Belmont on Unst. These boats leave about every half-hour, and the journey takes about 10 minutes and is free. For timetables and other details, go to www.shetland.gov.uk/ferries.

EXPLORING UNST

Hermaness Reserve ★★ NATURAL SIGHT   Britain goes out with a bang, or at least a squawk, along these dramatic cliffs overlooking the islet of Muckle Flugga, the northernmost point of land in the U.K. You're allowed to feel that you've found yourself at the edge of the world, since northing lies between Muckle Flugga and the North Pole. Kittiwakes, gannets, razorbills, guillemots, and puffins—as many as 23,000 of these amiable birds have been spotted here—roost on the cliffs, and great skuas are likely to dive-bomb walkers along the boardwalks and trails across the heather-covered moorland. They've been protected here since the 1830s. Plan on spending some time here, since it's a 3-mile walk from the car park to the cliff tops.

8 miles N of Baltasound. Free admission. Always open, best for bird watching in spring and summer, when the moors are a blaze of color.

Muness Castle ★ HISTORICAL SIGHT   The most northerly castle in Scotland was the seat and showplace of Laurence Bruce, sheriff of Shetland and half-brother of Robert Stewart, the tyrannical Earl of Orkney (see p. 398). Bruce built this castle to match the glory of Stewart's Earl's Palace in Orkney, possibly using the same craftsmen for the fine stonework, corbelling, and architectural showpieces that include a massive main hall and spiral stairs leading to now-vanished upper quarters. Like his Stewart relatives, Bruce was a despot, too, who oppressed the locals and made free use of young women, fathering 24 illegitimate children on the island during his brief tenure. French pirates burned the now-ruined, roofless castle in 1627, and the cellars and courtyards were used to store the salvage of shipwrecks.

5 miles east of Belmont. www.historic-scotland.gov.uk. Free admission. Always open. A sign informs visitors where to pick up the key.

WHERE TO EAT & STAY

Buness House ★★   It's a bit of a surprise, and a welcome one, to come across such a civilized retreat here in the far north, in a house built for an island laird in the 16th century. The genteel drawing room, shelf-lined library, and view-filled conservatory are ideal refuges when weather gets in the way of a walk across the nearby Hermaness Reserve, and even from these cozy perches you may spot otters, whales, and porpoises. Four bedrooms are as gracious and comfortable as everything else about this fine old house, where the hospitality extends to a four-course dinner served on request in the conservatory.

Baltasound. www.bunesshouseshetland.co.uk. ⓒ **01957/711-315.** 4 units. £122 double. Dinner £41. Discount for stays of 4 nights or more. **Amenities:** Free Wi-Fi.

Fair Isle ★★

45 miles S of Mainland

Birds and knitwear put this remote island on the map. Floating about halfway between Orkney and Shetland, Fair Isle is only 3 miles long and never more than 1½ miles wide, and the weather is often far from fair. Relentless seas pound the rocky coasts in winter, when westerly winds fling Atlantic spray from one side of the island to the other and shut the 70 or so residents off from the outside world for days and even weeks at a time. Birds—of an estimated 350 species—stop over on flights paths to and from Scandinavia, Iceland, and the Faroe Islands, to the delight of visiting birdwatchers. Knitwear has been a mainstay since island women traded gloves, socks, and underwear for goods with sailors on passing ships. The dapper Edward, Prince of Wales, began wearing distinctive Fair Isle V-neck sweaters under his tweed jackets in the 1920s, and the natty patterns have been a cool-weather favorite ever since.

ESSENTIALS

GETTING THERE   **Airtask** (www.airtask.com; ⓒ **01595/840-246**) flies to Fair Isle from Tingwall, 6 miles northwest of Lerwick, most days, with a weekly flight from Sumburgh Airport on Mainland. Flight time is 25 minutes.

The *Good Shepherd* sails at 11:30am on Tuesday, Thursday, and Saturday from Grutness Pier, Sumburgh Head, on Mainland; on alternate Thursdays in summer the boat sails from Lerwick at 3:30pm. For timetables, news of weather delays, and other details, go to www.shetland.gov.uk/ferries. The journey takes 2½ hours.

EXPLORING FAIR ISLE

Walking is the best (and unless you bring a car, only) way to get around the diminutive island, under the care of the National Trust for Scotland. A popular route is across moorlands on the northern end to North Stack lighthouse, a beacon that has greatly improved the safety of navigation in the surrounding seas, where more than 100 ships have foundered over the years. Among them was the longboat of Sigurd the Viking, shipwrecked off Fair Isle in 900. Off the eastern coast is distinctive Sheep Rock, a headland where sheet rock faces rise to 132m (433 ft.) to a grassy plateau. Shepherds used to raise and lower sheep up and down the cliffs on ropes to graze on these uplands. In spring and fall, the island is popular with birders from around the world, who have been known to fly into the tiny airport at news of a rare sighting. In summer, the moors are ablaze with color, and the island basks in almost perpetual light.

WHERE TO EAT & STAY

Fair Isle Bird Observatory Lodge ★★★   Ornithologist George Waterston established a bird observatory in 1948, and these well-kept lounges are still full of bird-watchers swapping notes. Guests who don't know a petrel from a puffin are welcome, too, and they might enjoy the lectures, bird walks, and joining rangers who ring migratory birds, keep logs, and collect date on migratory species. Accommodation in the bright, attractive, view-filled rooms comes with full board, and a good thing, since this is the only restaurant and bar on the island. The lodge is most busy during the spring and autumn bird migrations, when it's wise to reserve well in advance. Non-guests are welcome in the dining room and bar, and can also use shower facilities and a computer. The staff provides a wealth of information on the island and can steer you to local craftspeople who create the famous Fair Isle knitwear.

Fair Isle. www.fairislebirdobs.co.uk. ⓒ **01595/760-258.** 18 units. £150 double, full board. Closed Nov to late Apr. **Amenities:** Dining room, bar, laundry room.

PLANNING YOUR TRIP TO SCOTLAND

By Stephen Brewer

This chapter provides planning tools to help make your trip to Scotland go smoothly and help you get the most out of your time, including information on how to get there, how to get around, and how to arrange accommodations, along with local resources to tap.

GETTING THERE

By Plane

Scotland's two principal airports **Edinburgh Airport** (EDI; www.edinburghairport.com) and **Glasgow Airport** (GLA; www.glasgowairport.com) are served by nonstop flights, often seasonal, from several North American airports. These include Chicago (United); Newark (United); New York (Delta); Orlando (Virgin Atlantic); Philadelphia (American); and Toronto and Vancouver (Air Transat). If you're flying across the Atlantic, you can also go through London Heathrow or another European hub, often Amsterdam or Paris.

A recent Frommers.com study found that the websites www.momondo.com and www.skyscanner.net consistently come up with the best prices for transatlantic flights; they also will show you a myriad of possibilities when it comes to connections. An alternative for the truly budget conscious is to investigate the lowest transatlantic fares to European hubs and continue from there on one of the low-cost airlines that service Glasgow and Edinburgh (easyJet and Ryanair fly in and out of Glasgow and Edinburgh). Keep in mind, too, that Glasgow and Edinburgh Airports are only 39 miles apart, and the cities are well connected to both airports by bus, so it's worthwhile checking into the lowest fares to both. See p. 63 and p. 156 for info on how to get from the airport into Edinburgh and Glasgow.

By Car

If you're driving to Scotland from London or anywhere in eastern England to Edinburgh, the **A1** is the fastest route. This road heads directly north from the **M25,** London's ring road, and crosses into the Scottish Borders before leading into Edinburgh from the east. For Glasgow from London take the **M1,** which leads northwest from the M25. At junction 19 of the M1, head west to join the M6 to travel west through Birmingham before heading directly north up the west side of England into Scotland. If you're traveling from the southwest of England the **M5,** which begins at Exeter (Devon), leads into the M6 at Birmingham. As the M6 crosses the border into Dumfries and Galloway in Scotland, it becomes the M74 and heads directly north into Glasgow. All major routes into northern Scotland lead from either Edinburgh or Glasgow. Remember, Glasgow and Edinburgh are less than 40 miles apart and connected by the M8, so once you get near one you'll be within an easy drive of the other.

By Train

Two main rail lines link London to Scotland. The **East Coast Mainline** connects London's **King's Cross Station** with Edinburgh via York, Newcastle-upon-Tyne, and Durham. Trains depart at regular intervals throughout the day and cross from England into Scotland at Berwick-upon-Tweed. The journey from London to Edinburgh takes around 4¼ hours with some services traveling an additional hour on to Glasgow, and others continuing north to Dundee (an additional 1½ hr.) and Aberdeen (an additional 2½ hr.). The **West Coast Mainline** leads from London's **Euston Station** for Glasgow by way of Preston, Oxenholme in England's Lake District, and Carlisle. Trains depart roughly every hour throughout the day and take around 4½ hours to reach Glasgow. London North Eastern Railway (www.lner.co.uk) provides service along the East Coast Mainline; Virgin Trains (www.virgintrains.co.uk) provides service along the West Coast Mainline.

In addition, a **Cross Country** route leads from Penzance in Cornwall, England through Plymouth, Exeter, Bristol, Birmingham, Leeds, and other cities to Scotland. For more information on this service, contact ✆ **08477/369-123** (www.crosscountrytrains.co.uk).

If you're traveling to Scotland by train from continental Europe, you'll probably connect through London's **St Pancras Station**, hub for high-speed Eurostar train services (www.eurostar.com) from Paris, Brussels, and Amsterdam, traveling to the U.K. via the **Channel Tunnel.**

Train routes from Edinburgh and Glasgow lead across the rest of Scotland and are mostly operated by **ScotRail** (www.scotrail.co.uk; ✆ **08457/550-033**). ScotRail also operates **Caledonian Sleepers,** overnight trains between London's Euston Station and Scotland that offer both seated and sleeping berth accommodation. Services can be booked up to 12 weeks in advance either by telephone or online.

By Bus (Coach)

Long-distance buses, or "coaches" as they're known in Britain, are the least expensive means of reaching Scotland from other parts of the U.K. The majority of routes and services are operated by **National Express** (www.nationalexpress.com; ✆ **0871/781-8181**), which links with most decent-sized communities in the U.K. The budget operator **MegaBus** (www.megabus.com; ℂ **0871/352-4444**) also runs long-distance coach services to Scotland from a limited number of U.K. destinations. In London, most coaches depart from **Victoria Coach Station** at 164 Buckingham Palace Rd. and take 8 to 8½ hours to reach Edinburgh or Glasgow, and often make the trip at night. It's always wise to make reservations in advance, especially during peak times such as the summer months and over the festive season. National Express offers the Skimmer Pass for unlimited travel throughout Britain for 7 days, £69; 14 days, £119; and 28 days, £199.

GETTING AROUND

By Car

Driving in Scotland is straightforward and often enjoyable, once drivers from outside the U.K. become accustomed to driving on the left. A small network of motorways link the main urban areas, while "A" roads, often "dual carriageways" (divided highways), spread out over the rest of Scotland. In more remote areas—especially the islands of western Scotland—single-lane roads are often the only link to small communities. Passing places are provided but caution is important because many of these roads are unfenced and livestock often wanders into the road.

CAR RENTALS If you're considering hiring a car in Scotland try the website **Autoslash.com**. It will apply all of the discount codes available to your rental upon booking; and then it will continue to search for better rates until you pick up the car. If a better price is found, the site automatically re-books you. We have yet to find a better service for rental cars. Some companies require drivers to be at least 23 years old, although 21 is more standard. To rent a car in Scotland, you must present your passport and driver's license. Be aware that a further 20% VAT (Valued Added Tax) will be added to your bill.

Car-Rental Excess

It's illegal to drive without unlimited third-party insurance in the U.K., and the cost is included as standard in rental rates. This means you're covered if you cause damage or injury another person, vehicle, or property but you are not covered for damage to your vehicle. However, the excess (deductible) against this insurance is often as high as £1,000 unless you pay for a reduced excess which can, if you take the car rental company's policy, often be more than half the cost of the car rental. A number of companies offer slightly less-expensive insurance against car-rental excess. Under these policies you still have to pay the excess to the car rental company, but you then claim it back from the insurance company. You can often choose between annual and single trip coverage. Companies that provide this insurance include **Insurance 4 Car Hire** (www.insurance4carhire.com; ℂ **01883/724-001**) and **Car Hire Excess** (www.carhireexcess.com; ℂ **0818/444-447**).

BECOMING A leftie

Scots, like other residents of the U.K., drive on the left, so if you're coming from the U.S. or most other countries, you'll need to adjust. Here are some tips to help you do so.

○ Unless you're comfortable using a stick shift, ask for a car with an automatic transmission (for which you'll pay more). If you're not used to driving a manual, you don't want to add the challenge of changing gears and working a clutch to the rigors of driving on the left.

○ Become familiar with the car before getting onto the road. To keep distractions to a minimum, get to know the gears, switches, and controls so you can keep your eyes on the road.

○ Do some practice rounds in the rental car parking lot or on a less-traveled road before pulling onto busy highways. If you're staying in a rural location outside a city, it might pay to have your car delivered to you, so you can get in some practice away from traffic.

○ Enter roadways carefully. By instinct, you'll probably be tempted to look to the left when pulling out, and that's exactly opposite of what you should be doing—in most cases, oncoming traffic will be coming from the right.

○ Keep the centerline on your right. If you're driving on the left, the centerline will be to the right of the driver's side of the road. Of course, many roads in Scotland are single track and don't have centerlines, in which case you'll find pullouts you can use to allow an oncoming car to pass.

○ Be careful in roundabouts. They're everywhere in Scotland, and handy for traffic management as they are, Americans might need to take a little time to adjust to them. When approaching, remember that traffic in the roundabout always has the right of way. Once in, go slow and keep to the right so you can exit easily and safely. And of course, remember that traffic in a roundabout in Scotland or elsewhere in the U.K. will be moving in a clockwise direction.

○ Drive cautiously and keep your wits about you. Easy does it until you get used to left-side driving. Take heart, because with a little practice, driving on the left will soon seem natural to you.

PLANNING YOUR TRIP TO SCOTLAND | Getting Around

GASOLINE   There are plenty of gas ("petrol") stations in and around main urban areas, but in more remote locations they're few and far between and so always make sure you have a good supply before venturing away from larger towns and cities. At press time, prices charged for gasoline in the U.K. stand at around £1.20 per liter (1 U.S. gallon = 3.785 liters).

DRIVING RULES & REQUIREMENTS   In Scotland and the whole of the U.K., *you drive on the left* and pass on the right and always give way to traffic coming from the right at a roundabout. If you're driving on a single lane road, you must use the passing places on the left side of the road, give priority to

Look Both Ways!

Even if you adjust easily to driving on the left, don't trust your instincts. Always look both ways before pulling into traffic, to make sure you don't lapse into your right-oriented habits. Likewise, when on foot, always look both ways when crossing a street.

traffic traveling uphill, and never park in a passing place. Pedestrian crossings not controlled by traffic lights are marked by white striped lines (zebra striping) on the road and sometimes flashing lights near the curb. Drivers must stop and yield the right of way to any pedestrian waiting to cross or has already stepped out into the zebra crossing.

By Plane

To reach some of the farthest flung regions of the Highlands and Islands, an internal flight is often the quickest option. **Flybe** (www.flybe.com) and **Loganair** (www.loganair.co.uk) operate domestic routes from Glasgow and Edinburgh; for example, both fly to Stornoway on the Isle of Lewis and the northern airport of Wick John o' Groats, while Loganair serves the Shetland Islands and the Hebridean island of Tiree.

By Train

Traveling by train is one of the best ways to see Scotland and travel between different regions. The cost of rail travel within Scotland is generally quite low and services are normally frequent, punctual, and reliable, while the line from Glasgow to the West Highlands and other routes is among the most scenic in the world.

The main train operator in Scotland is **ScotRail** (www.scotrail.co.uk; © **0845/601-5929**), with a network of rail routes around the country. Some of the smaller stations are unstaffed and tickets must be purchased on the train from the conductor. In addition to standard single and return fares, ScotRail offers a number of ticket deals. With the Kids Go Free deal (www.scotrail.co.uk/kidsgofree), two children between ages 5 and 15 can travel free with an adult as long as you travel during off-peak hours and make the return journey on the same day. A number of attractions in Scotland are linked with this deal and allow free entry for one child traveling on these tickets. Tickets can be

Slow Sundays

We're not saying that when it comes to travel "never on Sunday" is the rule, but be forewarned that many train, bus, and ferry services are severely curtailed. A journey with transfers that might take a few hours on a weekday can take all day on a Sunday. So, check schedules carefully and plan accordingly. *A tip:* If you're using Traveline (p. 445) to plan a trip, always put in the exact date of travel, as schedules can vary daily, and almost always do so on Sundays.

Scotland can look at its scenic best from a train window, and some journeys put on an especially good show. Among the most scenic are the **West Highland Line,** from Glasgow to Oban or Fort William, alongside the Clyde estuary, through mountains, and along the shores of glimmering lochs; the **Kyle Line,** from Inverness through the moors and glens of the Highlands to Kyle of Lochalsh, gateway to the Isle of the Skye, for even more scenery; the **Far North Line,** from Inverness up the North Sea coast past salmon-filled rivers to Thurso and Wick; and the **Borders Railway,** from Edinburgh into the green vales and rolling hills of the beautiful Borders region.

bought in advance on the day of travel. Discounts of 33% are also available for groups of three to five adults traveling together; to find out more, ask about **GroupSave** for small groups when purchasing your tickets.

A Senior Railcard (www.senior-railcard.co.uk) slashes a third off rail travel for passengers 60 and older. Young adults between ages 16 and 25 can purchase an annual **16-25 Railcard,** which saves a third of the price on all rail tickets for a year. A yearlong pass costs £30, 3 years for £70; year-long passes can be bought online at www.16-25railcard.co.uk or at any staffed station, while 3-year passes may only be bought online.

The **Royal Scotsman** (www.belmond.com; ✆ **800/524-2420** or 401/884-0090) is on one of the most luxurious trains in the world. Known as "a country house hotel on wheels," it offers a choice of routes that depart from Edinburgh's Waverley station and sweep past ancient mountains and misty lochs and through glens and villages. The train carries a maximum of 36 guests, allowing each passenger plenty of sumptuous space to spread out, and travelers can expect plush beds and opulent en-suite bathrooms. Tours range from the 2-night Highland Journey at £3,100 per person to the 7-night Grand Western Journey Scenic Wonders Journey at £10,102 per passenger. Prices include all meals, drinks, and sightseeing excursions.

BRITRAIL TRAVEL PASSES BritRail Passes allow unlimited travel in England, Scotland, and Wales on any scheduled train on the network during the validity of the pass without restrictions. The Spirit of Scotland Pass, the Central Scotland Pass, and the Scottish Highland Pass provide options for travel within Scotland. **Consecutive passes** allow you to travel for a consecutive number of days for a flat rate; and **FlexiPasses** allow you to travel when you want during a set period of time that, depending on the pass, can vary from one week to a month. Prices can vary significantly depending on type of pass, length of travel, and class of service. Discounts are available for seniors age 60 and older, for children, and, with BritRail passes, passengers age 25 and under. Passes are available through www.britrail.com.

OTHER TRAIN PASSES FOR SCOTLAND **ScotRail** (www.scotrail. co.uk; ✆ **0845/601-5929**) offers a selection of passes across Scottish rail networks. The **Spirit of Scotland travel pass** allows unlimited travel across all routes in Scotland from Carlisle, England (near the western Scotland–England border) and from Berwick-upon-Tweed, England (near the eastern Scotland–England border). This pass also includes trips on **ferries** operated by Caledonian MacBrayne (www.calmac.co.uk), serving the Hebrides and other western islands, and travel on a limited selection of bus (coach) routes in Argyll, Skye, the Borders, and Northern Highlands, with Scottish CityLink, Stagecoach and West Coast Motors, as well as the Glasgow Subway and Edinburgh trams. The pass does not cover many bus routes, so check with the ticket office before boarding if you plan on using one. Passes for 4 days of unlimited travel over 8 consecutive days cost £139, and 8 days of unlimited travel over 15 consecutive days cost £179. Passes for children ages 5 to 15 are half the cost of adult passes, and under-5s travel for free.

Four other similar ScotRail touring passes are available, each covering a different section of the country and working with different ferry and bus operators. With a couple of exceptions, travel isn't permitted on any train before 9:15am Monday through Friday. Anyone planning to travel on ScotRail's Caledonian Sleeper trains with these passes is strongly advised to make reservations. More information is available on ScotRail's website Tickets can be bought online or from any staffed station.

By Bus (Coach)

Scottish CityLink (www.citylink.co.uk; ✆ **08705/505-050**) operates a frequent and inexpensive coach service for all Scotland's cities and large towns. The **Explorer Pass** allows unlimited travel on a set number of days within a consecutive time period; for example, 3 travel days within 5 days costs £49, 5 travel days within 10 days costs £74, and 8 travel days within 16 days costs £99. Tickets can be purchased on the CityLink website.

Stagecoach also runs many services across Scotland; for full details of its routes and timetables, visit www.stagecoachbus.com. **Megabus** (www.megabus.com) also operates routes between many of Scotland's towns and cities.

Tap & Ride

The good news: CityLink, Stagecoach, First Glasgow, Lothian, and many other Scottish bus networks now accept credit cards for onboard payment. The bad news: Most accept only contactless credit cards, in which you simply tap the card on a reader next to the driver. Trouble is, if you're American, you may not have a contactless card in your wallet, as they're only now being introduced to the U.S. market. You may ask your card issuer for a contactless card (American Express is among those that will issue them on request). Or, resort to some old-fashioned methods and buy your bus ticket in advance or pay in cash (but remember, drivers on some systems are not able to give change, and those who do often won't be able to accept large bills).

WHEN TO GO

Weather in Scotland is, in a word, changeable—sunny one moment, cloudy and gray the next. With some dramatic exceptions, you can expect fairly mod-erate temperatures and at least some light precipitation just about anytime, anywhere in Scotland. A word you need to learn is "dreich," referring to gray, gloomy weather, because Scots use it a lot. Even so, residents of Edinburgh like to point out that their annual rainfall is no higher than that of London, and in terms of total rainfall amounts (about 23 inches/584 millimeters in both), they're right, and Edinburgh is actually quite a bit drier than New York—just a lot mistier and grayer. Glasgow, only 40 miles west, gets twice as much rainfall. In fact, the western Highlands north of Glasgow catch moisture blow-ing in off the Atlantic and are the wettest place in Europe, with as much as 180 inches (4,570 millimeters) of rain a year. It rarely gets terribly warm in Scot-land, not much above the 60s, even in summer, or terribly frigid, though bit-terly cold air can blow in from the East from time to time, turning the precipitation to snow. The general packing rule is to bring some rain gear and warm clothes any time of year, and at least a light jacket in summer.

Average Temperature & Rainfall in Scotland

EDINBURGH	JAN	FEB	MAR	APR	MAY	JUNE	JULY	AUG	SEPT	OCT	NOV	DEC
Temp. (°F)	38	39	42	45	50	55	59	58	54	49	42	40
Temp. (°C)	3	3	5	7	10	12	15	14	12	9	5	4
Rainfall (in.)	2.2	1.6	1.9	1.5	2.0	2.0	2.5	2.7	2.5	2.4	2.5	2.4
ABERDEEN	JAN	FEB	MAR	APR	MAY	JUNE	JULY	AUG	SEPT	OCT	NOV	DEC
Temp. (°F)	38	38	41	44	49	54	58	57	53	48	42	39
Temp. (°C)	3	3	5	6	9	12	14	13	11	8	5	3
Rainfall (in.)	2.5	2.0	2.1	1.9	2.1	2.0	2.8	2.8	2.5	3.0	3.1	2.9

Scotland Calendar of Events

You can get details of specific events at many of the festivals below by going to **www. edinburgh-festivals.com**.

JANUARY

Celtic Connections, Glasgow. Beginning with a torchlight parade that lights up the wintry streets, the city comes to life with two weeks of concerts celebrating Celtic music

and dance. There are venues throughout the city, but most notably the Old Fruit Market, on Albion Street. For tickets and details, go to www.celticconnections.com. Mid-January to early February.

Burns Night, Ayr (near his birthplace) and Dumfries, where he died, and elsewhere. During Burns Night suppers to honor the poet and lyricist, there's much toasting with whisky and eating of haggis. Go to www.vis itscotland.com for information. January 25.

Up Helly Aa, Lerwick, in the Shetland Islands. The most northerly town in Great Britain stages an ancient Norse fire festival, the aim of which is to encourage the return of the sun after the pitch-dark days of winter. The highlight is the burning of a replica of a Norse longboat. See www.uphellyaa.org. Last Tuesday in January.

FEBRUARY

Six Nations Rugby Championship (aka NatWest 6 Nations), Edinburgh. Sixty-seven thousand fans cram into the Murray-field stadium for Scotland's home matches. Visit www.scottishrugby.org. Early February.

Fort William Mountain Festival. Films, lectures, music, and exhibitions are staged at the foot of Ben Nevis. See www.mountain filmfestival.co.uk. Late-February.

MARCH

Whuppity Scourie, Lanark. Residents of the Strathclyde get so tired of winter that they stage this traditional ceremony with processions and bell ringing, to chase it away. Find more information at www.lanark.co.uk. Mid-March.

Glasgow Comedy Festival. Glaswegians are certainly not shy in heckling some of comedy's biggest names. See www.glasgow comedyfestival.com. Two weeks in Mid-March.

APRIL

Kate Kennedy Procession & Pageant, St Andrews. A historic pageant with pipe bands and cross-dressed historical characters is staged annually at this ancient university. See www.calendarcustoms.com. Second Saturday in April.

Beltane Fire Festival, Edinburgh. Join the costumed revelers as they dance around the Calton hill, accompanied by drummers and musicians in this modern take on an ancient Celtic fertility ceremony. It's also a good excuse for a party. See www.beltane.org. End of April.

Spirit of Speyside Whisky Festival. Special tours and tastings are presented at various Speyside distilleries. See www.spiritofspey side.com. Late April and early May.

MAY

Scottish Motorcycle Trials, Fort William. The trials run for 6 days in the first part of the month, drawing enthusiasts from all over Europe. Visit www.ssdt.org. Early May.

Shetland Folk Festival, Lerwick and elsewhere on Mainland. Musicians from around the islands and the world gather for the U.K.'s most northerly folk festival and several nights of all-around fun. Visit www.shetland-folkfestival.com. Early May.

Royal Scottish Academy Annual Exhibition, Edinburgh. Showcase of the best of the academicians' painting, sculpture, photography, and architecture. See www.royalscottish academy.org. Early May to early June.

Pitlochry Festival Theatre, Pitlochry. Scotland's "theatre in the hills" launches its season in mid-May. Visit www.pitlochry.org.uk or call ✆ **01796/484-626.** Mid-May to October.

Gay Pride, Edinburgh. The annual gay-pride celebration includes a massive march through the city center. Contact Pride Edinburgh, www.prideedinburgh.org.uk. One Saturday in May or June.

JUNE

Lanimer Day, Lanark. A week of festivities features a procession around the town's boundaries, the election of a Lanimer Queen and a Cornet King, a parade with floats, and Highland dances and bagpipe playing. Visit www.lanarklanimers.co.uk. The Thursday between June 6 and 12.

Royal Highland Show, at the Ingliston Showground, outskirts of Edinburgh. This show is devoted to agriculture and country pursuits, with livestock displays and shows and more. Visit www.royalhighlandshow.org. Mid- to late June.

Selkirk Common Riding, Selkirk. Commemorating Selkirk's losses in the 1513 Battle of Flodden—only one Selkirk soldier returned alive from the battle to warn the town before dropping dead in the marketplace—some 400 horses and riders parade through the streets, and a young unmarried male is crowned at the sound of the cornet, representing the soldier who sounded the alarm. Visit www.returntotheridings.co.uk. Mid-June.

Peebles Beltane Festival. A town "Cornet" rides around to see if the boundaries are safe from the "invading" English, a young girl is elected Festival Queen, and her court is filled with courtiers, sword bearers, guards, and attendants. Children of the town dress in costumes for parade floats through the streets. Go to www.peebles-theroyalburgh. info. Mid-June.

Glasgow International Jazz Festival. Jazz musicians from all over the world come together to perform at various venues around the city. Visit www.jazzfest.co.uk. Late June to early July.

JULY

The Skye Festival/Fèis An Eilein, Isle of Skye. This series of concerts, ceilidhs, theatre performances, and children's events helps to maintain the vibrancy of Skye's culture. See www.isleofskye.com. Throughout July and August.

Hebridean Celtic Festival, Isles of Lewis and Harris. This music festival attracts the biggest names in the Scottish folk world. See www.hebceltfest.com. Mid-July.

Pride Glasgow, Glasgow. The city's largest Gay Pride event is a huge gathering in Kelvingrove Park. Visit http://festival.pride.scot. Mid-July.

AUGUST

Lammas Fair, St Andrews. Ferris wheels and whirligigs are hauled in and street performers arrive in force for Scotland's oldest surviving street fair. Visit www.event-standrews. co.uk. Five days in early August.

World Pipe Band Championships: Piping Live!, Glasgow. This weeklong festival of bagpiping takes place on Glasgow Green. Visit www.rspba.org or www.pipinglive. co.uk. Mid-August.

Edinburgh International Festival. Scotland's best-known festival is held for 3 weeks

(see chapter 5 for more information). More than 1,000 shows are hosted and 1,000,000 tickets sold. Numerous other festivals are also held in Edinburgh at this time, celebrating everything from books to jazz. Nothing tops the Military Tattoo against the backdrop of the floodlit Edinburgh Castle. For tickets, call ☎ **0131/473-2000** or visit www. eif.co.uk. Three weeks in August.

Edinburgh Festival Fringe. For more than 70 years this alternative the city's famous international festival has attracted comedians and all sorts of other performers, these days putting on 4,000 shows in 300 venues. Visit www.edfringe.com. Three weeks in August.

Cowal Highland Gathering, Dunoon, Cowal. The most famous and largest of the Highlands Games events showcases caber tossing, shot-putting, and hammer throwing, along with lots of dancing and piping. Visit www.cowalgathering.com. Late August.

SEPTEMBER

Ben Nevis Mountain Race, Fort William. A tradition since 1895, as many as 500 runners compete for the coveted MacFarlane Cup by running up the footpaths to the summit and back. Bagpipes rise in crescendos at the beginning and end of the race. See www.ben nevisrace.co.uk. First Saturday in September.

Braemar Gathering. The Queen and other members of the royal family often show up for this annual event, with its massed bands, dancing competitions, and trials of great strength by a tribe of gigantic men. Visit www.braemargathering.org. First Saturday in September.

Wigtown Book Festival, Wigtown. Booklovers flock to the remote corners of Galloway, where Scotland's National Book Town celebrates the written word with author talks and other events. Visit http://www.wigtown-bookfestival.com. Last week in September.

Camanachd Cup Final, different venue each year. The finale of the season's games of shinty (a sometimes-brutal hockey variant) is an extraordinary spectacle. Visit www.shinty. com. Late September or early October.

OCTOBER

Highland Autumn Cattle Show, Oban. Since the days of Rob Roy, Oban has been a marketplace for the distinctive Highland Cattle. Buyers and sellers descend on Oban to buy and sell at the industrial-looking Caledonian Auction Mart, 3 miles south of Oban. See www.highlandcattlesociety.com. Mid-October.

Sound Festival, Aberdeen. Performers from around the world and aficionados of avant-garde music gather at venues in and around the northern city. Visit www.sound-scotland. co.uk. Late October to early November.

NOVEMBER

Dundee Jazz Festival. Jazz musicians from around the world converge. See www.jazz dundee.co.uk. Throughout November.

Oban Winter Festival, Oban. The coastal city gets an early start to the holiday season with a Victorian market, reindeer parades, ceildihs, light shows, and 10 days of other events. Go to http://obanwinterfestival.com. From mid- to late-November.

DECEMBER

Flambeaux Procession, Comrie, Tayside. This torchlight parade takes place on New Year's Eve. For details, see www.gateway-to-the-scottish-highlands.com. December 31.

Hogmanay, Edinburgh. Hogmanay begins on New Year's Eve and merges into New Year's Day festivities. Events include a torch-light procession, a fire festival along Princes Street, a carnival, and a street-theatre spectacular. See www.edinburghshogmanay. com. December 31.

TIPS ON PLACES TO STAY
Keeping the Price Down

Accommodation prices quoted throughout this guide include breakfast unless otherwise noted. To save money, try these rules of thumb:

o **Choose your season carefully.** The cheapest time to travel to Scotland is off-season: **November 1 to December 12** and **early January to March 14.** In the past few years, airlines have been offering heavily discounted fares during these periods, with weekday flights even cheaper than weekend ones. Rates generally increase between March 14 and June 5 and in October, and hit their peak in the high seasons from June 6 to September 30 and December 13 to the end of December. Prices tend to be highest in July and August, are when most British people take their holidays. At many times throughout the year, you'll often find the lowest rates midweek, or conversely, in business-oriented hotels, on the weekend.

o **Buy a money-saving package deal.** A travel package that combines your airfare and your hotel stay for one price may be a good bargain, particularly for Edinburgh. In some cases, you'll get airfare, accommodations, transportation to and from the airport, plus extras—maybe an afternoon sightseeing tour—for less than the hotel alone would have cost. Be wary of packages that include meals and other extras, since these might be less expensive if purchased separately or outside the hotel. The usual booking websites (Priceline, Expedia) offer packages.

o **Shop around.** There are so many ways to save online and through apps that we've devoted an entire box to the topic. See below. Once you've done some shopping, contact the property directly and ask for the lowest possible rate—it's often that simple, and don't be shy about asking for a better deal

TURNING TO THE internet or apps FOR A HOTEL DISCOUNT

Before going online, it's important that you know what "flavor" of discount you're seeking. Currently, there are three types of online reductions:

1. **Extreme discounts on sites where you bid for lodgings without knowing which hotel you'll get.** You'll find these on such sites as **Priceline.com** and **Hotwire.com**, and they can be money-savers, particularly if you're booking within a week of travel (that's when the hotels resort to deep discounts to get beds filled). As these companies usually use major chains, you can rest assured that you won't be put up in a dump. For more reassurance, visit the website **BiddingTraveler.com**. On it, actual travelers spill the beans about what they bid on Priceline.com and which hotels they got. We think you'll be pleasantly surprised by the quality of many of the hotels that are offering these "secret" discounts. Keep in mind, though, that since you won't know the location of the hotel until you book, you can find yourself spending a lot of money and time reaching the hotel of choice—not necessarily a problem if you're traveling by car, but a potential hassle if you're relying on public transportation.

2. **Discounts on chain hotel websites.** Major chains reserve special discounts, ranging widely from a few dollars and going as high as $50, for travelers who book directly through their websites (usually in the portion of the site reserved for loyalty members). Our advice: Search for a hotel that's in your price range and ideal location (see below for where to do that) and then, if it is a chain property, book directly through the online loyalty portal.

3. **Use the right hotel search engine.** They're not all equal, as we at Frommers.com learned after putting the top 20 sites to the test in 20 cities (including Edinburgh) around the globe. We discovered that **Booking.com** listed the lowest rates for hotels in the city center, and in the under $200 range, 16 out of 20 times—the best record, by far, of all the sites we tested. And Booking.com includes all taxes and fees in its results (not all do, which can make for a frustrating shopping experience). For top-end properties, again in the city center only, both Priceline.com and HotelsCombined.com came up with the best rates, tying at 14 wins each.

4. **Last-minute discounts.** Booking last minute can be a great savings strategy, as prices sometimes drop in the week before travel as hoteliers scramble to fill their rooms. But you won't necessarily find the best savings through companies that claim to specialize in last-minute bookings. Instead, use the sites recommended in point 3 of this list.

It's a lot of surfing, we know, but this sort of diligence can pay off.

than the ones you've seen elsewhere. Then keep shopping—most reservations are fully refundable almost to time of check-in, so if you find a better price go back to the hotel of choice and renegotiate.

o **Choose a chain.** With some exceptions, we have not listed mass-volume chain hotels in this book. In our opinion, they tend to lack the character and

If you're planning to visit a number of Scotland's many historic properties, you could save money, especially if traveling with children, by purchasing a Historic Scotland **Explorer Pass** (www.historic-scotland.gov.uk; © **0131/668-8095**). Passes allow entry into many of Scotland's most visited historic attractions. There are two types of passes: The first is good for 3 days within a 5-day period and costs £31 for adults, £24.80 for seniors and students, £18.60 for children ages 5 to 15, and £62 for families of 2 adults and up to 6 children. The second pass is available for 7 days within a 14-day period and costs £42 for adults, £33.60 for seniors and students, £25.20 for children and £84 for families. Explorer Passes can be bought at any staffed Historic Scotland property, at **Tourist Information Centres (TICs)** across the country, or online at Historic Scotland's website.

the local feel that many independently run hotels give to the travel experience. That said, you may be able to use reward points or access some type of corporate discount at these chain hotels.

- **Avoid excess charges and hidden costs.** Use your own cellphone instead of dialing direct from hotel phones, which usually have exorbitant rates. And don't be tempted by minibar offerings: Most hotels charge through the nose for water, soda, and snacks. Finally, don't forget to factor in local taxes and service charges, which can increase the cost of a room by 15% or more.
- **Consider rentals and private B&Bs.** See below for more on this type of accommodation.
- **Stay longer.** Many hotels offer discounts of as much as 20% for week or sometimes even a few days.
- **Forego a private bathroom.** Many historic properties outside cities—castles, farmhouses, even lighthouses—have been converted to character-filled accommodations, in which not all of the rooms are en suite. These bathless rooms are often less expensive than others.
- **Join the club.** Some organizations, including AARP and AAA, offer hotel discounts to members, and these apply to some properties in Scotland and elsewhere abroad.

Classifications

In Britain, regional tourist boards classify the standard of accommodation through a star rating system, with five stars being the highest rating and one star the lowest. Each property is judged on categories that may make no difference to the stay of the traveler, though it's helpful to know that all establishments from two stars upward are required to provide en suite bathrooms, and in one-star accommodation hot and cold running water must be provided in all rooms. The ratings in this book go from one star to three stars and have nothing to do with the official rating system.

Bed & Breakfasts

A mainstay of accommodation in all areas of Scotland and the U.K. are bed-and-breakfasts. Sometimes this type of accommodation can be an extension of a family home; at other times the property can be a modern stylish guesthouse. What they all have in common is that they're small, typically offering between two and 15 rooms. They can be far friendlier than big large hotels, and some offer a homemade evening meal at a reasonable extra charge.

Bed and Breakfast Nationwide (www.bedandbreakfastnationwide.com; ✆ 01255/672-377) is an agency specializing in privately owned bed-and-breakfasts all over Britain. You'll also find B&Bs on **Wimdu.com. Airbnb. com,** and **Bed and Fed** (www.bedandfed.co.uk), networks of affordable guest rooms, often in private homes, for as little as £30 per night.

Farmhouses

Many farmhouses set aside rooms for paying guests on a bed-and-breakfast basis. These traditional farmhouses might not boast all the modern conveniences and luxuries of hotels, but they're packed with rural charm, provide a unique insight into Scottish life off the beaten track, and are famous for some of the best home-cooked breakfasts in Scotland. Staying in farmhouses, which are often also private homes, can be cheaper than many other types of accommodation, and many farms also offer self-catering accommodation in converted barns or cottages as well as camping and caravan sites on their land.

Farm Stay UK (www.farmstayuk.co.uk; ✆ 024/7669-6909) is the main national organization for accommodation of this type. The approximate prices range from £30 to £60 per person per night and include a full home-cooked breakfast and usually private facilities. Farm stay self-catering accommodation costs from £200 per week and usually include amenities such as dishwashers and central heating. Each property is inspected annually by both Farm Stay UK and regional tourist boards, and most are open year-round.

Holiday Cottages & Villages

Throughout Scotland, fully furnished studios, houses, cottages, "flats" (apartments), and even trailers suitable for couples, families, or groups can be rented by the day, week, or for longer periods. This type of holiday accommodation can often be an economical option, not least because you can cook all your own meals.

Alongside such multinational companies as Airbnb.com, Home-Away.com, and Fliplkey.com, U.K. companies that offer this type of accommodation include **Cottages. com** (✆ **0345/498-6900**), representing rental properties from thatch-roofed island cottages to

Scenic Scotland by Motor Home

When it comes to exploring Scotland, many visitors prefer to rent a motorhome. **Car Rental Scotland** (www. carrentalscotland.com; ✆ **0141/427-5475**) rents four-, five-, and six-berth motor homes and can arrange transfers from Edinburgh, Glasgow, and Prestwick airports.

hotels VS. RENTALS

It is impossible for us to include reviews for the thousands of apartments, houses and other "one-off" rentals that are available in Scotland through such online giants as **Airbnb.com, Wimdu. com, VRBO.com, Homeaway.com,** and others. But that doesn't mean you shouldn't consider them for your next vacation. The savings can be tremendous. Take for example a 1-week vacation in Edinburgh. If you'd booked a nice, midrange hotel for a week in the city you'd be looking at a something south of £800 for 6 nights in a double room with bathroom. Go to Airbnb, or one of its compatriots, and you'd be able to get not only a bedroom, but an entire flat for the week (including a kitchen, so you can save a bit of cash cooking) for almost half: £490.

Well, sort of. That's because you will likely have more fees to contend with on a rental than on a hotel stay. So before entering your credit card info, always factor in all costs, looking in particular for:

o The fee that the booking company charges. This can add 6% or more to the total cost.

o Cleaning fees: These come to an average of £40, so often the longer you rent, the more this cost can be amortized.

A big perk of this kind of stay: truly unique digs. Not only will you find rentable castles in Scotland (yes, actual ones), you'll also find a decommissioned church (in Urquhart, Morayshire), yurts in the Orkney Islands, a re-tooled giant whiskey vat turned house (in Findhorn), and even a cozy home on a 600-acre private island on Loch Sunart in Argyll.

castles; **Embrace Scotland** (© 01866/822-122); **Unique Cottages** (www. unique-cottages.co.uk; © 01835/822-277); and **Wilderness Cottages** (www. wildernesscottages.co.uk; © 01463/719-219). The perk of using U.K.-based properties is they vet the properties they rep, and will be on hand should anything go wrong with the rental.

The **National Trust for Scotland** (www.ntsholidays.com; © **0131/458-0200;** from outside U.K., **0131/458-0303**) also rents many incredible historic properties around the country from flats in old tenements on Edinburgh's Royal Mile to lighthouse cottages and castles. In addition, the **Landmark Trust** (www.landmarktrust.org.uk; © **01628/825-925**), a national building preservation charity, also has a large collection of historic buildings available for holiday lets.

[FastFACTS] SCOTLAND

Area Codes The telephone country code for Britain is **44.** The area code for Edinburgh is **0131;** for Glasgow, **0141;** for Aberdeen, **01224;** and for Inverness, **01463.**

Business Hours With many exceptions, business hours are Monday through Friday from 9am to 5pm. In general, stores are open Monday through Saturday from 9:30am to 5:30pm, and on Sunday from 11am to 5pm. In country towns, there's usually an early closing day (often on Wed or Thurs), when the shops close at 1pm, and most shops don't open at all on Sundays.

Customs Non-E.U. nationals can bring into Scotland duty-free 200 cigarettes, 100 cigarillos, 50 cigars, or 250 grams of smoking tobacco. You can also bring in 4 liters of wine and either 1 liter of alcohol over 22% proof or 2 liters of fortified wine under 22% proof. In addition, you can bring in up to £390 of other goods (including perfume) without having to pay tax or duty. Check www.hmrc.gov.uk/customs/arriving/arriving noneu.htm for further details.

There are no restrictions on the amount of goods (including alcohol and tobacco) that **E.U. nationals** may bring into Scotland. However, you must transport the goods yourself, the goods must be for your own use or intended as a gift (any form of payment received invalidates this claim), and the goods must be duty and tax paid in the E.U. country where they were acquired. Failure to meet any of these conditions may result in the goods being seized.

Disabled Travelers

Facilities for people with disabilities are improving all the time in Scotland. Legislation requires that new public buildings are fully accessible to wheelchairusers; new public buses and black taxis are generally wheelchair-friendly; and many theatres and cinemas offer induction loops for the hard of hearing. One

obstacle is that listed historic buildings are not allowed to widen entrances, build permanent ramps, or in many cases install elevators. A plus is that people with disabilities are often granted special discounts ("concessions") at attractions and entertainment venues. Free information and advice for people with disabilities traveling throughout Britain are available from **Tourism for All** (www.tourismforall.org.uk; ✆ **0845/124-9971**).

For international travel, **Accessible Journeys** (www.disabilitytravel.com; ✆ **800/846-4537** or 610/521-0339) caters specifically to slow walkers and wheelchair travelers and their families and friends. **Flying Wheels Travel** (✆ **877/451-5006**) offers escorted tours and cruises that emphasize sports, and private tours in minivans with lifts.

The **Moss Rehab Hospital** (www.mossresourcenet.org; ✆ **800/CALL-MOSS** [225-5667]) provides a library of accessible-travel resources online. **Flying with Disability** (✆ **877/451-5006**) is a comprehensive information source on airplane travel, and the **American Foundation for the Blind** (AFB; www.afb.org; ✆ **800/232-5463**) provides information on traveling with Seeing Eye dogs.

Drinking Laws The legal drinking age is 18. Children 15 and under aren't allowed in pubs, except in certain rooms,

and then only when accompanied by a parent or guardian. Pub opening hours are generally from 11am to 11pm, but within these limits there's wide variation, according to the discretion of the pub owner. Licensed premises in certain areas are allowed extended opening hours—up to 4am, on a "local need" basis. On Sundays, some pubs, particularly in city centers, are closed; those that do remain open usually do so from noon to 10:30 or 11pm. Restaurants are allowed to serve liquor during these hours, but only to people who are dining on the premises. The law allows an additional 30 minutes for "drinking-up time." In hotels, liquor may be served from 11am to 11pm to both guests and nonguests; after 11pm, only guests may be served. Supermarkets sell beer, wine, and liquor. Wherever you choose to drink, don't drink and drive—alcohol limits for drivers are much lower in Scotland than they are elsewhere in the U.K., and stiff penalties include license suspension, fines, and jail time.

Drug Laws Scotland, like the rest of Britain, takes a fairly relaxed view of the recreational use of marijuana in private, though possession of hard drugs such as heroin and cocaine may carry stiff penalties, including fines and imprisonment.

Drugstores There are very few 24-hour

pharmacies in Scotland. Some large in-store pharmacy counters in supermarkets remain open until very late. Police station in the country has a list of emergency chemists. Dial "0" (zero) and ask the operator for the local police, who will give you the name of one nearest you.

Electricity British electricity is 240 volts AC (50 cycles), roughly twice the voltage in North America, which is 115 to 120 volts AC (60 cycles). American plugs don't fit British wall outlets so you'll need an adapter to plug an American appliance directly into a European electrical outlet. While most electronic gear, phones and laptops included, are dual voltage, you'll also need a transformer to use a gadget that is not equipped with dual voltage.

Embassies & Consulates All embassies are in London. However, there's a **U.S. Consulate** in Edinburgh at 3 Regent Terrace (www.uk.usembassy.gov; ℭ **0131/556-8315**), open Monday through Friday from 1 to 5:30pm; appointment required. The **Canadian High Commission** is at 50 Lothian Rd. (www.travel.gc.ca; ℭ **0131/473-6320**), open Monday through Friday from 8am to 4pm. The **Irish Consulate** is at 6 Randolph Crescent (www.dfa.ie/irish-consulate/edinburgh; ℭ **0131/226-7711**), open Monday through Friday,

9:30am to 1pm and 2:30 to 5pm.

Emergencies For police, fire, or ambulance, dial ℭ **999.**

Family Travel Families are well catered to in Scotland. In fact, with such an abundance of outdoor scenery and activities, and a generally casual, family-friendly atmosphere prevailing even in the large cities, Scotland is unusually welcoming to young travelers. Many restaurants serve lower-priced child-size portions; many hotels are geared to accommodating families in large rooms with multiple beds or in family suites, often with kitchenettes; and museums and other attractions usually charge children 15 and younger a lower admission fee and have special rates for family groups.

Health Travel in Scotland does not pose any extraordinary health risks. If you need a doctor, your hotel can recommend one, or you can contact your embassy or consulate. U.S. visitors who become ill while in Scotland are eligible for free emergency care only. For other treatment, including follow-up care, you'll be asked to pay. Contact the **International Association for Medical Assistance to Travelers (IAMAT;** www.iamat.org) for tips on travel and health concerns, and for lists of local doctors.

Heritage Travel It's estimated that as many as 40 million people around

the world are of Scottish descent, and family history centers around the country help visitors trace their roots. Among them are the **Burns Monument Centre,** Kilmarnock, www.burnsmonumentcentre.co.uk; the **Highland Archive Service Family History Centre,** Inverness, www.highlifehighland.com; and **Family History at the Mitchell Library,** Glasgow, www.glasgowfamilyhistory.org.uk. **Solway Tours** (www.solwaytours.co.uk) arranges personalized itineraries geared to genealogical research and visits to associated family sights.

Holidays The following public holidays are celebrated in Scotland: New Year (Jan 1–2), Good Friday and Easter Monday, May Day (May 1), spring bank holiday (last Mon in May), summer bank holiday (first Mon in Aug), St Andrew's Day (Nov 30), Christmas Day (Dec 25), and Boxing Day (Dec 26). Almost everything is closed on Christmas Day, and most businesses (except pubs) are closed on New Year's Day. Many shops remain open on other public holidays.

Insurance For big ticket items, like home rentals, and medical emergencies, it's smart to get travel insurance. Chances are your Scottish travels won't be putting you at any special risks, but accidents do happen—lost luggage, scraped bumpers, emergencies that require a change of plans.

You may want to inform yourself about trip cancellation insurance, travellers' medical insurance, and general travel insurance, and good places to do so before heading to Scotland are **SquareMouth.com** and **InsureMyTrip.com**. Both are online marketplaces for travel policies that allow you to pick and choose which policy best suits your needs and budget.

Internet & Wi-Fi   There are abundant opportunities to connect to the Internet just about everywhere in Scotland, with Wi-Fi in most hotels, cafes, and other public spaces; if in need of a connection in a small town or village, the public library is always a good option.

LGBTQ Travelers
Same sex marriage is legal in Scotland, and Edinburgh and Glasgow have thriving gay communities, with bars, clubs, shops, and gyms. Gay and lesbian visitors may sometimes still experience bigoted attitudes in rural areas, but generally, visitors will find the Scots open and welcoming to all comers.

Mail   Most post offices and sub post offices are open Monday through Friday from 9am to 5:30pm and Saturday from 9:30am to noon. British mailboxes are painted red and carry a royal coat of arms. All post

offices accept parcels for mailing, provided they're wrapped properly and securely.

Mobile Phones   If your cellphone is on a GSM system, and you have a world-capacity multiband phone (most are these days) you can make and receive calls in Scotland. You'll need to opt for an "international roaming" plan with your carrier, and these are often available, providing voice and data, for about $10 a day. If you have an unlocked phone, you may also install a prepaid SIM card; a retailer who sells these inexpensive cards will usually install them for you. You'll be assigned a new number and be able to make and receive calls at much lower rates than those for international calls with many U.S.-based plans. You might also consider simply buying an inexpensive phone with a prepaid card to use while you're in Scotland. Many carriers also offer the capability to make calls via the internet, similar to Skype or other internet-based services; if your plan offers the service, your phone will switch to this mode as soon as you connect to Wi-Fi. The only drawback is that you need to be in Wi-Fi range to make calls; check

with your carrier about a Wi-Fi calling feature.

Money & Costs   Britain's monetary system is the pound Sterling (£). There are 100 pence (written as "p") to a pound. Colloquially, pounds are also referred to as "quid." Scotland issues its own pound notes, but English and Scottish money is interchangeable. Coins come in denominations of £2, £1, 50p, 20p, 10p, 5p, 2p, and 1p. Banknotes are issued in denominations of £5, £10, £20, and £50.

In Scotland, ATMs usually offer the best exchange rates. Avoid exchanging money at commercial exchange bureaus and hotels, which often have the highest transaction fees. You can find ATMs at almost all bank branches, as well as at most large supermarkets, some petrol stations, in shopping malls, and some post offices.

Chip & PIN is the system adopted in Scotland and the rest of Britain for the use of credit and debit cards, and with which the user inserts the card into a machine and enters a PIN number. American chip cards don't usually require a PIN, just a signature, but you should have no trouble using these cards in Scotland. Contactless credit

THE VALUE OF THE BRITISH POUND VS. OTHER POPULAR CURRENCIES

UK£	US$	Can$	Euro (€)	Aus$	NZ$
£1.00	US$1.27	C$1.66	1.12€	A$1.74	NZ$1.92

WHAT THINGS COST IN EDINBURGH

WHAT THINGS COST IN EDINBURGH	U.K.£
Airlink bus into the center of Edinburgh	4.50
Average bus fare within Edinburgh	1.70
Double room (expensive)	180.00
Double room (moderate)	120.00
Double room (inexpensive)	60.00
Dinner (expensive)	40.00
Dinner (moderate)	20.00
Dinner (inexpensive)	12.00
Average price of a drink in a nightclub	4.00
Average cover charge at a nightclub	5.00–12.00
Average theatre seat	15.00
Average movie ticket	12.00
Admission to Edinburgh Castle	18.50

14

Newspapers & Magazines

PLANNING YOUR TRIP TO SCOTLAND

cards are also widely used in Scotland; with these, the user simply holds the card near the terminal. However, unless your card is equipped with contactless technology, you will not be able to use it with these terminals.

Newspapers & Magazines While most towns of any size publish their own newspapers, and these are a good way to key into local concerns, *The New York Times* and *USA Today* are also widely available in major cities.

Packing Bring robust footwear and some waterproof clothing just about anywhere you're going in Scotland, whatever the season. You'll want to bring a light jacket, even in summer, when evenings can be nippy. Scots dress well when they go out, and many smarter restaurants request that customers don't wear jeans or trainers (sneakers). So bring nice clothing; a jacket for men and skirt or dress for women is not out of place in many restaurants.

Passports All U.S. citizens, Canadians, Australians, New Zealanders, and South Africans must have a passport with at least 2 months' validity remaining.

Police The best source of help and advice in emergencies is the police. For non-life-threatening situations, dial "0" (zero) and ask for the police; dial 999 for emergencies. If the local police can't assist, they'll usually have the contact details of a hospital or other agency that can. Losses, thefts, and other crimes should be reported immediately.

Safety Although rural Scotland is quite safe, the big cities are no more immune from crime than any other European city. If visitors do find themselves victims of a crime, it's likely to be one of pickpocketing; mugging; "snatch and grab" theft of mobile phones, watches, and jewelry; or theft of their unattended bags, especially at airports and from cars parked at restaurants, hotels, and resorts.

Pickpockets target tourists at historic sites and restaurants, as well as on buses and trains. Unattended cars are targeted, too. Visitors in Scotland aren't expected to produce identity documents for police authorities, so feel free to secure your passport in the hotel or room safe.

Senior Travel Many attractions offer discounts for seniors (sometimes that applies to someone as young as 60). Even if discounts aren't posted, ask if they're available. In most

456

cities, people over the age of 60 also qualify for discounted fares on public transport, and ScotRail offers a third off rail travel (see "Getting Around," above).

Smoking   Smoking has been banned in public places, including pubs, restaurants, workplaces, and public transportation. Ignoring the ban may incur a fine of £50.

Student Travel   The **International Student Identity Card (ISIC)** qualifies students for substantial savings on rail passes, entrance fees, and more. It also provides students with basic health and life insurance and a 24-hour helpline. The card is valid for a maximum of 18 months. You can apply for the card online or in person at **STA Travel** (www.sta travel.com; ✆ **800/781-4040** in North America; 132-782 in Australia; 087/1230-0040 in the U.K.). Check out the website to locate STA Travel offices worldwide. The agency **Travel CUTS** (www.travel cuts.com; ✆ **866/246-9762**) also issues the ISIC Card and offers services and discounts for U.S. and Canadian residents.

Taxes   A standard value-added tax (VAT) of 20% is imposed on most goods and services, and hotel rates and meals in restaurants are also taxed at 20%; the extra charge will usually show up on your bill. For non-EU residents, the VAT amount can be refunded if

you shop at stores that participate in the Retail Export Scheme (signs are posted in the window). When you make a purchase, show your passport and request a Retail Export Scheme form (VAT 407) and a stamped, pre-addressed envelope. Show the VAT form and your sales receipt to British Customs when you leave the country—they may also ask to see the merchandise, so keep them handy in a carry-on bag. After Customs has stamped the form, mail it back to in the envelope the shop has provided *before you leave the country.* Your VAT refund will be mailed to you. Or, in some larger airports you may be able to go to a VAT counter and receive your refund on the spot (Travelex offers this service in many U.K. airports).

Telephones   To call Scotland: If you're calling Scotland from outside of the U.K.:

1. Dial the international access code: 011 from North America; 00 from Ireland, Europe, or New Zealand; or 0011 from Australia.
2. Dial the country code 44.
3. Dial the local 3- or 4-digit area code (drop the initial "0").
4. Dial the 7-digit number. The whole number you'd dial for a number in Edinburgh would be 011-44-131-000-0000.

To make calls within Scotland: Cities and localities have area codes. If you're

calling within the same area code, simply dial the local 7-digit number. However, if you're calling from one area code to another, you must dial 0 and then the area code.

To make international calls: To make international calls from Britain, first dial 00 and then the country code (U.S. or Canada 1, Ireland 353, Australia 61, New Zealand 64, South Africa 27). Next, dial the area code and number.

For directory assistance: For U.K. directory enquiries, dial ✆ **118-500;** for international directory enquiries, dial ✆ **118-505.** Note that these are premium-rate numbers. Consult www.192. com for a free online service.

For operator assistance: If you need an international operator or to call collect, dial ✆ **155.**

Time   The United Kingdom follows Greenwich Mean Time (GMT), which is 5 hours ahead of Eastern Standard Time, with British summertime lasting (roughly) from the end of March to the end of October. For most of the year, including summer, Britain is 5 hours ahead of the time observed in the eastern United States. Because of different daylight-saving-time practices in the two nations, there's a brief period (about a week) in autumn when Britain is only 4 hours ahead of New York, and a brief period in spring when it's 6 hours ahead.

Tipping For **cab drivers,** add about 10% to 15% to the fare shown on the meter. If the driver personally unloads or loads your luggage, add 50p per bag.

You should tip hotel **porters** at least a pound or so even if you have only one small suitcase; give £5 if you have substantial amounts of luggage. Leave **maids** £1 per day.

In many **restaurants,** a 15% service charge is often added to the bill. To that, add another 3% to 5%, depending on the quality of the service. Tipping in **pubs** isn't common, although in cocktail bars the waiter or barmaid usually gets about £1 per round of drinks.

Barbers and **hairdressers** expect 10% to 15%. **Tour guides** expect £2, but it's not mandatory.

Water Tap water is considered safe to drink throughout Scotland.

Index

Accommodations

Restaurants

Map List

Photo Credits

Cover: chrisdorney / Shutterstock.com; p i: Shaiith; p ii: Katie Polockus Hughes; p iii: Nataliya Hora; p iv: Swen Stroop; p v, top: evenfh; p v, bottom left: lou armor / Shutterstock.com; p v, bottom right: matthi / Shutterstock.com; p vi, top left: David Fitzell / Shutterstock.com; p vi, top right: Brendan Howard / Shutterstock.com; p vi, bottom: Jeff Whyte / Shutterstock.com; p vii, top: Alessandro Storniolo / Shutterstock.com; p vii, middle: Skully / Shutterstock.com; p vii, bottom: lou armor / Shutterstock.com; p viii, top: meunierd / Shutterstock.com; p viii, bottom left: Soloviov Vadym / Shutterstock.com; p viii, bottom right: Sophie McAulay / Shutterstock.com; p ix, top: DrimaFilm / Shutterstock.com; p ix, middle: Tana888 / Shutterstock.com; p ix, bottom: Jane Rix; p x, top: WApted; p x, middle: travellight / Shutterstock.com; p x, bottom: GlennD; p xi, top: cornfield / Shutterstock.com; p xi, middle: Marek Masik; p xi, bottom: Alexey Fedorenko; p xii, top: Mikadun; p xii, bottom left: Tony Zaccarini / Shutterstock.com; p xii, bottom right: AK-Snapshot; p xiii, top left: Mark Cane; p xiii, top right: CL-Medien; p xiii, bottom: Georgi Djadjarov; p xiv, top: pitch00; p xiv, middle: Wozzie / Shutterstock.com; p xiv, bottom: Luca Quadrio; p xv, top: MarcAndreLeTourneux; p xv, bottom: Pecold; p xvi, top: duchy; p xvi, bottom left: Cristina Ortolani; p xvi, bottom right: Attila JANDI; Back Cover: Nataliya Hora.

Frommer's Scotland 2019, 16th Edition

Published by
FROMMER MEDIA LLC

ISBN 978-1-62887-400-6 (paper), 978-1-62887-401-3 (ebk)

Editorial Director: Pauline Frommer
Editor: Elizabeth Heath
Production Editor: Erin Geile
Cartographer: Roberta Stockwell
Photo Editor: Meghan Lamb
Cover Design: Dave Riedy

Front cover photo: Furry highland cow in Isle of Skye in Scotland: Shaiith.

For information on our other products or services, see www.frommers.com.

Frommer Media LLC also publishes its books in a variety of electronic formats. Some content that
appears in print may not be available in electronic formats.

Manufactured in the United States of America

5 4 3 2 1

ABOUT THE AUTHORS

Travel journalist **Stephen Brewer** became fascinated with Scotland a couple of decades ago when he ventured north during an extended stay in London and found himself wandering around the Borders. Since then he has been privileged to explore much of the rest of the country, and especially enjoys poking around quiet corners of Glasgow, hopping on a ferry to discover another small island in the Hebrides, or walking along lonely stretches of the Shetland coast. He totally agrees with what Paul McCartney said about mist rolling in from the sea and deer in the glen.

Lucy Gillmore is freelance journalist who specializes in food and travel. She was the deputy travel editor of The Independent newspaper but after 8 years on the travel desk left London to move up to Scotland. She now writes for newspapers such as *The Guardian*, *The Times*, and *the Daily Telegraph* along with magazines including *Condé Nast Traveller* and *House and Garden*. She currently writes a regular food and travel feature for *Olive* magazine and is the author of the *Wallpaper City Guide to Edinburgh*. She lives in the hills above Loch Ness in the Scottish Highlands.

ABOUT THE FROMMER TRAVEL GUIDES

For most of the past 50 years, Frommer's has been the leading series of travel guides in North America, accounting for as many as 24% of all guidebooks sold. I think I know why.

Though we hope our books are entertaining, we nevertheless deal with travel in a serious fashion. Our guidebooks have never looked on such journeys as a mere recreation, but as a far more important human function, a time of learning and introspection, an essential part of a civilized life. We stress the culture, lifestyle, history, and beliefs of the destinations we cover, and urge our readers to seek out people and new ideas as the chief rewards of travel.

We have never shied from controversy. We have, from the beginning, encouraged our authors to be intensely judgmental, critical—both pro and con—in their comments, and wholly independent. Our only clients are our readers, and we have triggered the ire of countless prominent sorts, from a tourist newspaper we called "practically worthless" (it unsuccessfully sued us) to the many rip-offs we've condemned.

And because we believe that travel should be available to everyone regardless of their incomes, we have always been cost-conscious at every level of expenditure. Though we have broadened our recommendations beyond the budget category, we insist that every lodging we include be sensibly priced. We use every form of media to assist our readers, and are particularly proud of our feisty daily website, the award-winning Frommers.com.

I have high hopes for the future of Frommer's. May these guidebooks, in all the years ahead, continue to reflect the joy of travel and the freedom that travel represents. May they always pursue a cost-conscious path, so that people of all incomes can enjoy the rewards of travel. And may they create, for both the traveler and the persons among whom we travel, a community of friends, where all human beings live in harmony and peace.

Arthur Frommer